SIXTH EDITION

Human Communication

University of Central Florida

Judy C. Pearson

Paul E. Nelson

Scott Titsworth

Lynn Harter

Jeff Butler

Stephen Ihde

Jim Katt

Burt Pryor

Mc
Graw
Hill
Education

5 6 7 8 9 0 SCI SCI 21 20 19

ISBN-13: 978-1-260-30414-5
ISBN-10: 1-260-30414-0

Solutions Program Manager: Tricia Wagner
Project Manager: Connie Kuhl

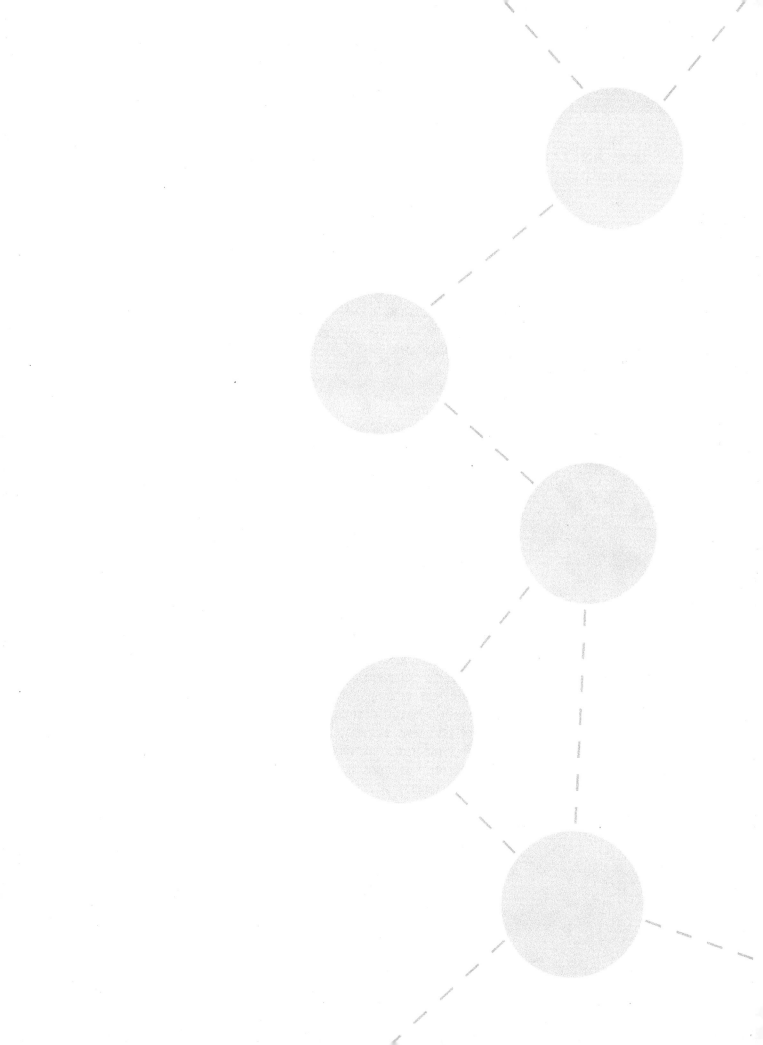

From the Authors

Your life is punctuated with critical moments in which communication plays an important role. Whether you are talking to a potential employer during a job interview, a loved one about an important issue facing your family, or an instructor about an assignment, what you say and how you say it can dramatically shape the outcome of an interaction. Our goal in writing *Human Communication* is to help you feel confident in any situation. We want you to have the knowledge, skills, and attitudes necessary to be a successful communicator.

We want you to be ready to

- **Communicate** effectively in novel and uncertain situations
- **Assess** who you are talking to and establish common ground
- **Listen** effectively and respond appropriately
- **Practice** the skills appropriate to a variety of relationships and cultures
- **Adapt** your communication using technologies that enhance, express, and transmit your messages
- **Speak** with confidence and clarity on important topics

Human Communication draws on the best available research to help you develop the knowledge you need to communicate effectively in a variety of situations. The research-based theories we present in this text, coupled with the street savvy you have developed over the course of your life, will equip you with a strong foundation for reading situations, acting appropriately, and adapting your communication behaviors.

As instructors in the field of communication, we believe that personal improvement in communication begins with a clear understanding of your own attitudes and of the relationships you build with others. *Human Communication* will help you develop the skills you need to tell the story of your life and serve as a foundation for lifelong success.

— *Judy C. Pearson*
— *Paul E. Nelson*
— *Scott Titsworth*
— *Angela M. Hosek*

brief contents

contents

"With SmartBook,
I remember more of
what I read."

> *"I like applying what I've read by answering the questions in SmartBook."*

"SmartBook helps me identify what we are going to be covering in class."

Chapter 4   Nonverbal Communication   64

"*SmartBook lets me know I am retaining the information.*"

> "SmartBook helps me feel more prepared for class."

Chapter 8   Small-Group Communication   154

> *"I am a big fan of how SmartBook emphasizes the topics I struggle with."*

"Reviewing with SmartBook about once a week is a good way to refresh my memory."

Part 3   Fundamentals of Public Speaking

> *"I feel the homework activities in SmartBook are most helpful because I need that extra push when learning."*

Chapter 12   Organizing Your Presentation   260

"I like the SmartBook assignments because they keep me on track."

Chapter 14   Persuasive Presentations   318

preface

McGraw-Hill Connect: An Overview

McGraw-Hill Connect offers full-semester access to comprehensive, reliable content and learning resources for the communication course. Connect's deep integration with most learning management systems (LMSs), including Blackboard and Desire2Learn (D2L), offers single sign-on and deep gradebook synchronization. Data from Assignment Results reports synchronize directly with many LMSs, allowing scores to flow automatically from Connect into school-specific grade books, if required.

The following tools and services are available as part of Connect for the communication course.

Tool	Instructional Context	Description
SmartBook	• SmartBook is an engaging and interactive reading experience for mastering fundamental communication content. • The metacognitive component confirms learners' understanding of the material. • Instructors can actively connect SmartBook assignments and results to higher-order classroom work and one-on-one student conferences. • Learners can track their own understanding and mastery of course concepts and identify gaps in their knowledge.	• SmartBook is an adaptive reading experience designed to change the way learners read and learn. It creates a personalized reading experience by highlighting the most impactful concepts a student needs to learn at that moment in time. • SmartBook creates personalized learning plans based on student responses to content question probes and confidence scales, identifying the topics learners are struggling with and providing learning resources to create personalized learning moments. • SmartBook includes a variety of learning resources tied directly to key content areas to provide students with additional instruction and context. This includes video and media clips, interactive slide content, mini-lectures, and image analyses. • SmartBook Reports provide instructors with data to quantify success and identify problem areas that require addressing in and out of the classroom. • Learners can access their own progress and concept mastery reports.

Connect Insight for Instructors	• Connect Insight for *Instructors* is an analytics resource that produces quick feedback related to learner performance and learner engagement.
	• It is designed as a dashboard for both quick check-ins and detailed performance and engagement views.
		• Connect Insight for *Instructors* offers a series of visual data displays that provide analysis on five key insights:
		  • How are my students doing?
		  • How is this one student doing?
		  • How is my section doing?
		  • How is this assignment doing?
		  • How are my assignments doing?

Connect Insight for Students	• Connect Insight for *Students* is a powerful data analytics tool that provides at-a-glance visualizations to help learners understand their performance on Connect assignments.	• Connect Insight for *Students* offers details on each Connect assignment to learners. When possible, it offers suggestions for the learners on how they can improve scores. These data can help guide learners to behaviors that will lead to better scores in the future.

Tool	Instructional Context	Description
Speech Capture	• Speech Capture provides instructors with a comprehensive and efficient way of managing in-class and online speech assignments, including student self-reviews, peer reviews, and instructor grading.	• The Speech Capture tool allows instructors to easily and efficiently set up speech assignments for their course that can easily be shared and repurposed, as needed, throughout their use of Connect. • Customizable rubrics and settings can be saved and shared, saving time and streamlining the speech assignment process from creation to assessment. • Speech Capture allows users, both students and instructors, to view videos during the assessment process. Feedback can be left within a customized rubric or as time-stamped comments within the video-playback itself.
Speech Preparation Tools	• Speech Preparation Tools provide learners with additional support and include Topic Helper, Outline Tool, and access to third-party Internet sites like EasyBib (for formatting citations) and Survey Monkey (to create audience-analysis questionnaires and surveys).	• Speech Preparation Tools provide learners with additional resources to help with the preparation and outlining of speeches, as well as with audience-analysis surveys. • Instructors have the ability to make tools either available or unavailable to learners.
Instructor Reports	• Instructor Reports provide data that may be useful for assessing programs or courses as part of the accreditation process.	• Connect generates a number of powerful reports and charts that allow instructors to quickly review the performance of a given learner or an entire section. • Instructors can run reports that span multiple sections and instructors, making it an ideal solution for individual professors, course coordinators, and department chairs.
Student Reports	• Student Reports allow learners to review their performance for specific assignments or for the course.	• Learners can keep track of their performance and identify areas with which they struggle.
Pre- and Post-Tests	• Instructors can generate their own pre- and posts-tests from the Test Bank. • Pre- and post-tests demonstrate what learners already know before class begins and what they have learned by the end.	• Instructors have access to two sets of pre- and post-tests (at two levels). Instructors can use these tests to create a diagnostic and post-diagnostic exam via Connect.
Tegrity	• Tegrity allows instructors to capture course material or lectures on video. • Students can watch videos recorded by their instructor and learn course material at their own pace.	• Instructors can keep track of which learners have watched the videos they post. • Learners can watch and review lectures by their instructor. • Learners can search each lecture for specific bites of information.
Simple LMS Integration	• Connect seamlessly integrates with every learning management system.	• Learners have automatic single sign-on. • Connect assignment results sync to the LMS's gradebook.

Instructor's Guide to Connect for *Human Communication*

When you assign **Connect** you can be confident—and have data to demonstrate—that the learners in your course, however diverse, are acquiring the skills, principles, and critical processes that constitute effective communication. This leaves you to focus on your highest course expectations.

TAILORED TO YOU. Connect offers on-demand, single sign-on access to learners—wherever they are and whenever they have time. With a single, one-time registration, learners receive access to McGraw-Hill's trusted content. **Learners also have *a courtesy trial period during registration.***

EASY TO USE. Connect seamlessly supports all major learning management systems with content, assignments, performance data, and LearnSmart, the leading adaptive learning system. With these tools you can quickly make assignments, produce reports, focus discussions, intervene on problem topics, and help at-risk learners—as you need to and when you need to.

Human Communication SmartBook

A Personalized and Adaptive Learning Experience with Smartbook. Boost learner success with McGraw-Hill's adaptive reading and study experience. The *Human Communication* SmartBook highlights the most impactful communication concepts the student needs to learn at that moment in time. The learning path continuously adapts and, based on what the individual learner knows and does not know, provides focused help through targeted question probes and learning resources.

Enhanced for the New Edition! With a suite of new learning resources and question probes, as well as highlights of key chapter concepts, SmartBook's intuitive technology optimizes learner study time by creating a personalized learning path for improved course performance and overall learner success.

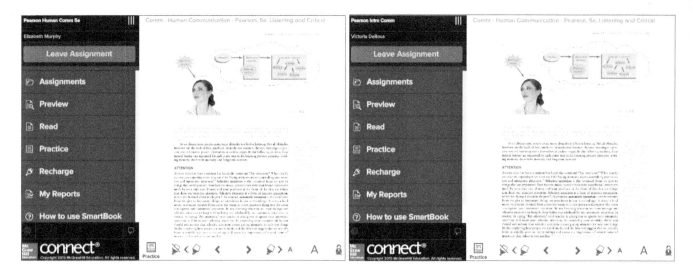

SmartBook highlights the key concepts of every chapter, offering the learner a high-impact learning experience (left). Here, highlighted text and an illustration together explain the listening process. Highlights change color (right) when a student has demonstrated his or her understanding of the concept.

Hundreds of Interactive Learning Resources. Presented in a range of interactive styles, *Human Communication* Learning Resources support learners who may be struggling to master, or simply wish to review, the most important communication concepts. Designed to reinforce the most important chapter concepts—from nonverbal communication cues and critical thinking skills to workplace interviewing techniques and organizing presentations—every Learning Resource is presented at the precise moment of need. Whether video, audio clip, or interactive mini-lesson, each of the 200-plus Learning Resources is new to the new edition and was designed to give learners a lifelong foundation in strong communication skills.

More than 1,000 Targeted Question Probes. Class-tested at colleges and universities nationwide, a treasury of engaging question probes—new and revised, more than 1,000 in all—gives learners the information on communication they need to know, at every stage of the learning process, in order to thrive in the course. Designed to gauge learners' comprehension of the most important *Human Communication* chapter concepts, and presented in a variety of interactive styles to facilitate student engagement, targeted question probes give learners immediate feedback on their understanding of the material. Each question probe identifies a learner's familiarity with the instruction and points to areas where additional remediation is needed.

The process of using messages to generate meaning _____ in a situation that allows mutual opportunities for both speaking and listening is defined as _____ communication.

Click the answer you think is right.

between at least two people; intrapersonal

within the self; interpersonal

within the self; mass

between at least two people; interpersonal

Do you know the answer?   🔲 Read about this

I know it   Think so   Unsure   No idea

Informed by the Latest Research. The best insights from today's leading communications scholars infuse every lesson and are integrated throughout *Human Communication*.

Fresh Examples Anchored in the Real World. Every chapter of *Human Communication* opens with a vignette exploring communication challenges in our everyday lives. Dozens of additional examples appear throughout the new edition, each demonstrating an essential element of the communication process. Whether learners are reading a chapter, responding to a question probe, or reviewing key concepts in a learning resource, their every instructional moment is rooted in the real world. McGraw-Hill research shows that high-quality examples reinforce academic theory throughout the course. Relevant examples and practical scenarios—reflecting interactions in school, the workplace, and beyond—demonstrate how effective communication informs and enhances students' lives and careers.

A Greater Emphasis on Creativity. A new feature, *Communicating Creatively*, illustrates ways in which originality—from effective collaboration strategies, to emphasizing one's personality, to using music to boost a message—can be used to augment the communication skills addressed in the chapters.

communicating creatively

Memorable Message About College

As a way to celebrate International Women's Day, YouTube encouraged people to empower young women with the *#DearMe* campaign. The *#DearMe* campaign asks digital creators around the world to upload "video letters" to their younger selves that provide the advice and encouragement that they wish they had heard when they were younger. The campaign encouraged people to use the hashtag *#DearMe* on social media to share their messages. Although the initial focus was on young girls, these video letters apply to anyone wishing to tell their younger selves or others a supportive, clarifying, and/or realistic message. A quick search of the videos yields an array of messages, perspectives, and identities. In this section, you have been learning about how your self-perceptions and others' perceptions of you have, in part, formed who you are. Perhaps you can take the time to create a video or write a handwritten letter to your younger self. What would your letter say? What part does perception play in your message to your younger self?

Source: Brouwer, B. (2015, March). YouTube launches #DearMe campaign for International Women's Day. *Tubefilter* (www.tubefilter.com/2015/03/03/youtube-dearme-campaign-international-womens-day/).

New Annotated Student Speech. The Informative Presentations chapter includes three compelling student speeches on contemporary topics, including an informative presentation new to the new edition. Each speech models how a speaker can increase audience members' awareness of an issue, integrate sources and other supporting material, and organize the message to help listeners better understand a topic.

Tips for Embracing Diverse Cultures. To help students navigate the communication challenges of a multicultural society, *Engaging Diversity* boxes offer guidance on topics such as nonverbal cues, disabilities, bilingualism, new technologies, and provocative speech.

Guidance for a Lifetime. The end-of-chapter feature, *Be Ready . . . for What's Next,* stresses the lifelong application of communication skills and how mastery of these skills can help learners in other classes, the workplace, and life.

Speech Capture

Designed for use in face-to-face, real-time classrooms, as well as online courses, Speech Capture allows you to evaluate your learners' speeches using fully customizable rubrics. You can also create and manage peer review assignments and upload videos on behalf of learners for optimal flexibility.

Persuasive Speech

instructor review   self review   peer review

video author:
Erik Linstrum

video title:
Linstrum

description:
No description given yet

Click the slider in the video player to add a time-stamped comment as you view the video.

Evaluate the student

Question 1 / 31   Answers (select one)

see all questions   Excellent (5)   Good (4)   Average (2)   Fair (2)   Poor (1)   N/A (0)
Gained attention and interest

Learners can access rubrics and leave comments when preparing self-reviews and peer reviews. They can easily upload a video of their speech from their hard drive or use Connect's built-in video recorder. Learners can even attach and upload additional files or documents, such as a works cited page or a PowerPoint presentation.

Peer Review. Peer review assignments are easier than ever. Create and manage peer review assignments and customize privacy settings.

Speech Assessment. Connect Speech Capture lets you customize the assignments, including self-reviews and peer reviews. It also saves your frequently used comments, simplifying your efforts to provide feedback.

Self-Reflection. The self-review feature allows learners to revisit their own presentations and compare their progress over time.

Data Analytics

Connect Insight provides at-a-glance analysis on five key insights, available at a moment's notice from your tablet device. The first and only analytics tool of its kind, Insight will tell you, in real time, how individual students or sections are doing (or how well your assignments have been received) so you can take action early and keep struggling students from falling behind.

Instructors can see how many learners have completed an assignment, how long they spent on the task, and how they scored.

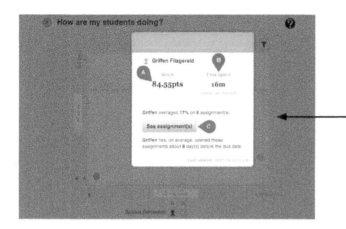

Instructors can see, at a glance, individual learner performance: analytics showing learner investment in assignments, and success at completing them, help instructors identify, and aid, those who are at risk.

Connect Reports

Instructor Reports allow instructors to quickly monitor learner activity, making it easy to identify which learners are struggling and to provide immediate help to ensure those learners stay enrolled in the course and improve their performance. The Instructor Reports also highlight the concepts and learning objectives that the class as a whole is having difficulty grasping. This essential information lets you know exactly which areas to target for review during your limited class time.

Some key reports include:

Progress Overview report—View learner progress for all modules, including how long learners have spent working in the module, which modules they have used outside any that were assigned, and individual learner progress.

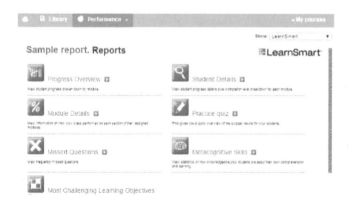

Missed Questions report—Identify specific probes, organized by chapter, that are problematic for learners.

Most Challenging Learning Objectives report—Identify the specific topic areas that are challenging for your learners; these reports are organized by chapter and include specific page references. Use this information to tailor your lecture time and assignments to cover areas that require additional remediation and practice.

Metacognitive Skills report—View statistics showing how knowledgeable your learners are about their own comprehension and learning.

Classroom Preparation Tools

Whether before, during, or after class, there is a suite of Pearson products designed to help instructors plan their lessons and to keep learners building upon the foundations of the course.

Annotated Instructor's Edition. The Annotated Instructor's Edition provides a wealth of teaching aids for each chapter in *Human Communication*. It is also cross-referenced with SmartBook, Connect, and other supplements that accompany *Human Communication*.

Powerpoint Slides. The PowerPoint presentations for *Human Communication* provide chapter highlights that help instructors create focused yet individualized lesson plans.

Test Bank. The Test Bank is a treasury of more than 1,000 examination questions based on the most important communication concepts explored in *Human Communication;* more than 100 of the questions are new or revised for this edition.

Support to Ensure Success

- **Digital Success Academy**—The Digital Success Academy on Connect offers a wealth of training and course creation guidance for instructors and learners alike. Instructor support is presented in easy-to-navigate, easy-to-complete sections. It includes the popular **Connect** how-to videos, step-by-step **Click through Guides,** and **First Day of Class** materials that explain how to use both the Connect platform and its course-specific tools and features. http://createwp.customer.mheducation. com/wordpress-mu/success-academy/

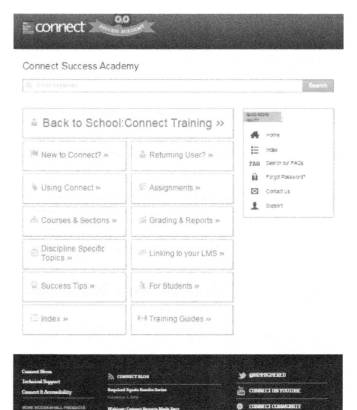

- **Digital Success Team**—The Digital Success Team is a group of specialists dedicated to working online with instructors—one-on-one—to demonstrate how the Connect platform works and to help incorporate Connect into a customer's specific course design and syllabus. Contact your digital learning consultant to learn more.

- **Digital Learning Consultants**—Digital Learning Consultants are local resources who work closely with your McGraw-Hill learning technology consultants. They can provide face-to-face faculty support and training. http://shop.mheducation. com/store/paris/user/findltr.html

- **Digital Faculty Consultants**—Digital Faculty Consultants are experienced instructors who use Connect in their classroom. These instructors are available to offer suggestions, advice, and training about how best to use Connect in your class. To request a Digital Faculty Consultant to speak with, please e-mail your McGraw-Hill learning technology consultant. http://connect.customer.mheducation.com/dfc/

- **National Training Webinars**—McGraw-Hill offers an ongoing series of webinars for instructors to learn and master the Connect platform as well as its course-specific tools and features. We hope you will refer to our online schedule of national training webinars and sign up to learn more about Connect! http://webinars.mhhe.com/

CONTACT OUR CUSTOMER SUPPORT TEAM

McGraw-Hill is dedicated to supporting instructors and learners. To contact our customer support team, please call us at 800–331–5094 or visit us online at http://mpss.mhhe.com/contact.php.

Chapter-by-Chapter Changes to the New Edition: Highlights

New and updated material in this edition of *Human Communication* reflects the latest research in the field, as well as McGraw-Hill Education's research identifying the skills and topics students find most challenging.

Chapter 2: New opening vignette on how language shapes perceptions and expectations; reframed focus on identity as a factor influencing perception; intergroup perspective added to theoretical framing of chapter; updated research on stereotyping; new coverage of technology's impact on perception, first impressions, online identity, and personal branding

Chapter 3: New opening vignette on how words become "real"; new examples of slang and clichéd language; reframed focus on gender-biased language and new discussion of trans* language; new coverage of vanishing languages, communicating personality, and using we-and-I statements during job interviews

Chapter 4: New coverage of communicating emotions, using adaptors, adapting nonverbal behaviors to digitally mediated communication, diversity, and nonverbal cues; updated research on the dangers of overemphasizing physical attractiveness

Chapter 6: New discussion of self-disclosure, communication privacy management, social media, and visible and nonvisible disabilities; updated research on grieving and social media

Chapter 7: New opening vignette on culture-based group conflict; updated statistics on diversity in the United States; new research on the importance of exposing college students to diversity; new coverage of the role of music in building cultural awareness

Chapter 8: New opening vignette on group work during community crises; updated research on group work, group think, and related tech apps; new *Emerging Technology and Group Roles* section; new coverage of collaborative co-working, the impact of physical structures on human interaction, managing privacy, and conflict in work groups; new *Adapted Competent Group Communication Evaluation Form*

Chapter 9: Updated statistics on U.S. workforce trends; new coverage of organizational communication, personal branding, and bilingual communication in the workplace; new table outlining workplace communication competence skills

Chapter 11: Chapter reorganized to emphasize strategies for locating information for presentations; new coverage of common ground, expertise, and credibility

Chapter 12: Enhanced coverage of audience feedback when creating the body of a speech

acknowledgments

The authors wish to extend a very sincere thank you to the many colleagues who assisted in the revision of this edition of *Human Communication*. Many of our communication faculty colleagues and students have provided feedback, both formal and informal, about how to improve both the substance and feel of this book. Such insight is critical, and we are very appreciative of your time and expertise. We are forever grateful to Judy Pearson, Paul Nelson, and Lynn Harter, who were co-authors on previous editions of this book. Your voices, spirit, and commitment to students are, and will forever be, integral parts of this project.

Reviewer Names

Gwen Dooley, *Jackson State University*
Amber Finn, *Texas Christian University*
Chris Goble, *Monmouth College*
Angela Johansson, *Kishwaukee College*
Katherine Lehman-Meyer, *St. Mary's University*
Amy Lenoce, *Naugatuck Valley Community College*
Yvette Lujan, *Miami Dade College, InterAmerican Campus*
Daniel McRoberts, *Northcentral Technical College*
Greg Ormson, *Northcentral Technical College*
Thomas Ruddick, *Edison Community College*
Shari Santoriello, *Suffolk County Community College, Eastern*
Patricia Smith, *Northcentral Technical College*
Susan Smith, *Broward College, South Campus*
Adam Vellone, *Miami Dade College, Homestead Campus*

Connect and LearnSmart Contributors

Jocelyn DeGroot Brown, *Southern Illinois University, Edwardsville*
Leah Bryant, *DePaul University*
Brady Carey, *Mt. Hood Community College*
Tim Chandler, *Hardin-Simmons University*
Denise Sperruzza, *St. Louis Community College*
Charlene Widener, *Hutchinson Community College*

Feature and Connect Plan Reviewers

Lawrence Albert, *Morehead State University*
Theresa Albury, *Miami Dade College, Wolfson Campus*
Brady Carey, *Mt. Hood Community College*
Nader Chaaban, *Montgomery College, Rockville*
Diane Egdorf, *Des Moines Area Community College*
Philip Lane, *Miami Dade College, Wolfson Campus*
Kara Laskowski, *Shippensburg University of Pennsylvania*
Linda Long, *North Lake College*
Xin-An Lu, *Shippensburg University of Pennsylvania*
Kay Mueller, *Des Moines Area Community College*
Renee Strom, *St. Cloud State University*
Anestine Theophile-LaFond, *Montgomery College, Rockville*

Survey Participants

Rebekah Pointer Adderley, *Tarrant County College*
Dr. Amy M. Atchley, *Baton Rouge Community College*
Manuel G. Avilés-Santiago, *Arizona State University*
Joseph Bailey, *Hardin-Simmons University*
Erin Begnaud, *South Louisiana Community College— Lafayette*
Tonya D. Bell, *Labette Community College*
Bryan Brown, *Northern Virginia Community College— Woodbridge*
Christy Burns, *Jacksonville State University*
Brady Carey, *Mt. Hood Community College*
Tim Chandler, *Hardin-Simmons University*
Gena Christopher, *Jacksonville State University*
Ingrid C Davis, *Central Piedmont Community College*
Kevin Ells, *Louisiana State University, Alexandria*
Diana Elrod-Sarnecki, *Des Moines Area Community College*
Jill Evans, *Kettering College*
John B. French, *Cape Cod Community College*
Chris Goble, *Monmouth College*
Mike Harsh, *Hagerstown Community College*
Daniel Hildenbrandt, *Owensboro Community and Technical College*
Sandy Humphries, *South Louisiana Community College*
Nancy A. Hutchinson, *Lipscomb University*
Khalil Islam-Zwart, *Eastern Washington University*
Tonya Blivens Kariuki, *Tarrant County College*
Carolyn Kershaw, *Charter Oak State College*
Amanda A. Knight, *Andrew College*
Erica Lamm, *Northern Virginia Community College*
Philip Lane, *Miami Dade College, Wolfson Campus*
Amy K. Lenoce, *Naugatuck Valley Community College*
Darren L. Linvill, *Clemson University*
Matthew Malloy, *Caldwell Community College and Technical Institute*
Anne McIntosh, *Central Piedmont Community College*
Jennifer Millspaugh, *Richland College*
Denny Morell, *Mass Bay Community College*

Robert Mott, *York College of Pennsylvania*
Terri Narrell, *Snead State Community College*
Lois B. Nemetz, *Louisiana State University, Eunice*
Steve "Butch" Owens, *Navarro College*
Trudi Peterson, *Monmouth College*
Paul E. Potter, *Hardin-Simmons University*
Danna Prather, *Suffolk County Community College*
Rebecca Putt, *Charter Oak State College*
Gary D. Reeves, *Baton Rouge Community College*
Maryanna Richardson, *Forsyth Technical Community College*
Rosemary Robertson-Smith, *Louisiana State University, Eunice*

Shari Santoriello, *Suffolk County Community College, Eastern*
Jesse Schroeder, *Northwestern Oklahoma State University*
Don Simmons, *Asbury University*
Patricia Spence, *Richland College*
Kari Stouffer, *University of Texas, Dallas*
Charlene Strickland, *Hardin-Simmons University*
Karol L. Walchak, *Alpena Community College*
Diana M. Withers, *Charter Oak State College*

We are also indebted to the outstanding team of McGraw-Hill Education colleagues who contributed their time and talent to this edition. Nancy Huebner and Lisa Pinto provided critical guidance as we developed a vision for this edition. Your wisdom and pragmatic approach provided us with confidence, while your enthusiasm and vision instilled excitement! There are many other individuals who worked on several essential aspects of this project, including Sally Constable, Samantha Donisi-Hamm, Sheila Frank, Laura Kennedy, Michael O'Loughlin, Jennifer Shekleton, Janet Smith, Linda Su, and Kim Taylo. Thank you for being part of the *Human Communication* team!

We were particularly blessed to work with a delightful editor, Victoria DeRosa. Victoria was a true collaborator on this project. Her eye for detail, insightful suggestions, understanding of our vision, and commitment to be inclusive to students was evident in the work she did with us. We are so thankful to have had you with us on this journey!

Finally, we are reminded that book projects are family endeavors. Scott would like to thank Lynn Harter for providing a creative sounding board and unending support for this project. Thanks also to Emma, Ned, and Cleo for their love and fun diversions from the computer! Angela would like to thank Scott for the opportunity to collaborate on this project and for his constant interest in new and bold ideas. She is also grateful for the endless support and patience of her partner, Timothy, and for the little hands and laughter of her children, Lillie and Ayden, that remind her to be still in the moment.

Human
Communication

an introduction to the *study* of communication

Jim Katt, University of Central Florida

When you have read and thought about this chapter, you will be able to:

1. Explain how the process of communication is pervasive, amoral, and agenda-advancing.

2. Describe logos, pathos, and ethos, and understand what speakers can do to enhance each of them in their presentations.

3. Explain the importance of the SMCRE variables.

4. Demonstrate ways to maximize the likelihood that your audience will be motivated and able to process your message.

5. Explain the various contexts in which communication takes place.

This chapter will introduce you to the study of human communication. First, we will look at some of the attributes of the process of communication. Next, we will explore some of the theories of communication and demonstrate how you can apply those theories to become a better communicator. We will preview the contexts in which communication occurs and discuss the opportunities and challenges of each area of study, and finally, we will talk about an ethical framework for communication.

Although we have been communicating all of our lives, most of us have not put a lot of thought into how the process of communication works. Before you begin your survey of various aspects of human communication, it will be good to have an overview of how the process works. Whether you are making a presentation for a college class or at work, or simply interacting with co-workers, friends and family, knowing about the process of communication can be helpful. Fortunately for you, there is a large body of knowledge just waiting to be tapped.

The study of communication has a theoretical basis that draws from contemporary empirical research as well as observations that date back centuries. This chapter makes no attempt to cover the body of knowledge that makes up communication theory, but instead looks at a few selected instances where some knowledge of communication theory can help you be a more effective communicator in your everyday life.

What Is Communication?

Communication is a complex process that, many would argue, is extraordinarily difficult to define. So, rather than attempting to define communication, let's examine some of the attributes of this process. Specifically, let's look at how communication is pervasive, amoral, and necessary to advancing our life-agenda.

pervasiveness
Communication takes place wherever humans are together because people tend to look for meaning, even when a message is not deliberately sent.

COMMUNICATION IS PERVASIVE

Many argue that humans in the presence of other humans cannot *not* communicate. Even when we try not to send any sort of message, it's likely that others will infer meaning from our lack of action. What do you think when someone doesn't call you back, doesn't look at you when you're talking, or doesn't answer your email? If you're like most people, you start making inferences about the other person's motives for not responding—she's doesn't like me; he's just a rude person; she's afraid to talk to me; he's probably really busy; and so on. People tend to look for meaning, even when there is no message. It's human nature. The problem is that, much of the time, the meaning assigned to the lack of an overt message simply isn't correct. Your voicemail is full and all of a sudden people think you don't like them, or you're rude, or you're fearful, or too busy to talk. But what does this inability to turn off the communication process mean for us as communicators? If we cannot *not* communicate, if people are going to assign meaning to our lack of sending messages, then maybe we would be better off trying to send clear messages that have a better chance of being received accurately. If the process of communication is going to continue whether we participate or not, it's better that we become active participants.

· What do you think when someone doesn't return your text message?

COMMUNICATION IS AMORAL

The word *amoral* is often misused. People use it when they really mean *immoral*. In the context of communication, **amoral** means ethically neutral—neither moral nor

amoral
The process of communication is ethically neutral.

Evaluate Your Own Communication Skills

We communicate in a variety of contexts. To improve your skill as a communicator, you should assess your own communication skills in each of the general communication contexts, so that you can identify your strengths and areas for growth. Read each of the following questions carefully, and respond using the following scale:

1 = Strongly disagree
2 = Disagree
3 = Neither agree nor disagree
4 = Agree
5 = Strongly agree

1. I can use communication to solve conflicts with friends.
2. I am able to express my ideas clearly when working in a group.
3. I am comfortable when giving public speeches.
4. I can use the Internet to locate highly reputable information.
5. Other people tell me that I am a good speaker.
6. My friends tell me that I am a good listener.
7. Others listen to my opinions in group meetings.
8. People rely on me to find information on the web.
9. I am good at delivering speeches.
10. I can effectively lead groups to discuss problems.
11. I make friends easily.
12. I am skilled at using computers to communicate with others (e.g., using Skype, IM, chat rooms, and other communication tools).

Note: This list has no "right" or "wrong" answers. It simply provides an overview of your communication skills at the beginning of the course. You might want to complete the survey again at the end of the course to determine whether your scores have changed. A guide for interpreting your responses appears at the end of this chapter.

immoral. Perhaps a quick analogy will help. Think about those one-celled amoebas you studied in high school biology. You may recall they reproduced *asexually*. Does this mean that the amoebas are sexually deficient or inferior? No, it means they are sexually neutral: neither male nor female. Scholars as far back as Aristotle have argued that the communication process is amoral. The morality, or lack of morality, comes from the people engaged in the process. Perhaps you've tried to persuade a roommate not to go out with a person you know is "bad news." Or, maybe you've tried to talk a friend out of using prescription drugs illegally to stay awake and be more mentally alert for finals. These are examples of moral, ethical communication behavior. In fact, many would argue that *failure* to attempt to influence your friend in these cases would be immoral. Unscrupulous scam artists, who try to sell worthless insurance policies to people who are poor and unknowledgeable, and drug dealers, who try to convince your kids to try their products, use those same methods of persuasion in immoral, unethical ways. The process is neutral—the people engaged in the process provide the morality, or lack of it. This brings us to another aspect of communication: what exactly do we do with it?

COMMUNICATION ALLOWS US TO ADVANCE OUR LIFE-AGENDA

Communication is the means by which each of us advances our life-agenda. As infants, we cried to be fed. Ever since, we have used whatever communication skills we could muster to influence others to think, feel, or act in ways that we believe they should. While such a statement may spark connotations of manipulation or coercion (see the Persuasion chapter to help distinguish "persuasion" from "coercion"), we must remind ourselves that the *process* of communication is ethically neutral and that advancing our life-agenda can be an ethical pursuit, enriching (or, at least, not harming) those around us. Or, it could be an unethical exploitation, advancing our agenda at the expense of others. Which one it is depends on the morality that we, as individuals, bring to the process.

If we acknowledge that communication is a pervasive process that happens with or without our active participation, that it is by this process that we advance our life-agenda, and that it is possible to engage in agenda-advancing behavior in an ethical manner, then communication becomes more than a college course requirement: it's an essential life skill. Becoming a more effective communicator is about more than getting a decent grade in your communication class—it's about becoming more effective at *life*.

What Can We Learn from Aristotle?

Twenty-five hundred years ago, long before anyone dreamed of printing presses, telephones, radio, television, the Internet, or texting, people had lives to live and agendas to advance. Public speaking was the primary mode of communication. Aristotle was a student of Plato, and wrote prolifically on many subjects. He was a keen observer of human behavior and lived in a culture where laws and societal issues were debated and decided orally. It was a society where the most effective orators usually had the most influence, so effective communication was important. Among the many things he wrote about, Aristotle (trans. 1932) identified three types of appeals one might use when sending a message. He called them logos, pathos and ethos.

LOGOS—"LISTEN TO MY MESSAGE BECAUSE IT MAKES SENSE"

First are logical appeals, or **logos**. Presenting a series of arguments supported by evidence can lead an audience to a "logical" conclusion. Some ways to increase the logical appeal of a message are to be well organized, to be sure that any claims that you might make are based on credible evidence, and that the evidence is clearly presented. On a basic level, if a message does not make logical sense, an audience is unlikely to be moved by it. Consistency is also important. If we compose a mostly logical message that includes a few weak or illogical arguments, there is a danger that the weak arguments will cast doubts on the strong arguments and impugn the entire message. The logos you communicate says to whomever is receiving your message, "Accept my message because it makes sense."

logos
Logical appeals.

PATHOS—"LISTEN TO MY MESSAGE BECAUSE OF THE FEELINGS IT EVOKES"

Aristotle also recognized the power of emotional appeals, or **pathos**. While sound logos attempts to influence what message receivers *think*, pathos is concerned with what they *feel*. Statistical data and facts help you to appeal logically, but specific examples and stories allow you to appeal emotionally—to make people receiving your message *feel* something about your topic. Some would suggest that while emotional appeals might be effective for some topics, informative or technical topics should not employ pathos. Although it would be difficult to imagine an effective presentation on a technical topic that used only emotional appeals, the absence of pathos would be of equal concern. Why should an audience care about a topic? How should they feel about the topic? Answering these questions provides an emotional component to go along with the logical one. The pathos in your message says to those receiving it, "Accept my message because of the feelings it evokes." Accepting it feels like the right thing to do, or rejecting it feels like the wrong thing to do.

pathos
Emotional appeals.

ETHOS—"LISTEN TO MY MESSAGE BECAUSE I AM A COMPETENT, TRUSTWORTHY, AND WELL-INTENTIONED PERSON"

The Greek word for the third type of appeal is **ethos**. Today we call that same concept "credibility." At the most basic level, credibility (ethos) can be defined as a receiver's perception of a sender's competence, trustworthiness, and goodwill (McCroskey & Teven, 1999). That definition seems simple enough, but let's unpack it. Notice that it is the receiver's *perception*, not reality, that determines ethos. As a message sender, your credibility is based on how competent, trustworthy, and well-intentioned those receiving your message think you are, not on how competent, trustworthy, and well-intentioned

ethos
The receiver's perception of a sender's competence and trustworthiness; credibility.

Being well-prepared, organized, and appropriately dressed for your presentation will increase your audience's perception of your competence.

© Jack Hollingsworth/Getty Images

you actually are. The receivers assign credibility. If you really are competent, but your receivers don't perceive you to be competent, they will not assign you high credibility. In a like manner, if you really are trustworthy, but your receivers don't perceive you to be trustworthy, they will not assign you high credibility. Goodwill has to do with your receivers' perception of your intentions toward them. Do they feel you have their best interests in mind? Or do they perceive you as self-serving, or someone who just doesn't care one way or the other about them? To be a truly credible communicator, your audience must perceive you as competent, trustworthy, and well-intentioned.

How can you maximize your credibility? In the case of competence, if you have expertise, let people know about it. Let's assume you were making a presentation about computer animation software and you have been involved with computer animation since you were 13 years old. You have already taken several courses in animation and spent one summer interning for an animation company. If your audience knows about your experience, they will undoubtedly see you as more competent than they would if they had no knowledge of your expertise. But they will not know unless you tell them.

Some presenters are reluctant to mention their qualifications or experience for fear of being perceived as boastful. It is, however, quite possible to present your expertise in a humble manner, thus increasing your audience's perception of your competence without coming across as a braggart. "While some kids were busy conquering Dungeons and Dragons, I was glued to my computer, trying to conquer pixels and polygons. The animation bug caught me when I was 13 years old, and since then I have devoted most of my time to learning animation. Here at the University, I have completed several courses in animation and was lucky enough to have spent last summer interning at Acme Animation."

Sometimes you may be speaking about a subject on which you are not an expert. In these cases, you may be able to "borrow" some expertise by citing the qualifications of

Figure 1

Tips for increasing the appeal of your message.

LOGOS

- be well organized
- use credible evidence
- clearly present your evidence
- maintain consistency by using sound arguments

PATHOS

- provide specific examples and stories
- tell your receivers why they should care about your message

ETHOS

- if you have expertise in your topic, describe it to your audience
- clearly cite the qualifications of your sources
- present your message in an honest and trustworthy fashion
- present your message in a prepared, organized manner
- adopt a caring attitude toward those receiving your message

the sources that you consulted in preparing your speech. For example, you might say, "I've been interested in growing my own herbs, but really didn't know very much about it until I read *The Secret Herb Garden* by Virginia Block, head of Harvard University's Herbal Horticulture Department." It's a way of saying, "I am competent to speak about this topic, because I have consulted expert sources."

In addition to their perceptions of your topical expertise, receivers also have perceptions about your competence as a communicator. A speaker's delivery can affect the receivers' perception of that speaker's competence (McCroskey, 2001). Being well-prepared, organized, and appropriately dressed for your presentation will also help increase your audience's perception of your competence.

Perceptions of trustworthiness are a little more difficult to influence. Just saying "I'm really trustworthy" tends to have a hollow ring. Fortunately, most people will assume you are trustworthy unless you give them evidence to the contrary. Once you give them reason to doubt your honesty or reliability, however, it is difficult to regain their confidence. For this reason, effective communicators are careful to present everything in an honest, trustworthy fashion. Many attorneys have won cases by catching opposing witnesses in a lie. Even if the lies had no direct impact on the cases, once it has been established that certain witnesses do not always tell the truth, their trustworthiness is damaged and their testimony is perceived as unreliable.

The perception of goodwill occurs when your audience feels that you care about them, that you have their best interests at heart, and that you are concerned with them. If you are making a presentation at work and you are ill-prepared or use visual aids that are crudely produced, these factors may send a message that you just don't care that much about your audience. Presenters who value their audiences go to the trouble of being well prepared. Also, a dismissive, flippant, or arrogant attitude (during a presentation or in every day interactions) may say, "I really don't care about you." Thoughtful communicators show their understanding and concern by adopting a caring attitude toward those receiving their messages.

If you can tell people about your competence, avoid giving them any reason to doubt your trustworthiness, and demonstrate that you have their best interests at heart, you maximize the possibility they will perceive you as credible. The ethos in your presentation says to your audience, "Accept my message because I am a competent, trustworthy, and well-intentioned person."

Over the years, there has been some disagreement over which type of appeal is most effective in different situations. Since no clear answers have emerged, perhaps the most practical advice is to utilize logos, pathos, and ethos in every situation. When making a formal presentation, keep your logic sound by making a series of clearly stated claims and by avoiding logical fallacies. Include credible statistics and other data to support those claims. Provide specific examples and stories to help your audience feel something about your topic. Be sure your audience knows about your personal expertise, and avoid giving them any reason to doubt your honesty. When communicating in a more informal setting, work on being clear and logical, and help those receiving your message to feel something about what you are saying. Know what you are talking about, be honest and trustworthy, and care about those with whom you interact—and allow that caring to show. Appeal to people with logic, emotion, and credibility—logos, pathos, *and* ethos.

The SMCRE Factors

In an effort to study the complex process of communication, scholars have found it helpful to categorize or group the many factors involved. One grouping is the SMCRE model, which identifies five groups of communication variables: Source, Message,

Channel, Receiver, and Environment. Although these categories can be applied to any communication situation, let's consider the context of public speaking as our example.

In a public speaking situation, the **source** is the speaker (including the speaker's perceptions), the **message** is the speaker's intended message (as opposed to any other, incidental messages that might become part of the transaction), the **channels** are sound and sight (in-person and in real time), the **receivers** are the audience (and their perceptions), and the **environment** is the situation or context in which the transaction takes place. It may be helpful to remember that these are variables we would see if we could "freeze frame" the communication process and study it in only one direction. In reality, the process of communication is transactional, meaning we "are engaged in sending (encoding) and receiving (decoding) messages simultaneously" (Wenberg & Wilmot, 1974, p. 5). So the SMCRE model is less helpful for understanding *how* the process of communication works, but it is very useful when studying what elements, or variables, make up the process of human communication. Below are brief descriptions of each category and some examples of variables that fit into each group. Bear in mind that the examples given are just a sampling. If we attempted to present an exhaustive list, there would be scores of variables for each category.

source
The person initiating the communication.

message
The message the speaker *intends* to send.

channel
The means through which the message is sent.

receivers
The audience to whom the message is delivered.

environment
The situation or context in which the transaction takes place.

SOURCE VARIABLES

The source is the person who initiates the communication transaction. In the case of speeches, it is the speaker. This model suggests that the overall effectiveness of the communication will be influenced by source factors such as age, gender, intelligence, education, attractiveness, personality, and voice quality as well as perceptual items such as attitudes, prejudices, and values. Furthermore, how these variables affect the process will depend on the situation. Take age, for example. Being a senior citizen may be a positive factor when making a presentation about the impact of the Korean War and a negative factor when making a presentation about which video gaming platform is best. Aristotle believed that arguments should be accepted (or rejected) solely on their own merits, but he recognized that "external matters do count for much, because of the sorry nature of an audience" (Aristotle, trans. 1932, 3, 1, 1404a). Some twenty-three hundred years later, his observation is still accurate—audiences can still be swayed by external matters. Aronson and Mills (1965) presented identical messages attributed to either physically attractive or physically unattractive sources. The audience was more persuaded by the message when it came from an attractive source. Since the topic had nothing to do with grooming, fashion, or fitness, the attractiveness of the source should not have made any difference—but it did.

An email is probably not the best channel of communication for a marriage proposal.

MESSAGE VARIABLES

All of the elements in a message can affect the communication process. Some of these variables would include length of message, organizational scheme, use of humor, types of appeals, types of arguments, or use of evidence. Again, the effects would vary with the situation. For example, using humor can often be an effective device, but it might be considered inappropriate and have a negative impact on a speech about world hunger.

CHANNEL VARIABLES

In older versions of this model, the channels were defined by the five senses: sight, sound, touch, taste, and smell. More recently, modalities (live, recorded, teleconferenced, computer-mediated, text-messaged, emailed) within the five senses have also been considered channel variables. Today, we have more choices than ever when it comes to communication channels. Certainly, some are preferable to others in a given situation. An email communication might be an effective way to announce an upcoming business meeting, but probably not the ideal channel for a marriage proposal. Most speeches are face-to-face endeavors featuring sounds and sights, but as businesses increase their use of internet and satellite technology, you may find yourself delivering an up-linked speech to an audience that is scattered across the globe.

RECEIVER VARIABLES

In this model, the receivers are people receiving the message. During a speech, the receivers are the audience. Each member of the audience brings his or her own variables (such as age, gender, cultural background, prior knowledge of topic, listening ability, and mood) and perceptual items (such as attitudes, values, and prejudices). The same topic may require a different approach based on receiver variables. For example, a presentation about the importance of cancer screenings might emphasize screenings for prostate cancer to an audience of men and breast cancer screenings to an audience of women. Effective communicators tailor their messages specifically to the audiences who will be receiving them.

ENVIRONMENT VARIABLES

Communication does not happen in a vacuum: it happens in places. Some places are noisy, some are crowded, some are attractively decorated, some have comfortable chairs, some are too cold, and some are messy. Research has shown that many of these "environmental" factors influence communication. Ask anyone who has tried to make a presentation on a hot, Florida afternoon in a room where the air-conditioning was not working, or tried to have a serious conversation with a close friend while a roommate's music was blasting at party levels—environmental factors make a difference.

WHICH VARIABLES CAN YOU CONTROL?

Although this question has implications for communication in any context, let's stay with our example of public speaking. Of the five groups of variables, which, as a speaker, do you have the most control over? Many would answer "source," since we like to think we have control over ourselves. While that may be partially true, there are a lot of source variables, like age, gender, height, ethnicity, and race, over which we have no control. Consider the source variable, attractiveness. Yes, we can spruce ourselves up a little, and even wear clothing that is appropriate to the rhetorical situation, but much of what others find attractive or unattractive in us is out of our control.

In real-world situations, we are usually assigned the channel through which we are to communicate. Occasionally your boss may say, "How do you think we can best get the message across?" but, more often, she'll say, "I'm sending you to Toledo to give a presentation to the sales force."

Our environments are usually assigned as well. Once we get there, we may be able to adjust the thermostat or the lighting, or re-arrange the chairs, but at best we have only partial control over our environment.

The variables over which we have the least control are the receiver variables. Speakers rarely have the opportunity to choose audience members with certain characteristics. An exception might be during political campaigns, when a candidate may speak to an audience made up entirely of loyal constituents who were handpicked by the politician's staff. This scenario, however, is the exception, not the rule. Most speakers speak to an audience they did not choose.

The variables over which we have the most control are the message variables. Sometimes speakers are assigned a topic, but rarely are the elements of the message prescribed. The message is the invention of the speaker. The speaker generally gets to choose what to include, what to leave out, how to order the information, what evidence to provide, and what words to use. This is true in non-public speaking contexts as well. Whether speaking, writing, emailing, or texting, the sender controls the message.

So, there are many, many variables affecting the process of communication, but, as message senders, we have little control over any except those that make up the message. If communicating effectively is important to us (and it is), can we focus more attention on our message and less on all of those other things we cannot control? How can we influence those receiving our message to pay more attention to our arguments and our evidence and less attention to our looks, the temperature of the room, or the fact that they are tired from partying last night? Another communication theory provides a possible answer to these questions.

The Elaboration Likelihood Model (ELM)

The Elaboration Likelihood Model is one of the most thoroughly researched communication theories. First described by Richard Petty and John Cacioppo (1986), the ELM is a comprehensive theory of persuasion. What is described here is a just a portion of the model, but it is a portion that has particular relevance to everyday communicating, including public speaking. The Persuasive Communication chapter will cover the ELM in greater depth and examine how to apply the theory to persuasive presentations. For now, let's examine aspects of the ELM that generalize to almost any communication situation.

CENTRAL ROUTE OR PERIPHERAL CUES?

elaboration
The degree to which a receiver scrutinizes a message.

central route processing
Receivers mentally elaborate on the elements of your message and carefully scrutinize your arguments and evidence.

peripheral route processing
Receivers give brief attention to the message without elaborated thought.

ELM researchers found that receivers expend a lot of mental energy processing some messages but very little energy processing others. More specifically, receivers sometimes mentally elaborate on elements of the message, scrutinizing the arguments and evidence, and at other times receivers give the message only cursory attention, often basing their decision to agree or disagree with the message on peripheral factors such as source attractiveness or the temperature of the room (Anderson & Pryor, 1992). Petty & Cacioppo (1986) termed the effortful scrutinizing of the message **central route processing,** and the casual, more cursory message reception **peripheral route processing.**

Their observation begs the question: "Why do receivers expend the effort to engage in central route processing sometimes, and other times process only peripherally?" Petty and Cacioppo (1986) suggest that people intrinsically want to hold correct attitudes, but don't have the time, inclination, or energy to carefully scrutinize every message they receive. Therefore, they must choose which messages they will process by the more effortful central route. According to their research, when people are *motivated* and *able* to scrutinize a message, they are likely to do so. Alternatively, people who lack either motivation or ability are more likely to be influenced by peripheral cues. The name "Elaboration Likelihood Model" is based on the premise that those who are both motivated and able are more likely to engage in elaborative processing.

ELM research also found that receiver attitudes based on central route processing are more persistent, more predictive of behavior, and more resistant to counter-persuasion (Petty & Cacioppo, 1986). So, if you make a speech and your audience changes their attitudes in the direction you advocate based on central route processing, they are more likely to retain those attitudes, more likely to act in accordance with those attitudes, and less likely to be un-persuaded by someone with an opposing view. If we think back to our examination of the SMCRE model, we notice that central route processing is focused primarily on the message variables, and peripheral route processing is focused more on sender, channel, receiver, and environment variables. If our audience is focused primarily on the message, they are basing their attitudes on the variables in the communication process over which we have the most control. If our audience is focused on peripheral cues, they are basing their attitudes on the elements over which we have very little control. All of this suggests that speakers who invent high quality messages have a better chance of being successful communicators if their audiences engage in central route processing.

MOTIVATION AND ABILITY

What can we, as speakers, do to increase the likelihood that our audience will engage in elaborative (central route) processing? Since we know that receivers are more likely to elaborate if they are motivated and able, the question becomes, "What can we do to maximize our audience's motivation and ability?"

⋅ Why do receivers expend mental energy processing some messages but not others?

© John Lund/Drew Kelly/ Blend Images LLC

Although a number of motivational factors have been studied, the factor most useful to message senders is relevance. If people believe a message is personally important (relevant) to them, they are more motivated to process that message carefully (Petty & Cacioppo, 1979). Anything that we, as speakers, can do to help our audience see how our message is important to them has the potential to increase their motivation. Aristotle observed that "men pay attention to things of importance, to their own interests, to anything wonderful, to anything pleasant; and hence you must give the impression that your speech has to do with the like" (Aristotle, trans. 1932, 3. 14. 1415b). If we can give that impression, and increase our audience's perceptions of relevance, we can increase their motivation, and thus their likelihood to elaborate. So, we should do what we can to make our messages relevant to our audience.

If you are making a presentation, tell your audience why your message will be important or useful to them. Moreover, tell them early, so the likelihood that they will engage in effortful processing of your entire message will be maximized. Sometimes the relevance of a message is unclear until late in the presentation. In these cases, it is too late for the audience to go back and re-process the message. When you send a message, make sure the answer to the "What's in it for me?" question is clear. If you are talking to your boss about an idea you have to make your job more efficient, help your boss see how it benefits the organization *and* how it benefits the boss. Even with something as simple as an email to a friend, a subject line that indicates why this email is important (as opposed to all of the others your friend receives that turn out to be unimportant) can help get your message read. To maximize your audience's motivation to process your message, make the case for relevance, and make it early.

Ability is the other variable that determines a receiver's likelihood to elaborate. But ability is a receiver variable and there is little we can do to change our audience's ability to process a message. We can, however, avoid doing things that might diminish their ability to process our messages. For example, when our messages include a lot of jargon that receivers are unfamiliar with, we will lessen their ability to process the message. If a message is spoken in Russian, only those who understand Russian will be able to process the message. Jargon can be a foreign language to the audience who is unfamiliar with it, and its overuse can interfere with their ability to process the message.

Another impediment to message processing is the inclusion of too many behaviors that distract from your message. In a written message, misspellings and grammatical errors can distract your audience and interfere with their message processing ability. In an oral presentation, including an occasional "ah" or "um" will probably not diminish your overall effectiveness. Sometimes, however, speakers include so many "ah's" and "um's" that audience attention is drawn away from the message. When this happens, the audience's ability to process the message in diminished. So, while we cannot increase our audience's innate ability to process our message, we can maximize that ability by *not* doing things that interfere with their ability.

In summary, those receiving your message are more likely to focus on your message (instead of peripheral cues) if they are motivated and able. Perceiving the relevance of your message can increase motivation, and eliminating interfering elements (jargon, technical references, distracting behaviors, etc.) can maximize their ability. Once engaged in the central route, your audience will be more influenced by the message that you invented, and less influenced by peripheral items over which you have no control.

Before leaving the ELM, three items need to be clarified. First, be reminded that this discussion has covered only a portion of the Elaboration Likelihood Model. There is much more to the model, but in this chapter we have covered only the basics to emphasize the importance of making your messages relevant and accessible.

Second, although the "route" metaphor suggests a receiver either takes one route or the other—that is, relies on central message processing or peripheral cues—the ELM is *not* an either/or model. Motivation and ability will cause the effect of peripheral cues to be diminished, but not eliminated. Under conditions of high elaboration likelihood, non-message factors will still be a part of the process, but they will be less influential than the message factors.

Third, having your audience focused on your message does not mean they will necessarily accept your message. Increased scrutiny will favor strong messages and expose weak messages (Petty & Cacioppo, 1984). If those receiving your message are following the central route, they may accept *or* reject your message, but they will do so based primarily on the message itself, not on peripheral cues. So, to increase the likelihood for successful communication, make your message relevant, avoid doing anything to impair your audience's ability, and create a strong, logically sound message.

Interpersonal communication
The process of using messages to generate meaning between at least two people in a situation that allows mutual opportunities for both speaking and listening.

Communication Contexts

Before we conclude this introduction to the study of communication, we should be aware of the various contexts in which communication takes place. In our discussion of the SMCRE model, we included communication environments, the physical places where senders and receivers exchange messages. When we speak of a communication *context*, however, we are looking at a broader concept. Let's take a brief look at some examples of communication contexts.

INTERPERSONAL COMMUNICATION

Some of the most important communication in our lives takes place between just two people. The messages exchanged between parent and child, husband and wife, brother and sister, or just between friends are all examples of **interpersonal communication**. Many scholars see interpersonal communication as

An interesting thing about communication theories is that there are often multiple theories at work simultaneously. For example, typing "**URGENT**" in the subject lines of emails that really aren't urgent may increase receivers' motivation to read your emails at first, but when they find out your claims of urgency are overstated, they may begin to doubt your trustworthiness, and that might motivate them to ignore your messages in the future. In this example, ethics, ethos, and the ELM are all happening at the same time, but they are not at odds with one another; a clear, truthful subject line can increase motivation without damaging your credibility.

a face-to-face transaction, but others argue that some mediated-by-technology exchanges can be considered interpersonal (Trenholm & Jensen, 2008). Interpersonal communication is the way we establish and maintain relationships and also the way we disengage from relationships. It is often the way we get into conflicts with others, and also the way we resolve (or don't resolve) those conflicts. Interpersonal communication is a big part of our establishing our own identities, of figuring out who we are and how we fit into the world around us. And once we figure out our personal concept of *self,* interpersonal communication is how we present our *self*, disclose our *self*, and defend our *self* (Canary, Cody, & Manusov, 2008).

· Some of the most important communication in our lives takes place between just two people.

The study of interpersonal communication includes topics like defining and communicating one's self, communicating verbally and non-verbally, listening, communicating in relationships, maintaining relationships, achieving intimacy and empathy, and managing interpersonal conflicts. The informal, unique, irreplaceable nature of interpersonal communication is characterized by the interdependence of the people involved and by their willingness to disclose to one another (Adler & Proctor, 2007). It is what makes interpersonal communication rewarding, and essential.

SMALL GROUP COMMUNICATION

When three or more individuals are interdependent, share goals, identify with one another, and interact, they are involved in **small group communication** (Keyton, 2006). Because small groups have communication dynamics that differ from other communication contexts, small group communication has become its own area of study. How do small groups make decisions? Solve problems? Assimilate new members? Achieve mutual goals? These are just some of the questions that the study of small group communication investigates.

small group communication
Communication that takes place among three or more individuals who are interdependent, share goals, identify with one another and interact.

organizational communication
The communication that is necessary to form and maintain an organization.

ORGANIZATIONAL COMMUNICATION

We can accomplish a lot as individuals, or in small groups, but we can accomplish much more when we join forces with many others and organize our efforts. The communication that is necessary to form and maintain an organization is the focus of the study of **organizational communication**. When individuals have a great idea, whether it is to produce a product or service, or to provide a non-profit service to society, how do they bring it to fruition? They organize. Organizations are established for some creative enterprise, but the very act of organizing constrains the creativity that the organizations intend to pursue. Balancing the competing interests of being creative and being organized is the mission of organizational communication (Eisenberg & Goodall, 2004). Over the years, different management theories have changed the way organizations operate, and those changes manifest themselves in the ways that organizations communicate. There are classical approaches, human relations approaches, human resources approaches, systems approaches, and cultural approaches to managing organizations; each affects the way an organization

· The study of small group communication investigates how groups of three or more work together to successfully accomplish their goals.

communicates. The study of organizational communication also includes the communication of leadership, the communication of assimilation, and the role communication plays in conflict resolution (Miller, 2006).

In today's world, managing an organization is increasingly difficult. Communication plays a key role in how organizations survive and thrive—or fail. It has been said that communication is the glue that holds organizations together. Today, more than ever, that glue needs to be strong. In today's world, managing an organization is increasingly difficult. Communication plays a key role in how organizations survive and thrive—or fail. It has been said that communication is the glue that holds organizations together. Today, more than ever, that glue needs to be strong.

PUBLIC SPEAKING

public speaking
The process of using messages to generate meanings in a situation in which a single source transmits a message to a number of receivers.

In spite of all of the technological advances we enjoy, and the plethora of communication modes from which we can choose, one of the oldest communication contexts remains one of the most important: **public speaking**. The ability to stand in front of a group of people and speak effectively has distinguished America's leaders from Lincoln and Roosevelt to Kennedy, Reagan, and Obama. And although many of us will not be called upon to communicate with the entire nation, there will be opportunities for each of us to speak publicly at work and in our communities. Effective oral communication consistently ranks among the top five skills employers look for in the people they hire (e.g., Hymowitz, 1990). You'll notice that several chapters in this book are devoted to public speaking—it's that important.

MASS-MEDIA COMMUNICATION

mass-media communication
The process of using messages to generate meaning in a mediated system, between a source and a large number of unseen receivers.

In Aristotle's time, the size of one's audience was limited by the number of people who could fit into the venue and the distance a speaker's voice could carry. Over the years, however, technology has made it possible to reach increasingly larger audiences. First, it was newspapers and magazines, then radio, and later television, and now we have the internet with its constantly changing modalities. All of these have made it possible for messages to be sent to millions of people simultaneously.

journalism
The communication of news, information about events in our communities, our nation, and our world; and commentary.

Journalism, with its roots in newspapers and magazines, deals with the communication of news, information about events happening in our communities, our nation, and our world, and commentary—the explication of what those events mean. Today, radio and television, the internet, and even cell phones join the traditional print media as outlets for journalism. The technology may change, but knowing and understanding what is happening around us continues to be integral to our personal lives, our communities, and our society as a whole.

Interpersonal, small group, organizational, public, and mass-media are the basic contexts for the study of communication, but some more specialized contexts have also emerged. Let's look at two of those specialized communication contexts.

HEALTH COMMUNICATION

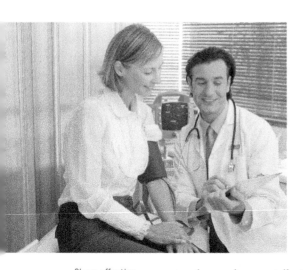

Clear, effective communication in health care is essential.

© Chris Ryan/age fotostock

Advances in medicine have given us health and treatment options that our grandparents could not have dreamed of, but these same advances have also contributed to a much more complicated (and expensive) health-care system. With that complication comes the need for clearer, more effective communication between patients and heath-care providers, and among health-care professionals. Because this type of communication has unique demands and serious consequences, health communication has become a communication context of its own. Scholars are researching health communication issues and universities are beginning to offer courses in health communication.

FAMILY COMMUNICATION

The complicated world we now live in has also taken its toll on families. The issues facing families today are more difficult that those that faced families a few decades ago. The traditional, nuclear family with one parent as bread-winner and the other as caretaker has been supplanted by two-income families, one-parent families, and an infinite variety of blended families. More than ever before, effective communication within the family is crucial. In recent years, scholars have begun to research and better understand the unique dynamics of communication within the context of the family.

Communication is a complex, pervasive process. Studying communication according to the context in which it occurs is just one way that we can better understand that process, and one more way that we can become more effective communicators.

The Ethics of Communicating

Early in this chapter, we talked about the process of communication being amoral (ethically neutral), and that the morality—or ethics—of communication comes not from the process, but rather from the *people* involved in that process. So what does it mean to communicate ethically? The National Communication Association's (NCA) "Credo for Ethical Communication" offers several principles to guide us in answering that question:

> Questions of right and wrong arise whenever people communicate. Ethical communication is fundamental to responsible thinking, decision making, and the development of relationships and communities within and across contexts, cultures, channels, and media. Moreover, ethical communication enhances human worth and dignity by fostering truthfulness, fairness, responsibility, personal integrity, and respect for self and others. We believe that unethical communication threatens the quality of all communication and consequently the well-being of individuals and the society in which we live. Therefore we, the members of the National Communication Association, endorse and are committed to practicing the following principles of ethical communication:

- We advocate truthfulness, accuracy, honesty, and reason as essential to the integrity of communication.
- We endorse freedom of expression, diversity of perspective, and tolerance of dissent to achieve the informed and responsible decision making fundamental to a civil society.
- We strive to understand and respect other communicators before evaluating and responding to their messages.
- We promote access to communication resources and opportunities as necessary to fulfill human potential and contribute to the well-being of families, communities, and society.
- We promote communication climates of caring and mutual understanding that respect the unique needs and characteristics of individual communicators.
- We condemn communication that degrades individuals and humanity through distortion, intimidation, coercion, and violence, and through the expression of intolerance and hatred.
- We are committed to the courageous expression of personal convictions in pursuit of fairness and justice.

- We advocate sharing information, opinions, and feelings when facing significant choices while also respecting privacy and confidentiality.
- We accept responsibility for the short- and long-term consequences of our own communication and expect the same of others.

Does your communication measure up to the standards set forth in the NCA Credo? How would your life be different if those with whom you regularly interact lived up to the standards set forth above? How would your life be different if *you* always lived up to those standards? The process is neutral. The rest is up to us.

What Have We Learned?

Although this chapter does not pretend to offer a complete overview of communication theory, we have tried to bring together a number of theoretical elements that can be useful in preparing and delivering oral presentations. We have seen the important and pervasive role communication plays in our lives. We have learned from Aristotle that our message might appeal to receivers' sense of logic, to their emotions, or to their willingness to accept a competent, trustworthy, and benevolent source. Rather than choosing among these three strategies, look for ways to utilize all three in your presentations. The SMCRE model reminds us that there are many factors that affect our attempts to communicate, but we have very little control over factors outside of the message itself. The Elaboration Likelihood Model helps explain why receivers sometimes focus on our message and sometimes focus on peripheral factors. Our discussion of the ELM also suggests some ways we might increase the likelihood of keeping our audience message-centered.

We introduced some of the contexts in which communication occurs, and we discovered that each type of communication—whether it takes place on the interpersonal level, in small groups, in organizations, in a public forum, or via one of the mass media—has its own unique opportunities and challenges. We also introduced the more specialized contexts of health communication and family communication.

Finally, we looked at the "NCA Credo for Ethical Communication" as a guide to communicating honestly and respectfully.

It has been said that nothing is more practical than a good theory. As you continue communicating in college and later in your careers, you should find many practical applications for the theories introduced in this chapter.

Chapter Review & Study Guide

Summary

In this chapter you learned the following:

1. Human communication is difficult to define but has characteristics that can be identified.
2. Among those characteristics are the following:
   - Communication is pervasive
   - Communication is amoral
   - Communication is how we advance our life-agenda
3. Aristotle suggested three ways message senders appeal to their audiences:
   - Logos—logical appeals
   - Pathos—emotional appeals
   - Ethos—source credibility, including
     - Competence
     - Trustworthiness
     - Goodwill
4. The SMCRE model defines five categories of communication variables:
   - Source variables
   - Message variables

- Channel variables
- Receiver variables
- Environment variables

5. As senders of messages, we generally have the most control over message variables.

6. The Elaboration Likelihood Model (ELM) offers insight into why receivers sometimes expend mental effort scrutinizing an incoming message, and why they process messages only superficially at other times.

7. The ELM identifies two types of message processing:
   - Central route—effortful, elaborative processing
   - Peripheral route—superficial processing

8. Two factors determine a receiver's likelihood to engage in elaborative, central route processing:
   - Motivation
   - Ability

9. Although the term "route" suggests an either-or relationship between the two types of processing, there is actually a continuum from wholly central to wholly peripheral processing.

10. Although the term "route" suggests an either-or relationship between the two types of processing, there is actually a continuum from wholly central to wholly peripheral processing.

11. When engaged in central route processing, receivers are focused on the message, and thus notice both strengths and weaknesses in the message.

12. Communication also occurs in various contexts. Communication contexts are studied because each presents unique opportunities and challenges. We introduced the following communication contexts:
   - Interpersonal communication
   - Small group communication
   - Organizational communication
   - Public communication
   - Mass communication
   - Health communication
   - Family communication

Key Terms

amoral	health communication	pathos
central route	interpersonal communication	peripheral route
channel	journalism	pervasiveness
communication context	logos	public communication
elaboration	mass communication	small group communication
Elaboration Likelihood Model	message	SMCRE
environment	motivation	source
ethos	organizational communication	transactional
family communication		

Study Questions

1. When we say communication is amoral, we mean
   a. There is no morality in communication
   b. Communication itself is ethically neutral
   c. Communication is everywhere
   d. Ethical communication is impossible to achieve

2. Logos could best be described by which of the following statements?
   a. Listen to my message because of the feelings it evokes
   b. Listen to my message because it will advance your life-agenda
   c. Listen to my message because it makes sense
   d. Listen to my message because I am a competent, trustworthy and well-intentioned person

3. By describing your topic expertise to your audience and citing the qualifications of the sources you use, you are using which of Aristotle's appeals?
   a. Logical   c. Pathos
   b. Ethos   d. Logos

4. We generally have the most control over which variable?
   a. Ourselves c. The environment
   b. The receivers d. The message

5. An audience is more likely to elaborate on your message if they are
   a. Motivated and able
   b. Paying attention to your appearance
   c. Comfortable and have a good attitude
   d. Neutral toward your message

6. Which of the following might diminish receivers' ability to process a message?

   a. Excessive use of logical appeals
   b. Interfering elements like jargon, technical references and distracting behaviors
   c. Using strictly central route processing
   d. Strong messages

7. Communication that takes place between two people is called

   a. Public speaking
   b. Organizational communication
   c. Interpersonal communication
   d. Family communication

8. Balancing the competing interests of being creative and being organized is the mission of

   a. Journalism
   b. Family communication

   c. Interpersonal communication
   d. Organizational communication

9. Which of the following ranks among the top five skills employers look for in the people they hire?

   a. Effective oral communication skills
   b. Central route processing skills
   c. The ability to use logical appeals
   d. The ability to defend our self concept

10. When three or more people are interdependent, share goals, identify with one another and interact they are involved in

    a. Mass communication
    b. Small group communication
    c. Central route communication
    d. Interpersonal communication

Answers:
1. (b); 2. (c); 3. (b); 4. (d); 5. (a); 6. (b); 7. (c); 8. (d); 9. (a); 10. (b)

Critical Thinking

1. Think about the last time you didn't hear back from someone when you thought you should. How did you react? What meaning did you assign to that lack of communication? What, if anything, did you do to resolve the situation?

2. Think about a recent presentation you heard in class. What did the presenter do or not do to enhance your ability and motivation to process the message?

Sizing Things Up Scoring and Interpretation

Evaluate Your Own Communication Skills

This chapter introduces the concept of communication competence. The survey you completed measures your competence. Each question in the survey asks you to indicate how effectively you can communicate within a particular context of communication (e.g., friendships or digitally mediated communication); some questions also target specific purposes for communicating (e.g., resolving conflict). You can use this scale either as a global Communication Competence Scale, in which case you should average together your answers for all questions to achieve an overall score, or as a way of analyzing particular communication contexts or processes. This latter approach would involve analyzing your responses to each statement. If your overall average or response to any individual question is below 3, you may be lower in self-perceived communication competence. A score near 3 is average, and a score higher than 3 suggests that you perceive yourself higher in communication competence.

References

1. Adler, R. B., & Proctor, R. F. (2007). *Looking out/Looking in* (12th ed.). Belmont, CA: Thomson.

2. Anderson, S., and Pryor, B. (1992). *Speech fundamentals: A contemporary approach*. Needham Heights, MA: Ginn.

3. Aristotle (trans. 1932). *The rhetoric of Aristotle* (L. Cooper, Trans.). New York: Appleton-Century-Crofts.

4. Canary, D. J., Cody, M. J., & Manusov, V. L. (2008). *Interpersonal communication: A goals-based approach*. Boston, MA: Bedford/St. Martin's.

5. Eisenberg, E. M., & Goodall, H. L., Jr. (2004). *Organizational communication: Balancing creativity and constraint*. Boston, MA: Bedford/St. Martin's.

6. Gurak, L. (2000). *Oral presentations for technical communication*. Needham Heights, MA: Allyn & Bacon.

7. Hymowitz, C. (1990, March 1). Managing. *Wall Street Journal* (Eastern Edition), p. B1. Retrieved March 29, 2009, from ABI/ INFORM Global database. (Document ID: 27584855).

8. Keyton, J. (2006). *Communicating in groups* (3rd ed.). New York: Oxford.

9. McCroskey, J. C. (2001). *An introduction to rhetorical communication* (8th ed.). Boston: Allyn and Bacon.

10. McCroskey, J. C., & Teven, J. J. (1999). Goodwill: A reexamination of the construct and its measurement. *Communication Monographs, 66*, 90–103.

11. Miller, K., (2006). *Organizational communication: Approaches and processes* (4th ed.). Belmont, CA: Thomson.

12. Mills, J., and Aronson, E. (1965). "Opinion change as a function of the communicator's attractiveness and desire to influence." *Journal of Personalityand Social Psychology, 1*, 173–177.

13. Petty, R., and Cacioppo, J. (1979). Issue involvement can increase or decrease persuasion by enhancing message-relevant cognitive responses. *Journal of Personality and Social Psychology, 37*, 1915–1926.

14. Petty, R., and Cacioppo, J. (1984). The effects of involvement on responses to argument quantity and quality: Central and peripheral routes to persuasion. *Journal of Personalityand Social Psychology, 46*, 69–81.

15. Petty, R., and Cacioppo, J. (1986). *Communication and persuasion: Central and peripheral routes to persuasion and attitude change*. New York: Springer Verlag.

16. Trenholm, S., & Jensen, A. (2008). *Interpersonal communication* (6th ed.). New York: Oxford.

17. Wenberg, J., & Wilmot W. (1973). *The personal communication process*. New York: Wiley.

chapter 2

© Frank Gaglione/Digital Vision/Getty Images RF

perception, self, and communication

When you have read and thought about this chapter, you will be able to

1. Describe what perception is.

2. Identify factors in the perceptual process.

3. Explain some of the reasons why people can perceive things differently.

4. Describe how selection, organization, and interpretation occur during perception and how they affect the way you communicate with others.

5. Differentiate among figure and ground, proximity, closure, and similarity in communication examples.

6. Identify errors you might make when you perceive others that affect your communication with them.

7. Recognize how the choices you make about whom you communicate with and how you communicate with them are influenced by your view of yourself.

8. Define identity management and describe how it influences your perception of self and others.

This chapter introduces you to the role of perception and the role of the self in communication. The chapter explains what perception is, the factors involved in making perceptions, how errors in perceptions occur and how you can check your perceptions, and why differences in perception occur. Next we explore our perceptions of others and the role of the self in communication.

How do perceptions affect communication? Kim was waiting for her instructor to arrive on the first day of her Spanish class. She was a transfer student so she did not know any of the other students yet. It was an 8 a.m. class and her classmates were clearly excited but tired. Kim didn't know anything about her instructor except for the name Justice. She thought the instructor would be a tall Latin male and was surprised when a short, Caucasian woman entered the room and said, "Hola, clase. Soy su profesora."

© Vincenzo Lombardo/Getty Images RF

Think back to the first day of this class. What had you heard, if anything, about this class? What had you heard through word of mouth, if anything, about the instructor? Did you look on websites like RateMyProfessor.com or YikYak to see what people were saying?

How did what you read on these websites or heard from word of mouth inform your feelings on the first day of class? What has changed or reinforced your perceptions since that first day of class? The way we see others and how others see us affects our communication. That is why this chapter focuses on the role of perception in communication.

Defining Perception

In this chapter we focus on perception, the self, and communication. Differences in perception affect the way we understand ourselves, situations, stories, events, and others. Consequently, perception affects the way we view ourselves and the way we present ourselves. In turn, perception acts like a filter that influences our experiences, our assessment of others, and our communication with them. The way you sense the world—the way you see, hear, smell, touch, and taste—is subjective, uniquely your own. Nobody else sees the world the way you do, and nobody experiences events exactly as you do.

The uniqueness of human experience is based largely on differences in **perception**—using the senses to process information about the external environment. Since our perceptions are unique, communication between and among people offers opportunities and challenges.

Contemporary approaches view perception as an active process. **Active perception** means that your mind selects, organizes, and interprets what you sense. Another way to think about this is to think about the last time you and your friends took pictures with your mobile devices. Perhaps you uploaded your picture to Instagram and changed the hues and colors and one of your friends used the fade-out setting to draw attention to a particular part of the image. Much like in this example, each person's perceptional lens is different; each person sees different colors; and each person picks up different sounds. Perception is subjective because you interpret what you sense; you make it your own, and you add to and subtract from what you see, hear, smell, and touch based on your lived experiences or lack thereof. **Subjective perception** is your uniquely constructed meaning attributed to sensed stimuli.

Consider how much your inner state affects your perceptions. If you have a bad headache, the pain probably will affect the way you treat your children, the way you respond

perception
The process of using the senses to acquire information about the surrounding environment or situation.

active perception
Perception in which your mind selects, organizes, and interprets that which you sense.

subjective perception
Your uniquely constructed meaning attributed to sensed stimuli.

to your co-workers, and even the way you see yourself in the mirror. Perhaps your general resting facial expression usually looks happy, but if you have an "off" day and are not smiling as much as usual, people may ask you repeatedly if you are okay. This might be frustrating to emotionally manage, especially if you are feeling fine. In contrast, some people have facial expressions that can be perceived as "grumpy" or "mean" when in fact that is not the case at all. For example, some might say that San Antonio Spurs head Coach Gregg Popovich always looks like he is in a bad mood or that music mogul Jay-Z looks unhappy. Both men have expressed during interviews that they sometimes don't like the media attention, so this may account for their facial expressions. Yet this doesn't mean that they are upset or mean people. Do you know anyone who frequently gets asked if he or she is "okay" just because of how people perceive that person's facial expressions? How have you reacted when people have misread your facial expressions?

Consider also how complicated communication becomes when you know that everyone has his or her own view, uniquely developed and varying according to what is happening both outside and inside the mind. Perception is a factor that increases the complexity of communication.

How do you see the world around you? Perhaps comparing the way your mind works to the way a computer works will help you answer this. Think of your conscious experiences as the images that appear on your iPad or tablet. Think of what you sense with your eyes, nose, tongue, ears, and fingertips as that which is read off your thumb drive. The picture you see on the screen is not the same as the bits on the disk; instead, an image is generated from the bits to create something you can see. "What we perceive in the world around us is not a direct and faithful representation of that world itself, but rather a 'computer enhanced' version based upon very limited data from that world," according to Wright.[1]

Differences in Perception

Perception is a subjective, an active, and a creative process. Differences in perception may be the result of identity factors, people's past experiences and roles, and their present feelings and circumstances.

IDENTITY FACTORS

You are not identical to anyone else. People differ from each other in biological sex, gender, height, weight, body type, senses, ableness, and ethnicity, to name a few factors that make up an individual's identity. How important these aspects of your identity are to you can influence how you perceive and communicate with others. You may be tall or short, have poor eyesight, or have impaired hearing; you may be particularly sensitive to smells; or your body temperature may be colder than those of the rest of your family. Similarly, age, hair color, height, and attractiveness greatly affect the way you feel about yourself and the way others treat you.

Biological sex is another identity factor that may lead to perceptual differences. One student explained the problem like this: "I am a younger white female. I do believe that because I am younger, white, and a female people tend to talk to me as though I am not capable of doing certain tasks. When older gentlemen or even older ladies speak to me, I do think they talk down to me because I do look younger, and to them I am just a young college student."[2]

gender identity
How you feel about and express your gender.

Gender identity is another factor that can influence perceptions. Gender identity relates to how you feel about and express your gender. Expressions of gender identity can occur through how we talk, act, and dress, which can challenge societal perceptions of gender. Yet experts have found no conclusive evidence establishing an anatomical difference between the brain structures of human females and males.

TEMPORAL CONDITIONS

Differences in perception also may arise from temporary conditions. A headache, fatigue, or a pulled muscle can cause you to perceive a critical comment when a friendly one is being offered. You may not see a stop sign if you are walking while texting or tweeting. Other physiological needs, such as hunger and thirst, may also affect your perceptive skills. Once you are aware of all the conditions that can affect your perceptions, you might be amazed that we can communicate with each other at all.

PAST EXPERIENCES AND ROLES

Just as your size, sex, and senses can affect your perceptions, so can your past experiences and your various roles. The concept that best explains the influence of your past experiences on your perceptions is **perceptual constancy**—the idea that your past experiences lead you to see the world in a way that is difficult to change; your initial perceptions persist. "A perceptual characteristic that affects my communication with others," said a male student, "is that I am very well-mannered. I am an only child, and my parents raised me very strictly to always tr eat others with respect, and put them before yourself. I also attended a Catholic elementary, middle, and high school where the golden rule of 'treat your neighbor as yourself' was always endorsed and upheld."[3] What happened to you in the past influences your current perceptions. A bad experience in a given situation may cause you to avoid that situation in the future. Your experiences affect how you respond to professors, police, and politicians.

Roles also influence perceptions. A **role** is the part you play in various social contexts. Jason observed that being "the boss" was effective at work, but not in his student role. "When I worked as a manager for a retail store, my assertiveness and confidence were viewed in a positive light. Many of my subordinates saw these characteristics [as] typical for a leader in my position. If I treated my fellow classmates with the same level of assertiveness that I did at work, I would come across as 'cocky' or 'full of it,' and my communication would be affected negatively."[4]

Your roles affect your communication: to whom you talk, how you talk to them, what language you use, and how you respond to feedback. A good example of how perceptual constancy and role are related is parents' treatment of their children. Even after some people become adults, their parents treat them as they did when they were growing up. Roles also tend to change with context: in your parents' home you are a son or daughter; in your own home you may be a roommate or a mother or father; in the classroom you are a student; and at work you may be a welder, a fry cook, or a retail associate.

PRESENT FEELINGS AND CIRCUMSTANCES

How you feel at the moment affects your perceptions and alters your communication. Your child kept you up all night, so you are tired and stressed. Your friend's "How are you?" releases a torrent of whiny complaints that are not your usual response. A headache, great news about your mother's health, a brief fight before class—all these life experiences influence with whom and how you communicate.

Now that you know why differences in perception occur, how can you apply this information to your communication skills? Imagine you are talking to a classmate about an assignment during class. She looks away from you, looks at her tablet, and does not respond to your attempts at conversation, but she does ask an occasional question. You might think that she is acting distant and disinterested. Yet she might be trying to listen

perceptual constancy
The idea that your past experiences lead you to see the world in a way that is difficult to change; your initial perceptions persist.

role
The part you play in various social contexts.

Differences in perception that are created by cultural differences can be overcome in our interaction with others.
© ASAP Agency/Science Source

to the instructor or trying to take notes on her tablet and is uncomfortable talking. Or maybe she has had the experience of helping other classmates with their work with no gratitude on their part. It turns out she is confused about the assignment as well and was hoping to ask the instructor to clarify what is due this week for the project. She also is waiting for a text message from her mom to hear if her sister is going to need eye surgery. As you can see, present circumstances and internal states influence your communication with others.

The Perceptual Process

You engage in three separate activities during perception: selection, organization, and interpretation. You are likely unaware of these processes because they occur quickly and all at once. Nonetheless, each plays a discrete role in perception. In turn, our perceptions affect our communication.

SELECTION

No one perceives all the stimuli in his or her environment at all times. Through selection, you neglect some stimuli and focus on others. For example, when you commute to school, you are bombarded with sights, sounds, smells, and other sensations. You don't remember every car you saw on the road, nor do you focus on every person you pass on the sidewalk. Instead, you choose to pay attention to some things while ignoring many others. At school you probably scan students passing by so that you can pick out any friends or classmates who deserve a nod, wave, or other greeting. While awake, you are always actively engaged in selecting which stimuli to which you will respond—or not.

You also select the messages to which you attend. You may tune out one of your teachers while you listen to the hard rainfall outside the classroom window or check your text messages during a break instead of reviewing your class notes. You might not listen to your roommate nagging you about cleaning the kitchen but listen to every word of praise from your boss. You hear and see thousands of ads, retweets on Twitter for Youtube videos, and news stories, but you choose to view only the ones that you find most interesting.

Four types of selectivity are selective exposure, selective attention, selective perception, and selective retention. In **selective exposure** you expose yourself to information that reinforces, rather than contradicts, your beliefs or opinions.[5] Selective exposure explains why you hide, block, or unfriend people on Facebook who have opinions that you don't agree with or want to be exposed to. In other words, conservative Republicans are more likely than liberal Democrats to listen to Rush Limbaugh on the radio, watch Fox News, and read articles in the *National Review*. Liberal Democrats, on the other hand, are more likely to watch Chris Matthews, Rachel Maddow, and John Oliver. Selective exposure has the value of reinforcing and validating our positions and the downside of protecting our biases.

In **selective attention,** even when you do expose yourself to information and ideas, you focus on certain cues and ignore others. On the train, you might notice the new outfit your friend is wearing but not the prosthetic leg the person in the next row is wearing. At a buffet table, you might be drawn to familiar foods while avoiding anything unfamiliar. In an elevator, you may notice the conversation between the two other passengers but not the music that's being piped in overhead.

In communication, you do not treat all sounds, words, phrases, and sentences equally. You almost always respond to your name or a command, such as "Watch out!" If there are certain words or phrases that you find offensive, you might respond negatively to television shows or people using those words. In classes you don't like, you drag through

selective exposure
The tendency to expose yourself to information that reinforces, rather than contradicts, your beliefs or opinions.

selective attention
The tendency, when you expose yourself to information and ideas, to focus on certain cues and ignore others.

the course without learning much at all, whereas in your favorite class you are highly attentive. Selective attention is in full-time operation during your waking hours, and your use of this aspect of perception affects your communication in many ways.

After you expose yourself to a message and pay attention to it, you see that message through your own lens. **Selective perception** is the tendency to see, hear, and believe only what you want to see, hear, and believe.[6] Suppose you are watching your favorite football team and your favorite player gets called out of bounds while diving for the end-zone pylon, rendering a reversal of a called touchdown. Despite the numerous rounds of instant replays, you insist to your roommate that the player was in bounds and the touchdown call should be upheld.

Perception is affected by our choice of which messages to attend to and which to ignore.

© Jupiterimages/Getty Images RF

selective perception
The tendency to see, hear, and believe only what you want to see, hear, and believe.

We see another example of selective perception in the way teachers observe signs of confusion or frustration from students. A study exploring how different types of teachers respond to the unique needs of people who are English language learners (ELLs) found that some are more adept than others at perceiving nonverbal signals of confusion from ELL students.[7] Teachers who tend to use more interaction and dialogue in their classroom are quick to observe nonverbal behaviors signaling a lack of understanding; in contrast, teachers who rely more on lecture tend to miss such signals. These findings illustrate how selective perception, perhaps driven by past experiences and roles, can cause some teachers to selectively perceive and react to such nonverbal signs while others do not. Although these findings point to the need for all teachers to be more observant of students' nonverbal behaviors, they may also suggest that ELL students can be more active in telling teachers when they have difficulty understanding specific terms or ideas.

Finally, you selectively remember some things while selectively forgetting others. **Selective retention** is the tendency to remember better the things that reinforce your beliefs than those that oppose them.[8] Even a loving parent or parental figure may have put you on "time out" now and then, but your dominant impression of that person as positive gets reinforced by your selectively remembering happy family holidays, vacations, and graduation. Often any negative events are suppressed, unless they were unusually traumatic.

selective retention
The tendency to remember better the things that reinforce your beliefs than those that oppose them.

How does selective retention function in your everyday communication? You unexpectedly meet someone at a coffee shop with whom you went to school some years ago. You immediately remember the person—as someone who was mean to you. Do you greet him or head in the other direction without a word? If you do speak, what do you say? Your selective retention of this person's past deeds greatly influences your choice.

You remember traumatic events and experiences that you found exciting or threatening. You remember when someone was unfairly critical of you, when someone of importance praised your work, or when a family member commented favorably about your Instagram post about donating to a charitable cause. You size up people every day. Based on your experience with them—your selective retention—you treat them with respect, talk with them, or avoid them. Such is the power of your selective retention. Next you will learn how organization functions in perceptions and affects communication.

ORGANIZATION

You organize what your senses tell you about your surroundings. **Organization** in perception is the grouping of stimuli into meaningful units or wholes. You organize stimuli in a number of ways, through figure and ground, closure, proximity, and similarity.

organization
The grouping of stimuli into meaningful units or wholes.

Figure and Ground

figure
The focal point of your attention.

ground
The background against which your focused attention occurs.

One organization method is to distinguish between figure and ground. **Figure** is the focal point of your attention, and **ground** is the background against which your focused attention occurs. When looking at figure 1, what do you see first? Some people might perceive a vase or a candlestick, whereas others perceive twins facing each other. People who see a vase identify the center of the drawing as the figure and the area on the right and left as the ground (background). Conversely, people who see twins facing each other identify the center as the ground and the area on the right and left as the figure.

How do figure and ground work in communication encounters? In your verbal and nonverbal exchanges, you perform a similar feat of focusing on some parts (figure) and distancing yourself from others (ground). When you hear your name in a noisy room, your name becomes figure and the remaining noise becomes ground; on a posted list for callbacks for a play, dance, slam poetry, or marching band audition, your name is figure and everyone else's name becomes ground.

Here's another example. During a job performance review your manager may talk about your areas in need of improvement and your strengths, but the so-called areas in need of improvement may make you so angry that you don't even remember the strengths. The messages about needed improvements are figure, and the ones about strengths are ground. Because of who and what you are and because of your unique perceptual processes, your attention focuses and fades, and you choose the figure or ground of what you see, hear, smell, touch, and taste.

Closure

closure
The tendency to fill in missing information in order to complete an otherwise incomplete figure or statement.

Another way of organizing stimuli is through **closure,** the tendency to fill in missing information to complete an otherwise incomplete figure or statement. If someone were to show you figure 2 and ask you what you see, you might say it is a picture of a cat. But as you can see, the figure is incomplete. You see a cat only if you are willing to fill in the blank areas.

Another example of closure happens with text. Can you read these lines?

I cdnuolt blveiee that I cluod aulacity uesdnatnrd waht I was rdanieg.
The phaonmneal pweor of the hmuan mnid! It deson't matter in what oredr the ltteers in a wrod are; the olny iprmoatnt tihng is that the frist and lsat ltteer be in the rghit pclae.[9]

Figure 1 (left)
An example of figure and ground: a vase or twins?

Figure 2 (right)
An example of closure: ink blobs or a cat?

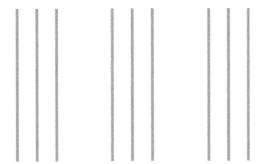

Figure 3

An example of proximity: three groups of lines or nine separate lines?

The reason you can read these words in spite of the crazy spelling is your mind's ability to achieve closure. Closure is the reason why you can make sense of the incorrectly worded text message your friend sends you when the auto-correct feature changes the words without asking for your approval.

Closure functions in your communication interactions. You see two people standing face-to-face and gazing deeply into each other's eyes, and you "fill in" your inference that they are lovers. A public speaker says, "We need to preserve our neighborhoods," and you assume she is against the proposed low-income housing. Visual closure might involve completing the circle or seeing the cat, but mental closure means filling in the meaning of what you hear and observe.

Proximity

You also organize stimuli on the basis of their proximity. According to the principle of **proximity,** people or objects that are close to each other in time or space are seen as meaningfully related. This principle is at work in figure 3. You are most likely to perceive three groups of three lines, rather than nine separate lines.

Proximity works verbally and nonverbally in communication. Nonverbal examples include thinking that anyone wearing a red shirt at Target is the cashier and that the two people arriving at a party or event at the same time are dating. And here is a verbal example: your boss announces that, due to an economic downturn, she is forced to lay off 25 employees. Fifteen minutes later, she calls you into her office. The proximity of the messages leads you to believe that you will be laid off.

Similarity

Similarity is probably one of the simplest means of organizing stimuli. On the basis of the principle of **similarity,** elements are grouped together because they resemble each other in size, color, shape, or other attributes. In figure 4, you probably perceive circles and squares, rather than a group of geometric shapes, because of the principle of similarity. The saying "Birds of a feather flock together" can hold true as well for human groups, who are often organized by ethnicity, religion, politics, or their interest in gaming, golfing, or NASCAR.

The **intergroup perspective** is one theory that guides research on how people identify and categorize themselves or others in terms of their social group membership (e.g., race and ethnicity) and how those categories shape perceptions and the ways people interact with others.[10] Typically, members of an **in-group**—a group that people belong to that gives them a source of pride, self-esteem, and sense of belonging to a social world—engage in activities and hold attitudes that promote a positive image for the in-group compared to the out-group. This theoretical lens also suggests that people want to view their own social groups positively and tend to favor those in their in-group.[11]

proximity
The principle that objects physically close to each other will be perceived as a unit or group.

similarity
The principle that elements are grouped together because they share attributes, such as size, color, or shape.

intergroup perspective
The theory that emphasizes the ways in which people in a social interaction identify and categorize themselves or others in terms of group membership and how these categorizations shape perceptions and interactions with others.

in-group
A group that people belong to that gives them a source of pride, self-esteem, and sense of belonging to a social world.

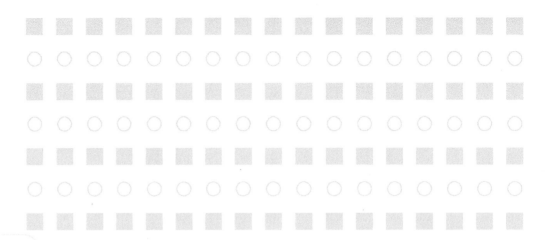

Figure 4

An example of similarity: squares and circles or a group of geometric shapes?

How does similarity work in our relationships and our interactions? Generally, we seek mates, friends, and work partners based on similarity. We choose to interact with those who are similar, on some dimension, to ourselves. Because our perceptions are egocentric, we choose to communicate with people we believe are similar to us. In other words, our friends tend to represent some part of ourselves.[12] We reject, or certainly are less interested in interacting with, people who are highly different from the way we see ourselves. The TV show *The Big Bang Theory* illustrates the concept nicely: Sheldon, Howard, and Raj hang out together because of their high IQs and their interest in physics and engineering. In other words, they perceive each other to be in the same common in-group of scientists, and being part of this group is important to their identities.

To understand the relationship between the organization of stimuli and communication, think about a classroom setting. When you enter the room, your tendency is to organize the stimuli, or people there, into specific groups. Your primary focus is on acquaintances and friends—the *figure*—rather than on the strangers—the *ground*. You talk to friends sitting near the doorway as you enter, due to their *proximity*. You then seat yourself near a group of students you perceive as having interests similar to yours, thus illustrating *similarity*. Finally, you see your instructor arrive with another professor of communication; they are laughing, smiling, and conversing enthusiastically. *Closure* is a result of your assumption that they have a social relationship outside the classroom.

INTERPRETATION

The third activity you engage in during perception is interpretation, the assignment of meaning to stimuli. **Interpretive perception,** then, is a blend of internal states and external stimuli. The more ambiguous the stimuli, the more room for interpretation. The basis for the well-known inkblot test lies in the principle of interpretation of stimuli. Figure 5 shows three inkblots that a psychologist might ask you to interpret. The ambiguity of the figures is typical.

When interpreting stimuli, people frequently rely on the context in which the stimuli are perceived, or they compare the stimuli to other stimuli. Sometimes context helps, but other times it can create confusion in interpretation.

You can become so accustomed to seeing people, places, and situations in a certain way that your senses do not pick up on the obvious. Perhaps this is why we have a false sense of security when we walk and text. We think we won't stumble because we know

the path in front of us so well. In a similar way, people who read the following sentence will overlook the problem with it:

The cop saw the man standing on the the street corner.

We achieve closure on the sentence and interpret its meaning without being conscious of the details, so we overlook the repeated *the*. Context provides cues for how an action, an object, or a situation is to be interpreted or perceived. Not seeing the double *the* in the sentence would be no problem for a reader trying to comprehend meaning, but a proofreader's job would be in jeopardy if such an error were missed often.

How does interpretation work in our interactions with others? Imagine that you are working in a group in one of your classes. One member of the group always comes prepared and seems to dominate the group interaction and to dictate the direction the project is taking. Another member of the group frequently misses agreed-upon group meeting times, arrives late when he does come, and is never prepared. How do you interpret the behavior of these two people?

Suppose you are more like the first group member than the second. You might feel that the first person is challenging your leadership in the group. On the other hand, you consider the enormous contributions she makes by bringing a great deal of research and planning each time. You dismiss the second person as lazy and unmotivated and as a poor student. You are worried that he will bring the group grade down.

Now suppose you are more like the second group member than the first. You miss meetings, arrive late, and do virtually nothing to prepare. You might interpret the first person's behavior as showing off, but, at the same time, you are glad she is going to lead the group to a good grade. You see the second person as laid-back and fun. In fact, you decide you would like to hang out with him. Thus, our own behavior can lead us to make very different interpretations.

Errors in Our Perceptions

Once we understand the active nature of perception and recognize that people hold unique perceptions as a consequence, we

building **behaviors**

First Impressions

Think about the first day of this class. Write down two initial impressions you had about the instructor who is teaching your first class of the week. What were these initial impressions based on? Think about the perceptual process and how your impression was formed as a result of each phase of the process.

can see that we might make errors when we perceive other people. Although many types of errors exist, we discuss only two of the most common errors here, stereotyping and relying on first impressions. Detailed discussions of the many types of errors are beyond the scope of this edition of *Human Communication,* but you may discuss them in class.

STEREOTYPING

stereotyping
Making a hasty generalization about a group based on a judgment about an individual from that group.

Stereotyping occurs when we offer a hasty generalization about a group based on a judgment about an individual from that group. How does stereotyping work? First, we categorize other people into groups based on a variety of criteria—age, sex, gender, race, sexual identity, occupation, nation of origin, region of the country, or physical abilities. Initially, this type of categorization is a natural process that helps people interpret their surroundings. Yet stereotyping becomes an issue when we refuse to let people move from these perceived categories. Next, we infer that everyone within that group has the same characteristics. For instance, we might conclude that all lesbians are masculine, that people on the East Coast are fast-talking, or that older adults don't know how to use social media. The trouble with stereotyping is that we practically insist that our stereotypes are correct through selective attention (we see what we want to see) and selective retention (we selectively sift through our past for memories that reinforce our stereotypes when they may not be accurate or true).

Our expectations and interpretations of the behavior of others are then guided by these perceptions. When we observe people from other groups, we exaggerate, or overestimate, how frequently they engage in the stereotypic behaviors we believe they engage in. We ignore, or underestimate, how frequently they engage in the behaviors that we do not believe they engage in. Although some stereotypes are positive (such as Asians and Indians are brilliant at math, engineering, and science), most are negative and harmful.

Unfortunately, our stereotypes of people from different groups are often negative.[13] Working dads may have negative views of dads who stay at home with their children. White Americans might incorrectly believe that Asian Americans are more qualified for higher education than they are. If you are able-bodied, you might not empathize with someone in a wheelchair. Hughes and Baldwin found that these negative stereotypes created different communication patterns when white and black individuals, for example, interacted. They suggest that "macrolevel interpretations between interracial speakers may be problematic."[14]

Our explanations for the expected and unexpected behaviors of people are frequently in error, as we assume situational reasons for unexpected outcomes and personal reasons for expected outcomes. Stereotypes can also be attributed to age differences. For example, if older generations believe that Millennials are lazy and entitled and if they view young peoples' perceived addiction to technology as having no real value, they may refuse to acknowledge the rebuttals to these negative stereotypes. This can be unfortunate because reports show that Millennials are changing the world in meaningful ways and have charitable goals. In fact, the 2014 Millennial Impact Report found that 94% of Millennials say they enjoy using their skills to benefit socially meaningful causes, 47% volunteer for nonprofit organizations, and 87% report donating money to charities and believe that social networking can spark social change.[15]

Finally, we differentiate ourselves from people whom we stereotype. A woman who has some African American heritage but does not identify with that heritage might view other black people as possessing qualities that are different from her own. A man who has only a little Hispanic background but is proud of this heritage may see people who are not Hispanic as boring and too cautious.

prejudice
An unfavorable predisposition about an individual because of his or her membership in a stereotyped group.

Stereotypes can lead to prejudices. **Prejudice** refers to an unfavorable predisposition about an individual because of his or her membership in a stereotyped group.

Although prejudice can be positive or negative, most often it reflects a harmful or hostile attitude about a person based on his or her membership in a particular social or ethnic group. Throughout history and around the world, people have held negative stereotypes, and they have been prejudiced against others. But such perceptional problems can stand in the way of fruitful communication among people who are different from each other.

Prejudice interferes with our accurate perceptions of others, and it can lead to discrimination. For example, women might not be hired for particular jobs because of prejudice against them. People may be disallowed housing because of their religious beliefs. People may fear others because of their racial or ethnic background. The color of people's skin, the texture of their hair, the shape and size of their facial features, and their clothing are sometimes used to identify an **out-group,** that is, a group marginalized by the dominant culture.

out-group
A group of people excluded from another group with higher status; a group marginalized by the dominant culture

FIRST IMPRESSIONS

When you meet someone for the first time, you seek to form a **first impression**—an initial opinion about people upon meeting them. Frequently, first impressions are based on other people's appearance and may form in as little as 3 seconds.[16] The nonverbal cues they offer are particularly powerful. We notice clothing, height and weight, physical attractiveness, and interaction skills. From these nonverbal cues we make judgments about others. Research suggests that our brains process a great amount of verbal and nonverbal cues when we meet someone, or simply look at their photo on Facebook, and we make fairly accurate first impressions based on this limited information. This means that the pictures you post (and even what you choose not to post) on Facebook, Instagram, or Tumblr convey a first impression of you to others who are viewing your social media sites for the first time. Now you have to ask yourself, is this the impression you want others to have of you? See the chapter on workplace communication to learn about personal branding and how to create the "brand" you want for yourself in your in-person and mediated interactions with others.

first impression
An initial opinion about people upon meeting them.

• First impressions are quick, powerful, and sometimes inaccurate.

© Laurence Mouton/Brand X Pictures/Getty Images RF

As we form our first impressions of others, we also compare the new person with ourselves. According to Sterling, we make certain comparisons and draw certain conclusions in business settings.[17] For example, if others appear to be of a business or social level comparable to our own, we decide they are worthy of further interaction. If they appear to be of a higher level, we admire them and cultivate them as a valuable contact. If they appear to be of lower status, we tolerate them but keep them at arm's length.[18] Studies have found that our initial judgments are typically about attractiveness and trustworthiness.[19]

Our first impressions are powerful, and sometimes they lead to errors in our assessment of others. Imagine a businessperson who has traveled all day and arrives late for a meeting. Her flight was delayed, her luggage was lost en route, and she arrives in jeans and a T-shirt. New business acquaintances might dismiss her simply on the grounds of her appearance.

First impressions can be affected by specific situations or circumstances that make our initial assessment inaccurate. Just the same, we tend to cling to these impressions in future interactions. Rather than altering our opinion, we filter out new information that disputes our original appraisal. According to Ambady and Skowronski in their book *First Impressions*, "a positive first impression may be easily reversed by information to the contrary, but a negative first impression may persist even in the face of contradictory information."[20]

A recent study on how facts don't change first impressions found that even when people were told the sexual orientation of someone, and it contradicted what they initially thought, the participants still identified whether the person was gay or straight based on their first impressions of how the person looked. Even though snap judgments are natural cognitive responses, they can lead to stereotyping, which we discussed earlier in the chapter.[21]

Our perceptions of others rest on a subjective, an active, and a creative perceptual process. Our perceptions of others are unique, and we perceive individuals in multiple ways through multiple interactions. We can more fairly appraise others and their behavior by understanding common attribution and perceptual errors and the extent to which we are engaged in them.

perception checking
A process of describing, interpreting, and verifying that helps us understand another person and his or her message more accurately.

Another important skill is **perception checking,** a process of describing, interpreting, and verifying that helps you understand another person and his or her message more accurately. Perception checking has three steps. *First,* you describe to the other person the behavior—including the verbal and nonverbal cues—that you observed. *Second,* you suggest plausible interpretations. *Third,* you seek verification through asking questions or observing for clarification, explanation, or amplification.

For example, imagine that you are assigned a group research project in one of your classes. Another member of the group asks you to share with the group all your primary sources for the project. You presented this source material weeks ago. You respond by saying, "I understand that you want me to give you my primary sources" (describe the behavior or the message). "I have a feeling that you do not trust me" (first interpretation). "Or maybe you just want to create the bibliography for the whole group" (second interpretation). "Can you explain why you want my primary sources?" (request for clarification).

Perception checking may be even more important in our personal or romantic relationships. Suppose a casual friend provides you with a very romantic birthday present. You begin by describing the behavior: "The gift you gave me was very romantic." You then suggest alternative interpretations: "Perhaps you want to change the nature of our relationship" (first interpretation). "Maybe this gift was for someone else" (second interpretation). "Maybe you don't view the gift as romantic" (third interpretation). Or you can just ask for clarification at the outset by inquiring: "Can you tell me what you intended?"

In perception checking, you must suggest interpretations that do not cause the other person to be defensive. In the first instance, imagine that you offered as one explanation "Maybe you want my primary sources so you can claim that you did all the research." The other person is most likely to become defensive. In the second instance, you could have offered "Maybe you don't realize that I don't want a romantic relationship with you." Most likely, embarrassment and a loss of face would follow.

Another example occurred in Falls Church, Virginia, at a medical clinic where patients from Central America did not keep their appointments. The healthcare workers had to do some follow-up to learn about the cultural differences. They needed to describe the behavior of keeping appointments, suggest

building **behaviors**

Check Your Perceptions

In the opening narrative to this chapter, Kim made perceptions of her instructor's gender based on the instructor's name. With a partner in class, name a physical feature of yourself that you think affects your communication with others, such as height, weight, skin color, age, hairstyle, clothing, jewelry, scars, tattoos, or even your name. First, say how you think this feature affects your communication with others. Next, let the other person say how he or she perceives this feature. Then switch roles and repeat. You are checking each other's perceptions about a feature that affects your communication.

an interpretation, but then allow the patients to explain the practice. Perception checks were also necessary when physicians learned that they could not look directly at a Hmong man and that breast self-exam programs for Muslim women needed to be conducted before regular hours, so that no men were on the property. Women from other countries report being surprised by the directness and invasiveness of male physicians' questions and sometimes do not answer these questions truthfully or fully.[22] The healthcare workers must continue to do perception checks to ensure that the women are receiving the best medical care possible.

Who Are You?

Discussing perception naturally leads us to look at self-perception. How you perceive yourself plays a central role in communication, regardless of whether the communication is on Facebook, in a text message, or on your smartphone. An early step in considering yourself a communicator is to think about who you are.

personal identity
Perception of what makes an individual unique with regard to various personality characteristics, interests, and values.

HOW YOU BECAME WHO YOU ARE

What you know about yourself includes your past, present, and future. Your family is one of the most influential factors in your life, and because of this your family helped shaped how you think, believe, and behave. When you were little, you may have stomped your feet when you didn't get your way, and your family reacted in a certain way to that behavior. Over time, your family members and other experiences have helped you learn to cope and express your frustration with words.

The **personal identity** that you have developed influences your perceptions of others.[23] If you see yourself as a shy person who keeps to yourself or likes to spend time with just a few close friends, then you may perceive others who are more outgoing as boisterous or attention seekers. Your self-perception will have a profound effect on your communication with others. Importantly, your self-perceptions are not static.

Personal identities can be changed, and people can improve their behavior as a result. For example, some low-income and minority teens who had low academic attainment were taught strategies that allowed them to develop a "new academic possible self." These students then achieved higher grades, scored higher on standardized tests, and showed greater academic initiative. At the same time, their levels of depression, absenteeism, and in-school misbehavior declined.[24] Also, students who perceive that their parents or parental figures are involved in their school experience are more satisfied with school, believe in their abilities, and perform significantly better on national exams like the ACT.[25]

sizing things up

What Messages Shaped You?

Most of the memorable messages college students receive about education come from their parents, and those messages help students make decisions during difficult or transitional times. Take a minute to write down the most memorable message that you can remember a parent or parental figure telling you about college. This can be a message about going to college, succeeding in college, or any other circumstance surrounding college.

Now take a look at this message. What is its main point? What does this message mean to you, personally?

The exercise you just engaged in was actually the same approach used in a research study by one of your textbook authors and her colleagues. We asked 419 college students the same question and found that parental messages about college are both meaningful and significant to college students. Overall, parents' messages about college are about working (and playing) hard, the necessity of attending college, and encouragement and support.

Does your message fit into one of these themes? If so, which one? How have you used this message, if at all, so far in your college experience? The lesson you can learn from this exercise is that others throughout our lives communicate with us about how we are supposed to think and behave. We are shaped by and act in ways that reflect the many messages we receive from parents, teachers, friends, and others.

Source: Kranstuber, H., Carr, K., Hosek, A. M. (2012). "If you can dream it, you can achieve it." Family socialization, memorable messages, and college student success. *Communication Education, 61*, 44–66.

How can personal identity research be applied to communication? When a speaker creates a message that highlights shared values with listeners, then the listeners perceive a social group identity match and are more likely to be persuaded by the message. Other factors may interfere with this cause–effect relationship, however. For example, if the shared values are unexpected because of someone's political party membership or other social group affiliations, the message may be rejected and the persuasive attempt may fail.[26]

Your awareness of who you are develops in your communication with yourself, that is, your intrapersonal communication. Shedletsky writes that intrapersonal communication includes "our perceptions, memories, experiences, feelings, interpretations, inferences, evaluations, attitudes, opinions, ideas, strategies, images, and states of consciousness."[27] Intrapersonal communication can be viewed as talking to ourselves; it is also synonymous with thinking. Intrapersonal communication appears to be the most common context of communication, the foundation for the other contexts.

Your awareness of who you are also develops in your communication with others. Once you mastered language, **symbolic interactionism**—the process of development of the self through the messages and feedback received from others[28]—shaped you in ways that made you what you are today. You may have been punished for acting up in class, rewarded for athletic skill, or ignored for saying too little. The result is the person you see in the mirror today.

symbolic interactionism
The process in which the self develops through the messages and feedback received from others.

To explore who you are, you may be assigned a speech of self-introduction. This speech may be the first one you deliver in class. Since you know more about yourself than does anyone else in the classroom, you will probably feel very little anxiety about this assignment. Of course, you will want to provide some basic information about yourself—your name, where you are from, and your current major in college—but this is also an opportunity to share aspects of your personal identity with your classmates.

Instead of beginning your speech of introduction with basic information, consider providing some information that is provocative and that will gain the attention of your audience. For example, one student began, "How many people do you know who fly an airplane and have also jumped out of one?" Another speaker stated, "I've been in 40 of the 50 states." A third noted, "I have never lived anyplace but in this city." These three students found some aspect about themselves to be unique. In one case, the student was adventuresome and a risk taker; the second student had enjoyed a great deal of travel with his family; and the third realized that her stability allowed her to nurture her roots.

communicating
creatively

Memorable Message About College

As a way to celebrate International Women's Day, YouTube encouraged people to empower young women with the #DearMe campaign. The #DearMe campaign asks digital creators around the world to upload "video letters" to their younger selves that provide the advice and encouragement that they wish they had heard when they were younger. The campaign encouraged people to use the hashtag #DearMe on social media to share their messages. Although the initial focus was on young girls, these video letters apply to anyone wishing to tell their younger selves or others a supportive, clarifying, and/or realistic message. A quick search of the videos yields an array of messages, perspectives, and identities. In this section, you have been learning about how your self-perceptions and others' perceptions of you have, in part, formed who you are. Perhaps you can take the time to create a video or write a handwritten letter to your younger self. What would your letter say? What part does perception play in your message to your younger self?

Source: Brouwer, B. (2015, March). YouTube launches #DearMe campaign for International Women's Day. *Tubefilter* (www.tubefilter.com/2015/03/03/youtube-dearme-campaign-international-womens-day/).

The speech of self-introduction will allow you to draw on the information in this chapter, and it will give you a relatively stress-free way to begin finding your voice in this class.

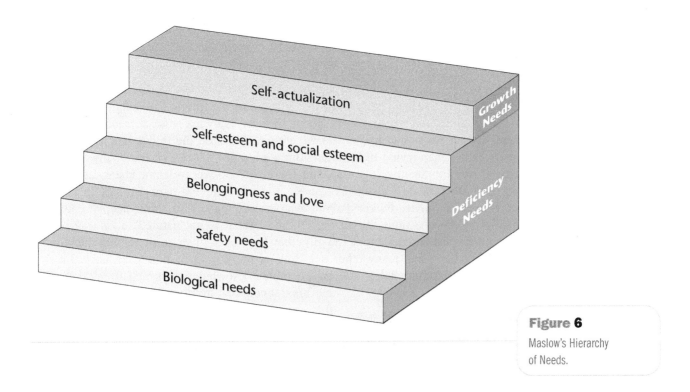

Figure 6
Maslow's Hierarchy of Needs.

NEEDS

Needs are physical and mental states that motivate us to behave in ways that lead to their satisfaction. Abraham Maslow wrote that we experience two sets of personal needs: deficiency needs and growth needs.[36] **Deficiency needs** are basic human needs. **Growth needs** are higher-order human needs. Maslow arranged these two sets of needs in the form of a hierarchy to show that our deficiency needs must be satisfied routinely before our growth needs become important to us.

As Figure 6 indicates, there are four sets of deficiency needs: (1) *biological needs*, such as food, water, and air; (2) *safety needs*, such as protection from physical harm; (3) *belongingness and love needs*, such as a child's need for the love of a parent; and (4) *self-esteem and social-esteem needs*, which involve believing in our self-worth and finding confirmation of that belief from others. Growth needs are not as straightforward as deficiency needs. They include self-actualization, knowledge and understanding, and aesthetic needs. Self-actualization is the most commonly discussed growth need. According to Maslow, *self-actualization* is the process of fully realizing one's potential. Self-actualized people not only understand themselves but also accept themselves for who they are and what they have achieved.

As you analyze your audience, consider how your speech can help audience members satisfy their likely needs. For example, many motivational speakers seek to help people satisfy their needs for self-actualization. On the other hand, someone selling home security equipment would appeal to safety needs.

deficiency needs
Basic human needs, which must be satisfied before higher-order needs can be met. They include needs for food, water, air, physical safety, belongingness and love, and self-esteem and social esteem.

growth needs
Higher-order human needs, which can be satisfied only after deficiency needs have been met. They include self-actualization (the process of fully realizing one's potential), knowledge and understanding, and aesthetic needs.

LEARNING MORE ABOUT YOURSELF

Perhaps you now understand why the ancients said, "Know thyself." They, like people today, believed that self-awareness is a discovery worth making. Accurate self-awareness helps you be ready to make sound choices now and in the future. If you dislike chemistry, you may not enjoy a career as a physician or pharmacist. If you like to write and are good at it, you may have a future as a writer or blogger. If you are skillful at athletics, perhaps you can take advantage of that talent with scholarships, varsity sports, and even professional sports. What you have learned about yourself in the past, and what you learn about yourself now, will affect your future.

Right now, as you go about your everyday activities, you should be aware of what kind of person you are and who you want to be in the future. Comedian Amy Poehler in her memoir, *Yes, Please!* talks about this as "knowing your currency." What she means is that we should know who we are and focus on the things that make us who we are rather than trying to be something we are not.[29] Are you timid, shy, and unassertive? Are you healthy, vigorous, and energetic? Do you welcome change, adventure, and risk? Do you see yourself as capable, unstoppable, and hard-driving? In his book *Let Your Life Speak,* Parker Palmer encourages readers to think deeply about the answers to the questions "What am I?" and "What is my nature?" as a way to find their inner voice and determine the gifts they have been given to share with the world.[30] Answering these and many other questions is the key to finding your authentic selfhood. As Will Schutz notes, "Given a complete knowledge of myself, I can determine my life; lacking that mastery, I am controlled in ways that are often undesirable, unproductive, worrisome, and confusing."[31]

New experiences may lead to increased self-knowledge.
© Matthius Engelien/ Alamy RF

Joseph O'Connor was a high school junior when he spent two weeks in the Sierra Nevada mountain range of northeastern California—a challenge that changed his level of self-awareness. Rain poured, hail pelted, and the beauty of dawn at 13,000 feet entranced him. Writing about his self-awareness in an article titled "A View from Mount Ritter: Two Weeks in the Sierras Changed My Attitude Toward Life and What It Takes to Succeed," O'Connor states:

> The wonder of all I'd experienced made me think seriously about what comes next. "Life after high school," I said to myself. "Uh-oh." What had I been doing the last three years? I was so caught up in defying the advice of my parents and teachers to study and play by the rules that I hadn't considered the effects my actions would have on me.[32]

O'Connor's experience changed his self-awareness, and he went from being a D student to one who made the honor roll.

You don't have to go to the mountains to come to a new awareness of yourself. If you want to learn more about yourself, you can take several steps to achieve that goal. If you want to learn more about your physical self, you can start a new workout program that pushes your physical strength in new ways. You can also talk to your relatives about people in your family. What health ailments do your parents and grandparents face? Are these problems inherited? How can knowing this information make you think differently about how you communicate or behave and the kinds of experiences you seek out or avoid? For example, if a close family member died of lung cancer due to years of smoking, do you avoid smoking cigarettes and people who smoke cigarettes? Do you advocate for antismoking initiatives on your campus?

If you want to learn more about your personality and how others perceive you, you can talk with your spouse or partner, friends, co-workers, bosses, and even your children if you are a parent. In what ways is your personality similar to and different from the personalities of your family members? For example, you may learn best by doing things hands-on just like your grandfather or lack patience like your mother. Consider other features of your life that will suggest how you are perceived. Do people seek you out as a relational partner? Do others ask you to participate in social events? Do friends ask you for advice?

If you want to know what type of employee you are, you can ask your supervisor, co-workers, and customers. Consider the type of environment that you thrive in and ones that you don't enjoy. Do you like to work alone or with others? What kinds of jobs have you held? Have you been given increasing amounts of responsibility in those jobs, or have you frequently lost jobs? Do you need motivation from others, or do you work to complete a task without reminders from others? Do others seek you out to partner with them on work or school projects?

Are you skillful in communication? Do you enjoy public speaking and receive invitations to talk to others at work or in the community? Can you listen to others uncritically and empathize with them? Are you adept at problem solving or conflict resolution? Are you an effective and adaptive leader? Are you apprehensive about communication? Are you argumentative? You can learn about your communication skills or deficits through a number of research methods. For example, the last three concepts can be found online by typing "Leader Effectiveness and Adaptability," "Personal Report of Communication Apprehension," and "Argumentativeness Scale," respectively, into a search engine. Many valid and reliable instruments measuring communication constructs can be found online, in communication journals, and in resource books.

engaging diversity

Differences in Memory

The dominant culture in the United States places the self in the spotlight, whereas most Asian cultures, such as the Chinese, emphasize the group over the individual. Notice that people in the United States write their given (first) name followed by the family name, whereas the Chinese start with the family name followed by their given name. For the Chinese, the group (family) comes before the self. These differences in emphasis extend even to the way people remember.

Research by Qi Wang and her associates shows that American adults and preschool children recall their personal memories differently than do indigenous Chinese. Since our self-concept is dependent on our self-awareness, these cultural differences are important.

"Americans often report lengthy, specific, emotionally elaborate memories that focus on the self as a central character," says Wang. "Chinese tend to give brief accounts of general routine events that center on collective activities and are often emotionally neutral. These individual-focused vs. group-oriented styles characterize the mainstream values in American and Chinese cultures, respectively."

Source: Han, J. J., Leichtman, M. D., & Wang, Q. (1998). Autobiographical memory in Korean, Chinese, and American children. *Developmental Psychology, 34*(4): 701–713.

How You Present Yourself

In this chapter we have shown the relationship among perception, self-perception, and communication. Communication and perception influence each other. Communication is largely responsible for our self-perceptions. Communication can also be used to change the perceptions that others have of us. We attempt to influence others' perceptions of ourselves through self-presentation, or impression management.

In our daily interactions, whether they be face-to-face or online, we present ourselves to people, both consciously and unconsciously. Self-presentation can be defined as the way we portray ourselves to others. Generally, our self-presentation is consistent with an ideal self-image, allows us to enact an appropriate role, influences others' views of us, permits us to define the situation in our terms, and/or influences the progress of an interaction.

Erving Goffman first described the process of self-presentation.[33] Goffman adopted the symbolic interactionist perspective mentioned earlier. He described everyday interactions through a dramaturgical, or theater arts, viewpoint. His theory embraces individual identity, group relationships, the context (the situation), and the interactive meaning of information. Individuals are viewed as "actors," and interaction is seen as a "performance" shaped by the context and constructed to provide others with "impressions" consistent with the desired goals of the actor. **Impression management** is sharing personal details in order to present an idealized self. Through impression management, people try to present an idealized version of themselves to reach desired ends.

impression management
Sharing personal details in order to present an idealized self.

It shouldn't be that difficult for you to realize that you engage in impression management in your face-to-face interactions and in your mediated interactions. Think about your use of social media and how you manage your privacy online. Maybe you hide or block your parents or children or let only friends of friends see certain pictures on Facebook. Or perhaps you use Snapchat to share pictures instead of posting them to Instagram. These are all ways you are actively managing the impression of you that can be perceived through the pictures and comments. Research on this topic suggests that when students know their teachers can view their social networking profiles, they are more apt to make sure their spelling is correct and their pictures are appropriate.[34]

Your understanding of verbal and nonverbal communication will be enhanced

sizing things up

Self-Esteem Scale

Below is a list of statements dealing with your general feelings about yourself. Read each statement carefully and respond by using the following scale:

1 = Strongly agree
2 = Agree
3 = Disagree
4 = Strongly disagree

1. On the whole, I am satisfied with myself.
2. At times I think that I am no good at all.
3. I feel that I have a number of good qualities.
4. I am able to do things as well as most other people.
5. I feel I do not have much to be proud of.
6. I certainly feel useless at times.
7. I feel that I am a person of worth, at least the equal of others.
8. I wish I could have more respect for myself.
9. All in all, I am inclined to feel that I am a failure.
10. I take a positive attitude toward myself.

This exercise has no right or wrong answers; instead, the answers will tell you something about how you feel about yourself. A guide for interpreting your responses appears at the end of the chapter.

Source: Rosenberg, M. (1989). *Society and adolescent self-image* (rev. ed.). Middletown, CT: Wesleyan University Press.

by your understanding of identity and impression management. Wiggins, Wiggins, and Vander Zanden suggest that three essential types of communication are used to manage impressions: manner, appearance, and setting.[35] Manner includes both verbal and non-verbal codes. Your manner might be seen as brusque, silly, businesslike, immature, friendly, warm, or gracious. Your appearance may suggest a role you are playing (administrative assistant), a value you hold (concern for the environment), your personality (easygoing), or your view of the communication setting (essential). The setting includes your immediate environment (the space in which you communicate) as well as other public displays of who you are (the kind of home in which you live, the type of automobile you drive).

be ready... for what's next

Online Presentation of Self

Have you ever "Googled" yourself? If you haven't, take a few minutes and do so now. What comes up when you search for yourself online? You will probably find links to any social media accounts you hold. Have you checked to see what types of pictures, comments, and content are available for the general public to see from your social media sites?

How do you feel about the level of access and privacy surrounding your information on these sites? What perception do you think this information conveys about your identity?

Now might be a good time to change some of your privacy settings on social media, delete unwanted comments, remove your name from photos, or ask friends to do the same who have tagged you in their social media posts.

It is important that you begin critically examining and managing your online reputation because it can impact your present and future opportunities. Many potential employers search online for information about potential employees before they request interviews, and many people work for employers who have policies about how they can present themselves online. At some point in your academic or professional career, you may even need to promote yourself online as part of your job.

Taking these few simple steps can help you manage your online reputation.

This chapter invited you to know and understand the link between perception and communication. You have learned now that everything from how you look to how you think can affect your communication with others—in regard to whether you communicate, with whom you communicate, and how you communicate. As part of your growing communication skills, you have to take seriously how you look, dress, and present yourself to others. You have learned the power of perception in communication.

are you "suit"ed for success?

By Gino Perrotte

"What should I wear?" You ask yourself this question as you look through your closet. The university's career fair is tomorrow and you want to be prepared to make a good first impression with potential employers. Perhaps the outfit you choose will give you a competitive advantage over other students at the fair. Can professional attire really make you stand out from the crowd? Yes, it can! According to Jacqueline Whitmore, author of the book "Business Class Etiquette Essentials for Success at Work," clothes can either detract from or enhance a person's appearance (2005, p. 34).

Just as you would want to make a good first impression with potential employers at a career fair, it is equally important to do so when speaking to an audience. That is why I require students to dress professionally for their presentations. Dressing well increases an audience's perception of a speaker's overall competence.

It is important to note that being well dressed is not a substitute for planning and delivering a good, solid speech. What it does mean is that having an appropriate style of dress allows you to step up to the next level of credibility with your audience. Appropriate attire says that you respect yourself (p. 33). Companies develop strict dress codes in order to create a respectable professional image for their business. Young professionals realize quickly that a formal style of business attire projects competence (Cardon & Okoro, 2009).

Obviously, it is important that your speech day attire enhances your appeal and credibility for the audience. The following tips inform you of the most common things that college students need to be aware of when it comes to presenting a professional, competent image on speech day.

These tips provided by both professionals and students should be your guide for dressing appropriately on your speech day. Remember that your professional look will add to your credibility as a speaker. If you commit yourself to dressing well, then you are on your way to being well "suit"ed for success.

Mr. Gino Perrotte (M.A., University of Central Florida) is a public speaking and interpersonal communication instructor at the University of Central Florida's Nicholson School of Communication. Mr. Perrotte's professional experience includes several HR functions such as interviewing, hiring and policy making.

© Courtesy of Gino Perrotte

Tips and Tactics	**Workplace Professionals**
What NOT to Wear:	
· Worn/scuffed shoes	· Flip flops
· Heavy perfume/cologne	· Mini-skirts
· Stained/wrinkled clothes	· Sleeveless shirts
· Excessive jewelry	· Jeans (Haefner, 2008)
· Sneakers	
· Night club attire (Whitmore, 2005, p. 37)	

This group of businesspeople illustrates business casual dress appropriate for most public speaking situations.
© Monalyn Gracia/ Fancy/age fotostock RF

Tips and Tactics	**Tips from Students**
Yes, Wear It!	**Don't Even Think About It!**
· Ties	· Stiletto heels
· Dress pants and a nice belt	· Excessive makeup
· 3 to 4 inch heels or flat dress shoes	· Distracting hair
· Collared shirts	· Hats
· Tailored skirts within 2 inches of the knee	· Too big or too tight clothing
· Suits	· Shorts

Chapter Review & Study Guide

Summary

In this chapter, you learned the following:

1. Perception is our use of our senses to gather information about the environment or the situation we are in.

2. Differences occur in perception for many reasons, including identity factors, past experiences, and our present feelings and circumstances.

3. Through selection, we neglect some stimuli in our environment and focus on others. Organization in perception is the grouping of stimuli into meaningful units or wholes. Interpretation is the way we assign meaning to stimuli.

4. Some ways in which we organize stimuli are figure and ground, closure, proximity, and similarity. Figure and ground refers to our focusing on some parts of an experience (figure) and distancing ourselves from others (ground). Closure is the tendency to fill in missing information. Proximity encourages us to perceive objects close in space or time as meaningfully related, and similarity is the basis on which we group elements that resemble each other in size, color, or shape.

5. Perceptual errors that affect communication include stereotyping and reliance on first impressions.

6. The way you see yourself affects how and to whom you communicate, regardless of the medium.

7. Impression management is a way for you to influence how others perceive you, usually as an idealized version of yourself.

Key Terms

Active perception
Closure
Deficiency needs
Figure
First impression
Gender identity
Ground
Growth needs
Impression management
In-group

Intergroup perspective
Interpretive perception
Organization
Out-group
Perception
Perception checking
Perceptual constancy
Personal identity
Prejudice
Proximity

Role
Selective attention
Selective exposure
Selective perception
Selective retention
Similarity
Stereotyping
Subjective perception
Symbolic interactionism

Study Questions

1. Which of the following may be the result of identity factors, past experiences and roles, and present conditions?

   a. selection
   b. similarity
   c. self-serving bias
   d. differences in perception

2. By neglecting some stimuli and focusing on other stimuli, you are engaging in which process of perception?

   a. organization
   b. selection
   c. classification
   d. interpretation

3. _____ is an organizational method whereby missing information is filled in to create the appearance of a complete unit, and _____ is another organizational technique whereby elements are grouped based on their similarities in size, color, and shape.

   a. Closure; similarity
   b. Proximity; figure and ground
   c. Similarity; proximity
   d. Closure; proximity

4. The more ambiguous the stimuli,

   a. the less room for confusion.
   b. the more room for interpretation.
   c. the less room for interpretation.
   d. the less you rely on context.

5. Perceptual constancy results because of

   a. identity factors.
   b. past experiences and roles.
   c. figure and ground.
   d. people's present feelings and circumstances.

6. A system of shared beliefs, values, customs, and behaviors is known as a

   a. person.
   b. communicator.
   c. role.
   d. culture.

7. Selection occurs in perception in all of the following ways *except*

   a. attention.
   b. exposure.
   c. distraction.
   d. retention.

8. Which of the following is a perceptual error frequently made by people?

   a. believing stereotypes about people who are different from themselves
   b. believing other people are courageous, whereas they, themselves, are cowardly
   c. believing that others are considerably older than themselves
   d. believing that uneducated people are happier than educated people

9. When people seek to present an ideal version of themselves, they are engaging in

   a. impression management.
   b. active perception.
   c. attribution.
   d. selection.

10. First impressions

    a. generally take weeks or more to develop.
    b. are based on people's sense of humor, their personality, and their religion.
    c. are frequently based on other people's appearance.
    d. are generally accurate and therefore are lasting impressions.

connect

To maximize your study time, check out CONNECT to access the SmartBook study module for this chapter, watch videos, and explore other resources.

Answers:
1. (d); 2. (b); 3. (a); 4. (b); 5. (b); 6. (d); 7. (c); 8. (a); 9. (a); 10. (c)

Critical Thinking

1. Researchers state that people's perceptions are largely learned because what people see, hear, taste, touch, and smell is conditioned by their culture. What parts of your culture are key factors in how you perceive events in day-to-day life?

2. The chapter discusses how people form impressions of who they are and how communication affects self-perceptions. How does this occur through social media? For instance, why do people follow the Instagram feeds of people they don't know? How are those popular Instagram users communicating a favorable perception of themselves through their posts that make people want to follow their feeds? How do you see yourself? How is this affected by your past, present, and projected future? How have conversations you have had with friends, co-workers, or other people at college altered the way you see yourself?

Sizing Things Up Scoring and Interpretation

Self-Esteem Scale

Self-esteem is a central component of self-perception. The Rosenberg Self-Esteem Scale is one of the most popular scales designed to measure your general positive or negative self-assessment. After completing and scoring this scale, talk with your teacher about self-esteem and how your communication behaviors are related to this self-perception.

Scoring of the Rosenberg Self-Esteem Scale is very straightforward. Items 2, 5, 6, 8, and 9 should be reverse-coded. This means that, if you answered with a 4 to one of those statements, your score should be reversed to be a 1 (if the original answer was 4) or a 2 (if the original answer was 3) and so on for the rest of the reverse-coded items. Reverse-coding will account for the fact that some questions are positively worded, whereas others are negatively worded. After reverse-coding, sum all items; values should range from 4 to 40, with higher values indicating more positive assessments of self-esteem.

References

1. Wright, R. (1994, July–August). That never really happened. *The Humanist,* 30–31.

2. Gilligan, M. (2011, Fall). Brief Paper One in Communication 114, Introduction to Human Communication, North Dakota State University.

3. Lutz, C. (2011, Fall). Brief Paper One in Communication 114, Introduction to Human Communication, North Dakota State University.

4. Bedsaul, J. (2011, Fall). Brief Paper One in Communication 114, Introduction to Human Communication, North Dakota State University.

5. Wilson, J., & Wilson, S. (Eds.). (1998). *Mass media/ mass culture.* New York: McGraw-Hill.

6. Ibid.

7. Curtin, E. (2005). Instructional styles used by regular classroom teachers while teaching recently mainstreamed ESL students: Six urban middle school teachers share their experiences and perceptions. *Multicultural Education, 12*(4): 36–42.

8. Wilson & Wilson, *Mass media/mass culture.*

9. Mentalblog.com. (2004). Retrieved from http://mentalblog.com/2004/12/cdnudtblveiee-that.html

10. Harwood, J., Giles, H., & Palomares, N. A. (2005). Intergroup theory and communication processes. In J. Harwood & H. Giles (Eds.), *Intergroup communication: Multiple perspectives* (pp. 1–17). New York: Peter Lang.

11. Tajfel, H., & Turner, J. C. (1986). The social identity theory of intergroup behavior. In S. Worchel & W. Austin (Eds.), *Psychology of intergroup relations* (pp. 7–24). Chicago: Nelson-Hall.

12. Leary, M. (2002). The self as a source of relational difficulties. *Self and Identity*, *1*, 137–142.

13. Hendrix, K. G. (2002). "Did being black introduce bias into your study?" Attempting to mute the race-related research of black scholars. *Howard Journal of Communication*, *13*, 153–171.

14. Hughes, P. C., & Baldwin, J. R. (2002). Communication and stereotypical impressions. *Howard Journal of Communication*, *13*, 113–128. (p. 113)

15. The Millennial Impact Report: A study on millennial alumni of four-year colleges in the United States. (2014). Retrieved from http://www.themillennialimpact.com

16. Gregoire, C. (2014, May). How to make the perfect first impression (according to science). The Third Metric. Retrieved from http://www.huffingtonpost.com/2014/05/30/the-science-and-art-of-fi_n_5399004.html

17. Sterling, M. (2006). Do you make your first impression your best impression? Retrieved from http://entrepreneurs.about.com/cs/marketing/a/uc051603a.htm

18. Ibid.

19. Willis, J., & Todorov, A. (2006). First impressions making up your mind after a 100-ms exposure to a face. *Psychological Science*, *17*, 592–598.

20. Ambady, N., & Skowronski, J. (Eds.). (2008). *First impressions*. New York: Guilford Press.

21. Society for Personality and Social Psychology. (2014, February 14). Even fact will not change first impressions. *Science Daily*. Retrieved March 7, 2015, from www.sciencedaily.com/releases/2014/02/140214111207.htm

22. Levine, S. (2006, March 20–26). Culturally sensitive medicine: Doctors learn to adapt to immigrant patients' ethnic and religious customs. *Washington Post National Weekly Edition*, 23(22): 31.

23. Seta, C. E., Schmidt, S., & Bookhout, C. M. (2006). Social identity orientation and social role attributions: Explaining behavior through the lens of self. *Self and Identity*, *5*, 355–364.

24. Oyserman, D., Bybee, D., & Terry, K. (2006). Possible selves and academic outcomes: How and when possible selves impel action. *Journal of Personality and Social Psychology*, *91*, 188–204.

25. Barwegen, L. M., Falciani, N. K., Putnam, J., Reamer, M. B., & Stair, E. E. (2004). Academic achievement of homeschool and public school students and student perception of parent involvement. *School Community Journal*, *14*, 39–58.

26. Nelson, T. E., & Garst, J. (2005). Values based political messages and persuasion: Relationships among speaker, recipient, and evoked values. *Political Psychology*, *26*, 489–515.

27. Shedletsky, L. J. (1989). The mind at work. In L. J. Shedletsky (Ed.), *Meaning and mind: An intrapersonal approach to human communication*. ERIC and the Speech Communication Association.

28. Mead, G. H. (1934). *Mind, self, and society*. Chicago: University of Chicago Press.

29. Poehler, A. (2014). *Yes, please!* New York: Dey Street.

30. Palmer, P. J. (1999). Let your life speak: Listening for the voice of vocation. Wiley.

31. Schutz, W. (1982). *Here comes everyone* (2nd ed.). New York: Irvington, p. 1.

32. O'Connor, J. T. (1998, May 25). A view from Mount Ritter: Two weeks in the Sierras changed my attitude toward life and what it takes to succeed. *Newsweek*, May 25, 1998, p. 17. © 1998 Newsweek, Inc. All rights reserved. Reprinted by permission.

33. Goffman, E. (1959). *The presentation of self in everyday life*. New York: Doubleday Anchor. Goffman, E. (1974). *Frame analysis: An essay on the organization of experience*. New York: Harper & Row. Goffman, E. (1981). *Forms of talk*. Oxford: Basil Blackwell.

34. DiVerniero, R., & Hosek, A. M. (2011). Students' perceptions and sense making of instructors' online self-disclosure. *Communication Quarterly*, *59*, 428–449.

35. Wiggins, J. A., Wiggins, B. B., & Vander Zanden, J. (1993). *Social psychology* (4th ed.). New York: McGraw-Hill.

36. Cardon, P. W., & Okoro, E. A. (2009). Professional Characteristics Communicated by Formal Versus Casual Workplace Attire. *Business Communication Quarterly*, 72(3), 355–360.

37. Haefner, R. (2008, July 30). *How to dress for success for work*. Retrieved January 26, 2011 from http://www.cnn.com/2008/LIVING/worklife/07/30/cb.dress.for.success/index.html

38. Whitmore, J. (2005). Business Class etiquette essentials for success at work. New York, NY: St. Martin's Press.

language and meaning

When you have read and thought about this chapter, you will be able to

1. Define language and understand how it works.

2. Understand the characteristics of language.

3. Use language effectively.

This chapter is about the importance of language and how language functions in communication. In this chapter you will learn about the world of language, including the definition of language and its many characteristics. You will learn how you can use language more effectively in your day-to-day interactions with others. Finally, we provide specific suggestions for improving your verbal skills.

Have you ever wondered why some words come into style and other words fade away? What makes slang words like "defriend," "on fleek," or "hangry" popular? In her TED talk "What Makes a Word 'Real,'" language historian Anne Curzan explores this question and how we make choices about language in our everyday lives.[1]

In fact, words change meaning all the time and in interesting ways. For example, did you know that early references to the word *silly* meant that something was worthy or blessed, but we now use it to refer to things that are foolish? Similarly, the term *flirt* used to mean flicking something away from you, but now we use it to mean trying to catch someone's attention or playing with emotions.[2]

You are probably wondering, "How can we ever communicate effectively if words change meaning all the time?" Well, you are in luck because Curzan notes that this has been happening as long as there has been language to express ideas. Through reading this chapter, you will come to understand the elements of language, identify common errors with language, and practice ways to use language more effectively in your personal and professional life.

Defining Language

Language is a collection of symbols, letters, or words with arbitrary meanings that are governed by rules and used to communicate. Language consists of words or symbols that represent things without being those things. People originally assigned arbitrary labels to objects in order to communicate ideas; as new objects are made, new words or symbols are created to aid communication. The word *automobile* is a symbol for a vehicle that runs on gasoline, but the symbol is not the vehicle itself. When you listen to others' verbal communication, you **decode,** or assign meaning to, their words to translate them into thoughts of your own. Because language is an imperfect means of transmission, the thoughts expressed by one person never exactly match what is decoded by another. In other words, language is an imperfect process that often requires corrections.

Verbal communication is essential in practically everything we do, from doing well at work to relating to friends and relatives. Both writing and speaking rely on the use of language. Verbal communication represents one of the two major codes of communication; the other is nonverbal communication.

Our definition tells you that language consists of words or symbols, has rules, and is arbitrary, but the definition does not reveal some of the other important characteristics of language. Language also is intertwined with culture, organizes and classifies reality, and is abstract. In this section we take a closer look at each of these characteristics.

LANGUAGE HAS RULES

Language has multiple rules. Three sets of rules are relevant to our discussion: semantic rules, syntactic rules, and pragmatic rules. **Semantics** is the study of the way humans

language
A collection of symbols, letters, or words with arbitrary meanings that are governed by rules and used to communicate.

decode
The process of assigning meaning to others' words in order to translate them into thoughts of your own.

semantics
The study of the way humans use language to evoke meaning in others.

use language to evoke meaning in others. Semantics focuses on individual words and their meaning. Semanticists—people who study semantics—are interested in how language and its meaning change over time.

Whereas semantics focuses on the definition of specific words, **syntax** is the way in which words are arranged to form phrases and sentences. For example, in the English language the subject is usually placed before the verb, and the object after the verb. Other languages have different rules of syntax, including reading from right to left. You **encode** by translating your thoughts into words. Syntax changes the meaning of the same set of words. For example, the declarative statement "I am going tomorrow" uses syntax to signal that someone is leaving the next day. If you change the word arrangement to "Am I going tomorrow?" the statement becomes a question and acquires a different meaning.

Pragmatics is the study of language as it is used in a social context, including its effect on the communicators. Messages are variable, depending on the situation. Ambiguous messages, such as "How are you?" "What's new?" and "You're looking good," have different meanings, depending on the context. For example, many people use such phrases as **phatic communication** or small talk—communication that is used to establish a mood of sociability rather than to communicate important information or ideas. Indeed, they would be surprised if someone offered serious or thoughtful answers to such questions or statements. For instance, have you ever asked a co-worker, "How's your day going?" and he responds, "This is the worst day ever," and then proceeds to tell you about the argument he had with his partner? More often than not, when we ask people these types of questions, we don't expect an in-depth answer. On the other hand, if you are visiting your grandmother who has been ill, your questions about how she is feeling are sincere and designed to elicit information. Similarly, you might genuinely be complimenting another person's new haircut or tattoo when you tell him he is looking good. Pragmatic rules help us interpret meaning in specific contexts.

LANGUAGE AND CULTURE ARE INTERTWINED

Culture may be defined as all of the socially transmitted behavior patterns, beliefs, attitudes, and values of a particular period, class, community, or population. We often think of the culture of a country (Greek culture), institution (the culture of higher education), organization (the Facebook culture), or group of people (the Hispanic culture). Culture and language are thus related as the transmission of culture occurs, in part, through language.

The relationship between culture and language is not as simple as it might first appear, however. Let us take the example of women and men and communication. In the recent past, books and articles were written on the differences between women and men in their communicative practices. As this research further developed, *gender* was expanded to refer to a complex social construct rather than simple biological sex. Some authors argued that gender was just as important as social class in understanding variations in communication.[3]

Language and culture are related in a second way. Culture creates a lens through which we perceive the world and create shared meaning. Language thus develops in response to the needs of the culture or to the perceptions of the world. Edward Sapir and Benjamin Lee Whorf were among the first to discuss the relationship between language and perception. The **Sapir-Whorf hypothesis,** as their theory has become known, states that our perception of reality is determined by our thought processes, our thought processes are limited by our language, and therefore language shapes our reality and our behaviors.[4] Language is the principal way that we learn about ourselves, others, and our culture.[5]

The Sapir-Whorf hypothesis has been illustrated in multiple cultures.[6] The Hopi language serves as an early example. The Hopi people do not distinguish between nouns and verbs. In many languages, nouns are given names that suggest that they remain static

---

syntax
The way in which words are arranged to form phrases and sentences.

encode
The process of translating your thoughts into words.

pragmatics
The study of language as it is used in a social context, including its effect on the communicators.

phatic communication
Communication that is used to establish a mood of sociability rather than to communicate important information or ideas.

culture
The socially transmitted behavior patterns, beliefs, attitudes, and values of a particular period, class, community, or population.

Sapir-Whorf hypothesis
A theory that our perception of reality is determined by our thought processes, our thought processes are limited by our language, and therefore language shapes our reality and our behaviors.

over time. For example, we assume that words such as *professor, physician, lamp,* and *computer* refer to people or objects that are relatively unchanging. Verbs are action words that suggest change. When we use words such as *heard, rehearsed, spoke,* and *ran,* we assume alterations and movement. The Hopi, by avoiding the distinction between nouns and verbs, thus refer to people and objects in the world as always changing.

In new ways, popular culture and social media regularly direct the creation of abbreviations.[7] For example, OMG and LOL are archaic. As acronyms become commonplace, people just use them in place of the things they are referencing. Therefore, the acronym becomes the thing it's referencing. Let's use the acronym *BAE* ("Before All Else") to illustrate this concept. As a traditional acronym, BAE would look like this: "You are my BAE!"—that is, "You are my before all else," meaning "You come before all else." Yet in contemporary phrasing it would look like this: "My BAE and I are hitting the town!" In this way, the acronym stands as the symbol for the original phrase.

People who speak different languages have different color terms than those who speak English. The color blue is familiar to most English speakers—both in their vocabulary and as a recognized color. English speakers use the word *blue* to refer to shades ranging from cyan to sky to navy to midnight blue. In Vietnamese and in Korean, a single word refers to blue or green. Japanese people use the word *ao* to refer to blue, but the color they are referencing is (for English speakers) green. Finally, Russian speakers do not have a single word for the range of colors that English speakers denote as blue; instead, they have one word for light blue and another for dark blue.

Waquet and Howe wrote an enlightening treatise on this topic of language and perception. In *Latin: A Symbol's Empire,* they trace the domination of Latin in the civic and religious worlds of Europe.[8] Latin's influence on the entire world followed as scholars, educational institutions, and the Roman Catholic Church adopted Latin as their official language. Like any other language, Latin affects perception and the development of culture. The domination of the language has surely shaped the cultures of many Western countries.

The Sapir-Whorf hypothesis, although complex, is not universally accepted by people who study language. For example, critics point out that Inuits may have a large number of words for snow because of their view of snow or because they actually have more varieties of snow in their world. Artists may have more color terms, and printers more words for different fonts, simply because of their work and environment. Thus, the critics note, thought and language may not be intimately related, but experience and language are. Our need to describe our environment and the items within it cause us to create language to do so.

LANGUAGE ORGANIZES AND CLASSIFIES REALITY

Because you cannot account for all the individual things in the world when you speak, you lump them into groups; thus, all four-legged pieces of furniture with seats and backs are called "chairs." Following is an example of how you might use classification when trying to identify someone in a crowd:

"See that person over there?"

"Which one?"

"The tall one."

"The one with short brown hair?"

"No, the shorter one with shoulder-length hair and glasses."

In this case, language is used to classify by height, hair color, and adornment.

You cannot think of your own identity without words because you are symbolically created through language. Your existence emerges through language, yet language is an inadequate means of describing you. You can describe yourself as "an Italian Roman Catholic," but those words say nothing about your height, weight, age, gender, personality, IQ, ambitions, or dreams. Thus, language creates us, without capturing the complexities of our identities.

LANGUAGE IS ARBITRARY

To understand language, you need to understand how words engender meaning. Words are arbitrary: They have no inherent meanings; they have only the meanings people give them. For example, in the English language, a person who has lived through cancer is often referred to as a "survivor." When many people use a word to represent an object or idea, the word is included in the dictionary. The agreed-upon meaning or dictionary meaning is called the **denotative meaning.** Including a word in the dictionary, however, neither keeps its meaning from changing nor tells you the **connotative meaning**—an individualized or personalized meaning that may be emotionally laden. Connotative meanings are meanings others have come to hold because of personal or individual experience. For example, the word *love* holds vastly different meanings for people because of their unique experiences with that concept, despite the agreed-upon denotative meaning that can be found in a dictionary.

To understand connotative meaning further, consider the language that relational couples create. In a romantic relationship you may have nicknames for each other, special terms for activities in which you participate, and unique ways to communicate private thoughts in public settings. Bruess and Pearson showed that heterosexual married couples are most likely to create such terms early in their relationships and that the creation of such terms is associated with relational satisfaction.[9]

Language is symbolic. The words we choose are arbitrary and based on an agreed-upon connection between them and the object or idea that we are referencing. Language varies based on a variety of features of the communicators, including their relational history. For example, you may call someone "Grandma" who biologically is not related to you, or you may choose to have your children call one of your best friends "Aunt" as a symbolic gesture to represent how close that person is to you and your family. Researchers have termed the persons outside blood and legal ties who are considered family *voluntary kin.*[10]

Language and its meaning are personal. Each person talks, listens, and thinks in a unique language (and sometimes several), which contains slight variations of its agreed-upon meanings and which may change each minute. It is shaped by your culture, country, neighborhood, job, personality, education, family, friends, recreation, gender, experiences, age, and other factors. The uniqueness of each individual's language provides valuable information as people attempt to achieve common, shared meaning. But because language is so personal, it can also present some difficulties in communication.

The meanings of words also vary when someone uses the same words in different contexts and situations. For example, *glasses* might mean "drinking glasses" if you are in a housewares store but most likely means "eyeglasses" if you are at the optometrist's office. Semanticists say that meaning emerges from context. But in the case of language, context is more than just the situation in which the communication occurs: context includes the communicators' histories, relationships, thoughts, and feelings.

• Words can have both denotative and connotative meanings.

© ballyscanlon/ Getty Images RF

denotative meaning
The agreed-upon meaning or dictionary meaning of a word.

connotative meaning
An individualized or personalized meaning of a word, which may be emotionally laden.

LANGUAGE IS ABSTRACT

Words are abstractions, or simplifications of what they stand for. Words stand for ideas and things, but they are not the same as those ideas and things. People who study meaning say "the word is not the thing." Semanticist S. I. Hayakawa introduced the "ladder of abstraction," which illustrates that words fall somewhere on a continuum from concrete to abstract.[11] Figure 1 shows an example of a ladder of abstraction for a dog named Bentley. The words used to describe him become increasingly abstract as you go up the ladder.

Language to Avoid When Speaking

When you are verbally communicating, it is important to avoid statements with grammatical errors and the use of slang, clichés, euphemisms, profanity, jargon, regionalisms, and gender-biased, racist, heterosexist, and ageist language. Overall, an important goal for the ways in which you use language should be to work to use language that is inclusive, rather than exclusive, of others.

engaging **diversity**

Vanishing Languages

Could you imagine if only 800 people in the world spoke your language? This is precisely what expedition teams recently discovered when they found a language called Koro, in northeastern India. The language was in danger of becoming extinct, in part because it had never been written down and very few people under 20 years of age speak the language. Linguists suggest that many languages are endangered due to cultural change, ethnic shame, and other factors. The National Geographic Enduring Voices project works to document vanishing languages.

Source: New language discovered in India. (2013, February). *Discovery News* (http://news.discovery.com/human/new-language-india.htm).

GRAMMATICAL ERRORS

Oral communication, in some situations, does not require the same attention to grammar as does written communication. For example, to hear people say, "Can I go with?" and "We're not sure which restaurant we're going to" are common, but neither of these sentences is desirable in written communication. "May I go with you?" and "We're not sure to which restaurant we're going" are correct but sound too formal when spoken in everyday conversation. Although we are often corrected for making grammatical errors in our writing, we are rarely corrected for poor grammar when speaking. On the other hand, some verbal grammatical errors are more obvious than others—for example, "I told him I ain't gonna do it" or "Could you pass them there peanuts?". Communicators who make such errors may find that others form negative opinions about them. Grammatical errors are thus particularly problematic in more formal situations or when another person is assessing your competence. When you are in a classroom, a job interview, or a new relationship, grammatical errors may result in negative perceptions about your credibility as a speaker.

Let's tackle a few of the most common grammatical errors in speaking *and* the correct way to say the same thing. These five come from Karen Bond's "Most Annoying Grammar Mistakes in English."

"He don't care about me anymore" should be "He doesn't care about me anymore."

The grocer's "Ten Items or Less" is incorrect because anything countable uses *fewer;* so "Ten Items or Fewer" is correct, as is "You should eat less meat" (not countable).

"I never would of thought he would act like that" should be "I never would have thought he would act like that."

"I'm not speaking to nobody in this class" should be "I'm not speaking to anybody in this class."

"I should have went to school yesterday" should be "I should have gone to school yesterday."[12]

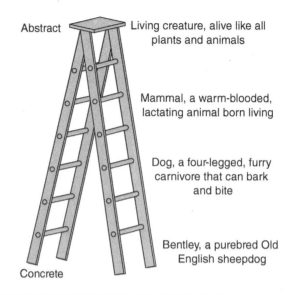

Abstract — Living creature, alive like all plants and animals

Mammal, a warm-blooded, lactating animal born living

Dog, a four-legged, furry carnivore that can bark and bite

Bentley, a purebred Old English sheepdog

Concrete

Figure 1

The ladder of abstraction. Source: Adapted from Hayakawa, S. I. (1978). *Language in thought and action.* Orlando, FL: Harcourt Brace Jovanovich.

We will look next at words that are a bit too casual for formal presentations but that can slip into your speech if you are not careful, because you may be accustomed to using them every day.

SLANG

slang
Informal, casual language used among equals with words typically unsuitable for more formal contexts.

Slang is informal, casual language used among equals with words typically unsuitable for more formal contexts. In other words, you certainly use slang among friends around campus, but such language may be very inappropriate in front of a more formal audience.

"OK, so don't *get bent out of shape*" is slang for "OK, so don't get angry."

"He was *decked* in a bar fight" is slang for "He was knocked down hard in a bar fight."

"My friend is *throwing me shade* on Twitter because I haven't texted him back yet" is slang for "My friend is saying disrespectful things about me on Twitter because I haven't texted him back in days."

"My co-worker is *cray cray*" can be slang for "My co-worker is crazy."[13]

Slang is frequently used in informal situations.
© Fancy/Alamy RF

If you want to see hundreds more examples of slang, just type the word *slang* into an online search engine.

CLICHÉS

A **cliché** is an expression that has lost originality and force through overuse. Common clichés include "No pain, no gain," "Beauty is only skin deep," "Another day, another dollar," and "If you love something, set it free." So many clichés exist that avoiding them would be impossible in your day-to-day conversations, and doing so is unnecessary. Clichés can be a shorthand way to express a common thought. But clichés may be unclear to individuals who are unfamiliar with the underlying idea, and they are usually ineffective in expressing ideas in fresh ways.

The following are a few examples of common American clichés. We provide them here not because we want you to use them, but because we want you to think of more original ways to express your ideas.

cliché
An expression that has lost originality and force through overuse.

all in a day's work

airing dirty laundry

ace in the hole

all's fair in love and war

all thumbs

ants in his pants

at the drop of a hat

as snug as a bug in a rug

barking up the wrong tree

If you want to see more examples of clichés, just type the word *cliché* into an online search engine.

EUPHEMISMS

Like clichés, euphemisms can confuse people who are unfamiliar with their meanings. A **euphemism** is a socially acceptable synonym used to avoid using language that would be offensive in a formal setting. Rothwell observes that euphemisms enter the language to "camouflage the naked truth."[14] Most people use euphemisms in their everyday language. Euphemisms are frequently substituted for short, abrupt words; the names of physical functions; or the terms for some unpleasant social situations. Although euphemisms are frequently considered more polite than the words for which they are substituted, they distort reality.[15] For example, you might hear people say "powder my nose," "see a man about a dog," "visit the little girls' room," or "go to the bathroom" instead of "urinate" or "defecate."

euphemism
A more polite, pleasant expression used instead of a socially unacceptable form.

Other examples from military, government, business, and sports contexts include

Military: "Friendly fire" means "killed by your own soldiers" (decidedly unfriendly)

Government: "undocumented worker" means "illegal alien" (worker can be deported)

Business: "preowned" means "used" (and possibly a "junker," a wrecked car)

Sports: "negative yardage" means "thrown for a loss" (an embarrassing reversal)

Euphemisms are not necessarily to be avoided. Although they can disguise the meaning a person is attempting to convey, they can also substitute for rude or obnoxious commentary. Euphemisms, especially unique euphemisms, can add interest to a conversation. They can also reinforce relational closeness as friends and colleagues regularly use similar euphemisms.

PROFANITY

The word *profane* comes from a Latin word meaning "outside the temple." Thus, **profanity,** or verbal obscenities, is a type of swearing that uses indecent words or phrases. Certainly, some people participate in groups in which profanity is common, as it is with the people on *Real Housewives*. But when you are speaking to people outside your "group"— especially in professional interviews, work teams, or public speaking situations—the use of profanity can offend. Profanity, like slang, may provide a vehicle for establishing group norms, gaining attention, or developing relational closeness in some settings, but it can also make you immediately lose credibility in other situations. Overall, remember that who the speakers are and where they use profanity can alter its effects.[16]

profanity
A type of swearing that uses indecent words or phrases.

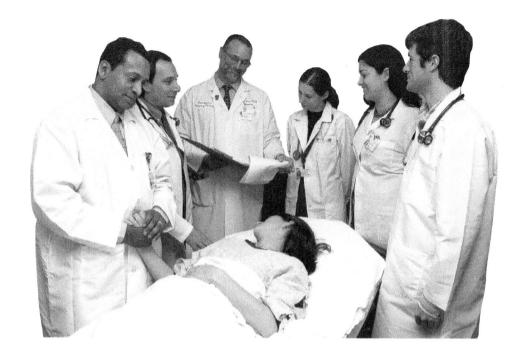

• Although medical jargon may obstruct communication with patients, nonverbal cues can provide comfort.

© David M. Grossman/ The Image Works

JARGON

jargon
Language particular to a specific profession, work group, or culture and not meant to be understood by outsiders.

Jargon is the language particular to a specific profession, work group, or culture and not meant to be understood by outsiders. Doctors, for example, often use medical jargon when they talk to each other about diseases, medications, and procedures. In most workplaces the technical support people are famous for their use of words that others do not understand. The *Hacker Dictionary*, available at catb.org/jargon/, reveals that the computer "hacker culture" uses jargon to overgeneralize grammatical rules. In other words, try not to sound like Dr. Sheldon Cooper, the physics Ph.D. on *The Big Bang Theory*, who confuses Penny in every conversation because he apparently cannot talk without using physics jargon.

If you want to see more examples of jargon, just type the word *jargon* into an online search engine.

You should also consider jargon that you use on the job and how you would translate that jargon to an audience of listeners who were unfamiliar with your work. Very likely, everyone in your class uses some jargon that is unfamiliar to others in the class, but in a communication course the idea is to know how to relate, define, and explain so that your audience learns what you are talking about.

REGIONALISMS

regionalisms
Words and phrases specific to a particular region or part of the country.

Regionalisms are words and phrases specific to a particular region or part of the country. The word *coke* in Texas has the same meaning as *soda* in New York and *pop* in Indiana. When people from different parts of the country try to talk with each other, clarity can break down. Some of us move with frequency from one region of the country to another; others tend to stay in one area. You may believe that you will never leave your home state but find that you are transferred for a new job. Careful listening, which is almost always a good idea, is especially important when you move to a new region. You can fairly easily identify and learn to use language that is particular to a location. Regionalisms encourage group membership for those who use them.

Perhaps the easiest way to illustrate regionalisms is to show the many ways in which people in different areas of the United States refer to those submarine sandwiches that become *hoagies* in Philadelphia, *po' boys* in New Orleans, *grinders* in Boston, *torpedoes* in Los Angeles, *wedgies* in Rhode Island, and *heros* in New York City.[17] Listen before you order your food or drink when you change locations, because your language can mark you as an outsider. Recently, the History Channel did a program on this very topic in a popular series called *How the States Got Their Shapes*. The entire season 1 episode titled "Mouthing Off" centers around regionalisms, such as why we have so many words for the same things.[18]

GENDER-BIASED, RACIST, HETEROSEXIST, AND AGEIST LANGUAGE

Language can communicate prejudice and even silence some members of marginalized groups while privileging other groups.[19] **Gender-biased language,** or gender-specific language, is language that privileges one gender over another; **racist language** is language that insults a group because of its race or ethnicity; **heterosexist language** is language that implies that everyone is heterosexual; and **ageist language** is language that denigrates people for being young or old. Whereas some of the other unique language choices have both positive and negative features, language that is gender-biased, racist, heterosexist, or ageist tends to have only negative consequences. In addition to avoiding these forms of language, you should also be mindful about language that privileges able-bodiedness.

Avoid generalizations and stereotypes—beliefs based on previously formed opinions and attitudes—that all members of a group are more or less alike. Your language can unintentionally suggest gender, as when you say, "A professor needs to read incessantly to keep up with his field," which hints that all professors are men. Say instead, "Professors need to read incessantly to keep up with their field." Also avoid gender-specific compound words, such as *chairman* and *salesman*. Finally, avoid gender-specific occupational titles when the gender is irrelevant. For example, instead of "Our clergyman is a great fisherman," say "Our pastor is a great angler."

The language used surrounding gender can recognize or silence the diverse landscape of gender identification. For example, people who identify with a gender or genders different from the one that was assigned to them at birth can fall under the *trans** umbrella. Using the term *trans** in spoken (and written) language recognizes the incredibly diverse community and widely varying self-identification.[20]

Most people have a good idea of what racist language is. Rather than using racist language, call people what they want to be called. White people should not decide what black people should be called, and straight people should not decide what gay and lesbian individuals should be called.

Homosexuality has always existed, in our culture and in other cultures. The visibility of gay, lesbian, transgender, and bisexual individuals has increased in the general cultural, political, and social stages; yet in many cultures language has masked that reality. An increasing number of gay and lesbian individuals have declared or shared their sexual orientation in recent years. Some are celebrities, possibly your friends or family members, or maybe even you yourself. At the same time, many people intentionally or unintentionally assume heterosexual orientations in their language choices. If you are not gay or lesbian and do not have close friends who have this sexual identity, you may not be sensitive to your language that privileges heterosexuality. Consider using terms such as *partner*, *companion*, and *significant other* instead of *husband*, *girlfriend*, and *spouse*.

Clearly, ageist language is problematic. Today many people in their sixties, seventies, and even eighties continue to have active lives, many of which include paid labor or service obligations. The workforce, partly because of the economy and partly because of the health of older people, is becoming more age-diverse. Ageist language in the workplace negatively affects worker productivity and corporate profitability.[21] In interpersonal communication, ageism is evident in language that infantilizes older persons and diminishes people's concepts of themselves as vigorous and vital. For example, perhaps you

gender-biased language
Language that privileges a certain gender over another.

racist language
Language that insults a group because of its race or ethnicity.

heterosexist language
Language that implies that everyone is heterosexual.

ageist language
Language that denigrates people for being young or old.

have overheard someone talking slower and louder to an older adult at the grocery store when it clearly wasn't necessary to do so. Communication Accommodation Theory (CAT) states that this is over accommodation, or adapting communication beyond what is needed in a given situation.[22] Finally, terms such as "Grandma," and "Gramps" for older people to whom you are not related signals a bias based on age.[23] In the workplace, ageism can occur when organizational practices are biased against younger employees.[24] This can be evident in language such as "kid," "girl," or "boy" or language that suggests people of a certain age are more qualified for leadership roles or opportunities than others.

descriptiveness
The practice of describing observed behavior or phenomena instead of offering personal reactions or judgments.

paraphrasing
Restating another person's message by rephrasing the content or intent of the message.

Improving Language Skills

To recognize that the names for different kinds of language are not mutually exclusive is important; that is, a particular expression can fit in more than one category. Can you see how the brief sentence "How's it going?" can be a cliché and perhaps even a regionalism? Nonetheless, these categories provide a vocabulary you can use to describe the language you hear every day.

building behaviors

Test Your Ability to Recognize Weaknesses in Language

To determine how well you understand the uses of language discussed in this section, complete the following quiz. Which of the following represent clichés, euphemisms, slang, jargon, regionalisms, or gender-biased, racist, heterosexist, or ageist language?

1. "This show gives me the feels."
2. "These kids today can't lead anything. They can't take their eyes off their screens."
3. "She's a cute chick."
4. "Don't add insult to injury."
5. "The rebel group advocates ethnic cleansing."
6. "I'll have a pop with my slice."
7. "Who is the reporting authority?"
8. "That old lady almost ran me over."
9. To a woman: "Who's your boyfriend?"
10. "How much spam do you receive every day?"
11. "Better late than never."
12. "No time for a thorough cleaning, so I will just clat over the floor."
13. "I can really burn rubber."
14. "The employer is engaged in right-sizing."

Answers:
1. Slang; 2. Ageism; 3. Gender-biased/heterosexist language; 4. Cliché; 5. Euphemism; 6. Regionalism; 7. Jargon; 8. Ageism; 9. Gender-biased/heterosexist language; 10. Jargon; 11. Cliché; 12. Regionalism; 13. Slang; 14. Euphemism

You can make specific changes in your language usage that will help you become a more effective communicator. The changes include being descriptive by checking your perceptions, paraphrasing, using operational definitions, and defining your terms. Another change is to be concrete in your use of language by using dating and indexing. Finally, you can change your use of language by understanding and practicing the difference between observation and inference.

USE DESCRIPTIVENESS

Descriptiveness is the practice of describing observed behavior or phenomena instead of offering personal reactions or judgments. You can be descriptive in different ways: by checking your perceptions, paraphrasing, using operational definitions, and defining terms.

Check Your Perceptions

One of the most common ways you can be descriptive is through simple perception checks. To communicate effectively with another person, you and the other person need to have a common understanding of an event that has occurred or a common definition of a particular phenomenon. You can check with another person to determine whether his or her perception is the same as yours.

Paraphrase

Paraphrasing can also help you improve your use of descriptive language. **Paraphrasing** is restating another person's message by rephrasing the content or intent of the message. Paraphrasing is not simply repeating exactly what you heard. Paraphrasing allows the other person—the original speaker—to make corrections, in case you misinterpreted what he or she said. The original speaker must actively listen to your paraphrase to determine whether you understood both the *content* and the *intent* of what he or she said.

It is likely that you have practiced paraphrasing regularly in your everyday life through texting, instant messaging, and tweeting, because these forms force you to paraphrase longer messages into very brief ones. But the important element about paraphrasing in general is not so much being brief as capturing the intended meaning of the other person's message. Thus, a paraphrase really requires a response about whether it was reasonably accurate. Even a simple statement such as "Do you want to celebrate tonight by going out to eat?" invites a paraphrase like "Do you mean you want to celebrate by eating tonight at an expensive restaurant?"—to which the original speaker says, "I do want to celebrate, and I do want to go out tonight, but not necessarily to an expensive restaurant." Through statements, paraphrases, and responses to another's paraphrase, the pair increasingly arrive at the intent and content of the original statement about going out to eat tonight.

operational definition
A definition that identifies something by revealing how it works, how it is made, or what it consists of.

Use Operational Definitions

Another kind of descriptiveness involves using **operational definitions**—that is, definitions that identify something by revealing how it works, how it is made, or what it consists of. Suppose a professor's syllabus states that students will be allowed an excused absence for illness. A student spends a sleepless night studying for an exam in another course, misses class, and claims an excused absence because of illness. The student explains that she was too tired to come to class, and the professor explains that illness is surgery, injury, vomiting, diarrhea, or a very bad headache. This operational definition of illness does not please the

• Define potentially confusing terms to help accurately convey your meaning.
© Laurence Mouton/PhotoAlto/PunchStock RF

student, but it does clarify what the professor means by "illness." In other examples, a cake can be operationally defined by a recipe, and a job by its description. Even abstractions become understandable when they are operationalized. Saying that someone is "romantic" does not reveal much, compared with saying that someone gave you flowers, invited you out for lunch, and took you to an event.

Define Your Terms

Confusion can also arise when you use unusual terms or use words in a special way. If you suspect someone might misunderstand your terminology, you must define the term. In such an instance, you need to be careful not to offend the other person; simply offer a definition that clarifies the term. Similarly, you need to ask others for definitions when they use words in new or unusual ways.

Many terms that we see every day are not necessarily well understood. One student gave a presentation on the

concrete language
Words and statements that are specific rather than abstract or vague.

dating
Specifying when you made an observation, since everything changes over time.

frozen evaluation
An assessment of a concept that does not change over time.

difference between "GMO" and "non-GMO" foods, terms that we see on food labels without knowing the difference. By defining the two terms, the student helped his audience to know terms they see often without understanding.

USE CONCRETE LANGUAGE

A person who uses **concrete language** uses words and statements that are specific rather than abstract or vague. "You have interrupted me three times when I have begun to talk. I feel as though you do not consider my point of view as important as yours" is concrete. In contrast, "You are being rude" is vague. The concrete statement describes the behavior being observed rather than evaluating the person engaging in the behavior.

Earlier in the chapter, semanticists were briefly mentioned. Count Alfred Korzybski started the field of general semantics with the noble purpose of improving human behavior through the careful use of language.[25] The general semanticists' contribution includes the use of more precise, concrete language to facilitate the transmission and reception of symbols as accurately as possible. Semanticists encourage practices that make language more certain to engender shared meanings. Two such practices are dating and indexing.

Dating

Dating is specifying when you made an observation, which is necessary because everything changes over time. Often, you view objects, people, or situations as remaining the same. You form a judgment or view of a person, an idea, or a phenomenon and maintain that view, even though the person, idea, or phenomenon may have changed. Dating is the opposite of **frozen evaluation,** in which you do not allow your assessment to change over time. An example of a frozen evaluation is always seeing someone as a bully because he or she once was. When using dating, instead of saying that something is always or universally a certain way, you state *when* you made your judgment and clarify that your perception was based on that experience.

For example, if you took a course with a particular instructor two years ago, any judgment you make about the course and the instructor must be qualified as to time. You may tell someone, "English 101 with Professor Jones is a breeze," but that judgment may no longer be true. Or suppose you went out with someone a year ago, and now your friend is thinking about going out with that person. You might say that this person was quiet and withdrawn when you dated, but that may no longer be accurate: time has passed, the situation is different, and the person you knew may have

sizing things up

Role Category Questionnaire

This chapter taught you how language can be used to create organization and classification. To illustrate this function of language, this survey asks you to describe two college instructors, one of whom you consider your favorite and one you consider your least favorite. For both persons, you should use sentences to describe what makes these people your favored and least favored teachers. Did you allude to their age, gender, race/ethnicity, physical features, and/or personality characteristics?

When researchers asked students to do this activity, they found that students commented on the age of least favored instructors more than that of favored instructors. Other researchers used 14 million student reviews on RateMyProfessor.com to create an interactive chart that allows users to search for any word and how often it appears by gender and discipline. Overall, words such as *brilliant* and *knowledgeable* are mostly attributed to men and *bossy, ugly,* and *helpful* are largely attributed to women. Ultimately, these unconscious biases go beyond students and teachers to feedback sessions and performance reviews. Benjamin Schmidt, author of the chart, points out that what people write is culture-bound, meaning that it is influenced by one's culture.

Now look at what words, phrases, and labels you used to describe your two instructors. If language shapes reality, then what meaning do you attribute to the number of sentences that were inspired by each person? This exercise has no right or wrong answers. A guide for interpreting your responses appears at the end of the chapter.

Sources: Edwards, C., & Harwood, J. (2003). Social identity in the classroom: An examination of age identification between students and instructors. *Communication Education, 52*(1), 60–65.

Miller, C. C (2015, February 7). Is the professor bossy or brilliant? Much depends on gender. *The New York Times* (http://mobile.nytimes.com/2015/02/07/upshot/is-the-professor-bossy-or-brilliant-much-depends-on-gender.html?_r=2&referrer=).

changed. You can prevent communication problems by saying "English 101 with Professor Jones was a breeze for me when I took it during the spring of 2015" or "Jamie seemed quiet and withdrawn when we dated last year, but I haven't really seen Jamie since."

Indexing

Indexing is identifying the uniqueness of objects, events, and people. Indexing simply means recognizing the differences among the various members of a group. Stereotyping, which was defined earlier in the chapter, is the opposite of indexing. People often assume that the characteristics of one member of a group apply to all members of a group. For example, you might assume that, because you have a good communication instructor, all instructors in the department are exceptional, but that may not be the case. Indexing can help you avoid such generalizations. You could say, "I have a great communication instructor. What is yours like?" Or instead of saying "Hondas get good gas mileage—I know, I own one," which is a generalization about all Hondas based on only one, try "I have a Honda that uses very little gas. How does your Honda do on gas mileage?" And rather than "Firstborn children are more responsible than their younger brothers or sisters," try using indexing: "My older brother is far more responsible than I. Is the same true of your older brother?"

Indexing
Identifying the uniqueness of objects, events, and people.

DIFFERENTIATE BETWEEN OBSERVATIONS AND INFERENCES

Another way to improve language skills is to discern between observations and inferences. Observations are descriptions of what is sensed; inferences are conclusions drawn from observations. For example, during the day you make observations as to where objects in a room are placed. Later at night, when you walk through the room, although you cannot see where the objects are placed, you conclude that they are still where they were during the day, and you are able to walk through the room without bumping into anything. You have no problem with this kind of simple exchange of an inference for an observation—unless someone has moved the furniture or placed a new object in the room, or unless your memory is inaccurate. Even simple inferences can be wrong. Many shins have been bruised because someone relied on inference rather than observation.

If you speak English as a second language, you know that language skills take time and effort to develop. Although much work still needs to be done to better understand how to help

communicating
creatively

Personality Communicated

Are you an introvert? Or are you more of an extrovert? Or better yet, are you an ambivert? You may think that all the loudest people at a party are extroverts and all the quiet people reading books alone at the coffee shop are introverts. Although some people fall neatly into the introverted or extroverted personality spectrums, psychologist Robert McCrae suggests that 38% fall somewhere in between. These people are known as *ambiverts*—people who enjoy the solitude and focus of introversion and engage in the outgoing side of extroversion. Psychologist Dan Pink called the ability to draw on the positives of both the "ambivert advantage." Research has shown that ambiverts are more effective at closing sales than both introverts and extroverts and that companies may want to invest in training extroverted people to model the reserved tendencies of introverts. These labels are somewhat arbitrary because levels of extroversion have more to do with how stimulated you are in the neocortex of the brain than how friendly you are in social settings. Extroverts tend to need more excitement to be stimulated; introverts have lower thresholds for stimulation and tend to seek out more solitude for this reason. Ambiverts are right in the middle in terms of how much arousal they need—they can go back and forth between calmer environments and more exciting settings. Although the psychological explanation of these ideas is interesting, think about where you believe you fall on the introversion–ambiversion–extroversion spectrum and how that reflects in your communication behaviors.

Sources: Yes, it's possible to be both an introvert and an extravert. (2014, November). *Huffington Post* (www.huffingtonpost.com/2014/11/24/both-introvert-and-extravert-ambivert_n_6177854.html). Grant, A. M. (2013). Rethinking the extraverted sales ideal: The ambivert advantage. *Psychological Science, 24*(6), 1024–1030.

non-native speakers build their language skills, the Teachers of English to Speakers of Other Languages (www.tesol.org) provides this advice:

1. *Keep language functional.* Rather than initially learning a second language through vocabulary lists and formal rules of grammar, you should try to learn how to use language in conversation. By learning the functional rules of language, you will develop skills more quickly.

2. *Be aware of language nuances.* As you learn the English language, recognize that how it functions differs, depending on whom you are talking to and in what context. As with your native language, the English language has many nuances. As you pay attention to slight variations in how English is used, your skills in English will accumulate rapidly. Being flexible, observant, and patient is important as you learn about these differences.

3. *Recognize that language learning is long-term.* Native speakers begin learning language from infancy, so it should be no surprise that non-native speakers need time to develop skills. Many non-native speakers may take five to seven years to attain proficiency with English. You can try to speed your learning by engaging in consistent, meaningful interactions with native speakers.

4. *Develop language processes interdependently.* Old views of language acquisition assumed that language learning was linear—that you learned first to listen, then to speak, and finally to read in a second language. Newer views suggest that these processes happen at the same time. Thus, to develop your skills more quickly, you should engage in all of these activities consistently.

5. *Use your own language to help.* Your intuitive understanding of your native tongue can assist you in learning English. For example, your native language has some differences between spoken and written language. Using those differences as a guide, can you discover similar differences in English? By comparing and contrasting your language with English, you will more quickly develop an automatic understanding of how to use English appropriately in different situations.

be ready... for what's next

Is It All About You or Us in the Job Interview?

At this point in the chapter you should feel more confident in knowing how to use language more effectively in your everyday life. Yet it's also important that you think about how this knowledge can promote or hinder your next step in your professional career.

As you are probably well aware, there are more qualified job applicants than there are jobs and you need to set yourself apart from the rest. One way is through the words you use to answer interview questions. Leading business executives offer the following advice for answering the following questions:

Interviewer Question

1. What has been your greatest success so far, and why?

The interviewer wants to hear *we*, rather than *I*, because *we* highlights that you are a team player.

2. What has been your greatest failure so far, and why?

The interviewer wants to hear *I*, rather than *they*, because *I* signals accountability and ownership on your part rather than blaming.

Using pronouns correctly can reveal what kind of employee and team member you are likely to be for the company. Therefore, be mindful of how you respond to these questions.

Source: Fischer, A. (2015, March). How candidates use of two pronouns can reveal (almost) everything you need to know. *Fortune* (http://time.com/3728845/job-interview-words/).

Chapter Review & Study Guide

Summary

In this chapter you learned the following:

1. Language is a collection of symbols, letters, and words with arbitrary meanings that are governed by rules and are used to communicate. It is arbitrary, organizes and classifies reality, is abstract, and shapes perceptions.

2. People sometimes use language poorly, which can present a barrier to communication. Examples include

   - Grammatical errors
   - Slang
   - Clichés
   - Euphemisms
   - Profanity
   - Jargon
   - Regionalisms
   - Gender-biased, racist, heterosexist, and ageist language

3. You can change and improve your use of language by
   - Being more descriptive
   - Being more concrete
   - Differentiating between observations and inferences

Key Terms

Ageist language	Euphemism	Pragmatics
Cliché	Frozen evaluation	Profanity
Concrete language	Gender-biased language	Racist language
Connotative meaning	Heterosexist language	Regionalisms
Culture	Indexing	Sapir-Whorf hypothesis
Dating	Jargon	Semantics
Decode	Language	Slang
Denotative meaning	Operational definition	Syntax
Descriptiveness	Paraphrasing	
Encode	Phatic communication	

Study Questions

1. Which of the following is *not* a characteristic of language?
   a. classifies reality
   b. organizes reality
   c. is arbitrary
   d. is concrete

2. Because messages can vary depending on the situation, to examine the context of the communication is important. This concept is called
   a. syntax.
   b. pragmatics.
   c. semantics.
   d. encoding.

3. Which statement reflects the relationship between language and culture?
   a. Language does not progress in response to the needs of the culture, but culture does progress in response to language.
   b. Language is a minor way that we learn about our culture.
   c. Culture creates a lens through which we perceive the world and create shared meaning.
   d. Language and culture are not related.

4. When doctors communicate with technical language, they are using
   a. profanity.
   b. euphemisms.
   c. clichés.
   d. jargon.

5. One way to improve language skills is to restate the content of the other person's message, a process called
   a. defining your terms.
   b. paraphrasing.
   c. using concrete language.
   d. indexing.

6. A word's dictionary definition is its _____ meaning, and an individualized or personalized definition is its _____ meaning.
   a. denotative; connotative
   b. denotative; abstract
   c. connotative; denotative
   d. concrete; connotative

7. Communication may be hindered in all the following cases *except* when we use
   a. improper grammar.
   b. descriptive language.
   c. clichés.
   d. gender-biased language.

8. Dating is important because
   a. you tend to view objects, people, or situations as remaining the same.
   b. situations change little or not at all over time.

   c. you are saying that something is always static, or universally staying a certain way.
   d. you clarify a perception based on a particular experience in a specific context.

9. Which of the following terms refers to disrespectful language?
   a. profanity
   b. jargon
   c. clichés
   d. regionalisms

10. When you describe observed behavior instead of offering personal reactions, you are
   a. drawing inferences.
   b. being concrete.
   c. using descriptiveness.
   d. being judgmental.

Answers:
1. (d); 2. (b); 3. (c); 4. (d); 5. (b); 6. (a); 7. (b); 8. (d); 9. (a); 10. (c)

Critical Thinking

1. Think hard about some things for which we have no words. If we have no words for something, can we still think about that thing?

2. The Whorf-Sapir hypothesis says that our language shapes our reality. One fact about language is that we have many more negative words to describe women than to describe men. What does that fact say about how English-speaking people in the United States think about women?

3. In what ways, if any, does the use of anonymous posting on social media contribute to the negative and positive use of language?

4. Your culture uses abbreviations and acronyms frequently. Does this practice reduce or enhance group identification? Does this practice reduce or enhance relationship development and intergenerational communication?

Sizing Things Up Scoring and Interpretation

Role Category Questionnaire

One way that language might influence how you perceive the world around you is through implicit categories and hierarchies found in language systems. For instance, you might comment that a dog is "cute" and "friendly." Those terms indicate that you place the dog into certain categories and perhaps even rank the dog into some sort of hierarchy. The role category questionnaire (RCQ) provides one mechanism through which you can identify such hierarchies in how you use language.

The traditional method of scoring the RCQ involves circling and then counting each separate construct used to identify the "liked" person and the "disliked" person. A construct is any adjective or other description that you use to describe the people you analyze. All constructs should be counted, even duplicates, although you should not count descriptions of physical appearance. The total value represents a differentiation score; higher scores represent higher levels of cognitive complexity.

To further explore the hierarchical nature of language, think about the following questions:

1. Are the numbers of constructs you identified for "liked" and "disliked" people generally the same or different for both people? Why?

2. In comparing your scores with others in your class, or even friends you ask to complete the RCQ, are there differences between male and female students in their numbers of constructs? Are there differences between you and students with other characteristics, such as those who are older, are younger, or have different ethnic backgrounds?

3. Do differentiation scores differ depending on whether the person being described is male or female?

You may develop other ways of analyzing results. For instance, you may observe that there are clusters (i.e., hierarchies) of constructs that people use to describe others.

References

1. Curzan, A. (2014, March). What makes a word "real?" [Video file]. Retrieved from http://www.ted.com/talks/anne_curzan_what_makes_a_word_real/transcript?language=en

2. Curzan, A. (2014). 20 words that once meant something very different. Retrieved from http://ideas.ted.com/20-words-that-once-meant-something-very-different/

3. Schilling-Estes, N. (2002). American English social dialect variation and gender. *Journal of English Linguistics, 30,* 122–137.

4. Whorf, B. L. (1956). Science and linguistics. In J. B. Carroll (Ed.), *Language, thought and reality* (pp. 207–219). Cambridge, MA: MIT Press.

5. Bakhurst, D., & Shanker, S. G. (Eds.). (2001). *Jerome Bruner: Language, culture, and self.* Kent, UK: Saunders. Cragan, J. F., & Shields, D. C. (Eds.). (1995). *Symbolic theories in applied communication research: Bormann, Burke and Fisher.* Cresskill, NJ: Hampton Press. Wood, J. T. (1997). *Communication theories in action.* Belmont, CA: Wadsworth.

6. Samovar, L. A., & Porter, R. E. (2000). *Intercultural communication: A reader* (9th ed.). Belmont, CA: Wadsworth. Whorf, Science and linguistics.

7. Walsh, H. (2014, July). 33 cool abbreviations you should know (JIC you didn't already). *The Huffington Post.* Retrieved from http://www.huffingtonpost.com/2014/07/24/dictionary-of-modern acronyms_n_5614544.html

8. Waquet, F., & Howe, J. (2001). *Latin: A symbol's empire.* New York: Verso Books.

9. Bruess, C. J. S., & Pearson, J. C. (1993). "Sweet pea" and "pussy cat": An examination of idiom use and marital satisfaction over the life cycle. *Journal of Social and Personal Relationships, 10,* 609–615.

10. Braithwaite, D. O., Bach B. W., Baxter, L. A., DiVerniero, R., Hammonds, J., Hosek, A. M., Willer, E., & Wolf, B. (2010). Constructing family: A typology of voluntary kin. *Journal of Social and Personal Relationships, 27,* 388–407.

11. Hayakawa, S. I. (1978). *Language in thought and action.* Orlando, FL: Harcourt Brace Jovanovich.

12. Bond, K. (2011). Most annoying grammar mistakes in English. Retrieved from http://www3.tellus.net/linguisticissues/commonerrorsinenglish.html

13. urbandictionary.com. (2015). Retrieved from http://www.urbandictionary.com

14. Rothwell, J. D. (1982). *Telling it like it isn't: Language misuse and malpractice/what we can do about it.* Englewood Cliffs, NJ: Prentice-Hall, 93.

15. Euphamisms. (2015, July 20). Retrieved from http://literarydevices.net/euphemism/

16. Rothwell, J. D. (1971). Verbal obscenity: Time for second thoughts. *Western Speech, 35,* 231–242.

17. Nordquist, R. (2011). Regionalisms. Retrieved from http://grammar.about.com/od/rslg/regionalismterm.htm

18. Sondreal, C. (Writer), & Konschnik, D. (Director). (1986). Mouthing off [Television series episode]. In C. Sondreal (Producer), *How the states got their shapes.* New York: Halfyard Productions.

19. Hecht, M. L. (Ed.). (1998). *Communicating prejudice.* Thousand Oaks, CA: Sage. Taylor, A., & Hardman, M. J. (Eds.). (1998). *Hearing muted voices.* Cresskill, NJ: Hampton Press.

20. Trans* Guide (2015). Retrieved from http://www.ohio.edu/lgbt/resources/transgender.cfm

21. When words get old: Ageist language. (2008, September 9). *NewsBlaze.* Retrieved from http://newsblaze.com/story/2008090913190200009.wi/topstory.html

22. Giles, H., Coupland, N., & Coupland, J. (1991). Accommodation theory: Communication, context, and consequence. In H. Giles, J. Coupland & N. Coupland (Eds.), *Contexts of accommodation: Developments in applied sociolinguistics* (pp. 1–68). New York: Cambridge University Press.

23. Nuessel, F., & Stewart, A. V. (1999). Research summary: Patronizing names and forms of address used with older adults. *Names, 47,* 401–409.

24. McNamara, T. K., & Williamson, J. B. (2012). Is age discrimination ever acceptable. Public Policy & Aging Report, 22(3), 9–13.

25. Korzybski, A. (1994). *Science and sanity.* Forest Hills, NY: Institute of General Semantics.

nonverbal communication

When you have read and thought about this chapter, you will be able to

1. Define nonverbal communication.

2. Describe how verbal and nonverbal codes work in conjunction.

3. Identify two problems people have in interpreting nonverbal codes.

4. Define and identify nonverbal codes.

5. Recognize the types of bodily movement in nonverbal communication.

6. Describe the role of physical attraction in communication.

7. State the factors that determine the amount of personal space you use.

8. Understand how objects are used in nonverbal communication.

9. Utilize strategies for improving your nonverbal communication.

This chapter focuses on the role of nonverbal codes in communication. The chapter first looks at the problems that can occur in interpreting nonverbal codes. Next, some of the major nonverbal codes are identified and defined, including bodily movement and facial expression, bodily appearance, space, time, touching, and vocal cues. The chapter concludes with a discussion of some solutions to the problems you might encounter in interpreting nonverbal codes.

Cultures differ greatly in their rituals and customs associated with communication. Whereas learning other languages can require years of study, picking up on nonverbal rituals can take but a few hours of careful observation. Both of these observations were experienced by one of the authors, who recently visited Thailand for a semester abroad.

In Thai culture, it is common to greet others using a nonverbal gesture that is visually similar to praying—hands pressed together below the chin, with a slight bow of the head.

© ranplett/Getty Images, RF

Most generally, that nonverbal behavior is accompanied by a phrase that has the same meaning as "hello" in English-speaking countries. Later in the chapter you will learn that this accompaniment of verbal and nonverbal symbols is called complementing.

After carefully observing several female colleagues use the gesture and say, "Sawadee-Kha," I felt confident enough to do the same. After several introductions over the course of several days, one of my colleagues mentioned that females end the greeting with "Sawadee-**KHA**," whereas males end the greeting with "Sawadee-**KRAB**." Despite careful observation, the nonverbal behavior was much easier to master than the accompanying verbal symbols. In this chapter you will learn about various nonverbal behaviors, including how nonverbal cues and verbal symbols work alongside one another to create meaning.

Defining Nonverbal Communication

This chapter focuses on nonverbal communication and the relationship between nonverbal and verbal communication. The chapter should help you make sense of the most frequently seen nonverbal codes, as well as provide you with some suggestions for improving your nonverbal communication. Let us begin with a definition of nonverbal communication and a brief discussion of its significance.

Nonverbal communication is the process of using messages other than words to create meaning with others. Nonverbal communication can include behaviors that you see, like facial expressions and gestures; things that you hear, like vocal volume or the speed of talking; and even nonword vocalizations, like "ahh" and "umm." Although precise estimates of how much communication is verbal or nonverbal are difficult, researchers estimate that between 60% and 90% of our daily communication behaviors are conducted nonverbally.[1] Indeed, when we are not certain about another person's feelings or our feeling about him or her, we may rely far more on nonverbal cues and less on the words that are used.[2] You know the importance of nonverbal communication in your own life. Imagine how difficult communication would be if you could not see the people with whom you are communicating, hear their voices, or sense their presence. Actually, this is what occurs when you send e-mail or instant messages or chat with others online. As electronic forms of communication have become more prevalent, people have found creative ways to communicate feeling and

nonverbal communication
The process of using messages other than words to create meaning with others.

emotions. In fact, mobile devices and social networking sites like Facebook offer special keyboards and other tools allowing you to use emojis, or special visual characters, to express emotions and carry on nonverbal conversations. These tools illustrate our need to use symbols and behaviors other than words to convey certain types of messages.

How Verbal and Nonverbal Communication Are Related?

Both verbal and nonverbal communication are essential for effective interactions with others. How are the two related? In a recent study, the roles of verbal and nonverbal elements were examined to determine which was most important in a persuasive message. The results showed that the content (verbal portion of the speech) was most important in determining the effect of the speech. Emphasis and gestures, however, added to some aspects of the presentation and caused the speech to be viewed as lively and powerful.[3] In other words, both the verbal and the nonverbal elements of the speech were important.

Nonverbal communication works in conjunction with the words that we utter in six ways: to repeat, to emphasize, to complement, to contradict, to substitute, and to regulate. Let us consider each of these briefly.

Repeating occurs when the same message is sent verbally and nonverbally. For example, you say that you are "excited" while also displaying a big smile and using animated hand gestures. Or you point to a paper when saying to your instructor, "I need to turn this assignment in early because I will be gone during our next class meeting."

Emphasizing is the use of nonverbal cues to strengthen your message. Hugging a friend and telling him that you really care about him is a stronger statement than using either words or bodily movement alone.

Complementing is different from repeating in that it goes beyond duplication of the message in two channels. It is also not a substitution of one channel for the other. The verbal and nonverbal codes add meaning to each other and expand the meaning of either message alone. For example, during an intense conversation you might hold up your palm to signal "stop" while you are making a point, signaling to the other person to avoid interrupting you. The verbal and nonverbal messages are independent, but add meaning to each other for the listener.

repeating
Sending the same message both verbally and nonverbally.

emphasizing
The use of nonverbal cues to strengthen verbal messages.

complementing
Using nonverbal and verbal codes to add meaning to each other and to expand the meaning of either message alone.

contradicting
Sending verbal and nonverbal messages that conflict.

substituting
Using nonverbal codes instead of verbal codes.

communicating creatively

Repeating and Emphasizing with Slides

When using PowerPoint or Keynote, you are often advised to not have slides simply repeat what you say (or vice versa). One way to effectively and creatively use slides to both repeat and emphasize is to use a minimalist approach with words. Pick a few key words that emphasize points you will make in your presentation, and place those words by themselves on slides. You can use simple text effects like coloring and opacity to improve the aesthetic look of each word on the separate slides. As you move through your presentation, the displayed words will repeat and emphasize, but will do so in a creative way that will not appear as if you are reading to the audience.

Contradicting occurs when your verbal and nonverbal messages conflict. Often this occurs accidentally. If you have ever been angry at a teacher or parent, you may have stated verbally that you were fine—but your bodily movements, facial expression, and use of space may have "leaked" your actual feelings. Contradiction occurs intentionally in humor and sarcasm. Your words provide one message, but your nonverbal delivery tells how you really feel.

Substituting occurs when nonverbal codes are used instead of verbal codes. You roll your eyes, you stick out your tongue, you gesture thumbs down, or you shrug. In most cases your intended message is fairly clear.

Regulating occurs when nonverbal codes are used to monitor and control interactions with others. For example, you look away when someone else is trying to talk and you are not finished with your thought. You walk away from someone who has hurt your feelings or made you angry. You nod your head and encourage another person to continue talking.

regulating
Using nonverbal codes to monitor and control interactions with others.

As we communicate, we naturally allow our verbal and nonverbal communication to interact using these techniques. However, they are not perfectly distinct categories. The raised-palm "stop" signal used while talking is both a complementary message and a regulating message. A tone of voice to suggest sarcasm is both complementing and contradicting. So, while you should understand how these relationships between verbal and nonverbal messages work, you should not assume that they represent perfectly distinct categories of behavior.

Although verbal and nonverbal codes often work in concert, they also exhibit differences, which we will consider next.

The Ambiguity of Nonverbal Codes

Just as people have difficulty interpreting verbal symbols, so do they struggle to interpret nonverbal codes. The ambiguity of nonverbal communication occurs for two reasons: people use the same code to communicate a variety of meanings, and they use a variety of codes to communicate the same meaning.

ONE CODE COMMUNICATES A VARIETY OF MEANINGS

The ambiguity of nonverbal codes occurs in part because one code may communicate several different meanings. For example, the nonverbal code of raising your right hand may mean that you are taking an oath, you are demonstrating for a cause, you are indicating to an instructor that you would like to answer a question, a physician is examining your right side, or you want a taxi to stop for you. Also consider how you may stand close to someone because of a feeling of affection, because the room is crowded, or because you have difficulty hearing.

Although people in laboratory experiments have demonstrated some success in decoding nonverbal behavior accurately,[4] in actual situations receivers of nonverbal cues can only guess about the meaning of the cue.[5] Our accuracy in interpreting nonverbal codes can be influenced by factors such as the communication context, our familiarity with the person with whom we are interacting, and our skills in listening to and observing others.

A VARIETY OF CODES COMMUNICATE THE SAME MEANING

Nonverbal communication is not a science; any number of codes may be used to communicate the same meaning. One example is the many nonverbal ways by which adults communicate love or affection. You may sit or stand more closely to someone you love. You might speak more softly, use a certain vocal intonation, or alter how quickly you speak when you communicate with someone with whom you are affectionate. Or perhaps you choose to dress differently when you are going to be in the company of someone you love.

Cultural differences are especially relevant when we consider that multiple cues may be used to express a similar message. How do you show respect to a speaker in a public speaking situation? In some cultures listeners show respect when they avert their eyes; in other cultures listeners show respect and attention by looking directly at the speaker. You may believe that showing your emotions is an important first step in resolving conflict, whereas a classmate may feel that emotional responses interfere with conflict resolution.

You must know a person in order to interpret his or her nonverbal communication.

© Sigrid Olsson/PhotoAlto/ Corbis RF

nonverbal codes
Messages consisting of symbols that are not words, including nonword vocalizations.

kinesics
The study of bodily movements, including posture, gestures, and facial expressions.

emblems
Nonverbal movements that substitute for words and phrases.

Nonverbal Codes

Nonverbal codes are messages consisting of symbols that are not words, including nonword vocalizations. Bodily movement, facial expression, physical attraction, the use of space, the use of time, touch, vocal cues, and clothing and artifacts are all nonverbal codes. Let us consider these systematic arrangements of symbols that have been given arbitrary meaning and are used in communication.

BODILY MOVEMENT AND FACIAL EXPRESSION

The study of bodily movements, including posture, gestures, and facial expressions, is called **kinesics,** a word derived from the Greek word *kinesis,* meaning "movement." Some popular books purport to teach you how to "read" nonverbal communication, so that you will know, for example, who is sexually aroused, who is just kidding, and whom you should avoid. Nonverbal communication, however, is more complicated than that. Interpreting the meaning of nonverbal communication is partly a matter of assessing the other person's unique behavior and considering the context. You don't just "read" another person's body language; instead, you observe, analyze, and interpret before you decide the probable meaning.

Assessing another person's unique behavior means that you need to know how that person usually acts. A quiet person might be unflappable even in an emergency situation. A person who never smiles may not be unhappy, and someone who acts happy might not actually be happy. You need to know how the person expresses emotions before you can interpret what his or her nonverbal communication means.

To look more deeply into interpreting nonverbal communication, let us consider the work of some experts on the subject: Albert Mehrabian, Paul Ekman, and Wallace Friesen.

Mehrabian studied nonverbal communication by considering its connection to how we display liking, status, and responsiveness.[6]

- We express *liking* by forward leaning, a direct body orientation (such as standing face-to-face), close proximity, increased touching, relaxed posture, open arms and body, positive facial expression, and direct eye contact. Liking is essential in communication. For example, people who work for supervisors who engage in these kinds of behaviors tend to have higher self-reported satisfaction than do people who work for managers who do not use these behaviors.[7] Indeed, babies as young as two to five days of age prefer faces that offer a direct gaze rather than those that look to one side.[8]

- *Status,* especially high status, is communicated nonverbally by bigger gestures, relaxed posture, and less eye contact. During a conversation, an individual with higher status might feel more comfortable using forceful gestures than would someone in a lower-status role.

- *Responsiveness* is exhibited by movement toward the other person, by spontaneous gestures, by shifts in posture and position, and by facial expressiveness. In other words, the face and body provide positive feedback to the other person.

Ekman categorized movement on the basis of its functions, origins, and meanings.[9] The categories include emblems, illustrators, affect displays, regulators, and adaptors.

- **Emblems** are nonverbal movements that substitute for words and phrases. Examples of emblems are a beckoning first finger to mean "come here," an open hand held up to mean "stop," and a forefinger and thumb forming a circle to mean "OK." Be wary of emblems; they may mean something else in another culture.

- **Illustrators** are nonverbal movements that accompany or reinforce verbal messages. Examples of illustrators are nodding your head when you say yes, shaking your head when you say no, stroking your stomach when you say you are hungry, and shaking your fist in the air when you say, "Get out of here." These nonverbal cues tend to be more universal than many in the other four categories of movement.

- **Affect displays** are nonverbal movements of the face and body used to show emotion. Watch people's behavior when their favorite team wins a game, listen to the door slam when an angry person leaves the room, and watch men make threatening moves when they are very upset with each other but don't really want to fight.

- **Regulators** are nonverbal movements that control the flow or pace of communication. Examples of regulators are starting to move away when you want the conversation to stop, gazing at the floor or looking away when you are not interested, and yawning and glancing at your watch when you are bored. Turn taking in conversations is generally managed with gestures, gaze, and touch. However, turn taking regulators vary from one culture to another.[10]

- **Adaptors** are nonverbal movements that usually involve the unintended touching of our bodies or manipulations of a body artifact that serves some physical or psychological need.[11] Some people habitually play with their hair, others adjust their glasses, and some even constantly rub or scratch their hands. We often use these adaptors without knowledge, but they could signal deep thought, anxiety, or distraction to observers.

Finally, Ekman and Friesen determined that a person's facial expressions provide information to others about how he or she feels.[12] Consider the smile. Findings are overwhelming that a person who smiles is rated more positively than a person who uses a neutral facial expression. Indeed, you are more likely to be offered a job if you smile.[13]

Perhaps a more provocative finding is that people are more likely to attend to faces that are angry or threatening than they are to neutral facial expressions. When adults were presented with multiple faces, including some that appeared threatening, they were more likely to attend to the angry faces than they were to others. Recently, it was shown that children have the same bias, and they observed angry and frightened faces more rapidly than they did happy or sad faces.[14] This response to threatening stimuli may have evolved as a protective means to help people avoid danger.

What is the effect of showing disagreement with a negative facial expression and head shaking, compared to using a neutral facial expression? In a study investigating opponents who stood behind a political speaker and displayed neutral facial expression, occasional negative facial expression, constant negative expression, or both negative and positive expression, surprising results were found. When either negative or

illustrators
Nonverbal movements that accompany or reinforce verbal messages.

affect displays
Nonverbal movements of the face and body used to show emotion.

regulators
Nonverbal movements that control the flow or pace of communication.

adaptors
Nonverbal movements that usually involve the unintended touching or manipulating of our bodies or artifacts to fulfill some physical or psychological need.

building **behaviors**

It's All About the Face

Most of our emotions are conveyed through our face. Whether we are happy, sad, excited, or bored, our face most likely gives our emotions away. To learn about this connection, take 15 minutes to carefully observe another person during a lecture or during conversation. During that time, attempt to record and describe each facial expression that you observe. What conclusions can you draw about the emotions that person was experiencing. Do you think the observed emotions were authentic? Why or why not? Learning to read emotions during conversations can help you become better at sharing meaning with and responding to others.

Ask a classmate to record a video of you giving a presentation, engaging in conversation, or taking part in a group discussion. When watching the video, take note of how you use facial expressions, gestures, movement, and other nonverbal features. By intentionally focusing on how you use a few of those behaviors, how can you best improve your nonverbal communication?

negative and positive expressions were used, respondents viewed the speaker as less credible, less appropriate, and less skillful in debate.[15] In other words, some positive facial expressions did not lessen the negative response toward the speaker.

Research on bodily movement today includes considerations of how the body and mind work together. Although we have known for some time that bodily movement has some basis in the brain and in our neurological functioning, a new focus combining these areas has shown promise. For example, groups of psychologists, neuroscientists, dancers, and choreographers have worked together to explore how the act of dancing affects both performers and spectators. One study reported that when spectators watch dance, they become emotionally excitable and have a sense of connection to the dancer.[16] This suggests that our minds actively process and draw meaning from a variety of bodily movements.

Facial expressions are important in conveying information to others and in learning what others are feeling. Bodily movement and orientation add to that information by suggesting how intense the feeling might be. When you are able to observe and interpret both facial expression and bodily movement, you gain a fuller understanding of the other person's message.

PHYSICAL ATTRACTION

Beauty, it has been noted, is in the eye of the beholder. However, some research has suggested that particular characteristics—bright eyes, symmetrical features, and thin or medium build—are generally associated with physical attraction.[17] Moreover, such characteristics may not be limited to our culture but may be universal.[18]

Physical attractiveness affects many aspects of our lives. Generally, people who are physically attractive are privileged over those who are not physically attractive. This bias is stronger for women than for men.[19] In other words, in our culture it is more important that women are physically attractive than are men.

Physical attractiveness has been studied over the life course. Jaeger's comprehensive study found that taller men have higher earnings than do shorter men, that attractive women who are not overweight have higher socioeconomic status late in their careers, and that both women and men who are attractive are more likely to be married at younger ages.[20]

The influence of physical appearance begins when we are young. By age four, children are treated differently based on their physical appearance by their daycare teachers.[21] When children misbehave, their behavior is viewed as an isolated, momentary aberration if they are physically attractive but as evidence of a chronic tendency to be bad if they are unattractive. These patterns continue throughout childhood and adolescence.[22]

Physical attractiveness generally leads to more social success in adulthood. Women who are attractive report a larger number of dates in college. Attractiveness may be affected by skin tone and hair color. Swami, Furnham, and Joshi found that men clearly prefer brunettes over blondes, and they slightly prefer women who have light skin tones.[23] Both women and men who are attractive are seen as more sociable and sensitive.[24]

Do people change their view of mate preferences over time? Eastwick and Finkel found that men ideally desire a physically attractive mate whereas women ideally desire a mate who has strong earning prospects.[25] In real-life potential partners, women and men did not evidence these preferences or differences. Stereotypes may exist in abstract thinking about potential mates, but they do not appear to be realized in actual behavior.

The "matching hypothesis" suggests that women and men seek others who are of similar attractiveness. Lee, Loewenstein, Ariely, Hong, and Young demonstrated this consistent finding, although they did find that men were more oblivious to their own physical attractiveness in selecting a woman to date, whereas women were keenly aware of their "physical attraction quotient."[26] They also asked whether less attractive people delude themselves when they are dating less attractive people with the sense that they are more attractive than others view them. They found that this is not the case. People have a fairly objective sense of their own, and their partner's, attractiveness.

Similarly, people who are obese are less likely to have physically attractive partners than are people of normal weight. Body type is not the only factor in mate selection; obese people are seen as more attractive if they have a good education, good grooming, and more attractive personalities. Nonetheless, similarity in body type remains the strongest predictor in mate selection among these qualities.[27]

Physical attractiveness affects both credibility and one's ability to persuade others. Attractive people receive higher initial credibility ratings than do those who are viewed as unattractive.[28] Women have more success in persuading the opposite sex when they are attractive than men have in persuading the opposite sex when they are attractive, but attractive women find that this effect dissipates as they grow older.[29] When two attractive women interact, they compete dynamically for status, which suggests that they feel they have more social status or interactional power as a result of their physical beauty.[30]

Physical attractiveness is also relevant in relationships that are formed and maintained through digitally mediated communication channels. Social networking sites like Instagram allow individuals to use selfies, which are a way we represent our physical appearance to others. The ways we represent ourselves might differ online, but the role of attractiveness in communication does not.

Although there are several potential benefits of being physically attractive, we must also remember that an overemphasis on physical attraction can be damaging. Writing in her senior thesis at Claremont McKenna College, Kendyl Klein pointed out that advertising and social media work together to perpetuate an idealized body image. Such images are used by some as a measure of their own attractiveness, which can lead to serious negative outcomes like body dissatisfaction, eating disorders, and disordered eating, which includes behaviors similar to eating disorders but lesser in frequency or degree.[31]

Physical attractiveness is an important nonverbal attribute, but the media may distort realistic views of physical attractiveness.

© Antonio de Moraes Barros Filho/WireImage/Getty Images

SPACE

Anthropologist Edward T. Hall introduced the concept of **proxemics**—the study of the human use of space and distance—in his book *The Hidden Dimension*.[32] This researcher and others, such as Werner,[33] have demonstrated the role space plays in human communication. Two concepts considered essential to the study of the use of space are territoriality and personal space.

proxemics
The study of the human use of space and distance.

• *Territoriality* refers to your need to establish and maintain certain spaces as your own. In a shared residence hall room, items on a common desk area mark territory. For example, you might place your notebook, pens and pencils, and tablet charger on the right side of the desk and your roommate might place books, a cell phone, and a laptop on the left side. While the desk is shared, you are each claiming part of the area. On a cafeteria table the placement of the plate, glass, napkin, and eating utensils marks the territory. In a neighborhood it might be fences, hedges, trees, or rocks that mark the territory. All are nonverbal indicators that signal ownership.

- *Personal space* is the personal "bubble" that moves around with you. It is the distance you maintain between yourself and others, the amount of space you claim as your own. Large people usually claim more space because of their size, and men often take more space than women. For example, in a lecture hall, observe who claims the armrests as part of their personal bubbles.

Hall was the first to define the four distances people regularly use while they communicate.[34] His categories have been helpful in understanding the communicative behavior that might occur when two people are a particular distance from each other. Beginning with the closest contact and the least personal space, and moving to the greatest distance, Hall's categories are intimate distance, personal distance, social distance, and public distance.

- *Intimate distance* extends from you outward to 18 inches, and it is used by people who are relationally close to you. Used more often in private than in public, this intimate distance is employed to show affection, to give comfort, and to protect. Burgoon noted that the use of intimate distance usually elicits a positive response because individuals tend to stand and sit close to people to whom they are attracted.[35]

- *Personal distance* ranges from 18 inches to 4 feet, and it is the distance used by most Americans for conversation and other nonintimate exchanges.

- *Social distance* ranges from 4 to 12 feet, and it is used most often to carry out business in the workplace, especially in formal, less personal situations. The higher the status of one person, the greater the distance.

- *Public distance* exceeds 12 feet and is used most often in public speaking in such settings as lecture halls; churches, mosques, and synagogues; courtrooms; and convention halls. Professors often stand at this distance while lecturing.

Distance, then, is a nonverbal means of communicating everything from the size of your personal bubble to your relationship with the person to whom you are speaking or listening. A great deal of research has been done on proxemics.[36] Virtual environments allow researchers to study the human use of space in relatively unobtrusive ways.[37] Sex, size, and similarity seem to be among the important determiners of personal space.

Gender affects the amount of space people are given and the space in which they choose to communicate.[38] Men tend to take more space because they are often larger than women.[39] Women take less space, and children take and are given the least space. Women exhibit less discomfort with small space and tend to interact at closer range.[40] Perhaps because women are so often given little space, they come to expect it. Also, women and children in our society seem to desire more relational closeness than do men.

Your relationship to other people is related to your use of space. You stand closer to friends and farther from enemies. You stand farther from strangers, authority figures, high-status people, physically challenged people, and people from racial groups different from your own. You stand closer to people you perceive as similar or unthreatening because closeness communicates trust.

The physical setting also can alter the use of space. People tend to stand closer together in large rooms and farther apart in small rooms.[41] In addition, physical obstacles and furniture arrangements can affect the use of personal space. We even use space when online. By friending, following, or connecting with people on social media, you invite them into your virtual space through your timeline or personal profile. Connecting online is similar to taking a step closer to someone in a face-to-face situation. Some apps even use location tagging to help us know when we are in proximity to contacts and friends.

The cultural background of the people communicating also must be considered in the evaluation of personal space.[42] Hall was among the first to recognize the importance of cultural background when he was training American service personnel for service overseas. He wrote:

> Americans overseas were confronted with a variety of difficulties because of cultural differences in the handling of space. People stood "too close" during conversations, and when the Americans backed away to a comfortable conversational distance, this was taken to mean that Americans were cold, aloof, withdrawn, and disinterested in the people of the country. USA housewives muttered about "waste-space" in houses in the Middle East. In England, Americans who were used to neighborliness were hurt when they discovered that their neighbors were no more accessible or friendly than other people, and in Latin America, exsuburbanites, accustomed to unfenced yards, found that the high walls there made them feel "shut out." Even in Germany, where so many of my countrymen felt at home, radically different patterns in the use of space led to unexpected tensions.[43]

Cultural background can result in great differences in the use of space and in people's interpretation of such use. As our world continues to shrink, more people will be working in multinational corporations, regularly traveling to different countries and interacting with others from a variety of backgrounds. Sensitivity to space use in different cultures and quick, appropriate responses to those variations are imperative.

TIME

Temporal communication, or **chronemics,** is the way that people organize and use time and the messages that are created because of their organization and use of that time. Time can be examined on a macro level. How do you perceive the past, future, and present? Some people value the past and collect photographs and souvenirs to remind themselves of times gone by. They emphasize how things have been. Others live in the future and are always chasing dreams or planning future events. They may be more eager when planning a vacation or party than they are when the event arrives. Still others live in the present and savor the current time. They try to live each day to its fullest and neither lament the past nor show concern for the future.

chronemics
Also called temporal communication; the way people organize and use time and the messages that are created because of their organization and use of that time.

One distinction that has been drawn that helps us understand how individuals view and use time differently is the contrast between monochronic and polychronic people. *Monochronic* people view time as very serious and they complete one task at a time. Often their jobs are more important to them than anything else—perhaps even including their families. Monochronic people view privacy as important. They tend to work independently, and they rarely borrow or lend money or other items. They may appear to be secluded or even isolated. Although we cannot generalize to all people, we may view particular countries as generally monochronic. They include the United States, Canada, Germany, and Switzerland. In contrast, *polychronic* people

building **behaviors**

Time Flies

We become better communicators as we are able to distinguish between others' varying behaviors. In the next week, observe at least three of your friends. Describe how each of them uses time differently. Do they tend to be more monochronic or polychronic? What cues did you use to make this assessment? How can you be more effective in your communication with them if they are monochronic? If they are polychronic? Consider adaptations that you can make when you encounter a person who is more monochronic than polychronic.

work on several tasks at a time. Time is important, but it is not revered. Interpersonal relationships are more important to them than their work. Polychronic individuals tend to be highly engaged with others. Again, without generalizing to all people, countries such as Egypt, Saudi Arabia, Mexico, and the Philippines tend to include people who are polychronic.

Time is viewed dissimilarly in different cultures.[44] In the United States, two recent applications of the use of time—one in electronic communication and one in the workplace—have been studied. The first is the effect of relatively slow or quick responses to e-mail. Earlier research suggested that delayed e-mail messages could cause perceptions of decreased closeness. More recently, though, it appears that several factors interact to produce feelings of increased closeness or more distance. In addition to reply rate are biological sex and emotional empathy. People who demonstrate concern for the other person may offset feelings of detachment that a delayed e-mail message could ordinarily signal.

The second study looked at how several features of time affected worker job satisfaction and worker satisfaction with their communication. The researchers learned that the highest job satisfaction occurred among people who viewed their work as more punctual and oriented toward the future. When workers experienced delayed time, they were least satisfied with their interactions.[45]

TOUCHING

tactile communication
The use of touch in communication.

Tactile communication is the use of touch in communication. Because touch always involves invasion of another person's personal space, it commands attention. It can be welcome, as when a crying child is held by a parent, or unwelcome, as in sexual

Touch commands attention and is essential to many rituals.

© AP Images/Shawn Baldwin

harassment. Our need for and appreciation of tactile communication start early in life.[46] Psychologist William Schutz observed:

> The unconscious parental feelings communicated through touch or lack of touch can lead to feelings of confusion and conflict in a child. Sometimes a "modern" parent will say all the right things but not want to touch the child very much. The child's confusion comes from the inconsistency of levels: if they really approve of me so much like they say they do, why don't they touch me?[47]

Insufficient touching can lead to health disorders, such as allergies and eczema, speech problems, and even death. Researchers have found that untouched babies and small children can grow increasingly ill and die.[48]

For adults, touch is a powerful means of communication.[49] Usually, touch is perceived as positive, pleasurable, and reinforcing. The association of touch with the warmth and caring that began in infancy carries over into adulthood. People who are comfortable with touch are more likely to be satisfied with their past and current lives. They are self-confident, assertive, socially acceptable, and active in confronting problems. Think about how you use nonverbal communication. Are you comfortable touching and being touched? Do you frequently hug others or shake hands with others?

Touch is part of many important rituals. In baptism, the practice can range from as little as a touch on the head during the ceremony to as much as a total immersion in water. In some churches, prayers are said with the pastor's hand touching the person being prayed for. In some fundamentalist Christian churches, the healer might accompany the touch with a mighty shove, right into the hands of two catchers. Physician Bernie Siegel wrote the following in his book on mind–body communication:

> I'd like to see some teaching time devoted to the healing power of touch—a subject that only 12 of 169 medical schools in the English-speaking world deal with at all . . . despite the fact that touch is one of the most basic forms of communication between people. . . . We need to teach medical students how to touch people.[50]

Siegel's appeal did not go unheard. A number of medical schools are now training their students to decode patients' nonverbal cues and to provide nonverbal communication, including touch, to their patients.[51] The results of the training are mixed, however; as students' awareness of nonverbal communication increases, their actual performance does not.[52] Religion and medicine are just two professions in which touch is important for ceremonial and curative purposes.

Touch varies by gender.[53] The findings relating touch with gender indicate the following:

- Women value touch more than men do.[54]
- Women are touched more than men, beginning when they are six-month-old girls.[55]
- Women touch female children more often than they touch male children.[56]
- Men and their sons touch each other the least.[57]
- Female students are touched more often and in more places than are male students.[58]
- Males touch others more often than females touch others.[59]
- Males may use touch to indicate power or dominance.[60]

On the last point, to observe who can touch whom among people in the workplace is interesting. Although fear of being accused of sexual harassment has eliminated a great deal of touch except for handshaking, the general nonverbal principle is that the higher-status individual gets to initiate touch, but touch is not reciprocal: the president might pat you on the back for a job well done, but in our society you don't pat back. We even see the importance of touch in online communication. Take a look at your Instagram feed and count how often you see pictures of people touching. Indeed, new communication tools provide opportunities for hundreds or even thousands of people to witness our use of touch with others.[61]

Further, both co-culture, such as gender, and culture determine the frequency and kind of nonverbal communication. People from different countries handle nonverbal communication differently—even something as simple as touch.[62] Sidney Jourard determined the rates of touch per hour among adults from various cultures.[63] In a coffee shop, adults in San Juan, Puerto Rico, touched 180 times per hour, whereas those in Paris, France, touched about 110 times per hour, followed by those in Gainesville, Florida, who touched about 2 times per hour, and those in London, England, who touched only once per hour.

Touch sends such a powerful message that it has to be handled with responsibility. Touch may be welcomed by some in work or clinical settings, but it is equally likely that touch is undesirable or annoying. Certainly, touch can be misunderstood in such settings.[64] When the right to touch is abused, it can result in a breach of trust, anxiety, and hostility. When touch is used to communicate concern, caring, and affection, it is welcome, desired, and appreciated.

VOCAL CUES

Nonverbal communication includes some sounds, as long as they are not words. We call them **paralinguistic features**—the nonword sounds and nonword characteristics of language, such as pitch, volume, rate, and quality. The prefix *para* means "alongside" or "parallel to," so *paralinguistic* means "alongside the words or language."

The paralinguistic feature examined here is **vocal cues**—all of the oral aspects of sound except words themselves. Vocal cues include

- **Pitch:** the highness or lowness of your voice
- **Rate:** how rapidly or slowly you speak
- **Inflection:** the variety or changes in pitch
- **Volume:** the loudness or softness of your voice
- **Quality:** the unique resonance of your voice, such as huskiness, nasality, raspiness, or whininess
- **Nonword sounds:** "mmh," "huh," "ahh," and the like, as well as pauses or the absence of sound used for effect in speaking
- **Pronunciation:** whether or not you say a word correctly
- **Articulation:** whether or not your mouth, tongue, and teeth coordinate to make a word understandable to others (such as a lisp)
- **Enunciation:** whether or not you combine pronunciation and articulation to produce a word with clarity and distinction so that it can be understood; a person who mumbles has an enunciation problem
- **Silence:** the lack of sound

These vocal cues are important because they are linked in our mind with a speaker's physical characteristics, emotional state, personality characteristics, gender characteristics, and even credibility. For example, when you talk to strangers on the telephone, you form an impression of how they look and how their personality might be described. In addition, vocal cues, alone, have a persuasive effect for people when they are as young as 12 months.[65]

According to Kramer, vocal cues frequently convey information about the speaker's characteristics, such as age, height, appearance, and body type.[66] For example, people often associate a high-pitched voice with someone who is female, younger, and/or smaller.

---

paralinguistic features
The nonword sounds and nonword characteristics of language, such as pitch, volume, rate, and quality.

vocal cues
All of the oral aspects of sound except words themselves.

pitch
The highness or lowness of the voice.

rate
The pace of your speech.

inflection
The variety or changes in pitch.

volume
The loudness or softness of the voice.

quality
The unique resonance of the voice, such as huskiness, nasality, raspiness, or whininess.

nonword sounds
Sounds like "mmh," "huh," and "ahh," as well as the pauses or the absence of sounds used for effect.

pronunciation
Saying a word correctly or incorrectly.

articulation
Coordinating one's mouth, tongue, and teeth to make words understandable to others.

enunciation
Combining pronunciation and articulation to produce a word with clarity and distinction.

silence
The lack of sound.

You may visualize someone who uses a loud voice as being big or someone who speaks quickly as being nervous. People who tend to speak slowly and deliberately may be perceived as being high-status individuals or as having high credibility.

A number of studies have related emotional states to specific vocal cues. Joy and hate appear to be the most accurately communicated emotions, whereas shame and love are among the most difficult to communicate accurately.[67] Joy and hate appear to be conveyed by fewer vocal cues, and this makes them less difficult to interpret than emotions such as shame and love, which are conveyed by complex sets of vocal cues. "Active" feelings, such as joy and hate, are associated with a loud voice, a high pitch, and a rapid rate. Conversely, "passive" feelings, which include affection and sadness, are communicated with a soft voice, a low pitch, and a relatively slow rate.[68]

Personality characteristics also have been related to vocal cues. Dominance, social adjustment, and sociability have been clearly correlated with specific vocal cues.[69] Irony, on the other hand, cannot be determined on the basis of vocal cues alone.[70]

Although the personality characteristics attributed to individuals displaying particular vocal cues have not been shown to accurately portray the person, as determined by standardized personality tests, our impressions affect our interactions. In other words, although you may perceive loud-voiced, high-pitched, fast-speaking individuals as dominant, they might not be measured as dominant by a personality inventory. Nonetheless, in your interactions with such people, you may become increasingly submissive because of your perception that they are dominant. In addition, these people may begin to become more dominant because they are treated as though they have this personality characteristic.

Vocal cues can help a public speaker establish credibility with an audience and can clarify the message. Pitch and inflection can be used to make the speech sound aesthetically pleasing, to accomplish subtle changes in meaning, and to tell an audience whether you are asking a question or making a statement, being sincere or sarcastic, or being doubtful or assertive. A rapid speaking rate may indicate you are confident about speaking in public or you are nervously attempting to conclude your speech. Variations in volume can be used to add emphasis or to create suspense. Enunciation is especially important in public speaking because of the increased size of the audience and the fewer opportunities for direct feedback. Pauses can be used in a public speech to create dramatic effect and to arouse audience interest. Vocalized pauses—"ah," "uh-huh," "um," and so on—are not desirable in public speaking and may distract the audience.

Silence is a complex behavior steeped in contradictions. During interpersonal conversations, public speeches, and group discussions, silence can be used strategically to your advantage. Intentionally being silent can create a dramatic pause to build drama or punctuate a point.[71] When presenting or discussing difficult information, silence can

engaging **diversity**

An International Education at Home

Colleges and universities in the United States remain a destination of choice for international college students. During the 2013–2014 academic year, a record 886,052 international students enrolled in American higher education, according to a study conducted by the Institute of International Education in partnership with the U.S. Department of State. Because this trend is expected to continue, you will increasingly work alongside students from other cultures.

How will you learn to work with these students in teams? Should you ask them about their home customs, dress, and use of nonverbal symbols to say hello? While you could simply ignore those issues and interact with international students as if they were Americans, you would be missing an opportunity to learn. By talking about nonverbal and other communication behaviors with your international peers, you could gain valuable information that could improve your communication when you have opportunities to travel abroad or eventually work with people from other cultures. Culturally based nonverbal behaviors are among the most interesting and easily learned communication behaviors in other cultures.

Source: 2014 Open Doors Report (2014, November 17). Institute for International Education (www.iie.org/en/Research-and-Publications/Open-Doors).

allow listeners time to process and give meaning to your statements. On the other hand, silence may signal the dark side of communication. People in power, in dominant cultures, or in positions of authority may silence others. Those with whom they come in contact may be marginalized or embarrassed and feel that they must remain silent because of sexism, racism, taboo, incidents of violence or abuse, shame, or a hostile environment.[72]

CLOTHING AND ARTIFACTS

objectics
Also called object language; the study of the human use of clothing and artifacts as nonverbal codes.

artifacts
Ornaments or adornments you display that hold communicative potential.

Objectics, or object language, is the study of the human use of clothing and artifacts as nonverbal codes. **Artifacts** are ornaments or adornments you display that hold communicative potential, including jewelry, hairstyles, cosmetics, automobiles, canes, watches, shoes, portfolios, hats, glasses, tattoos, body piercings, and even the fillings in teeth. Your clothing and other adornments communicate your age, gender, status, role, socioeconomic class, group memberships, personality, and relation to the opposite sex. Dresses are seldom worn by men, low-cut gowns are not the choice of shy women, bright colors are avoided by reticent people, and the most recent Paris fashions are seldom seen in the small towns of America.

These cues also indicate the time in history, the time of day, the climate, and one's culture.[73] Clothing and artifacts provide physical and psychological protection, and they are used to spur sexual attraction and to indicate self-concept. Your clothing and artifacts clarify the sort of person you believe you are.[74] They permit personal expression,[75] and they satisfy your need for creative self-expression.[76]

Many studies have established a relationship between an individual's clothing and artifacts and his or her characteristics. Conforming to current styles is correlated with an individual's desire to be accepted and liked.[77] In addition, individuals feel that clothing is important in forming first impressions.[78]

Perhaps of more importance are the studies that consider the relationship between clothing and an observer's perception of that person. In an early study, clothing was shown to affect others' impressions of status and personality traits.[79] People also seem to base their acceptance of others on their clothing and artifacts. In another early study, women who were asked to describe the most popular women they knew cited clothing as the most important characteristic.[80]

What do you conclude about this person based on the artifacts?

© Medioimages/Photodisc/Getty Images RF

Clothing also communicates authority and people's roles. Physicians have historically worn a white coat to indicate their role. For many people the white coat signified healing and better health. As the white coat has begun to be phased out, however, the physician's ability to persuade patients to follow advice may have declined as well. Thus, physicians may need to learn alternative symbolic means of persuasion.[81]

As the world has become more interconnected, we have become increasingly aware of how people dress in other cultures. The dress of the Muslim woman, which tends to be modest and consist of loose and fairly heavy materials, is distinctive. Some Muslim women cover their entire bodies, including the face and/or hands, whereas others wear a simple hijab on their heads, with long sleeves and long skirts. Others modify this look with head scarves and Western-style clothing. Muslim women in Saudi Arabia are among the most conservatively dressed, with dark colors and bodies totally covered by abayas and chadors, whereas Muslim women in Malaysia wear bright colors, jewelry, makeup, and scarves in place of the traditional head pieces, and they may sport long skirts with slits up the side.

Indian people are well represented in universities, technology fields, and medicine in the United States. Some women from India who are Hindu may wear dhotis and saris, at least for formal occasions.

Although the skirts are long, frequently the middle area of the body can be glimpsed in these outfits. Additionally, because a number of Mormons have been actively engaged in politics, including running for the U.S. presidency, their unique clothing has been discussed.

Christian crosses have been banned in most public elementary schools in the United States and Europe.[82] The cross has become associated with gangs, and the reasoning is that by prohibiting the cross, schools might curtail gang behavior. In some schools, religious symbols of other major religions are allowed, whereas other schools have banned all religious symbols. Needless to say, parents and school boards have been vocal in their debates over such prohibitions.

Body modifications are a type of artifact. They include tattoos and piercing, which have been popular in recent years. Although they can be removed, the procedures may be both costly and time-intensive. What do tattoos signal to others? Most people probably choose to adorn themselves with tattoos and piercings because they believe such artifacts add to their overall attractiveness. A recent study, however, showed some different findings. Men with tattoos were viewed as more dominant than nontattooed men, and women with tattoos were seen as less healthy than women without tattoos. These findings hold implications for a biological signaling effect of tattoos.[83]

Ways to Improve Nonverbal Communication

Skills in being able to effectively interpret and respond to nonverbal cues vary greatly among individuals.[84] You can improve your understanding of nonverbal communication, though, by being sensitive to context, audience, and feedback.

The *context* includes the physical setting, the occasion, and the situation. In conversation, your vocal cues are rarely a problem unless you stutter, stammer, lisp, or are affected by some speech pathology. Paralinguistic features loom large in importance in small-group communication, in which you have to adapt to the distance and to a variety of receivers. These features are perhaps most important in public speaking because you have to adjust volume and rate, you have to enunciate more clearly, and you have to introduce more vocal variety to keep the audience's attention. The strategic use of pauses and silence is also more apparent in public speaking than it is in an interpersonal context in conversations or small-group discussion.

The occasion and physical setting also affect the potential meaning of a nonverbal cue. For example, when would it be appropriate for you to wear a cap over unwashed, uncombed hair and when would doing so be interpreted as inappropriate? The distance at which you communicate may be different based on the setting and the occasion: you may stand farther away from people in formal situations when space allows but closer to family members or to strangers in an elevator.

The *audience* makes a difference in your nonverbal communication, so you have to adapt. When speaking to children, you must use a simple vocabulary and careful enunciation, articulation, and pronunciation. With an older audience or with younger audiences whose hearing has been impaired by too much loud music, you must adapt your volume. Generally, children and older people in both interpersonal and public-speaking situations appreciate slower speech. Also, adaptation to an audience may determine your choice of clothing, hairstyle, and jewelry. For instance, a shaved head, a facial piercing, and a shirt open to the navel will not go over well in a job interview unless you are trying for a job as an entertainer.

Your attention to giving *feedback* can be very important in helping others interpret your nonverbal cues that might otherwise distract your listeners. For example, some pregnant women avoid questions and distraction by wearing a shirt that says, "I'm not fat, I'm pregnant"; such feedback prevents listeners from wondering instead of listening. Similarly, your listeners' own descriptive feedback—giving quizzical looks, staring, or nodding off—can

sizing things up

Berkeley Nonverbal Expressiveness Questionnaire

In this chapter you learned that your nonverbal communication is used to express meaning generally and emotion in particular. Each statement below describes ways in which you express your emotions through nonverbal communication. Respond to each statement using the following scale. A guide for interpreting your responses appears at the end of the chapter.

1 = Strongly disagree
2
3
4 = Neutral
5
6
7 = Strongly agree

1. Whenever I feel positive emotions, people can easily see exactly what I am feeling.
2. I sometimes cry during sad movies.
3. People often do not know what I am feeling.
4. I laugh out loud when someone tells me a joke that I think is funny.
5. It is difficult for me to hide my fear.
6. When I'm happy, my feelings show.
7. My body reacts very strongly to emotional situations.
8. I've learned it is better to suppress my anger than to show it.
9. No matter how nervous or upset I am, I tend to keep a calm exterior.
10. I am an emotionally expressive person.
11. I have strong emotions.
12. I am sometimes unable to hide my feelings, even though I would like to.
13. Whenever I feel negative emotions, people can easily see exactly what I am feeling.
14. There have been times when I have not been able to stop crying even though I tried to stop.
15. I experience my emotions very strongly.
16. What I'm feeling is written all over my face.

Source: Copyright © 1997 by the American Psychological Association. Reproduced with permission. Gross, J. J., & John, O. P. (1997). Revealing feelings: Facets of emotional expressivity in self-reports, peer ratings, and behavior. *Journal of Personality and Social Psychology, 72*, 435–448.

signal you to talk louder, introduce variety, restate your points, or clarify your message.

If your conversational partner or audience does not provide you with feedback, what can you do? Practice asking questions and checking on the perceptions of others with whom you communicate. Silence has many meanings, and you sometimes must take great effort to interpret the lack of feedback in a communicative setting. You can also consider your past experience with particular individuals or a similar audience. Do they ever provide feedback? Under what circumstances are they expressive? How can you become more accurate in your interpretation of their feedback?

Although this chapter only introduces you to nonverbal communication, you know that your success in college and in the workplace is dependent on your sensitivity to nonverbal cues and your ability to alter familiar nonverbal cues, given the context and the situation. The following are some suggestions offered by professors and employers:

1. Establish eye contact and demonstrate interest through bodily movement and the use of space. Both professors and employers observe that students and new workers appear to be tied to their handheld devices. How much time do you spend on Facebook, Twitter, and YouTube? Do you plan on "media-free" time while in class, while studying, and while at work? In a recent study, professors attempted to curtail the use of text messaging in class by using positive facial expression, standing closer to the students, using a relaxed stance, and speaking in an animated manner, but these behaviors did not discourage the use of handheld devices.[85] If your professors cannot influence your behavior, consider what you might do to show interest and to avoid being distracted.

2. Recognize that others may use time differently than you do. It is always important to attend class and to be on time. Your professor probably offers office hours. Take advantage of meeting with him or her during these scheduled times, rather than

waiting until the last minute and then demanding an emergency meeting or having an electronic "meltdown."

3. Manage your time just as your professors and employers do. Find time to do your homework, to study for exams, to write papers, and to meet with your study groups. Similarly, go to work on time or earlier, stay until your shift or time is completed, and do your job while you are at work.

4. Manage your time in your interactions with others. Allow others to share their experiences, and be willing to exchange talk time. Do you tend to interrupt or overlap your professors or employers? Allow other people a full hearing.

5. Be aware that most professors and most employers are not interested in a personal relationship. Do not engage in romantic behaviors with either one. Touching, using intimate physical space, requiring time alone after hours, and engaging in other such behaviors are generally inappropriate.

6. Dress appropriately for school and for work. Students have assumed very relaxed standards for classroom attire. If your college allows revealing casual clothes, you may be able to dress similarly. However, you will want to consider dressing more conservatively for your job. Some work sites do not even allow jeans.

7. Avoid using overly dramatic nonverbal behaviors to intentionally or unintentionally signal disagreement with a professor, employer, or friend. Most people appreciate hearing about differences in opinions, but they do not value sneers or being mocked.

engaging **diversity**

Understanding Differences in Nonverbal Communication

A variety of characteristics can be used to identify distinctions among cultures—many of which include nonverbal differences in how we use gestures, space, touch, and even time. If you come from a country other than the United States, the amount of nonverbal adaptation you will need to undertake depends on how similar your culture is to U.S. culture. Although many nonverbal characteristics will likely be similar—the use of facial expression to convey emotion, for instance—there are also likely to be several differences. Understanding those differences can help you avoid misperceiving others and potentially avoid creating misperceptions yourself. Key considerations include the following:

- *Americans tend to expect consistent uses of space.* In normal conversations, U.S. speakers tend to stay in Hall's personal distance zone. Standing closer can violate expectations and cause discomfort and unease; standing farther apart can be perceived as unfriendly. Unless you are very close to another person, touching is generally considered a violation of space rather than a signal of warmth, particularly among adults.

- *A greater emphasis is placed on verbal messages.* Although most communication is still done nonverbally during interactions, U.S. speakers tend to be verbally explicit in terms of describing feelings, opinions, and thoughts. A non-native speaker may need to be more explicit and should not assume that such explicitness is rude—such directness is simply a cultural characteristic.

- *U.S. uses of emblems are often for less formal messages.* Commonly used emblems range from obscene gestures to specific emblems representing athletic teams. Unlike emblems in other cultures, very few U.S. emblems signify status or respect.

- *Eye contact is expected.* In nearly every communication situation, consistent eye contact is viewed positively as a signal of confidence, warmth, and attentiveness. Even in situations in which there are strong power differences, such as the communication between a supervisor and an employee, eye contact is desirable; a lack of consistent eye contact can cause you to be viewed as untrustworthy or noncredible.

- *For vocal characteristics, bigger tends to be better.* Listeners tend to react positively to speakers who have strong volume, good vocal variety, and forceful projection and articulation.

As a general principle, U.S. speakers tend to be expressive with most nonverbal behaviors, though such expressiveness is typically not found with respect to space and touch. You will notice many other cultural characteristics of U.S. nonverbal behavior as you gain more experience observing native speakers. You may integrate some of those differences into your own communication repertoire; others you may dismiss. Being observant and asking native speakers about their use of various nonverbal behaviors, as well as their expectations for how others use those behaviors, will help non-native speakers develop their own skills more quickly.

be ready... for what's next

Learning to Say It Like It Is

As you progress through your college and professional career, you will have opportunities to take on greater levels of responsibility. For example, you will work in teams with individuals who are perhaps older and have more experience. Learning to sound confident in those situations could impact how people perceive you. Being confident is communicated through your nonverbal behaviors. One of the best ways to improve perceptions of your confidence is through your use of paralanguage. You can practice paralanguage by reading text out loud at least once a week, recording yourself, and then critiquing how well you enunciate, use vocal variety, rate, and other paralinguistic vocal cues. Learning to use paralanguage effectively will cause people to perceive you as more confident, which will likely open new opportunities for growth for you.

Chapter Review & Study Guide

Summary

In this chapter, you learned the following:

1. Nonverbal communication is defined as the process of using messages other than words to create meaning with others.

2. Verbal and nonverbal codes work in conjunction with each other in six ways: to repeat, to emphasize, to complement, to contradict, to substitute, and to regulate.

3. People often have difficulty interpreting nonverbal codes because

   - They use the same code to communicate a variety of meanings.

   - They use a variety of codes to communicate the same meaning.

4. Nonverbal codes consist of nonword symbols, such as the following:

   - Bodily movements and facial expression include posture, gestures, and other bodily movements and facial expressions, known as kinesics.

   - Bodily appearance includes how physically attractive one is.

   - Proxemics is the study of the human use of space and distance.

   - Temporal communication, or chronemics, is the way people organize and use time and the messages that are created because of their organization and use of that time.

   - Tactile communication is the use of touch in communication.

   - Paralinguistic features include the nonword sounds and nonword characteristics of language, such as pitch, volume, rate, and quality.

   - Objectics, or object language, is the study of the human use of clothing and artifacts as nonverbal codes.

5. The types of bodily movement are posture, gestures, and facial expression.

6. Physical attraction affects how other people treat us, how socially successful we are, with whom we have a relationship, how credible we are, and how persuasive we are.

7. Personal space is affected by one's size and one's biological sex.

8. Objects are used in communication to indicate one's age, gender, status, role, socioeconomic class, group memberships, personality, and relationship to the opposite sex.

9. You can solve some of the difficulties in interpreting nonverbal codes if you

   - Consider all the variables in each communication situation.

   - Consider all the available verbal and nonverbal codes.

   - Use descriptive feedback to minimize misunderstandings.

Key Terms

Adaptors
Affect displays
Articulation
Artifacts
Chronemics
Complementing
Contradicting
Emblems
Emphasizing
Enunciation
Illustrators

Inflection
Kinesics
Nonverbal codes
Nonverbal communication
Nonword sounds
Objectics
Paralinguistic features
Pitch
Pronunciation
Proxemics

Quality
Rate
Regulating
Regulators
Repeating
Silence
Substituting
Tactile communication
Vocal cues
Volume

Study Questions

1. What is included in nonverbal communication?

   a. only vocalized cues
   b. only nonvocalized cues
   c. nonword vocalizations as well as nonvocalized cues
   d. vocalized words

2. Nonverbal codes work together with vocalized words to

   a. generalize and broaden.
   b. analyze and synthesize.
   c. confuse and distinguish.
   d. contradict and substitute.

3. One of the difficulties of interpreting nonverbal codes is

   a. one code may communicate several different meanings.
   b. no two nonverbal codes communicate the same meaning.
   c. each nonverbal cue has only one perceived meaning.
   d. observers can easily distinguish meaning from specific nonverbal cues.

4. Bodily movement, facial expression, the use of time, and vocal cues, among other actions, are examples of

   a. kinesics.
   b. complementation.
   c. nonverbal codes.
   d. adaptors.

5. What type of nonverbal cue is most likely to be used to fulfill a personal psychological need?

   a. emblem
   b. adaptor
   c. illustrator
   d. chronemic

6. Pointing to your wrist while asking for the time is an example of a(n)

   a. adaptor.
   b. illustrator.
   c. regulator.
   d. emblem.

7. Compared with those who are unattractive, physically attractive people

   a. tend to be snobbish.
   b. never learn how to work well with others.
   c. are more likely to wait until they are older to marry.
   d. are treated differently as children.

8. Shaking hands while saying "hello" is an example of

   a. regulating.
   b. repeating.
   c. emphasizing.
   d. complementing.

9. In relation to gender and tactile communication, which of the following is true?

   a. Females and their daughters touch each other the least.
   b. Men value touch more than women do.
   c. Women are touched more than men.
   d. Females touch others more often than males touch others.

10. Which of the following provide physical and psychological protection, permit personal expression, and communicate age, gender, socioeconomic class, and personality?

    a. vocal cues
    b. affect displays
    c. illustrators
    d. artifacts

connect

To maximize your study time, check out CONNECT to access the SmartBook study module for this chapter, watch videos, and explore other resources.

Answers:

1. (c); 2. (d); 3. (a); 4. (c); 5. (b); 6. (b); 7. (d); 8. (c); 9. (c); 10. (d)

Critical Thinking

1. When speaking verbally, we use paralanguage to supply important information about syntax that would normally be visible in written text. How do you naturally relay syntax using such paralinguistic vocal cues? What errors could you potentially make with paralanguage that could make your syntax difficult to follow? Besides paralanguage, are there other ways to use nonverbal behaviors to make spoken syntax easier to follow?

2. When you are at the library or other public place, note how people "mark their territory." Do they use their backpack or purse, books, or nothing at all? Also observe the size of people's personal space. Does one gender have a smaller space than the other? Does age make a difference? In what situations does that distance decrease?

Sizing Things Up Scoring and Interpretation

Berkeley Nonverbal Expressiveness Questionnaire

Simple observation suggests that some people are just more nonverbally expressive than others. Whereas one person may remain stiff and deadpan, another may appear to be landing planes based on the nature of how he or she naturally gestures. The nonverbal expressiveness questionnaire assesses the extent to which a person "leaks" implicit meanings (especially emotional) through nonverbal behaviors. Although this scale is typically used to assess expressiveness, you will notice that expressivity is enacted, based on these statements, through nonverbal cues.

The expressivity scale taps three dimensions of nonverbal/emotional expressivity. To achieve a score for each dimension, simply average the values for each item after reverse-coding the items below with the "(R)" next to the item number; higher values indicate higher levels for that dimension. To reverse-code items indicated below, take your original responses and make a 1 become a 7, a 2 become a 6, or a 3 become a 5. If you answered initially with a 7, 6, or 5,

do the opposite. After reverse-coding your answers, average all questions related to each of the three dimensions.

- *Negative expressivity*. The extent to which others observe you feeling negative emotions, such as nervousness, fear, and anger. The following items are included in this dimension: 9(R), 13, 16, 3(R), 5, and 8(R).

- *Positive expressivity*. The extent to which others can observe you experiencing positive emotions, such as happiness and joy. The following items should be averaged for this dimension: 6, 1, 4, and 10.

- *Impulse strength*. The extent to which you can control, diminish, or manage your emotional expression. Items for this dimension are 15, 11, 14, 7, 2, and 12.

You can also average all questions to obtain an overall expressiveness value. Higher overall scores indicate, regardless of positive or negative emotions, how expressive you are.

References

1. Eastman, B. (2015, February 12). How much of communication is really nonverbal? The Nonverbal Group Blog [webpage]. Available from http://www.nonverbal-group.com/2011/08/how-much-of-communication-is-really-nonverbal/

2. Grahe, J. E., & Bernieri, F. J. (1999). The importance of nonverbal cues in judging rapport. *Journal of Nonverbal Behavior, 23,* 253–269. Vedantam, S. (2006, October 2–8). A mirror on reality: Research shows that neurons in the brain help us understand social cues. *Washington Post National Weekly Edition, 23*(50): 35.

3. Nikolaus, Jackob, Roessing, Thomas, & Petersen, Thomas. (2011). The effects of verbal and nonverbal elements in persuasive communication: Findings from two multi-method experiments. *Communications: The European Journal of Communication Research, 36,* 245–271.

4. Horgan, T., & Smith, J. (2006). Interpersonal reasons for interpersonal perceptions: Gender-incongruent purpose goals and nonverbal judgment accuracy. *Journal of Nonverbal Behavior, 30,* 127–140.

5. Motley, M. T., & Camden, C. T. (1988). Facial expression of emotion: A comparison of posed expressions versus spontaneous expressions in an interpersonal communication setting. *Western Journal of Speech Communication, 52,* 1–22.

6. Mehrabian, A. (1971). *Silent messages.* Belmont, CA: Wadsworth.

7. Teven, Jason J. (2010). The effects of supervisor nonverbal immediacy and power use on employees' ratings of credibility and affect for the supervisor. *Human Communication,13,* 69–85.

8. Bower, B. (2002, July 6). The eyes have it. *Science News, 162*(1): 4.

9. Ekman, P. (1997). Should we call it expression or communication? *Innovations in Social Science Research, 10,* 333–344. Ekman, P. (1999). Basic emotions. In T. Dalgleish & T. Power (Eds.), *The handbook of cognition and emotion* (pp. 45–60). Sussex, UK: Wiley. Ekman, P. (1999). Facial expressions. In T. Dalgleish & T. Power (Eds.), *The handbook of cognition and emotion* (pp. 301–320). Sussex, UK: Wiley.

10. Yang, Ping. (2011). Nonverbal aspects of turn taking in Mandarin. *Language and Discourse, 2,* 99–130.

11. Fujiwara, K., & Daibo, I. (2014). The extraction of nonverbal behaviors: Using video images and speech-signal analysis in dyadic conversation. *Journal of Nonverbal Behavior, 38,* 377–388.

12. Ekman, P., & Friesen, W. V. (1967). Head and body cues in the judgment of emotion: A reformulation. *Perceptual and Motor Skills, 24,* 711–724.

13. Krumhuber, E., Manstead, A., Cosker, D., Marshall, D., & Rosin, P. (2009). The effects of dynamic attributes of smiles in human and synthetic faces: A simulated job interview setting. *Journal of Nonverbal Behavior, 33,* 1–15.

14. LoBue, V. (2009). More than just another face in the crowd: Superior detection of threatening facial expressions in children and adults. *Developmental Science, 12,* 305–313.

15. Seiter, John S., Weger, Harry, Jensen, Andrea, & Kinzer, Harold J. (2010). The role of background behavior in televised debates: Does displaying nonverbal agreement and/or disagreement benefit either debater? *Journal of Social Psychology, 150,* 278–300.

16. Jola, C., Ehrenberg, S., & Reynolds, D. (2012). The experience of watching dance: Phenomenological-neuroscience duets. *Phenomenology and the Cognitive Sciences, 11,* 17–37.

17. Cash, T. F. (1980, July 7). If you think beautiful people hold all the cards, you're right, says a researcher. *People Weekly, 14,* 74–79. Kowner, R. (1996, June). Facial asymmetry and attractiveness judgment in developmental perspective. *Journal of Experimental Psychology, 22,* 662–675.

18. Brody, J. E. (1994, March 21). Notions of beauty transcend culture, new study suggests. *The New York Times,* A14.

19. Rhode, Deborah L. (2010). *The beauty bias: The injustice of appearance in life and law.* New York: Oxford University Press.

20. Jaeger, Mads Meier. (2011). "A thing of beauty is a joy forever": Returns to physical attractiveness over the life course. *Social Forces, 89,* 983–1003.

21. Cash, If you think beautiful people hold all the cards, you're right, says a researcher.

22. Knapp, M. L., & Hall, J. A. (2010). *Nonverbal communication in human interaction* (7th ed.). Boston: Wadsworth.

23. Swami, V., Furnham, A., & Joshi, K. (2008). The influence of skin tone, hair length, and hair colour on ratings of women's physical attractiveness, health and fertility. *Scandinavian Journal of Psychology, 49,* 429–437.

24. Knapp & Hall, *Nonverbal communication in human interaction.*

25. Eastwick, P. W., & Finkel, E. J. (2008). Sex differences in mate preferences revisited: Do people know what they initially desire in a romantic partner? *Journal of Personality and Social Psychology, 94,* 245–264.

26. Lee, L., Loewenstein, G., Ariely, D., Hong, J., & Young, J. (2008). If I'm not hot, are you hot or not? Physical attractiveness evaluations and dating preferences as a function of one's own attractiveness. *Psychological Science, 19,* 669–677.

27. Carmalt, J. H., Cawley, J., Joyner, K., & Sobal, J. (2008). Body weight and matching with a physically attractive romantic partner. *Journal of Marriage and Family, 70,* 1287–1296.

28. Widgery, R. N. (1974). Sex of receiver and physical attractiveness of source as determinants of initial credibility perception. *Western Speech, 38,* 13–17.

29. Davies, A. P. C., Goetz, A. T., & Shackelford, T. K. (2008). Exploiting the beauty in the eye of the beholder: The use of physical attractiveness as a persuasive tactic. *Personality and Individual Differences, 45,* 302–306.

30. Haas, A., & Gregory, S. (2005). The impact of physical attractiveness on women's social status and interactional power. *Sociological Forum, 20,* 449–471.

31. Klein, K. M. (2013). Why don't I look like her? The impact of social media on female body image. Unpublished manuscript. Claremont McKenna College. Available from http://scholarship.claremont.edu/cgi/viewcontent.cgi?

32. Hall, E. T. (1966). *The hidden dimension.* New York: Doubleday.

33. Werner, C. M. (1987). Home interiors: A time and place for interpersonal relationships. *Environment and Behavior, 19,* 169–179.

34. Hall, *The hidden dimension.*

35. Burgoon, J. K. (1978). A communication model of personal space violations: Explication and an initial test. *Human Communication Research, 4,* 129–142.

36. See, for example, McMurtray, J. W. (2000). Exploring that other space. *Ad Astra, 12*(1): 38–39; and Terneus, S. K., & Malone, Y. (2004). Proxemics and kinesics of adolescents in dual-gender groups. *Guidance and Counseling, 19,* 118–123.

37. Bailenson, J. N., Blascovich, J., Beall, A. C., & Loomis, J. M. (2001). Equilibrium theory revisited: Mutual gaze

and personal space in virtual environments. *Presence: Teleporters and Virtual Environments, 10,* 583–598.

38. Ro'sing, I. (2003). The gender of space. *Philosophy and Geography, 6,* 189–211.

39. Argyle, M., & Dean, J. (1965). Eye contact, distance, and affiliation. *Sociometry, 28,* 289–304.

40. Leventhal, G., & Matturro, M. (1980). Differential effects of spatial crowding and sex on behavior. *Perceptual and Motor Skills, 51,* 111–119.

41. Sommer, R. (1962). The distance for comfortable conversation: A further study. *Sociometry, 25,* 111–116.

42. Burgoon, Judee K., & Hubbard, Amy Ebesu. (2004). Cross-cultural and intercultural applications of expectancy violations theory and interaction adaptation theory. In William B. Gudykunst (Ed.), *Theorizing about intercultural communication* (pp. 149–171). Thousand Oaks, CA: Sage.

43. Hall, E. T. (1963). Proxemics: The study of man's spatial relations and boundaries. In I. Galdston (Ed.), *Man's image in medicine and anthropology* (pp. 422–445). New York: International Universities Press.

44. Bruneau, T. J. (2007). Time, change, and sociocultural communication: A chronemic perspective. *Sign Systems Studies, 35,* 89–117.

45. Ballard, D. I., & Seibold, D. R. (2006). The experience of time at work: Relationship to communication load, job satisfaction, and interdepartmental communication. *Communication Studies, 57,* 317–340.

46. Cecchini, Marco, Baroni, Eleonora, Di Vito, Cinzia, & Lai, Carlo . (2011). Smiling in newborns during communicative wake and active sleep. *Infant Behavior & Development, 34,* 417–423.

47. Schutz, W. C. (1971). *Here comes everybody.* New York: Harper & Row, 16.

48. Hertenstein, M. J. (2002). Touch: Its communicative functions in infancy. *Human Development, 45,* 70–94. Loots, G., & Devise, I. (2003). The use of visual-tactile communication strategies by deaf and hearing fathers and mothers of deaf infants. *Journal of Deaf Studies and Deaf Education, 8,* 31–43.

49. Aguinis, H., Simonsen, M. M., & Pierce, C. A. (1998). Effects of nonverbal behavior on perceptions of power bases. *Journal of Social Psychology, 138*(4): 455–475.

50. Siegel, B. S. (1990). *Peace, love and healing: Bodymind communication and the path to self-healing: An exploration.* New York: Harper Perennial, 134.

51. Molinuevo, Beatriz, Escorihuela, Rosa M., Fernandez-Teruel, Albert, Tobena, Adolf, & Torrubia, Raphael. (2011). How we train undergraduate medical students in decoding patients' nonverbal clues. *Medical Teacher, 33,* 804–807.

52. Ishikawa, Hirono, Hashimoto, Hideki, Kinoshita, Makoto, & Yano, Eliji. (2010). Can nonverbal skills be taught? *Medical Teacher, 32,* 860–863.

53. Lee, J. W., & Guerrero, L. K. (2001). Types of touch in cross-sex relationships between coworkers: Perceptions of relational and emotional messages, inappropriateness, and sexual harassment. *Journal of Applied Communication Research, 29,* 197–220.

54. Fisher, J. D., Rytting, M., & Heslin, R. (1976). Hands touching hands: Affective and evaluative effects of interpersonal touch. *Sociometry, 3,* 416–421.

55. Goldberg, S., & Lewis, M. (1969). Play behavior in the year-old infant: Early sex differences. *Child Development, 40,* 21–31.

56. Ibid.

57. Jourard, S., & Rubin, J. E. (1968). Self-disclosure and touching: A study of two modes of interpersonal encounter and their inter-relation. *Journal of Humanistic Psychology, 8,* 39–48.

58. Jourard, S. M. (1966). An exploratory study of body accessibility. *British Journal of Social and Clinical Psychology, 5,* 221–231.

59. Henley, N. (1973–1974). Power, sex, and nonverbal communication. *Berkeley Journal of Sociology, 18,* 10–11.

60. McDaniel, E., & Andersen, P. A. (1998). International patterns of interpersonal tactile communication: A field study. *Journal of Nonverbal Behavior, 22,* 59–76.

61. Immergut, M., & Kosut, M. (2014). Visualizing charisma: Representations of the charismatic touch. *Visual Studies, 29,* 272–284.

62. Jourard, S. M. (1968). *Disclosing man to himself.* Princeton, NJ: Van Nostrand.

63. ibid.

64. Kane, M. N. (2006). Research note: Sexual misconduct, non-sexual touch, and dual relationships: Risks for priests in light of the code of pastoral conduct. *Review of Religious Research, 48,* 105–110. Lee & Guerrero, Types of touch in cross-sex relationships between coworkers. Strozier, A. L., Krizek, C., & Sale, K. (2003). Touch: Its use in psychotherapy. *Journal of Social Work Practice, 17,* 49–62.

65. Vaish, A., & Striano, T. (2004). Is visual reference necessary? Contributions of facial versus vocal cues in 12-month-olds' social referencing behavior. *Developmental Science, 7,* 261–269.

66. Kramer, E. (1963). The judgment of personal characteristics and emotions from nonverbal properties of speech. *Psychological Bulletin, 60,* 408–420.

67. Laukka, P., Juslin, P. N., & Bresin, R. (2005). A dimensional approach to vocal expression of emotion. *Cognition and Emotion, 19,* 633–653. Planalp, S. (1996). Varieties of cues to emotion in naturally occurring situations. *Cognition and Emotion, 10,* 137–154.

68. Kramer, The judgment of personal characteristics and emotions from nonverbal properties of speech.

69. Bateson, G., Jackson, D. D., Haley, J., & Weakland, J. H. (1956). Toward a theory of schizophrenia. *Behavioral Science, 1,* 251–264.

70. Bryant, G. A., & Tree, J. E. F. (2005). Is there an ironic tone of voice? *Language and Speech, 48,* 257–277.

71. Genard, G. (2013, August 25). Public speaking tips: Silence is one of your most powerful tools. Speak for Success [webpage]. Available from http://www.genard-method.com/blog-detail/view/25/public-speaking-tips-silence-is-one-of-your-most-powerful-tools#.VN9PZOJwXlk

72. Olson, L. C. (1997). On the margins of rhetoric: Audre Lorde transforming silence into language and action. *Quarterly Journal of Speech, 83,* 49–70.

73. Frith, K. T., Hong, C., & Ping Shaw, K. T. (2004). Race and beauty: A comparison of Asian and Western models in women's magazine advertisements. *Sex Roles, 50*(1/2): 53–61.

74. Fisher, S. (1975). Body decoration and camouflage. In L. M. Gurel & M. S. Beeson (Eds.), *Dimensions of dress and adornment: A book of readings.* Dubuque, IA: Kendall/Hunt.

75. Boswell, R. (2006). Say what you like: Dress, identity, and heritage in Zanzibar. *International Journal of Heritage Studies, 12,* 440–457.

76. Laurie, Alison. (2000). *The language of clothes.* New York: Holt.

77. Taylor, L. C., & Compton, N. H. (1968). Personality correlates of dress conformity. *Journal of Home Economics, 60,* 653–656.

78. Henricks, S. H., Kelley, E. A., & Eicher, J. B. (1968). Senior girls' appearance and social acceptance. *Journal of Home Economics, 60,* 167–172.

79. Douty, H. I. (1963). Influence of clothing on perception of persons. *Journal of Home Economics, 55,* 197–202.

80. Williams, M. C., & Eicher, J. B. (1966). Teenagers' appearance and social acceptance. *Journal of Home Economics, 58,* 457–461.

81. Panja, Ayan. (2004, January 3). The death of the white coat? *British Medical Journal, 328* (7430): 57.

82. Dress, religion, identity. (2010). *Material Religion, 6,* 371. Laurie, *The language of clothes.*

83. Wohlrab, Silke, Fink, Bernhard, Kappeler, Peter M., & Brewer, Gayle. (2009). Differences in personality attributions toward tattooed and nontattooed virtual human characters. *Journal of Individual Differences, 30*(1): 1–5.

84. Rosenthal, R., Hall, J. A., Matteg, M. R. D., Rogers, P. L., & Archer, D. (1979). *Sensitivity to nonverbal communication: The PONS Test.* Baltimore: Johns Hopkins University Press.

85. Wei, Fang-Yi Flora, & Wang, Y. Ken. (2010). Students' silent messages: Can teacher verbal and nonverbal immediacy moderate student use of text messaging in class? *Communication Education, 59,* 475–496.

5

listening

Stephan Ihde

When you have read and thought about this chapter, you will be able to

1. Define listening.

2. Identify five ways to listen.

3. Identify four listening styles.

4. Understand how to improve your listening skill.

5. Understand how to facilitate audience listening during a speech.

In a successful communication transaction, listening is just as important as speaking.

s speakers, men have become schooled in the arts of persuasion, and without the counter-art of listening a man can be persuaded—even by his own words—to eat foods that ruin his liver, to abstain from killing flies, to vote away his right to vote, and to murder his fellows in the name of righteousness. The art of listening holds for us the desperate hope of withstanding the spreading ravages of commercial, nationalistic and ideological persuasion.

—Wendell Johnson

You might be surprised to find a chapter on listening in a speech textbook. You may be even more surprised to learn just how crucial listening is to the communication process. Face-to-face communication is the primary communication channel we use at school, at work, and in interpersonal situations (even though mediated communication channels such as e-mail and texting have increased in percentage) (Janusik & Wolvin, 2009). However, *successful* face-to-face communication requires that both the speaker and the listener are actively participating in the process. According to research by Janusik & Wolvin (2009) summarized in Figure 1 we spend more of our time listening each day (about 24%) than we spend speaking (about 20%) (see also Emanuel et al., 2008). But it is rare to find students who have had any formal training in listening. We spend the least amount of time writing (9%) and reading (8%) but those are the skills you have probably practiced the most in school.

College students tend to believe that they are naturally good listeners (Sargent & Weaver, 2003). In one study, students who received formal instruction in listening realized at the end of that instruction that their listening skills were not very strong (Zabava Ford, Wolvyn, & Chung, 2000). In this chapter we cannot provide extensive instruction in listening but we can help you understand the concept of listening the way listening scholars do. We will define listening, examine different goals of listening

Figure 1

Research Indicates that We Spend More of Our Time Listening Than in Any Other Communication Activity.

Source: (Janusik & Wolvin, 2009)

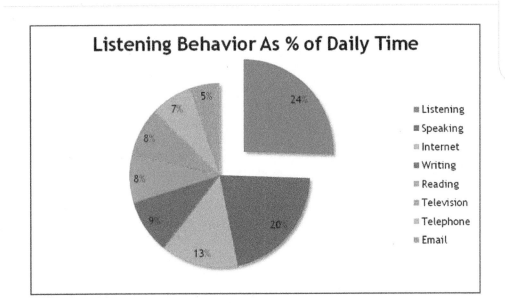

Listening Behavior As % of Daily Time

- Listening 24%
- Speaking 20%
- Internet 13%
- Writing 9%
- Reading 8%
- Television 8%
- Telephone 7%
- Email 5%

in different situations, look at four distinct listening styles, and discuss some specific strategies to help you become a better listener as well as a better speaker.

As you learned in the chapter on Communication Theory, one way to characterize communication is as a set of variables. According to the SMCRE model, receivers (R) have a significant part to play in the public speaking process because they decode the messages senders give to them. Decoding requires a listener to translate messages into understandable symbols. These symbols are interpreted as part of the listening process. You might be thinking at this point that decoding is just a matter of having a large vocabulary. In reality, we have more than one vocabulary. We tend to have different vocabularies for reading, writing, speaking and listening. For example, when was the last time you used the word "pulchritudinous" in a conversation? As a college student you could probably recognize the definition of this word or interpret it from the context of a story. You might have a harder time understanding it when listening to a lecture. The vocabulary, syntax, and grammar we use to write or read are usually larger than those we use to speak or listen. (By the way, this is one reason why writing out your speech word-for-word is not a good idea for most speaking situations. It doesn't sound natural.) In our early years, our primary vocabulary comes from listening to others speak and experiencing concrete forms (for example, "ball," "house," and "dog") (Nagy & Herman, 1987). But at grades 4 or 5, we shift from learning only concrete words to learning more abstract ones as our abstract reasoning capacities begin to develop (Chall, 1987). So in our childhood, our listening vocabulary is paramount, but then later our primary vocabulary comes from our reading and we learn terms that we don't always use in everyday speech. Interestingly, the average high school senior's vocabulary is probably somewhere around 40,000 words (Nagy & Herman, 1987). This is not very large given the fact that the Oxford English Dictionary catalogs upwards of 295,000 distinct English words! That does not even include many specialized and technical terms that would be considered the *jargon* of certain professions. Nor does it take into account the various **connotative meanings** of many words. So, it should be obvious that simply having a college-level vocabulary does not ensure that you are a good listener. Being a good listener requires an understanding of what listening is, how it is improved, and how it can be made easier during the communication transaction.

Denotative meaning
the literal or explicit definition of a word

Connotative meaning
the implied meaning of a word based upon its use within a given context

What Is Listening?

listening
the process of receiving, attending to, and assigning meaning to aural and visual stimuli

Andrew Wolvyn and Carolyn Coakley (1996), listening researchers at the University of Maryland, state that **listening** is "the process of receiving, attending to, and assigning meaning to aural and visual stimuli" (p. 69). *Receiving*: we take in lots of information, but we only *attend* to some of the information. Exercise 1 at the end of this chapter illustrates that sound and activity may be happening all around you, and your brain is aware of it at some level, but you only notice it when you literally pay attention to it. Listening requires mental energy. First, you must give selective attention. That is, you must decide what sound you want to hear. Second, you must *assign meaning* to the sound. And finally, you must decide how to associate it and store it if you want to recall it later. So the process might go something like this: sound waves hit our ears, we pay attention to the sound, we recognize it as the song of a mockingbird because we have heard these before, and then we decide what to do with it. In this case, we decide to listen and enjoy it. We can say we *listened* to the mockingbird. Note also that listening required more than simply *hearing*, which is only the physical process of receiving sound.

It is significant the Wolvyn and Coakley definition includes *visual stimuli*. Listening is not only done with your ears, but also with your *eyes*. Consider this example: through the evening news, you just found out that your best friend won the lottery. Then you see your friend enter the room where you are, and you exclaim, "Wow! Congratulations! I just heard the news! That's incredible!" Your friend replies with a sad, morose face: "Thanks. I'm really happy to have won." What do you conclude from this conflicting information? Your friend *said* they were happy, but their *nonverbal communication* says otherwise. Which do you believe? According to traditional research (e.g., Mehrabian & Ferris, 1967), you'd believe the sad face over the words spoken. Early research on contradictory messaging suggested that we tend to believe nonverbal communication when it directly contradicts the verbal message. However, some recent research has suggested that we decide whether to believe the verbal, vocal, or visual cues (Telfer & Howe, 1994) based on the situation. The more "dominant" channel of communication given the situation and context (Walker & Trimboli, 1989) will determine how we assign meaning to the message. Thus, maybe your friend truly *is* excited (verbal component—what was said) but you understand that the context of your friend's response allows for a flat emotional response (vocal component—how it was said) and also for a sad face (visual component—what was seen) due to the shock of the event. What's important to note here is that communication involves more than just *what* is said. It also involves *how* something is said. Good listeners pay attention to *all* channels of a message.

A Systems Model of Listening

The idea that listening occurs against a larger backdrop than simply the speaker-listener interaction is gaining traction with listening researchers. More than conceptualizing listening as simply information processing, researchers now see multiple factors in play, as illustrated by this process chart (Imhof and Janusik, 2006). This *systems model* characterizes listening as more than simply the interaction of a sender and a receiver. Factors such as personality, cultural norms, abilities, and goals are also considered. When any of these is altered, the listening process is affected.

As shown in Figure 2, listening *presage* includes the things listeners bring to a listening situation and the context in which listening occurs, including the listener's culture, the norms governing conversations in that culture, and the listening styles the person has. The *process* of listening is the actual mechanics of listening, including converting sound into electrical impulses and then into meaning (decoding), and accessing memories in order to prepare effective responses. Additionally, the behaviors of

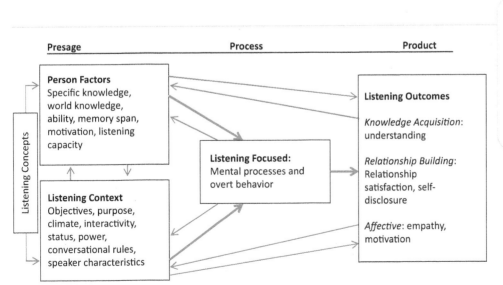

Figure 2

The Systems Model of Listening Characterizes Listening as More than Simply the Interaction of a Sender and a Receiver.

Source: (Imhof and Janusik, 2006)

listening such as head nods and eye contact are seen here. Finally, the *product* of listening is the outcomes of the process, such as a strengthened relationship between friends, a personal feeling of satisfaction or accomplishment, or a deeper understanding of a particular concept or idea.

Five Ways of Listening

Wolvyn and Coakley (1996) identify ways to listen that anyone can do: people can listen discriminatively, cognitively, therapeutically, critically, and appreciatively. Each of these involves different goals and can be thought of as a different way of listening, much like there are different flavors of ice cream at an ice cream shop.

DISCRIMINATIVE LISTENING

We use Discriminative listening when we "distinguish the auditory and visual stimuli" (p. 152). We are able to distinguish the sound of a bird from a human voice, the sound of a fan from the sound of a car. Discriminative listening answers the question, "What is that sound?" Exercise 1 at the end of the chapter helps you focus and listen for different sounds. This type of listening is also used to identify languages. Discriminative listening allows us to know how a language *sounds*. You may not understand Spanish or Chinese but you can probably distinguish between these languages simply by the way they sound. Moreover, we recognize questions from statements in English given the speaker's inflection and tone of voice. Discriminative listening allows us to distinguish among sounds and stimuli.

COMPREHENSIVE LISTENING

Comprehensive listening is used to "understand the message in order to retain, recall, and, possibly, use that information at a later time" (p. 152). If you are actively listening to a lecture, you are utilizing comprehensive listening. That is, you are seeking to understand the information so you can pass the exam, gain personal knowledge, appeal to a personal interest. There are a whole host of other reasons why we listen in this way. Comprehensive listening refers to the process of information acquisition, storage, and retrieval.

THERAPEUTIC LISTENING

Therapeutic listening provides "help to a person who needs to talk through a concern" (p. 153). Typically, therapeutic listening helps others process their feelings. Everyone faces a time when they need someone to help them through a difficult experience, and it can be invaluable to "be with" someone as they walk through those times. Therapeutic listening requires "being with" another person by reflecting thoughts back accurately to the other, sharing information without judging or "flinching," accepting the other person, or helping them make sense of difficult information (Myers, 2000). While trained counselors do this professionally for deeply troubling issues, friends and family do this quite often for much lesser ones. Therapeutic listening is a big part of the human experience: very often, we simply need to be heard and validated by another human being.

CRITICAL LISTENING

We use Critical listening to "evaluate the merits of the message" (p. 154). Critical listening arrives at an informed judgment regarding an idea, situation, or argument.

For example, suppose it is election time and you are evaluating the candidates in order to decide how to vote. This is the first election in which you can vote, so you want to make your vote count. You might listen to each candidate and, considering your own biases, evaluate your vote based on the merits of the candidates' arguments, the *messages* they offer. This kind of listening will be used when you and your classmates present persuasive speeches. You will need to listen critically to each one. Are the speaker's arguments sound? Are there logical fallacies? Does the message make sense? Does the message appeal to you? These are questions critical listeners employ when listening to a message. By the same token, as a speaker, you must be aware that others are using critical listening to process your arguments. You will want to make sure your arguments are sound and that there is no reason for anyone to dismiss your arguments on logical grounds. (For more on logical fallacies. For a more expansive treatment, see Warburton, 2003, which is available online through the UCF library or in print form).

Appreciative Listening

Finally, **appreciative** listening serves "to obtain sensory stimulation or enjoyment through the works and experiences of others" (p. 362). Appreciative listening is not simply putting on the headphones and listening to your favorite MP3 from "Petrified Remains." Sure, you can passively "veg-out" to music or mindlessly flop in front of the television to watch a favorite show; but these aren't examples of listening actively. Appreciative listening is actively listening to and engaging with the sound, music, words, and the blends that the sounds produce. Imagine taking in the blends of sound that make up a musical piece: the drums, the singers and their specific harmonies, the guitars, the bass, and so on. As you listen to the music in your headphones, are you aware in which ear the person who mastered the mix put most of these sounds? Does it switch from ear to ear at given points? Can you make out the individual harmonies? Do the toms of the drums sound as if they were around you as the drummer fills in a measure with a drum riff? Of course, appreciative listening isn't limited to music: it can just as well be talk, sounds, song, music, theatre, or film. Wherever you go to take in listening for enjoyment and pleasure, you can listen appreciatively.

Figure 3 shows a model of listening developed by Wolvyn and Coakley (1996, p. 153) which illustrates the interdependence of different ways to listen. If we interpret this model in terms of the ways to listen described above we might substitute the labels as follows: Discriminative listening is at the root of the listening process; how we distinguish among stimuli orients us to what we do next with the stimuli. The trunk of the tree in this illustration reflects Comprehensive listening: we listen to understand across a variety of contexts, and need to understand a message before we can act on it appreciatively, therapeutically, or critically. Finally, the branches reflect Appreciative, Critical, and Therapeutic listening. These "higher order" levels of listening are possible only once a solid foundation of Comprehensive and Discriminative listening has been achieved.

By now, you should see that true listening is an active process. Yes, there is "couch potato" listening where messages go in one ear and out the other, but, in those cases, no real information typically lands anywhere to plant and take root. To listen actively to a friend, a lecture, a song, a sermon, or to distinguish among different sounds requires mental effort, and that is something we're not always ready to give. Let's face it: it's much easier to pretend as if we're listening than to truly listen. So, if you want to improve your listening habits, one of the first things you need to do is understand what kind of listener you are. This brings us to the concept of *listening styles*.

Appreciative, Critical, and Therapeutic listening

Comprehensive Listening

Discriminative Listening

Figure 3
Source: (Wolvyn and Coakley, 1996)

What Kind of Listener Are You?

Researchers have long wanted to have a way to measure differences in the ways people listen, to identify preferred individual *listening styles*, in order to help people improve their listening behavior. While everyone practices the five ways to listen, it is not difficult to see that some people prefer to listen to facts and figures; some prefer the content of a message; some prefer stories and illustrations; and some prefer concise, succinct information. While several tests have been created, one of the more recent and empirically grounded measurement tools is called the Listening Styles Profile-16 (LSP-16), developed by Kittie Watson at Tulane University and Larry Barker and James Weaver III at Auburn University (1995). These researchers wanted to help conceptualize differences in listening—"the how, where, when, who and what part of the information reception and encoding process" (p. 2). The research by Watson, Barker, and Weaver suggests that listening patterns can be characterized as four main *listening styles*: people-oriented, action-oriented, content-oriented, and time-oriented.

If you have a **people-oriented** listening style you tend to have a high regard for another person's feelings and seek to find common ground with the speaker. These individuals respond keenly to the emotions of others and particularly enjoy harmony and commonality. Listeners with this style are often labeled as "relationally oriented." **Action-oriented** listeners like to receive concise, succinct information that is free from mistakes. These individuals are particularly frustrated by disorganized presentations since they get in the way of commencing action. Individuals with this style are often thought of as "task oriented." If you have a **Content-oriented** listening style you prefer challenging and complex messages. Someone who is content-oriented is more drawn to evaluate facts and strengths of arguments. These listeners are frequently called "unbiased" since they are willing to listen to both sides of an argument before rendering judgment. Finally, if you are a **time-oriented** listener, you prefer brief listening encounters. A time-oriented person will let others know they have limited time to spend in an interaction and prefer interactions to move along swiftly, sometimes even interrupting others in order to move the interaction along (Bodie & Villaume, 2003; Johnston, Weaver, Watson, & Barker, 2000; Watson, Barker, & Weaver, 1995).

What do we know about people who have these different listening styles? Many research studies have asked this question with interesting results:

- In a large survey done by Watson, Barker, & Weaver, 40% of respondents had two or more listening styles, 36% of respondents had only one listening style, and 24% had no particular listening style (Watson, Barker, & Weaver, 1995). Of those who had a single listening style preference, people-oriented was most popular (11.6%); followed by action-oriented (8.5%), content-oriented (8.3%), and time-oriented (7.7%).

- Listening styles may change depending on the situation. For example, a person may be more people-oriented when talking with friends, but more content-oriented when listening to a lecture (Imhof, 2004). So, don't be surprised if your LSP changes with a given situation.

- People-oriented jurors in a mock trial concerning a failed savings and loan found the plaintiffs less at fault, whereas time-oriented listeners awarded higher damages to the defense (Worthington, 2001).

- First-year medical students had a strong, majority people-oriented listening style upon entering medical school. At the end of their first year of medical school, however, people-oriented listening styles in those same students dropped dramatically. Also, at the end of schooling there were more students with no distinct listening style than with any one style (Watson, Lazurus, & Thomas, 1999).

- Bodie and Villaume (2003) measured nine dimensions of communication style (such as dominant, animated, and relaxed) against the four listening styles. They found that

  - People with a high people listening orientation are more relationally oriented. They attend to and affirm the other person and feel less receiver apprehension when speaking.

  - People with high content and action listening orientations tend to have a precise and attentive style of arguing the issues that leaves a strong impression on other people.

  - People with high time and action listening orientations tend to feel higher receiver apprehension and tend to be dramatic, forceful, and animated. Additionally, these individuals tend to dominate others in conversation.

- People- and content-oriented listeners are more conversationally sensitive than the other listening types (although the strength of the association found in this study was weak for content-oriented listeners) (Chesebro, 1999).

- People-oriented listeners are more extraverted (i.e., they are more sociable and have a positive self-concept); they are less psychotic (where psychotic individuals deviate from social norms and have a stronger, more independent sense of self), and also less neurotic (where neurotic individuals are more anxious and have a more negative self-concept) (Villaume & Bodie, 2007).

  - Additionally, they found that individuals with high time- and content-orientations more psychotic and have a friendlier communication style. "In other words, they seem to say what they want and do not necessarily worry about the effect on others that may run counter to their expectations" (p. 119).

- People- and content-oriented listeners have slightly less communication apprehension in group, meeting, and interpersonal settings (however, all styles were somewhat apprehensive about public speaking) (Sargent, Kiewitz, & Weaver, 1997).

- Content-oriented listeners are more likely to have a higher "need for cognition," or a greater tendency to think and enjoy the thinking process (Worthington, 2008).

- Content- and action-oriented listeners are more likely to question the information they hear than the other listening types (Kirtley & Honeycutt, 1997).

- A study of international students suggests that Israeli students favor the content and action listening orientations, German students favor an action listening orientation, and American students favor both people and time listening orientations (Kiewitz, Weaver, Brosius, & Weimann, 1997).

So we can see that there are quite a number of distinctions among these four listening styles. But how else does this relate to us as individuals? We can compare these styles to familiar personality characteristics, how we utilize empathy with others, and our gender.

LISTENING STYLES AND PERSONALITY

Some particularly fascinating relationships occur between these four listening styles and personality types. One familiar personality inventory, the Myers-Briggs Type Indicator (MBTI®), measures personality across five bipolar dimensions: introversion (e.g., you "recharge your batteries" by being alone) versus extraversion (e.g., you "recharge your batteries" by being around other people); intuiting (e.g., you gather and process information through a strong internal sense and awareness) versus sensing (e.g., you gather and process information most readily by the five senses); thinking (e.g., you make decisions by careful thought and logical processes) versus feeling (e.g., you make decisions by based on emotional sensitivity to others); and judging (e.g., you prefer structure and predictability) versus perceiving (e.g., you prefer open-endedness and possibilities) (see, e.g., Quenk, 2000; Keirsey, 1998). These personality traits are often very consistent with listening styles. (If you don't know your Myers-Briggs personality type and you want to find out what it is, a reliable facsimile may be obtained via the Keirsey Temperament Sorter on-line at http://www.keirsey.com or at http://www.humanmetrics.com/cgi-win/jtypes2.asp.)

The results of Worthington's (2003) study [Table 2] show that Feelers and Intuitors are more strongly related to the people-oriented listening style while Thinkers have a small relation to action-, content-, and time-oriented listening styles. It makes some sense to think that those who are interested in relationships, community and harmony will have a listening style that reflects this while those who value efficiency and action will also reflect this in their listening. Similarly, Bommelje, Houston, & Smither, (2003) conducted a personality-listening styles study using different personality measures (intellectance, adjustment, prudence, sociability, likeability, ambition and school success) and using a different listening inventory (the Watson-Barker Listening Test). In their results, however, they found that only "school success," the degree to which a person values educational achievement and academics, was a predictor of effective listening.

Table 2 Listening Styles and Myers-Briggs Personality Types Associations
(Adapted from Worthington, 2003)

	People Orientation	Action Orientation	Content Orientation	Time Orientation
Introversion (I)				weak
Extraversion (E)	weak			
Intuiting (N)	moderate			
Sensing (S)		weak		weak
Thinking (T)		small	small	small
Feeling (F)	moderate			
Perceiving (P)	small			
Judging (J)		weak		

(Based on Pearson Product Moment Correlations significant at p<.05)

LISTENING STYLES AND EMPATHY

Another study looked at the LSP-16 and how people display empathy via empathetic responsiveness. Empathetic responses include *congruent emotional responses* (a friend feels sad, so you feel sad), *perspective taking* ("walking in the other person's shoes"), and *sympathetic responsiveness* (feelings of sorrow or compassion for others in distress). Weaver and Kirtley (1995) found that individuals with a people-oriented listening style showed a great deal of sympathetic responsiveness to others in difficult situations (that is, they generally have a great deal of concern and compassion for the well-being of others) but not much empathetic responsiveness. This seems to suggest that people-oriented listeners can feel pity and compassion for others but don't tend to feel the emotions that another may feel. Additionally, action and time listening styles showed the least amount of sympathetic responsiveness toward others in difficult situations, perhaps because in communication scenarios, they prefer a simple, get-to-the-point approach that doesn't deal so much with the feelings of others. Interestingly, however, there was a level of moodiness and nervousness to which action- and time-oriented listeners sympathized. Finally, content-oriented individuals (perhaps due to their objectivity) seemed to have an ability to interact with others who were emotionally upset without becoming emotionally upset themselves. As mentioned earlier, it could well be that empathy and listening styles are context dependent, so that an "active emotional commitment, acceptance of role-taking as a necessity, and identification with the other" (Walker, 1997, p. 134) may arise from any type of listener in a particular situation.

So, a variety of studies show links between the four listening styles and personality types and empathy styles. Hopefully, you will see these as more tools at your disposal to help you learn more about who you are and how you can become a more effective listener. It should be noted, however, that the research indicates it is somewhat difficult (but not impossible) to change your listening style once you have yours, even when you are presented with better and more efficient options of listening (Wolvyn & Coakley, 1996). Worthington's study suggests some links between personality and listening styles and we know that personality is something deeply ingrained in us. It would follow that our listening style would be resistant to change, although, as we saw earlier, some of your listening styles may well be context dependent. Before we look at some specific

Table 3 Male and Female Differences in Listening Styles and Behaviors

Males	Females
Specialize in vocal communication: are better at judging and expressing information through the voice (Hall, 1984)	Specialize in visual communication: are better and judging and expressing information in the face and body (Hall, 1984)
Perceive head nods as feedback to be indicators of agreement (Maltz & Borker, 1982)	Perceive head nods as feedback to be indicators of "I'm listening" (Maltz & Borker, 1982; Doohan, 2007)
Interrupt more frequently in conversation (Hall, 1984)	Display more complexity and differentiation in how they describe emotional experiences (Barrett, Lane, Sechrest, & Schwartz, 2000)
Emit more errors in speech (such as filled pauses) (Hall, 1984)	Use more body movements to communicate involvement (Hall, 1984)
Favor the task-oriented listening styles (content-, action-, and time-oriented) (Johnston, Weaver, Watson & Barker, 2000)	Favor "communal" or people-oriented listening styles (Johnston, Weaver, Watson & Barker, 2000), but can also favor content-oriented (Watson, Barker, & Weaver, 1995)
Rate themselves as more content-oriented (Sargent & Weaver, 2003)	Rate themselves as more people-oriented (Sargent & Weaver, 2003)

ways you might work to improve your listening skills, let's turn to another deeply engrained trait that shows some connections to our listening behavior–our gender.

LISTENING AND GENDER

It turns out that men and women are somewhat different when it comes to listening styles. The data summarized in Table 3 show that women tend to prefer conversations with others, particularly where feelings are involved and common ground is evident. Men tend to prefer listening for complex information that is to the point, free from error, and brief. Men make more errors in communication and are more likely to use "uh" and "um." Women use more body language and movement to communicate; however, they tend to perceive head nods in communication differently!

From where do all these differences come? Are we born with them or do we learn them? Johnston, Weaver, Watson, & Barker (2000) suggest that these listening differences may be a function of learning or socialization rather than biology. Maltz and Borker (1982) suggest that men and women perceive head nods differently due to the fact that they are from different *cultures*. Bryden (1980) argues that how men's and women's brains are organized could be as much biology or learning strategies. And finally, Canary and Hause (1993) would argue with all of these results, suggesting that very little gender difference can be accounted for statistically when communication research is taken as a whole. Well, it doesn't seem like researchers have much consensus on this particular question. What do *you* think? Do you think the difference in men's and women's communication and listening behavior is something innate, something learned, or both?

How Can You Improve Your Own Listening Skills? (Receiver)

Now that you have a good handle on what listening is; on different ways to listen; on what your particular listening style is; and how your style of listening relates to your personality, gender, and the way you display empathy; let's look at some ways you can improve your listening skills.

Poor listening skills can be costly. The space shuttle *Challenger* disaster can be traced, in large part, to communication breakdowns—spoken and listening—between managers and subordinates (Moore, 1992; Winsor, 1988). Unclear messages sent or received may result in such consequences as misunderstandings, loss of business, injury, or even death (Ihde, Katt, & Bosley, 2000). Even physicians who do not listen are more likely to be sued for malpractice if something goes wrong (Hickson, Clayton, Githens, & Sloan, 1992). Let's face it: the technical professions demand precision, and errors can be costly. Fortunately, there are proven ways to improve our listening skills, and these can have great benefits—for example, as Virshup, Oppenberg, and Coleman (1999) discuss, physicians who listen to their patients are less likely to be sued (see also Coy & Stratton, 2002) and patients are more likely to be happier with their doctors (Harris & Templeton, 2001).

ASK PRE-QUESTIONS

Listening researcher Margarete Imhof (2001) states that "intentional and meaningful learning can only take place when a person has identified a specific learning goal" (p. 4). Imagine coming to class with a list of questions for things *you* wanted to learn rather than simply writing down what the instructor or speaker gave to you! It would change your focus about what you learned for the class. King (1994) found that students who could ask their own questions about an upcoming lecture did better on a posttest than those who were simply given questions to consider. Look on the syllabus for this class and ask yourself: "What do *I* want to get out of this class today?"

CONSIDER YOUR INTEREST LEVEL

How much interest you have for a given topic seems to suggest a greater ability to recall that information at a later time (Schiefele & Krapp, 1996). Intuitively, this makes sense: we attend to things we want to learn, and so are willing to devote more mental energy to those things. You're less likely to retain information you're "forced" to learn. While there's little you can do to change the interest level you have for something, you *can* change your perception and evaluation of a given topic. Instead of saying, "How boring!" what would it be like to approach an uninteresting topic with, "What can I learn from this?"

USE ELABORATION STRATEGIES

Elaboration strategies (Imhof, 2001) involve relating new knowledge in some meaningful way to existing knowledge (such as creating new examples, contrasting the information, and mentally "seeing" the concept). Taking good notes with these elements in mind also falls into this category. According to Imhof, when these methods were used, "participants consistently reported more comprehensive understanding, deeper level of processing, more reflective assessment of the new material, facilitated integration of new information into existing knowledge structures, and improved processing characteristics (e.g., sustaining attention and selective focus, better retention)" (p. 16). Practice putting the information you hear into your knowledge framework in a way that makes it more meaningful for you.

AS A LISTENER, TAKE 51% OF THE RESPONSIBILITY FOR THE COMMUNICATION TRANSACTION

Researchers Wolvyn & Coakley, (1996) have suggested that effective communication is more than half the responsibility of the listener. Imagine how different your communication interactions would be if you saw yourself as having slightly more responsibility than the speaker for clear communication! Rather than letting the speaker do all the work, imagine being actively engaged in the entire process. In this class, take 51% of the burden of communication during student speeches, during lectures, and when you speak to your classmates. If there's something you don't understand, ask questions!

CHOOSE TO FOCUS

This is easier said than done, but well worth the effort. Thinking speed (about 500 words per minute) is typically substantially faster than speaking speed (about 125 to 175 words per minute) (Wolvyn & Coakley, 1996; Foulke, 1968). The question, then, is what do we do with the difference in words and time? Our minds do something with the difference. For example, in the middle of a speaker's sentence, we might predict the end of the speaker's sentence and then devote our mental energy toward something else, figuring that we already know what the speaker will say. Instead, if we should choose to focus our full attention on the speaker and the message we might use our extra thought energy for elaborating on the message.

BE AWARE OF LOGICAL FALLACIES, SOURCE CREDIBILITY, AND APPEALS

These are especially relevant for the persuasive speeches. Thinking critically will help you analyze a speaker's message and make you more likely to accept or reject it based on carefully-considered, well-reasoned grounds, rather than peripheral factors or fallacious arguments (Wolvyn & Coakley, 1996). Pay attention to that little voice inside you when it says that something isn't quite right with the speaker's message. Chapter 15 will discuss the logical fallacies in detail. In Chapter 14 you will learn more about persuasive appeals and what types of appeals are typically used to increase persuasion.

KEEP A LISTENING JOURNAL

Johnson, Barker, & Pierce (1995) suggest that you keep track of your listening behaviors by writing down what you did, assessing what you learned from those behaviors, and writing how you felt as a result. It can be an eye-opening experience to see what we actually do—and do poorly—as listeners. Also, it may make you more aware of how your listening style affects others and how others' listening styles affect you.

BE WILLING TO LISTEN

Researchers Roberts & Vinson (1998) found that a person's willingness to listen positively correlated with communication skills and negatively correlated with communication fears of receiving messages, sending messages, and always being right ("dogmatism"). It's possible that simply being willing to listen may make the whole process of communication work better.

If you are struggling with extemporaneous delivery, take heart: Having a message that has high relevance to your audience also helps ensure that listeners will be less affected by areas of your delivery that still need improvement and may still respond positively to the highly relevant verbal content of your message (Marsh, Hart-O'Rourke, & Julka, 1997).

How Can You Facilitate Increased Listening in the Audience? (Sender)

As speakers, we can also help our listeners make the communication transaction a more profitable experience for them. Here are some key strategies:

HAVE A STRONG MESSAGE THAT IS RELEVANT TO YOUR AUDIENCE

Let's be honest: Have you heard speeches in this class that you thought were a waste of time? Well, here's an even tougher question: Do you wonder if your speeches have wasted the class's time? More than likely, if you don't care about your message, your audience won't, either. Having a message that you care about and that has strong sources and utilizes good logos increases the chances that that your audience will care about the message also. Have you made your messages relevant to them? Recall that we tend to remember and process things in which we have an interest (Schiefele & Krapp, 1996). This is a good time to practice "perspective taking," one characteristic of empathy discussed previously: think about how your audience will perceive your message. And why not specifically refer to one or two members of your audience in your introduction and, topic permitting, show how your topic might be relevant to them?

USE CONFIDENT LANGUAGE

In a study by Holtgraves & Lasky (1999), subjects used both central and peripheral routes to persuasion when the speaker used confident ("strong") language instead of hedging language (e.g., "I suppose that...", "It's kinda true that...", and frequent vocal pauses). Make sure your purpose and thesis statements are crystal clear for your speech so you know exactly what you want to say and how you want to say it. When you give a speech think about specific techniques and word choices that will make the language of your persuasive speech more confident and assertive.

DEFINE ANY UNFAMILIAR TERMS AND USE STANDARD ENGLISH

Make sure you clearly explain any terms that your audience doesn't understand. Using vocabulary or concepts that your audience doesn't know is much like speaking a foreign language (Reimann, 2001). When asked how professors could improve speaking to foreign students, Chinese students responded with answers like, "avoid using colloquial and slang expressions," "speak clearly and loudly in the classroom," "use formal English to deliver lectures," and "try to get rid of strong accent and strange pronunciation" (Huang, 2004). Expressions and idioms are among the most difficult things for new speakers to a language to understand accurately (e.g., "It's raining cats and dogs!"). Consider your specific audience's language capacity and vocabulary base, and use terms with which they will be familiar.

OFFER OPPORTUNITIES FOR CLARIFICATION

While your speeches in this class may not have the time or format to do this, remember this when you're giving presentations in the "real world." Take the time to make sure your audience understands your message. If you are a people-oriented listener, you will know quickly if your audience doesn't understand your message by their reactions and nonverbal expressions to your message. Build in opportunities for feedback if the situation allows, and allow for questions. As we saw earlier, when students could generate their own questions regarding a topic, they did better on recall (King, 1994).

ASSUME THAT YOUR AUDIENCE MAY NOT HAVE THE SAME LISTENING STYLE AS YOU

You may enjoy connecting with an audience and making everyone feel good but there may be audience members who prefer a succinct and direct message. Similarly, if your points are not in logical order and you are speaking to content-oriented listeners who are strongly uncomfortable with disorganization, this will spell trouble. And if you are an action-oriented speaker whose audience is primarily people-oriented, you may need to relate to them on levels of connectivity. Utilizing good audience analysis skills is a key element of planning a strong message.

Chapter Review & Study Guide

Summary

In this chapter you learned the following:

1. listening is crucial to our communication patterns but it is a subject which is rarely taught in depth in the grade school or college curriculum

2. listening is "the process of receiving, attending to, and assigning meaning to aural and visual stimuli" and it is distinct from hearing

3. a systems model of listening (presage, process, and product) suggests that changing individual elements affects the entire process

4. how to listen discriminatively, comprehensively, therapeutically, critically, and appreciatively, which define the differing listening goals we might have at a given time

5. four styles of listening (people-, content-, action-, and time-oriented) which have direct correlations with personality, gender, and styles of empathy

6. specific ways to improve listening habits both as a receiver and as a sender.

Key Terms

action-oriented listening style
appreciative listening
comprehensive listening
content-oriented listening style
critical listening

decoding
discriminative listening
listening
people-oriented listening style
selective attention

therapeutic listening
time-oriented listening style
verbal cues
visual cues
vocal cues

Check Your Understanding: Exercises and Activities

1. Do a listening experiment. Before you begin reading this chapter:

   Close your eyes
   Silently count to ten
   Listen—Take in all the sounds around you.

   What did you experience? What did you notice? What did you hear? Did you become aware of any new sounds around you? Did you hear an air conditioning fan, a radio, a television, conversations, a bird, an automobile, your own breathing? Now, do the same thing one more time—close your eyes, silently count to ten, and listen—but this time, try to listen for a sound you didn't hear the first time. Were you aware of these sounds before you closed your eyes the first time? If not...how is it that you became aware of them now? Why did you notice them now and not before?

2. Keep a listening journal. For the next two weeks, keep daily accounts of how you listened, whom you listened to, and in what situations you chose to listen. Which ways to listen did you employ most frequently? Did you encounter people with different listening styles than you? What happened when there were differences? How did you feel about the ways that you listen? When you complete your two weeks, look back over your journal. Did you see any areas in which you need to improve?

3. Rent a British/Irish/Scottish movie that has a strong dialect difference from American English. (Some examples include "Trainspotting," "Snatch," "Becoming Jane," and "About a Boy." The movie "About a Boy" has an "English to English" translation section in the special features of the DVD that highlights British English idioms and expressions that American audiences would probably not recognize.) Practice your discriminative listening skills by first watching the film without subtitles and then watching the film with subtitles.

4. Expand your critical and content-listening skills by visiting an open trial in a courthouse. Many courts are open to the public, and sitting in an actual trial can be quite instructive. Listen to the lawyers as they state their arguments, and listen especially when the opposing lawyer shouts "Objection!" and the judge responds. You can also read ahead to chapter 15 concerning logical fallacies.

5. Expand your therapeutic listening by practicing with a friend. Enlist a friend to tell a real story that either positively or negatively influenced them. Practice empathy simply by "being in the other person's shoes." As they are telling their story, what do you think they are feeling? How do you think they felt when the event happened to them? Test what you're feeling by asking your friend, "I can imagine when ___ happened, you felt ___. Am I right?" What else can you do to support what the person is feeling? *Special note to men: Avoid the stereotypical temptation to "fix" your friends, especially if your friends are female. For example, if a female*

friend says she is upset, a male might stereotypically respond "Well, here's what you need to do." Instead, try listening and validating what your friend is feeling. A better response might begin "I see how sad you are when you're telling your story."

6. Scan the radio dial and stop on stations that you normally don't listen to. Practice appreciative listening by engaging with what you hear.

References

1. Barrett, L. F., Lane, R. D., Sechrest, L., & Schwartz, G. E. (2000). Sex di erences in emotional awareness. *Personality and Social Psychology Bulletin, 26(11),* 1027–1035.

2. Bodie, G. D. and Villaume, W. A. (2003). Aspects of receiving information: The relationship between listening preferences, communication apprehension, receiver apprehension, and communicator style. *International Journal of Listening, 17,* 47–67.

3. Bodie, G. D., Worthington, D., Imhof, M., & Cooper, L. O. (2008). What would a unified field of listening look like? A proposal linking past perspectives and future endeavors. *International Journal of Listening, 22,* 103–122.

4. Bommelje, R., Houston, J. M., & Smither, R. (2003). Personality characteristics of e ective listeners: A five factor perspective. *International Journal of Listening, 17,* 32–46.

5. Bryden, M. P. (1980). Sex di erences in brain organization: Different brains or different strategies? *The Behavioral and Brain Sciences, 3,* 230–232.

6. Canary, D. J. & Hause, K. S. (1993). Is there any reason to research sex differences in communication? *Communication uarterly, 41,* 129–144.

7. Chall, J. S. (1987). Two vocabularies for reading : Recognition and meaning. In M. G. McKeown & M. E.Curtis (Eds.), *The nature of ocabulary acquisition* (pp. 7–17). Hillsdale, NJ: Lawrence Erlbaum Associates.

8. Chesebro, J. L. (1999). The relationship between listening styles and conversational sensitivity. *Communication Research Reports, 16 (3),* 233–238.

9. Coy, K. & Stratton, R. (2002). Avoiding your greatest fear—malpractice. *Journal of the Oklahoma Dental Association, 93(2),* 18–27.

10. Doohan, E. (2007). Listening behaviors of married couples: An exploration of nonverbal presentation to a relational outsider. *International Journal of Listening, 21 (1),* 24–41.

11. Edwards, R. (2011). Listening and message interpretation. *International Journal of Listening, 25(1),* 47–65.

12. Emanuel, R., Adams, J., Baker, K., Daufin, E. K., Ellington, C., Fitts, E., Himsel, J., Holladay, L., & Okeowo, D. (2008). How college students spend their time communicating. *International Journal of Listening, 22(1),* 13–28.

13. Foulke, E. (1968). Listening comprehension as a function of word rate. *Journal of Communication, 18,* 198–206.

14. Hall, J. A. (1984). *Nonverbal sex differences.* Baltimore, MD: The Johns Hopkins University Press.

15. Harris, S. R. & Templeton, E. (2001). Who's listening? Experiences of women with breast cancer in communicating with physicians. *The Breast Journal, 7(6),*444.

16. Holtgraves, T. & Lasky, B. (1999). Listening power and persuasion. *Journal of Language and Social Psychology, 18(2),* 196–205.

17. Huang, J. (2004). Voices from Chinese students: Professors' use of English a ects academic listening. *College Student Journal, 38(2),* 212–223.

18. Ihde, S. K., Katt, J., & Bosley, A. (2000). *Technically Speaking: A guide for technical communicators.* Dubuque, IA: Kendall-Hunt.

19. Imhof, M. (2004). Who are we as we listen? Individual listening profiles in varying contexts. *International Journal of Listening, 18,* 36–45.

20. Imhof, M. (2001). How to listen more efficiently: Self-monitoring strategies in listening. *International Journal of Listening, 15,* 2–17.

21. Imhof, M. & Janusik, L. A. (2006). Development and validation of the Imhof-Janusik Listening Concepts Inventory to measure listening conceptualization differences between cultures. *Journal of Intercultural Communication Research, 35,* 79–98.

22. Janusik, L. A. & Wolvin, A. D. (2009). 24 hours in a day: A listening update to the time studies. *International Journal of Listening, 23(2),* 104–120.

23. Johnson, I. W., Barker, R.T., & Pearce, C. G. (1995). Using journals to improve listening behavior: An exploratory study. *Journal of Business and Technical Communication, 9(4),* 475–483.

24. Johnston, M. K., Weaver, III, J. B., Watson, K. W., & Barker, L. B. (2000). Listening styles: Biological or psychological di erences? *International Journal of Listening, 14,* 32–46.

25. Keirsey, D. (1998). Please understand me II: *Temperament, character, intelligence.* Del Mar, CA: Prometheus Nemesis.

26. Kiewitz, C., Weaver, III, J. B., Brosius, H. B., & Weimann, G. (1997). Cultural di erences in listening styles preferences: A comparison of young adults in Germany, Israel, and the United States. *International Journal of Public Opinion Research, 9(3),* 233–247.

27. King, A. (1994). Autonomy and question asking: The role of personal control in guided student-generated questioning. *Learning and Individual Differences, 6,* 163–185.

28. Kirtley, M. D., & Honeycutt, J.M. (1996). Listening styles and their correspondence with second guessing. *Communication Research Reports, 13(2),* 174–182.

29. Maltz, D. N, & Borker, R. A. (1982). A cultural approach to male-female miscommunication. In J. J. Gumperz (Ed.), *Language and Social Identity* (pp. 196–216). Cambridge: Cambridge University Press.

30. Marsh, K. L., Hart-O'Rourke, D. M., & Julka, D. L. (1997). The persuasive effects of verbal and nonverbal information in a context of value relevance. Personality and Social Psychology Bulletin, 23(6), 563–579.

31. Mehrabian, A. & Ferris, S. R. (1967). Inference of attitudes from nonverbal communication in two channels. *Journal of Consulting Psychology, 31,* 33–41.

32. Moore, P. (1992). When politeness is fatal: Technical communication and the *Challenger accident. Journal of Business and Technical Communication, 3(3),* 269–292.

33. Myers, S. (2000). Empathic listening: Reports on the experience of being heard. *Journal of Humanistic Psychology, 40(2),* 148–173.

34. Nagy, W. E., & Herman, P. A. (1987). Breadth and depth of vocabulary knowledge: Implications for acquisition and instruction. In M.G. McKeown & M.E.Curtis (Eds.), *The nature of ocabulary acquisition* (pp.19–35). Hillsdale, NJ: Lawrence Erlbaum Associates.

35. Quenk, N. L. (2000). *Essentials of Myers-Briggs type indicator assessment.* New York, NY: John Wiley & Sons.

36. Reimann, P. (2001). Jargon, abbreviations cloud message being conveyed. *Ophthalmology Times, 26(8),* 76.

37. Roberts, C. V., & Vinson, L. (1998). Relationship among willingness to listen, receiver apprehension, communication apprehension, communication competence, and dogmatism. *International Journal of Listening, 12,* 40–56.

38. Sargent, S. L., Kiewitz, C., & Weaver, J. B. (1997). Correlates between communication apprehension and listening style preferences. *Communication Research Reports, 14(1),* 74–78.

39. Sargent, S. L. & Weaver, III, J.B. (2003). Listening styles: Sex di erences in perceptions of self and others. *International Journal of Listening, 17,* 5–18.

40. Schiefele, U. & Krapp, A. (1996). Topic interest and free recall of expository text. *Learning and Individual Di erences, 8,* 141–160.

41. Telfer, K. E., & Howe, C. J. (1994). Verbal, vocal, and visual information in the judgment of interpersonal a ect: A methodological limitation of some in uential research. *Journal of Language and Social Psychology, 13(3),* 331–344.

42. Villaume, W. A., Bodie, G. D. (2007). Discovering the listener within us: The impact of trait-like personality variables and communicator styles on preferences for listening style. *International Journal of Listening, 21(2),* 102–123.

43. Virshup, B. B., Oppenberg, A. A., & Coleman, M. M. (1999). Strategic risk management: Reducing malpractice claims through more e ective patient-doctor communication. *American Journal of Medical uality, 14(4),* 153–159.

44. Walker, K. L. (1997). Do you ever listen? Discovering the theoretical underpinnings of empathic listening. *International Journal of Listening, 11(1),* 127–137.

45. Walker, M. B. & Trimboli, A. (1989). Communicating a ect: The role of verbal and nonverbal content. *Journal of Language and Social Psychology, 8(3,4),* 229–248.

46. Warburton, N. (2003). *Thinking from A to Z.* New York, NY: Taylor & Francis.

47. Watson, K. W., Barker, L. L, & Weaver, III, J. B. (1995). The listening styles profile (LSP-16): Development and validation of an instrument to assess four listening styles. *International Journal of Listening, 9,* 1–13.

48. Watson, K. W., Lazarus, C. J., & Thomas, T. (1999). First-year medical students' listener preferences: A longitudinal study. *International Journal of Listening, 13,* 1–11.

49. Weaver, III, J. B. & Kirtley, M. D. (1995). Listening styles and empathy. *The Southern Communication Journal, 60,* 131–140.

50. Winsor, D. A. (1988). Communication failures contributing to the Challenger accident: An example for technical communicators. *IEEE Transactions on Professional Communication, 31(3),* 101–107.

51. Wolvin, A. & Coakley, C. G. (1996). *Listening* (5th ed). Brown & Benchmark: Dubuque, IA.

52. Worthington, D. L. (2008). Exploring the relationship between listening style and need for cognition. *International Journal of Listening, 22(1),* 46–58.

53. Worthington, D. L. (2003). Exploring the relationship between listening style preference and personality. *International Journal of Listening, 17,* 68–87.

54. Worthington, D. L. (2001). Exploring juror's listening processes: The effect of listening style preference on juror decision making. *International Journal of Listening, 15,* 20–37.

55. Zabava Ford, W. S., Wolvyn, A. D., & Chung, S. (2000). Students' selfperceived listening competencies in the basic speech communication course. *International Journal of Listening, 14,* 1–13.

interpersonal communication

When you have read and thought about this chapter, you will be able to

1. Define interpersonal communication.

2. Define interpersonal relationships.

3. Explain the importance of interpersonal relationships.

4. Describe how self-disclosure affects relationships.

5. Describe friendships and how they have changed.

6. Explain the importance of cross-cultural relationships.

7. Name and explain the three stages in interpersonal relationships.

8. Explain a motive for initiating, maintaining, and terminating relationships.

9. Name three essential interpersonal communication behaviors.

10. Describe how bargaining and behavioral flexibility can be used to improve interpersonal communication skills.

Interpersonal relationships can be immensely rewarding and they take effort to build and maintain. This chapter highlights some of the basic elements of interpersonal relationships and interpersonal communication. You will learn why people start, maintain, and end relationships. You will also study essential skills such as self-disclosing, using affectionate and supportive communication, influencing others, and developing a unique relationship.

Both students and professors believe that improving interpersonal communication skills is a top priority for college students. Sometimes the problems that students experience are not expected. Ashley, for example, is a well-adjusted first-year college student. However, she wrote,

One problem I faced coming to college was not so much making my own adjustment, but helping a friend adjust. I came to school with a few people from my high school, and although I didn't room with any of them, my friend Kate lives right down the hall from me. She and her boyfriend broke up right before she came to college and her two best friends went to other Minnesota schools. She misses the way high school was structured; she misses her house and our home town and just being somewhere that she feels comfortable and connected. As a result, she hasn't really put a lot of effort into making new friends here.

© LittleBee80/Getty Images, RF

This has made it hard for me because, while she's my friend and I enjoy hanging out with her, I feel like she is always around me. Instead of making her own friends she's just tagged along with mine, so she isn't particularly close to any of them. I want to be there for her when she's upset, but she's upset a lot and that burden falls on me. Coming to college has brought along with it a lot of responsibilities I hadn't expected.

Major changes in interpersonal relationships and new challenges in interpersonal communication are things many college students face. What would you suggest for Ashley and Kate? What can Ashley do to improve her situation? What about Kate? At the end of the chapter, we'll come back to Ashley and consider what steps she might take to address her communication challenge with Kate.

How do you rate your own skills at interpersonal relationships and communication? Do you disclose information about yourself to others? How do you handle conflict? In this chapter, you'll learn more about improving your communication in interpersonal relationships.

What is a friend? With whom do you share a sexual relationship? These questions were not so difficult to answer in the past, but today they have become complicated with social networking sites, such as Facebook, and online dating apps like Tinder and OkCupid. In the past, a friend was a person with whom we had face-to-face conversations and with whom we shared details of our lives. Sexual partners may have been restricted to one person, or to a relatively small number of people, with whom we had first established a loving and trusting relationship and whom, perhaps, we intended to be committed to for an extended period of time.

Today our definitions of interpersonal relations are more complex and variable. People may count dozens, or even hundreds, of others as their "friends." College students may experience a sexual relationship with someone they consider to be a friend but with whom they have no long-term commitment. One advantage of these new relationships is the ease with which they can be begun or ended. The disadvantage is that they may be shallow or unfulfilling.

Scholars are fascinated by these new developments. They see them as raising some important issues about the definitions of interpersonal relationships and interpersonal communication. For what reasons do people form their online relationships? How do they know whom they can trust to have a sexual relationship with? How do people interact when a relationship is exclusively online rather than in face-to-face settings? What is their relationship with a friend with whom they have had a sexual relationship after the sex is gone? Can people manage to move between online and offline friendships? Can they move into and out of sexual relationships with friends?

These questions are part of the fabric of our society today. In this chapter you will learn about interpersonal communication among a variety of relational forms. You will discover what interpersonal communication is, what constitutes interpersonal relationships, how we communicate within them, and how relationships are maintained and enriched.

The Nature of Communication in Interpersonal Relationships

DEFINING INTERPERSONAL COMMUNICATION

Interpersonal communication is defined by the context, or the situation. In other words, interpersonal communication is the process of using messages to generate meaning between at least two people in a situation that allows mutual opportunities for both speaking and listening. Defined in this manner, interpersonal communication includes our interactions with strangers, with salespeople, and with waiters, as well as with our close friends, our lovers, and our family members. This definition is very broad.

We can also think of interpersonal communication as communication that occurs within interpersonal relationships.[1] This idea suggests that interpersonal communication can be limited to those situations in which we have knowledge of the personal characteristics, qualities, or behaviors of the other person. Indeed, Miller and Steinberg assert that, when we make guesses about the outcomes of conversations based on sociological or cultural information, we are communicating in a noninterpersonal way. When we make predictions based on more discriminating information about the other specific person, we are communicating interpersonally. When we communicate with others on the basis of general social interaction rules, such as engaging in turn taking, making pleasantries, and discussing nonpersonal matters, we are engaging in impersonal, or nonpersonal, communication. For instance, when you engage in small talk with the barista at your favorite coffee shop, this can be viewed as a form of impersonal communication. When we communicate with others based on some knowledge of their uniqueness as individuals and a shared relational history, we are communicating interpersonally.

None of our interpersonal relationships are quite like any of our other interpersonal relationships. A friendship you might have had in high school is not the same as your new friendships in college. Your relationship with one of your parents or parental figures is uniquely different from your relationship with the other. Likewise, if you have multiple siblings, your relationship with each of them will be different. Even if you have several intimate relationships with people, you will find that none of them is quite like the others. On the one hand, our interpersonal relationships are mundane; on the other, they can also be the "sites for spiritual practice and mystical experience."[2]

Nonetheless, we have accumulated a great deal of knowledge about how to communicate more successfully in our interpersonal relationships.[3] This chapter will explore that knowledge by first defining what interpersonal relationships are and why we form them. Then you will learn about the skills needed to develop and maintain relationships.

DEFINING INTERPERSONAL RELATIONSHIPS

On the simplest level, relationships are associations or connections. Interpersonal relationships, however, are far more complex. **Interpersonal relationships** may be defined as associations between at least two people who are interdependent, who use some consistent patterns of interaction, and who have interacted for an extended period of time. Consider the various elements of this definition in more detail:

communicating creatively

Describing Your Relationships Visually

In his book *Relational Communication,* William Wilmot discusses various metaphors we have for relationships. For instance, relationships can be described as work, in that two people must negotiate and engage in a process of give-and-take; as a journey, in that people progress along a path as they move through a relationship; and as a game, in that romance and perhaps friendship are viewed as play and competition. Consider what your relationship would look like as a picture. Take out a piece of paper and draw an image that represents your relationship. Would you draw an image of a safe place, dangerous territory, or a novel adventure? Are there bright colors or muted hues? How would you describe in words the image you've drawn.

Source: Wilmot, W. W. (1995). *Relational communication.* New York: McGraw-Hill.

- *Interpersonal relationships include two or more people.* Often, interpersonal relationships consist of just two people—a dating couple, a single parent and a child, a married couple, two close friends, or two co-workers. Interpersonal relationships can also include more than two people—a family unit, a group of friends, or a social group.

- *Interpersonal relationships involve people who are interdependent. Interdependence* refers to people's being mutually dependent on each other and having an impact on each other. When individuals are independent of each other, we typically do not define the resulting association as an interpersonal relationship. Friendship easily illustrates this concept. Your best friend, for example, may be dependent on you for acceptance and guidance, whereas you might require support and admiration. If you did not care about your best friend's well-being or needs, then you would not offer her guidance, and therefore you would not truly have an interpersonal relationship.

- *Individuals in interpersonal relationships use some consistent patterns of interaction.* These patterns may include behaviors generally understood across a variety of situations, as well as behaviors unique to the relationship. For example, your partner may always greet you with a kiss. This kiss is generally understood as a sign of warmth and affection. On the other hand, you may have unique nicknames for your partner that are not understood outside the relationship.

- *Individuals in interpersonal relationships generally have interacted for some time.* When you nod and smile at someone as you leave the classroom, or when you place an order at a fast-food counter, you do not have an interpersonal relationship. Although you use interpersonal communication to accomplish these activities, one-time interactions do not constitute interpersonal relationships. That said, these interactions could be the beginnings of an interpersonal relationship, should the other elements we've discussed occur. We should note, however, that interpersonal relationships might last for varying lengths of time—some are relatively short but others continue for a lifetime.

interpersonal relationships
Associations between at least two people who are interdependent, who use some consistent patterns of interaction, and who have interacted for an extended period of time.

THE IMPORTANCE OF INTERPERSONAL RELATIONSHIPS

According to psychologist William Schutz, we have three basic interpersonal needs that are satisfied through interaction with others:

1. The need for inclusion, or becoming involved with others

2. The need for affection, or holding fond or tender feelings toward another person

3. The need for control, or having the ability to influence others, our environment, and ourselves[4]

Although we may be able to fulfill some of our physical, safety, and security needs through interactions with relative strangers, we can fulfill the other needs only through our interpersonal relationships.

The interdependent nature of interpersonal relationships suggests that people mutually satisfy their needs in this type of association. Interdependence suggests that one person is dependent on another to have some need fulfilled and that the other person (or

• Interpersonal relationships fulfill basic needs.

© Floresco Productions/ Corbis RF

persons) is dependent on the first to have the same or other needs fulfilled. For example, a child who is dependent on a parent may satisfy that parent's needs for inclusion and belonging. The parent, in turn, may supply the child's need for affection in hugging, kissing, or listening to the child.

Complementary relationships—those in which each person supplies something the other person or persons lack—provide good examples of the manner in which we have our needs fulfilled in interpersonal relationships. An example is a friendship between an introverted individual and an extroverted one. The introvert may teach her friend to be more self-reflective or to listen to others more carefully, whereas the extrovert might, in exchange, encourage her to be more outspoken or assertive.

Our needs also may be fulfilled in **symmetrical relationships**—those in which the participants mirror each other or are highly similar. A relationship between two intelligent individuals may reflect their need for intellectual stimulation. Two people of similar ancestry might marry in part to preserve their heritage.

Conflict is inevitable and normal in interpersonal relationships; indeed, conflict can be constructive and creative. Conflict can be healthy when it is used to resolve differences and to "clear the air." On the other hand, it can also be dysfunctional. You might have grown up in a family in which sequences of conflict were ever present, and the only way you know how to have a conversation is by fighting. Or you might have had parents who never discussed differences, and the only way you know to manage conflict is to walk away or not talk about what bothers you.

Conflict is dysfunctional when you avoid talking about problems, withdraw, or become sullen. Conflict is also dysfunctional when you take any criticism or suggestions as a personal attack. Do you fight fairly, or do you attack the other person rather than raising the issue that is at stake? If you feel out of control when you are engaged in an argument with a family member, you may experience conflict as dysfunctional. Finally, conflict can be dysfunctional when you store up many complaints and then attack your roommate with all of them.

If you have experienced conflict as dysfunctional, you can begin to experience it more positively when you follow some straightforward guidelines. First, you need to remain calm. You should also express your feelings in words rather than in actions such as breaking objects, driving recklessly, or using alcohol. Try to be specific about what is bothering you. Rather than bringing up multiple grievances of the past, try to deal with only one issue at a time. Consider your language and avoid words such as *never* and *always* in describing the problem—particularly when it is about your roommate's actions. Do not exaggerate or invent additional problems that are not central to the discussion. Finally, you may find that it is important to establish some ground rules that both you and your partner adopt.

complementary relationships Relationships in which each person supplies something the other person or persons lack.

symmetrical relationships Relationships in which participants mirror each other or are highly similar.

sizing things up

Interpersonal Motives

We enter into interpersonal relationships for a variety of reasons. Below you will read several statements that describe possible reasons for joining interpersonal relationships. Indicate how likely you are to enter into an interpersonal relationship for each reason using the following scale:

1 = Never
2 = Unlikely
3 = Likely
4 = Frequently

I enter into interpersonal relationships . . .

1. Because I can have influence over others.
2. So that I can share emotions with others.
3. To feel part of a group.
4. To be involved in things with other people.
5. To gain affection from others.
6. To bring control to my life.
7. So that I can have more influence over my surroundings.
8. Because I need to know that people like me.
9. Because I want to be included in different activities.

A guide for interpreting your responses appears at the end of this chapter.

Successful interpersonal relationships are based on effective communication.

© Kristy-Anne Glubish/ Design Pics RF

self-disclosure
The process of making intentional revelations about yourself that others would be unlikely to know and that generally constitute private, sensitive, or confidential information.

THE DARK SIDE OF INTERPERSONAL RELATIONSHIPS

Conflict is only one aspect of interpersonal relationships that seems to represent a "dark side" to these most personal affiliations. Although your interpersonal relationships are generally pleasurable and positive, you might also have experienced painful and negative liaisons. Spitzberg and Cupach have provided the most comprehensive treatment of the shadowy side of relationships.[5] What are some of the qualities of negative relationships? Obsession that includes fatal attraction and jealousy certainly creates negative outcomes. Similarly, misunderstanding, gossip, conflict, and codependency can lead to harmful results. Abuse, which includes sexual, physical, mental, and emotional abuse, is truly harmful to individuals and destroys relationships.

In addition, some of the qualities we associate with healthy relationships—self-disclosure, affectionate communication, mutual influence, and the development of a unique relationship—can all become extreme and therefore unhealthy. Effective communication, as you have been learning, is very challenging, and interpersonal communication may be the most challenging context of all. This chapter focuses primarily on positive interpersonal relationships and how to improve them.

SELF-DISCLOSURE IN THE DEVELOPMENT OF INTERPERSONAL RELATIONSHIPS

One change that occurs as relationships become deeper and closer is an increasing intentional revealing of personal information. **Self-disclosure** is the process of making intentional revelations about yourself that others would be unlikely to know and that generally constitute private, sensitive, or confidential information. Pearce and Sharp distinguish among self-disclosure, confession, and revelation.[6] They define self-disclosure as voluntary, confession as forced or coerced information, and revelation as unintentional or inadvertent communication.

Jourard suggests that self-disclosure makes us "transparent" to others, that disclosure helps others to see us as a distinctive human being.[7] Self-disclosure goes beyond self-description. More specifically, your position on abortion, your close relationship with your grandfather, your sexual history, your deepest fears, your proudest moments, and your problems with drugs or alcohol are considered self-disclosure by most definitions. Self-disclosure is not always negative, but it is generally private information.

Sandra Petronio's communication privacy management (CPM) theory provides a useful framework for helping people think about the rules they create regarding when they will and will not share private information and how they manage privacy boundaries once they have shared private information.[8] Have you ever told someone something in confidence and then said, "Now don't tell anyone else about that." According to CPM, this is an example of how people intentionally make rules surrounding who has access to their private information. Privacy rules are created to control the permeability of the boundary.[9]

Why Is Self-Disclosure Important?

Self-disclosure is important for three reasons. First, it allows us to develop a greater understanding of ourselves. Consider the Johari window depicted in figure 1. Joseph Luft and Harrington Ingham created this diagram to depict four kinds of information about a person. The open area (I) includes information that is known to you and to other people, such as your approximate height and weight, and information you freely disclose, such as your hometown, major, or age. The blind area (II) consists of information known to

	Known to self	Not known to self
Known to others	I Open area	II Blind area
Not known to others	III Hidden area	IV Unknown area

Figure 1

Johari window.

Source: Luft, J. (1984). *Group Processes: An Introduction to Group Dynamics.* NY: Mayfield Publishing Company. Copyright 1984, 1970, and 1969 by Joseph Luft. © The McGraw-Hill Companies, Inc. Used by permission.

others but unknown to you, such as your personality characteristics that others perceive but you do not recognize or acknowledge. The hidden area (III) includes information that you know about yourself but others do not. Any information that is hidden and that you do not self-disclose lies here. Finally, the unknown area (IV) comprises information that is unknown to you *and* to others. For instance, neither you nor others know when you will pass on (assuming that you have not been diagnosed with a terminal disease).

The quadrants of the Johari window can expand or contract in size. The quadrants can also have different shapes with different family members, friends, or acquaintances. For example, you might have a very large open area when you are considering the relationship between you and your closest friend. On the other hand, the hidden area may be very large when you consider the relationship between you and your employer. As the size of one of the quadrants changes, so do the sizes of all the others.

Self-disclosure allows you to develop a more positive attitude about yourself and others, as well as more meaningful relationships. Have you ever experienced a problem or faced a difficult situation? Most of us have, and we know that sharing our fears or telling others about our anguish provides comfort. For example, imagine that you vandalized property in high school and were caught. You might feel very guilty for having done the wrong thing, for having to pay a large fine, and for damaging someone else's property. If you can find the courage to talk about your feelings to a friend, you might find that you are not alone, that almost everyone gets into trouble at one time or another. Similarly, if you have recently experienced the loss of a family member, you may find that talking about your feelings and sharing your grief will lead to positive growth for you. Hastings found that self-disclosure is a powerful form of communication in grieving and in healing a fractured identity.[10] In addition, self-disclosing on social media provides a possible place for grieving, support, and coping after the loss of a loved one.[11]

Self-disclosure is one way relationships grow in depth and meaning. Partners in romantic relationships, for example, report greater feelings of security when self-disclosure between them is intentional and honest.[12] When you self-disclose more to others, they will most likely disclose more to you. Without the opportunity for self-disclosure and active listening, relationships can be based on superficiality, which can lead to relational termination.

At the same time, self-disclosure can be used inappropriately. Have you ever sat on an airplane next to a stranger who revealed highly personal information to you? Have you ever dated someone who insisted on sharing private information too early in the relationship? In the next section we will consider some of the findings about self-disclosure that may provide guidelines for your self-disclosing behavior.

What Factors Affect Appropriate Self-Disclosure?

Disclosure generally increases as relational intimacy increases. We do not provide our life story to people we have just met. Instead, in the developing relationship, we gradually reveal an increasing amount of information. We might begin with positive information that is not highly intimate and then begin to share more personal information as we learn to trust the other person. In this way our disclosure tends to be incremental, to increase over time.

Disclosure tends to be reciprocal. This conclusion is related to the previous one. When people offer us information about themselves, we tend to return the behavior in kind. Indeed, when people reciprocate self-disclosure, we tend to view them positively; when they do not, we tend to view them as incompetent. Dindia, Fitzpatrick, and Kenny studied dyadic interaction between women and men and strangers and spouses. They concluded that, in conversations, the disclosure of highly intimate feelings was reciprocal.[13]

Reciprocal disclosure generally does not occur in families. Although parents have an expectation of self-disclosure from their children and adolescents, they do not perceive a need to reciprocate. A variety of factors affect adolescents' disclosures to their parents. Adolescents do not generally feel the need to disclose to their parents, and they are even more reluctant to disclose if their behavior is not sanctioned by their parents.[14] Grandparents may become the target of self-disclosures, since they are sometimes seen as more empathic and positive.[15]

Negative disclosure is directly related to the intimacy of the relationship; however, positive disclosure does not necessarily increase as the relationship becomes more intimate. What does this mean? As we become closer to another person, we are more likely to reveal negative information about ourselves. Positive information, on the other hand, flows through conversations from the earliest developmental stages throughout the lifetime of the relationship. Hence, negative information increases over time, but positive disclosure does not necessarily increase.

Disclosure may be avoided for a variety of reasons. Self-disclosure does not flow freely on all topics. Indeed, relational partners may avoid self-disclosure for reasons of self-protection, relationship protection, partner unresponsiveness, and social appropriateness. As Afifi and Guerrero observe, "Some things are better left unsaid."[16] At the same time, topics that are taboo under some conditions may be appropriate later, when conditions change.[17]

People do not always avoid self-disclosure for noble reasons. College students who were in close relationships were asked whether they disclosed their sexual histories before engaging in sex. Although nearly all the students surveyed felt they were knowledgeable about safe sex, over 40% did not realize that revealing one's sexual history is a safe-sex practice. One-third of those who were sexually active had not disclosed their sexual history to at least one partner prior to becoming sexually involved. And at least one-fifth of the sexually active students purposefully misrepresented their sexual history to their sex partners.[18]

Disclosure varies across cultures. Self-disclosure is not uniformly valued or disvalued around the world. For example, Chinese professionals view interpersonal communication differently in Chinese organizations and in American businesses. They view Chinese interactions to be characterized by blunt assertiveness, smooth amiability, and surface humility. They view American workplaces as composed of sophisticated kindness, manipulative "stroking," and casual spontaneity.[19] Koreans and Americans avoid making requests of others for different reasons. Koreans are concerned with avoiding negative evaluation from the hearer and avoiding hurting the other person's feelings, whereas Americans are more concerned with clarity.[20] These differences most likely transfer to differences in disclosures as well.

Relational satisfaction and disclosure are curvilinearly related. Satisfaction is lowest with no disclosure and with excessive disclosure; it is highest when self-disclosure is provided at moderate levels. Consider your own personal relationships. Does this conclusion appear to be accurate?

Friendship

Friendship contributes to our well-being. People who have harmonious sibling relationships and same-gender friends report the highest levels of well-being.[21] Whereas we celebrate romantic relationships, we do not similarly honor friendships. Rawlins notes that we ought to have a "friendship day," because our friendships are at least as important as our romantic relationships.[22]

THE VALUE OF FRIENDSHIPS

What does friendship mean? Friendships can be based on shared activities or on the level of information we exchange with others. Young adolescents report that their friendships are based on shared activities, whereas for emerging adults they are based on self-disclosure.[23] The communication of private information appears to gain in importance as people mature. Most people identify both family and nonfamily members as friends.

Friendships also change over time. As people age, family members become more salient as friends.[24] For many older men, their only friend is their wife,[25] although the same is not true for older women. Do friendships actually improve over time? Although we cannot be sure, we do know that people *perceive* that they do.[26] Perhaps people come to better understand the importance of friendship as they mature.

The quality of friendships is affected by psychological predispositions, such as attachment styles. People who are securely attached to others have lower levels of conflict with their friends and are able to rise above problems in their friendships. People who are avoidant, or not attached, experience higher levels of conflict and lower levels of companionship.[27]

Rawlins provides a six-stage model of how friendships develop.[28] The first stage, role-limited interaction, includes an encounter in which individuals are polite and careful with their disclosures. Second, friendly relations occur when the two people determine that they have mutual interests or other common ground. Third, moving toward friendship allows them to introduce a personal topic or to set up times to get together. Fourth, in nascent friendship they think of themselves as friends and begin to establish their own private ways of interacting. Fifth, the friends feel established in each other's lives, in what is termed a stabilized friendship. Finally, friendships may move to a waning stage, when the relationship diminishes. Not all friendships reach this sixth stage.

Friendships are maintained differently, depending on the intent of the relational partners. Rawlins notes that issues of romantic attraction must be negotiated early in a relationship.[29] Guerrero and Chavez studied friends who both wanted the relationship to become romantic (mutual romance), friends neither of whom wanted the friendship to

building behaviors

Guidelines for Self-Disclosure

Try the following strategies for appropriate self-disclosure in interpersonal relationships.

1. Gradually increase disclosure as your relationship develops.

2. Reveal information to others as they reveal information to you.

3. Do not disclose negative information until your relationship is established.

4. Do not disclose information that will cause you personal harm.

5. Be sensitive to cultural differences in your self-disclosure.

6. Be aware of non-dominant cultural differences in self-disclosure.

7. Be willing to self-disclose in interpersonal relationships.

Consider how, if at all, these guidelines change or remain the same when self-disclosing in online or other digitally mediated contexts.

become romantic (platonic), and friends of whom one desired romance but felt that the partner did not (desiring or rejecting romance).[30] People in the mutual-romance situation generally reported the most relationship maintenance behavior. Those in the platonic or the rejecting-romance situation had fewer routine contacts and activities, were more likely to talk about other romantic situations, and were less flirtatious. People in the desiring-romance and mutual-romance situations reported the most relationship talk. Clearly, friendships are dynamic and may lead to romantic relationships.

Partners behave differently in their communication with friends and romantic partners. For example, the scope of the "chilling effect," or the suppression of grievances, depends on whether you see the other person as a friend or a romantic partner. One study used binge drinking as the topic to determine whether friends or romantic partners would confront the other person. The researchers found that college students would not talk with their friends about their excessive drinking but they would do so with their romantic partners. In other words, the chilling effect on this topic affected only friendships.[31]

Friendships are not necessarily defined the same way in all cultures. People in collectivist cultures tend to have more intimate but fewer friendships. As people have more contact with other cultures, however, these patterns are showing signs of change. For example, Indonesian people, traditionally from a collectivist culture, now display extensive social contacts.[32]

A new development, made possible by mediated communication, is friendships on the Internet. However, these friendships are perceived as less close and less supportive than are friendships that originate with face-to-face contact. Internet friends are also less likely to be engaged in joint activities.[33]

FRIENDSHIPS AND NEW TECHNOLOGY

Social networking sites, such as Facebook, Twitter, Instagram, Meetup, Snapchat, Meerkat, and LinkedIn, have made new kinds of friendships possible by allowing people to communicate with each other online.

Facebook claims over 1.39 billion monthly active users, 890 million of whom log on during any given day. More than 1.9 billion active users access Facebook through a mobile device. Although we might believe Facebook is distinctly American, more than 223 million current users are outside the United States and use more than 70 languages on the site. Finally, the average Facebook user has 190 Facebook friends.[34]

Twitter was created in March 2006 and boasted 289 million active users in 2015. Like Facebook, Twitter is an online social network, and "tweets" are limited to 140 characters. Twitter's use multiplies when prominent events occur. For example, during Beyoncé's performance at the MTV Video Music Awards, when she announced she was pregnant, tweets reached 8,868 per second, and when Osama Bin Laden was killed, Twitter recorded 5,000 tweets per second.[35] However, the greatest spike to date occurred at the passing of Apple's founder Steve Jobs, when 10,000 tweets per second were exchanged.[36]

Why do people choose to have online friends? Although extraversion and openness to new experiences have some predictive power in identifying people who are likely to use social networking, no clear personality factors distinguish social networkers from others.[37] Perhaps people are motivated to form online friendships because they have a sense of safety and security—they do not need to meet the other person in a face-to-face setting. Others might perceive that online friendships are more exciting than day-to-day relationships. Finally, some people might be attracted to social networking sites because they can create a more idealized self—someone who is more attractive and has a different personality than they actually have.

Although people may have dozens of online friends, they rarely have large numbers of friends with benefits. Friends with benefits (FWB) are those who are not romantically involved but who have agreed to have a sexual relationship. Although studies vary regarding the percentage of college students who engage in such relationships, the most conservative study suggested that over half (51%) of college students are or have been in an FWB relationship.[38] One study found that women are more interested in having a friend, whereas men are more interested in the benefits of such a relationship.[39]

How do FWB relationships conclude? Bisson and Levine found that about 36% of the couples quit having sex but remained friends; 28% stayed friends and remained sexually active; 26% claimed that they were no longer either friends or lovers; and about 10% of the couples had a relationship that became completely romantic.[40] Generally, FWB do not talk at all about romance or the possibility of falling in love, but it is important for people who wish to engage in this kind of relationship to set clear rules and boundaries. They also need to be clear with their friend about their goals with the relationship. Finally, they need to choose their partner wisely: someone they trust, someone they enjoy being with, and someone who is looking for a similar experience.

Social networking sites provide opportunities for new kinds of interpersonal relationships.

© James Woodson/Digital Vision/Getty Images RF

CROSS-CULTURAL RELATIONSHIPS

Because our culture is increasingly diverse, the likelihood that you will be part of a cross-cultural friendship, or even romantic relationship, is far greater now than ever before. In many respects, cross-cultural relationships work like any other type of relationship—we enter into them for many of the same reasons; the processes of self-disclosure work the same; we even initiate and maintain them using many of the same skills.

One difference is that we may feel more tentative in initiating a dialogue with a person from another culture. Perhaps we are afraid of language barriers or of accidentally saying something wrong. In other situations, such as when two people are assigned to a residence hall room as roommates, the relationship may be forced upon them. In either case, one approach to establishing a relationship is to view it as a cooperative learning opportunity in which both participants work together to achieve a mutually shared understanding while learning about each other's culture.[41] In approaching the relationship in this way, try to do the following:

1. *Have meaningful personal interaction.* If you feel uncomfortable in the initial stages of interaction, you may be tempted to stick to very safe topics of conversation. Try to talk about some more personal and meaningful topics as well. For instance, what are the similarities and differences between your families? What religions do you practice? What are your hometowns like? What work experiences have you had? By talking about more personal topics like these, you will begin to learn about each other and start the self-disclosure cycle.

2. *Maintain equal status.* Research shows that, when one person assumes a role of "leader" or "teacher," the relationship will have more trouble developing. Both members of the relationship should recognize that each has something unique to offer in terms of knowledge, creativity, openness, listening, and so on. Remembering to keep the new relationship focused on interpersonal closeness rather than task concerns can help prevent a perception of inequality in the early stages of the relationship.

3. *Find ways to build interdependence.* Any relationship will be stronger if both individuals bring something to it. If each can find ways to help the other, interdependence will form, and the bond of the relationship will grow stronger.

4. *Respect individual differences.* People from different cultures are like anyone else. Some are shy, whereas others are outgoing; some are very cerebral, and others are very practical; some like romantic comedies, whereas others like action shows. Such differences and even disagreements over them do not mean you cannot make a cross-cultural relationship work; it may simply mean that you don't like certain personality characteristics. Just as with friends from your own culture, you occasionally have to overlook minor disagreements in light of the many areas of agreement.

The Stages in Interpersonal Relationships

Communication and relationship development are symbiotic; that is, communication affects the growth of relationships, and the growth of relationships affects communicative behavior.[42]

DEVELOPING RELATIONSHIPS

relational development
The initial stage in a relationship that moves a couple from meeting to mating.

Relational development does not occur overnight, although many couples in long-term relationships recall falling in love "at first sight." College students outline a general pattern for the developing relationship. When college students first meet, they exchange names, majors, and hometowns. They might begin using social media and text each other from time to time. This early investigative stage lasts a fairly short time and allows the couple to determine whether they have anything in common.

If the couple finds they are compatible, they may begin to spend more time together and go to parties, movies, dinners, and other social events together. They meet each other's friends and eventually engage in intimacy. Because intimacy is an emotional step in a relationship, couples may assess the cost as well as the benefits of becoming intimate with someone to whom they are not committed.[43] As a result of differences in opinion about the desirability of intimacy or the meaningfulness of it, the first fight might ensue shortly after intimacy has occurred. Too, partners are sometimes not equally astute at understanding the nonverbal and verbal cues that lead to intimacy, and one may be baffled while the other is keenly aware of the likelihood of engaging in a sexual relationship.[44] Assuming the fight has cleared the air and not ended the relationship, they next meet each other's family. At this point, the two become exclusive. They are no longer interested in dating others, or "playing the field." They develop mutual concerns, shared jokes, and a bit of a common history.

About this time they express their affection verbally, as one or both disclose, "I love you." Additional shared experiences, such as working on projects or traveling together, might occur next. The two develop rituals to manage both work and play. They might have a common language that allows them to communicate with each other without strangers understanding. They share each other's friends and perhaps eliminate other relationships.

Commitment is the final stage of relational development. Some couples exchange a promise ring or other pieces of jewelry next, to suggest to others that they are now a couple. They begin to spend increasing amounts of time at each other's apartment or room, and one member might suggest moving in together. A proposal of marriage may follow or precede this suggestion. The two may determine whether they can provide steady and dependable care for another live being by buying plants together or getting a pet. Some couples remain at this point for years, whereas others marry, or marry and have children. Couples who do not choose to marry may host a public event that tells others of the bond they share.

MAINTAINING RELATIONSHIPS

relational maintenance
The stage in a relationship after a couple has bonded and in which they engage in the process of keeping the relationship together.

Once individuals have bonded in a relationship, they enter a stage of **relational maintenance,** in which they begin establishing strategies for keeping the relationship together. Wilmot suggests that relationships stabilize when the partners reach a basic level of agreement about what they want from the relationship.[45] This can occur at any level of intimacy, and even "stabilized" relationships have internal movement.

The relational maintenance stage is not like a plateau. Instead, people become more intimate or closer at some periods and more distant and less close at other times, usually describing a jagged rather than a straight line. Maintained relationships are in motion, and healthy relationships are always changing. A relationship that is static is probably dead, or dying.

Baxter and her colleagues, as well as other researchers, have developed and demonstrated the importance of dialectic theory in interpersonal relationships.[46] **Dialectic** refers to the tension that exists between two conflicting or interacting forces, elements, or ideas. When dialectic theory is applied to interpersonal relationships, we acknowledge that relationships often incorporate contradictions or contrasts within them and that relationships are always in process. By **contradictions,** we mean that each person might have two opposing desires for maintaining the relationship—you want to be with your partner, but you also have a need for space and time away from him or her. *Process* means that relationships are always changing. Thus, relational maintenance cannot be depicted as a flat line but, rather, one that has peaks and valleys.

What are some of the primary dialectics that Baxter identifies? Three emerged in the early work. The dialectic of *integration/separation* suggests the tension between wanting to be separate entities and wanting to be integrated with another person. The dialectic of *stability/change* suggests the tension between wanting events, conversations, and behavior to be the same and desiring change. The dialectic of *expression/privacy* suggests the tension between wanting to self-disclose and be completely open and wanting to be private and closed. Table 1 summarizes Baxter's primary dialectics.

The use of media has multiple effects on relationships and may play a greater role than we suspect. For example, people who consume a great deal of television and play video games frequently use fewer relational maintenance strategies than those who are modest or moderate media users. In one study, this difference was particularly strong for those who showed high dependence on video games, perhaps due to the competition games provide for relational development and maintenance time.[47]

dialectic
The tension that exists between two conflicting or interacting forces, elements, or ideas.

contradictions
In dialectic theory, the idea that each person in a relationship might have two opposing desires for maintaining the relationship.

Table 1 Baxter's Dialectic Tensions	
Integration	**Separation**
"Let's move in together."	"When we get married, I would like us to keep separate bank accounts."
Stability	**Change**
"I'm glad we've never moved."	"I'm feeling restless. I think it is time to plan a vacation!"
Expression	**Privacy**
"I did absolutely the dumbest thing last night. Let me tell you."	"I would rather not explain how I spent the weekend."

On the other hand, college students regularly use texting and instant messaging to connect with others who are in both long-distance and geographically close relationships with them. With family and friends, students tend to use self-disclosure (directly discussing the nature of their relationship), positive comments (being cheerful and upbeat), and discussions of social networks (attempting to involve them in a variety of activities) in their messages. When interacting with romantic partners, they also use assurances that include stressing commitment and love.[48]

WHEN RELATIONSHIPS DETERIORATE

relational deterioration
The stage in a relationship in which the prior bond disintegrates.

Although all relationships go through a period of development, and many go through the maintenance stage, some deteriorate. **Relational deterioration** may occur because of the pressures of external events, because of differences that develop within the couple, or because of relationships with other people. Couples may first observe that they are spending increasing amounts of time away from each other and they prefer this time of separation.

The couple may begin to physically, emotionally, and communicatively pull away from each other. Perhaps they do not attend public events together. They might decide to sleep in separate rooms or separate beds. They no longer appear to be a couple to each other or to others.

The parties may begin to look for others with whom to share their thoughts and feelings. They might find spending time with each other to be boring, stifling, and awkward. If they have children, they may attend the children's events but arrive and leave in separate vehicles. They may arrange events so that they do not have to be alone together.

Next, the couple avoids spending any time at all together. One person may move out. One might reschedule activities so he or she is gone when the other awakens or comes home sufficiently late that the other partner is already sleeping. Communication may actually increase at this point, but it is marked with anger and negative intent.

Finally, the couple takes legal action to end their relationship, if it has been legally sanctioned. They might engage in outright hostility and dissociation. They may divide their common property, returning jewelry and other sentimental gifts to the partner and shedding any symbols of their relationship. Common friends are now divided between the two. One member of the couple may assert him- or herself by taking a new job at a great geographic distance. The relationship is clearly over.

Not all relationships go through these stages, particularly deterioration or termination. People experience movement as they reconnect after periods of little intimacy. They may question their relationship but not move to dissolve it. Sometimes couples move back to the dating stage as they renew their love, perhaps after the children have left home or after retirement.

Communication skills can also alter the trajectory of a relationship. In relationships that are dysfunctional or deteriorating, communication can help heal or remedy problems. In new relationships it can stimulate relational development and growth. Communication skills thus allow us to subscribe to realistic hope in our relationships.

Finally, individuals do not move through each of these stages with everyone they meet. Research has shown that people base decisions to develop relationships on such factors as physical attractiveness, personal charisma, and communication behaviors.[49] In general, we are more likely to attempt to develop relationships with people who are attractive, emotionally expressive, extroverted, and spontaneous. In the next section we will consider some of the theories that

Relational deterioration is marked by differentiating behavior.

© Radius Images/Corbis RF

suggest why we select some people with whom to relate and why we neglect, or even reject, other people.

Motivations for Initiating, Maintaining, and Terminating Relationships

Most relationships go through definable stages of development, maintenance, and deterioration.

MOTIVATIONS FOR INITIATING RELATIONSHIPS

How do you determine which people you will select to be your friends, lovers, or family members? Why do you cultivate relationships with them? How does communication figure into the equation?

First, **proximity**—the location, distance, or range between persons and things—is obvious but important. You are probably not going to have relationships with people from places you have never been. You are most likely to find others where you spend most of your time. For this reason a roommate or co-worker can easily become a friend.[50] People who attend the same religious services, belong to the same social clubs, or are members of the same gang are most likely to become friends. People who share a major or a dormitory, cafeteria, car pool, or part of the seating chart in a class are also likely candidates. To underline the power of proximity, consider that changes in location (high school to college and college to job) often change relationship patterns.

Second, from all the people we see, we select the ones we find high in **attractiveness,** which includes physical attractiveness, how desirable a person is to work with, and how much "social value" the person has for others.[51] In other words, a person who is desirable to work with, in whom others also show interest, and who physically looks good to us is attractive.[52] Attractiveness is not universal, however; it varies from culture to culture[53] and person to person. Because of perceptual differences, you will not be looking for the same person as everyone else.

Responsiveness describes the reason we tend to select our friends and loved ones from people who demonstrate positive interest in us. Few people are more attractive than those who actively listen to us, think our jokes are funny, find our vulnerabilities endearing, and see our faults as amusing. In short, we practically never select our friends from among those who dislike us.

Similarity, the idea that our friends and loved ones are usually people who like or dislike the same things we do, is another feature of attractiveness. Whatever we consider most important is the similarity we seek, so some friends or people in loving relationships are bound by their interests, others by their ideology, and still others by their mutual likes and dislikes. Thousands of people find their friends in the same circle where they work: clerical workers with clerical workers, managers with managers, and bosses with bosses. Similarity is a powerful source of attraction.

Complementarity is the idea that we sometimes bond with people whose strengths are our weaknesses. Whereas you may be slightly shy, your friend may be assertive. In situations that call for assertiveness, she may play that role for you. A math-loving engineer may find friendship with a people-loving communication major, who takes care of the engineer's social life while the engineer helps his friend with math courses. Complementarity seems to occur in fiscal matters, too. Those who spend more than they should tend to marry those who spend less than is ideal. However, these marriages tend to result in a great deal of conflict over fiscal matters, and the couples report diminished marital happiness.[54] At the same time, having a friend or spouse who is too much like us may also have negative effects on the relationship.

proximity
The location, distance, or range between persons and things.

attractiveness
A concept that includes physical attractiveness, how desirable a person is to work with, and how much "social value" the person has for others.

responsiveness
The idea that we tend to select our friends and loved ones from people who demonstrate positive interest in us.

similarity
The idea that our friends and loved ones are usually people who like or dislike the same things we do.

complementarity
The idea that we sometimes bond with people whose strengths are our weaknesses.

We select friends from among people who are responsive to us.

© Don Hammond/Design Pics RF

MOTIVATIONS FOR MAINTAINING RELATIONSHIPS

After you have gotten to know someone, why do you continue to relate to him or her? You may begin to relate to dozens of people, but you do not continue friendships, family relationships, or love relationships with everyone with whom you start a relationship. Let us consider some of the motivators that encourage continuing a relationship.

Although we initially develop a relationship on the basis of such factors as attractiveness and personal charisma, we maintain relationships for different reasons. Maintained relationships invite certain levels of predictability, or certainty.[55] Indeed, we attempt to create strategies that will provide us with additional personal information about our relational partners.[56] We also are less concerned with partners' expressive traits (such as being extroverted and spontaneous) and more concerned with their ability to focus on us through empathic, caring, and concerned involvement.[57] Indeed, as relationships are maintained, partners not only become more empathic but also begin to mirror each other's behavior. Did you know that most research suggests that maintaining social relationships is the main reason we use social networking sites?[58]

Gender and Cultural Differences

Motivations for maintaining relationships are not simple. Many differences between women and men affect maintenance behaviors. For example, women tend to use more maintenance strategies than do men.[59] People with different ethnicities express different primary needs in their interpersonal relationships. According to Collier, "Latinos emphasized relational support, Asian Americans emphasized a caring, positive exchange of ideas, African Americans emphasized respect and acceptance, and Anglo Americans emphasized recognizing the needs of the individual."[60] People from different generations view intergenerational communication differently.[61] In addition, people display different levels of nonverbal involvement and intimacy with their romantic partners.[62]

Satisfying Relationships

Couples can achieve satisfying and long-term relationships, however. Pearson looked at couples who had been happily married for more than 40 years. She found that many of these marriages were characterized by stubbornness ("This marriage will succeed no matter what"), distortion ("She is the most beautiful woman in the world"), unconditional acceptance (regardless of faults), and the continuous push and pull of autonomy or independence versus unity or interdependence.[63] Maintaining positive, satisfying relationships is not easy, but the people who are the most satisfied with their relationships are probably those who have worked hardest at maintaining them. Communicatively, people in long-term and satisfied relationships are distinctive from those in short-term or unhappy relationships. Sillars, Shellen, McIntosh, and Pomegranate found that people in long-term and satisfied relationships are more likely to use joint rather than individual identity pronouns ("we" and "us" rather than "I" or "me").[64]

MOTIVATIONS FOR TERMINATING RELATIONSHIPS

Although our goal may be to maintain satisfying relationships, this outcome is not always possible. Relationships do not last. About half of all marriages end in divorce, and in second and third marriages the failure rate is even higher. Why do interpersonal relationships end? What factors encourage people to seek the conclusion, rather than the continuation, of a relationship? We consider a few of those factors here.

Hurtful messages create emotional pain or upset. They fall into 10 categories of behavior: accusation, evaluation, directive, advise, express desire, inform, question, threat, joke, and lie.[65] Among the most common are accusations (that imply or state fault or offense), evaluation (describe value, worth, or quality), and inform (those that disclose feelings that involve the partner).

hurtful messages
Messages that create emotional pain or upset.

Hurtful messages occur in most relationships, even those in which couples are very satisfied. They do not always end in disruption of the relationship, but they can if they become a pattern or are so intense that one partner cannot forget them. Why do some hurtful messages create significant relational problems, whereas others do not? Duck and Pond suggest that the relational history, the closeness of the couple, and their satisfaction with the relationship all affect how they perceive and respond to their own interaction.[66]

Vangelisti and Crumley determined that people respond in one of three ways: active verbal responses (for example, attacking the other, defending oneself, or asking for an explanation), acquiescent responses (for example, apologizing or crying), and invulnerable responses (for instance, laughing or ignoring the message).[67] People who felt extremely hurt were more likely to use acquiescing responses. Those who were less hurt used invulnerability more than did those who felt extremely hurt. The researchers also found that people expressed more satisfaction with the relationship when verbal responses were used.

Deceptive communication—the practice of deliberately making somebody believe things that are untrue—can also lead to relational dissatisfaction and termination. All relational partners probably engage in some level of deception from time to time. The "little white lie," the nonrevelation of the "whole truth," and the omission of some details are commonplace. However, deliberate and regular deception can lead to the destruction of trust and the end of the relationship.

deceptive communication
The practice of deliberately making somebody believe things that are not true.

People may tell familiar lies (stories that are manufactured and that they tell again and again) or unfamiliar lies (untruths that are constructed on the spot). They vary the length of their pauses, their eye gaze, and the amount of smiling and laughing in which they engage, depending on whether they are telling familiar or unfamiliar lies. Observers, however, cannot detect these alterations.[68] In short, we do not seem to be very able to accurately identify deceptive behaviors.

aggressiveness
The assertion of one's rights at the expense of others and caring about one's own needs but no one else's.

Aggressiveness occurs when people stand up for their rights at the expense of others and care about their own needs but no one else's. Aggressiveness might help you get your way a few times, but ultimately others will avoid you and let their resentment show. People who engage in aggressive behavior may do so because they have a negative self-concept or because they have learned this pattern of behavior growing up. Martin and Anderson show that both sons and daughters have patterns of verbal aggression that are similar to their mother's.[69]

argumentativeness
The quality or state of being argumentative; synonymous with contentiousness or combativeness.

Aggressiveness is not the same as argumentativeness. **Argumentativeness**, defined as the quality or state of being argumentative, is synonymous with being contentious or combative. People who are argumentative are not verbally aggressive.[70] Indeed, argumentative people may value argument as a normal social communicative activity. Argumentation varies across the life span.[71] Argumentativeness patterns are shown to be similar between mothers and their children.[72]

defensiveness
The response that occurs when a person feels attacked.

Defensiveness occurs when a person feels attacked. Jack Gibb suggests that trust is essential to healthy relationships.[73] But trust must be established between individuals and not be based on their roles, positions, or status. In other words, people should come to relationships without all the trappings of the roles they play. Reducing defensiveness is essential to building trust.

Gibb distinguished between behaviors that encourage defensiveness and those that reduce defensiveness. He identified evaluation, control, neutrality, superiority, certainty, and strategy as promoting defensive behaviors in others:

- *Evaluation* occurs when an individual makes a judgment about another person or his or her behavior.

- *Control* suggests that the speaker does not allow the second person to join in the discussion of how a problem should be solved.

- *Neutrality* means that the originator of the message does not show concern for the second person.

- *Superiority* occurs when the first person treats the second as a person of lower status.

- *Certainty* denotes a lack of openness to alternative ideas.

- *Strategy* refers to the employment of manipulative and premeditative behavior.

Gibb then categorized the following behaviors as reducing defensiveness: description, problem orientation, empathy, equality, provisionalism, and spontaneity. People who use *description* report their observations rather than offering evaluative comments. People with a *problem orientation* do not act as though they have the solution but are eager to discuss multiple ideas. *Empathy* implies concern for others, as shown through careful listening for both the content and the intent of the other's message. *Equality* means that the communicator demonstrates that he or she is neither superior nor inferior to the second person. *Provisionalism* suggests that the communicator does not communicate certainty or a total conviction but is open to other ideas. *Spontaneity* implies naturalness and a lack of premeditation.

building **behaviors**

Reducing Defensiveness

Rewrite the following statements in a way that would decrease defensiveness. Use the categories generated by Gibb. For example, you would replace evaluation with description.

1. "What's wrong with you, anyway?"
2. "Who's responsible for the mess in our room?"
3. "I don't really care what you do."
4. "We're not leaving here until I say we're leaving."
5. "We don't need to meet. I know how to solve the problem."
6. "I don't need your help."

Table 2 Jack Gibb's Contribution to Reducing Defensiveness

Create Defensiveness	Reduce Defensiveness
Evaluation	Description
Control	Problem orientation
Neutrality	Empathy
Superiority	Equality
Certainty	Provisionalism
Strategy	Spontaneity

Gibb suggests that people replace those behaviors that create defensiveness with those that reduce it. Table 2 depicts the paired concepts. For example, rather than telling someone he is late for a meeting and you do not appreciate waiting, you might note the time he arrived and inquire empathically about his circumstances. Rather than being indifferent toward others and nonverbally suggesting you are superior, inquire about them and express your multiple similarities.

Essential Interpersonal Communication Behaviors

In interpersonal communication you need to be aware of factors such as perception, to have a good self-concept, to provide clear verbal and nonverbal cues to others, and to listen and empathize as others provide messages to you. In an interpersonal relationship you also show affection and support, influence others, and develop the unique nature of the relationship. In this section we consider three interpersonal communication areas: affectionate communication; influence, which includes compliance-gaining and interpersonal dominance; and the development of the distinctive relationship.

USING AFFECTIONATE AND SUPPORTIVE COMMUNICATION

Affection, the holding of fond or tender feelings toward another person, is essential in interpersonal relationships. You express your affectionate feelings for others in a variety of ways, often nonverbally as you touch, hug, kiss, or caress the person. You also use verbal statements of affection, such as "I care about you," "I really like being with you," or "I love you."

Affectionate communication can be risk-laden, and a number of variables affect its appropriateness, such as your own and the other person's sex, the kind of relationship you have (platonic or romantic), the privacy and emotional intensity of the situation, and your predispositions.[74] Telling another person you love him or her may hold significantly different meanings, depending on any of these factors.

Although the expression of affection is generally positive, if the receiver of the message does not reciprocate, the sender may be embarrassed or feel that he or she has lost face. Floyd and Burgoon found that, indeed, expressions of liking do not always result in positive relational outcomes.[75] In general, when people have particular expectations about communicative behavior and they are not met, they might rethink their relationship or they might change their behavior.[76]

Supportive communication is also important in interpersonal communication. Support includes giving advice, expressing concern, and offering assistance and can vary as a result of the receiver's age[77] and the support provider's goals.[78] In times of distress, comforting messages, such as suggesting a diversion, offering assistance, and expressing

engaging **diversity**

Maintaining "Positive Face"

One of your textbook authors has a good friend named Kelly who is the mother to five-year-old Addison. Addison was born with vascular malformations and sinus pericranii. For Addison, her condition, in part, results in blue-type markings on her forehead and a blue nose. Often when Kelly meets new parents, she knows it's only a matter of time before one of them asks about Addison's marks or makes a joke (thinking she colored on her face with a marker) or one of their children says to the parent, "What's on Addy's face?" Kelly values the chance to bring awareness to Addison's condition, but at times the tone or the words people use to ask questions can be face-threatening to Kelly or Addison, even when people don't mean to cause this. In other words, new friends ask questions or react in ways that can damage Kelly's or Addison's "positive face," or their self-esteem (K. Meyers, personal communication, April 7, 2015).

In what ways are people, even children, with visible and nonvisible disabilities treated and communicated with at the early stages of a relationship? Does this change as the relationship progresses? If you met Kelly and Addison at the park, how might you go about asking questions about Addison's condition in ways that preserved positive face for both of them?

optimism, encourage people to feel less upset. At the same time, the recipients of such messages may also feel demeaned. The distressed person is most likely to feel less upset when the comforting message is offered by a close friend rather than an acquaintance.[79] Comfort, then, is viewed as most positive in close interpersonal relationships rather than in more distant ones.

INFLUENCING OTHERS

Influence is the power to affect other people's thinking or actions. It has been studied widely in the context of interpersonal communication. One body of research has focused on compliance-gaining and compliance-resisting. **Compliance-gaining** is a person's attempts to influence a target "to perform some desired behavior that the target otherwise might not perform."[80] It occurs frequently in interpersonal communication. We ask a friend for advice, we ask a parent for financial assistance, or we encourage a relational partner to feel more committed. Children become more skillful at identifying situational and personal cues in possible compliance-gaining as they develop, with girls showing more sensitivity than boys.[81]

compliance-gaining
Attempts made by a source of messages to influence a target "to perform some desired behavior that the target otherwise might not perform."

compliance-resisting
The refusal of targets of influence messages to comply with requests.

Compliance-resisting occurs when targets of influence messages refuse to comply with requests. Targets often offer reasons for their refusal.[82] People who are more sensitive to others and who are more adaptive are more likely to engage in further attempts to influence.[83] Indeed, they may address some anticipated obstacles in their original request, and they may adapt later attempts by offering counterarguments.

For example, if you are asking a friend to let you borrow his car, you might consider some of the reasons he might refuse. He might state that he needs his car at the same time, that the last time you borrowed his car you returned it with no gas, or that the only time he ever hears from you is when you want something from him. In your initial message you might suggest to him that you believe you have been neglecting him, that you want to spend some time together, and that you have not been as considerate as you could be with him. When he suggests that he needs his car at the same time that you do, you might offer to use his car at a different time.

DEVELOPING A UNIQUE RELATIONSHIP

personal idioms
Unique forms of expression and language understood only by individual couples.

rituals
Formalized patterns of actions or words followed regularly.

Interpersonal relationships are defined by their uniqueness. Bruess and Pearson found that couples who created **personal idioms**—or unique forms of expression and language understood only by them—expressed high relational satisfaction.[84]

In a similar way, through playful interaction and the creation of **rituals**—formalized patterns of actions or words followed regularly—couples create a shared culture. Rituals may become so routine that we do not realize that they are part of the fabric of a relationship. However, if a relational partner does not enact them, uneasiness often follows. For example, can you recall a time when your partner failed to call you, say "I love you," or enact another regular behavior? Although the importance of the ritual might never have been verbalized, you probably felt hurt or neglected.

Bruess and Pearson suggest that the following rituals are important characteristics of long-term interpersonal relationships:

- *Couple-time rituals*—for example, exercising together or having dinner together every Saturday night
- *Idiosyncratic/symbolic rituals*—for example, calling each other by a special name or celebrating the anniversary of their first date
- *Daily routines and tasks*—for example, if living together, one partner always preparing the evening meal and the other always cleaning up afterward
- *Intimacy rituals*—for example, giving each other a massage or, when apart, talking on the telephone before going to bed
- *Communication rituals*—for example, saying "I love you" before they go to sleep
- *Patterns, habits, and mannerisms*—for example, meeting her need to be complimented when going out for a fancy evening and meeting his need to be reassured before family events
- *Spiritual rituals*—for example, attending services together or doing yoga together in the evening[85]

The Possibilities for Improvement

Can you improve your communication in interpersonal relationships? Most individuals feel it's possible. Are such changes easy? Generally, they are not. You should not expect that an introductory course in communication will solve all your relational problems. Self-help books that promise instant success will probably result only in disillusionment. Courses on assertiveness training, relaxation techniques, and marital satisfaction provide only part of the answer. Improving relationships is a lifelong process that nobody perfects but that many people can pursue for their own benefit.

bargaining
The process in which two or more parties attempt to reach an agreement on what each should give and receive in a transaction between them.

BARGAINING

Often we engage in bargaining in our interpersonal relationships. **Bargaining** occurs when two or more parties attempt to reach an agreement on what each should give and receive in a transaction between them. Bargains may be explicit and formal, such as the kinds of agreements you reach with others to share tasks, to attend a particular event, or to behave in a specified way. Bargains may also be implicit and informal. For example, in exchange for receiving a compliment from your boyfriend every day, you might agree not to relate embarrassing stories about him. You may not even be aware of some of the unstated agreements you have with others with whom you communicate.

A study on interpersonal bargaining identified three essential features of a bargaining situation:

1. All parties perceive the possibility of reaching an agreement in which each party would be better off, or no worse off, than if no agreement were reached.

2. All parties perceive more than one such agreement that could be reached.

3. Each party perceives the others as having conflicting preferences or opposed interests.[86]

• Couple-time rituals help maintain long-term interpersonal relationships.

© Peter Cade/Iconica/Getty Images

What are some examples of bargaining situations? You may want to go out with friends when your spouse would prefer a quiet evening at home. One person could use the word *forever* to mean a few days or weeks, whereas another assumes the word refers to a much longer period of time. In each of these instances, the disagreement can be resolved through bargaining.

Thibaut and Kelley underlined the importance of bargaining in interpersonal communication:

> Whatever the gratifications achieved in dyads, however lofty or fine the motives satisfied may be, the relationship may be viewed as a trading or bargaining one. The basic assumption running throughout our analysis is that every individual voluntarily enters and stays in any relationship only as long as it is adequately satisfactory in terms of rewards and costs.[87]

MAINTAINING BEHAVIORAL FLEXIBILITY

behavioral flexibility
The ability to alter behavior to adapt to new situations and to relate in new ways when necessary.

In addition to applying your understanding of communication concepts, skills, and settings, you can enhance your interactions by using **behavioral flexibility**—the ability to alter behavior to adapt to new situations and to relate in new ways when necessary. Behavioral flexibility allows you to relax when you are with friends or to be your formal self while interviewing for a job. The key to behavioral flexibility may be self-monitoring, always being conscious of the effect of your words on the specific audience in a particular context.

Behavioral flexibility is especially important in interpersonal communication because relationships between people are in constant flux. For example, the family structure has gone through sharp changes in recent years, the United States has an increasingly older population, and changes in the labor force also require new skills and ways of interacting with others. People travel more often and move more frequently. Millions of people cohabit. As a result of these types of changes, people may interact differently today.

What kinds of changes can you expect in your own life that will affect your relationships with others? You may change your job 10 or more times and move your place of residence even more frequently. You may marry at least once and have one child or more. You will experience loss of family members through death and the dissolution of relationships. When your life appears to be most stable and calm, unexpected changes will occur.

How can behavioral flexibility assist you through life's changes? A flexible person is confident about sharing messages with others, understands the messages others provide, self-discloses when appropriate, and at the same time demonstrates good listening skills. Flexibility lets us show concern for a child who needs assistance, be assertive on the job, yield when another person needs to exercise control, and be independent when called upon to stand alone. A flexible person is not dogmatic or narrow-minded. In short, flexibility means drawing on a large repertoire of communication behaviors as appropriate to the situation.

Changes are not always negative. In fact, many are positive. For instance, when you graduate from college, the changes that occur are generally perceived as positive. When you enter into new relationships, you generally feel better about your life.

But even positive change can be stressful. Gail Sheehy, author of *Passages: Predictable Crises of Adult Life,* wrote:

> We must be willing to change chairs if we want to grow. There is no permanent compatibility between a chair and a person. And there is no one right chair. What is right at one stage may be restricting at another or too soft.[88]

be ready... for what's next

Improving Interpersonal Communication Skills

It is likely that you will experience some relational changes with your friends from high school as you enter college. Similarly, if you are entering college for the first time after starting your career or coming back to college after taking time off, your relationships with your co-workers and your family may change as you balance new routines.

Consider Hannah, a sophomore, who listened to Ashley's tale of her friend from high school. Her response was philosophical:

> *College students face many obstacles in their first year. Difficult classes, lots of freedom, and the pressure to commit to a major can complicate a college experience, but the most crucial experiences have to do with interpersonal relationships. The right roommate, group of friends, and significant other can make or break a college experience.*

Hannah, who had taken a course in interpersonal communication, urged Ashley to slowly cut her ties with her high school friend.

> *Interpersonal relationships are complicated in high school. In college, they are even more difficult to maintain and keep healthy. Some students struggle enormously with social issues in college, but others adapt to their surroundings with ease. Choosing the right relationships and learning to deal with difficult issues are all part of growing up and learning more about communication.*

What do experts identify as key strategies for improving interpersonal communication? Here is some advice that can help both Ashley and her friend:

1. *Listen first.* Communication is a two-way process; getting your message across depends on understanding the other person.

2. *Be interested* in the people with whom you are communicating. Remember, people are more attracted to those who are interested in them and will pay more attention to what they are saying.

3. *Be relaxed.* Bad body language, such as hunched shoulders, fidgeting, toe-tapping or hair-twiddling, gives the game away.

4. *Smile and use eye contact.* It's the most positive signal you can give.

5. *Ask questions.* It's a great way to show people that you are really interested in them.

6. *Respect different points of view.* If the other person has a different point of view from yours, find out more about why he or she thinks that way. The more you understand the reasons behind the person's thinking, the more you can understand his or her point of view or can help the person better understand your point of view.

7. *Be assertive*—try to value the other person's input as much as your own. Don't be pushy but don't be a pushover. Try for the right balance.

8. *Be enthusiastic, when appropriate.* Use both your voice and body language to demonstrate interest.

9. *Make it about the other person first and then you.* Let the other person share his or her story before you jump in and tell your story. Avoid immediately latching onto something someone has just said, as in "Oh, yes, that happened to me," and then immediately telling your story. Make sure you ask enough questions of the other person first, and be careful when or if you give your story, so as not to sound like it's a competition.

10. *Learn from your interactions.* If you had a really good conversation with someone, try to determine why it went well and remember the key points for next time. If it didn't go so well, again try to learn something from it.[89]

Chapter Review & Study Guide

Summary

In this chapter, you learned the following:

1. Interpersonal communication is the process of using messages to generate meaning between at least two people in a situation that allows mutual opportunities for both speaking and listening.

2. Interpersonal relationships provide one context in which people communicate with each other. Interpersonal relationships are associations between at least two people who are interdependent, who use some consistent patterns of interaction, and who have interacted for a period of time. Interpersonal relationships are established for a variety of reasons.

3. Interpersonal relationships are important because they allow us to fulfill our needs for inclusion, affection, and control. Most interpersonal relationships are positive, but they also may have a dark side, which could include obsessions, jealousy, misunderstanding, gossip, conflict, codependency, and abuse.

4. Self-disclosure is fundamental to relationships.

5. Friendships are important, but they have changed over time largely due to social media.

6. Cross-cultural relationships are increasingly common.

7. Most relationships go through definable stages of development, maintenance, and deterioration.

8. Interpersonal communication includes affectionate and supportive communication, influence behaviors, and behaviors that allow people to develop unique relationships.

Key Terms

Aggressiveness
Argumentativeness
Attractiveness
Bargaining
Behavioral flexibility
Complementarity
Complementary relationships
Compliance-gaining
Compliance-resisting

Contradictions
Deceptive communication
Defensiveness
Dialectic
Hurtful messages
Interpersonal relationships
Personal idioms
Proximity
Relational deterioration

Relational development
Relational maintenance
Responsiveness
Rituals
Self-disclosure
Similarity
Symmetrical relationships

Study Questions

1. Which is *not* an element of an interpersonal relationship?

    a. It includes at least two people.
    b. It involves people who are interdependent.
    c. Its patterns of interaction are inconsistent.
    d. Individuals in an interpersonal relationship have interacted for some time.

2. Interpersonal relationships are important because

    a. they fulfill our needs for inclusion, affection, and control.
    b. physical, safety, and security needs cannot be met elsewhere.
    c. dependence is vital.
    d. we need to interact with people having similar interests.

3. An extrovert being friends with an introvert demonstrates which type of relationship?

    a. symmetrical
    b. complementary
    c. negotiated
    d. no relationship

4. Obsession, jealousy, gossip, and mental abuse are examples of

    a. healthy interpersonal communication.
    b. most marital relationships.
    c. possible negative qualities of some interpersonal relationships.
    d. positive problem-solving techniques and skills to develop.

5. Which of the following statements regarding friendship is true?
   a. Friendships remain unchanged over time.
   b. All friendships are maintained identically, regardless of relational partners' intent.
   c. The quality of friendship is affected by other psychological predispositions.
   d. For many older women, their only friend is their husband.

6. If two people in a relationship start to merge their social circles and purchase items together, they are exhibiting actions in the
   a. relational development stage.
   b. relational maintenance stage.
   c. relational deterioration stage.
   d. relational dialectic stage.

7. We may begin a relationship with someone based on how desirable that person is to work with in the classroom. This type of motivation is called
   a. responsiveness.
   b. similarity.
   c. complementarity.
   d. attractiveness.

8. A motivation for terminating a relationship by deliberately making somebody believe untrue things is labeled
   a. deceptive communication.
   b. aggressiveness.
   c. argumentativeness.
   d. defensiveness.

9. Your childhood nickname and the pet name your significant other calls you are examples of
   a. compliance-gaining.
   b. personal idioms.
   c. rituals.
   d. contradictions.

10. Which of the following is very important in interpersonal communication, given that relationships between people are constantly changing?
    a. bargaining
    b. self-concept
    c. behavioral flexibility
    d. dialectic tensions

Answers:
1. (c); 2. (a); 3. (b); 4. (c); 5. (c); 6. (a); 7. (d); 8. (a); 9. (b); 10. (c)

Critical Thinking

1. Consider a friendship you have or had. Explain that friendship in terms of the interpersonal relationship stages. Give examples that describe each stage.

2. How have you maintained your relationships with various people over time? If you have come close to terminating a relationship, how was it regained? Using terminology from the chapter, what was the reason for the near-termination?

3. How, if at all, has social media impacted your ability to initiate conversations with new people?

4. What are the strengths and weaknesses of the stages of interpersonal relationships? When you use this model to understand how relationships progress, are some relationship forms more or less visible?

Sizing Things Up Scoring and Interpretation

Interpersonal Motives

You might have various motives for entering into interpersonal relationships with others. Although the list of motives could be very specific, you learned about inclusion, affection, and control in this chapter. The interpersonal motives questionnaire created for this chapter helps students assess whether one or more of those motives are more dominant in explaining why they enter into relationships. You responded to three questions for each of the three motives. To calculate scores for each motive, sum or average responses as follows:

- *Inclusion.* This motive suggests that we enter into interpersonal relationships to feel part of a group or to be included with others: items 3, 4, and 9.

- *Affection.* Affective motivation stems from our need to share emotion and support with others: items 2, 5, and 8.

- *Control.* To have more instrumental control over our lives and our surroundings, a motivation to control may cause us to enter into relationships: items 1, 6, and 7.

This scale is not designed to generate an overall score; you should calculate scores for each dimension separately. For a variation on this scale, change the target from multiple relationships to a particular relationship, such as the selection of your roommate, your best friend, and so on. When analyzing response patterns, your motives could be multidimensional with high scores for each dimension, or you could emphasize or de-emphasize one or more motives.

References

1. Miller, G. R., & Steinberg, M. (1975). *Between people: A new analysis of interpersonal communication.* Chicago: Science Research Associates.

2. Crawford, L. (1996). Everyday Tao: Conversation and contemplation. *Communication Studies, 47,* 25–34. (p. 25)

3. Julien, D., Chartrand, E., Simard, M. C., Bouthillier, D., & Begin, J. (2003). Conflict, social support, and relationship quality: An observational study of heterosexual, gay male, and lesbian couples' communication. *Journal of Family Psychology, 17,* 419–428.

4. Schutz, W. (1976). *The interpersonal underworld.* Palo Alto, CA: Science and Behavior Books.

5. Spitzberg, B. H., & Cupach, W. R. (2007). *The dark side of interpersonal communication* (2nd ed.). Mahwah, NJ: Lawrence Erlbaum.

6. Pearce, W. B., & Sharp, S. M. (1973). Self-disclosing communication. *Journal of Communication, 23,* 409–425.

7. Jourard, S. M. (1964). *The transparent self: Self-disclosure and well-being.* New York: Van Nostrand Reinhold.

8. Petronio, S. (2002). *Boundaries of privacy: Dialectics of disclosure.* Albany: State University of New York Press.

9. Hosek, A. M., & Thompson, J. (2009). Communication privacy management and college instruction: Exploring the rules and boundaries that frame instructor private disclosures. *Communication Education, 58,* 327–349. doi: 10.1080/03634520902777585

10. Hastings, S. O. (2000). Self-disclosure and identity management by bereaved parents. *Communication Studies, 51,* 352–371.

11. Rossetto, K. R., Lannutti, P. J., & Strauman, E. C. (2014). Death on Facebook: Examining the roles of social media communication for the bereaved. *Journal of Social and Personal Relationships,* 1–21. doi: 10.1177/0265407514555272

12. LePoire, B. A., Haynes, J., Driscoll, J., Driver, B. N., Wheelis, T. F., Hyde, M. K., Prochaska, M., & Ramos, L. (1997). Attachment as a function of parental and partner approach—avoidance tendencies. *Human Communication Research, 23,* 413–441.

13. Dindia, K., Fitzpatrick, M. A., & Kenny, D. A. (1997). Self-disclosure in spouse and stranger interaction. *Human Communication Research, 23,* 388–412.

14. Darling, N., Cumsille, P., Caldwell, L. L., & Dowdy, B. (2006). Predictors of adolescents' disclosure to parents and perceived parental knowledge: Between- and within-person differences. *Journal of Youth and Adolescence, 35,* 659–670. Smetana, J. G., Metzger, A., Gettman, D. C., & Campione-Barr, N. (2006). Disclosure and secrecy in adolescent–parent relationships. *Child Development, 77,* 201–217.

15. Tam, T., Hewstone, M., Harwood, J., Voci, A., & Kenworthy, J. (2006). Intergroup contact and grandparent–grandchild communication: The effects of self-disclosure on implicit and explicit biases against older people. *Group Processes and Intergroup Relations, 9,* 413–429.

16. Afifi, W. A., & Guerrero, L. K. (1998). Some things are better left unsaid II: Topic avoidance in friendships. *Communication Quarterly, 46,* 231–249. (p. 231)

17. Roloff, M. E., & Johnson, D. I. (2001). Reintroducing taboo topics: Antecedents and consequences of putting topics back on the table. *Communication Studies, 52,* 37–50.

18. Lucchetti, A. E. (1999). Deception in disclosing one's sexual history: Safe-sex avoidance or ignorance? *Communication Quarterly, 47,* 300–314.

19. Wang, S. H.-Y., & Chang, H.-C. (1999). Chinese professionals' perceptions of interpersonal communication in corporate America: A multidimensional scaling analysis. *Howard Journal of Communications, 10,* 297–315.

20. Kim, M.-S., & Bresnahan, M. (1994). A process model of request tactic evaluation. *Discourse Processes, 18,* 317–344.

21. Sherman, A. M., Lansford, J. E., & Volling, B. L. (2006). Sibling relationships and best friendships in young adulthood: Warmth, conflict, and well-being. *Personal Relationships, 13,* 151–165.

22. Rawlins, W. (1992). *Friendship matters: Communication, dialectics, and the life course.* New York: Aldine de Gruyter.

23. Radmacher, K., & Azmitia, M. (2006). Are there gendered pathways to intimacy in early adolescents' and emerging adults' friendships? *Journal of Adolescent Research, 21,* 415–448.

24. Pahl, R., & Pevalin, D. J. (2005). Between family and friends: A longitudinal study of friendship choice. *British Journal of Sociology, 56,* 433–450.

25. Rawlins, *Friendship matters.*

26. Way, N., & Greene, M. L. (2006). Trajectories of perceived friendship quality during adolescence: The patterns and contextual predictors. *Journal of Research on Adolescence, 16,* 293–320.

27. Saferstein, J. A., Neimeyer, G. J., & Hagans, C. L. (2005). Attachment as a predictor of friendship qualities in college youth. *Social Behavior and Personality, 33,* 767–775.

28. Rawlins, *Friendship matters.*

29. Ibid.

30. Guerrero, L. K., & Chavez, A. M. (2005). Relational maintenance in cross-sex friendships characterized by different types of romantic intent: An exploratory study. *Western Journal of Communication, 69,* 339–358.

31. Neary Dunleavy, K., & Booth-Butterfield, M. (2008). Chilling effects and binge drinking in platonic and romantic relationships. *Human Communication, 11,* 39–51.

32. French, D. C., Bae, A., Pidada, S., & Okhwa, L. (2006). Friendships of Indonesian, South Korean, and U.S. college students. *Personal Relationships, 13,* 69–81.

33. Mesch, G., & Talmud, I. (2006). The quality of online and offline relationships: The role of multiplexity and duration of social relationships. *Information Society, 22,* 137–148.

34. Zephoria (2015, February). The top 20 valuable Facebook statistics. Retrieved from https://zephoria.com/social-media/top-15-valuable-facebook-statistics/

35. Smith, C. (2011, May 2). Osama Bin Laden's death leaked via Twitter. *The Huffington Post* (www.huffingtonpost.com).

36. Gaudin, S. (2011, October 5). Twitter, Facebook flooded with reaction to Jobs' death. *Computerworld* (www.computerworld.com).

37. Ross, C., Orr, E. S., Sisic, M., Arseneault, J. M., Simmering, M. G., & Orr, R. R. (2009). Personality and motivations associated with Facebook use. *Computers in Human Behavior, 25,* 578–586.

38. Puentes, J., Knox, D., & Zusman, M. E. (2008). Participants in "friends with benefits" relationships. *College Student Journal, 42,* 176–180.

39. McGinty, K., Knox, D., & Zusman, M. E. (2007). Friends with benefits: Women want "friends," men want "benefits." *College Student Journal, 41,* 1128–1131.

40. Bisson, M. A., & Levine, T. R. (2009). Negotiating a friends with benefits relationship. *Archives of Sexual Behavior, 38,* 66–73.

41. Ronesi, L. M. (2003). Enhancing postsecondary intergroup relations at the university through student-run ESL instruction. *Journal of Language, Identity, and Education, 2,* 191–210.

42. Miller, G. R. (1976). *Explorations in interpersonal communication.* Beverly Hills, CA: Sage.

43. La France, B. H. (2010). Predicting sexual satisfaction in interpersonal relationships. *Southern Communication Journal, 75,* 195–214.

44. La France, B. H. (2010). What verbal and nonverbal communication cues lead to sex? An analysis of the traditional sexual script. *Communication Quarterly, 58,* 297–318.

45. Wilmot, W. W. (1995). *Relational communication.* New York: McGraw-Hill.

46. Baxter, L. (1993). The social side of personal relationships: A dialectical perspective. In S. Duck (Ed.), *Understanding relationship processes: Vol. 3. Social context and relationships* (pp. 139–165). Newbury Park, CA: Sage. Baxter, L., & Montgomery, B. (1996). *Relating: Dialogues and dialects.* New York: Guilford Press. Dindia, K., & Baxter, L. A. (1987). Strategies for maintaining and repairing marital relationships. *Journal of Social and Personal Relationships, 4,* 143–158.

47. Chory, R. M., & Banfield, S. (2009). Media dependence and relational maintenance in interpersonal relationships. *Communication Reports, 22,* 41–53.

48. Johnson, A. J., Haigh, M. M., Becker, J. A. H., Craig, E. A., & Wigley, S. (2008). College students' use of relational management strategies in email in long-distance and geographically close relationships. *Journal of Computer-Mediated Communication, 13,* 381–404.

49. Friedman, H. S., Riggio, J. R. E., & Casella, D. F. (1988). Nonverbal skill, personal charisma, and initial attraction. *Personality and Social Psychology Bulletin, 14,* 203–211.

50. Sias, P. M., & Cahill, D. J. (1998). From coworkers to friends: The development of peer friendships in the workplace. *Western Journal of Communication, 62,* 273–299.

51. McCroskey, J. C., & McCain, T. A. (1974). The measurement of interpersonal attraction. *Speech Monographs, 41,* 267–276.

52. Pearson, J. C., & Spitzberg, B. H. (1990). *Interpersonal communication: Concepts, components, and contexts.* Dubuque, IA: Brown.

53. Hetsroni, A., & Bloch, L.-R. (1999). Choosing the right mate when everyone is watching: Cultural and sex differences in television dating games. *Communication Quarterly, 47,* 315–332.

54. Rick, S. I., Small, D. A., & Finkel, E. J. (2011). Fatal (fiscal) attraction: Spendthrifts and tightwads in marriage. *Journal of Marketing Research, 48,* 228–237.

55. Perse, E. M., & Rubin, R. B. (1989). Attribution in social and parasocial relationships. *Communication Research, 16,* 59–77.

56. Berger, C. R., & Kellermann, K. (1989). Personal opacity and social information gathering. *Communication Research, 16,* 314–351.

57. Davis, M. H., & Oathout, H. A. (1987). Maintenance of satisfaction in romantic relationships: Empathy and relational competence. *Journal of Personality and Social Psychology, 53,* 397–498.

58. Ellison, N. B., Steinfield, C., & Lampe, C. (2011). Connection strategies: Social capital implications of Facebook-enabled communication practices. *New Media & Society, 13,* 873–892. http://dx.doi.org/10.1177/1461444810385389

59. Ragsdale, J. D. (1996). Gender, satisfaction level, and the use of relational maintenance strategies in marriage. *Communication Monographs, 63,* 354–369.

60. Collier, M. J. (1996). Communication competence problematics in ethnic friendships. *Communication Monographs, 63,* 314–336.

61. Harwood, J., McKee, J., & Lin, M.-C. (2000). Younger and older adults' schematic representations of intergenerational communication. *Communication Monographs, 67,* 20–41.

62. Guerrero, L. K. (1996). Attachment-style differences in intimacy and involvement: A test of the four-category model. *Communication Monographs, 63,* 269–292.

63. Pearson, J. C. (1996). Forty-forever years? Primary relationships and senior citizens. In N. Vanzetti & S. Duck (Eds.), *A lifetime of relationships* (pp. 383–405). Pacific Grove, CA: Brooks/Cole.

64. Sillars, A., Shellen, W., McIntosh, A., & Pomegranate, M. (1997). Relational characteristics of language: Elaboration and differentiation in marital conversations. *Western Journal of Communication, 61,* 403–422.

65. Vangelisti, A. L., & Crumley, L. P. (1998). Reactions to messages that hurt: The influence of relational contexts. *Communication Monographs, 65,* 173–196.

66. Duck, S., & Pond, K. (1989). Friends, Romans, countrymen, lend me your retrospections: Rhetoric and reality in personal relationships. In C. Hendrick (Ed.), *Close relationships* (pp. 17–38). Newbury Park, CA: Sage.

67. Vangelisti & Crumley, Reactions to messages that hurt.

68. di Battista, P. (1997). Deceivers' responses to challenges of their truthfulness: Difference between familiar lies and unfamiliar lies. *Communication Quarterly, 45,* 319–334.

69. Martin, M. M., & Anderson, C. M. (1997). Aggressive communication traits: How similar are young adults and their parents in argumentativeness, assertiveness, and verbal aggressiveness? *Western Journal of Communication, 61,* 299–314.

70. Semic, B. A., & Canary, D. J. (1997). Trait argumentativeness, verbal aggressiveness, and minimally rational argument: An observational analysis of friendship discussions. *Communication Quarterly, 45,* 355–378.

71. Schullery, N. M., & Schullery, S. E. (2003). Relationship of argumentativeness to age and higher education. *Western Journal of Communication, 67,* 207–224.

72. Martin & Anderson, Aggressive communication traits.

73. Gibb, J. R. (1991). *Trust: A new vision of human relationships for business, education, family, and personal living* (2nd ed). North Hollywood, CA: Newcastle.

74. Floyd, K. (1997). Affectionate communication in nonromantic relationships: Influences of communicator, relational, and contextual factors. *Western Journal of Communication, 61,* 279–298. Floyd, K. (1997). Communicating affection in dyadic relationships: An assessment of behavior and expectancies. *Communication Quarterly, 45,* 68–80. Floyd, K., & Morman, M. T. (1998). The measurement of affectionate communication. *Communication Quarterly, 46,* 144–162. Floyd, K., & Morman, M. T. (2000). Reacting to the verbal expression of affection in same-sex interaction. *Southern Communication Journal, 65,* 287–299.

75. Floyd, K., & Burgoon, J. K. (1999). Reacting to nonverbal expressions of liking: A test of interaction adaptation theory. *Communication Monographs, 66,* 219–239.

76. LePoire, B. A., & Yoshimura, S. M. (1999). The effects of expectancies and actual communication on nonverbal adaptation and communication outcomes: A test of interaction adaptation theory. *Communication Monographs, 66,* 1–30.

77. Caplan, S. E., & Samter, W. (1999). The role of facework in younger and older adults' evaluations of social support messages. *Communication Quarterly, 47,* 245–264.

78. MacGeorge, E. L. (2001). Support providers' interaction goals: The influence of attributions and emotions. *Communication Monographs, 68,* 72–97.

79. Clark, R. A., Pierce, K. F., Hsu, K., Toosley, A., & Williams, L. (1998). The impact of alternative approaches to comforting, closeness of relationship, and gender on multiple measures of effectiveness. *Communication Studies, 49,* 224–239.

80. Wilson, S. R. (1998). Introduction to the special issue on seeking and resisting compliance: The vitality of compliance-gaining research. *Communication Studies, 49,* 273–275. (p. 273)

81. Marshall, L. J., & Levy, V. M., Jr. (1998). The development of children's perceptions of obstacles in compliance-gaining interactions. *Communication Studies, 49,* 342–357.

82. Saeki, M., & O'Keefe, B. (1994). Refusals and rejections: Designing messages to serve multiple goals. *Human Communication Research, 21,* 67–102.

83. Ifert, D. E., & Roloff, M. E. (1997). Overcoming expressed obstacles to compliance: The role of sensitivity to the expressions of others and ability to modify self-presentation. *Communication Quarterly, 45,* 55–67.

84. Bruess, C. J. S., & Pearson, J. C. (1993). "Sweet Pea" and "Pussy Cat"? An examination of idiom use and marital satisfaction over the life cycle. *Journal of Social and Personal Relationships, 10,* 609–615.

85. Bruess, C. J. S., & Pearson, J. C. (1997). Interpersonal rituals in marriage and adult friendship. *Communication Monographs, 64,* 25–46.

86. Deusch, M., & Kraus, R. M. (1962). Studies of interpersonal bargaining. *Journal of Conflict Resolution, 6,* 52.

87. Thibaut, J. W., & Kelley, H. H. (1959). *The social psychology of groups* (p. 37). New York: John Wiley.

88. Sheehy, G. (1976). *Passages: Predictable crises of adult life.* New York: Dutton.

89. A to Z of world: Top ten tips for good interpersonal communication skills. Retrieved from http://z-from-a. blogspot.com/2009/08/top-ten-tips-for-good-interpersonal.html

© SilviaJansen/Getty Images, RF

intercultural communication

When you have read and thought about this chapter, you will be able to

1. Explain why the study of intercultural communication is important for you.

2. Distinguish between dominant and non-dominant cultures.

3. State the characteristics of various cultures, such as individualism, certainty, and time.

4. Practice some strategies for improving intercultural communication.

This chapter introduces you to intercultural communication. Being an effective communicator means interacting positively with people from various racial, ethnic, and cultural backgrounds. The chapter stresses the importance of communicating effectively in an ever-changing world. It reveals strategies used by ethnic groups and marginalized people to interact with dominant cultures, identifies broad characteristics of several cultures, and provides strategies for improving intercultural communication. When you have completed this chapter, you should feel more confident about communicating successfully with others.

In the fall of 2014, the city of Ferguson, Missouri, became a flashpoint for civil strife and public discourse surrounding race relations in America as protestors challenged police over the shooting of Michael Brown, an African American. Although a grand jury decided to not convict the Ferguson police officer with a crime over the shooting, a subsequent investigation by the U.S. Department of Justice found troubling patterns in how African Americans had been treated by police in the city. For example, 85% of the traffic stops made by police were of residents who were black. Additionally, 88% of the instances in which police used force to subdue someone involved people who were black.[1]

© Scott Olson/Getty Images

Public discourse surrounding the situation in Ferguson did consider the merits of the case against the police officer who shot Brown. However, discourse also focused on a broader cultural issue related to how citizens who are black are treated by police. Much of that discourse characterized typically white police officers as part of a dominant white culture that acts with distrust and disrespect toward black individuals. Such discourse is part of a larger dialogue about race that can be traced back to the civil rights movement and even the abolition of slavery.

The events in Ferguson illustrate that the United States, like many other countries around the world, is made up of many different types of individuals who perceive themselves as part of distinct subcultures. Just as countries around the world must negotiate political differences, various cultures within countries must also navigate real and perceived differences. Whether communication is occurring between two countries or two subcultures, intercultural communication is necessary.

What cultures and subcultures do you belong to? How do you perceive your cultures as interacting with other cultures? How do you personally navigate being part of your culture as you interact with others? Understanding intercultural communication can help you become more effective at communicating with people from other cultures that might be very similar to yours or very different.

For centuries the United States looked to the United Kingdom and Western Europe as its main cultural and economic interest. But today the BRIC countries—Brazil, Russia, India, and China—are rapidly gaining power and influence. Because their economies are booming, many Americans will be interacting with their counterparts in those countries. U.S. college and universities have been and still are a magnet for international students.

How well can you actually talk to and learn from students at your own college who are immigrants, refugees, and international students? Do you know some of the basics of how to greet, meet, and eat with people from cultures besides your own? Can you understand the different ways that people from other cultures think and behave: their way of meeting and marrying; their religious beliefs; their family, tribe, or clan relationships; and their means of establishing trust in each other for personal or business reasons?

When you have finished studying this chapter, you will know much more about how to understand and communicate with people from other cultures.

The Importance of Studying Intercultural Communication

intercultural communication
The exchange of information between individuals who are unalike culturally.

Martin and Nakayama define **intercultural communication** as "the interaction between people from different cultural backgrounds."[2] Not long ago, intercultural communication involved only missionaries, jet-setting business executives, foreign correspondents, and political figures. Now, however, developments in technology and shifts in demographics have created a world in which intercultural communication is common. More people are exposed to different global cultures through vacation travel, transnational jobs, international conflicts, military and humanitarian service, and the presence of immigrants, refugees, and new citizens in the United States.

More people are also exposed to groups that operate outside the dominant culture: immigrant populations of a distinct ethnic heritage, undocumented individuals from other nations, and gay, lesbian, or transsexual individuals. You may work and live every day with people different from yourself. Or you might only occasionally encounter unfamiliar groups. But today chances are excellent that you will need to know the basics of intercultural communication presented in this chapter. The first reason, then, that you should study intercultural communication is that communication with people from other cultures is increasingly common.

A second reason to study intercultural communication is economic. Today we sell our corn, wheat, and cars in Asia; we buy coffee from Colombia, bananas from Costa Rica, and oil from Africa, the Middle East, and South America. Our clothing comes from China and Panama, our shoes are made in Mexico, and our cars may have been assembled in Germany, Hungary, or Canada. Business that was previously domestic is now global. You will likely find yourself working with people from many different cultures because of our global economy.

A third reason to study intercultural communication is our curiosity about others. We are curious about people who don't look like us, sound like us, or live like us. We wonder why one woman always wears a long dress and veil, why someone would prefer polkas to rap, why a man wears a turban, and why some people do not eat pork or beef. We are curious about arranged marriages, rituals such as funerals and weddings, and sports such as sumo wrestling, kick boxing, and cricket. We express disbelief that fanatics in an otherwise peace-loving religion promise heaven to suicidal followers as a reward for murdering

engaging **diversity**

The Value of Silence

One of the more striking differences among cultures is the value of silence. The dominant European American culture in the United States practically fears silence; people perceive silence as unintended and even embarrassing. But many East Asian cultures, such as the Japanese; autonomous cultures in the United States, such as the Amish; and Native American cultures, such as the Western Apache of Arizona, see silence as an important way to know and understand another person through intuition and quietly figure out the other person. Here are some sayings that illustrate the idea:

- It is what people say that gets them in trouble. (Japan)
- A loud voice shows an empty head. (Finland)
- To be always talking is against nature. (Taoist saying)
- One who speaks does not know. (Taoist saying)
- The cat that does not mew catches rats. (Japan)

Compared with some other cultures in the world, the dominant culture in North America consists of a bunch of chatterboxes who may or may not know what they are talking about. In any case, most European Americans do not use or respect silence as a means of communicating.

Source: Kim, Min-Sun. (2002). *Non-Western perspectives on human communication: Implications for theory and practice.* Thousand Oaks, CA: Sage, pp. 135, 137.

people. We do not understand religious fanatics and paramilitary groups in our own country who stockpile weapons to attack our own government. Intercultural communication includes better understanding of cultural friends and enemies.

A fourth reason to study intercultural communication is the convergence of technologies. Using cell phones and the Internet, people can instantaneously broadcast events from around the world even before major news outlets know they are occurring. Individuals who are thousands of miles apart can remain in close contact using Skype or other communication tools. New technologies have transformed interpersonal and face-to-face communication and have made possible instant communication across the world.

A fifth reason to study intercultural communication is the influx of foreign-born immigrants, aliens, and refugees that has changed the face of the United States. In communities across the country, the people we encounter on a daily basis are from distinct international cultures other than our own. Whereas coastal cities like New York, Washington D.C., and Los Angeles have long been culturally diverse, we now witness similar trends in midwestern communities like Minneapolis–St. Paul, Minnesota; Columbus, Ohio; and Kansas City, Missouri. Indeed, the United States is growing in its cultural diversity. In fact, by the end of this decade, no single ethnic or racial group will have a majority of children under the age of 18; by the early 2040s, no single group will constitute a majority in the country.[3] Being able to navigate the growing melting pot in the United States will require intercultural communication.

Defining Cultures

You have just learned that intercultural communication is the exchange of information between people of different cultures, but you may be uncertain about the definition of a culture. A **culture** is a unique combination of rituals (such as greeting and parting), religious beliefs, ways of thinking (such as how the Earth was created), and ways of behaving (such as women can marry at 14 years of age in Iran) that unify a group of people. Often we perceive cultural differences (see the chapter on perception, self, and communication) as emerging from nation-states (France, the Czech Republic), religious groups (Muslims, Buddhists, Amish), tribal groups (Kurds, Ibos, Potawatomi Nation), or even people united by a cause (Palestinians, the Taliban, ISIS).

A **dominant culture** is determined by who has the power and influence in traditional social structures like politics, religious institutions, schools, and businesses. For example, in the United States the dominant culture is white, male, able-bodied, straight, married, and employed.

Despite the two-term election of Barack Obama, the U.S. Congress remains representative of the dominant culture. For instance, the senators and representatives serving at the start of 2015 were 80% white, 80% male, and 92% Christian.[4] In big business, men hold 82% of the positions on corporate boards, with both women and minorities losing ground in recent years. Among Fortune 500 companies, 24 have women as their chief executive officer.[5] Despite some progress for women, a recent poll by Pew Social Research observed that 4 in 10 Americans believe that there are double standards for women seeking to break the glass ceiling in business or politics. In essence, women must do more to prove themselves in comparison to their male peers.[6]

If you have persistent bodily or mental deficiencies, you are no longer in the dominant culture, as indicated by the fact that you receive federal protection in the job market. Despite the recent Supreme Court of the United States ruling that legally recognizes same-sex marriage, no federal laws exist to protect LGBTQ individuals in

culture
A unique combination of rituals, religious beliefs, ways of thinking, and ways of behaving that unify a group of people.

dominant culture
A culture determined by who has the power and influence in traditional social structures like politics, religious institutions, schools, and businesses; in the United States the dominant culture is white, male, able-bodied, straight, married, and employed.

the workplace.[7] The military remains white and male dominated (80%).[8] Higher education is still the bastion of white male professors, and most pastors and ministers, all imams, and all Roman Catholic cardinals, bishops, and priests are males.

To connect the issue of the dominant culture to communication, consider the burgeoning number of under- and unemployed. Lose your job and you find out quickly that the United States is a capitalist culture that strongly favors workers and casts the unemployed into a situation where they are devoid of power or influence. In fact, you end up in a dependent situation where you have to get unemployment, food stamps, and the like from government agencies. In the dominant U.S. culture, individual identity is tightly tied to occupation. When strangers meet, one of the first questions they ask each other is "What do you do?"

In Korea and some of the other Pacific Rim countries, the exchange between strangers is quite different. First, Korea is a country of 100 clans, so your name, whether it be Kim, Min, or Choi, tells the other person something of your lineage. But the first question people ask is not about what you do for a living. Instead, Koreans want to know whom you know in common. In other words, Koreans value human relationships, the linkage with others, over occupation.

non-dominant culture
A term that includes people of color, women, gays/lesbians/bisexuals, people with disabilities, the lower/working class, the unemployed, the underemployed, the bankrupt, the young, and the elderly.

A **non-dominant culture** exists within a larger, dominant culture but differs from the dominant culture in some significant characteristic. For instance, an Afghani who comes to the United States moves from a dominant culture (an Afghani in Afghanistan) to a non-dominant culture (an Afghani in the United States). An able-bodied, wealthy white male could move from the dominant culture to a non-dominant culture if he became disabled in an automobile accident. Non-dominant cultures are based on varied criteria: females because they are not equal to men in pay, power, or prestige; poor people because they are united in powerlessness; and gays and lesbians because they lack certain rights and privileges. An individual can belong to many non-dominant cultures. A U.S. adolescent female immigrant from Panama who is a Roman Catholic earning minimum wage belongs to at least five non-dominant cultures, and no one would say she is of the dominant U.S. culture.

Next we are going to explore some methods used by non-dominant cultures to communicate with dominant cultures. Consider a gay male working in an office with a dominant culture of straight men and women. What choices does he have in relating to other workers? The next section explains the goals of assimilation, accommodation, and separation.

THE GOALS OF NON-DOMINANT CULTURAL COMMUNICATION

Some of the earlier studies of non-dominant cultures focused on how little influence women had, even when they were part of workforce teams. Kramarae, for instance, called women a "muted group" because their ideas were undervalued, underestimated, and sometimes unheard.[9]

◦ Cultural identity is maintained by distinctive clothing and other adornments.

© Mike Segar-Pool/Getty Images News/Getty Images

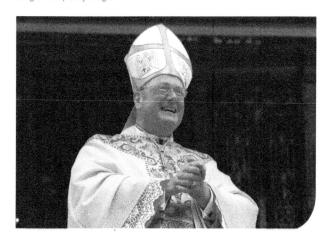

Non-dominant cultures are often called "marginalized groups" because they live on the edges of the dominant culture; in other words, they exist on the margins. Who are the marginalized groups? Orbe calls them "non-dominant groups" and categorizes them as "people of color, women, gays/lesbians/bisexuals, people with disabilities, lower/working class, and the young and the elderly."[10] To these groups we could now add others: people who are bankrupt, who have lost their jobs, who are unemployed or underemployed, or who have lost their homes due to the economic downturn.

Who are the likely members of the dominant culture? Orbe quotes Folb's list of the dominant as male,

European American, heterosexual, able-bodied, youthful, middle/upper class, and/or Christian groups.[11] Others dominant in our culture are the college-educated, people in the professions, business owners, home-owners, married couples, and people paid by the month instead of by the hour.

Usually, marginalized, non-dominant groups seek three possible goals to relate to dominant groups: assimilation, accommodation, or separation. The **assimilation goal** means that the marginalized group attempts to fit in with the dominant group. They wear suits; you wear a suit. They don't have body piercing or visible tattoos; you forgo the ear, lip, and eyebrow rings and body art. They talk sports; you learn the names of the teams and players.

The **accommodation goal** means that the marginalized group manages to keep its identity while striving for positive relationships with the dominant culture. For example, a woman takes her lesbian partner to the company picnic, makes no secret of the relationship at work, but does not discuss her lesbianism with her heterosexual colleagues. A fundamentalist Christian woman always wears long dresses and never cuts her hair or wears makeup, but she respects the right of co-workers to have their own religious beliefs without interference from her.

A **separation goal** is achieved when the marginalized group relates as exclusively as possible with its own group and as little as possible with the dominant group. A number of very conservative religious groups, such as Hasidic Jews, the Amish, and Black Muslims, are examples. But marginalized individuals can live separate lives in the midst of the dominant culture by relentlessly focusing on work, studiously avoiding any but the most necessary interactions, and never socializing outside work with any colleagues.

Certain events can cause marginalized groups to cycle in and out of these different goals. For example, the events surrounding high-profile killings of black men in Ferguson, Missouri, and New York sparked protests that, when nonviolent, appeared to focus on assimilation or accommodation. Chants of "black lives matter" certainly carried those tones. However, when protests turned violent, the "us versus them" antagonism between police and protesters certainly appeared to be more separatist in orientation.

Intercultural Communication Problems

Intercultural communication is subject to all the problems that can hamper effective interpersonal communication. Intercultural relationships are especially hindered by many perceptual distortions (see the chapter on perception, self, and communication). How we

building **behaviors**

Relating to the Dominant Culture

It is likely that you are aware of the dominant and non-dominant cultures in society. Yet, regardless of where you are positioned within them, it is important to critically examine how communication may be enacted differently depending on your relation to these cultures.

How does your standpoint as part of the dominant culture or non-dominant culture influence how you feel about the situations listed below? For example, if you are an able-bodied, white, Christian, straight male, how may you encounter these situations differently from or similarly to a nonwhite, non-Christian, GLBTQ+ woman or non-able-bodied person? As you read each situation, think about how you would feel and how you would act. Then discuss the situations with someone significant in your life.

- Exchanging an item for money at a pawn shop, where the clerk is an older white man
- Seeking to meet an attractive person from the dominant culture at a party full of them
- Realizing the person sitting next to you is dressed in what you perceive to be "masculine" clothing but identifies as female
- Meeting your lover's dominant-culture parents at their home in a suburban gated community
- Buying a used car from a white man whose pickup sports a Confederate flag
- Buying a small pistol in a state that allows you to carry a concealed weapon
- Being stopped by the highway patrol when you are quite sure you have broken no laws

assimilation goal
The marginalized group attempts to fit in with the dominant group.

accommodation goal
The marginalized group manages to keep its identity while striving for positive relationships with the dominant culture.

separation goal
The marginalized group relates as exclusively as possible with its own group and as little as possible with the dominant group.

select, organize, and interpret visual and message cues is even more important between cultures than among friends. Attribution and perceptual errors are more likely to occur between persons with many differences. Several additional problems may occur during intercultural interactions. Becoming aware of these issues can help you avoid them or reduce their effects. Keep in mind that, although the barriers identified here can be problematic, they do not occur in every exchange.

ETHNOCENTRISM

ethnocentrism
The belief that your own group or culture is superior to other groups or cultures.

cultural relativism
The belief that another culture should be judged by its own context rather than measured against your culture.

stereotype
A generalization about some group of people that oversimplifies their culture.

The largest problem that occurs during intercultural communication is that people bring the prejudices of their culture to the interaction. **Ethnocentrism** is the belief that your own group or culture is superior to all other groups or cultures. You are ethnocentric if you see and judge the rest of the world only from your own culture's perspective. Some common examples include thinking that everyone should speak English, that people in the United States should not have to learn languages other than English, that the U.S. culture is better than Mexico's, and that the Asian custom of bowing is odd.[12] Each of us operates from an ethnocentric perspective, but problems arise when we interpret and evaluate other cultures negatively compared with our own. Generally, a lack of interaction with another culture fosters high levels of ethnocentrism and encourages the notion of cultural superiority. Ethnocentrism makes others feel defensive.

In ethnocentrism you use your own culture as the measure that others are expected to meet; **cultural relativism** is the belief that another culture should be judged by its own context rather than measured against your culture. Saying that the Asian custom of bowing is odd overlooks the long history of bowing to one another as a sign of respect. To communicate effectively with people from different cultures, you need to accept people whose values and norms may be different from your own. An effective communicator avoids ethnocentrism and embraces cultural relativism. In the box "Cultural Relativism in Gestures Around the Globe," you will find some examples of behaviors that make sense only in the context of another culture.

engaging diversity

Cultural Relativism in Gestures Around the Globe

As you consider the ideas of cultural relativism, look at this list of nonverbal behaviors from around the world. Each of these behaviors needs to be judged not in comparison with what people do in the United States but in terms of its meaningfulness in another culture.

- *China:* Chinese always use both hands when passing food, a gift, or a business card.
- *Italy:* The U.S. indication of "one" (the index finger) means "two" in Italy.
- *Thailand:* Do not linger in the doorsill where Thais believe a spirit lives.
- *Greece and Turkey:* A small upward nod that means "yes" in the United States is the way to say "no."
- *Brazil:* The OK sign in the United States (circle made with thumb and forefinger) is obscene.
- *Japan:* Laughter in certain situations signals embarrassment, not amusement.
- *Kenya:* Pointing with the index finger is regarded as very insulting.

Source: Mancini, M. (2003). *Selling destinations: Geography for the travel professional.* Clifton Park, NY: Thompson/Delmar Learning.

STEREOTYPING

Ethnocentrism is not the only perceptual trap you can fall into in intercultural communication. Equally dangerous is the tendency to stereotype people in cultural groups. Rogers and Steinfatt define a **stereotype** as "a generalization about some group of people that oversimplifies their culture."[13] The stereotype of a gay male is an effeminate fellow, but gay people are just as likely to be truckers, physicians, and athletes. Similarly, Jews are both wealthy and poor, Asians are both gifted at math and not, and some black Americans are great athletes but some are not.

Why do people stereotype? Bruno observes, "The tribal drum beats in all societies, warning members of the tribe against the dangers of the others, those who are not members of the tribe, even those who are different within a society. The drum's messages result in different tribal behavior, from religious warfare in Northern Ireland and the Middle East, ethnic cleansing in Yugoslavia and Rwanda, to Neo-Nazi racial purification in Germany and America."[14] Bruno notes that prejudice may be bold or subtle and can even occur among physicians against the disabled people they treat.

Allport originally observed that people are more likely to stereotype individuals and groups with whom they have little contact.[15] For example, you might have a whole set of beliefs about Middle Eastern Muslim women, many of whom cover their body and face and walk well behind their husband. You may not realize that one of your neighbors is actually Muslim but does not follow some of the strict traditions of her religion.

Sometimes stereotyping occurs because people have had a negative or positive experience with a person from another culture. In one investigation, people stereotyped African Americans after only one observation of a negative behavior. In another, simply hearing about an alleged crime was sufficient to stereotype African Americans.[16] Clearly, people are willing to stereotype with very little evidence.

What stereotypes come to mind when you see this image?
© Tanya Constantine/Brand X Pictures/PunchStock

How do people feel about receiving either negative or positive comments that reflect on their social group rather than on them as individuals? In general, people respond adversely to negative comments that are about them either as an individual or as a member of a social group. They also respond negatively if the comment is positive but reflects a stereotype. Participants in this study reported that even positive stereotypes caused increased anger and a desire to avoid or attack the speaker.[17]

What can an individual do who feels that another is stereotyping him or her? A study that tested the effectiveness of confrontation found that the following strategy helps. Although confrontations elicited negative emotions and evaluations toward the person doing the confronting, they also resulted in fewer stereotypic comments from the initial speaker. This change in behavior may be due to the negative self-directed affect that was felt by the stereotyping speaker.[18]

PREJUDICE

Whereas ethnocentrism is thinking your culture is better than others and stereotyping is acting as if all members of a group were alike, **prejudice** is a negative attitude toward a group of people just because they are who they are. Often the groups on the receiving end of prejudice are marginalized groups—people in poverty, people of color, people who speak a language other than English, and gay men and lesbian women. People who are accustomed to being on the receiving end of prejudice can become highly aware of that prejudice. One study showed that African Americans could identify previously identified prejudiced people in only 20 seconds, a much higher degree of accuracy than measured in whites.[19]

Sometimes the group experiencing the prejudice is actually larger than the group that exhibits it. For example, many countries, including the United States, show prejudice against women (lower pay, the glass ceiling) even though they are a majority. Women experience sexist incidents—demeaning and degrading comments and sexual objectification—much more than men, and they suffer from depression, anger, and lower self-esteem because of such incidents.[20] In still other countries, people who are a numerical minority control the fates and show prejudice toward a group that is larger but weaker. Some of the countries that deposed their leaders in the Arab Spring of 2011 were led by rulers from minority groups in their own country.

prejudice
A negative attitude toward a group of people just because they are who they are.

engaging **diversity**

Meeting, Greeting, and Eating

- U.S. citizens and Europeans shake hands in greeting, whereas an even larger number of Chinese, Taiwanese, and Japanese bow when meeting.

- In China and other Pacific Rim countries, hosts/hostesses and guests exchange small, nicely wrapped presents, especially in formal visits.

- Men and women in Russia, Italy, and France give each other a cheek-to-cheek hug and even a kiss on the cheek when greeting.

- Citizens of Pacific Rim countries exchange business cards on meeting by using both hands as if handing off a delicate gift. They look at and even comment on the card.

- The Chinese and other Asians eat with chopsticks, whereas many countries influenced by the British eat with the fork in the left hand and the knife in the right hand. North Americans hold the fork in the right hand.

- Muslim men in Malaysia and in some other countries touch their heart after shaking hands as if to say their greeting is "from the heart."

- Whereas many North Americans have alcoholic drinks before a big meal, millions of Muslims in the world shun alcohol at any time.

- Jews eat kosher food that has been blessed by a rabbi; Muslim people eat halal foods prepared by custom by a butcher who faces east and says the name of Allah while draining the animal's blood. Neither Jews nor Muslims eat pork.

- Whereas North Americans are famous for their "fast foods," much of the rest of the world takes time to eat, to savor the food, and to enjoy conversations with others.

Prejudice is often based on ignorance. That is, the dominant culture chooses not to know much about the target of its prejudice, or the dominant group sees the objects of their prejudice as being in the place they belong. Women and African Americans have made some headway against prejudice, but "mistakes" indicate that prejudices persist: the man—not a woman—must be the manager or owner, the African American man by the luxury car must be someone's driver, and that Mexican must be a day laborer. Education may be the best route to reducing prejudice, so one of the goals of this course is to help educated people overcome ethnocentrism, stereotyping, and prejudice. That will not occur, however, if you protect your prejudices against any outside interference.

Characteristics of Different Cultures

Accepting that your own culture is not superior to another person's culture is one way to improve intercultural communication. Another way is by understanding some of the values and norms of other cultures. For example, suppose you are an American teaching in Japan. Your students' first assignment is to give a speech before the class. After you give them the assignment, they automatically form groups, and each group selects a spokesperson to give the speech. In the United States, students would be unlikely to turn a public-speaking assignment into a small-group activity unless specifically directed to do so. If you don't know anything about the norms and customs of the Japanese culture, you might be totally baffled by your students' behavior. Before launching into some broad characteristics of international cultures, review the box "Meeting, Greeting, and Eating."

In this section you will learn about three characteristics of cultures: individualistic versus collectivist cultures, uncertainty-accepting versus uncertainty-rejecting cultures, and On-time versus Sometime cultures. Keep in mind that the characteristics discussed here are general tendencies. They are not always true of a culture, and they are not true of everyone in a culture.

INDIVIDUALISTIC VERSUS COLLECTIVIST CULTURES

individualistic cultures Cultures that value individual freedom, choice, uniqueness, and independence.

Much of what is known about individualistic and collectivist cultures comes from a study by Hofstede that involved more than 100,000 managers from 40 countries.[21] Although neither China nor Africa was included, the study is a classic in its comprehensiveness.

Individualistic cultures value individual freedom, choice, uniqueness, and independence. These cultures place "I" before "we" and value competition over cooperation, private property over public or state-owned property, personal behavior over group behavior, and individual opinion over what anyone else might think. In an individualistic society, people are likely to leave the family home or the geographic area in which they were raised to pursue their dreams; their loyalty to an organization has qualifications; they move from job to job; and they may leave churches that no longer meet their needs. Loyalty to other people has limits: individualistic cultures have high rates of divorce and illegitimacy. According to the Hofstede study, the top-ranking individualistic cultures are the United States, Australia, Great Britain, Canada, and the Netherlands.[22] Table 1 charts the broad cultural characteristics of individualistic cultures; we discuss its other comparisons next.

building **behaviors**

Interpret the Meaning of Common Sayings

Carefully examine the following sayings, and by yourself or with classmates determine whether they reflect a collectivist or an individualistic culture:

1. When spider webs unite, they can tie up a lion.
2. God helps those who help themselves.
3. The squeaky wheel gets the grease.
4. The ill-mannered child finds a father wherever he goes.

Answers:

1. An Ethiopian proverb, collectivist. 2. An American saying, individualistic. 3. An American saying, individualistic. 4. An African saying, collectivist.

Source: Samovar, L. A., Porter, R. E., & Stefani, L. A. (1998). *Communication between cultures* (3rd ed.). Belmont, CA: Wadsworth.

Table 1 Summary of Cultural Characteristics

Individualistic Cultures Tend to:	Collectivist Cultures Tend to:
Value individual freedom; place "I" before "we."	Value the group over the individual; place "we" before "I."
Value independence.	Value commitment to family, tribe, and clan.
Value directness and clarity.	Value cooperation over competition.
Examples: United States, Australia, Great Britain	*Examples:* Venezuela, Pakistan, Taiwan, Thailand

Uncertainty-Accepting Cultures Tend to:	Uncertainty-Rejecting Cultures Tend to:
Be willing to take risks.	Be threatened by ideas and people from outside.
Avoid rules, seek flexibility, and reject hierarchy.	Establish formal rules for behavior; prefer stability, hierarchy, and structure.
Value individual opinion, general principles, and common sense.	Embrace written rules, regulation, and rituals.
Examples: United States, Great Britain, Denmark	*Examples:* Japan, France, Spain, Greece, Argentina

On-Time Cultures Tend to:	Sometime Cultures Tend to:
Compartmentalize time.	Factor in time as one element of a larger context.
Say that they can waste or save time.	Value social relationships and time considerations together.
Separate work and social time, task and relational time.	Orchestrate family and social responsibilities and task dimensions.
Examples: North America, Northern Europe	*Examples:* Latin America, Middle East, Asia, France, Africa

Source: Adapted from Dodd, Carley. (1998). *Dynamics of intercultural communication.* New York: McGraw-Hill. © 1998 The McGraw-Hill Companies, Inc. Used by permission.

collectivist cultures
Cultures that value the group over the individual.

Collectivist cultures, on the other hand, value the group over the individual. These cultures place "we" before "I" and value commitment to family, tribe, and clan; their people tend to be loyal to spouse, employer, community, and country. Collectivist cultures value cooperation over competition, and group-defined social norms and duties over personal opinions.[23] An ancient Confucian saying captures the spirit of collectivist cultures: "If one wants to establish himself, he should help others to establish themselves first." The highest-ranking collectivist cultures in Hofstede's study were Venezuela, Pakistan, Peru, Taiwan, and Thailand,[24] to which we can easily add China and Japan.

UNCERTAINTY-ACCEPTING VERSUS UNCERTAINTY-REJECTING CULTURES

uncertainty-accepting cultures
Cultures that tolerate ambiguity, uncertainty, and diversity.

Uncertainty-accepting cultures tolerate ambiguity, uncertainty, and diversity. Some of these cultures already have a mixture of ethnic groups, religions, and races. They are more likely to accept political refugees, immigrants, and new citizens from other places. They are less likely to have a rule for everything and more likely to tolerate general principles. Uncertainty-accepting cultures include the United States, Great Britain, Denmark, Sweden, Singapore, Hong Kong, Ireland, and India.[25] Interestingly, Singapore is a city-state that is more tolerant of uncertainty and diversity, but it has many rules, including one prohibiting chewing gum. This oddity should serve as a reminder that these characteristics are generalizations and therefore are not found consistently in every culture.

uncertainty-rejecting cultures
Cultures that have difficulty with ambiguity, uncertainty, and diversity.

Uncertainty-rejecting cultures have difficulty with ambiguity, uncertainty, and diversity. These cultures are more likely to have lots of rules, more likely to want to know exactly how to behave, and more likely to reject outsiders, such as immigrants, refugees, and migrants who look and act differently than they do. Among the most common uncertainty-rejecting cultures are Japan, France, Spain, Greece, Portugal, Belgium, Peru, Chile, Russia, China, and Argentina.[26]

This uncertainty-rejection can lead to communication problems. For example, an increasing number of Asian people now reside in the United States. Teachers who are conferring with Asian parents may find that their communicative style is different from that of European Americans with whom they meet. Lee and Manning report that Asian parents do not start talking immediately in a teacher–parent conference.[27] Instead, they rely on the teacher's tone of voice, gestures, facial expressions, posture, walk, and treatment of time and space to learn about how the teacher feels about their child. The nonverbal cues help the Asian parents reduce their uncertainty.

ON-TIME VERSUS SOMETIME CULTURES

On-time
The time schedule that compartmentalizes time to meet personal needs, separates task and social dimensions, and points to the future.

The last intercultural characteristic we will consider here is time concepts for differentiating among cultures of the world. **On-time** cultures compartmentalize time to meet personal needs, to separate task and social dimensions, and to point to the future.[28] On-time is dominant in Canada, the United States, and Northern Europe.

These cultures see time as something that can be controlled, wasted, or saved. Americans might schedule times to work out, to keep appointments, to go to meetings, and to take the family to a fast-food restaurant. Time is segmented, dedicated to work or social experiences (but usually not both), and plotted toward future events and activities. Within this scheme, getting to any appointment on time is given considerable importance.

Sometime
The time schedule that views time as "contextually based and relationally oriented."

If you travel to other parts of the world, including most countries in Latin America and the Middle East, you will probably experience being an On-time person in a **Sometime** world. You may feel psychologically stressed, as others always seem to be late. On the other hand, you may note that Sometime people focus only on you when they are conversing with you. They are not distracted by schedules or other commitments.

Sometime cultures view time as "contextually based and relationally oriented."[29] For Sometime cultures, time is not saved or wasted; instead, it is only one factor in a much larger and more complicated context. Why halt a conversation with an old friend to hurry off to an appointment on a relatively unimportant issue?

Relationships in some contexts trump time considerations. Sometime cultures orchestrate their relational and task obligations with the fluid movements of jazz, whereas On-time cultures treat life like a march in which people strive mainly to stay on schedule, be efficient, and value tasks over relationships. Typical Sometime cultures are found in Latin America, the Middle East, Asia, France, Africa, and Greece. The United States is predominantly an On-time culture because of the strong European influence, but some non-dominant cultures within the United States exhibit Sometime tendencies.

Businesspeople in Sometime cultures do conduct business, but they do it very differently than those in On-time cultures. A businessperson might have a large waiting room outside his or her office. Several people will be in that waiting room, and they will use the space and time to meet with each other and resolve issues. A great deal of business in Sometime cultures is conducted in public rather than in a series of private meetings.

communicating creatively

Music as Intercultural Dialogue

In an unpublished paper for a class at Dublin City College, Judith McKimm-Vorderwinkler pointed out that music can play an important role in helping individuals from different cultures find common ground from which to communicate. As she noted, when individuals create music together, they are in a "space free of power structures, based on symmetry and empathic understanding." On your campus, or in your community, there are likely opportunities for you to engage in musical exploration with individuals from other cultures. By participating in, or at least witnessing, these activities, you can learn to interact with individuals from other cultures through an aesthetic, creative medium. Such opportunities will better prepare you to interact with people from other cultures in various types of situations.

Source: McKimm-Vorderwinkler, J. (2010, April 30). Can music play a role in intercultural dialogue? Unpublished manuscript. Dublin City College (www.culturaldiplomacy.org/acd/content/articles/2011loam/participant-papers/Can_music_play_a_role_in_intercultural_dialogue.pdf). (p. 11)

Strategies for Improving Intercultural Communication

Effective intercultural communication often takes considerable time, energy, and commitment. The strategies presented here should provide you with some ways to improve intercultural communication and avoid potential problems. Having some strategies in advance will prepare you for new situations with people from other cultures and will increase your confidence in your ability to communicate effectively with a variety of people.

1. *Conduct a personal self-assessment.* How do your own attitudes toward other cultures influence your communication with them? One of the first steps toward improving your intercultural communication skills is an honest assessment of your own communication style, beliefs, and prejudices.

2. *Practice supportive communication behaviors.* Supportive behaviors, such as empathy, encourage success in intercultural exchanges; defensive behaviors tend to hamper effectiveness.

3. *Develop sensitivity toward diversity.* One healthy communication perspective holds that you can learn something from all people. Diverse populations provide ample opportunity for learning. Take the time to learn about other cultures before a communication situation, but don't forget that you will also learn about others simply by taking a risk and talking to someone who is different from you. Challenge yourself. You may be surprised by what you learn.

4. *Avoid stereotypes.* Cultural generalizations go only so far; avoid making assumptions about another's culture, and get to know individuals for themselves.

sizing things up

Cultural Orientation Scale

As we grow in experience, we naturally become accustomed to particular cultural orientations. For some of us this process begins at birth, and for others it can "restart" when we move from one culture to another. Using the scale below, provide a number for each statement that best indicates how well the statement describes your own orientation.

1 = Does not describe me at all
2 = Does not describe me very well
3 = Describes me somewhat
4 = Describes me well
5 = Describes me very well

1. I am a very independent minded person.
2. I have a strong preference to always follow certain rituals.
3. I dislike planning my day in a very structured way.
4. I prefer to promote cooperation and collaboration among those with whom I interact.
5. I dislike having to follow a bunch of rules.
6. It really annoys me when people waste my time.
7. The groups I belong to are more important than me as an individual.
8. New ways of doing things make me feel uncomfortable.
9. I like to carefully manage my work time, family time, and social time.
10. I value my individual freedom to do things my own way.
11. I am excited to travel to new places.
12. I easily lose track of time when talking with others.

This exercise has no right or wrong answers. A guide for interpreting your responses appears at the end of the chapter.

5. *Avoid ethnocentrism.* You may know your own culture the best, but that familiarity does not make your culture superior to all others. You will learn more about the strengths and weaknesses of your own culture by learning more about other cultures.

6. *Develop code sensitivity.* **Code sensitivity** refers to the ability to use the verbal and nonverbal language appropriate to the cultural norms of the individual with whom you are communicating. The more you know about another's culture, the better you will be at adapting.

7. *Seek shared codes.* A key ingredient in establishing shared codes is being open-minded about differences while you determine which communication style to adopt during intercultural communication.

8. *Use and encourage descriptive feedback.* Effective feedback encou-rages adaptation and is crucial in intercultural communication. Both participants should be willing to accept feedback and exhibit supportive behaviors. Feedback should be immediate, honest, specific, and clear.

9. Open communication channels. Intercultural communication can be frustrating. One important strategy to follow during such interactions is to be patient as you seek mutual understanding.

10. *Manage conflicting beliefs and practices.* Think ahead about how you might handle minor and major differences, from everyday behavior to seriously different practices, such as punishments (beheading, stoning), realities (starvation, extreme poverty), and beliefs (male superiority, female subjugation).

Of course, the most effective strategy for improving your intercultural communication competence is practice. Fortunately, the increasing diversity of our own culture means that intercultural communication practice can take place with the people at the corner market, at your place of employment, or even with the student sitting next to you in class. To learn from these many instances of intercultural communication, you must learn to be reflexive. **Reflexivity** means being self-aware and learning from

code sensitivity
The ability to use the verbal and nonverbal language appropriate to the cultural norms of the individual with whom you are communicating.

reflexivity
Being self-aware and learning from interactions with the intent of improving future interactions.

▫ Freedom of expression and a diversity of perspectives are fundamental to a civil society.

© Francis Dean/Dean Pictures/The Image Works

interactions with the intent of improving future interactions. That is, you are able to assess the interaction, identify what went well in the conversation and what could have been done better, and then learn from those observations. Through reflexivity not only will you improve your intercultural communication skills but you will also become a more effective communicator in nearly every situation.

be ready... for what's next

Getting Involved with Other Cultures

Did you know that spending time with people who are from different ethnic groups has a positive effect on your ethnic attitudes during your college years? Researchers have shown that when college students had a large percentage of friends from different ethnic groups, especially during sophomore and junior years of college, they tended to be less biased in favor of their own ethnic group. Additionally, students tended to feel less anxious when interacting with members of different ethnic groups by the end of their senior year.[30]

In an effort to develop new friendships with people from different cultures or gain new understanding of cultural practices, make it a point to ask questions and attend events at your school or in your community. Below is a list of questions to help get the conversation started:

1.   How do people in your culture greet friends, strangers, or business partners?

2.   What do people in your culture do to establish trust in someone with whom they plan to have future dealings?

3.   What religion, celebrations, and holidays does your culture recognize?

4.   How is language in your culture different from English in the United States?

5.   How does the dominant culture in your country differ from that in the United States?

Chapter Review & Study Guide

Summary

In this chapter you learned the following:

1. The study of intercultural communication is important because we are increasingly exposed to people of other cultures. We also are curious about and have an economic need to relate to others.

2. Non-dominant cultures communicate with the dominant culture in dealing with different goals. The three goals of non-dominant groups with the dominant culture are separation, accommodation, and assimilation.

3. Ethnocentrism, stereotyping, and prejudice result in communication problems in intercultural interactions.

4. You can strive to improve your own communication competence by

   - Conducting a personal self-assessment
   - Practicing supportive communication behaviors

   - Developing sensitivity toward diversity
   - Avoiding stereotypes
   - Avoiding ethnocentrism
   - Developing code sensitivity
   - Seeking shared codes
   - Using descriptive feedback
   - Opening communication channels
   - Managing conflicting beliefs and practices
   - Practicing reflexivity

Key Terms

Accommodation goal
Assimilation goal
Code sensitivity
Collectivist cultures
Cultural relativism
Culture
Dominant culture

Ethnocentrism
Individualistic cultures
Intercultural communication
Non-dominant culture
On-time
Prejudice
Reflexivity

Separation goal
Sometime
Stereotype
Uncertainty-accepting cultures
Uncertainty-rejecting cultures

Study Questions

1. Which of the following statements is *not* true?

   a. The convergence of technologies has created global connectedness.
   b. Communication with people from other cultures is becoming increasingly uncommon.
   c. The influx of foreign-born immigrants, aliens, and refugees has changed the face of America.
   d. Intercultural communication is vital because we are increasingly exposed to people from other cultures.

2. How does the dominant culture differ from a non-dominant culture?

   a. The non-dominant culture is always smaller in number.
   b. The non-dominant culture has the power and authority.
   c. The dominant culture makes the rules.
   d. The dominant culture is always larger in number.

3. When marginalized groups try to fit in with the dominant group, they are attempting to achieve

   a. accommodation.
   b. separation.
   c. distinction.
   d. assimilation.

4. When people bring prejudices of their culture to intercultural interactions, they are being

   a. ethnocentric.
   b. stereotypic.
   c. accommodating.
   d. collectivist.

5. When people stereotype, they
   a. judge another person's culture by its own context.
   b. make a generalization about a group of people that oversimplifies their culture.
   c. believe their own culture is superior to other cultures.
   d. avoid making degrading comments with relation to sexual objectification.

6. Cultures that are more concerned with individuality, competition, and private property are which type of culture?
   a. collectivist
   b. relativistic
   c. individualistic
   d. assimilated

7. An example of a non-dominant culture that does not try to fit into the dominant culture in the United States is
   a. the Amish.
   b. women.
   c. Protestants.
   d. the U.S. Army.

8. When you have a negative attitude about other people just because they are who they are, you are demonstrating
   a. prejudice.
   b. ignorance.
   c. ethnocentrism.
   d. stereotyping.

9. Those who schedule their days, are early for appointments, and plan for the future are probably members of a(n)
   a. On-time culture.
   b. Sometime culture.
   c. uncertainty-accepting culture.
   d. collectivist culture.

10. If you are trying to improve your intercultural communication, you should do which of the following?
    a. Be ethnocentric.
    b. Avoid shared codes.
    c. Close communication channels.
    d. Conduct a personal self-assessment.

Answers:
1. (b); 2. (c); 3. (d); 4. (a); 5. (b); 6. (c); 7. (a); 8. (a); 9. (a); 10. (d)

Critical Thinking

1. In the spring of 2015, controversy erupted surrounding a religious freedom law that opened the door for private businesses to potentially deny services to people who are gay, based on religious grounds. How do you think the topics of intercultural communication and dominant/non-dominant subcultures played a role in this controversy?

2. What are the dominant and non-dominant cultures where you live? By what means does the dominant culture in your area reinforce its rules for living? How does it communicate its rules to all others?

Sizing Things Up Scoring and Interpretation

Cultural Orientation Scale

Your responses to these statements can help you assess your preferences for individualism/collectivism, uncertainty-accepting/uncertainty-rejecting, and On-time/Sometime cultural orientations. You can score your responses by following these directions:

- Individualism (add responses to Q1 and Q11) vs. Collectivism (add responses to Q4 and Q7)

- Uncertainty Accepting (add responses to Q5 and Q11) vs. Uncertainty Rejecting (add responses to Q2 and Q8)

- On-time (add responses to Q6 and Q9) vs. Sometime (add responses to Q3 and Q12)

On each dimension, which side yielded the higher score? Were your scores very close together (one or two points) or very far apart (5 or more points)? Which cultural orientations do you lean toward?

References

1. Schuppe, J. (2015, March 3). U.S. finds pattern of biased policing in Ferguson. *NBC News*. Available from http://www.nbcnews.com/storyline/michael-brown-shooting/u-s-finds-pattern-biased-policing-ferguson-n316586

2. Martin, J. N., & Nakayama, T. K. (2011). *Experiencing intercultural communication: An introduction*. New York: McGraw-Hill.

3. Cooper, M. (2012, December 12). Census officials, citing increasing diversity, say U.S. will be a "plurality nation." *The New York Times*. Available from http://www.nytimes.com/2012/12/13/us/us-will-have-no-ethnic-majority-census-finds.html

4. Bump, P. (2015, January 5). The new Congress is 80 percent white, 80 percent male and 92 percent Christian. *The Washington Post*. Available from http://www.washingtonpost.com/blogs/the-fix/wp/2015/01/05/the-new-congress-is-80-percent-white-80-percent-male-and-92-percent-christian/

5. Fairchild, C. (2014, June). Number of Fortune 500 women CEOs reaches historic high. *Fortune*. Retrieved from http://fortune.com/2014/06/03/number-of-fortune-500-women-ceos-reaches-historic-high/

6. Women and leadership. (2015, January 14). *Pew Research Center*. Available from http://www.pewsocialtrends.org/2015/01/14/women-and-leadership/

7. Fidas, D. & Cooper, L. (2005, May). The cost of the closet and the rewards of inclusion: Why the workplace environment for LGBT people matters to employees. Human Rights Campaign. Retrieved from http://www.catalyst.org/knowledge/lesbian-gay-bisexual-transgender-workplace-issues#footnote10_ub1si5u

8. *Women in the military*. (2011). Retrieved from http://usmilitary.about.com/od/womeninthemilitary/Women_in_the_United_States_Military.html

9. Kramarae, C. (1981). *Women and men speaking*. Rowley, MA: Newbury House.

10. Orbe, M. P. (1996). Laying the foundation for co-cultural communication theory: An inductive approach to studying "non-dominant" communication strategies and the factors that influence them. *Communication Studies, 47*, 157–176.

11. Folb, E. (1994). Who's got the room at the top? Issues of dominance and nondominance in intracultural communication. In L. A. Samovar & R. E. Porter (Eds.), *Intercultural communication: A reader* (pp. 119–127). Belmont, CA: Wadsworth.

12. Dodd, C. H. (1998). *Dynamics of intercultural communication* (5th ed.). New York: McGraw-Hill.

13. Rogers, E. M., & Steinfatt, T. M. (1999). *Intercultural communication*. Prospect Heights, IL: Waveland Press.

14. Bruno, R. L. (1999). "Beating" the tribal drum: Rejecting disability stereotypes and preventing self-discrimination. *Disability and Society, 14*, 855–857. (p. 855)

15. Allport, G. W. (1954/1958). *The nature of prejudice*. Cambridge, MA: Addison-Wesley; Garden City, NY: Doubleday.

16. Henderson-King, E., & Nisbett, R. E. (1996). Anti-black prejudice as a function of exposure to the negative behavior of a single black person. *Journal of Personality and Social Psychology, 71*, 654–664.

17. Garcia, A. L., Miller, D. A., Smith, E. R., & Mackie, D. M. (2006). Thanks for the compliment? Emotional reactions to group-level versus individual-level compliments and insults. *Group Processes and Intergroup Relations, 9*, 307–324.

18. Czopp, A. M., Monteith, M. J., & Mark, A. Y. (2006). Standing up for a change: Reducing bias through interpersonal confrontation. *Journal of Personality and Social Psychology, 90*, 784–803.

19. Richeson, J., & Shelton, J. N. (2005). Brief report: Thin slices of racial bias. *Journal of Nonverbal Behavior, 29*, 75–86.

20. Swim, J. K., Hyers, L. L., Cohen, L. L., & Ferguson, M. J. (2001). Everyday sexism: Evidence for its incidence, nature, and psychological impact from three daily diary studies. *Journal of Social Issues, 57*, 31–53.

21. Hofstede, G. (1980). *Culture's consequences: International differences in work-related values*. Newbury Park, CA: Sage.

22. Ibid.

23. Coleman, D. (1998, December 22). The group and self: New focus on a cultural rift. *The New York Times*, 40.

24. Hofstede, *Culture's consequences*.

25. Ibid.

26. Samovar, L. A., Porter, R. E., & Stefani, L. A. (1998). *Communication between cultures* (3rd ed.). Belmont, CA: Wadsworth.

27. Lee, G.-L., & Manning, M. L. (2001). Treat Asian parents and families right. *Education Digest, 67*, 39–45.

28. Ting-Toomey, S. (1997). Managing intercultural conflicts effectively. In L. A. Samovar & R. E. Porter (Eds.), *Intercultural communication: A reader* (8th ed., pp. 392–404). Belmont, CA: Wadsworth.

29. Ibid., 395.

30. Sidanius, J., Levin, S., van Laar, C., & Sears, D. O. (2008). *The diversity challenge: Social identity and intergroup relations on the college campus.* New York: Russell Sage Foundation.

chapter 8

© Comstock Images/SuperStock RF

small-group communication

When you have read and thought about this chapter, you will be able to

1. Explain what characterizes small-group communication.

2. Explain how culture develops in small groups.

3. Clarify the two functions of small groups.

4. Compare and contrast task, maintenance, and self-centered roles in groups.

5. Describe how effective leadership is accomplished in small groups.

6. Enact a process for group problem solving and decision making.

7. Discuss two technology tools that can be used to facilitate small-group communication.

8. Utilize skills necessary for effective and ethical group communication.

Small groups permeate nearly all facets of our lives. Our families, our jobs, our courses, and our friends are all invigorated and driven by small groups of people. In this chapter we address several issues related to small-group communication. After discussing generally what small-group communication is, we turn to theories explaining concepts such as leadership, group culture, and small-group decision making. The chapter concludes by discussing several processes related to small-group effectiveness: cohesiveness, the use of technology, and skills used by ethical group communicators.

Boston Strong.[1] It was a mantra that echoed across a devastated city and nation shortly after the Boston Marathon bombing on April 15, 2013. You may have seen the blue and yellow block-letter shirts or many of its variations, but do you know how the catchphrase started? "Boston Strong" was coined by Nicholas Reynolds (class of 2014), a visual and media arts major, and Chris Dobens (class of 2016), a marketing communication major, from Emerson College in Boston, Massachusetts. Nick and Chris were sitting in dorm rooms, less than a mile from the marathon site, and felt the need to do something to help their local community. One of your *Human Communication* authors was a faculty member at Emerson College during this time and remembers the feeling of energy that arose from the tragedy as an entire community rallied in support of fellow classmates, marathon runners, and fellow citizens.

© Steve Lipofsky/Corbis Sports/Corbis

In an interview, Nick stated, "We wanted something everyone could rally behind." These inexpensive shirts provide a way for college students and others to support their community in remembrance of the tragedy because a portion of the proceeds from their sales goes to victims of the marathon bombing through the One Fund. The campaign has raised over $1 million, and people from all over the world post pictures of themselves wearing their Boston Strong T-shirts on the Boston Strong website.[2]

Nick and Chris partnered with Lane Brenner (class of 2013), a communication studies major, to manage the social media presence by creating Twitter hashtags and promoting a Facebook page. Lane shared the following about working in this small group:

> Working with only two other people on such a large undertaking was stressful at times, but had a multitude of benefits. Nick, Chris, and I were easily able to hash out ideas in a casual setting where each of us felt heard and had a chance to contribute. Due to this, we could make decisions quickly and efficiently and implement them without needing to go through any red tape.[3]

What do you think were some of the challenges Nick and Chris faced as they initially created the catchphrase together? What can you guess were the reasons for bringing Lane in to be part of the small group? How can decision making and problem solving occur when multiple voices need to be heard? As you consider these questions you will begin to recognize many of the issues surrounding group communication.

Has something in your community or on your campus compelled you to act, but you were unsure how to do so? Small groups help provide ideas and energy for addressing those types of situations. Nick, Chris, and Lane had only experience, a computer, an idea, and a phrase . . . it was simple and made a lasting difference. It worked because a small group of like-minded college students made it happen.

Groups are all around us; they are inescapable, and as you've read, they can accomplish extraordinary things. In this chapter, you will explore the characteristics of groups, how communication works within groups, the various roles within groups, how leaders use their skills, and how group members can ethically and effectively make decisions and solve problems.

The Importance of Learning About Small Groups

Small groups are the basic building blocks of our society. Families, work teams, support groups, religious circles, and study groups are all examples of the groups on which our society is built. In organizations, the higher up you go, the more time you will spend working in groups. Membership in small groups is both common and important. In fact, most types of jobs increasingly rely on team-based work, and an increasing number require working in teams that meet online rather than face-to-face.[4] Although the demand and expectation to use technology is apparent, a recent article in *Forbes,* "The Top 10 Skills Employers Most Want in 2015 Graduates," indicated that working in teams and communicating well with others are more important than technology skills.[5] Of course, not all teamwork happens smoothly. For example, recent reports refer to the "black holes of the workday"[6] in response to polls showing that 75% of workers say that time spent in meetings could be more productive. That's why learning about group communication skills is important—you will have to work in groups, so why not do it well?

Small groups are important for four reasons. First, working in groups is an aspect of nearly every human activity. William Schutz, a psychologist who studied group interaction, said that humans have needs for inclusion, affection, and control.[7] The need for **inclusion**— the state of being involved with others—suggests that we need to belong to, or be included in, groups with others. As humans, we derive much of our identity, our beliefs about who we are, from the groups to which we belong. Starting with our immediate families, because they are one of the most influential social groups in our lives,[8] and including such important groups as members of a neighborhood church, mosque, or synagogue; interest groups such as those concerned with preventing sexual assault on campus; and social groups such as book clubs—all these help us define who we are. The need for **affection**—the emotion of caring for others and/or being cared for—means that we humans need to love and be loved, to know that we are important to others who value us as unique human beings. Finally, we have a need for **control**—the ability to influence our environment. We are

inclusion
The state of being involved with others; a human need.

affection
The emotion of caring for others and/or being cared for.

control
The ability to influence our environment.

- Being a part of a group gives us feelings of inclusion and affection.

© BananaStock/ JupiterImages, RF

better able to exercise such control if we work together in groups. One person cannot build a school, bridge, or new business. We need others to meet our needs.

Second, because group work is expected to increase in the future, particularly in business and industry, knowing how groups function and having the ability to operate effectively in them will be highly valued skills. A survey of college graduates showed that oral communication, problem-solving skills, and the ability to motivate and manage others were three of the top four skills taught in college classes that were essential for workplace success—the fourth was written communication.[9] A Pew Research Center poll conducted in October 2014 found that 78% of college-educated adults believed teamwork skills are necessary for children to get ahead in the world. Communication skills, in general, were ranked number one, followed by reading, logic, writing, and teamwork.[10]

Third, being an effective group or team member is a skill you can learn about, develop, and master. As helpful as groups can be to any organization, they often fail because group leaders have not thought through exactly what they want the groups to accomplish or because group members have not been trained in how to behave appropriately as part of a team.[11] Group members need training to understand the dynamics of small-group interaction.

Finally, groups can be an important way for Americans to participate in the democratic process. By talking in groups, we can become more confident in articulating our own beliefs, which, in turn, may lead us to be more vocal about our beliefs in a variety of contexts.[12] During the 2014 election, small groups played a key role in increasing voter turnout. At Illinois State University (ISU), a small group of communication instructors created assignments in their public-speaking classes designed to get students more involved in civic issues. As a result of this effort, students engaged in an annual "issues fair" at which small groups of students presented information about local, state, and national issues by setting up tables and booths on their campus quad. These students helped raise awareness of how political issues were relevant to other college students. Those efforts not only significantly increased student-voter turnout but also persuaded the county board of elections to expand early voting locations to the campus.

Most recently, ISU created the Social Media Analytics Command Center (SMACC) that hosted a campus watch party for the 2015 State of the Union address. At this event, students worked in small groups to analyze the social media chatter about the SOTU

engaging diversity

Groups Help Us Maintain Culture

If you travel 10 minutes northeast of Hermann Park in central Houston, you will find yourself in the middle of the greater Third Ward. Houston's Third Ward is distinctive for many reasons: that area is the home of Texas Southern University, it is one of the original political subdivisions of Houston, and it is just adjacent to downtown Houston and the world-renowned Texas Medical Center campus. The Third Ward has also been the home for much of Houston's African American community. As an article in the *Houston Business Journal* points out, the Third Ward has been threatened with losing its historic identity because of gentrification, or the influx of higher-income development within lower-income areas. Lower-income residents who can no longer afford the rent or property taxes mainly feel the effects of gentrification—those residents often become displaced and the historical roots of the area are ripped apart.

Small groups of residents in Houston's Third Ward are doing their part to combat the negative effects of gentrification. A group of artists created Project Row Houses (www.projectrowhouses.org) in 1993 as a way to use art to build community. Today, Project Row Houses embraces the philosophy that communities created through art can revitalize inner-city neighborhoods like the Third Ward. Recently, artists Ashley Hunt and Bree Edwards spearheaded a Row House project called "communograph," which uses art to create representations of community life. Through the communograph initiative, artists can help community members and other interested individuals understand the culture of the Third Ward through art. Both the Row House project as a whole and the communograph initiative in particular started with small groups of people working together to effect positive change in their community.

Sources: Bradford, N. (2007, July 22). Houston's Third Ward battles an identity crisis. *Houston Business Journal* (www.bizjournals.com/houston/stories/2007/07/23/focus1).html?page=all. Community, creative arts come together with "communograph." (2011, September 19). *The Cypress Times* (www.thecypresstimes.com/article/News/Local_News/COMMUNITY_CREATIVE_ARTS_COME_TOGETHER_WITH_COMMUNOGRAPH/50755).

A social network map of the cliques formed by Twitter accounts that either used or were mentioned in conjunction with the #iSOTU hashtag during President Obama's 2015 State of the Union address.

Source: Social Media Analytics Command Center (SMACC) at Illinois State University.

in real time. The small groups analyzed 1,688 posts that contained the #iSOTU hashtag and they found that the tweets had the following relationships:

- *Cliques*—groups of Twitter handles that frequently mentioned each other or were mentioned together.
- *Degree*—the number of connections to other Twitter handles by means of retweets or mentions.
- *Betweenness*—the extent to which a Twitter handle serves as a connection between other handles in the network. A Twitter handle with a high level of betweenness has influence over what flows and does not flow through the social network.
- *Authority*—the extent to which a Twitter handle is a definitive source of information. A Twitter handle with a large amount of authority is frequently retweeted or mentioned by other Twitter handles or groups of Twitter handles.[13]

This example illustrates how groups can organize and voice opinions through social media.

Defining Small-Group Communication

small-group communication
Interaction among three to nine people working together to achieve an interdependent goal.

Small-group communication is the interaction among three to nine people who are working together to achieve an interdependent goal.[14] This definition implies several things:

- Groups must be small enough that members are mutually aware that the group is a collective entity. Groups typically contain between three and nine people but may be larger if members perceive the group as an entity. Research does show that groups of three or four people are more productive than are larger groups of five or more people.[15] So, if given a choice, working with a smaller group may produce better results.

- The substance that creates and holds the group together is the interaction between members.

- Group members are interdependent—they cannot achieve their goals without the help of other group members. If you watch reality TV shows, such as *The Amazing Race,* you have seen examples of how groups of people must work as interdependent units to achieve success.

Based on this definition, *communication* is the essential process within a small group. Communication creates a group, shapes each group in unique ways, and allows the group to function. As with other forms of human communication, small-group communication involves sending verbal and nonverbal signals that are perceived, interpreted, and responded to by other people. Group members pay attention to each other and coordinate their behavior in order to accomplish the group's assignment. In fact, group communication is like any other form of communication; however, the greater number of people makes communication even more challenging.

The Types and Functions of Small Groups

Think for a moment about the different groups to which you belong. You may regularly study with other students from your accounting class, you may belong to an acappella singing group on campus, you may be assigned to participate in a student service learning group, and you likely have a group of friends with whom you socialize. What are the key differences between these groups? In answering that question, you might think about differences that point to the type of group or the function that the group serves in your life. For instance, there are two types of groups:

- **Assigned groups** occur when individuals are appointed to be members of the group. A student union advisory board is an example of an assigned group.

- **Emergent groups** occur when a group of individuals decide to form a cohesive group out of personal need or desire, but they are not appointed to be part of the group. A group of friends who meet at college are an emergent group.

assigned groups
Groups that evolve out of a hierarchy whereby individuals are assigned membership to the group.

emergent groups
Groups resulting from environmental conditions leading to the formation of a cohesive group of individuals.

◦ A family is an example of a relationship-oriented group.

© Hill Street Studios/Crystal Cartier/Blend Images/Getty Images, RF

We can also classify groups according to the function they serve:

- **Task-oriented groups** are formed for the purpose of completing tasks, such as solving a problem or making a decision. A group of students studying for an exam are taking part in a task-oriented group.
- **Relationship-oriented groups** are usually long-term and exist to meet our needs for inclusion and affection. Your family is an example of a relationship-oriented group.

Classifying groups according to whether they are task-oriented, relationship-oriented, assigned, or emergent is important because a primary tension felt in groups is balancing the task and the interaction (relational) side of group work. Because people form groups, and because groups can grow and change through communication, lines between these types and functions can easily blur. Members of relationship-oriented groups, such as families, engage in work, make decisions, and must cooperate to complete tasks. Members of task-oriented groups forge strong personal bonds and provide each other with affection and recognition. In fact, some of the best task-oriented groups are those that benefit from strong relational bonds, so members feel appreciated and valued. If positive relationships are established among group members, an assigned group can start to look and feel like an emergent group. As we interact with members of that group, a relationship-oriented social group may emerge. Just as our personal relationships can go through several turning points, our group membership is also constantly in flux.

Establishing Culture in Small Groups

When small groups are created, they immediately begin developing a unique group culture. Some group cultures are pleasant, empowering, and motivating, whereas others are aggressive, hostile, and demeaning. In this section you will learn how group culture develops as a result of group norms, role structures enacted by group members, group cohesiveness, and diversity.

THE DEVELOPMENT OF GROUP NORMS

The first time group members communicate, they begin to establish the **norms**—informal rules for interaction created and sustained through communication—that

will eventually guide the members' behaviors. Norms for group behavior tell us implicitly, and sometimes explicitly, how we are to act and behave with others in the group. At first, the full range of human behavior is available to members. For example, they may greet each other formally ("Director," "Dr.," "Professor," and so on), or they may speak informally and use first names. Some group members may shake hands when they first meet, whereas others may hug or bow. The initial pattern of behavior tends to set the tone for subsequent meetings and to establish the general norms that members will follow. The norms of any group tend to mirror the norms of broader cultures in which the group exists. Such norms are also created and altered through communication between group members. As the group interacts, and as leaders exercise authority, the norms of the group can be modified to help the group function more effectively. Of course, sometimes bad norms also develop, which can negatively affect the group's outcomes.

Most norms are not established directly. For example, if Ali comes late to a meeting and no one seems bothered, other members may get the message that coming to meetings on time is unnecessary. By saying nothing to Ali, the group, without consciously thinking about it or formally "deciding," has begun to establish a norm that members need not be on time.

Norms often develop rapidly, without members consciously realizing what is occurring. For example, repeated behaviors, such as members always sitting in the same seats, show how easily norms can emerge through communication. Groups naturally use feedback to enforce norms. If a group member continually texts during meetings, another group member or a leader might say, "We need to put our devices away and focus," to indicate that a norm has been violated.

Members should pay attention to group norms to ensure that they are appropriate to the group task. As teachers we often observe students working in groups. As we walk around the classroom, groups seem to notice we are standing near them and quickly stop talking about the band playing at a local club and turn to the topic we asked them to discuss. As we walk away, discussion soon returns to music and fun. Such norms for playfulness, although important for relationship development, may begin to distract the group from assigned tasks. We certainly do not advocate having no "fun time" in groups. Nevertheless, a norm that emphasizes all "fun time" and no "work time" can prevent the group from reaching its goal.

sizing things up

Leadership Power in Groups

When we enact leadership in small groups, we use a variety of methods to create and enact power that is used to influence others. Below are several statements to help you assess which types of power you typically use during your small group interactions. Respond to each statement using the following scale.

0 = Never
1 = Rarely
2 = Occasionally
3 = Often
4 = Very Often

During group interactions, I generally attempt to influence others' opinions by

1. Showing benefits for agreeing with my viewpoint.
2. Threatening to not work as hard if they do not agree with me.
3. Being open and friendly with everyone in the group.
4. Showing that I have a lot of knowledge or information about the topic.
5. Telling them that my assigned or volunteered role should allow my opinion to carry weight.
6. Offering to help them with their tasks if they follow my way of thinking.
7. Using subtle threats if they do not agree with me.
8. Demonstrating that I am honest and trustworthy.
9. Explaining how my background and experiences give me a uniquely qualified perspective.
10. Pointing out that I was told to lead the discussion, project, or task.

This exercise has no right or wrong answers. A guide for interpreting your responses appears at the end of the chapter.

THE DEVELOPMENT OF ROLES FOR GROUP MEMBERS

role
A consistent pattern of interaction or behavior exhibited over time.

Every group member enacts a unique **role,** which is a consistent pattern of interaction or behavior exhibited over time. In movies, characters enact roles to drive the story; in small groups, members enact roles to drive the interaction of the group. Whereas actors learn their roles from scripts, group members create their roles spontaneously during interactions with others and while drawing on their unique skills and attitudes. Just as an actor plays different roles in different scripts, individuals enact many diverse roles in the numerous groups to which they belong.

The Types of Group Roles

formal role
Also called positional role; an assigned role based on an individual's position or title within a group.

Two major types of group roles are formal and informal. A **formal role** (sometimes called a *positional role*) is an assigned role based on an individual's position or title within a group. You may have a job in which you are assigned to send an e-mail reminding group members about tasks to complete before the next meeting. Your job duty could even state that your role is to keep track of finances or to record agenda items for future meetings. As a result of your formal role, other group members might expect you to behave in certain ways: they might expect you to be organized and have the ability to locate information quickly and without warning. Formal roles bring expectations, and your job is to understand and meet those expectations.

informal role
Also called behavioral role; a role that is developed spontaneously within a group.

An **informal role** (sometimes called a *behavioral role*) is a role that develops naturally, or spontaneously, within a group. The role of each group member is worked out through interactions with the rest of the group and changes to meet emerging needs of the group. Informal roles strongly reflect members' personality characteristics, habits, and typical ways of interacting within a group. If you are the type of person who likes to talk in front of others, you might take on the role of a facilitator. On the other hand, if you are less talkative, you might be a person who takes on behind-the-scene roles, such as conducting research or creating documents for the group. If you are the most competent social media user in your group, you might create a Facebook group for the members or coordinate Google hangouts for meetings. Informal roles allow you to play to your strengths; of course, to develop informal roles you may need to talk to other group members about your preferences and abilities.

Behaviors That Define Roles

Roles enacted by group members create a set of behaviors that help the group achieve its objectives. An effective group is like a jigsaw puzzle; each group member performs a slightly different role, but each set of behaviors is coordinated to work with the others, so that a complete picture is formed.

task functions
Behaviors that are directly relevant to the group's purpose and that affect the group's productivity.

maintenance functions
Behaviors that focus on the interpersonal relationships among group members.

self-centered functions
Behaviors that serve the needs of the individual at the expense of the group.

One way of understanding the various types of behaviors performed by group members is to classify them as task, maintenance, or self-centered behaviors. **Task functions** are behaviors that are directly relevant to the group's purpose and that affect the group's productivity; their purpose is to focus group members productively on their assignment. **Maintenance functions** are behaviors that focus on the interpersonal relationships among group members; they are aimed at supporting cooperative and harmonious relationships. Both task and maintenance functions are considered essential to effective group communication. On the other hand, **self-centered functions** are behaviors that serve the needs of the individual at the expense of the group. The person performing a self-centered behavior implies, "I don't care what the group needs or wants. *I* want . . ." These group members use self-centered functions to manipulate other members for selfish goals that compete with group goals. Examples of statements that support task,

Table 1 Examples of Task, Maintenance, and Self-Centered Statements

TASK FUNCTIONS AND STATEMENTS

Initiating and Orienting	"Let's make a list of what we still need to do."
Information Giving	"Last year, the club spent $150 on publicity."
Information Seeking	"John, how many donations did the Child and Family Advocacy Center report last year?"
Opinion Giving	"I don't think the cost of parking stickers is the worst parking problem students have."
Clarifying	"Martina, are you saying that you couldn't support a proposal that increased student fees?"
Extending	"Another thing that Toby's proposal would let us do is . . ."
Evaluating	"One problem I see with Cindy's idea is . . ."
Summarizing	"So we've decided that we'll add two sections to the report, and Terrell and Candy will write them."
Coordinating	"If Carol gets everyone's sources by Monday, then Jim and I can prepare the references page for Tuesday's meeting."
Consensus Testing	"We seem to be agreed that we prefer the second option."
Recording	"I think we decided at our last meeting. Let me check the minutes."

MAINTENANCE (RELATIONSHIP-ORIENTED) FUNCTIONS AND STATEMENTS

Establishing Norms	"It doesn't help to talk about other group members when they aren't here. Let's stick to the issues."
Gatekeeping	"Pat, you look like you want to say something about the proposal."
Supporting	"I think Victoria's point is well made, and we should look at it more closely."
Harmonizing	"Jared and Sally, I think there are areas where you are in agreement, and I would like to suggest a compromise that might work for you both."
Tension Relieving	"We're getting tired and cranky. Let's take a 10-minute break."
Dramatizing	"That reminds me about one time last year when . . ."
Showing Solidarity	"We've really done good work here!" or "We're getting this done!"

SELF-CENTERED FUNCTIONS AND STATEMENTS

Withdrawing	"Do whatever you want; I don't care" or not speaking at all.
Blocking	"I don't care if we've already voted; I want to discuss it again!"
Status and Recognition Seeking	"I have a lot more experience fund-raising than many of you, and I think we should do it the way I know works."

maintenance, and self-centered functions are shown in table 1. The list is not exhaustive, however; many more functions could be added.

Behaviors are the building blocks for roles. These behavioral functions combine to create a member's informal role, which is a comprehensive, general picture of how a particular member typically acts in a group. An example of how individual functions combine to create a role is shown in figure 1. As you can see, information-giving and information-seeking behaviors primarily characterize the information specialist role. The storyteller role comprises several behaviors, including dramatizing, relieving tension, supporting, summarizing, and clarifying. Numerous other informal roles can be created through combinations of behaviors.

Emerging Technology and Group Roles

New technology and social media are changing the ways groups interact as well as the amount and frequency of their interactions. Studies show that students who participate in

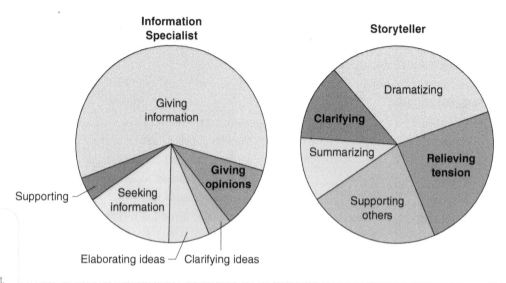

Figure 1

Behavioral functions combine to create roles.

Source: Galanes, G. J., & Brilhart, J. K. (1993). Communicating in groups: Applications and skills. Madison, WI: Brown & Benchmark. Copyright © 1993. Times Mirror Higher Education Group, Inc. All rights reserved. Reprinted by permission.

© PictureNet/Corbis RF

social media as part of a class feel more connected to their peers than do students who do not participate in social media. Using social media creates a more collaborative and engaging learning environment for people to discuss ideas.[16] Did you know that research shows that collaborating with classmates on a given topic through social media can help groups develop a stronger sense of community?[17] And with increased accessibility to news and media, everyone can now be an information giver and an information seeker. As a result, we may have to rethink how group roles are derived and assigned. For example, perhaps it may be a disadvantage or no longer necessary for only one person to be tasked with being an information giver.

GROUP COHESIVENESS

group climate
The emotional tone or atmosphere members create within the group.

Another important element that helps shape a group's culture is the **group climate,** which is the emotional tone or atmosphere members create within the group. For example, you have probably attended a group meeting where the tension silenced everyone. That atmosphere of tension describes the group's climate. Three factors that contribute heavily to group climate are trust, cohesiveness, and supportiveness.

- *Trust* means that members believe they can rely on each other. Two types of trust relevant to group work are task trust and interpersonal trust. Task trust develops when you have confidence that others will get their jobs done in support of the group's goals. Interpersonal trust emerges when you perceive that others are working in support of the group rather than trying to achieve personal gain or to accomplish hidden agendas.

- *Supportiveness* refers to an atmosphere of openness in which members care about each other and create cohesiveness. Examples of both supportive and defensive statements are found in table 2.

- *Cohesiveness* is the attachment members feel toward each other and the group. Highly cohesive groups are more open, handle disagreement more effectively, and typically perform better than less cohesive groups.[18]

groupthink
An unintended outcome of cohesion in which the desire for cohesion and agreement takes precedence over critical analysis and discussion.

Although cohesiveness is generally desirable for groups, dangers arise from too much cohesion. **Groupthink** happens when the desire for cohesion and agreement takes precedence over critical analysis and discussion. According to sociologists, groupthink can destroy effective decision making. Several historical decision-making blunders have

Table 2 Examples of Defensive and Supportive Statements

Behavior	Description	Sample Statement
DEFENSIVE BEHAVIORS AND STATEMENTS		
Evaluation	Judging another person	"That's a completely ridiculous idea."
Control	Dominating or insisting on your own way	"I've decided what we need to do."
Manipulation	Trying to verbally push compliance	"Don't you think you should try it my way?"
Neutrality	Not caring about how others feel	"It doesn't matter to me what you decide."
Superiority	Pulling rank, maximizing status differences	"As group leader, I think we should . . ."
Certainty	Being a "know-it-all"	"You guys are completely off base. I know exactly how to handle this."
SUPPORTIVE BEHAVIORS AND STATEMENTS		
Description	Describing your own feelings without making those of others wrong	"I prefer the first option because . . ."
Problem Orientation	Searching for the best solution without predetermining what that should be	"We want to produce the best results, and that may mean some extra time from all of us."
Spontaneity	Reacting honestly and openly	"Wow, that sounds like a great idea!"
Empathy	Showing you care about the other members	"Jan, originally you were skeptical. How comfortable will you be if the group favors that option?"
Equality	Minimizing status differences by treating members as equals	"I don't have all the answers. What do the rest of you think?"
Provisionalism	Expressing opinions tentatively and being open to others' suggestions	"Maybe we should try a different approach . . ."

been attributed to groupthink, including the escalation of the Vietnam conflict, the space shuttle *Challenger* disaster, and potentially the *Columbia* shuttle disaster over Texas.[19] More recently, the BP Deepwater Horizon oil spill in 2010 in the Gulf of Mexico can be viewed as an example of groupthink because workers ignored automated warnings since they happened frequently on the rig.[20] Although groupthink may be difficult to detect when you are in a group, researchers have identified the following observable signs of groupthink:

- An illusion of invulnerability by the group
- An unquestioned belief in the morality of the group
- Collective efforts by group members to rationalize faulty decisions
- Stereotypic views of enemy leaders as evil, weak, or ineffective
- Self-censorship of alternative viewpoints
- A shared illusion that all group members think the same thing
- Direct pressure on group members expressing divergent opinions
- The emergence of "mind guards" to screen the group from information contradictory to the prevailing opinion

Although Janis's original description of groupthink suggests that these characteristics lead to groupthink, and consequently result in bad decisions, recent studies suggest that

Group members must make counterviewpoints known to help the group avoid groupthink.
© Color-Blind Images/ Blend Images LLC RF

Janis's groupthink characteristics actually occur after the group has already made a poor decision.[21] Once groups make decisions, group members try to create and reinforce a consensus in support of the decision, even in the face of evidence that the decision is a poor one. The desire for consensus then leads to all of the groupthink characteristics identified by Janis.

Groupthink is possible in nearly every group. To prevent groupthink from occurring, groups should

- seek all pertinent information,
- carefully assess the credibility of information relevant to the decision at hand,
- assign members to present counterarguments, and
- maintain a commitment to finding the best possible outcome as supported by the available evidence.

THE EFFECT OF DIVERSITY ON GROUP CULTURE

group culture
The socially negotiated system of rules that guide group behavior.

Although we typically think of culture as belonging to very large groups of people, small groups also develop cultures. **Group culture** is the socially negotiated system of rules that guide group behavior. Group culture differs from national and ethnic cultures in that group cultures are relatively unstable and short-term phenomena. Group cultures are constantly in flux, and they disappear when the group dissolves. National and ethnic cultures change slowly and are relatively persistent. If you compare two groups from your own life, you can easily understand the concept of group culture. Your group of friends has implicit rules for behavior—inside jokes, slang, norms for touching, and shared objectives. Your group likely has a culture different from that of an assigned group of students you work with in one of your classes. Classroom groups are typically more formal, less cohesive, and more task-oriented. The two groups reflect different cultures that have emerged.

The culture of a group can be influenced by many things. The norms and behaviors of group members can influence culture; so, too, can the diversity among group members.

Table 3 Observable and Implicit Within-Group Diversity

	Observable	**Implicit**
Definition	Within-group diversity based on physical characteristics that can be seen	Within-group diversity based on individuals' worldviews, perspectives, and other personality characteristics
Example	Ethnicity, sex, able/non-able-bodiedness	Religious orientation, educational background

Within-group diversity is the presence of observable and/or implicit differences among group members. We observe within-group diversity when group members differ based on visible characteristics. For example, to visually distinguish between able-bodied and non-able-bodied group members or between members of certain ethnic groups is easy. Group diversity can be implicit when members of a group have differing values, attitudes, and perspectives—personal characteristics that cannot be seen. Table 3 shows common examples of observable and implicit within-group diversity.

Differences between group members can have an impact on how they interact with one another and how effectively the group functions. To illustrate the effects of group diversity on group members' behaviors, here are several research findings on differences between how men and women interact in groups:

- In online discussion groups and other forms of digitally mediated communication, women tend to use more exclamation points as markers of friendliness—thus emphasizing the relational aspects of group communication.[22]

- Although men are typically more influential in standard communication contexts, this difference diminishes in groups, especially when more than one woman is present. In such situations the influence of women is roughly equal to that of men.[23]

- Recent research has observed no differences in perceived leadership ability regardless of whether the group is primarily task- or relationship-oriented; previous research had shown that women were better leaders in relationship-oriented groups.[24]

In addition to gender differences, cultural differences can also influence group dynamics. For instance, it is likely that work groups and even classroom groups will have at least one member who is an English language learner (ELL). You might assume that group members who speak English with different levels of proficiency can diminish the cohesiveness of the group. That assumption would be incorrect, however. Research shows that having various primary languages represented in a group does not impede group cohesiveness as long as members continue to have frequent interactions.[25]

In such situations, all group members should make sure that ELL members are fully included. Strategies for helping non-native speakers feel included are (1) providing written information in advance of discussions, (2) asking someone in the group to take notes that can be copied and distributed to all group members, (3) viewing difference as a strength of the group, and (4) matching tasks to members' abilities. Particularly with the last suggestion, finding out the strengths of all group members is important. Second-language speakers often do not speak as frequently as native English speakers, but this does not mean that they do not have highly developed skills in other areas, such as computers, artwork, record keeping, and so on.

If you are a second-language speaker who is part of a group with mostly native speakers, you must practice being assertive. You should ask questions to clarify the

within-group diversity
The presence of observable and/or implicit differences among group members.

activities of the group or points made during discussion. You should also let group members know about skills you have that could be useful to the group. Finally, try to recognize that in most situations group discussions are as much about relationship building as task accomplishment. Taking time to get to know other members of your group will not only help all of you build confidence in each other but can lead to meaningful friendships outside class or the workplace.

The Role of Leadership in Small Groups

For most groups to work effectively, some structure is necessary. Noted group communication scholar Gloria Galanes observed that group leaders must attend to four issues: (1) identifying the task of the group; (2) creating cohesiveness among the group members; (3) monitoring and adapting the behaviors of the group members as needed to accomplish tasks; and (4) keeping the group focused on the task at hand.[26]

DEFINING LEADERSHIP

leadership
A process of using communication to influence the behaviors and attitudes of others to meet group goals.

designated leader
Someone who has been appointed or elected to a leadership position.

emergent leader
Someone who becomes an informal leader by exerting influence toward the achievement of a group's goal but does not hold the formal position or role of leader.

power
Interpersonal influence that forms the basis for group leadership.

Hackman and Johnson define **leadership** as a process of using communication to influence the behaviors and attitudes of others to meet group goals.[27] A leader is a person who influences the behavior and attitudes of others through communication. In small groups, two types of leader are designated and emergent. A **designated leader** is someone who has been appointed or elected to a leadership position (such as a chair, team leader, coordinator, or facilitator). An **emergent leader** is someone who becomes an informal leader by exerting influence toward the achievement of a group's goal but does not hold the formal position or role of leader. Groups benefit from having a designated leader because designated leaders add stability and organization to the group's activities. An emergent leader can be any group member who helps the group meet its goals. Groups work best when all members contribute skills and leadership behaviors on behalf of the group.

How do leaders, designated or emergent, gain their ability to influence others? Wilmot and Hocker suggest that group leaders may gain interpersonal influence over groups through the use of **power,** which is the interpersonal influence that forms the basis for small-group leadership.[28] According to Wilmot and Hocker's perspective, group leaders likely use one of three types of power:

- *Distributive power,* whereby the leader exerts influence over others.
- *Integrative power,* which highlights interdependence with another person or persons to achieve mutually agreed-upon goals.
- *Designated power,* which reflects the importance of relationships between people. Marriages, families, and groups often hold such power for us.

Whereas Wilmot and Hocker describe how power influences us, a classic study by French and Raven describes different ways in which group members enact power:

- *Reward power*—the ability to give followers what they want and need.
- *Punishment power*—the ability to withhold from followers what they want and need. An extreme form of punishment power is *coercion,* in which compliance is forced through hostile acts.
- *Referent power*—power based on others' admiration and respect. Charisma is an extreme form of referent power that inspires strong loyalty and devotion from others.
- *Expert power*—power that arises when the other members value a person's knowledge or expertise.
- *Legitimate power*—power given to a person because of a title, position, or role.[29]

Table 4 Tensions Present for Group Leaders

Tension	Description
Leader-centered vs. group-centered	Does the leader maintain complete control over the group, or are aspects of group control given to members of the group?
Listening vs.talking	Does the group leader spend more time talking, to set an agenda for group action, or listening, to build trust and cohesiveness?
Task vs. nontask emphasis	Does the group focus primarily on task-related behaviors or primarily on nontask behaviors? One focus could get the job done quicker; the other could build cohesiveness.
Process vs. outcome focus	Does the group focus only on outcomes, or does it also focus on getting tasks done "the right way"?

Source: Based on Galanes, G. (2009). Dialectical tensions of small group leadership. *Communication Studies, 60,* 409–425.

Understanding how to use power to influence small groups is not easy. Galanes describes the process of leadership as a balancing act, where leaders must learn to manage various tensions, identified in table 4. Group leaders must understand how to use power in ways that balance several of these tensions in an effort to push the group to achieve its goals while building and maintaining a positive culture.

WAYS OF ENACTING LEADERSHIP

Since Aristotle's time, people have been interested in what makes a good leader. Is leadership a skill you are born with? Can you learn to be a leader? In this section you will learn about three ways of thinking about effective leadership: leadership as style, leadership as communication competence, and leadership as planning. Although they are presented as separate perspectives, effective leaders learn to embrace key elements from each simultaneously.

Leadership Styles

Style approaches to studying leadership focus on the patterns of behavior that leaders exhibit in groups. Considerable research has examined three major styles of designated leader: democratic, laissez-faire, and autocratic. **Democratic leaders** encourage members to participate in group decisions, even major ones: "What suggestions do you have for solving our problem?" **Laissez-faire leaders** take almost no initiative in structuring a group discussion; they are nonleaders whose typical response is "I don't care; whatever you want to do is fine with me." **Autocratic leaders** maintain strict control over their group, including making assignments and giving orders: "Here's how we'll solve the problem. First, you will . . ." Autocratic leaders ask fewer questions but answer more than democratic leaders; they make more attempts to coerce and fewer attempts to get others to participate.[30]

Groups vary in the amount of structure and control their members want and need, but research findings about style have been consistent.[31] Most people in the United States prefer democratic groups and are more satisfied in democratically rather than autocratically led groups.

The style approaches imply a single leadership style good for all situations. However, most scholars believe that the style should match the needs of the situation. For example, if you are in a group working on a class project and the deadline is tomorrow, a democratic leadership style might be ineffective, because it takes longer to make decisions.

democratic leaders
Leaders who encourage members to participate in group decisions.

laissez-faire leaders
Leaders who take almost no initiative in structuring a group discussion.

autocratic leaders
Leaders who maintain strict control over their group.

Democratic groups allow group members to take part in decision making.

© Hybrid Images/Cultura/ Getty Images RF

The Communication Competencies of Leaders

Communication scholars who adopt the communicative competencies approach have tried to focus on the communicative behaviors of leaders as they exercise interpersonal influence to accomplish group goals. They ask such questions as "What do effective leaders do?" The Communication Competency Model of Group Leadership, developed by Barge and Hirokawa,[32] is one of the most comprehensive models to address this question. This model assumes that leaders help a group achieve its goals through communication skills (competencies). Two competencies include the task and interpersonal, or relationship, distinctions discussed earlier. Leaders must be flexible to draw from a personal repertoire of such competencies. Some of the most important leader competencies are described briefly here:

- Effective leaders are able to clearly and appropriately communicate ideas to the group without dominating the conversation.
- Effective leaders communicate a clear grasp of the task facing the group.
- Effective leaders are skilled at facilitating discussion.
- Effective leaders encourage open dialogue and do not force their own ideas on the group.
- Effective leaders place group needs over personal concerns.
- Effective leaders display respect for others during interaction.
- Effective leaders share in the successes and failures of the group.

The Planning Skills of Leaders

In addition to exhibiting an appropriate style and being a competent communicator, effective leaders must learn to plan. Although planning cannot prevent all problems from occurring, some up-front work can increase the likelihood of successful outcomes. Here are some tips for planning effective meetings:

1. *Know the task at hand.* Later in the chapter you will learn about the group problem-solving model. Effective leaders should understand the problem facing the group and take care to communicate that task to group members.

2. *Know the people.* As you will learn, individual group members have different skills, motivations, frames of reference, and knowledge bases. Understanding how to draw on group members' strengths and manage interpersonal dynamics is a key role of the group leader.

3. *Collect information.* The group leader should attempt to become knowledgeable on all issues facing the group. If you are knowledgeable, you will know when discussions are off track.

4. *Distribute leadership.* In certain situations, leadership should be distributed among all group members. The designated leader may need to delegate responsibility, especially when smaller tasks need to be assigned to individual group members.

GROUP AGENDA
DATE

I. *Approval of minutes from previous meeting(s).* The group facilitator should determine if there are any changes to the minutes and have group members vote to approve the minutes.

II. Announcements. Members of the group should make announcements relevant to the group but not necessarily tied to group business. For example, a group member might read a thank-you note from a person the group helped or might provide personal announcements that may be of interest to group members. Such announcements should be brief.

III. Reports. Individuals assigned to collect information or carry out tasks should report on their progress. If a report results in an action item—that is, something the group should discuss and vote on—the report should be included under new business. Reports in this segment of the meeting should be informative, but they do not necessarily require action at this time.

IV. New business. Items in this part of the agenda can include important discussions and/or action items. Discussions may or may not result in a vote, but action items should be voted on by the group.

V. Old business. Occasionally, action items and discussion from previous meetings may not be complete. In such cases those items should be listed under old business and approached in the same way as new business, with appropriate discussion and voting as necessary.

Figure 2

Standard group agenda template.

Distributed leadership, whereby all members share in leadership responsibilities, can result in highly productive group outcomes.[33]

5. *Organize the discussion.* Although some types of group discussions may not need much organization—a short class discussion assigned by your teacher, for instance—most discussions need more structure. The group leader should plan an agenda for the discussion. The agenda should be adapted to the task at hand; however, a general template for the agenda is provided in figure 2. As you can see, the typical agenda requires group members to agree on minutes from the past meeting to clear up any confusion or disagreement, make announcements, hear reports, consider new business, and reconsider old business as necessary.

Problem Solving and Decision Making

A primary task facing many groups is solving problems: student clubs need to raise money, church groups need to plan activities, and social groups must find fun things to do. Group members must be both creative and critical to arrive at the best solutions to these problems. Groups are usually (but not always) better problem solvers than individuals, because several people can provide more information than one person. Group members can bring greater resources to bear on a problem, can collectively have a broader perspective, and can more easily spot flaws in each other's reasoning. However, trade-offs occur. Group problem solving takes longer, and sometimes personality, procedural, or social problems make working as a team difficult for members. Group problem solving is usually more effective when the process is systematic and organized, because a group that does not have an overall plan for decision making is more likely to make a poor decision.[34] In this section you will learn techniques for making group problem-solving efforts more systematic and organized, as well as other work you can accomplish in groups.

EFFECTIVE GROUP PROBLEM SOLVING

When groups succeed, it is, in part, because they have followed a coordinated process for analyzing and discussing the problem and its solutions. Effective problem solving is systematic and follows a procedure. Typically the problem-solving process includes determining the discussion question, identifying the criteria, identifying potential solutions, and evaluating potential solutions.

Determining the Discussion Question

Problem-solving groups typically handle three basic types of discussion questions. Questions of *fact* deal with whether something is true or can be verified. Questions of *value* ask whether something is good or bad, better or worse. Cultural and individual values and beliefs are central to questions of value. Questions of *policy* ask what action should be taken. The key word *should* is either stated or implied in questions of policy. Examples of each type of question are presented in figure 3.

Regardless of the type of discussion question guiding a problem-solving group, the leader must state the question appropriately. Remember, a key task of effective leaders is to help focus the group on what is being discussed. First, the language and terminology should be concrete rather than abstract. If ambiguous terms such as *effective, good,* or *fair* are used, providing examples helps each group member have as close to the same meaning as possible. Second, a well-stated discussion question helps group members know when the solution has been achieved. For example, a task force charged

Figure 3

Examples of questions of fact, value, and policy.
(top): © Burke/Triolo/Brand X Pictures/PunchStock RF
(middle): © Comstock/ Jupiterimages RF;
(bottom): © Siede Preis/ Photodisc/Getty Images RF

FACT

How has the divorce rate changed in the past 15 years?

How many Hispanic students graduate from high school each year?

What percentage of college students graduate in four years?

How often, on average, does a person speak each day?

What occupations earn the highest annual incomes?

VALUE

Why should people seek higher education?

How should Americans treat international students?

Does our legal system provide "justice for all"?

How should young people be educated about AIDS?

What is the value of standardized tests for college admission?

POLICY

What courses should students be required to take?

Should the state's drunk-driving laws be changed?

What are the arguments for and against mandatory retirement?

Should the United States intervene in foreign disputes for humanitarian reasons?

What advantages should government provide for businesses willing to develop in high-risk areas of a city?

PROBLEM QUESTIONS

How can we reduce complaints about parking on campus?

What can we do to increase attendance at our club's activities?

How can we make Ginny Avenue safer to cross?

© PNC/Photodisc/Punchstock, RF

SOLUTION QUESTIONS

How can we increase the number of parking spaces in the campus lots?

How can we improve publicity for our club's activities?

How can we get the city council to reduce the speed limit on Ginny Avenue?

Figure 4

Problem questions versus solution questions.

with "completing a report by May 15 on why membership has dropped from 100 to 50 members" knows exactly what to do by what deadline. Finally, a group should start its problem solving with a problem question rather than a solution question. Problem questions focus on what is wrong and imply that many solutions are possible for resolving the problem. Problem questions do not bias a group toward one particular solution. Solution questions, on the other hand, slant the group's discussion toward one particular option. They may inadvertently cause a group to ignore creative or unusual options because they blind members to some alternatives. Examples of problem and solution questions appear in figure 4.

Identifying Criteria

Criteria are the standards by which a group must judge potential solutions. For example, a solution's likely effectiveness ("Will it work?"), acceptability ("Will people vote for our proposal?"), and cost ("Does this option keep us within the budget?") are common criteria. Group members should discuss and agree on criteria before adopting a solution. Because criteria are based on the values of group members, two members, each using rational tools of decision making, can arrive at different conclusions. The more similar group members are in age, gender, ethnicity, background, attitudes, values, and beliefs, the more easily they can agree on criteria.

criteria
The standards by which a group must judge potential solutions.

Two kinds of criteria are common. Absolute criteria are those that *must* be met; the group has no leeway. Important criteria are those that *should* be met, but the group has some flexibility. Group members should give the highest priority to criteria that must be met. Ideas that do not meet absolute criteria should be rejected, and the rest should be ranked on how well they meet important criteria. Examples of absolute and important criteria are presented in figure 5.

Figure 5

Absolute criteria versus important criteria for a new student union.

© Thinkstock/Jupiterimages RF

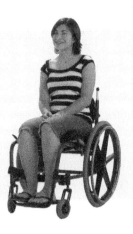

ABSOLUTE CRITERIA

(*Must* be met)

· Must not cost more than $2 million

· Must be wheelchair-accessible

· Must include flexible space that can be arranged in different ways

IMPORTANT CRITERIA

(*Should* be met)

· Should be centrally located

· Should have stage space for concerts

· Should be attractive to all campus constituencies, including traditional and nontraditional students, faculty, and staff

Identifying Potential Solutions

One of the most important jobs a leader has is to encourage group creativity. One technique that can promote innovation and creative thought among groups is brainstorming.[35] Brainstorming is most effective when group members are free to identify multiple ideas, they are asked to defer any judgment (positive or negative) until all ideas have been identified, and the ideas are succinct. Critical evaluation kills creativity, so the main rule of brainstorming is "no evaluation," at least during the brainstorming process. Evaluation of the ideas takes place *after* the group has exhausted its options.

As a leader, you must carefully guide the brainstorming phase of group discussions. You should start with a specified time period in which brainstorming will occur. Before starting dialogue, providing group members with a few minutes to consider the question before responding can help them start individual brainstorming. As ideas are presented to the group, they should be recorded and displayed for all to see; doing so can generate additional ideas. The initial time period for brainstorming can be modified based on the discussion. If ideas start to become repetitive, you may need to stop sooner; if ideas are still unique and interesting, you may need to slightly extend the time. In research this is called "looking for saturation." When all the new ideas have been tapped out (saturated), that is a good time to stop.

Evaluating Potential Solutions

After group members have adequately brainstormed potential solutions, the final task is to evaluate the ideas. At this stage in the discussion, the criteria the group has identified are used to judge the efficacy of each idea generated through brainstorming. Before proceeding to this step, it may be useful to determine whether various ideas can be organized together in some way. Solutions failing to meet absolute criteria are quickly eliminated. Once the nonviable alternatives are eliminated, group members must evaluate each alternative based on the remaining important criteria. Eventually, the group must determine which alternative best meets the set of important criteria they identified.

OTHER WORK TO ACCOMPLISH IN GROUPS

Although this section has highlighted the role of problem solving in small groups, other important types of work are also accomplished in group settings. In fact, groups serve multiple functions, sometimes simultaneously. In addition to helping us perform task functions, such as solving problems, groups also allow us to do the following:

1. *Make decisions.* Many groups exist to make decisions that are unrelated to specific problems. For example, student groups on your campus make daily decisions, such as planning events, launching community outreach projects, and maintaining facilities. These decisions do not necessarily solve problems; rather, they sustain the day-to-day functions of the groups.

2. *Effect change.* Some groups want to influence society but do not have the power to make decisions. You might belong to a community association or the student government organization on your campus. Those groups attempt to influence change even though they may not have the power to make final decisions on that change.

3. *Negotiate conflict.* Groups are often created to resolve conflict. In Los Angeles, small groups were used to bring Latino American and Armenian American high school students together to resolve racial tensions. In fact, the National Communication Association in partnership with the Southern Poverty Law Center has used this strategy across the nation to promote intercultural understanding and to help resolve racial conflict.

4. *Foster creativity.* Groups help us achieve a level of creativity not possible when working alone. The idea that "two heads are better than one" is magnified in groups. People working together to identify creative ideas will likely be more successful than one person working alone.

5. *Maintain ties between stakeholders.* A final function for small groups is to bring together stakeholders. **Stakeholders** are groups of people who have an interest in the actions of an organization. For example, most schools have parent–teacher organizations. The principal of a school might bring together selected teachers and parents to discuss issues facing the school so that open lines of communication between the stakeholders (parents, teachers, and administrators) can be maintained. Various organizations, including businesses, government agencies, and nonprofit organizations, use groups to establish and maintain communication among multiple groups of stakeholders.

As you can see, groups exist for many reasons. Although the heart of group activity may indeed be problem solving, not all groups exist solely for that purpose.

Technology and Group Communication Processes

Throughout this course you have learned how technology impacts various forms of human communication, and group communication is no different. Groups of all types use technology to find and analyze information, to facilitate interaction among group members, and even to aid in the decision-making process.

As Web 2.0 technology has advanced, many other tools have become available to help support the work of groups by allowing people to collaborate and share information online. Consider how the following resources can help groups work more efficiently:

- *Facebook.* Besides helping group members stay connected as friends, Facebook allows you to create a group page for any group to which you belong. On the group page you can post information, links to other resources, agendas, and other information that may help group members stay prepared. You can also create events to alert group members to upcoming meetings.

- *Dropbox.* Dropbox is a free file-sharing service that allows you to create shared folders, so that group members can all store, have access to, and edit group documents, such as word processing files, presentation files, and other documents.

- *Evernote.* This free resource can be used for **content curation,** the collection and storage of information from across the web. Your group might locate several webpages, videos, and other resources and use Evernote to maintain a research file

stakeholders
Groups of people who have an interest in the actions of an organization.

content curation
The collection and storage of documents and other multimedia from the web, covering a specified topic.

communicating creatively

Collaborative Co-working

What images and feelings arise in you when you think about working in a cubicle? Like many people, you may think it reflects an outdated way of organizing a workspace and limits co-worker interaction. Initially, organizations thought creating open workspaces was the answer, but it turns out that open workspaces promote less productivity, increase the use of sick days, and reduce morale.

Now consider the images and feelings that arise in you when you think about working in a collaborative common area that includes space for meetings and casual gatherings among co-workers. Many contemporary organizations are turning to a design approach that considers employee work and privacy needs. For example, designers are creating team rooms but also quiet spaces, where people can make personal calls and have one-on-one meetings, that encourage some degree of privacy. Frank Chalupa, president and cofounder of Amata Office Solutions, indicates that

> a circular or rectangular layout is one way to achieve this, as it avoids dead-end hallways that workers might not pass through if their offices are located elsewhere. It's also important to scatter amenities throughout a workplace so employees aren't walking by the same offices or workstations each day.

When you think about the type of physical environment that you want to work in, what does it look like? What types of communication and collaboration opportunities do you want with your co-workers? You may want to begin implementing some of these workspace plans into the task-oriented groups that you are currently part of. This will help you get a sense of how you work and communicate best in groups and teams.

Source: Chalupa, F. (2015, March). Coworking 2.0: Collaborating meeting privacy in the workplace. *The Huffington Post* (www.huffingtonpost.com/frank-chalupa/coworking-20-collaboration-meets-privacy-in-the-workplace_b_6858952.html).

Computers can be used to facilitate group communication.

© Ariel Skelley/The Agency Collection /Getty Images RF

in shared notebooks. Evernote is also a powerful note-taking tool, so you can use the service to record and publish notes from meetings. You can collaborate on notes, and the Work Chat feature allows you to instant-message with people who are working on the project. This ensures your notes and comments about the project are organized in one place.

- *Google Documents.* Google provides a free version of office programs used for word processing, spreadsheets, and presentations. You can create, collect, and analyze online forms using Google Docs. All files can be shared and edited by other members of your group.

- *Skype and Google Hangout.* These free resources can be used for online videoconferencing so that group members can meet remotely to share ideas, images, screens, and folders.

- *Asana.* This is one of many free web and mobile-based applications created to allow teams to plan and manage projects and tasks online without e-mail. Each group gets a workspace where members can assign tasks to users and include notes, comments, attachments, and tags.

- *Texting.* Although you are probably well versed in using text messaging for social interactions, many students find it easy to use text messages for quick reminders and general announcements. For example, if a room change occurs a half hour before a meeting, one group member can text the entire group with the update.

- *Mural.ly.* This is a visual collaboration and communication tool that allows multiple users to visually collaborate and storyboard ideas. Users can upload photos, insert videos and figures, and create Post-it notes on the board. Unlike the other applications that have been discussed, this one requires subscription fees.

These resources show several options available online that can be used to facilitate the work of groups. Of course, how you use the web for group work is limited only by your imagination. A variety of services and social media sites can be readily adapted to support the work of your group.

group decision support
system (GDSS)
An interactive network of
computers with
specialized software,
allowing users to
generate solutions for
unstructured problems.

One form of group communication technology is a **group decision support system,** or **GDSS.** A GDSS system uses networked computers, so group members can anonymously communicate with one another through text messages, and it allows anonymous voting to help make decisions. If you have ever taken a class in which "clickers," or student response systems, are used, you have seen GDSS technology in action. Clickers allow teachers to ask students practice quiz questions and have a summary of anonymous responses displayed for the class. More advanced GDSS systems (and, in fact, more advanced student response systems) simply add the element of anonymous texting. Research shows that GDSS technology has the potential to increase interactions because it allows anonymity for group members, can increase the efficiency of decision making, and can reduce the potential that groupthink will influence outcomes.[36]

Regardless of which resources a group uses, it is important that group members create rules surrounding how they will and will not share private information created as a result of these tools. For example, if the group determines that individual group members cannot use the research summaries created for the current project for other courses, then the group members must be accountable and uphold this rule. Similarly, group members may decide that they will not share with nongroup members any private information generated during group texts (e.g., text messages).

Of course, not all group technology automatically improves group communication. As communication researcher Paul Turman points out, groups communicating entirely through technology may find that group norms and basic structures for how the group operates are more difficult to create in computer-mediated environments.[37] He cautions that computer-mediated groups must take more time to explicitly talk about how the group will function and about various norms for communication among group members.

How to Communicate in Small Groups

Each member of a group must take personal responsibility to help support the functions of the group. How can you best do that? The ability to speak fluently and with polish is not essential, but the ability to speak clearly is. Other members of the group will understand your views more easily if you follow this advice:

1. *Relate your statements to preceding remarks.* Public speakers do not always have the opportunity to respond to remarks by others, but small-group members do. Your statement should not appear irrelevant. Clarify the relevance of your remark to the topic under discussion by linking your remark to the preceding remark:

    - Briefly note the previous speaker's point that you want to address—for example, "I want to piggyback on Bill's comment by noting that we can meet our goal by . . ."

    - State your point clearly and concisely.

    - Summarize how your point adds to the comments made by others—for example, "So, I agree with Bill. We need to fund-raise, but we can't get so caught up in raising money that we forget about our goal of volunteering."

2. *Use conventional word arrangements.* When you speak, you should use clear, common language, so that people can understand you. Consider this comment: "I unequivocally recognize the meaningful contribution made by my colleague." Although the language might impress some, a simple "I agree" would work just as well. Here are some ways to improve your verbal clarity while in group discussions:

    - After connecting your idea to the discussion or previous speaker, state your point and then provide one piece of supporting information or additional explanation.

    - Explain to group members how you perceive the importance of what you are saying. Not all comments are critical; some are just ideas. Letting others know how important you think something is may influence how they react and respond.

    - When done, ask if anyone needs you to clarify your point.

3. *Speak concisely.* The point here is simple: don't be long-winded. The main advantage of small groups is their

building behaviors

Harnessing Technology for Your Group

Digital tools to support the work of a group are a valuable resource that can help you with any group to which you belong. Go to google.com/docs and explore the various ways in which you can create word processing, spreadsheet, and presentation files. Using this chapter as a guide, create a three-slide presentation explaining what you feel are the three most important technology resources you read about in this chapter. In your presentation, identify the resource, present its key features, and explain why groups should use this tool or application rather than others. After creating the presentation, share the file with your teacher or at least one other student in your class.

sizing things up

Adapted Competent Group Communication Evaluation Form

Think about a problem-solving-type group you are currently involved in. For each of the eight competencies listed below, decide whether you believe you are performing the behavior unsatisfactorily, satisfactorily or excellently.

Group Task Competencies (1–5)

1. *Defines and analyzes the problem*—appropriately defines and analyzes the problem that confronts the group
2. *Identifies criteria*—appropriately participates in the establishment of the group goal and identifies criteria for assessing the quality of the group outcome
3. *Generates solutions*—appropriately generates solutions or alternatives
4. *Evaluates solutions*—appropriately evaluates the solutions or alternatives identified by group members
5. *Maintains task focus*—appropriately helps the group stay on the task, issue, or agenda item the group is discussing

Group Relationship Competencies (6–8)

6. *Manages conflict*—appropriately manages disagreements and conflict
7. *Manages climate*—appropriately provides supportive comments to other group members
8. *Manages interaction*—helps manage interaction and appropriately invites others to participate

Source: Beebe, S. A., Barge, J. K., & McCormick, C. (1995). *The competent group communicator: Assessing essential competencies of small group problem solving.* Presented at the annual meeting of the Speech Communication Association, San Antonio, TX.

ability to approach a problem interactively. If you monopolize the discussion, that advantage may be diminished or lost completely. To learn to speak concisely, try the following:

- Write down your idea before speaking. Those who are wordy during group discussions often spend much of their time trying to figure out what they want to say.
- Try to talk for no more than one minute at a time. Of course, this time limit is arbitrary; however, one minute should be enough time to get an idea out for consideration, and you can always answer questions to clarify as needed.

4. *State one point at a time.* Sometimes this rule is violated appropriately, such as when a group member is presenting a report to the group. However, during give-and-take discussion, stating only one idea promotes efficiency and responsiveness. To ensure this practice, try the following strategies:

- As a group, appoint a process observer to be in charge of keeping the group discussion moving along and preventing any member from bringing up more than one idea at a time. After using the process observer a few times, these behaviors become second nature.
- If you have several ideas that vary in importance, provide some of the less important points to group members in written form for later reflection. Save discussion time for the most important ideas.

Being an Ethical Group Member

The unique nature of small groups requires attention to special ethical concerns regarding the treatment of speech, people, and information. First, as noted in the NCA Credo of Ethics, the field of communication strongly supports the value of free speech. Many secondary groups are formed because several heads perform better than one, but that advantage will not be realized if group members are unwilling or afraid to speak freely in the group. An important ethical principle for small groups is that group members should be willing to share their unique perspectives. But they should also refrain from saying or doing things that prevent others from speaking freely. Members who are trustworthy and supportive are behaving ethically.

Second, group members must be honest and truthful. In a small group they should not intentionally deceive one another or manufacture information or evidence to persuade other members to adopt their point of view.

Third, group members must be thorough and unbiased when they evaluate information. Groups are used to make any number of decisions, both large and small. Such decisions will be only as good as the information on which they are based and the reasoning the members use to assess the information. Group members must consider *all* relevant information in an open-minded, unbiased way by using the best critical thinking skills they can; otherwise, tragedies can result.

Fourth, group members must behave with integrity. That is, they must be willing to place the good of the group ahead of their own goals. Some individuals cannot be team players because they are unable or unwilling to merge their personal agendas with those of the group. Groups are better off without such individuals. If you make a commitment to join a group, you should be the kind of team member who will benefit rather than harm the group. If you cannot in good conscience give a group your support, you should leave the group rather than pretend to support the group while sabotaging it.

Finally, group members must learn to manage **group conflict,** which is an expressed struggle between two or more members of a group.[38] Although some conflict can actually help groups make better decisions because ideas are debated and tested more vigorously, too much conflict may result in decreased group cohesiveness and can cause the group to cease functioning. To manage conflict, group members must be ethical in the way they approach disagreement and be willing to listen to and compromise with others. Ethical disagreement happens when you express your disagreement openly, disagree with ideas rather than people, base your disagreement on evidence and reasoning, and react to disagreement positively rather than defensively.[39]

group conflict
An expressed struggle between two or more members of a group.

be ready... for what's next

Resolving Group Conflicts

Our hope is that you engage in meaningful group work like Lane, Chris, and Nick did with the Boston Strong campaign. Yet it's inevitable that you will also find yourself engaged in difficult group experiences. Difficult group experiences occur because of the task at hand and/or relationships among the group members. Perhaps you are currently experiencing problems with a group project. Maybe group members are missing meetings or regularly come late to meetings. What are you and the other members doing as a group about these problematic behaviors, if anything? What would you do if your group's final presentation occurred and one of your group members failed to show up? Perhaps you'd talk to your instructor about it, who says that it's up to the group to decide what to do about the group member's grade in light of the missed presentation. Does the group member get the same grade as the rest of the group for the project? Or does the group determine that a reduction in grade is warranted for his or her absence? If you experience these situations as part of class projects, they are actually important opportunities for you to build the behaviors you've read about in this chapter. For example, though it may be uncomfortable to tell a group member that the rest of the group is frustrated with his or her habitual lateness, it is far better to deal with it early on rather than let the behavior continue.

If you find yourself in situations like this, talk to your group members about the problem and perhaps seek the advice of your instructor. It is likely that your instructor will want you and the other members to try to work these problems out as a group. This is a good thing because it will ultimately provide you with real examples of how you've handled conflict in groups that you can talk about during future job interviews. Remember, one of the top skills employers want college graduates to have is team-building skills, and having experiences to highlight how you have managed conflict—rather than avoided it—provides evidence of your ability to work effectively in groups and teams.

Chapter Review & Study Guide

Summary

In this chapter, you learned the following:

1. Small-group communication is the interaction of a small group of people working together to achieve a common goal. Small groups can be classified as task-related, relationship-related, assigned, or emergent. Many groups can blur boundaries among these types of groups.

   - Task groups are formed to accomplish something, such as solving a problem.
   - Relationship groups are formed to meet our needs for inclusion and affection.
   - Assigned groups occur because individuals are appointed to the group by someone else.
   - Emergent groups occur naturally as individuals meet and decide to become interdependent.

2. Groups form unique cultures as members interact with one another.

   - From the first time group members talk, they start to develop norms for how the group will interact. As those norms develop, individual group members begin to take on certain roles in the group.
   - Strong group cultures can lead to greater cohesiveness, which can more strongly tie group members together. Groups must take care that cohesiveness does not lead to groupthink.
   - Diversity among group members can influence, both positively and negatively, the culture of a group.

3. Leadership is the process of using communication to influence the behaviors and attitudes of people to meet group goals. Various theories discuss how leadership affects small-group communication.

   - The most effective leaders are able to adapt their leadership skills to the needs of the group. All members of the group can share leadership responsibilities.

   - Leaders must learn to manage various tensions within a group, such as the tension between task and relational goals.

4. Group decision making has four steps:

   - Determining the discussion question
   - Discussing criteria for evaluating potential solutions
   - Brainstorming possible solutions
   - Evaluating possible solutions

5. Small-group communication can utilize technology to help facilitate communication and decision making.

   - Group decision support systems use special software to facilitate brainstorming and decision making. Group members are able to anonymously present ideas to other members and are able to anonymously rate and vote for specific alternatives.
   - A variety of free web services and tools can be used to facilitate group communication and group work.

6. To effectively communicate in small groups, you must use clear language and make concise comments that are related to the comments of other group members. You should try to keep your comments limited to one issue at a time.

7. Ethical behaviors in group contexts include allowing others to speak without fear, being honest and truthful, carefully evaluating alternatives, acting with integrity, and managing conflict ethically.

Key Terms

Affection
Assigned groups
Autocratic leaders
Content curation
Control
Criteria
Democratic leaders
Designated leader
Emergent groups
Emergent leader
Formal role

Group climate
Group conflict
Group culture
Group decision support system
  (GDSS)
Groupthink
Inclusion
Informal role
Laissez-faire leaders
Leadership
Maintenance functions

Norms
Power
Relationship-oriented groups
Role
Self-centered functions
Small-group communication
Stakeholders
Task functions
Task-oriented groups
Within-group diversity

Study Questions

1. "Groups meet needs," "Groups are everywhere," and "Working effectively in groups requires training" are statements that explain
   a. types of small groups.
   b. reasons for studying small-group communication.
   c. ways of interacting in small groups.
   d. methods of studying small-group communication.

2. What is true of small groups?
   a. They are comprised of three to nine people.
   b. Members are interdependent.
   c. Group members work toward a common goal.
   d. All of the above are correct.

3. A group that meets via Skype to discuss integrated urban housing developments for cities near Los Angeles is an example of a
   a. relationship-oriented group.
   b. task-oriented group.
   c. cluster-oriented group.
   d. meeting-oriented group.

4. A process of using communication to influence the behaviors and attitudes of others to meet group goals and to benefit the group is
   a. groupthink.
   b. inclusion.
   c. leadership.
   d. role.

5. According to French and Raven, referent power is
   a. power based on others' admiration and respect.
   b. the ability to give followers what they want and need.
   c. power that arises when other members value a person's knowledge or expertise.
   d. the ability to withhold from followers what they want and need.

6. Informal rules for group interaction, the emotional tone created within a group, and group member roles are comprised in
   a. leadership skills.
   b. brainstorming techniques.
   c. maintenance functions.
   d. a group's culture.

7. Creating a discussion question, evaluating prospective solutions, and brainstorming and evaluating possible solutions are steps in
   a. group conflict.
   b. group diversity.
   c. group decision making.
   d. groupthink.

8. Which of the following statements is true?
   a. Groups exist solely for problem solving.
   b. Effective leaders do not adapt their leadership skills to the needs of the group.
   c. Technology can be utilized to help facilitate communication within small groups.
   d. Groupthink is a helpful and effective method of decision making.

9. When communicating with other group members, you should
   a. use technical language, so that you appear more credible.
   b. state numerous points at a time.
   c. be long-winded.
   d. relate your remarks to previous statements.

10. To manage group conflict ethically, members must
    a. be willing to listen to and compromise with others.
    b. base their disagreements on feeling and intuition.
    c. disagree with people rather than ideas.
    d. defend their ideas and refuse to listen to others' ideas.

Answers:
1. (b); 2. (d); 3. (b); 4. (c); 5. (a); 6. (d); 7. (c); 8. (c); 9. (d); 10. (a)

Critical Thinking

1. Think of the groups to which you belong. Do they mesh with the text's definition of a small group? What are the groups' functions? What type of leader does each group have? What group norms are you expected to abide by?

2. What are the benefits and drawbacks to group processes when groups attempt to implement technology resources like Evernote, Asana, and Google Hangout to aid in their workflow? Have you experienced any of these benefits or drawbacks personally?

Sizing Things Up Scoring and Interpretation

Leadership Power in Groups

The Leadership Power in Groups scale assesses your use of French and Raven's categories of power. You can assess your use of power along these dimensions by averaging together (add your responses together and then divide by 2) your responses to the following statements:

- Reward Power: Statements 1 and 6
- Punishment Power: Statements 2 and 7
- Referent Power: Statements 3 and 8 .

- Expert Power: Statements 4 and 9
- Legitimate Power: Statements 5 and 10

Averages for your responses to any particular category of power that are above 3 suggest that you rely on that type of power frequently. Averages of 2 or below indicate that you use that type of power infrequently, if at all. Your results may show that you rely on several types of power frequently, that you typically focus on only one, or that you generally rely on none. Any of these outcomes can help you better understand your leadership approach in group situations.

References

1. Students coin "Boston Strong," raise $800k, Emerson College. (n.d.). Retrieved March 7, 2015, from http://www.emerson.edu/news-events/emerson-college-today/students-coin-boston-strong-raise-800k#.VKihwVaaT3o

2. Boston Strong, Charity T-Shirts. (n.d.). Retrieved March 7, 2015, from http://www.staystrongbostonstrong.org

3. L. Brenner, personal communication, January 20, 2015.

4. Terris, D. (2011, October 14). Teaching virtual teamwork. *Inside Higher Education.* Retrieved from www.insidehighered.com/views/2011/10/14/essay_calls_for_more_of_an_emphasis_on_teaching_virtual_teamwork.

5. Adams, S. (2014, November). The 10 skills employers most want in 2015 graduates. *Forbes.* Retrieved from http://www.forbes.com/sites/susanadams/2014/11/12/the-10-skills-employers-most-want-in-2015-graduates/

6. Herring, H. B. (2006, June 18). Endless meetings: The black hole of the workday. *The New York Times,* 2.

7. Schutz, W. C. (1958). *FIRO: A three-dimensional theory of interpersonal behavior.* New York: Rinehart.

8. Braithwaite, D. O., Bach, B. W., Baxter, L. A., DiVerniero, R., Hammonds, J., Hosek, A. M., . . . , & Wolf, B. (2010). Constructing family: A typology of voluntary kin. *Journal of Social and Personal Relationships, 27,* 388–407.

9. Zekeri, A. A. (2004). College curriculum competencies and skills former students found essential to their careers. *College Student Journal, 38,* 412–423.

10. Goo, S. (2015, February). The skills Americans say kids need to succeed in life. Pew Research Center. (p. 161). Retrieved from http://www.pewresearch.org/fact-tank/2015/02/19/skills-for-success/

11. Vengel, A. (2006). Lead your team to victory: The dos and don'ts of effective group influence. *Contract Management, 46,* 69–70.

12. Zorn, T. E., Roper, J., Broadfoot, K., & Weaver, C. K. (2006). Focus groups as sites of influential interaction: Building communicative self-efficacy and effecting attitudinal change in discussing controversial topics. *Journal of Applied Communication Research, 34,* 115–140.

13. Carpenter, N. J., & Soti, P. (2015). *#iSOTU social media analysis report.* Unpublished report, Social Media Analytics Command Center, School of Communication, Illinois State University, Normal, Illinois.

14. Galanes, G. J., & Adams, K. H. (2009). *Effective group discussion.* New York: McGraw-Hill.

15. Whelan, S. A. (2009). Group size, group development, and group productivity. *Small Group Research, 40,* 247–262.

16. Jackson, C. (2011). Your students love social media . . . and so can you. *Teaching Tolerance, 39,* 38–41. Retrieved from http://www.tolerance.org/magazine/number-39-spring-2011/your-students-love-social-media-and-so-can-you

17. Top, E. (2012). Blogging as a social medium in undergraduate courses: Sense of community best predictor of perceived learning. *Internet and Higher Education, 15,* 24–28. doi:10.1016/j.iheduc.2011.02.001

18. Barker, D. B. (1991, February). The behavioral analysis of interpersonal intimacy in group development. *Small Group Research, 22,* 76–91. Kelly, L., & Duran, R. L. (1985). Interaction and performance in small groups: A descriptive report. *International Journal of Small Group Research, 1,* 182–192.

19. Ferraris, C. (2004). Investigating NASA's intergroup decision-making: Groupthink and intergroup social dynamics. International Communication Association Convention, May 2004, New Orleans, LA.

20. Corrigan, T. (2010, August). So many warnings, so little action ahead of BP's Deepwater disaster. *The Telegraph*. Retrieved from http://www.telegraph.co.uk/finance/comment/tracycorrigan/7966587/So-many-warnings-so-little-action-ahead-of-BPs-Deepwater-disaster.html

21. Henningsen, D. D., Henningsen, M. L., Eden, J., & Cruz, M. G. (2006). Examining the symptoms of groupthink and retrospective sense making. *Small Group Research, 37*, 36–64.

22. Waseleski, C. (2006). Gender and the use of exclamation points in computer-mediated communication: An analysis of exclamation points posted to two electronic discussion lists. *Journal of Computer Mediated Communication, 11*, 1012–1024.

23. Carli, L. L. (2001). Gender and social influence. *Journal of Social Issues, 57*, 725–742.

24. Won, H. L. (2006). Links between personalities and leadership perception in problem-solving groups. *Social Science Journal, 43*, 659–672.

25. Lauring, J., & Selmer, J. (2010). Multicultural organizations: Common language and group cohesiveness. *International Journal of Cross Cultural Management, 10*, 267–284.

26. Galanes, G. (2003). In their own words: An exploratory study of bona fide group leaders. *Small Group Research, 34*, 741–770.

27. Hackman, M. Z., & Johnson, C. E. (2003). *Leadership: A communication perspective* (4th ed.). Prospect Heights, IL: Waveland Press.

28. Wilmot, W. W., & Hocker, J. L. (2007). *Interpersonal conflict* (7th ed.). New York: McGraw-Hill.

29. French, J. R. P., & Raven, B. (1981). The bases of social power. In D. Cartwright & A. Zander (Eds.), *Group dynamics: Research and theory* (3rd ed.). New York: McGraw-Hill.

30. Foels, R., Driskell, J. E., Mullen, B., & Salas, E. (2000). The effects of democratic leadership on group member satisfaction. *Small Group Research, 31*, 676–702.

31. See Brown, M. E., & Trevino, L. K. (2006). Socialized charismatic leadership, values congruence, and deviance in work groups. *Journal of Applied Psychology, 91*, 954–962.

32. Barge, J. K., & Hirokawa, R. Y. (1989). Toward a communication competency model of group leadership. *Small Group Behavior, 20*, 167–189.

33. Ibid.

34. Gouran, D. S., & Hirokawa, R. Y. (1986). Counteractive functions of communication in effective group decision-making. In R. Y. Hirokawa & M. S. Poole (Eds.), *Communication and group decision-making*. Beverly Hills, CA: Sage.

35. Blomstrom, S., Boster, F. J., Levine, K. J., Butler, E. M., & Levine, S. L. (2008). The effect of training on brainstorming. *Journal of the Communication, Speech, & Theatre Association of North Dakota, 21*, 41–50.

36. Craig, R. (2004). Benefits and drawbacks of anonymous online communication: Legal challenges and communicative recommendations. *Free Speech Yearbook, 41*, 127–141.

37. Turman, P. (2005). Norm development, decision-making, and structuration in CMC group interaction. *Communication Teacher, 19*, 121–125.

38. Galanes & Adams, *Effective group discussion*. Wilmot & Hocker, *Interpersonal conflict*.

39. Galanes & Adams, *Effective group discussion*.

workplace communication

When you have read and thought about this chapter, you will be able to

1. Describe the structures of workplace communication as they are created within diverse types of organizations.

2. Create and communicate your personal brand in preparation for a job search.

3. Take steps to effectively prepare for employment interviews.

4. Enact communication behaviors that will demonstrate communication competence in the workplace.

5. Recognize and practice ethical workplace communication behaviors.

The very fabric of our social, cultural, and economic worlds is intertwined with various organizations, including schools, clubs, places of worship, and the workplace. Our ability to communicate effectively and ethically within these various organizations determines, in large part, our opportunities for personal, social, and economic advancement. In this chapter you will learn about various skills related to workplace communication.

I n March 2015, former First Lady Laura Bush celebrated the fifth year of her Women's Initiative Fellowship program. The Women's Initiative Fellowship is "designed to enhance the leadership skills of women around the world with an initial focus on women in the Middle East and North Africa." According to the Women's Initiative website,[1] women who develop strong professional networks are able to thrive economically and contribute to the social institutions that promote prosperity and empowerment. The program pairs prominent American women as mentors to women from other nations so that they can expand their network and gain valuable knowledge on how to build lasting change in their home countries.

Like many other organizations, the Women's Initiative is reliant on communication for success. As the primary spokesperson, Laura Bush must explain the objectives of the organization to potential supporters and other stakeholders. Once the mission is clear, communication must be used to organize the efforts of volunteers and others to support opportunities for women entrepreneurs, activists, and leaders throughout the world. To achieve success, these communication efforts must be organized and executed carefully.

© Ingram Publishing/Super Stock RF

The Women's Initiative teaches us two important lessons. First, organizations of all types rely on effective communication for success. The Women's Initiative is not unlike your university, a local small business, a church, or a community group in this regard—communication is used to accomplish strategic objectives. From this example we also learn that organizational communication is carefully planned in many instances. For the celebration of the Women's Initiative, a speech by Mrs. Bush was combined with press releases and other information published on the organization's website to launch a new cohort of women who would participate in the program. Effective organizational communication requires strategic planning for both the message and how the message will be disseminated to various stakeholders and audiences. In this chapter, you will learn more about the nature of organizational communication, both for the success of the organization itself and for your personal success as you seek employment or other forms of involvement with organizations.

Defining Workplace Communication

Each of us belongs to several different **organizations,** which are social collectives, or groups of people, in which activities are coordinated to achieve both individual and collective goals. According to the U.S. Census Bureau, 72% of the 19.7 million college students in the United States in 2011 worked at least part-time to help pay for their education and living expenses.[2] You may belong to a church, student clubs, and community service organizations, and, of course, we are all members of local, state, and national government organizations. To contribute meaningfully to these organizations, you must have some understanding of how communication functions in these settings, as well as understanding the skills that are most salient to organizational contexts. We

organizations
Social collectives, or groups of people, in which activities are coordinated to achieve both individual and collective goals.

organizational communication
The ways in which groups of people both maintain structure and order through their symbolic interactions and allow individual actors the freedom to accomplish their goals.

economic orientation
Organizations that manufacture products and/or offer services for consumers.

political orientation
Organizations that generate and distribute power and control within society.

integration orientation
Organizations that help mediate and resolve discord among members of society.

define **organizational communication** as the ways in which groups of people both maintain structure and order through their symbolic interactions and allow individual actors the freedom to accomplish their goals. From this definition you should be aware of the following points. First, we use verbal and nonverbal communication to create structure. Through organizational communication, hierarchy is established among people. For instance, there are supervisors and subordinates, with formal or informal rules about how they communicate with each other. Second, we use communication to create order. How we discuss problems, how we arrive at decisions, and how we celebrate successes are all organizational processes that are created in and through organizational communication. Third, we use organizational communication to accomplish personal goals. Through the structure and order found in most organizations, we have an ability to use communication to demonstrate our creativity, ability, and potential so that we are better able to accomplish personal goals in support of the organization. Consequently, communication simultaneously creates structure and freedom as we enact our roles within the organization. In this section you will learn about organizational communication as it flows through communications networks in various types of organizations.

TYPES OF ORGANIZATIONS

Talcott Parsons classified organizations into four primary types: economic, political, integration, and pattern maintenance.[3] Although some organizations might overlap these categories, we usually can classify organizations according to their primary functions in society. For instance, a labor union has a primarily political function as it represents members' interests to management, local and state governments, and other unions. At the same time, unions obviously have an interest in promoting economic vitality. Although they span more than one organization type, unions have a primary function that allows clear classification.

Organizations with an **economic orientation** tend to manufacture products and/or offer services for consumers. Small businesses, which according to the U.S. Small Business Administration account for 99.7% of all U.S. employer firms and employ about half of private sector employees, are examples of organizations with an economic orientation.[4] Of course, large corporations, banks, and media organizations also have economic orientations.

Organizations with a **political orientation** generate and distribute power and control within society. Elected local, state, and federal officials and police and military forces are political organizations. Of course, there are Democrats and Republicans who form organizations with political orientations, but did you know that as of April 2015 there were 39 national third-party political organizations in the United States, with an additional 221 operating

Schools are pattern-maintenance organizations because they teach people how to effectively participate in society.
© Jonathan Kirn/The Image Bank/Getty Images

within various states?[5] Political organizations must adhere to rules established in formal documents, such as the U.S. Constitution, while they attempt to influence the ideology of the electorate. You have witnessed the attempts of the Tea Party and the Occupy Wall Street movement to use the media and social networks to promote particular positions on issues.

Organizations with an **integration orientation** help mediate and resolve discord among members of society. Our court system, public interest groups, and conflict management centers are all examples of integration-oriented organizations. One unique characteristic of communication within integrative organizations is the necessity for impartiality. A judge, for example, must not be biased in the way he or she talks to criminal defendants, and public interest groups must demonstrate that their objective benefits all of society, not just a few individuals.

Organizations with a **pattern-maintenance orientation** promote cultural and educational regularity and development within society. Organizations that teach individuals how to participate effectively in society, including families, schools, and religious groups, promote pattern maintenance. Communication within organizations focused on pattern maintenance emphasizes social support. Your family or your church, for instance, provides you with personal and spiritual support. Even schools support individuals by helping them learn.

pattern-maintenance orientation
Organizations that promote cultural and educational regularity and development within society.

COMMUNICATION NETWORKS

Competent workplace communicators understand that the workplace comprises multiple communication networks. **Communication networks** are patterns of relationships through which information flows in an organization. Stohl describes communication networks as capturing "the tapestry of *relationships*—the complex web of *affiliations* among individuals and organizations as they are woven through the collaborative threads of communication."[6] Communication networks can take many forms, depending on the complexity of the organization. However, we typically classify these networks as formal or informal in nature.

communication networks
Patterns of relationships through which information flows in an organization.

Formal communication consists of messages that follow prescribed channels of communication throughout the organization. The most common way of depicting formal communication networks is with organizational charts like the one in figure 1. Organizational charts provide clear guidelines as to who is responsible for a given task and which employees

formal communication
Messages that follow prescribed channels of communication throughout the organization.

Figure 1
Formal communication flow.

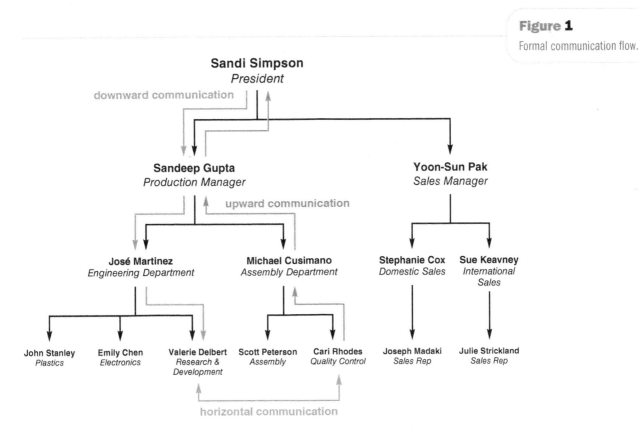

are responsible for others' performance. When communicating occurs in formal networks, information typically flows in three ways:

- **Downward communication** occurs whenever superiors initiate messages to subordinates. Ideally, downward communication should include such things as job instructions, job rationale, policy and procedures, performance feedback, and motivational appeals.

- **Upward communication** occurs when messages flow from subordinates to superiors. Obviously, effective decision making depends on timely, accurate, and complete information traveling upward from subordinates.

- **Horizontal communication** flows between people who are at the same level of the organizational hierarchy. It influences organizational success by allowing members to coordinate tasks, solve problems, share information, and resolve conflict.

Informal communication consists of interactions that do not follow the formal upward and downward structures of the organization but emerge out of less formal interactions among organizational members.[7] For example, co-workers who work from home might use private e-mail accounts, Facebook, or other noncompany mechanisms to have informal discussions about other employees, their boss, or other issues about their jobs.[8] These informal networks, sometimes referred to as "grapevine communication," are typically very accurate, with between 80% and 90% of the information being correct.[9] An understanding of formal and informal networks within organizations is critical as you join and try to fit in at a new organization.

Communication networks can also extend beyond organizations. **Organizational communities** are established when *several organizations—similar businesses, clubs, or community service organizations—have overlapping interests and become networked together to provide mutual support and resources.*[10] For example, a group of organic farms in your area might act together to make connections with local restaurants and grocery stores to sell their goods. If the farmers and the restaurants form networks to coordinate menus with seasonal local foods, or "30-mile meals," those networks can evolve as the organizational community grows. Social media helps facilitate organizational communities. When one organization follows another, information can be shared. For organizational communities to thrive, key individuals must step forward to be boundary spanners. A **boundary spanner** not only shares information between groups but also provides strategic vision for how the groups can actively work together and form a community.

Preparing for the Job Market

According to the Bureau of Labor Statistics, 19 of the 30 fastest-growing occupations through 2022 will require an associate degree or higher; those occupations project more rapid wage growth than occupations that do not require any form of postsecondary education.[11] The implication is clear: your qualifications matter when you are looking for a job. To have success in the job market, you must define and communicate your personal brand. A **personal brand** is a set of attributes and values that can be used to consistently represent yourself to others (see the chapter on perception, self, and communication). You might think of personal branding as a particular type of identity management focused on your public and professional identity. In this section you will learn how to present your personal brand throughout the job search process.

CONDUCTING A SELF-INVENTORY

What do you really know about yourself? When was the last time you took inventory of your assets and liabilities as a potential employee? Could you express these qualities

downward communication
Messages flowing from superiors to subordinates.

upward communication
Messages flowing from subordinates to superiors.

horizontal communication
Messages between members of an organization who have equal power.

informal communication
Interactions that do not follow the formal upward and downward structures of the organization but emerge out of less formal interactions among organizational members.

organizational communities
Groups of similar businesses or clubs that have common interests and become networked together to provide mutual support and resources.

boundary spanner
An individual who shares information between groups and establishes strategic vision for collaboration.

personal brand
Your personal attributes and values that can be consistently communicated to others.

intelligently? Analyzing answers to these questions will help you discover the attributes and values that define your personal brand. Although you will want to gain feedback from others, defining your personal brand begins with a careful self-inventory based on qualities like these:

- Your work and educational experiences
- Your motivations and goals
- Your strengths and weaknesses
- Your likes and dislikes
- Your skills
- Your roles in campus extracurricular activities
- Your professional experience, if any (including co-op programs and internships)
- Your interests and hobbies
- Your talents, aptitudes, and achievements
- What is important to you in a position and an organization

After answering these questions, you will be armed with a series of fact statements and value statements. For example, a fact statement might be that you have had a variety of leadership experiences in student organizations and part-time employment positions. A value statement might be that you enjoy work settings where you have the opportunity to interact with others. By combining fact and value statements, you can articulate your personal brand through a statement like, "I am an experienced leader who values solving problems by communicating with co-workers and clients."

communicating creatively

Blogging Your Personal Brand

In addition to using a self-inventory to better understand your personal brand, you should also actively create and manage your brand. Lindsey Shoemake, a student at Georgia College & State University, created a blog called *That Working Girl* to engage readers about young women who want to develop careers in public relations and media. Through her blog she was able to gain a substantial number of followers, which helped her gain a valuable internship. Creating a blog is free and easy, but the maintenance requires ongoing attention. The work you put into your blog can show that you are actively engaged in your profession while also demonstrating that you have valuable digital skills.

Source: Duis, S. (2013, July 15). Experts to students: Build your brand now, get hired later. *USA Today College* (http://college.usatoday.com/2013/07/15/experts-to-students-build-your-brand-now-get-hired-later/).

personal network
A web of contacts and relationships that can help you gain job leads and can provide referrals.

Volunteering is a great way to make connections and expand your personal network.

© Ariel Skelley/Blend Images/Corbis RF

CREATING A PERSONAL NETWORK

Many people assume that the key to landing a good job is having a good résumé. Though partly true, this conventional wisdom is also incomplete: the key to finding a great job is getting your résumé into the hands of the right people, and that requires having a great personal network. A **personal network** is an intricate web of contacts and relationships designed to benefit the participants—including identifying leads and giving referrals.[12] People in your network, including family, friends, people you have met at social functions, and people with whom you have worked and studied, can assist you in identifying job leads and introducing you to others who can become a part of your network.

Because many college students have not yet had significant work experience, developing a

network is critical to postcollege employment. Here are strategies you can use to develop your network:

1. *Create an inventory of your network.* Using your phone list, e-mail list, set of Facebook friends, and other sources, inventory the people in your social network who could assist you in your job search. Talk with those who have significant work experience to make them aware that you are in the job market.

2. *Contact the career services office on your campus.* Most campuses offer several job fairs throughout the academic year or provide other networking opportunities. Taking advantage of these face-to-face meeting opportunities can be a very productive use of your time.

3. *Contact and join student chapters of professional organizations on your campus.* In communication, for instance, students often join clubs such as the National Communication Association, the Association for Women in Communication, the Public Relations Society of America, or the Society for Professional Journalists. Campus chapters of these organizations provide very useful networking opportunities for members.

4. *Consider an internship.* If you are early in your academic career, an internship can provide valuable networking opportunities. Most colleges and universities offer options for students to earn course credit for internships—you should talk with your academic adviser about such options on your campus.

5. *Volunteer.* Simply taking the time to volunteer in your community can open many doors. Besides giving you the satisfaction that comes from helping others, your hard work and dedication will be noticed by others. Volunteering for a community organization will allow you to get to know many different types of people in your community, thus expanding your network.

SEARCHING FOR A JOB

Once you have defined your personal brand and created your network, you can embark on the exciting, and sometimes frustrating, journey of a job search. With millions of potential employers, how can you possibly begin the process of narrowing your focus? In addition to the traditional methods of meeting with your career-services center on campus, reading job advertisements, contacting your personal network, and attending career and job fairs, you can use a variety of online tools.

One key to successful online searching is to use regional job sites that allow you to focus your efforts by geographic location. The U.S. Bureau of Labor Statistics maintains an employment information database for each state that you can find online. Using this resource, you can find links to state employment statistics bureaus, as well as job and employment projections broken down by state. Such information can help you identify potentially good leads in areas where you want to live. Likewise, the Riley Guide, also available online, provides links to several domestic and international job databases. Using those databases, coupled

engaging **diversity**

Being Bilingual Helps the Job Search

As a result of globalization, organizations increasingly function in a bilingual world. Even small businesses routinely work in a global market. As a result, language skills can significantly benefit you as you seek employment. For private sector jobs, Asian languages, Scandinavian languages, and Portuguese could provide you with the biggest payoff. For government jobs, East Asian, South Asian, and Near East languages may be most in demand.

Source: Burrow, G. (2013, November 14). Hot job skill: Fluency in a foreign language. Economic Modeling Specialists International [blog] (www.economicmodeling.com/2013/11/14/hot-job-skill-fluency-in-a-foreign-language/).

with statistical information, you will have a data-driven starting point for finding potential jobs. Newspaper websites and other sites such as www.localhelpwanted.net can also help you target your search to specific cities and careers.

U.S. adults born between 1957 and 1964 (the youngest group of baby boomers) held an average of 11 jobs from age 18 to 44, more than half of them before they were 27, according to the Bureau of Labor Statistics National Longitudinal Survey of Youth.[13] This trend has changed very little in subsequent generations; people still hold several different types of jobs. If you have held previous jobs, one search strategy is to identify similar or related career fields, which you can do on the My Skills My Future website (www.myskillsmyfuture.org). For example, assume that you have previous experience as a retail salesperson. If you enter that into the My Skills database, it will point out that a related position in meeting, conference, and event planning has a bright outlook for bachelor-degree holders.

There are thousands of online websites designed to help you search for jobs. Some are free. Before using any online source, particularly one that costs money, consult with professors, individuals from your career-services office, and professionals in the field. You should not waste time or money joining a site that has little relevance to your field(s) of interest.

PREPARING COVER LETTERS

A **cover letter** is a short letter to an interviewer persuasively introducing you and your credentials in relationship to the job description, and it typically accompanies your résumé. Cover letters help ensure that your résumé is read and let you target your appeal for a particular job. Typical cover letters have four main sections or paragraphs designed to achieve the following: (1) attention, (2) interest, (3) desire, and (4) action.[14]

After headings that contain your address and the interviewer's address, your cover letter should gain the *attention* of the reader. At this point you should specify the position for which you are applying, indicate how you heard about it, and provide a general overview of your qualifications. The introductory paragraph is where you should provide a clear but brief description of your personal brand. In the second paragraph you need to arouse the reader's *interest* and demonstrate your desire for the job. At this point you want to describe your major experiences and strengths as they relate to the job. If possible, mention one or two accomplishments that illustrate your proficiency and effectiveness. The main idea is to create interest and show how your skills and qualifications can be of value to the organization. You can refer the reader to the enclosed résumé for more detail on your qualifications and experience. In the third paragraph you need to suggest action. Restate your *desire* to learn more about the organization and to have a face-to-face meeting, which is the *action* you are hoping for. Finally, express your appreciation for the reader's time and/or consideration.

A cover letter is an opportunity to demonstrate your writing skills. Take care with respect to grammar, spelling, and other mechanics that could turn off a potential employer. You would be surprised at how easily a perfectly credible applicant is dismissed simply because of correctable errors. If you opt to send e-mail queries to potential employers, remember that the e-mail will act as your cover letter. Make it persuasive and include your résumé as an attachment. If you receive a reply to your e-mail inquiry, you should carefully follow the directions about what to do next.

PREPARING RÉSUMÉS AND OTHER CREDENTIALS

Although human resource professionals use a variety of employment screening tools to screen job applicants, ranging from surveys to background checks, the professional

cover letter
A short letter introducing you and your résumé to an interviewer.

SAMANTHA BRADSHAW

14 35th St South, Lowland, SC 34567
| (123) 456-7890 | bradshaw@llmail.com

www.sam-makes-media.com

OBJECTIVE

To obtain an entry-level position in social media communication strategy and analytics.

EXPERIENCE

Social Media Intern   Transpar, LLC (Charleston, SC)   2015–Present

- Create cross-platform social media messages
- Track views, impressions, and click-throughs across social media platforms
- Develop cross-platform communication strategy
- Provide briefings to CEO, CFAO and Director of Communications

Web Designer   Low Country Tours (Beaufort, SC)   2013–2015

- Developed website architecture using Wordpress
- Created page templates to implement user interface design

Tour Guide   Low Country Tours (Beaufort, SC)   2012–2013

- Assisted boat captain with safety preparations and monitoring during cruises
- Gave public presentations on historic landmarks and ecology
- Provided direct customer service to clients while on tours

EDUCATION

B.A. in Strategic Communication, Georgetown River University (Georgetown, SC)   2007–2013

- GPA 3.85
- Certificate in Digital Media Production

SKILLS

Outstanding in oral and written communication. Proficient in Wordpress CMS, HTML Coding, Nuvi Social Media Analytics, Adobe Creative Cloud Suite, Final Cut Pro, and Microsoft Office.

Figure 2

Sample chronological résumé.

résumé remains the foundational source of information.[15] A good résumé is your starting point in any job search, and it is likely to be critical to securing an interview and an eventual offer of employment. To create a successful résumé, you must consider style, content, and format.

Style

Style refers to the way you use language and grammar to construct your written materials. It can range from very informal to very formal in tone. A sample résumé is shown in figure 2. Notice it uses several stylistic approaches that are uncommon in other forms of writing.

First, complete sentences and the pronoun "I" are unnecessary in résumés. Descriptive clauses are sufficient as long as they are understandable. Many experts recommend beginning descriptive clauses with action verbs, such as *planned, supervised,* and *conducted.*[16]

Table 1 Action Verbs for Résumés

Accomplished	Formulated	Ordered	Succeeded
Adapted	Generated	Participated	Supervised
Administered	Handled	Performed	Supplied
Analyzed	Headed	Persuaded	Supported
Balanced	Identified	Prepared	Tabulated
Disbursed	Managed	Revised	Uploaded
Examined	Modified	Searched	Verified
Executed	Notified	Selected	Volunteered
Explained	Obtained	Sponsored	Won
Filed	Offered	Streamlined	Wrote

These words catch employers' attention because they are concrete and indicate what you have done. Some commonly used action verbs are listed in table 1. Should you use past- or present-tense verbs? The tense depends on whether you are currently performing the particular job duties. Use present-tense verbs for present employment and activities, and use past-tense verbs for past jobs.

Whenever possible, you should quantify information to illustrate the scope of your accomplishments. Here are some examples:

Managed a $30,000 budget for Lambda Chi Alpha

Supervised 10 customer service representatives

Increased sales by 200%

Employers look for accomplishments like these because they are concrete, measurable, and significant.

Be consistent. Whenever you make stylistic decisions, adhere to them. If you use bullets to present your job duties, use bullets throughout your résumé. If you put periods at the end of your bulleted descriptions, make sure you do so consistently. If you indent one job title five spaces and underline, make sure all your job titles are indented five spaces and underlined.

Be concise. Remember that you do not have to put everything in a résumé. In fact, view your résumé as an appetizer. You can tell about the main course in the interview. Unless you have more than seven years of work experience, most experts agree that your résumé should not be longer than one page.[17]

Be neat. Given that employers have very limited time to spend reading your résumé, the overall impression it creates is important. Employers judge you and your capabilities based in part on the physical appearance of your résumé. Hiring managers will have a hard time ignoring poor proofreading and sloppiness, and your chances of securing an interview will significantly decrease.

Content

The content of résumés for college students typically includes contact information as well as your objectives, education, experience, skills, and campus activities or community involvement. Without contact information the rest of your résumé is useless. Include links to your LinkedIn profile or creative portfolio if available.

An **objective statement,** or an articulation of your goals, is usually the first information on the résumé, just below your contact information. Objective statements are important because they allow you to tailor your credentials and goals to the needs of a particular organization and job description.[18] In addition to describing your personal goals, you should consider what the organization needs or what types of issues it faces when you are writing your objective statement. The following are examples of objective statements:

- To apply programming skills in an environment with short deadlines and demanding customers.
- To achieve observable increases in return on investment of information technology expenditures.

Employers also want to see your educational credentials. Your credentials show that you had the intellect to go to college, the determination to complete high school, and the capability of learning new things and finishing complex projects. In summarizing your education, you should include degrees awarded, completion dates (or anticipated completion dates), schools attended, majors and minors, and honors or scholarships. Employers always look at your education, but the further along you are in your career, the smaller the role it plays on your résumé. Instead, experience becomes more important.

With few exceptions, employers will focus much of their attention on your past jobs, whether you are a freshly minted college graduate or an experienced individual changing jobs or careers. Employers look at the types of jobs you have held, as well as your job tenure, job duties, and accomplishments. When describing your work experience, make sure you include a job title, the name of the organization, the dates of employment, and a description of your major responsibilities and achievements. Remember to use action verbs (see table 1) and to quantify accomplishments whenever possible.

When adapting your résumé to a particular job, include key words and phrases from the actual job description. In larger organizations, electronic databases are used to search through hundreds of résumés to find perfect matches between jobs and people—much as what happens when you use Google to search for a webpage.[19] As a result, if your résumé contains more key terms from the job advertisement, the chance that an actual person will review it is increased.

Most résumés also include a skills section highlighting abilities, ranging from the ability to use specialized computer applications to fluency in multiple languages. The skills section of your résumé should be tailored to the job description of the position for which you are applying.

Many college students end their résumé with a list of their campus activities and/or community involvement. Don't stop there. Rather, indicate your level of involvement, including participation on committees and leadership positions. Involvement in campus and community organizations is important because, in the mind of many employers, it translates to workplace citizenship.

Traditional Formats

Traditional résumés are designed to be printed. These types of résumés are used for mass interviews, job fairs, and other face-to-face meetings. Traditional résumés typically rely on chronological or functional formatting.

The **chronological résumé,** which organizes your credentials over time, is what most people envision when they think of a résumé. A résumé based on time has long been the standard and, despite technological advances allowing for electronic résumés, continues to be the most widely accepted format.[20] To refer to a résumé as "reverse chronological" is actually more accurate, because in describing your work experience (and education), you begin with your present or most recent job and continue back to past jobs. Figure 2 is an example of a chronological résumé.

Whereas the chronological format organizes your experience based on when you acquired it, the **functional résumé** organizes your experience by type of function performed. If you have held a variety of jobs (such as teaching, sales, and advertising), the functional résumé allows you to group them by the skills you developed and the duties you performed. Graduating college students will use a functional résumé to group "professional experience" separately from "other work experience," which may include jobs that do not directly relate to your career goal but nonetheless illustrate your work ethic.

functional résumé
A document that organizes your credentials by type of function performed.

Electronic Résumés

A preference for electronic résumés is increasing in most businesses, regardless of their size or type of industry. Research reported in *Business Communication Quarterly* showed that 71% of the companies surveyed preferred standard résumés following the chronological or functional format.[21] The majority, 41%, preferred that résumés be submitted as e-mail attachments, followed closely by 34% preferring they be uploaded to a website. One reason why electronic résumés are so popular is that they are searchable. One efficient way to evaluate candidates is to search for similarities in wording between a job description and résumés submitted for the job. Résumés that have a better match with the job description based on such an analysis may rise to the top of an interview list more easily. Take care to adapt your résumé and cover letter to the job for which you are applying.

Portfolios

Some fields, including technical writing, web design, graphic arts, and even public relations, may require development of a professional portfolio as you enter the job market. A professional portfolio provides examples of your knowledge, skills, and abilities to perform specific field-related tasks.[22] Because the format and design of portfolios will vary by field, your best source of information for how to create yours will be your professors and mentors. However, if you are in a creative field, or any field where you create products that can be shown to others, you should plan early to build your portfolio.

A good rule of thumb is to save everything and to make notes to yourself indicating what skill you mastered or perfected on each project that you save. Later, when you are applying for an internship or a job, your mentor can assist you in compiling the materials into an acceptable portfolio. Having a portfolio can be valuable for any type of profession—keeping papers and other projects from all your courses could come in handy as you attempt to illustrate the broad repertoire of skills, particularly communication skills, you accumulated in college. You can see what portfolios look like by visiting Seelio.com and reviewing one of the many portfolios on that site. Such portfolios provide more concrete information than a simple résumé or LinkedIn account and are more professional than simply using Facebook or other informal social media outlets.

Preparing for the Interview

Your written credentials will rarely be sufficient to obtain employment. Nearly every job search will require some sort of personal interview. Like any formal communication situation—including speeches and presentations—job interviews start with careful

Study the job description carefully so that you can learn the exact skills needed to succeed.

© Peopleimages/Getty Images, RF

job description
A document that defines a job in terms of its content and scope.

planning and practice. In this section you will learn various strategies for guiding that preparation.

GATHER INFORMATION

Your initial step in preparing for a job interview is carefully researching the organization. Although you may not have much time for this step, knowing about the organization and the position for which you applied is critical to successfully answering questions during the interview. Your research efforts can be focused around three general goals:

1. *Understand the job.* A **job description** defines the position in terms of its content and scope. Although the format can vary, job descriptions may include information on job duties and responsibilities; the knowledge, skills, and abilities necessary to accomplish the duties; working conditions; relationships with co-workers, supervisors, and external stakeholders; and the extent of supervision required. You will likely find the formal job description online, either on the company website or as part of a job search database. Besides providing you with information about the job expectations, the job description serves as the legal basis upon which the job interview is conducted, including the focus of interview questions. If you have sufficient time, you can use your professional/social network to try to solicit others' perspectives on the type of job for which you applied.

2. *Understand the organization.* Job applicants and interviewees lose all credibility when they cannot demonstrate even superficial knowledge of the organization to which they are applying. Besides using obvious sources of information, such as the organization's website, check your library for specialized resources, such as the LexisNexis Company Insight database or the BusinessWeek Company Insight Center, to find information about the company's finances, executive officers, and other pertinent facts. Of course, small businesses may not be indexed in such databases. A local library or chamber of commerce may have information about these.

3. *Understand the field.* To present yourself as a mature candidate for any job, you will want to illustrate knowledge of your chosen field by demonstrating awareness of new trends, market forces, and other matters. Keep current on all aspects of your field, because employers will view you more positively if you are conversant with these issues. Professional trade magazines are helpful for this type of research. Of course, by virtue of your major you should be keeping up with this type of information well before a job interview.

Remember that the primary purpose of an interview is to analyze the knowledge, skills, and abilities of a particular applicant in relationship to the required and desired skills in the job description. Taking time to learn about these issues will help you advocate for a close fit between your qualifications and those specified by the employer.

GENERAL INTERVIEWING STRATEGIES

During the interview you must present yourself as a potential asset to the organization. Doing so requires using verbal and nonverbal communication; specifically, you want to (1) create a good first impression, (2) speak with clarity, and (3) demonstrate interest.

Just as your written credentials should reflect a professional and competent image, so should you. One of the most obvious ways to create a good first impression is to dress appropriately. The general rule is to match the style of dress of the interviewer. For professional positions, conservative dress is typically appropriate (dark suits, white shirts or blouses, standard ties for men, dark socks or neutral hose, dark shoes). Be sure to wear clothes that fit and are comfortable but not too casual. Be modest in your use of jewelry and cologne. Of course, you need to arrive on time and learn to take cues from the interviewer on how to act, while trying to present yourself in an honest, positive way.

The way you use grammar can deeply influence the impressions others form about you in professional settings, such as job interviews.[23] Even if you have to pause before responding, organize your answer and avoid slurring your words, using potentially offensive language, or using grammatically incorrect sentences. Many applicants do not convey clear messages because their sentences include vocalized pauses ("uh," "um"), verbal fillers ("you know"), and repetitive phrases ("things like that"). By practicing beforehand

building **behaviors**

Practicing Interview Questions

Practice answering these typical job interview questions with a partner:

1. Why would you like to work for us?
2. What do you know about our products or services?
3. How have your previous work positions prepared you for this position?
4. What do you think your previous supervisors would cite as your strengths? Weaknesses?
5. Describe a typical strategy that you would use in a customer service call.
6. What criteria do you use when assigning work to others?
7. How do you follow up on work assigned to others?
8. Which aspect of your education has prepared you most for this position?
9. Which course did you like most in college?
10. If you had your education to do over again, what would you do differently, and why?
11. Why did you choose _____ as your major?
12. What do you think is the greatest challenge facing this field today?
13. Which area of this field do you think will expand the most in the next few years?

Be prepared to both answer and ask questions effectively during your interviews.
© MBI/Stockbroker/Alamy RF

and thinking quickly on your feet, you should be able to speak with clarity and precision. In sum, the employment interview is a context in which to practice the verbal and nonverbal communication skills you have been learning about and developing in this course. You should also use the interview as an opportunity to expand on your personal branding statement. If you say that you are an experienced leader, how can you demonstrate that through your previous experiences? If you value working with others to solve problems, what examples of group problem solving can you relate? How can you demonstrate that you attempt to improve your communication skills across a variety of settings?

To be interpersonally effective in interviews, you must also demonstrate interest. One of the most important and meaningful ways to do so is by maintaining strong eye contact with the interviewer.[24] Although you may be tempted to focus on responding to questions as the central interviewing skill, listening can also improve your responses. Use body language to show interest. Smile, nod, and give nonverbal feedback to the interviewer. Although you want to remain engaged, being confident and somewhat relaxed is ideal. Be sure to thank the interviewer for his or her time and consideration of you as a candidate.

ANSWERING QUESTIONS EFFECTIVELY AND ETHICALLY

Answering questions effectively is critical for interviewees. Research has shown that various strategies are associated with successfully answering questions.[25] Four key guidelines emerge from that body of research: (1) offer relevant answers, (2) substantiate your claims with evidence, (3) provide accurate answers, and (4) be positive.

Your answers should be relevant to the question asked and to the job description. As an interviewee you should never evade questions; rather, you should respond to them thoroughly and directly. In discussing your skills and abilities, try to relate them to the specific position for which you are interviewing. Whenever possible, specify how and why you think you are well suited to the job. By so doing, you demonstrate your knowledge of the position and illustrate the transferability of your knowledge and skills to the job at hand.

Whatever claims you make about your experience, always provide support. Some interviewees give terse, underdeveloped responses, forcing the interviewer to probe endlessly. Presenting claims without evidence can sound self-serving. If you offer evidence for your assertions, the objective facts and supporting examples will confirm your strengths. Take care to avoid talking for too long when responding. After you have provided a direct answer and presented an example or other form of evidence, summarize your point and wait for a response or the next question. A long, rambling answer can be just as negative as an underdeveloped one.

All employers are searching for honest employees, so always provide accurate information. If an employer finds out you have misrepresented yourself during the interview by exaggerating or lying, everything you do and say will become suspect. Successful interviews feature candid conversation. If you are asked a question you cannot answer, simply say so and do not act embarrassed. An interviewer will have more respect for an interviewee who admits to ignorance than for one who tries to fake an answer.

Being accurate does not mean confessing to every self-doubt or shortcoming. In fact, be as positive as possible during interviews, because in a sense you are "selling" yourself to the employer. To volunteer some limitations or claim personal responsibility for past events is fine, especially in the context of challenges you have met or problems you have encountered. However, avoid being overly critical of others and yourself. You can highlight your strengths and downplay your weaknesses, but always be honest.

Table 2 provides examples illustrating these suggestions. Notice how the effective answers demonstrate honesty while presenting the best case possible for your attributes as an employee.

Table 2 Answering Questions Effectively

Ineffective	Effective
Question: "Describe your best attribute as an employee."	
"I'm really organized."	"I take time to ensure that materials and documents are put away before leaving my desk. This promotes security and allows me to stay organized."
Question: "Have you ever coded HTML?"	
"I think that I had to do something with HTML when working on my Facebook page."	"I have not actually coded HTML, but I am comfortable working on webpages that use plain text content management systems like you find on social media sites."
Question: "Have you experienced conflict in the workplace?"	
"Yes! One of my previous bosses was always mad at everyone and it was always horrible to go to work!"	"I did experience conflict with a co-worker, but I was able to resolve the problem amicably by communicating less by e-mail and more through face-to-face interactions where we could clarify our perceptions more effectively."

ASKING QUESTIONS EFFECTIVELY AND ETHICALLY

Any potential employer will recognize that you have questions about the job and/or organizational environment. After answering the interviewer's questions, you should be prepared to ask questions. This gives you the insight you need to decide if you want this particular job, shows your interest in the job, and demonstrates communication skills.

Recognize that your questions make indirect statements about your priorities, ambitions, and level of commitment. Consequently, avoid overreliance on questions that focus on financial issues such as salary, vacation time, and benefits. Devise questions that elicit information about the company and/or job that you were unable to obtain through your research. Arrange questions so that the most important ones come first, because you may not get a chance to ask all of your prepared questions. Although your questions will need to be tailored to the organization, here are general types of questions relevant in most interview situations:

"Do you assign mentors to help new employees fit in with the culture of the company while learning their new job roles?"

"What is the average length of time that an employee works for the company?"

"What percentage of entry-level employees stay with the company and get promoted?"

"Does the company offer financial support for continuing education?"

PREPARING FOR ILLEGAL QUESTIONS

Legally, employers must approach the hiring process with reference to the laws that govern employment. These laws, known as equal employment opportunity (EEO) laws, are written and enacted by Congress and individual state legislatures. Although a variety of laws can exist at the state level, the pertinent federal statutes are

- *Title VII of the Civil Rights Act.* This law prevents employment discrimination based on race, color, sex, religion, or national origin.
- *Equal Pay Act.* This act, passed in 1963, prevents unequal pay for men and women for equal work.
- *Pregnancy Discrimination Act.* This law makes it illegal to discriminate, either through hiring or promotion, based on pregnancy or related medical issues.

- *Age Discrimination Act.* According to this law, employers cannot refuse to hire applicants who are 40 years of age or older because of age alone.
- *The Americans with Disabilities Act.* This act prevents discrimination against qualified applicants because of a disability and requires employers to make reasonable accommodations to help them apply and perform work.[26]

The purpose of such laws is to ensure that individuals are selected for employment without bias.

To comply with these laws, employers should (1) describe the qualities and skills needed for the position they hope to fill, (2) construct questions that relate to those attributes, and (3) ask the same questions of all candidates for the position. These questions are known as "bona fide occupational qualification (BFOQ) questions." BFOQ questions should be about skills, training, education, work experience, physical attributes, and personality traits. With rare exceptions, questions should not be about age, gender, race, religion, physical appearance, disabilities, ethnic group, or citizenship.

Even with carefully planned BFOQ questions, employers will occasionally pose questions to interviewees that are intentionally or unintentionally illegal. For example, an employer might ask, "Are you married?" or "How old are your children?" when, in fact, he or she should really ask, "Is there anything that would prevent you from being able to travel frequently?" Often, illegal questions are unintentionally asked by untrained interviewers who are trying to be polite. In any circumstance you must carefully consider how to respond to the illegal question(s), using one or more of these strategies:

1. *Weigh the severity of the violation against your desire for the job.* If you really want the job and the violation was minor, you may opt to provide a short answer or tactfully try to rephrase the question to avoid being forced to provide irrelevant information.

2. *Ask for clarification.* If you suspect that the illegal question is actually attempting to reference a BFOQ for the job, you can clarify what skills, knowledge, or attitudes the interviewer is attempting to assess.

3. *Be assertive.* You can tell the interviewer that the question is not related to the attributes specified in the job description or that the question, as phrased, asks for information you do not have to provide. A less aggressive option is to politely decline to answer the question as phrased.

4. *Report the violation.* If the interviewer continues to ask illegal questions or is otherwise offensive, you might consider reporting the violation to a superior and/or to the federal Equal Employment Opportunity Commission (www.eeoc.gov) or a similar state agency.

THE POSTINTERVIEW STAGE

Most interviews end with some plan for future action on the part of both the interviewee and the interviewer. The interviewer will typically explain the criteria for selection as well as a time frame for the decision. As an interviewee, make certain you carry out appropriate responsibilities, including writing to reconfirm your interest in the position and thanking the interviewer for his or her time. Be prepared to deal with various interview outcomes.

A letter of appreciation is appropriate after an interview and should be sent within one or two days following the interview. If a company has been corresponding with you using e-mail, then you should send an e-mail thank-you letter. If you are still interested in the position, express that interest in the letter. If you are not interested, a letter is still appropriate for withdrawing your candidacy.

After the employment interview you may receive a job offer. Making a final decision about accepting a job involves careful consideration of multiple pieces of information. Here are tips for conducting negotiations with your potential employer and making a final decision:

1. *Wait for the appropriate time.* The interview is not the ideal place to discuss salary expectations and other points of negotiation. In the interview you have little bargaining power. Once the company makes an offer, you are *in demand* and have a better chance of negotiating various items.

2. *Know what you want in advance.* Once you have been offered the job, you should immediately be prepared to begin the negotiation process. Conduct research to determine common salary ranges for your type of position. Online salary databases, such as www.salary.com, provide national and regional salary profiles for different types of jobs. Depending on the type of position, you may also be able to negotiate moving expenses, the start date, continuing education funding, and other types of benefits.

3. *Understand the implications of taking the job.* If the job requires moving, you may want to investigate the living expenses of the new community. Try using an online cost-of-living calculator to compare where you live now with the place you will live if you accept the job.

4. *Get it in writing.* Be aware that a job offer and your acceptance of it are legally binding documents. Take care to ensure that all negotiated items are included in the offer letter, and do not write an acceptance letter until you have a correct offer letter in hand.

5. *Be tactful in your response.* Regardless of whether you are accepting or declining the job offer, your official response should be professional. If you accept the position, your acceptance letter should thank the interviewer and formally state that you are accepting the position as described in the offer letter. If you decline the offer, you should state your reason(s) for not accepting the offer, explicitly decline the offer, and end on a pleasant note.

Communication Skills Needed on the Job

Previous sections of this chapter provided you with general information about organizations and taught you the skills necessary for obtaining a job. This section emphasizes skills relevant to your role as an employee or organizational member. We begin by identifying several behaviors representing competent workplace communication and then discuss specific skills, such as conflict management and customer service effectiveness.

WORKPLACE COMMUNICATION COMPETENCE

Before turning to specific communication skills, we begin by discussing the general nature of communication competence in the workplace. Communication competence is the extent to which you are able to be effective at a broad range of verbal and nonverbal communication skills in particular settings. A study by Joann Keyton and colleagues reviewed literature on workplace communication and synthesized over 300 communication behaviors into the four general categories listed in table 3. According to their research, competent workplace communicators effectively share information by asking and answering questions, providing feedback, and engaging in discussions with others. They engage in relationship maintenance by appropriately using humor, engaging in small talk with others, and creating positive relationships. To engage in organizing behaviors, competent communicators are clear on how they schedule tasks and actions and manage others, while also being very effective listeners. Finally, competent communicators avoid complaining and continual displays of frustration.[27]

SPECIFIC WORKPLACE COMMUNICATION SKILLS

Whereas the previous discussion of communication competence provides a broad strategy for improving your workplace communication skills, this section concludes by highlighting seven specific behaviors that will help you improve your workplace communication in a variety of settings: immediacy, supportiveness, strategic ambiguity, interaction management, cross-cultural skills, conflict management, and customer service.

Immediacy

immediacy
Communication behaviors intended to create perceptions of psychological closeness with others.

When people engage in communication behaviors intended to create perceptions of psychological closeness with others, they are enacting **immediacy.** Immediacy can be both verbal and nonverbal. Smiling, reducing physical distance, and using animated gestures and facial expressions are all examples of nonverbally immediate behaviors, whereas calling people by their first names, using "we" language, and telling stories are examples of verbal immediacy behaviors. Using immediacy has been shown to have positive effects in the workplace. For instance, it can improve the relationship between supervisors and subordinates[28] and encourage people to engage in higher levels of self-disclosure.[29] In sales situations, higher levels of self-disclosure can be helpful, because they create more rapport between the salesperson and the customer, and the salesperson can learn valuable information that gives a product or service more value for that customer.

Supportiveness

supportive communication
Listening with empathy, acknowledging others' feelings, and engaging in dialogue to help others maintain a sense of personal control.

People engage in **supportive communication** when they listen with empathy, acknowledge the feelings of others, and engage in dialogue to help others maintain a sense of personal control. Of course, supportive communication is an important skill in any context, including workplace settings. Research reviewed by Hopkins suggests that supportive supervisor communication is one of the most significant factors influencing employee morale.[30]

Table 3 Workplace Communication Competence Categories

Category	Definition
Information sharing	Effectively sending and receiving job-related content to and from others
	Representative behaviors: Giving and receiving feedback, asking others for opinions, asking and answering questions, showing respect, engaging in discussion
Relationship maintenance	Creating and continuing positive workplace connections with others
	Representative behaviors: Creating relationships, engaging in small talk, using humor appropriately
Avoiding negative emotion	Reducing continual outward displays of negativity surrounding your job or the organization
	Representative behaviors: Avoiding displays of frustration and anger, reducing complaints about your job or co-workers
Organizing	Using communication to promote coherent work flow
	Representative behaviors: Discussing schedules, making decisions, resolving problems, planning, managing others effectively

Source: Adapted from Keyton, J., Caputo, J. M., Fore, E. A., Fu, R., Leibowitz, S. A., Liu, T., Polasik, S. S., Gosh, P., & Wu, C. (2013). Investigating verbal workplace communication behaviors. *Journal of Business Communication, 50,* 152–169.

To enhance your supportive communication skills, consider the following strategies adapted from Albrecht and Bach's discussion of supportive communication:

1. *Listen without judging.* Being judgmental while listening to a co-worker's explanation of a problem can cause you to lose your focus on what he or she is really saying.

2. *Validate feelings.* Even if you disagree with something your co-workers say, validating their perceptions and feelings is an important step in building a trusting relationship.

3. *Provide both informational and relational messages.* Supportive communication involves both helping and healing messages. Providing a metaphorical "shoulder to cry on" is equally as important as providing suggestions and advice.

4. *Be confidential.* When co-workers share feelings and personal reflections with you, maintaining their trust and confidence is essential. Telling others or gossiping about the issue will destroy your credibility as a trustworthy co-worker.[31]

Professional touch, such as a handshake, can help establish immediacy between people.

© DCA Productions/The Image Bank/Getty Images

Strategic Ambiguity

When learning to be competent communicators, we often assume that being competent always means being clear. Eisenberg disagrees with this assumption and points out that clarity is essential for competent communication only when clear communication is the objective of the communicator.[32] Professional and workplace communication often features the use of **strategic ambiguity**—the purposeful use of symbols to allow multiple interpretations of messages. You have probably witnessed instances of strategic ambiguity on your college campus. At the beginning of each year, various student organizations undertake recruitment drives to gain new members. When presenting their organization, whether a student club or a Greek organization, members are often strategically ambiguous about some aspect of it. After all, recruiting would be difficult if we knew there were really only a few members or there was significant political infighting in the club. When you enter the workforce, you will encounter new examples of strategic ambiguity. During orientation, for example, you might learn about your new company's mission statement. Such mission statements are often strategically ambiguous so that all stakeholders (employees, managers, owners, and so on) can find relevant meaning in them. Of course, competent communicators must not only be skillful in recognizing the use of strategic ambiguity but also be able to use it themselves when necessary.

strategic ambiguity
The purposeful use of symbols to allow multiple interpretations of messages.

Interaction Management

Workplace communication is somewhat different from other types of communication situations because conversations tend to flow between the technical jargon associated with the workplace and other topics brought up to relieve stress and pass time. Thus, computer technicians might talk about megabytes and megapixels one minute and speculate about next week's episode of *Game of Thrones* the next. Competent workplace communicators engage in **interaction management** to establish a smooth pattern of interaction that allows a clear flow between topics and ideas. Using pauses, changing pitch, carefully listening to the topics being discussed, and responding appropriately are skills related to interaction management.

interaction management
Establishing a smooth pattern of interaction that allows a clear flow between topics and ideas.

Being an effective communicator with co-workers and clients requires carefully observing how they prefer to talk. Recognizing that one co-worker always talks about technical matters related to the job, whereas another always likes to chit-chat about family, is important; adapting your conversational style to the different styles of these individuals will help you fit in more easily. If you aspire to managerial positions in your company, the ability to communicate well with various individuals is critical.

Cross-Cultural Skills

The changing nature of the U.S. workplace makes it increasingly a cross-cultural setting. If you speak English as a second language, develop cross-cultural skills to aid your transition to the workplace. Because you have both a new language and a new set of technical terms to learn in your workplace, questions are the most effective strategy for avoiding misunderstanding. Ask questions as needed to clarify instructions or expectations, and pay careful attention to your co-workers. By observing them and asking questions if necessary, you can learn not only important vocabulary but also skills for interacting with customers or clients. Finally, keeping a journal of your daily activities is a good idea. The first few days and weeks may seem overwhelming, but you will learn a great deal. Keeping a journal can help you retain vocabulary, directions, and other important pieces of information more easily.

If you are a native speaker who works with a second-language speaker, you will also have to adapt your communication behaviors. You can help ease your co-worker's transition through some relatively easy steps. First, provide important directions, policies, and procedures in writing. Second-language speakers often find written information easier to process because the pace of spoken language can be challenging. Second, take time to explain. You can help your co-worker(s) learn vocabulary and interaction skills more quickly if you take a few moments to explain how and why you communicate the way you do. Finally, be patient. Becoming impatient and frustrated will introduce new

Cross-cultural skills are necessary in today's global economy.

© Andersen Ross/Blend Images LLC RF

problems and make the situation worse for everyone. Patience makes the transition easier and will likely prevent problems from recurring.

Conflict Management Skills

Communicating in organizations is not an easy task. In fact, a pervasive part of organizational life is conflict—both destructive and productive. Destructive conflict can destroy work relationships, whereas productive conflict can create a needed impetus for organizational change and development. Workplace conflict can occur because of mundane issues, such as one person playing a radio too loudly in her cubicle, or serious issues, such as office politics pitting one faction of employees against another. Indeed, conflict management skills are not just desirable but necessary for effective workplace communication.

People often view conflict negatively because they associate it with anger. However, conflict occurs anytime two or more people have goals they perceive to be incompatible. When one employee wants to work late to finish a joint project and another wants to go home to be with his or her family, conflict can occur. In short, workplace conflict is a fact of life—the rule rather than the exception.

You can use a variety of techniques to manage conflict productively. Wilmot and Hocker suggest several approaches:

- *Avoidance.* With the avoidance style, you deny the existence of conflict. Although avoidance can provide you with time to think through a situation, continued avoidance allows conflict to simmer and flare up with more intensity.

- *Competition.* With the competition style, you view conflict as a battle and advance your own interests over those of others. Although the competition style can be necessary when quick decisions must be made or when you are strongly committed to a position, it can also be highly detrimental to your relationships with your co-workers.

- *Compromise.* With a compromise style, you are willing to negotiate away some of your position as long as the other party in the conflict is willing to do the same. Compromise can be an effective strategy because it

sizing things up

Conflict in the Workplace

Workplace contexts create potential for conflict because they force us to accomplish important task outcomes while managing relationships with others. The way we manage conflict can influence how effective we are as organizational communicators. Below you will find several statements; for each one, indicate how well the statement describes you by using the following scale:

1 = Does not describe me at all
2 = Does not describe me very well
3 = Describes me somewhat
4 = Describes me well
5 = Describes me very well

1. When working on problems, I try to win arguments to support my opinion.
2. When communicating at work, I generally let others have their way.
3. If I sense a conflict brewing, I would rather find a way to leave.
4. When in a conflict with a co-worker, I work to find common ground to resolve the conflict.
5. When I disagree with someone, I am willing to give up some of my own position as long as others are willing to do the same.
6. I am quick to give up on my opinion when I sense conflict coming.
7. I am generally willing to meet others halfway to resolve conflict.
8. When in a conflict, my interests are most important.
9. I generally avoid conflict in the workplace.
10. When involved in a conflict, talking things through is the best way to find a solution.
11. I generally resolve conflict by compromising with the other person.
12. I often try to find ways to delay having to face a conflict situation.
13. When in a conflict, having dialogue can often resolve the situation.
14. I tend to give up on my views to resolve conflicts with others.
15. When in a conflict, I approach the other person ready for battle.

There are no right or wrong answers to these questions. A guide for interpreting your responses appears at the end of this chapter.

is a win–win proposition for both parties, but when used too often, it can become a sophisticated form of conflict avoidance.

- *Accommodation.* With the accommodation style, you set aside your views and accept those of others. Accommodation can maintain harmony in relationships, but it is problematic in many situations, because tacit acceptance of others' views can stifle creative dialogue and decision making.

- *Collaboration.* A collaborative style relies on thoughtful negotiation and reasoned compromise whereby both parties agree that the negotiated outcome is the best possible alternative under the circumstances. Although collaboration takes more time and effort to enact, it typically results in the best possible outcome for all parties.[33]

Customer Service Skills

We often hear that we now live in a "service economy," in which U.S. companies increasingly make money by providing services rather than goods. In this kind of business environment, one of the most important forms of external communication occurs in providing service to organizational customers. Bitner, Booms, and Tetreault define the **customer service encounter** as "the moment of interaction between the customer and the firm."[34] During this moment the organizational representative provides professional assistance in exchange for the customer's money or attention.

Customer service means different things to different people. For some it means being friendly, shaking hands warmly, and initiating pleasant conversations with clients. For others, customer service means processing customers efficiently and quickly. Still others view it as listening intently to identify individual needs and providing sufficient information and/or support to meet those needs. All these perspectives are legitimate; however, the *customer* is the ultimate judge of whether customer service interactions are satisfying.

Regardless of how employees understand the concept of customer service, most providers have the goal of influencing their customers' behaviors. An extensive body of research covers communication techniques for gaining compliance. In her book *Communicating with Customers: Service Approaches, Ethics, and Impact,* W. Z. Ford reviews compliance-gaining strategies used by customer service representatives. Her work is summarized in table 4.

customer service encounter
The moment of interaction between the customer and the firm.

Table 4 Compliance-Gaining Strategies Used by Customer Service Representatives

Promise: Promising a reward for compliance (e.g., "If you purchase this car, I'll give you tickets to a football game.")

Threat: Threatening to punish for noncompliance (e.g., "If you don't buy the car before the end of the week, I cannot guarantee the 1 percent interest rate.")

Pre-giving: Rewarding the customer before requesting compliance (e.g., "I will give you $50 just for test-driving this new car.")

Moral appeal: Implying that it is immoral not to comply (e.g., "Since you have small children, you should be looking at our crossover utility model with more safety features.")

Liking: Being friendly and helpful to get the customer in a good frame of mind to ensure compliance (e.g., "Good afternoon; my, how nice you look today. How can I help you?")

Source: Adapted from Ford, W. Z. (1998). *Communicating with customers: Service approaches, ethics, and impact.* Cresskill, NJ: Hampton Press. Used by permission of Hampton Press, Inc.

A wide range of occupations require interactions between employees and clients or customers. In many of these, the provision of service often involves some degree of emotional content.[35] Nurses interact with dying patients in a hospice, ministers counsel troubled parishioners, and social workers help physically abused women. Emotional communication also characterizes other, less obvious occupations. Flight attendants must appear happy and attentive during flights,[36] and bill collectors must remain stern and avoid any trace of sympathy in interactions.[37]

Arlie Hochschild was the first scholar to deal with this phenomenon, in her book *The Managed Heart.*[38] She uses the term **emotional labor** to refer to jobs in which employees are expected to display certain feelings in order to satisfy organizational role expectations. Research has indicated that, although emotional labor may be fiscally rewarding for the organization and the client, it can be dangerous for the service provider and can lead to negative consequences, such as burnout, job dissatisfaction, and turnover.[39]

emotional labor
Jobs in which employees are expected to display certain feelings in order to satisfy organizational role expectations.

Ethical Dimensions in the Workplace

In this section we are concerned with the ethical dimensions of workplace communication. In particular, we focus on aggressive communication, honesty, and sexual harassment.

AGGRESSIVE COMMUNICATION

Verbal aggressiveness is communication that attacks the self-concepts of other people in order to inflict psychological pain.[40] It is on the rise in organizational settings, though sometimes unrecognized by management. A recent summary of literature on workplace aggression identified the following types:

- *Abusive supervision* occurs when a supervisor engages in sustained behaviors via hostile verbal and nonverbal messages but does not rise to the level of physical aggression.

- *Bullying* occurs when one person is subjected to ridicule, offensive statements, teasing, social isolation, or other abuse by one or more individuals over an extended period of time.

- *Incivility* is frequent rude behavior that may or may not have the intent of being harmful. Uncivil people may or may not know they are being rude.

- *Social undermining* is action meant to socially isolate another person from a larger group. Whereas incivility can occur unwittingly, social undermining is intentional and often planned.[41]

Any problems with workplace aggression should be reported to a trusted manager or a representative of human resources or the appropriate union.
© Olix Wirtinger/Fancy/ Corbis RF

The psychological pain produced by verbal aggression and other aggressive behaviors includes embarrassment, feelings of inadequacy, humiliation, hopelessness, despair, and depression. If you feel you are the victim of workplace aggression, consult a human resources manager, a union representative, or a trusted manager for advice.

HONESTY

Political figures and other prominent individuals are constantly scrutinized for the honesty and accuracy of their statements. When you speak to others, whether for personal or professional reasons, they rely on you to be honest. One might assume that for communication to work effectively, all parties must both enact and assume honesty. Is it appropriate for you to misrepresent information to your supervisor to make your performance appear better? Is it ethical to integrate key words into your résumé so electronic search engines will highlight them, even if you do not truly possess the requisite skills for that job? Amare and Manning observe that individuals at all levels of organizations have a personal responsibility to act with integrity and to be honest.[42] Even deciding with whom you should be honest is important. If you know a fellow employee is under-performing, should you confront your peer first or go straight to your supervisor?

Honesty is at the heart of personal ethics and must begin with open communication and trust. The fears that drive people to dishonest behaviors at work can often be countered by establishing open communication with co-workers.

SEXUAL HARASSMENT

Sexual harassment includes a set of behaviors that constitute workplace aggression. Unfortunately, instances of sexual harassment litter the news, and sexual harassment has been a problem in the workplace for decades.

What is sexual harassment? The Equal Employment Opportunity Commission (EEOC) defines **sexual harassment** as

> unwelcome sexual advances, requests for sexual favors, and other verbal or physical conduct of a sexual nature if (1) submission to the conduct is made a condition of employment, (2) submission to or rejection of the conduct is made the basis for an employment decision, or (3) the conduct seriously affects an employee's work performance or creates an intimidating, hostile, or offensive working environment.[43]

sexual harassment
Unwelcome, unsolicited, repeated behavior of a sexual nature.

Simply put, sexual harassment is unwelcome, unsolicited, repeated behavior of a sexual nature.

The EEOC definition outlines two different, although sometimes overlapping, types of sexual harassment. The first type, **quid pro quo sexual harassment,** occurs when an employee is offered a reward or is threatened with punishment based on his or her participation in a sexual activity. For example, a supervisor might tell her employee, "I'll give you Friday off if you meet me at my place tonight." The second type is **hostile work environment sexual harassment,** or conditions in the workplace that are sexually offensive, intimidating, or hostile and that affect an individual's ability to perform his or her job. For example, if two males talk explicitly about the physical features of a female colleague in her presence, sexual harassment has occurred.

quid pro quo sexual harassment
A situation in which an employee is offered a reward or is threatened with punishment based on his or her participation in a sexual activity.

hostile work environment sexual harassment
Conditions in the workplace that are sexually offensive, intimidating, or hostile and that affect an individual's ability to perform his or her job.

A major obstacle to ending sexual harassment is the tendency of victims to avoid confronting the harasser. Most instances of sexual harassment are neither exposed nor reported. Instead, the victim usually avoids the situation by taking time off, transferring to another area, or changing jobs. The perpetrator is usually someone in the organization with authority and status—with power over the victim—and the victim feels exposure or confrontation will backfire.

Clearly, the EEOC's definition indicates that a wide range of communication behaviors can constitute sexual harassment, although many men and women see only serious offenses (for example, career benefits in exchange for sexual favors) as harassment. However, although harassment is judged by its effects on the victim, not on the intentions of the harasser, a person need not suffer severe psychological or work outcomes to be a victim. The courts use the "reasonable person rule" to determine whether a reasonable person would find the behavior in question offensive. One limitation of this rule, however, is evidence that men and women view sexual harassment differently.[44] In particular, sexual overtures that women typically view as insulting are viewed by men, in general, as flattering.

Sexual harassment is a serious and pervasive communication problem in modern organizational life, with both the victims and the perpetrators (and even falsely accused perpetrators) suffering personal and professional anguish. Note that, even though in a majority of cases women are victims, the EEOC guidelines apply equally to men.

be ready... for what's next

Building Your Personal Brand

Earlier in this chapter you learned about the concept of personal branding. Your personal brand is something that you use to define yourself to others by representing who you are and what you stand for. Brands, whether they are for products or for people, must be built.

One way that you can develop your personal brand is to strategically use social media. Statistics reported by *Ad Week* show that 92% of companies use social media for recruiting. In addition, 1 out of 3 employers reported that candidates were rejected for employment because of something observed on social media accounts.[45] How can you use social media to effectively build your personal brand?

1. *Strategically use platforms.* LinkedIn is the most popular social media service for employers to recruit and evaluate candidates. Other platforms like Twitter or Pinterest are gaining in relevance.

2. *Demonstrate engagement in serious matters.* Using social media to state observations or opinions on topics related to your profession can show potential employers that you are developing thought leadership skills that help promote innovation in the organization.

3. *Connect.* A key benefit of social media rests in the connections you can make. Follow and friend respected professionals in your field.

4. *Be personal, but remember it is public.* You have seen the stereotype of college students who emphasize "party hard" over "work hard." Although your social media branding should show your human side, it should not create a one-sided caricature of who you are.

Chapter Review & Study Guide

Summary

In this chapter, you learned the following:

1. Workplace communication takes place within the context of an organization.

   - Organizations are generally classified as having one of four primary functions in society: economic production, political participation, integration, and pattern maintenance.

   - Communication within organizations follows networks. These networks provide for formal communication flow, including upward communication, downward communication, and horizontal communication. Networks also allow informal, or "grapevine," communication.

2. To prepare for your job market, you create a personal brand to represent who you are and what you stand for as a potential employee.

   - A cover letter should persuasively establish your qualifications in relation to the job description.

   - The résumé should be concise and stylistically reflect your personality in a professional way.

   - Your résumé should highlight your work qualifications and experiences.

   - Certain professions may require a professional portfolio to illustrate your mastery of key skills.

3. Effective strategies for preparing for a job interview include gathering information about the organization, answering questions appropriately, asking questions, and conducting postinterview negotiations.

4. Workplace communication competence involves using verbal and nonverbal communication effectively in a variety of organizational settings.

   - Specific behaviors that contribute to your communication competence include immediacy, supportive communication, strategic ambiguity, interaction management, cross-cultural skills, conflict management, and customer service skills.

   - Cross-cultural understanding requires that you act with sensitivity toward those who are different, including those who do not speak your language well.

   - Conflict management approaches include avoidance, competition, compromise, accommodation, and collaboration. Each approach may have utility in specific situations; however, the collaborative approach works best in most situations.

   - Customer service interaction skills include using compliance-gaining strategies with customers while engaging in emotional labor.

5. Unethical workplace communication includes aggressive communication and sexual harassment.

   • Workplace aggression occurs when individuals intentionally or unintentionally use verbal or nonverbal aggressive behaviors toward others.

   • Sexual harassment is the abuse of power involving either quid pro quo harassment or a hostile work environment.

Key Terms

Boundary spanner
Chronological résumé
Communication networks
Cover letter
Customer service encounter
Downward communication
Economic orientation
Emotional labor
Formal communication
Functional résumé
Horizontal communication

Hostile work environment sexual
   harassment
Immediacy
Informal communication
Integration orientation
Interaction management
Job description
Objective statement
Organizational communication
Organizational communities
Organizations

Pattern-maintenance orientation
Personal brand
Personal network
Political orientation
Quid pro quo sexual harassment
Sexual harassment
Strategic ambiguity
Supportive communication
Upward communication

Study Questions

1. An organization with this orientation generates and distributes power and control within society.

   a. economic   c. political
   b. pattern maintenance   d. integration

2. Information flows in an organization through patterns of relationships known as

   a. communication networks.
   b. organizational communication.
   c. objective statements.
   d. pattern maintenance.

3. When information is transferred formally between a worker and his or her boss, which type of communication takes place?

   a. horizontal   c. societal
   b. political   d. upward

4. When preparing for and taking part in an interview, you should

   a. dress a bit more casually than you expect the interviewer to dress.
   b. ignore the job description, because the interviewer will tell you about the job's duties.
   c. avoid using strong eye contact.
   d. ask and answer questions effectively and ethically.

5. Which workplace communication competence category includes behaviors surrounding giving and receiving feedback?

   a. organizing
   b. immediacy
   c. relationship maintenance
   d. information sharing

6. By smiling, gesturing, and using facial expressions in the workplace to create perceptions of psychological closeness with others, you are enacting

   a. immediacy.
   b. management.
   c. ambiguity.
   d. preparation.

7. Which technique of conflict management is used to maintain relationship harmony but stifles creative dialogue and decision making?

   a. compromise
   b. accommodation
   c. avoidance
   d. collaboration

8. Customer service representatives may use which of the following compliance-gaining strategies, in which the representative implies that it is immoral not to comply?

   a. promises   c. pre-giving
   b. threats   d. moral appeals

9. Conflict in the workplace can be

   a. destructive.   c. neither a nor b.
   b. productive.   d. both a and b.

10. If your boss tells you that you can leave work early on Fridays if you go on a date with him or her, he or she is utilizing a type of sexual harassment called

   a. quid pro quo sexual harassment.
   b. hostile work environment sexual harassment.
   c. emotional labor.
   d. nothing; it is not sexual harassment.

connect

To maximize your study time, check out CONNECT to access the SmartBook study module for this chapter, watch videos, and explore other resources.

Answers:

1. (c); 2. (a); 3. (d); 4. (d); 5. (d); 6. (a); 7. (b); 8. (d); 9. (d); 10. (a)

Critical Thinking

1. Pick one of your friends and analyze several months of his or her social media presence. Based on your review, what would you identify as the attributes, values, and principles that define your friend's observable personal brand. What feedback would you provide your friend to work toward improving his or her brand?

2. Think about some of your past jobs. In the workplace, did people display immediacy, supportiveness, strategic ambiguity, or interaction management? What did they do to demonstrate these behaviors? What conflict management skills did your supervisors use? Were they successful?

Sizing Things Up Scoring and Interpretation

Conflict in the Workplace

People have different natural orientations toward how conflict should be resolved. Although most people adapt to their circumstances to select approaches to conflict resolution, predispositions might make some options more likely than others. The Conflict in the Workplace Scale assesses your predispositions toward five approaches for managing conflict.

You should sum and average responses to determine scores for each one of the five dimensions:

- *Avoidance*: attempting to deny the existence of conflict; items 3, 9, and 12

- *Competition*: viewing conflict as a battle; items 1, 8, and 15

- *Compromise*: being willing to negotiate away some things if others will as well; items 5, 7, and 11

- *Accommodation*: setting aside your views and accepting the views of another; items 2, 6, and 14

- *Collaboration*: using dialogue to reach a mutually beneficial solution; items 4, 10, and 13

As worded, this scale can be used to assess a general predisposition toward conflict resolution. You can adapt the scale by tying it to various scenarios of conflict to determine whether approaches toward conflict resolution differ from situation to situation or because of the source of conflict, and so on. For example, you could complete the scale once when thinking about conflict with your roommate and again when thinking about conflict with your parents or another family member.

References

1. Women's Initiative. (2015, March 6). George W. Bush Presidential Center. Available from http://www.bushcenter.org/womens-initiative/womens-initiative-fellowship

2. Davis, J. (2012, October). School enrollment and work status: 2011. U.S. Census Bureau. Available from http://www.census.gov/prod/2013pubs/acsbr11-14.pdf

3. Parsons, T. (1963). *Structure and process in modern societies.* New York: Free Press.

4. Small Business Administration. (2014, March). Frequently asked questions. Available from https://www.sba.gov/sites/default/files/FAQ_March_2014_0.pdf

5. Ballotpedia. (2015, April 16). List of political parties in the United States. Available from http://ballotpedia.org/List_of_political_parties_in_the_United_States

6. Stohl, C. (1995). *Organizational communication: Connectedness in action.* Thousand Oaks, CA: Sage. (p. 18)

7. Susskind, A. M., Schwartz, D. F., Richards, W. D., & Johnson, J. D., (2005). Evolution and diffusion of the Michigan State University tradition of organizational communication network research. *Communication Studies, 56,* 397–418.

8. Fay, M. J., & Kline, S. L. (2011). Coworker relationships and informal communication in high-intensity telecommuting. *Journal of Applied Communication Research, 39,* 144–163.

9. Caudron, S. (1998). They hear it through the grapevine. *Workforce, 77,* 25–27.

10. Monge, P., Heiss, B., & Margolin, D. (2008). Communication network evolution in organizational communities. *Communication Theory, 18,* 449–477.

11. Bureau of Labor Statistics. (2013, December 19). Employment projections: 2012–2022 summary. Available from http://www.bls.gov/news.release/ecopro.nr0.htm

12. See Boase, J. (2008). Personal networks and the personal communication system. *Information, Communication & Society, 11,* 490–508.

13. Bureau of Labor Statistics. (2011, June 6). *National Longitudinal Survey of Youth.* Available from http://www.bls.gov/nls/nlsy79.htm

14. Krizan, A., Merrier, P., & Jones, C. (2002). *Business communication* (5th ed.). Cincinnati: South-Western.

15. Wright, E. W., Domagalski, T. A., & Collins, R. (2011). Improving employee selection with a revised resume format. *Business Communication Quarterly, 74,* 272–286.

16. Henricks, M. (2000). *Kinko's guide to the winning résumé.* United States of America: Kinko's.

17. Ibid.

18. Bennett, S. (2005). *The elements of résumé style: Essential rules and eye-opening advice for writing résumés and cover letters that work.* New York: AMACOM.

19. Amare, N., & Manning, A. (2009). Writing for the robot: How employer search tools have influenced resume rhetoric and ethics. *Business Communication Quarterly, 72,* 35–60.

20. Henricks, *Kinko's guide to the winning résumé.*

21. Schullery, N. M., Ickes, L., & Schullery, S. E. (2009). Employer preferences for résumés and cover letters. *Business Communication Quarterly, 72,* 163–176.

22. Belicove, M. E. (2011, March). The master of your domain. *Entrepreneur, 39,* 58.

23. Lipovsky, C. (2006). Candidates' negotiation of their expertise in job interviews. *Journal of Pragmatics, 38,* 1147–1174.

24. Young, M. J., Behnke, R. R., & Mann, Y. M. (2004). Anxiety patterns in employment interviews. *Communication Reports, 17,* 49–57.

25. See, for example, Tey, C., Ang, S., & Van Dyne, L. (2006). Personality, biographical characteristics, and job interview success: A longitudinal study of the mediating effects of interviewing self-efficacy and the moderating effects of internal locus of causality. *Journal of Applied Psychology, 91,* 446–454.

26. Lawsuit free hiring: The 5 laws you need to know & 4 steps you need to take. (2010, January). *HR Specialist: Employment Law, 40,* 4.

27. Keyton, J., Caputo, J. M., Fore, E. A., Fu, R., Leibowitz, S. A., Liu, T., . . . & Wu, C. (2013). Investigating verbal workplace communication behaviors. *Journal of Business Communication, 50,* 152–169.

28. Teven, J. J., McCroskey, J. C., & Richmond, V. P. (2006). Communication correlates of perceived Machiavellianism of supervisors: Communication orientations and outcomes. *Communication Quarterly, 54,* 127–142.

29. Lee, D. & LaRose, R. (2011). The impact of personalized social cues of immediacy on consumers' information disclosure: A social cognitive approach. *CyberPsychology, Behavior, & Social Networking, 14,* 337–343.

30. Hopkins, K. M. (2001). Manager intervention with troubled supervisors: Help and support at the top. *Management Communication Quarterly, 15,* 83–99.

31. Albrecht, T. L., & Bach, B. W. (1997). *Communication in complex organizations: A relational approach.* New York: Harcourt Brace.

32. Eisenberg, E. M. (1984). Ambiguity as strategy in organizational communication. *Communication Monographs, 51,* 227–242.

33. Wilmot, W. W., & Hocker, J. L. (2005). *Interpersonal conflict* (7th ed.). New York: McGraw-Hill.

34. Bitner, M. J., Booms, B. H., & Tetreault, M. S. (1990). The service encounter: Diagnosing favorable and unfavorable incidents. *Journal of Marketing, 54,* 71–84. (p. 71)

35. Waldron, V. R. (1994). Once more, with feeling: Reconsidering the role of emotion in work. In S. A. Deetz (Ed.), *Communication yearbook* (Vol. 17, pp. 388–416). Thousand Oaks, CA: Sage.

36. Murphy, A. (2001). The flight attendant dilemma: An analysis of communication and sensemaking during in-flight emergencies. *Journal of Applied Communication Research, 29,* 30–53.

37. Rafeili, A., & Sutton, R. I. (1990). Busy stores and demanding customers: How do they affect the display of positive emotion? *Academy of Management Journal, 33,* 623–637.

38. Hochschild, A. (1983). *The managed heart: Commercialization of human feeling.* Berkeley: University of California Press.

39. Tracy, S. (2005). Locking up emotion: Moving beyond dissonance for understanding emotional labor discomfort. *Communication Monographs, 72,* 261–283.

40. Infante, D., Riddle, B., Horvath, G., & Tumlin, S. (1992). Verbal aggressiveness: Messages and reasons. *Communication Quarterly, 40,* 116–126.

41. Herschovis, M. S. (2011). "Incivility, social undermining, bullying . . oh my!": A call to reconcile constructs within workplace aggression research. *Journal of Organizational Behavior, 32,* 499–519.

42. Amare & Manning, Writing for the robot.

43. Equal Employment Opportunity Commission. (n.d.). *Sexual Harrassment*. Available from http://www.eeoc.gov/laws/types/sexual_harassment.cfm

44. Solomon, D., & Williams, A. (1997). Perceptions of social-sexual communication at work: The effects of message, situation, and observer characteristics on judgments of sexual harassment. *Journal of Applied Communication Research, 25,* 196–216.

45. Bennett, S. (2013, October 16). 92% of companies use social media for recruitment. Social Times [blog]. Adweek.com. Available from http://www.adweek.com/socialtimes/social-media-recruiting/492059?red=at

© Mike Kemp/Getty Images

understanding communication apprehension

Jeff Butler, University of Central Florida

When you have read and thought about this chapter, you will be able to:

1. Understand the differences between normal anxiety and communication apprehension.

2. Identify and explain the four potential causes of communication apprehension.

3. Understand how culture can affect a person's level of communication apprehension.

4. Identify the current research findings regarding high communication apprehension and academics.

5. Understand and use the skills that have been shown to reduce the effects of communication apprehension.

Communication apprehension can affect all areas of our lives–academic, personal and professional. This chapter will introduce you to this common phobia, and explain the differences between communication apprehension and normal speaker anxiety. Next, it will examine some of the causes of communication apprehension, including genetic and environmental factors, cultural influences and personality traits. Then, it will discuss the effects it has on your academic career. Finally, you will learn some skills to reduce communication apprehension.

Normal Speaker Anxiety

This chapter is about a common phobia called communication apprehension. Before discussing details about this phobia, it's important that we distinguish between normal anxiety and communication apprehension.

Most people, even experienced communicators, feel some anxiety before (or during) a speech, presentation, or even just a normal conversation with someone new. This anxiety often takes the form of "butterflies" in your stomach, a quaver in your voice, or adrenaline—induced symptoms such as trembling hands or increased heart rate. These symptoms are usually comparatively mild and typically diminish. They're a bit like the chill you feel when you first jump into the water when you go swimming. It's a little uncomfortable at first, but the discomfort fades quickly. Most of the American population experiences some form of this mild anxiety in some circumstances. If these symptoms are similar to how you have felt, then you have experienced normal levels of anxiety about communication. The rest of this chapter will focus on the more severe form of anxiety called "communication apprehension."

Even if you don't experience communication apprehension yourself, you will encounter people who do. Consequently, the rest of this chapter should prove valuable because it promotes an understanding of this common phenomenon. Such an understanding is important for two reasons. First, we often discount other people's phobias. A common reaction to another person's report of extreme nervousness about communicating is the reply, "Oh yeah, I get nervous, too." Non-phobic individuals who make this or a similar response often think they feel the same way as a genuine apprehensive, but they don't. Think of your own worst phobia (for me, it's fear of heights). Perhaps you're afraid of flying, or snakes, or clowns. The stark terror these phobias inspire in affected persons is the same way most high apprehensives feel about communicating with others. It's not mild anxiety, it's gut-wrenching fear, and people who are not apprehensive need to understand how truly traumatic that fear is.

Second, forcing someone who is phobic about communicating with others into a situation where they must interact can actually increase the intensity of their phobia. This is important in light of another common response to persons who experience communication apprehension. Often, victims of apprehension are urged to "just do it." While this sort of sink-or-swim approach may work for some activities, it usually doesn't work for high apprehensives and can make the apprehension worse. I often wonder how much damage has been caused by well-intentioned instructors who forced apprehensive students to "get up there like everyone else." High apprehension can often be overcome through the use of techniques discussed later in this chapter, but forcing someone to speak when they're afraid is usually ineffective and often counterproductive.

What Is Communication Apprehension?

Communication apprehension (CA) is a type of anxiety that involves the fear and avoidance of communication with other people (McCroskey, 1993). It's widespread, with various surveys identifying components of CA, such as fear of public speaking, as the most common phobia in the United States (Motley, 1997). Millions of Americans experience some form of CA. In fact, about 16% of the American population experiences anxiety based on high levels of communication apprehension (Daly & McCroskey, 1984).

communication apprehension
Fear and avoidance of communication with other people.

Communication apprehension has many forms. For example, some people don't usually feel nervous about speaking, but may find a specific situation threatening. Such a person might normally feel comfortable talking with a supervisor, but would be anxious about conversing with that supervisor during an annual evaluation. Others might be relaxed during normal conversations but experience anxiety about a forthcoming public speech. In contrast to these situation—specific forms of CA, other people experience **generalized anxiety** about almost all communication in almost all settings with almost all people (Daly & McCroskey, 1984). This generalized anxiety is regarded as the most serious form of CA.

generalized anxiety
Feelings of anxiety associated with communication in nearly all situations.

While, this chapter focuses primarily on anxiety related to oral presentations, please remember this fear is only one aspect of the phenomenon we label "communication apprehension." In other words, CA is not just a new term for "stage fright." It encompasses a fear of public speaking, but it also includes anxiety about other communication settings and situations.

What Are the Causes of Communication Apprehension?

The cause of communication apprehension is the subject of considerable debate among communication scholars. Although individual researchers may support certain causes and disagree with others, most would agree that the available evidence centers around four potential causes of apprehension: genetic contributors, environmental reinforcers, personality traits, and cultural factors.

GENETIC CONTRIBUTORS

communibiology
The study of the biological bases of human communication.

Researchers subscribing to **communibiology** as a cause of anxiety suggest that CA may have a predominantly hereditary basis. Citing studies of identical twins who were raised together and comparing them with identical twins who were separated at birth, they have discovered commonalities in personality and behavior which suggest people may inherit preferences (temperaments) to behave in certain ways. Temperament traits don't mandate specific behaviors (you aren't genetically destined for a certain occupation, for example), but combinations of inherited proclivities may exert powerful influences on our behavioral preferences. A person who inherits a tendency to be high in extraversion and low in self-doubt, for example, is unlikely to experience CA, while someone who has inherited high introversion and high self-doubt has a higher probability of feeling anxiety about communicating (Beatty, McCroskey, & Valenic, 2001). Communibiology is the newest research category and probably the most controversial, but it raises legitimate questions about the role of **genetic contributors** in human behavior.

ENVIRONMENTAL REINFORCERS

genetic contributors
Combinations of inherited tendencies that may exert influences on our behavioral preferences.

environmental reinforcers
Factors within our environment that contribute to our fear of speaking.

Rewards, punishments, and negative **environmental reinforcers** are also likely contributors to communication apprehension. Researchers who believe that environmental factors contribute to the fear of communicating with others suggest that behavior that is rewarded is likely to be repeated while behavior that is punished will be decreased or extinguished (Richmond & McCroskey, 1998). Consider two children raised in different environments. Rita was raised in a home where communication was encouraged and rewarded. Since her communication ability was reinforced, she improved her communication skills. Rita would be an unlikely candidate for high CA. Burt, on the other hand, was raised to believe that "children should be seen, not heard." His early attempts at communication were criticized and ridiculed. Since Burt's communication behavior was punished, he engaged in less of it and did not develop into a competent communicator. Because competence and confidence are often linked together, Burt would be more likely to develop high communication apprehension.

Another environmental contributor to communication apprehension involves uncertainty about the outcome of communication. **Learned helplessness** occurs if a person'scommunication behavior is rewarded one time and punished the next, since it makes it difficult for that person to predict the consequences of communication (Richmond & McCroskey, 1998). Poor Jim never knew what reaction he would receive when he talked to his mother. One day he would be told how smart he was, and the next he would be called "stupid" and told to keep his mouth shut. Since he couldn't predict the outcome of his communication behavior, he withdrew from communication whenever possible. Because he withdrew, he failed to develop skill and confidence in his communication ability. These circumstances placed Jim at risk for developing high CA.

Researchers who believe environmental factors are primary contributors to communication apprehension probably represent the majority of communication scholars. Still, their findings are sometimes questioned because they offer only a partial explanation for the overall cause of communication apprehension. Critics argue that even their best research accounts for only a comparatively small percentage of the reasons people experience CA (Beatty, et al., 2001).

learned helplessness
A person feels unable to predict whether a behavior will result in a reward or punishment, therefore he or she avoids the behavior all together if possible.

PERSONALITY TRAITS

Certain personality traits appear to be associated with high CA. When researchers compared mean scores of groups of people with high CA with mean scores of groups of people with low CA, they found high CAs tended to have lower tolerance for uncertainty, less self-control, less adventurousness, lower emotional maturity, higher introversion, lower self-esteem, and lower assertiveness (Richmond & McCroskey, 1998).

These results should be interpreted carefully. First, correlation alone can never imply causality. Sometimes something that is correlated with something else is actually a casual factor (people who smoke are more likely to develop cancer because cigarette smoking is one of the causes of lung cancer), but other times two phenomena can occur together and have nothing to do with each other (every serial killer in history has had a mother, but it does not follow that motherhood causes serial killers). Since all the research cited in this section is correlational, it would be dangerous to imply causality. Consider the research on high communication apprehension and self-esteem, for example. When researchers suggest a correlation between low self-esteem and high CA, we don't really know if low self-esteem causes high CA, high CA causes low self-esteem, some other factor causes both of them, or whether they occurred together but are totally unrelated.

Questions can also be raised about the framework of comparison used for this research. Although most researchers tend to view high CAs as disadvantaged when compared to their low CA counterparts, an equally good argument is that low CAs are uniquely gifted, and high CAs are no different in personality than the normal population. There is credible research in support of this argument (Butler, 1986).

CULTURAL FACTORS

Scholars of intercultural communication argue that the culture in which we are raised can affect our level of CA. These researchers suggest that some cultures, such as those found in many Asian, Arab, and some South American countries, are comparatively collectivistic. **Collectivistic cultures** tend to discourage individual assertiveness and stress group harmony. Other cultures, such as those found in the United States and other western countries, are comparatively **individualistic cultures**,

collectivistic cultures
Cultures that discourage individual assertiveness and stress group harmony.

individualistic cultures
Societies that stress individual assertiveness over group harmony.

Communication apprehension is serious and can have a negative impact on your academic career.
© Andersen Ross/Blend Images LLC

stressing individual assertiveness over group harmony. A growing body of research suggests a strong correlation between high CA and collectivistic cultures, probably because collectivistic cultures discourage assertiveness and often value silence (Zhang, Butler, & Pryor, 1996; Sarquisse, Butler, & Pryor, 2003).

SUMMARY: CAUSES OF COMMUNICATION APPREHENSION

Most communication researchers would agree that the factors discussed in this section represent significant contributors to high communication apprehension, but many would argue over which factors are most predominant. Controversies such as these are characteristic of scientific inquiry, since competing claims are tested against each other until research reveals which are most strongly supported by the evidence.

Please also note that the above categories are not necessarily discrete. Culture, for example, can be viewed as a part of one's environment, and personality characteristics may contain an hereditary component. Nevertheless, most researchers would agree that heredity, environment, personality, and culture all contribute to communication apprehension.

What Are the Effects of Communication Apprehension?

The effects of communication apprehension have been widely studied, with research results generally painting a gloomy picture of the effects of high CA. These effects are widespread, affecting people in virtually every aspect of their lives, including self-perception, relationships, work satisfaction, occupational choices, and academic success (Daly & McCroskey, 1984).

Since this chapter is designed for college students, academic effects will be primarily emphasized. Persons curious about effects unrelated to the classroom should consult the references cited above for a more comprehensive review. From an academic standpoint, high communication apprehension appears to be detrimental to success. Some of its specific effects are described below.

CA AND STANDARDIZED TEST SCORES

Although research has revealed no significant difference in intelligence between high and low CAs, scores on standardized tests such as the ACT tend to be significantly lower for high CAs than for their low CA counterparts (Daly & McCroskey, 1984).

CA AND GRADES

Some (but not all) studies have found that high CAs have lower mean grade point averages than low CAs. This is particularly true in courses that require oral participation (Daly & McCroskey, 1984).

CA AND CLASS SELECTION

High and low CAs differ in their choice of classes. Low CAs prefer small classes with lots of participation while high CAs prefer large classes with little participation

(Daly & McCroskey, 1984). High CAs also tend to select classes where they can use their seating preferences to avoid communication. While most low CAs choose seats in the front, middle section of a typical classroom, high CAs tend to select seats that are out of the instructor's normal zone of participation, such as seats in the back or on the sides of the room (Daly & McCroskey, 1984).

High CAs try to avoid classes that involve group projects and discussions. When they are required to take such classes, they choose obscure seating positions and minimize participation. Their comments are often irrelevant, and they seldom disagree with other group members. They are also less likely to engage in productive brainstorming (Daly & McCroskey, 1994).

CA AND COLLEGE GRADUATION

Perhaps as a result of the factors discussed earlier in this section, graduation rates for high CAs are lower than those for low CAs. Research by Ericson and Gardner (1992), for example, found that "high communication apprehensives had tendencies to not complete their degrees" (p. 132). In fact, 50% of the high apprehensives they studied failed to graduate, and incoming freshmen with high CA were more likely to drop out of school than those with low CA.

SUMMARY: EFFECTS OF COMMUNICATION APPREHENSION

Research on the academic effects of high CA paints a bleak picture for those affected by this form of anxiety. Highly apprehensive students have comparatively lower test scores, grades, and graduation rates than their low apprehension counterparts. In spite of these findings, high CA students can take encouragement from three observations.

First, remember the previously cited research was comparative in nature. For example, high CAs have lower grades only when compared with low CAs. Such a comparison *could* demonstrate that low CAs average uniquely high grades—not that high CAs average uniquely low grades. A more telling comparison could have been made by comparing the mean GPAs of high and low CAs with the GPAs of students with normal levels of apprehension, but such comparisons were not examined in the research cited in this section. This lack of data makes it hard to determine whether high CAs are truly disadvantaged.

Second, the research cited in this section draws its conclusions by comparing mean group scores and is not designed to be applied to individual students. Pretend, for example, that researchers compare groups of engineering majors and computer science majors and conclude that engineering majors have higher mean IQ scores than computer science majors. Would this research prove that every engineering major is smarter than every computer science major? Of course not! In spite of the differences in group means, there would still be plenty of engineering majors with low scores, and lots of computer science majors with high scores. Research conducted on groups simply can't be generalized to individuals, and those who make such generalizations are committing a classic research fallacy known as the ecological fallacy. Conclusion? Even though mean group GPAs differ, there are still plenty of high CA students with excellent grades.

Third, the negative effects of high communication apprehension can be mitigated. The next section will discuss ways individual students can reduce their anxiety. These are methods I have used and found to be effective in nearly two decades of working with highly apprehensive students.

How Do We Reduce the Effects of Communication Apprehension?

There are a number of different strategies for reducing high communication apprehension. We will concentrate on the ones that do not require professional supervision and that have proven effective for most high CA students.

USE POSITIVE SELF-TALK

self-talk
Silent communications with oneself that influence our perceptions of reality.

negative self-talk
Destructive self-criticism.

The first strategy focuses on a phenomenon called **self-talk.** We probably talk to ourselves more than we talk to other people, and the nature of our self-talk often influences our perceptions of reality. Researchers have discovered that persons with high communication apprehension often engage in **negative self-talk,** which is critical and negative (Bullard & Carroll, 1993). When thinking about a forthcoming speech for example, high CAs often bombard themselves with criticism. Typical thoughts include, "My speech will be boring," "People will think I'm stupid," or "I'll lose my place and people will laugh at me." Unfortunately, thoughts like these can easily turn into self-fulfilling prophecies, so many high CAs literally become their own worst enemies.

From a physiological standpoint, the thoughts we have about ourselves trigger interesting reactions in our brains. Physicists who study electrical activity in the human brain report that thoughts about ourselves trigger up to 100 times more neuronal firings than random thoughts, and thoughts about ourselves spoken out loud generate up to 1,000 times more neuronal firings than random thoughts (Bullard & Carroll, 1993). In other words, our brains devote considerable energy to processing our self-talk, especially when we say things about ourselves out loud. When we talk, our brains listen.

Most high CAs who engage in negative self-talk learned this self-destructive habit from someone else, usually parents, teachers, or even friends. Unfortunately, many high CAs incorporate these descriptions by others into their self-perceptions and come to believe that that's just the way they are. Then they perpetuate their negative self-images by engaging in self-criticism and self-doubt. Over time, these people *become* their own negative descriptions. If you call yourself a loser enough times, chances are you will become what you say you are.

Luckily, self-talk doesn't have to be negative. Furthermore, *you* are in charge of how you talk to yourself! Picture yourself walking across campus. As you walk, you encounter a friend who greets you. Undoubtedly, you will respond with a "good morning" or some similar greeting instead of something that makes no sense. "Good morning" is seldom followed with a nonsensical response like "prune juice for dinner." This illustration is silly, but it makes a crucial point, namely that you are in charge of what you say to other people. You have the ability to control your conversational responses. You also have the power to control what you say to yourself! If you are busily talking yourself into being a poor communicator, there is only one person on the planet who can reverse that trend. You see that person every time you look into the mirror.

This is not to suggest that reversing negative self-talk is easy. Old habits are hard to break—but they can be broken. The next time that inner voice tells you you're a loser, tell it to shut up! Replace negative self-descriptions with **positive self-talk.** Think, "I am an interesting person," or "People will enjoy what I have to say." Better yet, say these things to yourself out loud (your car is a good place for this, even if other drivers think you are crazy). Remember, when you speak, your brain listens, and you—not old habits—are in charge of what you say.

USE POSITIVE VISUALIZATION

Positive self-talk mainly affects the verbal areas of the brain. Other parts of the brain are primarily influenced by visual images. Consequently, we can influence our visual perceptions with visualized images. One could label these images **proactive imagination.** Things that we imagine can have a very real impact on how our brain processes information. Remember, your brain receives visual data only in the form of electrical impulses, and these impulses seem real to your brain whether they come from actual or imagined events. That's why movies (or nightmares) can trigger strong emotional and physical responses in us even though nothing "real" is actually happening.

Many athletes use visualization to improve their game.

© MichaelSvoboda/ Getty Images

You can use this property of your brain to help overcome high CA. Let's say you are giving a speech. Picture yourself speaking confidently to a smiling, interested audience. Visualize yourself giving an articulate, informative presentation—the more detail, the better. Combining visualization with self-talk allows you to positively influence both the visual and verbal areas of your brain. Visualization is best practiced with your eyes closed while you are lying down. Closing your eyes helps eliminate most competing visual information, so it is easier for you to picture what you are trying to proactively imagine (Bullard & Carroll, 1993). It's also a good idea to prepare a "script" to guide your visualization (Bullard & Carroll, 1993). You might picture yourself standing and walking to the front of the room, then visualize yourself speaking articulately to a smiling, interested audience. Visualization is a powerful technique for reducing high CA, especially when used in conjunction with positive self-talk.

UTILIZE KINESIC INPUTS

Kinesics is the study of body movement and facial expressions. Researchers who investigate the impact of kinesics on our moods have made an interesting discovery: our facial expressions can influence how we feel. Most of us think that facial expressions are usually the result of our feelings, and we're right. In general, expressions are the result, not the cause, of emotions. But nonverbal reactions also perform a second, more subtle function. In addition to reflecting our feelings, they also influence them. Communication researchers have discovered that changing facial expressions can alter our state of mind (Kleinke, Peterson, & Rutledge, 1998). High CAs can use this discovery to their advantage. Never mind how you feel inside, when it's your turn to give a speech, interact with a group, or meet with your professor, smile, and walkconfidently into the room, and then sound and act as if you are interested in your topic. You can literally reduce some of your anxiety by acting confidently.

Changing your facial expressions can alter your state of mind. Smile!

© Shutterstock/ SnowWhiteimages

kinesics
The study of body movement and facial expressions.

CHANGE YOUR PERSPECTIVE

Remember the last time you watched individual competitive events like diving or figure skating during the Olympics? The contestant would finish and then nervously wait for his or her evaluation. Eventually, the judges would each hold up a card with a number on it and the numbers would be tallied for a final score. That system works fine for Olympic competition, but it can't accurately be applied to many speaking situations. The trouble is that some high CAs don't realize that. Consider the plight of Sally, who needed to give a presentation to her classmates.

Poor Sally regarded her audience as a group of critics. She felt they were keenly focusing on every word she said and every movement she made. Any tiny error she committed would be recorded and deducted from her score. Since she regarded her audience as a group of hostile critics, she anticipated her presentation with trepidation.

Sally's classmate, Burt, cultivated a different attitude about his presentation. Instead of regarding it as a performance, he saw it as an opportunity to share information about his topic with his audience. He was excited to exchange information about his home state of Ohio and his favorite football team, the Buckeyes, with his classmates, and pictured them not as critics, but as interested receivers of his message. Burt wanted to do a good job, but he recognized that most human communication contains a few errors and figured that if he made a mistake, his audience would get over it. He wasn't too worried about his upcoming presentation.

As you can see from these examples, your attitude about the purpose of any presentation and the role of the audience can play a significant part in how much anxiety you feel. If you have unrealistic attitudes about your job as a presenter or the perspective of the audience, you will probably experience increased anxiety.

Let's go back and analyze Sally's position. Sally's first mistake was to regard her presentation as a performance. The truth is that most contemporary presentations don't sound much like rehearsed performances; they are more like enlarged conversations. In the early days of our country, speeches were seen as entertainment, and speakers were applauded for their oratorical skills. Renowned speakers like Daniel Webster and William O. Douglas gave flawless, moving performances—some over three hours long. We still have vestiges of that style. You see it in a few evangelists, and in the State of the Union Address. Most speeches though, are comparatively informal. Think of a presidential news conference, a Pentagon briefing, or a college lecture. These events just *aren't* performances.

Sally's second mistake involved her misinterpretation of the audience's expectations. As you listen to other student's presentations, monitor your own attentiveness and behavior. Are you listening with critical attention, ready to pounce on the smallest error, or are you listening in a more detached way, trying to understand the main points the speaker is trying to make? In fact, do you really care all that much about what the other speakers are saying at all? How much time do you spend agonizing over other students' presentations out of class? Do you discuss them in detail with your friends or lay awake at night thinking about them? Probably not.

The bottom line is this: most of your small mistakes will hardly be noticed by your classmates, and even if you really blow it, other people won't think about it all that much. Thinking otherwise places you in an imaginary world—a place where presentations are like theater performances and audiences are like predatory tigers ready to pounce.

Sally's classmate, Burt, was considerably closer to the truth. He recognized that if he offered his audience interesting, relevant information, delivered with reasonable articulation and enthusiasm, he would probably be okay. When it comes to your perspective on communication, you want to be more like Burt than Sally.

BE PREPARED

This section is last because it is probably the least important component of anxiety reduction for high CAs. Still, it deserves some consideration. Most anxiety doesn't seem to be linked to how well prepared a person is. You may recall that lack of preparation was not one of things discussed in the *Causes of Communication Apprehension* section of this chapter. There are two ways, however, that lack of preparation can lead to increased apprehension.

First, a person who is already nervous certainly doesn't need any additional negative baggage. In other words, if the poor guy is predisposed to be anxious about communicating, comes from a background that was punishing and critical, has personality characteristics associated with apprehension, and comes from a culture that discourages speaking, he sure doesn't need anything else to contribute to his anxiety. Being unprepared can do just that. I have won state championships for college impromptu and extemporaneous speaking (never mind what year), yet I still feel a little nervousness when I'm unprepared, so pity the poor high CA who is unprepared.

Second, one specific type of nervousness is clearly linked to the lack of preparation. Although it may sound tautological, lack of preparation definitely leads to nervousness about not being prepared. I personally cherish the fine art of procrastination and am an ardent practitioner, but if you're already nervous, putting off preparing for a presentation is a poor move. Likewise, if you have a meeting, you might benefit by finding out as much as you can about the people you'll be meeting with. Think about the kinds of questions they might ask you and then prepare some answers for those questions. If you're going to an interview, have a mock interview with a friend to prepare. All of these activities can ease your anxiety.

From the Author: *Some Final Thoughts for Persons Who Experience High Communication Apprehension*

Please don't mistake these suggestions about coping with apprehension for a panacea. The solutions offered here are the best answers we currently have, but they aren't miracle cures. There are at least three problems with what I've suggested.

First, the solutions I've proposed usually reduce apprehension, but they seldom eliminate it. If you experience uncommonly high anxiety about communicating with others, the methods I've discussed should lower your discomfort to tolerable levels, but you'll still probably experience some nervousness. Ideally, I'd like to offer you a method that would completely eliminate your discomfort, but it's probably more realistic for you to expect to reduce it. Even a *reduction* in anxiety can be important. It can make a significant difference in your college grades, your career success, and your relationships after you graduate.

Second, reducing anxiety can be a slow process. Don't expect one week of positive self-talk and proactive imagination to undo years of habituated anxiety. Your nervousness will decrease gradually, and you may not experience a meaningful decline in it for a while. Anxiety reduction is a bit like working out or losing weight. It works, but it's slow.

Third, these methods won't work effectively for everyone. Over the years, I've known a few people (probably fewer than 5% of my high CA students) who diligently used the methods I've recommended without much effect. These students lie at the extreme end of the high CA spectrum. They're the people who can't sleep for days prior to giving a speech, become physically ill before class, pass out while speaking, and repeatedly register for and then drop the basic speech class. I had one student who dropped the course three times before I met him.

If you think you are one of the students who fall into this extreme category, I strongly urge you to consider seeking professional assistance. This may sound like an extreme solution to overcoming apprehension, especially since college is so filled with short-term deadlines and obligations that it's hard to think of long-term consequences. When I admitted that we can't always help people with extremely high CA, I was speaking with a degree of candor that you don't often find in college texts or popular self-improvement manuals. I'm speaking with that same blunt honesty now. The consequences of high CA reach far beyond your college education. In this chapter, I restricted my discussion of the results of high communication apprehension to the college environment, partly because a complete discussion would have at least doubled the length of this chapter, but mostly because I didn't want to bury you under an avalanche of bad news. I won't bury you now either, but I want to make it abundantly clear that communication apprehension affects more things—and bigger things—than a few college classes. People with extremely high communication apprehension don't do well in relationships, in employment, in life. High CA is seriously bad stuff, and deciding to "just live with it" should only be a last ditch option. I'm not overstating when I say that if you don't overcome it now, you may pay for it for the rest of your life.

In the end, more than anything else, it comes down to courage. Are you going to give in to the apprehension monkey on your back, or are you going to go to war with it? The war isn't easy, but you'll carry the consequences of your choice for the rest of your life. Both Abraham Lincoln and Winston Churchill suffered from high communication apprehension. If they had lacked the courage to overcome it, I wonder if their names would mean anything to us today.

Make good choices and don't give up. And remember that you have plenty of good resources at your disposal—your instructors, your friends and fellow classmates are all there to help you. Good luck!

JUST B-R-E-A-T-H-E!
By Shari Hodgson

According to the National Association of Colleges and Employers (2009), the number one skill on employers' wish lists for college graduates is the ability to effectively speak publically. Unfortunately, speaking publically is also the number one fear of most people (Motley, 1997). While teaching public speaking at the University of Central Florida, I have helped students cope and reduce their speaker anxiety by incorporating a systematic process called "BREATHE" while preparing for speech assignments.

The B-R-E-A-T-H-E Process
B = Brain and the F.E.A.R. (false evidence appearing real) response process

More than 100 billion nerve cells comprise a network of neural pathways that begin the process of everything we think, feel and do (LeDoux, 1991). The brain's fear response is autonomic so we don't know what's happening until it is too late to reduce (Behnke & Sawyer, 1999). The following sequence exhibits the physical phenomenon on our body during the fear response.

When you experience fear, the blood rushes to the parts of the brain that alert the body to take action; NOT, to the part of the brain that remembers your speech. To reduce this effect, you must **reframe** the way to think of yourself and the public speaking situation to reduce fear and produce successful results.

Shari Hodgson has been an instructor at UCF, Nicholson School of Communication, since 1990 as an Associate Instructor. She has taught several courses in Interpersonal and Organizational Communication, as well as the basic public speaking course. Ms. Hodgson has also been a private consultant to businesses and attorneys.

© Courtesy of Shari Hodgson

Parts of the Brain Involved in Fear Response

R = Reframe with new thoughts

You may not always choose <u>what</u> situations you face but you can choose <u>how</u> you will experience these situations. Your beliefs about giving a speech are scaring you, NOT, the actual upcoming speech event (Lefkoe, 2001). Your thoughts create your feelings that trigger actions that will lead to your demise.

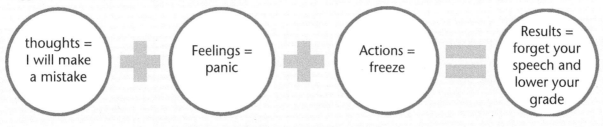

As you plan and practice your speech, use this 4-step process to help you **reframe** your thinking.

1. First, acknowledge you're fear thoughts and think, "Wow, I just scared myself."

2. Second, accept that these thoughts are based on old beliefs about being judged or ridiculed and think, "Is this fear really real for the speech situation today?"

3. Third, know that you have new skills and say, "I am prepared and ready to speak!"

4. Fourth, state these new beliefs and repeat 10 times a day, "I am a good speaker!" With this new thought your results will begin to change. Confident people simply *believe* that they are competent. While you are reframing old beliefs into new beliefs, you can further manage the brain's fear response by **envisioning** yourself as successful.

E = Envision yourself successful by reprogramming your brain

The next two techniques will help you reprogram the old vision of making mistakes during your speech to seeing yourself successful and confident (Bandler & Grinder, 1981).

1. *Relaxation Techniques:* Get into a relaxed state, preferably with eyes closed and in a quiet place. REPEAT the new message you used when reframing your thoughts, "I am prepared and excited about..." Because you are relaxed, the new message is programmed directly to your sub-conscious mind. When you associate this positive message with speaking, the message will work at a deeper internal level to quickly alleviate your anxiety and increase your chances for success and a higher grade. (Lefkoe, 2001).

2. *Natural Programming:* Every day of your life you go through some natural programming of your brain. Can you ever get away from the messages constantly transmitted by the media, music, texting, your friends, family, and school outcomes? This constant barrage may be preventing you from engaging in the process of thinking positively about yourself. Monitor the messages you are listening and programming into your brain. By more carefully selecting messages, you will naturally create new positive thought patterns. However, this reprogramming does take **practice and repetition** (Butler, Chapman, Forman, & Beck, 2006).

A = Apply through practice

Repetition of a skill causes the brain to assign extra neurons to the practice of this skill (Sousa, 2001) much the same way that a computer assigns more memory for more complex software. If you want your speaking ability to improve, you will need to practice your speeches in a way that increases the effectiveness of your practice sessions. Here are a few tips:

1. Be motivated to practice and plan. I recommend 15 practice sessions and in front of classmates!

2. Your instructor will provide you with a grading rubric. Use this rubric to develop speech content and evaluate your progress during practice sessions.

3. Know what extemporaneous delivery components are required and practice <u>all</u> of them. For example, if your speech requires that you use PowerPoint or another visual aid, make sure you include appropriate gestures and movement associated with PowerPoint in your practice.

4. Get help and appropriate feedback to help you analyze your practice progress. Practice with classmates familiar with speech requirements and able to give constructive criticism that ***tests*** your level of anxiety.

T = Test your plan for speech day

Test all of your speech day activities to reduce any unexpected disasters. Plan your clothing, complete your note cards, and check your PPT slides the night before speaking. On the day of your speech, plan extra time for traveling to class. While in route, practice your new *positive self-talk and visualize* yourself giving a successful speech. When you arrive, check the classroom technology.

H = Handle your negative thoughts

But what if things don't go exactly as planned? Even the most planned speeches are not perfect. *While you are waiting to speak,* remember to reprogram your negative thoughts to positive: "I am prepared and excited about giving my speech. *During the speech* if something unexpected happens, acknowledge it and remind yourself: "No one knows what I don't know and I am well prepared." *After your speech*, if you think negative self-talk like, "I forgot my facts and looked dumb," *immediately reframe and repeat* positive thoughts: "I enjoyed giving my speech and I did my best. "No matter what happens, *CELEBRATE yourself*. Repeat this statement 15 times: "I did the best job possible when giving my speech!"

E = End your fear cycle

By understanding your brain's fear response, reframing your thoughts, envisioning your success, applying yourself through practice, testing your speech plan, and handling *negative thoughts* before, during and after your speech, you can end the fear response cycle. You will actually change your brain and reduce your fear of the public speaking experience.

(NOTE: If you experience severe symptoms of anxiety such as shortness of breath, disorientation, heart palpitations, numbness, or nausea you may suffer from 'communication apprehension' which is estimated to affect about 16% of the American population. Communication Apprehension (CA) sometimes extends to other speaking situations like meeting new people or participating in class discussions. A Self-Assessment of CA and an in-depth discussion of possible causes and coping strategies.)

Chapter Review & Study Guide

Summary

In this chapter you learned the following:

1. Communication apprehension is a type of anxiety involving the fear of communicating with others. It is not the same as normal speaker anxiety that many people have when they give presentations.

2. Most communication scholars agree that there are four potential causes of communication apprehension: genetic contributors, environmental reinforcers, personality traits, and cultural factors.

3. While communication apprehension impacts all areas of life, it affects student's academic careers in several ways.

   - High CAs tend to have lower scores in standardized tests, for example the ACT.

   - High CAs tend to have lower GPAs.

   - High CAs prefer larger classes that require little or no participation.

   - College graduation rates are lower for people with high communication apprehension

4. There are several strategies students can employ to manage communication apprehension.

   - Changing self-talk from positive to negative influences your perception of yourself as a communicator.

   - Visualizing yourself giving a successful presentation is especially effective when used in conjunction with positive self-talk.

   - Looking and acting confident, regardless of how you feel, can reduce some of your anxiety.

- Perfection is rarely expected. Allowing yourself to be human and understanding that the people you're communicating with are not looking for every little mistake you make will change your attitude toward communication.

- Not being prepared can raise your level of anxiety. It's wise to plan ahead for any presentation.

- Although deciding to tackle your fear of communication may seem daunting, your efforts will benefit you for the rest of your life.

5. There are many good reasons to study and practice public speaking. Among them are these:

   - Personal reasons, including personal satisfaction, empowering yourself and others.

   - Professional reasons, including self-promotion, presenting ideas to decision makers, creating positive change in the workplace, and contributing worthwhile ideas in meetings.

Key Terms

Collectivistic cultures
Communibiology
Communication apprehension
Cultural factors
Environmental reinforcers

Generalized anxiety
Genetic contributors
Individualistic cultures
Kenesics
Learned helplessness

Negative self-talk
Positive self-talk
Proactive imagination
Self-talk

Study Questions

1. A quavering voice, shaking hands, increased heart rate and the feeling of "butterflies" in your stomach are all symptoms of

   a. Communication apprehension.
   b. Positive visualization.
   c. Communibiology.
   d. Normal speaker anxiety.

2. A person who is _____ in extraversion and _____ in self-doubt is unlikely to experience communication apprehension.

   a. High, high.
   b. High, low.
   c. Low, high.
   d. Low, low.

3. Which of the following occurs when a person's communication behaviors are rewarded one time and punished the next?

   a. Learned helplessness.
   b. Proactive imagination.
   c. Increased self-esteem.
   d. Positive self-talk.

4. Students with high communication apprehension

   a. Prefer smaller classes.
   b. Usually disagree with others in group discussions.
   c. Have lower graduation rates.
   d. Have higher scores on standardized tests.

5. Collectivist cultures

   a. Usually have lower levels of communication apprehension than individualistic cultures.
   b. Encourage assertiveness.
   c. Are more likely to engage in positive self-talk.
   d. Value group harmony

6. If you imagine yourself delivering a successful presentation, you are engaging in

   a. Kinesics.
   b. Positive visualization.
   c. Self-talk.
   d. Environmental reinforcement.

7. Which of the following does not contribute to high communication apprehension?

   a. Environmental factors.
   b. Genetic contributors.
   c. Proactive imagination.
   d. Personality traits.

8. Which of the following is true of kinesics?

   a. Our nonverbal reactions can influence our feelings.
   b. Our facial expressions have no impact on communication apprehension.
   c. Acting confidently will not change how you feel about communication apprehension.
   d. Changing facial expressions only help if you are interacting with individualistic cultures.

Answers:
1. (d); 2. (b); 3. (a); 4. (c); 5. (d); 6. (b); 7. (c); 8. (a)

Critical Thinking

1. Take the self-assessment survey called the Personal Report of Public Speaking Anxiety found online at: www.jamescmccroskey.com/measures/prpsa.htm What are your scores? Do they accurately represent your levels of communication apprehension?

2. Based on what you have learned in this chapter, what are some specific steps you can take to prepare for your next presentation?

References

1. Bandler, R., & Grinder, J. (1981). TRANCE-formations: *Neuro-Linguistic Programming and the structure of Hypnosis.* Salt Lake City, UT: Real People Press.

2. Beatty, M. J., McCroskey, J. C., & Valenic, K. (2001). *The biology of communication: A communibiological perspective.* Cresskill, NJ: Hampton Press.

3. Behnke, R. R., and Sawyer, C. R. (1999). The prediction of a state of uneasiness as perceived by individuals. *Journal of Applied Communication, 8,* 98–102.

4. Bullard, B., & Carnol, K. (1993). *Communicating from the inside out.* Dubuque, Iowa: Kendall/Hunt.

5. Butler, A. C., Chapman, J. D., Forman, E. M., & Beck, A. T. (2006). The empirical status of cognitive-behavioral therapy, *Clinical Psychology Review, 26,* 17–31.

6. Butler, J. F. (1986). Personality characteristics of subjects high and low in apprehension about communication. *Perceptual and Motor Skills, 62,* 895–898.

7. Cameron-Bandler, L., Gordan, D., & Lebeau, M. (1985). *The Emprint Method: a Guide to Reproducing Competence.* San Rafael, CA: The Future Press.

8. Clements, K., and Turpin, G. (1996) Physiological effects of public speaking assessed using a measure of palmar sweating. *Journal of Psychophysiology, 10,* 238–290.

9. Daly, J. A., & McCroskey, J. C. (1984). *Avoiding communication.* Beverly Hills, CA: Sage.

10. Ericson, P. M., & Gardner, J. W. (1992). Two longitudinal studies of communication apprehension and its e ects on college students' success. *Communication quarterly, 40,* 127–137.

11. "Fear and the Amygdala," http://www.sfn.org. Society for Neuroscience: *Brain Briefings. Web. 10 December 2010.*

12. Kleinke, C. L., Peterson, T. R., & Rutledge, T. R. (1998). E ects of self generated facial expressions on mood. *Journal of Personality and Social Psychology, 74,* 272–279.

13. *LeDoux, J. (1991). Emotion and the limbic system concept. Concepts in Neuroscience, 2, 169–99.*

14. *Lefkoe, M. (2001a). Behavior change doesn't have to be difficult. California Psychologist, 34, 24–25.*

15. *Lefkoe, M. (2001b). Everyone knows that you can't eliminate fundamental beliefs: are you sure? California Therapist, May, 54–60.*

16. McCroskey, J. C. (1993). *An introduction to rhetorical communication,* 6th ed. Englewood Cli s, NJ: Prentice-Hall.

17. Motley, M. T. (1997). *Overcoming your fear of public speaking: a proven method.* Boston, MA: Houghton Mifflin.

18. NACE (2009). *Employers site qualities, attributes of "perfect" job candidate.* Retrieved December 10, from http://www.naceweb.org/Press/Release/Employers.

19. Richmond, V. P., & McCroskey, J. C. (1998). *Communication: Apprehension, avoidance, and e effectiveness,* 5th ed. Boston, MA: Allyn and Bacon.

20. Richmond, V. P., & McCroskey, J. C., (1995). *Communication: Apprehension, avoidance, and effectiveness* (4th Ed.). Scottsdale, AZ: Gorsuch Scarisbrick.

21. Sarquisse, V., Butler, J., & Pryor, B. (2003). A comparison of communication apprehension scores between Americans and Argentineans. *North American Journal of Psychology, 5,* 223–228.

22. Sousa, D. (2001). How the Brain Learns (2nd ed.). Thousand Oaks, CA: Sage.

23. Zang, Y., Butler, J., & Pryor, B. (1996). A comparison of apprehension about communication in China and the United States. *Perceptual and Motor Skills, 82,* 1168–1170.

© Marc Romanelli/Blend Images LLC

being credible and using evidence

When you have read and thought about this chapter, you will be able to

1. Explain the importance of source credibility in public presentations.

2. Use four dimensions of credibility to improve how audience members perceive you.

3. Develop a research strategy for finding support for your presentation.

4. Use research to identify eight types of supporting materials for your ideas.

5. Correctly attribute information to sources, both verbally and in writing.

6. Ground your use of credibility and supporting materials in core ethical principles surrounding honesty.

Effective public presentations are an artfully drafted combination of you, your ideas, and the ideas and opinions of others. How you present yourself, your ideas, and your evidence will determine how much trust the audience places in the points you make. In this chapter you will learn about source credibility and the ways that you can increase your credibility by using strong evidence.

In September 2014, actor Emma Watson delivered an address at the United Nations in support of the HeForShe campaign. The worldwide campaign promoted solidarity between men and women in support of gender equality, an end to gender-based discrimination, and an end to violence against women and girls. Watson's challenge was to establish common ground with men and boys whom she was asking to support the movement. Without such common ground, her message would likely lack impact and could potentially alienate those she was trying to reach.

Midway through her speech, Watson addressed this issue directly by saying:

© Getty Images/Wavebreak Media

> We don't often talk about men being imprisoned by gender stereotypes, but I can see that they are. . . . If men don't have to be aggressive in order to be accepted, women won't feel compelled to be submissive. . . . If we stop defining each other by what we are not and start defining each other by what we are—we can all be freer, and this is what HeForShe is about.[1]

In this message, Watson was able to broaden gender stereotypes to be relevant to both men and women. In so doing, she was able to establish common ground with male listeners and create a sincere message—that both men and women need to be part of the solution in promoting equality and freedom of opportunity for all. Watson was more credible as a result.

This chapter will help you learn various strategies, like using common ground, to establish your credibility as a speaker.

Source Credibility and Its Importance

The most important resource you have for convincing an audience is yourself. Audiences do not want to hear from someone they do not trust or respect. They will not listen to or retain information from someone who has not earned the right to talk about that subject. Finding ways to convince your audience that you are trustworthy and qualified is among the most important objectives for any speaker. In the public speaking classroom you are the source of the message. You need to be concerned about your **source credibility**—the audience's perception of your effectiveness as a speaker. You may feel that you do not have the same credibility as a high public official, a great authority on a topic, or an expert in a narrow field. Nonetheless, you can be a very credible source to your classmates, colleagues, or friends. Source credibility is not something a speaker possesses, like a suit of clothes. Instead, the audience determines credibility. Credibility is like many other subjective perceptions—just as each person might have a slightly different impression of whether a song is good, each person may also have a slightly different perception of a speaker's credibility.

source credibility
The audience's perception of your effectiveness as a speaker.

College students can use their personal experiences to establish credibility. For instance, a soldier who served as a medic could establish strong credibility to speak on medical issues.
© DoD photo by Lt. Col. Leslie Pratt, U.S. Air Force

As you begin thinking about how you can convince audience members of your credibility, consider the following questions you need to specifically address during your presentation:

- What are your motives for speaking on this topic?
- Why are you qualified to speak on this topic?
- What work have you done to ensure that your information is correct?
- In what ways will the audience benefit from your information?
- Why did you choose to present the information in the way that you did?
- What are you *not* telling the audience, and does omitting that information create an unbalanced or biased perspective?

These questions are not a checklist you should run through as you speak. Effective speakers find ways to address these questions more subtly, through the natural course of their presentation. The results add up to the kind of credibility that means audience members are more likely to trust and respect what the speaker has to say.

Credibility is a challenging issue for beginning speakers. Whereas highly experienced speakers typically have a lifetime of experience from which to establish credibility, most college students lack significant expertise on many topics. Fortunately, students can establish credibility through their sincerity and goodwill, resources available to anyone. And credibility is essential. If you have it, the audience will listen and likely remember much of what you say; speakers who lack or fail to establish credibility during their presentation have little chance of having any impact other than boredom.

The audience's perception of a speaker's credibility arises from a combination of factors, including the speaker, the topic, the situation, and the message. Focusing for a moment on the speaker, have you served in the armed forces overseas? You may have earned the right to speak on national defense, the price of being in the National Guard, and the inside story of war. Did you grow up in another country? You may have earned the right to speak on that country's culture, food, or customs. Your qualifications influence the audience's perceptions about your credibility.

How do you establish your qualifications? Students often state that they have done research on the topic—usually a heavy dose of the first three to five hits on Google. Do you think that makes them credible? Probably not. Rather than relying on "I did research," a sincere statement about why you are interested in a particular topic might be convincing for a group of peers in a college classroom. The same approach may not suffice if you are giving the same speech to a group of community activists or business professionals. What it takes to be credible depends on the audience you are addressing, so you'll want to anticipate what each audience will expect.

A final factor influencing your credibility is your message. It should be obvious that a poorly conceived message will lack credibility. Besides relying on research, therefore, you should also focus on relevance. Messages that are connected to the lives of your audience will be perceived as more credible than messages they see as unimportant or disconnected.[2] Stated simply, if audience members perceive the topic as important, they are more likely to perceive you as important and therefore credible.

Dimensions of Credibility

What do audience members perceive that signals speaker credibility? If individuals in the audience base credibility on judgments, what is the basis for those judgments? On what will your classmates be rating you when they judge your credibility? According to research, four of the most important dimensions of credibility are competence, trustworthiness, dynamism, and common ground. Three of these relate to you, the speaker.

COMPETENCE

The first aspect of credibility is **competence**—the degree to which a speaker is perceived as skilled, qualified, experienced, authoritative, reliable, and informed. A speaker does not have to live up to all these adjectives; any one of them, or a few, might make the speaker credible. A machinist who displays her metalwork in a speech about junk sculpture as art is as credible as a biblical scholar demonstrating his ability to interpret scripture. They have different bases for their competence, but both can demonstrate expertise in their areas of specialization.

Words, skillful use of technology, and an air of authority convey your own competence as a speaker. What can you build into your speech that will help the audience perceive your competence? What experience have you had that is related to the subject? What training or knowledge do you have? How can you suggest to your audience that you have earned the right to speak about the subject? The most obvious way is to tell the audience of your expertise, but a creative speaker can think of dozens of ways to hint and suggest competence without being explicit and without seeming arrogant.

There are several things you can do to improve your competence as a speaker. First, you should become familiar enough with your information and speech that you do not have to rely on extensive notes. Constantly referring to notes for every point can lead audience members to perceive that you really do not understand the information. Second, focus on translating ideas. If you are able to take relatively complex ideas and make them understandable for audience members by using metaphors, vivid descriptions, visual aids, and other resources, you will appear more competent. Third, make yourself comfortable with the speaking situation. If you plan to use technology, make sure that you know how to use the computer, the software, and other resources. Finally, audience members will perceive you as more competent if you deliver the speech well (see the chapter on delivery and visual resources).

TRUSTWORTHINESS

The second aspect of credibility is **trustworthiness**—the degree to which a speaker is perceived as honest, fair, sincere, friendly, honorable, and kind. These perceptions are also earned. We judge people's honesty by their past behaviors and whether we perceive them to have

competence
The degree to which the speaker is perceived as skilled, qualified, experienced, authoritative, reliable, and informed; an aspect of credibility.

trustworthiness
The degree to which the speaker is perceived as honest, fair, sincere, friendly, honorable, and kind; an aspect of credibility.

goodwill toward their listeners. In a study exploring perceived credibility of the 2008 presidential candidates, communication researcher Jason Teven found that goodwill was the strongest predictor of perceived credibility among the leading candidates in the primary elections.[3] So, too, your classmates will judge your trustworthiness based on how you represent your past behaviors and establish goodwill.

You may have to reveal to your audience why you are trustworthy. Have you held jobs that demanded honesty and responsibility? Have you been a cashier, a bank teller, or a supervisor? Have you given up anything to demonstrate you are sincere? The person who pays his or her own way through college ordinarily has to be very sincere about education. Being respectful of others' points of view can be a sign of fairness. What can you say or do that signals trustworthiness?

Trustworthiness and goodwill are difficult to establish in a short speech. After all, the trust we give to others typically develops after we have known them for some time. During a speech, both what you say and how you say it can affect audience members' perceptions of your trustworthiness. First, you should take care to present fair and balanced information. Using reliable sources and presenting other viewpoints can show audience members that the conclusions you draw are accurate. Talking with a confident tone and maintaining eye contact are also important tools in building trust at the beginning of your speech.

DYNAMISM

The third aspect of credibility is **dynamism**—the extent to which an audience perceives the speaker as bold, active, energetic, strong, empathic, and assertive. Audiences value behavior described by these adjectives. Perhaps when we consider their opposites—timid, tired, and meek—we can see why dynamism is attractive. People who exude energy and show the passion of their convictions impress others. Watch television evangelists and note how they look and sound. You can learn to be dynamic. Evidence indicates that the audience's perception of your dynamism will enhance your credibility.

dynamism
The extent to which the speaker is perceived as bold, active, energetic, strong, empathic, and assertive; an aspect of credibility.

Dynamism is exhibited mainly by voice, movement, facial expressions, and gestures. A person who speaks forcefully and rapidly and with considerable vocal variety; a speaker who moves toward the audience, back behind the lectern, and over to the visual aid; and a speaker who uses facial expressions and gestures to make a point are all exhibiting dynamism. What can you do with your voice, movement, facial expressions, and gestures to show the audience you are a dynamic speaker?

COMMON GROUND

Common ground occurs when you and your audience share an understanding of the world, either in broad terms or in relationship to specific issues.[4] Common ground comes about in two ways. First, you and your audience might share common ground prior to your speech. If you have significant commonality—you are similar in age, you have the same general education level, or you have similar socioeconomic backgrounds—you are likely to have much in common. Common ground is also created through the act of communicating. As you begin to speak, you express a certain way of looking at the world or a particular topic. Do you take a stance on whether there is too much national debt? Do you assume people value health over personal freedom? As you present information, you begin staking claims

building **behaviors**

Establishing Common Ground with Classmates

Common ground is best established when you can show relationships between yourself, your audience, and the topic, as illustrated in figure 1. Using knowledge of your classmates, list ideas that could establish common ground. For example, if giving a speech on the need for increased state support for education funding, you could point out that you and your classmates share in the experience of needing to pay higher and higher tuition bills.

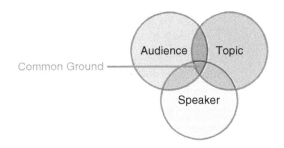

Figure 1

Common ground is best established when you can show connections between the topic, your audience, and yourself.

for particular ways of thinking about issues. In so doing, you will establish greater common ground with some audience members and reduce it with others.

Making a connection with your audience can mean simply establishing a shared trajectory—showing that we are all doing something together. In a March 2011 speech at an awards ceremony for young scientists, Mary Sue Coleman established common ground in this way:

> *America has long been recognized as a global leader in science and technology. But we know . . . that our nation is slipping in how we prepare and nurture the talent of tomorrow. Your hard work shows us what is possible. . . . Your ideas and theories are going to lead our country to new cures, solutions and technologies. That is why I am so happy to be here tonight: to congratulate you, encourage you, and provide a little advice about being a scientist in a country that absolutely must place more value on discovery, innovation and the creation of new knowledge.[5]*

Speaking as a scientist, Coleman was able to create common ground with her audience by pointing to a shared objective—to elevate the training of future scientists. Coleman's approach recognized that she and her audience, who were not yet in college, let alone college presidents, would share a perspective at some future time when the students matured into scientists like her. Her approach established common ground in the present by pointing to where her audience would eventually be. Other approaches to building common ground can include pointing to past shared experiences or present shared circumstances.

STRATEGIES FOR IMPROVING CREDIBILITY

Credibility is influenced by topics, messages, audiences, and circumstances. You may hold the speaker in high regard before the speech, but during the speech your perception of him or her may diminish, and then after the speech you may think better of the speaker again because you decide the message has merit. Here are practical approaches for improving your credibility during your presentation:

- Speeches with higher-quality arguments convey more credibility on the speaker.[6] Be sure to carefully research your topic and use sound reasoning.

- Sometimes a **sleeper effect** occurs when source and message get separated in the listener's mind over time: a low-credibility speaker's message can gain influence, whereas a high-credibility speaker's message

common ground
The degree to which the speaker's values, beliefs, attitudes, and interests are shared with the audience; an aspect of credibilty.

sleeper effect
A change of audience opinion caused by the separation of the message content from its source over a period of time.

· What actions did the Occupy Wall Street protesters engage in that helped or hurt their credibility?

© Erica Simone Leeds

can diminish long after a particular message.[7] Crafting a clear and persuasive message can help capitalize on the possibility of a positive sleeper effect.

- Self-disclosure can increase credibility, even through mechanisms such as Facebook;[8] however, inappropriate self-disclosure can harm it. Use self-disclosure appropriate to the topic, and don't overrely on it.

- Speakers who appear younger may be perceived as less credible than those who appear older.[9] Dress professionally when speaking to help increase your perceived age.

- Presenting a message that favors one side of an issue often looks like bias to listeners, resulting in lower perceived credibility.[10] Present a balanced representation of issues, even if you personally take a stand on one side.

- People who are perceived to use referent and expert power are seen as more competent, trustworthy, and likable.[11] Build rapport with your audience, and stress your personal knowledge of and careful research on the topic (see the chapter on small-group communication).

- Speaking with fluency can increase perceptions of credibility, including competence, character, and caring.[12] Take care to speak at a moderate pace, enunciate your words, and practice your delivery.

- Your use of evidence, the audience's perception of the topic's importance, and your competence as a speaker interact to influence your credibility. Reinard and Myers found that, although the use of any type of evidence increases your credibility, the effects are even greater when the audience perceives the topic to be important and you to be competent.[13]

- When someone else introduces you to your audience, the timing and content of the introduction are important to your credibility. Mike Allen and colleagues found that, if you do not have automatic credibility based on your qualifications, it may be best to delay letting the audience know your qualifications until after you have spoken.[14]

Orally Citing Sources, by Christine Hanlon

Why Cite Sources?

There are several reasons why we should cite sources. According to Carol Bledsoe (former Coordinator of public speaking at University of Central Florida), there are three main reasons why we should cite sources:

- To establish credentials of the source and the data
- To enable the audience to retrieve the material
- To give credit to others

Establishing the Credentials of the Source and the Data

The first reason we should cite sources is to establish the credentials of the source and the data. If we, the audience, do not know why the source is credible, why should we believe that the information is valid? Let's take the following excerpt from a speech as an example:

According to the CDC, there weren't any monkey pox cases in the United States until the 2003 outbreak.

The speaker has identified the CDC as the source of the data. Although many of us in the United States know that "CDC" is the acronym for Centers for Disease Control, you cannot assume that everyone is familiar with it. If you want to use the acronym for an organization, be sure to first identify what that acronym stands for. For example, state "the Centers for Disease Control, also known as the CDC . . ." Analyzing your audience will help you to determine if there is a time when you can break this rule. There will be times in the workplace when you will use acronyms. However, if you are ever in doubt, explain the acronym so your audience understands it.

Furthermore, there may be audience members who don't know what the CDC is. Be sure to briefly explain the purpose of the organization so your audience understands why the source is credible. Using this example, an appropriate explanation of the CDC could be, "The CDC is the United States' lead federal agency that investigates health problems and conducts research to prevent infectious diseases." Again, you want to analyze your audience to determine if an explanation is necessary.

Enabling the Audience to Retrieve the Material

By indicating where you found the information, you can enable the audience to retrieve the material. In the previous example, the speaker did not clarify where the information about the CDC was located. Was the information located on the CDC's official Web site or in a pamphlet distributed by the CDC, or did it come directly from a researcher who works for the CDC? To enable the audience to retrieve the material, speakers need to be clear about where the information can be found. Let's take some of these examples individually.

Where the information was found	Oral citation that enables the audience to retrieve the material
CDC's official Web site	"According to the CDC's Monkey pox factsheet posted online . . ."
CDC pamphlet	"The CDC's pamphlet entitled 'Tuberculosis: What you need to know' states that . . ."
Researcher who works for the CDC	"In a recent study, CDC researcher Jane Smith found that. . ."

Giving Credit to Others

It is important to give credit to others for their ideas. Many academics and scientists consider their ideas, their intellectual property, as their greatest contribution. There is even an international organization that works to uphold worldwide standards for intellectual property. According to the World Intellectual Property Organization (2004), "these works— intellectual property—are expanding the bounds of science and technology and enriching the world of the arts." If you use others' ideas during your presentation and fail to cite them, you are essentially *stealing* the ideas of others. There are two important reasons why you should orally cite your sources while presenting speeches, and they are both directly tied to credibility. Failing to cite a source can decrease your credibility, whereas orally citing a source can add to your credibility as a speaker.

There can be serious consequences for speakers who fail to orally cite their sources properly. First, they can be charged with plagiarism. Whenever students fail to orally cite a source in a speech, they are guilty of plagiarism. The reality is that there are consequences to plagiarism, whether or not it was intentional. The bottom line is always to orally cite your sources so you can avoid the situation altogether.

Christine Hanlon (Ph.D., University of Central Florida) is a public speaking instructor at the University of Central Florida's Nicholson School of Communication. She is also a past president of the Florida Communication Association. Her research interests include family violence and popular culture. She has presented scholarly papers at regional and national conferences for communication, sociology, women's studies, and popular culture associations. Additionally, she has published in past volumes of *Teaching Ideas for the Basic Communication Course*.

Adapted from Christine Hanlon, "Speaking of . . . Orally Citing Sources." Between One and Many, Nicholson School Edition, McGraw-Hill. Reprinted by permission of Christine Hanlon.

How to Be Strategic in Finding Information

Your credibility is determined, in part, by your delivery. Credibility is also influenced by the quality of the information you present in the speech. To build your credibility, audience members must perceive that you have selected and presented high-quality information to support your ideas. This section helps you better understand the process through which you develop and implement a research strategy for your presentations.

PRINCIPLES FOR EFFECTIVE RESEARCH

Students at all levels generally understand that research is important. Few recognize that research is the foundation for everything else you do in your speech. Table1 analyzes how a good research plan can help nearly every aspect of the speechmaking process, even delivery. This section explains approaches you should embrace and those you should avoid when planning your research strategy.

Refine Your Topic

Poor research strategies often result from poorly worded thesis statements or vague ideas for topics. Take time to think carefully about what your topic is and how others might think of it. After collecting some initial research, do you have information that might help you narrow your topic further? Finding ways to reduce the amount of information you need to review and evaluate will speed up your workflow and help you find higher-quality sources.

Think of Research as a Process

Experts rarely assume they have many answers. In fact, many professors who conduct research will claim that at the conclusion of a research project they have more questions than answers. You should embrace the same philosophy when conducting research. Start early, research repeatedly while integrating ideas into your presentation, then do more research, and so on. Waiting until the last minute to start your research, viewing it as just another hoop to jump through for your assignment, locks you into an outcome of ineffective research.

Use a Variety of Sources

Not all sources tell you the same thing. On any given speech topic—global poverty, for example—you can obtain information from each type of source: personal experience, library resources, the Internet, and even personal interviews. Each type of source will yield a different type of information. Personal experience might tell you how poverty is felt in our

Table 1 Research and the Speech Preparation Process

Preparation Step	Benefit of Research
1. Selecting a topic	Research helps you discover and narrow topics.
2. Organizing ideas	Research helps you identify main and subordinate points.
3. Researching support materials	Research provides facts, examples, definitions, and other forms of support to give substance to your points.
4. Preparing an introduction and a conclusion	Research may reveal interesting examples, stories, or quotes to begin or end the speech.
5. Practicing and delivering the speech	Because your speech is well researched, you will feel more confident and will seem more credible.

own lives, either directly or indirectly; magazine and newspaper articles might give general background about regions where poverty is most rampant; scientific journals might provide detailed statistics showing how poverty is linked to disease, famine, and even conflict; and webpages might describe groups committed to reducing poverty and its effects.

When devising your research plan, be committed to locating a variety of types of sources. Using only Google will skew your research base to certain types of information while excluding others. Likewise, finding one really good book on poverty and relying only on that resource will limit the details you can integrate into your presentation. Using table 3 (presented later in the chapter) as a guide, try to locate one of each type of source on your topic. Does this seem like a lot of work? Maybe, but given the importance of research to your success in this class and well into the future, the effort will pay off.

heuristics
Mental shortcuts used to make decisions—for instance, evaluating sources.

• Start your research early and use more than one source. Research is a process, not a step.
© Image Source/Getty Images RF

Evaluate Sources Carefully

Merely finding sources does not ensure that you have effectively researched your speech. Regardless of what type of source you have found, apply critical criteria to evaluate its quality. Table 2 describes several **heuristics,** or *mental shortcuts,* that people use when evaluating sources. Using these is definitely better than simply selecting the first five sources from a Google search. For instance, a poorly constructed site or sloppy article could be indicative of sloppy work overall, so the aesthetic appeal heuristic, though weak, could be useful. However, these shortcuts can lead to faulty conclusions about the quality of any given source and should not be used alone.

Rather than using shortcuts, try these more robust criteria for evaluating sources of all types:

1. *Is the supporting material clear?* Does the source present information in a clear and simple manner? Sources that lack clarity could indicate a lack of true understanding on the part of the creator.

Table 2 Heuristics Used by College Students to Evaluate Research

Heuristic	Description
1. Reputation	Trusting a source because it has a recognizable name or brand (For example, you might trust CNN because it is a large media organization.)
2. Endorsements	Believing information because others say it is believable (For example, you might trust a source because reader comments attached to a story are positive.)
3. Consistency	Trusting one source because it says something similar to what other sources say (For example, you might believe one website because another website says the same thing.)
4. Expectancy violation	Mistrusting a source because it says something contrary to what you thought or contrary to what other sources say
5. Persuasive intent	Mistrusting a source because it makes an obvious attempt to be persuasive
6. Aesthetic appeal	Trusting a source because it is well designed and visually appealing

Source: Items 1–5 are adapted from Metzger, M. J., Flanagan, A. J., & Medders, R. B. (2010). Social and heuristic approaches to credibility evaluation online. *Journal of Communication, 60,* 413–439.

2. *Is the supporting material verifiable?* Whereas the consistency heuristic simply suggests that sources are OK if they all say the same thing, verifiability means that you can confirm the source's facts and details. In journalism this process is called *independent verification,* meaning you can confirm details independently from the source you are using.

3. *Is the source of the supporting material competent?* For each source you should be able to determine qualifications. If your source is a person, what expertise does the person have in the topic? If your source is an organization, what connection does the organization have to the issue? For instance, would you trust a statement on a small business website supporting conceal and carry laws? Your answer might depend on the type of small business and its connection to the issue.

4. *Is the source objective?* All sources—even news reports—have some sort of bias. The National Rifle Association has a bias against gun control; Greenpeace has a bias in favor of environmental protections; TV news programs have a bias toward vivid visual imagery. What biases do your sources have, and how might those biases affect the way the source frames information?

5. *Is the supporting material relevant?* Loading your speech with irrelevant sources might make it *seem* well researched; however, critical listeners will see through this tactic. Include only sources that directly address the key points you want to make.

6. *Is the supporting material current?* Knowledge changes on a daily basis. What we thought was true about the war on drugs, the Internet, health, and the economy a few years ago is now irrelevant. Use older sources sparingly, and attempt to find up-to-date information.[15]

These criteria are not yes or no questions. Sources will meet some criteria well and fail others. Your job as speaker is to weigh the benefits and drawbacks of each source and determine whether to include it in your speech. Indeed, you have an ethical responsibility to carefully evaluate your sources.

LOCATING INFORMATION FOR YOUR PRESENTATION

Although audience members look at several factors to determine your credibility, you have control over only some of them. For instance, you can practice your delivery to avoid mispronunciations, you can work to improve your gestures, and you can take care to create a well-organized speech. In addition, you can improve your own credibility by borrowing on the credibility of others. In this section you will learn how to conduct research and gather supporting material from personal experience, other people, written and visual resources, and the Internet. We also show how to evaluate those sources and use them effectively in your speeches.

Personal Experience

personal experience
Your own life as a source of information.

The first place you should look for materials for the content of your speech is within yourself. Your **personal experience**—your own life as a source of information—is something about which you can speak with considerable authority. One student had been a "headhunter," a person who finds employees for employers willing to pay a premium for specific kinds of workers. This student gave a speech from his personal experience concerning what employers particularly value in employees. Another student had a brother who was autistic. In her informative speech she explained what autism is and how autistic children can grow up to be self-reliant and successful. Your special causes, jobs, and family can provide you with firsthand information to use in your speech.

However, you should ask yourself some critical questions about your personal experience before you use it in your speech. Some experiences may be too personal or too intimate to share with strangers or even classmates. Others may be interesting but irrelevant to the topic of your speech. You can evaluate your personal experience as evidence, or as data on which proof may be based, by asking yourself the following questions:

1. Was my experience typical?
2. Was my experience so typical that it will bore an audience?
3. Was my experience so atypical that it was a chance occurrence?
4. Was my experience so personal and revealing that the audience may feel uncomfortable?
5. Was my experience one that this audience will appreciate or from which this audience can learn a lesson?
6. Does my experience really constitute proof or evidence of anything?

Also consider the ethics of using your personal experience in a speech. Will your message harm others? Is the experience your own or someone else's? Experience that is not firsthand is probably questionable, because information about others' experiences often becomes distorted as the message is passed from one person to another. Unless the experience is your own, you may find yourself passing along a falsehood.

Other People

Speakers often overlook the most obvious sources of information—the people around them. The easiest way to secure information from other people is to ask them in an informational interview.

How do you find the right people? Your instructor might have some suggestions about whom to approach. Good and accessible sources of information are professors and administrators who are available on campus. They can be contacted during office hours or by appointment. Government officials, too, have an obligation to be responsive to your questions. Even big business and industrial concerns have public relations offices that can help you with information. Your objective is to find someone, or a few people, who can provide you with the best information in the limited time you have to prepare your speech.

sizing things up

Research Attitudes Scale

You have a variety of sources in which you can locate evidence and information. Read each statement below and respond using the following scale. There are no right or wrong answers to these questions. A guide for interpreting your responses appears at the end of the chapter.

1 = Strongly disagree
2 = Disagree
3 = Neither agree nor disagree
4 = Agree
5 = Strongly agree

1. I feel confident when using the Internet to find good information.
2. I like to use journals to find good articles on a topic.
3. I find it easy to locate good books on a given topic.
4. I have confidence in using reference materials to find good research on topics.
5. I find it easy to locate good popular press articles on topics.
6. I like to look for good books when researching a topic.
7. I find it easy to locate good journal articles on topics.
8. I like to use good reference materials when researching.
9. The Internet is easy to use when looking for good information.
10. I am confident in my abilities to find good popular press articles on topics.
11. I am confident in my ability to find good books on a topic.
12. It is easy to use the reference section in the library to find good information.
13. I like to search for good popular press articles on topics.
14. I like to use the Internet to search for good information.
15. I am confident in my ability to locate good journal articles on a topic.

An interview can be an important and impressive source of information for your speech—if you conduct it properly. After you have carefully selected the person or persons you wish to interview, follow these suggestions:

1. *On first contact with your interviewee or the interviewee's assistant, be honest about your purpose.* For example, you might say, "I want to interview Dr. Schwartz for 10 minutes about the plans for student aid for next year, so that I can share that information with the 20 students in my public speaking class." Notice that this request tells the person how much time the interview will take.

2. *Prepare specific questions for the interview.* Think ahead about exactly what kind of information you will need to satisfy yourself and your audience. Conducting at least some research before the interview is often advisable—you will be able to ask better questions. Keep your list of questions short enough to fit the time limit you have suggested to the interviewee.

3. *Be respectful toward the person you interview.* Remember, the person you interview is doing you a favor. You do not need to question aggressively like a talk show host. Instead, dress appropriately for the person's status, ask your questions politely, and thank your interviewee for granting you an interview.

4. *Tell the interviewee you are going to take notes so you can use the information in your speech.* If you are going to record the interview, you need to ask the interviewee's permission. Be prepared to take notes in case the interviewee does not wish to be recorded. Even if you record the interview, it's a good idea to take notes as a backup in case something happens to the recording.

5. *When you quote the interviewee or paraphrase his or her ideas in your speech, use oral footnotes to indicate where you got the information.* Here's an example: "According to Dr. Fred Schwartz, the director of financial aid, the amount of student financial aid for next year will be slightly less than it was this year."

Sometimes the person you interview will be a good resource for additional information. For example, one student interviewed the director of disability services on campus for her informative speech about learning disabilities. The director not only answered her questions but also gave her an extensive packet of information about the topic. Of course, even with an expert, you should also use other types of resources, so that differing opinions and alternate explanations can be identified.

Written and Visual Resources from the Library

Modern libraries, such as the ones found at most colleges and universities, are portals to digital information. So, rather than helping you find a particular book or article, a **reference librarian**—someone specifically trained to help you locate sources of information—is far more likely to teach you how to use your school's particular library system and one or more of the available electronic databases.

Here are some practical principles of library research that you can adapt to your unique situation:

1. *Start at the center and work your way out.* The reference desk is the practical "center" of your library. To find anything, you will start with a search of some type; the reference desk is there to help you conduct that search, so start by asking for help there. In addition to starting at the center of the library, you should begin by searching at the center of your topic. Following the principle that topics will be

reference librarian
A librarian specifically trained to help you find sources of information.

narrowed as you conduct research, start by researching the broad and typical elements of your topic. As you gain more information, you will be able to narrow your search to more specific (and possibly off-center) aspects of your topic.

2. *Understand that not all sources are equal.* Modern libraries offer access to many different types of sources, ranging from books and academic journals to newspapers and trade magazines. Each will provide you with different types of information, and each will likely be indexed in a different database. Table 3 identifies several different types of sources and suggests how you might use them as evidence. A key principle when conducting good research is that source variety is important—finding and using a variety of types of sources from this list is wise.

3. *Know your databases!* Some university libraries can provide access to hundreds of electronic databases. With so many options, figuring out which databases to use can seem daunting. Following the principle that you should start at the center, generalized databases such as Academic Search Premier and Lexis-Nexis are excellent places to begin. The library computer catalog will also help you locate

Table 3 Types of Sources

Source	Uses
Fiction books	Some plots or characters can be used to illustrate points you are making in your speech.
Nonfiction books	Nonfiction books include historical, political, social, and scientific studies. Research reported in books tends to be very detailed but can also be somewhat out of date.
Academic journal articles	Most academic journal articles undergo careful editorial review and blind peer review, which can help ensure high-quality information. Academic articles tend to report the results of very specific studies.
Government documents	The federal government produces publications ranging from compilations of congressional testimony to the results of million-dollar scientific studies. Many university libraries have a separate department for government documents.
Trade journal articles	Trade journals are targeted toward professionals in a particular profession or discipline. Trade journals tend to be practical but based on solid research.
Reference books	Your library reference department will have a number of reference books ranging from dictionaries and biographies to atlases. Depending on your speech topic, such sources can be very useful.
Encyclopedias	Encyclopedias are excellent places to start researching topics about which you know absolutely nothing. Encyclopedia entries provide short, easy-to-read explanations but tend to be dated and too general.
Magazine articles	Magazine articles provide timely information and tend to provide more in-depth coverage. The disadvantage of magazine articles is that they are typically written by journalists with little or no expertise on the topics they write about.
Newspaper articles	Newspaper articles are among the timeliest sources of print information. Although they are up to date, they are written by journalists who may have little or no expertise on the topics they write about. They also tend to provide few details.
Webpages	Webpages are hard to describe because they come in so many variations. Later you will learn about how to locate effective websites. For now, understand that, although websites provide easy access to current information, the quality of information on the web must always be verified.

Google can be a good starting point for research, but relying only on that resource can limit the types of information that you locate. Using multiple search portals is a better strategy.

books and other resources in your library. Once you have located initial information, you may wish to consult more specific and specialized databases. For example, if you are doing a presentation about a medical topic, you may wish to consult MEDLINE. And if you are doing a persuasive speech, you may wish to consult the Opposing Viewpoints Resource Center to find "pro" and "con" articles on topics ranging from adoption to welfare reform. Remember that the reference librarian is trained to help you select and use the right databases for your topic.

4. *Recognize that good research requires reading, thinking, and doing more research.* Many students assume their research task is over with one quick Google search or a quick trip to the library. Although the "one trip fits all" approach is appealing, it does not work well. Once you have obtained initial research on your topic, the best thing you can do is to spend time reading those sources, revising your outline, and conducting more research to fill in gaps and find more specific information. Good research takes time, but the end result is outstanding evidence that is sure to impress.

The Internet

The Internet has been integrated into nearly every aspect of our lives, appearing on our cell phones, televisions, and even upscale refrigerators. We have access to more information than ever, but not all of it is useful, and filtering through the garbage can be overwhelming.

Good web searches start with a plan, and we provide a general strategy here. Depending on the nature of your topic and your specific assignment, you might need to perform additional steps.

1. *Use search engines and other portals.* A **search engine** is a webpage designed to help you search for information; Google is the prime example. Although search engines will locate thousands of sites that contain the word or phrase you are searching for, they also return hundreds of irrelevant websites. An alternative approach is to use a more specialized search engine. For instance, for some topics Google Scholar might be much better than the standard Google search engine. In addition, there are thousands of other types of information portals on the web. YouTube and TED provide portals for finding video; iTunes is a portal for finding podcasts; and Visual.ly is a portal for interesting information graphics. Using a variety of search engines and other portals can diversify your research base and help you find better information.

   search engine
   A program on the Internet that allows users to search for information.

2. *Refine your search.* Many students assume one search will be sufficient. As you discover more information, try using different combinations of search terms. Sometimes adding a few words or rearranging words can make an important change in what your search engine returns. Also, try using more advanced techniques, such as Boolean operators, to narrow searches. Table 4 provides recommendations on how to more effectively narrow your searches. Searching for information is easy; being smart about your searches is more challenging. Your objective should be to narrow the search until you have separated the junk from the gold.

Table 4 Tools for Narrowing Your Web Search

Type	Description	Example
Exact-word searching	By default, browsers return any webpage containing the word you asked it to search for. For example, if you want to search for the informal speech abbreviation *inform*, the search engine would return sites with the words *informative, information, informal, informing,* and so forth. To prevent this problem, type your search term enclosed in double quotations marks.	*"inform"*
Exact-phrase searching	If you are looking for a phrase, put the phrase in quotation marks. For example, simply typing in *public speaking* would return all sites that contain the two -words anywhere on the site. Placing the phrase in quote marks will return only sites using the phrase.	*"public speaking"*
Excluding terms	Sometimes you may want to search for a word or phrase but, because it is used in multiple contexts, you need to exclude some types of pages. Suppose you wanted to search for the word *apple* with the intention of finding out about the fruit, not the company. One way of accomplishing that search is to type in *apple* followed by words you want to exclude, preceded by minus signs.	*Apple −computer −iPhone −iPad*
Using wildcards	Wildcards, or symbols (usually an asterisk) that stand in for an unknown character, can expand your search. For example, suppose you wanted to search for state laws pertaining to voter registration. You could search for each state separately (e.g., *state of Alaska voter registration laws*), or you could combine the wildcard with quotation marks to search for all states, simultaneously, while keeping your search narrowed to documents containing the exact phrase you are interested in.	*"state of * voter registration laws"*

Source: Adapted from Google (www.google.com/support/websearch/?hl=en).

3. *Evaluate carefully all sources of information found on the Internet,* especially when you use sources outside your university's web domain. Later in the chapter we focus specifically on this issue, but it cannot be stated too many times. The critical skills in research are both locating *and* evaluating sources of information. Perhaps you are picky about your clothes or your food. You should be equally picky about the information you consume and, in this case, serve to others.

Keep in mind that people have different motives for creating webpages. Some websites are intended to be informative, others are intended to persuade, and still others are out to make money. Some are designed to conceal their true motive: a website might look informative but actually tell only part of a story to lure you into making an uninformed decision. One way to understand the motive of websites is to pay attention to the server extension. Figure 2 explains the parts of a web address and the characteristics of web addresses with different server extensions. No single type of web address—based on the server extension— is necessarily better than another. However, you can make initial judgments about the credibility of a site by looking at the extension. Remember that ".com" sites are trying to

Figure 2

Breaking down web addresses.

Elements of a Web Address

http://www.nws.noaa.gov/om/hazstats.shtml

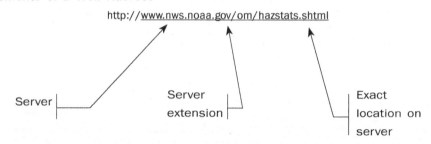

Server | Server extension | Exact location on server

Common Server Extensions

Extension	Description	Example
.edu	Primarily college and university websites	www.ohio.edu website for Ohio University
.com	Primarily commercial or for-profit websites	www.mhhe.com website for McGraw-Hill Higher Education
.gov	Government websites	www.ed.gov website for the U.S. Department of Education
.net	Primarily Internet service provider public sites, sometimes used as an alternative when a ".com" name has already been taken	www.maui.net website for island of Maui Tourism Bureau
.org	Primarily not-for-profit organizations	www.helping.org resource site for volunteerism and nonprofit organizations

make money, ".gov" sites are maintained by the government and are typically oriented toward public service, and ".edu" sites are associated with universities. Although only a start, this information can help you sift through certain types of sites that have the potential to present misleading or even deceptive information.

Types of Supporting Material

Now that you know where to look for information, the next step is pulling key facts, quotations, stories, and other details out of those sources to use in your presentation. Such details are called **supporting material,** which consists of details you can use to substantiate your arguments and to clarify your ideas. In this section you will learn about examples, narratives, surveys, testimony, numbers and statistics, analogies, explanations, and definitions.

EXAMPLES

Examples—specific instances used to illustrate your point—are among the most common supporting materials found in speeches. Sometimes a single example helps convince an audience; other times a relatively large number of examples may be necessary to achieve your purpose. For instance, you could support the argument that a university gives admission priority to out-of-state students by showing the difference between the numbers of in-state and out-of-state students who are accepted in relation to the number of students who applied in each group. Likewise, in a persuasive speech designed to motivate everyone to vote, you could present cases in which a few more votes would have meant a major change in election results.

You should be careful when using examples. Sometimes an example is so unusual that an audience will not accept the story as evidence or proof of anything. For instance, would you find information obtained from Hawaii a good example for illustrating the price of consumable goods? Probably not, because Hawaii is geographically isolated and requires many of its consumable goods to be transported to the islands. A good example must be plausible, typical, and related to the main point of the speech.

Two types of examples are factual and hypothetical: a *hypothetical* example is fictional but realistic, whereas a *factual* example is based on real circumstances. Either type can be brief or extended. The following is a brief factual example:

> Several online memorial sites on Facebook illustrate how social networking sites have started to serve a larger role than simply helping people connect.

Here is an extended hypothetical example:

> An example of a good excuse for a student missing class is that he or she has a serious auto accident on the way to class, ends up in the hospital, and has a signed medical statement from a physician to prove hospitalization for a week. A poor excuse for a student missing class is that the student, knowing beforehand when the final examination will be held, schedules a flight home for the day before the exam and wants an "excused absence."

building **behaviors**

Verbally Citing Sources

Making verbal citations is one of the most important skills you will learn in this course, and it will benefit you for years to come. Start by drafting possible ways to state your sources in written form. For each source you plan to use in your presentation, write down statements similar to those in table 5 (later in the chapter) that you could use when identifying your sources. You should not read aloud from these drafts during your presentation, but planning the wording ahead of time will help you state the information more effectively. When writing your drafts, take care to emphasize the credentials, expertise, and timeliness of the sources.

supporting material
Information you can use to substantiate your arguments and to clarify your position.

examples
Specific instances used to illustrate your point.

The brief factual example is *verifiable,* meaning it can be supported by a source that the audience can check. The extended hypothetical example is not verifiable and is actually a composite of excuses.

NARRATIVES

narratives
Stories to illustrate an important point.

Whereas examples are primarily intended to present factual information, **narratives**—stories to illustrate an important point—focus more on telling a human story. Think about the difference between hearing that Michael J. Fox has Parkinson's disease (an example) and hearing a detailed story about how his acting career has been affected by the disease—narratives provide richer detail and dimension to people's lives.

Narratives are important parts of speeches. Major elections like the one in 2016 turn on the power of narrative—the ability of a particular candidate to describe a vision that a majority of the electorate can buy into with their vote. When using narratives in your speech, take care to focus on the human element, to be truthful in telling the story, and to help the audience understand what can be learned from the story. Because they tend to draw us into human dramas, narratives can sometimes cause audience members to lose sight of potential implications and outcomes.

surveys
Studies in which a limited number of questions are answered by a sample of the population to discover opinions on issues.

SURVEYS

Another source of supporting material commonly used in speeches is **surveys,** studies in which we ask a sample of the population a limited number of questions to discover public opinions on issues. Surveys are found most often in magazines or journals and are usually seen as more credible than an example or one person's experience, because they synthesize the experience of hundreds or thousands of people. One person's experience with alcohol can have an impact on an audience, but a survey indicating that one-third of all U.S. adults abstain, one-third drink occasionally, and one-third drink regularly provides better support for an argument. As when dealing with personal experience, you should ask some important questions about the evidence found in surveys:

Telling narratives can bring issues to life by introducing characters and emotions into your speech.

© U.S. Coast Guard photo by Petty Officer 1st Class Susan Blake

1. *How reliable is the source?* A report in a professional journal of sociology, psychology, or communication is likely to be more thorough and more valid than one found in a local newspaper.

2. *How broad was the sample used in the survey?* Did the survey include the entire nation, the region, the state, the city, the campus, or the class? Larger samples allow the survey to be more precise in representing a broader viewpoint. In political and other polls you have heard mention of a "margin of error." Larger sample sizes reduce the margin of error, which can boost confidence in the accuracy of a poll's results.

3. *Who was included in the survey?* Did everyone in the sample have an equally good chance of being selected, or were volunteers asked to respond to the questions? If people are randomly selected to be in a survey, the results are less likely to be biased by a particular viewpoint. If you conducted a poll only through Facebook, responses to questions could be very different from those in a paper-and-pencil survey conducted at a shopping mall. Although those approaches to sampling are used all the time, they do risk biasing results in a certain way, because certain types of people had greater opportunity to participate than did others.

4. *How representative was the survey sample?* For example, *Playboy*'s readers may not be typical of the population in your state.

5. *Who performed the survey?* Was the survey firm nationally recognized, such as Lou Harris or Gallup, or did the local newspaper perform the survey? Did professionals such as professors, researchers, or management consultants administer the survey?

6. *Why was the survey done?* Was the survey performed for any self-serving purpose—for example, to attract more readers—or did the government conduct the study to help establish policy or legislation?

TESTIMONY

Testimonial evidence, a third kind of supporting material, consists of written or oral statements of others' experience used by a speaker to substantiate or clarify a point. One assumption behind testimonial evidence is that you are not alone in your beliefs, ideas, and arguments: other people also support them. Another assumption is that the statements of others should help the audience accept your point of view because those other people may have additional credibility that can transfer to your argument. The three kinds of testimonial evidence you can use in your speeches are lay, expert, and celebrity.

Lay testimony is statements made by an ordinary person that substantiate or support what you say. In advertising, this kind of testimony shows ordinary people using or buying products and stating the fine qualities of those products. In a speech, lay testimony might be the words of your relatives, neighbors, or colleagues concerning an issue. Such testimony shows the audience that you and other ordinary people support the idea. Other examples of lay testimony are proclamations of faith by fundamentalist Christians at a church gathering and statements about the wonderful qualities of their college by alumni at a recruiting session.

Expert testimony is statements made by someone who has special knowledge or expertise about an issue or idea. In your speech you might quote a mechanic about problems with an automobile, an interior decorator about the aesthetic qualities of fabrics, or a political pundit about the elections. The idea is to demonstrate that people with specialized experience or education support the positions you advocate in your speech.

Celebrity testimony is statements made by a public figure who is known to the audience. Celebrity testimony occurs in advertising when someone famous endorses a particular product. In your speech you might point out that a famous politician, a syndicated columnist, or a well-known entertainer endorses the position you advocate.

Although testimonial evidence may encourage your audience to adopt your ideas, you need to use such evidence with caution. An idea may have little credence even though many laypeople believe in it; an expert may be quoted on topics well outside his or her area of expertise; and a celebrity usually is paid for endorsing a product. To protect yourself and your audience, ask yourself the following questions before using testimonial evidence in your speeches:

1. Is the person you quote an expert whose opinions or conclusions are worthier than most other people's opinions?

2. Are you quoting someone's statements about his or her own area of expertise?

3. Is the person's statement based on extensive personal experience, professional study or research, or another form of firsthand proof?

4. Will your audience find the statement more believable because you got the quotation from this outside source?

NUMBERS AND STATISTICS

A fourth kind of evidence useful for clarification or substantiation is numbers and statistics. Because numbers are sometimes easier to understand and digest when they appear in print, the public speaker often has to simplify, explain, and translate their meaning in

testimonial evidence
Written or oral statements of others' experience used by a speaker to substantiate or clarify a point.

lay testimony
Statements made by an ordinary person that substantiate or support what you say.

expert testimony
Statements made by someone who has special knowledge or expertise about an issue or idea.

celebrity testimony
Statements made by a public figure who is known to the audience.

a spoken presentation. For example, instead of saying "There were 323,462 high school graduates," say "There were more than 300,000 graduates." You can also simplify a number like 323,462 by writing it on a visual aid like a PowerPoint slide and making a comparison, such as "Three hundred thousand high school graduates are equivalent to the entire population of Lancaster."

statistics
Numbers that summarize numerical information or compare quantities.

Statistics—numbers that summarize numerical information or compare quantities—are also difficult for audiences to interpret. For example, an audience will have difficulty interpreting a statement such as "Honda sales increased 47%." Instead, you could round off the figure to "nearly 50%," or you could reveal the actual dollar value of Honda car sales this year and last year. You can also help the audience interpret the significance with a comparison such as "That is the biggest increase in sales experienced by any domestic or imported car dealer in our city this year."

You can greatly increase your effectiveness as a speaker if you illustrate your numbers by using visual resources, such as pie charts, line graphs, and bar graphs. Both say and show your figures. Try using visual imagery—for example, "That amount of money is greater than all the money in all our local banks" or "That many discarded tires would cover our city 6 feet deep in a single year."

analogy
A comparison of things in some respects, especially in position or function, that are otherwise dissimilar.

explanation
A clarification of what something is or how it works.

Using graphs and tables can help you present statistics and numbers more effectively.
© Shutterstock/Rawpixel.com

ANALOGIES

Another kind of supporting material used in public speeches is analogies. An **analogy** is a comparison of things that are otherwise dissimilar. For instance, one government official said that trying to find Osama bin Laden in Afghanistan was like trying to find one particular rabbit in the state of West Virginia. Similarly, analogies can be used to show that ancient Roman society is analogous to U.S. society and that a law applied in one state will work the same way in another.

An analogy also provides clarification, but it is not proof, because the comparison inevitably breaks down. Therefore, a speaker who argues that U.S. society will fail just as Roman society did can carry the comparison only so far because the form of government and the institutions in the two societies are quite different. Likewise, you can question the rabbit-in-West-Virginia analogy by pointing out the vast differences between the two things being compared. Nonetheless, analogies can be quite useful as a way to illustrate or clarify.

EXPLANATIONS

Explanations are another important means of clarification and persuasion that you will often find in written and visual sources and in interviews. An **explanation** clarifies what something is or how it works. A discussion of psychology would offer explanations and answers, as well as their relationship to the field—for example, "How does Freud explain our motivations?" "What is *catharsis,* and how is it related to aggression?" or "What do *id, ego,* and *superego* mean?"

A good explanation usually simplifies a concept or an idea by explaining the idea from the audience's point of view. If you have ever watched Sanjay Gupta from CNN or other medical correspondents, you've seen them attempt to explain highly technical medical procedures in ways that lay audiences can understand. Likewise, legal reporters must use explanations to simplify detailed legal issues. Explanations are the lifeblood of great journalism; they are also critical for great speeches.

DEFINITIONS

Some of the most contentious arguments in our society center on **definitions,** or determinations of meaning through description, simplification, examples, analysis, comparison, explanation, or illustration. Experts and ordinary citizens have argued for years about definitions. For instance, when does art become pornography? Is euthanasia murder or mercy? The way you define a concept can make a considerable difference.

> **definitions**
> Determinations of meaning through description, simplification, examples, analysis, comparison, explanation, or illustration.

Definitions in a public speech enlighten the audience by revealing what a term means. Sometimes you can use definitions that appear in standard reference works, such as dictionaries and encyclopedias, but simply trying to explain the word in language the audience will understand is often more effective. For example, suppose you use the term *subcutaneous hematoma* in your speech. *Subcutaneous hematoma* is jargon used by physicians to explain a blotch on your flesh, but you could explain the term in this way: "*Subcutaneous* means 'under the skin,' and *hematoma* means 'swelled with blood,' so the words mean 'blood swelling under the skin,' or what most of us call a 'bruise.'"

THINK ABOUT THE MIX

When selecting supporting material for your presentation, you should think carefully about the various types of material that you integrate. Using an analogy, you are creating a meal from scratch without a recipe, which means that you must anticipate how the ingredients will work together to make a tasty dish. In public speaking, there are no rules on the types or mixtures of supporting material. However, some principles to follow are listed below:

1. *Balance your supporting material.* Because supporting material differs in presentation and tone, relying on a single type of supporting material can result in perceptions that your presentation is incomplete. For example, using only quotations can diminish your voice, and using only statistics can become overwhelming for audience members. Emphasize some variety.

2. *Match your support to the topic.* If your topic is emotionally charged, examples and narratives will assist you in conveying the emotion. If your topic is highly controversial, statistics can impose a greater sense of rationality to perhaps tone down polarized viewpoints.

3. *Match supporting material to your purpose.* Use of narratives and examples may increase the vividness of your presentation, which may diminish the impact of statistics. Contrarily, using many statistics can potentially diminish the effect of narratives.[16] Although you should have some variety, you should determine your primary objective and emphasize supporting material that is consistent with that objective.

4. *Tie supporting material together.* A detailed statistic may need to be followed by an explanation so that audience members can better understand the information. A survey might be paired with a quotation from an expert to discuss implications from the survey.

In summary, there are many types of supporting material that you can include in any type of presentation. Selecting and integrating supporting material must be done with care. You should consider your objective, your audience, and your message to identify the best possible mix of support to help you achieve your goals as a speaker.

communicating creatively

Identifying Sources Visually

Inexperienced speakers often struggle with citing sources during their presentations. Many forget to cite sources altogether. Those that remember often have difficulty in effectively identifying sources of information for audience members. A creative way to identify sources is to use visual aids (see the chapter on delivery and visual resources). For example, when using a quotation from an individual, create a slide showing his or her picture and use text to briefly describe your source's title or other qualifications. By showing the source visually, you will establish the source's qualifications. In fact, when you use a picture, your audience will likely connect better with the source and perceive the source, and you, as more credible.

How to Cite Sources of Information

All the work you put into conducting great research will be lost if you do not find ways to explain well the sources that you used. When reading or watching the news, how often have you heard reports from anonymous sources? It turns out that the use of anonymous sources lowers both the credibility and the believability of news stories.[17] The same holds true for speeches. If you do not identify your sources and show why they are credible, you can damage your own credibility.

bibliographic references
Complete citations that appear in the "references" or "works cited" section of your speech outline.

internal references
Brief notations indicating a bibliographic reference that contains the details you are using in your speech.

verbal citations
Oral explanations of who the source is, how recent the information is, and what the source's qualifications are.

You will provide references for your sources both on your outline and during your presentation. **Bibliographic references** are complete citations that appear in the "references" or "works cited" section of your speech outline (or term paper). Your outline should also contain **internal references,** which are brief notations of which bibliographic reference contains the details you are using in your speech. Internal and bibliographic references help readers understand what sources you used to find specific details, such as statistics, quotations, and examples. Ask your instructor whether you should use a particular format for references. See the chapter on organizing your presentation for more on how you should prepare a bibliography for your outline using common style guidelines.

In addition to citing sources in your outline, you must provide verbal citations during your presentation. **Verbal citations** tell listeners who the source is, how recent the information is, and what the source's qualifications are. The examples in table 5 illustrate how to orally cite different types of sources.

Students often have the most difficulty citing webpages. Remember that the web address is only that—an address. Although you should list it in the references or works cited page of your outline, giving the address during your presentation is seldom necessary unless you want your audience to visit that website.

Table 5 Examples of Verbal Citations

Type of Source	Example
Magazine article	"According to an article by Hannah Beech in the April 13, 2009, edition of *Time* magazine, scores of people have been injured during antigovernment protests in Bangkok, Thailand."
Research study	"Erika Kirby, a communication researcher, found in a 2006 study that businesses are starting to take on more family-like roles that blur the separation between family life and work life."
Webpage	"According to a statement on the American Red Cross website, which I visited on April 13, 2009, that organization had to battle three simultaneous disasters—tornadoes, wildfires, and floods—during the week of April 9th."
Graphic or picture	"As you can see in this picture, taken from the ESPN website yesterday, fans ridiculed players for what they tweeted prior to their game."

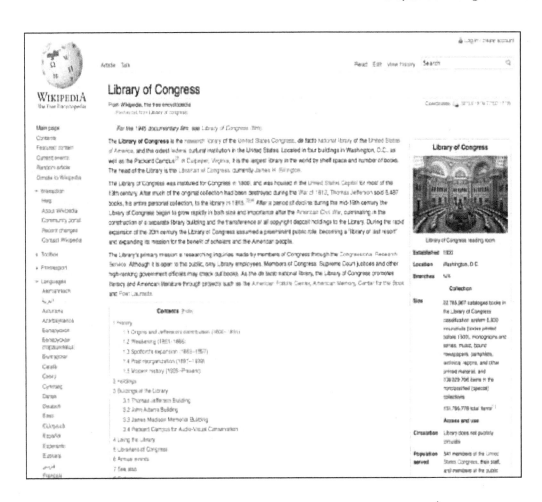

> The decision to use some web resources, such as Wikipedia, is controversial. The appropriateness of these sites is determined by your speaking situation, for which your professor's opinion is important.

Ethical Principles to Follow for Credibility and Research

As you have learned, credibility is a perceptual variable that is not based on external, objective measures of competence, trustworthiness, dynamism, and common ground. However, you retain an ethical obligation to project an honest image of yourself to your audience. The well-known adage that you can fool all the people some of the time may be accurate, but an ethical communicator avoids fooling anyone.

ETHICS AND SOURCE CREDIBILITY

To determine whether you are behaving ethically, answer the following questions:

1. *Are your speech's immediate purpose and long-range goal sound?* Are you providing information or recommending change that would be determined worthy by current standards? Attempting to sell a substandard product or to encourage people to injure others would clearly not be sound; persuading people to accept new, more useful ideas and to be kinder to each other would be sound.

2. *Does your end justify your means?* This time-honored notion suggests that communicators can have ethical ends but may use unethical means of bringing the audience to a particular conclusion. You want listeners to join the armed forces, but should you use scare tactics to achieve your goal?

3. *Are you being honest with your audience?* Are you well informed about the subject instead of being a poseur who only pretends to know? Are you using good evidence and reasoning to convince your audience? Are your passions about the subject sincere?

engaging **diversity**

Building Credibility Across Cultures

How we define credibility depends on many factors, some of which are determined by our culture. When communicating with audiences from cultures other than your own, what steps should you take to build trust and credibility? The answer to that question could depend on the cultures involved. For instance, required trust-building behaviors may differ when speaking in front of an Asian audience in comparison to a Scandinavian audience. Knowledge of customs and rituals within each culture is necessary to understand which behaviors will have the most positive effect on audience members' perceptions of you. Some suggestions on how to understand these differences follow:

1. If possible, observe local customs to understand how strangers greet one another, how individuals display emotion, and how non-verbal behaviors are used to display sincerity.

2. Interview a classmate from the culture to understand the common mistakes made by non-native speakers.

3. Cultures differ on expectations associated with individualism, un-certainty, and use of time. Respecting these cultural differences will dramatically improve your credibility, even if you cannot emulate many of the particular cultural customs and norms. Trying a little can gain a lot (see the chapter on intercultural communication).

4. Let your actions speak first. In U.S. culture, we often use words—our qualifications or our work—to establish credibility. In many cross-cultural situations, you must establish credibility first through deeds. For instance, when formal presentations are made to individuals from an Asian culture, it is often customary to exchange small gifts. Failing to abide by that behavioral norm could potentially diminish your credibility.

Your credibility does lie in the audience's perception of you, but you also have an ethical obligation to be the sort of person you project yourself to be. In addition, you must consider the influence of your message on the audience. Persuasive speeches, particularly, may lead to far-reaching changes in others' behaviors. Are the changes you are recommending consistent with standard ethical and moral guidelines? Have you thoroughly studied your topic, so that you are convinced of the accuracy of the information you are presenting? Are you presenting the entire picture? Are you using valid and true arguments? In short, are you treating the listeners in the way you wish to be treated when someone else is speaking and you are the listener?

ETHICS AND SUPPORTING MATERIAL

Throughout this edition of *Human Communication* we have emphasized various ethical requirements for communication that stem from the NCA Credo on Ethics. And at various points in this chapter, we have pointed out ethical obligations faced by speakers when searching for and using supporting materials. Recall that the first point in the NCA Credo on Ethics states that accuracy and honesty are essential for ethical communication. In this final section we summarize the ethical obligations faced by speakers when working with supporting materials:

- *Speakers have an ethical obligation to find the best possible sources of information.* The Internet and full-text databases certainly provide us with easier research options; however, these tools do not necessarily improve the quality of our research. Nor are the best sources of information always available online or in full-text form. When you speak, your audience depends on you to present the best and most accurate information possible. As a result, many communication instructors emphasize the importance of using *high-quality* sources of information during a presentation. That's why selecting a variety of sources, including print, Internet, and possibly even interviews, can help improve the overall quality of your presentation.

- *Speakers have an ethical obligation to cite their sources of information.* Of course, one reason to cite sources of information is to avoid **plagiarism,** which is the intentional use of information from another source without crediting the source. All universities have specific codes of conduct that identify sanctions levied against those who are caught plagiarizing. Although we see relatively few cases of full plagiarism, we often see students mistakenly commit **incremental plagiarism,** which is the

plagiarism
The intentional use of information from another source without crediting the source.

incremental plagiarism
The intentional or unintentional use of information from one or more sources without fully divulging how much information is directly quoted.

intentional or unintentional use of information from one or more sources without fully divulging how much information is directly quoted. We commonly see students use large chunks of information from webpages and other sources—many times this information is directly copied and pasted from the website. Failing to clearly identify what is directly quoted, even accidentally, is a form of plagiarism. Moreover, your instructor will likely evaluate your speech more favorably if you interpret the meaning of short quotations for the audience rather than over-relying on very large quotations.

- *Speakers have an ethical obligation to fairly and accurately represent sources.* How often have you heard politicians and other public figures complain that the media take their comments "out of context"? To avoid unfair and inaccurate representations of sources, whether they are newspaper articles, webpages, books, or even interviews, you must ensure that you fully understand the points being made by the source. Remember, for example, that two-sided arguments are often used to present a point. A **two-sided argument** is one in which a source advocating one position presents an argument from the opposite viewpoint and then goes on to refute that viewpoint. To take an excerpt from a source in which the opposing argument is being presented for refutation and to imply that the source was advocating the opposing argument is unethical. As a speaker you are free to disagree with points made by the sources you consult; however, you may not misrepresent them.

> **two-sided argument**
> A source advocating one position presents an argument from the opposite viewpoint and then goes on to refute that argument.

Locating, understanding, and incorporating supporting material is one of the most important tasks you will undertake as a presenter of information and argument. As illustrated by table 1, research affects every step in the process of preparing and delivering a presentation. Taking care to effectively and ethically use your information will make you a better speaker and will garner the respect of your peers and teachers.

be ready... for what's next

How to Be an Expert

As a college student, you are just starting to build a portfolio, or set of credentials, to establish your credibility in a particular area. You should not think of credibility as something that is there or not there. Rather, there are degrees of credibility.[18] Some people are more credible than others. So, if you are in the early stages of building credibility, what should it look like several years, or even decades, later?

In fact, there is a good deal of research exploring the characteristics of experts—those who are at the highest levels of credibility in a particular area. These studies have explored expertise in many different domains, ranging from chess playing to medicine and sports. Common to all of these areas are the following characteristics of experts:

1. There is a certain quantity of time that is necessary to achieve expertise. Literally thousands of hours of practice or study are necessary to reach expert status.

2. The quality of how you spend your time is important. Simply rehearsing something to maintain a skill is not sufficient to reach expert status. You must calibrate practice to continually advance your skill in performing a task, recognizing clues, and drawing conclusions.

3. Your practice should allow for instant feedback and for opportunities to repeat newly learned tasks until you do them correctly. Professional athletes have natural skills, but the very best athletes carefully challenge themselves to improve through multiple sources of critique and feedback from others.

4. Experts are self-aware. Rather than being satisfied with maintaining a set level of performance, experts always have an understanding of what the next level of proficiency could be. There is always another goal that is established.

Based on these typical characteristics of experts, what can you do to go beyond being credible and develop strong expertise? Your journey down that path has already started, but it is up to you to determine how far and how quickly you want to take that journey.

Chapter Review & Study Guide

Summary

In this chapter, you learned the following:

1. Source credibility is important because it helps audience members understand why you are qualified and trustworthy enough to present on the topic in question.

   - Source credibility is the audience's perception of your qualifications and effectiveness as a speaker. Although you must provide information that establishes your credibility, audience members ultimately decide the degree to which you are credible.

   - Your credibility is determined by a combination of the topic, the situation, and your qualifications. To analyze credibility, you should ask the question "Why am I credible to speak on this topic in this situation?"

2. Source credibility is created from the audience's perceptions of four dimensions of credibility.

   - Competence is the speaker's qualifications to speak on a topic.

   - Trustworthiness is the perceived dependability and ethics of the speaker.

   - Dynamism is the extent to which the speaker appears confident and comfortable to the audience. A lack of dynamism can make the speaker appear less competent and less trustworthy.

   - Common ground exists when there is perceived shared understanding between the speaker and the audience. The shared understanding or experience can happen in the past, present, or future.

3. Because your credibility is influenced by the information you use to support your ideas, you must develop a good strategy for identifying and selecting high-quality information that can later be used as supporting material.

   - To be most effective, you should think of research as a process in which you select a variety of high-quality sources to present information on a carefully focused topic.

   - Your research strategy should consider use of multiple types of sources, including your own personal experience, information from interviews that you conduct with others, various types of library resources, and online resources.

   - You should carefully evaluate all types of sources to determine whether they are clear, verifiable, competent, objective, relevant, and current.

4. There are eight types of supporting material that you can use to support ideas in your speech: examples, narratives, surveys, testimony, numbers and statistics, analogies, explanations, and definitions.

5. When using supporting material from sources that you have found, you must correctly reference those sources, both in writing on your outline and orally during your presentation.

   - Your outline should contain a reference section at the end where complete bibliographic references are provided. You should consult with your teacher about specific requirements for the formatting of those citations.

   - In the text of the outline, you should use internal citations to indicate where information from other sources is integrated.

   - During your speech, you should use verbal citations to tell audience members about your sources.

6. You should follow core ethical principles to establish your credibility and in the use of evidence.

   - You have an obligation to be honest with your audience by using good evidence. Your purpose in speaking should be reasonable and sound, and you should use methods of presenting information that are justified.

   - You have an ethical obligation to find the best possible sources to use in your presentation, to cite those sources during the presentation, and to accurately represent what those sources say.

Key Terms

Analogy	Definitions	Heuristics
Bibliographic references	Dynamism	Incremental plagiarism
Celebrity testimony	Examples	Internal references
Common ground	Expert testimony	Lay testimony
Competence	Explanation	Narratives

Personal experience
Plagiarism
Reference librarian
Search engine
Sleeper effect

Source credibility
Statistics
Supporting material
Surveys
Testimonial evidence

Trustworthiness
Two-sided argument
Verbal citations

Study Questions

1. Which of the following statements regarding source credibility is *not* true?

   a. Source credibility is the audience's perception of the effectiveness of a speaker.
   b. Source credibility depends on the speaker, the subject discussed, the situation, and the audience.
   c. Source credibility is something a speaker possesses.
   d. The audience determines credibility.

2. Which aspect of source credibility is the degree to which a speaker is perceived as honest, friendly, and honorable?

   a. competence
   b. trustworthiness
   c. dynamism
   d. common ground

3. If a person speaks with vocal variety, moves toward the audience, or uses facial expressions and gestures, he or she is exhibiting which aspect of credibility?

   a. competence
   b. trustworthiness
   c. dynamism
   d. common ground

4. Which of the following results in higher credibility?

   a. disorganized speeches
   b. people perceived as low in status
   c. fumbling over words
   d. effective delivery skills

5. Which of the following cannot be effectively utilized when gathering evidence for your speeches?

   a. personal experience
   b. library resources
   c. the Internet
   d. a friend's speech

6. Which type of source undergoes blind peer review to ensure high-quality information and contains specified studies?

   a. nonfiction books
   b. academic journal articles
   c. government documents
   d. trade journal articles

7. Brief notations in your outline that indicate a reference used in your speech are called _____ references, whereas _____ references are complete citations that appear in the "references" section of the speech outline.

   a. internal; bibliographic
   b. verbal; internal
   c. bibliographic; external
   d. external; verbal

8. When evaluating sources, you should ensure that the supporting material

   a. contains jargon and technical explanations.
   b. includes relevant and irrelevant information.
   c. contains bias and is subjective.
   d. is verifiable.

9. Which type of supporting material includes written or oral statements of others' experiences?

   a. examples
   b. testimonial evidence
   c. numbers and statistics
   d. definitions

10. To develop high expertise, research suggests that your experience should

   a. take as few hours as possible.
   b. involve instant feedback.
   c. maintain basic skills.
   d. avoid repetition.

Answers:

1. (c); 2. (b); 3. (c); 4. (d); 5. (d); 6. (b); 7. (a); 8. (d); 9. (b); 10. (b)

connect

To maximize your study time, check out CONNECT to access the SmartBook study module for this chapter, watch videos, and explore other resources.

Critical Thinking

1. Using the Internet, pick a topic and find two sources that could be used to provide information on the topic. One source should be high in credibility, and the other should be low in credibility. Discuss the differences between the sources, and explain why you selected them to illustrate high and low credibility.

2. Using a news site like CNN, Fox, or MSNBC, watch a video of a news story. List each source that was identified in the story, and take note of how the source was introduced to the viewer. How did the news report establish credibility of the sources that were used or referenced? Did you find this effective? How could you use similar techniques in your presentation?

Sizing Things Up Scoring and Interpretation

Research Attitudes Scale

Effective speakers use a variety of types of supporting materials and research in their speeches. The scale created for this chapter helps you assess your strengths and weaknesses in using various types of research resources. After completing and scoring the scale, you can use the results as a diagnostic tool to determine strategies for which you may need additional assistance from your teacher or a reference librarian.

The Research Attitudes Scale assesses your comfort and ability in using five different types of research resources: the Internet (items 1, 9, and 14), journals (items 2, 7, and 15), books (items 3, 6, and 11), reference materials (items 4, 8, and 12), and popular press sources (items 5, 10, and 13). You should sum the responses to questions for each resource to find specific scores. Scores of 3 to 6 indicate areas needing greater attention or assistance.

References

1. Watson, E. (2014, November). Be the he for she. *Vital Speeches of the Day, 80,* 348–349.

2. Heikkilä, H., Kunelius, R., & Ahva, L. (2010, August). From credibility to relevance. *Journalism Practice, 4,* 274–284.

3. Teven, J. (2008). An examination of perceived credibility of the 2008 presidential candidates: Relationships with believability, likeability, and deceptiveness. *Human Communication, 11,* 391–407.

4. Kecskes, I., & Zhang, F. (2009). Activating, seeking, and creating common ground. A socio-cognitive approach. *Pragmatics & Cognition, 17,* 331–355.

5. Coleman, M. S. (2011). I was a teenage scientist. *Vital Speeches Of The Day, 77*(5), 181–184.

6. Hosman, L. A., & Siltanen, S. A. (2011). Hedges, tag questions, message processing, and persuasion. *Journal of Language & Social Psychology, 30,* 341–349.

7. Kleinnijenhuis, J., van Hoof, A. J., & Oegema, D. (2006). Negative news and the sleeper effect of distrust. *Harvard International Journal of Press/Politics, 11,* 86–104.

8. Mazer, J. P., Murphy, R. E., & Simonds, C. J. (2009). The effects of teacher self-disclosure via Facebook on teacher credibility. *Learning, Media & Technology, 34,* 175–183.

9. Masip, J. (2003). Facial appearance and judgments of credibility: The effects of facial babyishness and age on statement credibility. *Genetic, Social & General Psychology Monographs, 129*(3): 269–311.

10. Fico, F., Richardson, J. D., & Edwards, S. M. (2004). Influence of story and structure on perceived story bias and news organization credibility. *Mass Communication & Society, 7,* 301–318.

11. Teven, J. J. (2010). The effects of supervisor nonverbal immediacy and power use on employees' ratings of credibility and affect for the supervisor. *Human Communication, 13,* 69–85.

12. Myers, S. A., & Bryant, L. E. (2004). College students' perceptions of how instructors convey credibility. *Qualitative Research Reports in Communication, 5,* 22–27.

13. Reinard, J., & Myers, K. (2005, May). *Comparisons of models of persuasive effects of types of evidence introductions*. Paper presented at the International Communication Association Convention, New York.

14. Allen, M. (2002). Effect of timing of communicator identification and level of source credibility on attitude. *Communication Research Reports, 19,* 46–55.

15. Bourhis, J., Adams, C., Titsworth, S., & Harter, L. (2008). *A style manual for communication studies* (3rd ed.). New York: McGraw-Hill.

16. Han, B. & Fink, E. L. (2012). How do statistical and narrative evidence affect persuasion? The role of evidentiary features. *Argumentation and Advocacy, 49,* 39–58.

17. Sternadori, M. M., & Thorson, E. (2009). Anonymous sources harm credibility of all stories. *Newspaper Research Journal, 30,* 54–66.

18. Guest, C. B., Regehr, G., & Tiberius, R. G. (2001). The life-long challenge of expertise. *Medical Education, 35,* 78–81.

© Hero Images/Getty Images, RF

organizing your presentation

When you have read and thought about this chapter, you will be able to

1. Present an effective introduction that captures the interest of your audience in your topic, the purpose of the speech, and the development of the talk.

2. Write an effective outline for a presentation.

3. Describe the most frequently used patterns of organization in public presentations.

4. Use transitions and signposts that link ideas and indicate direction to the audience.

5. Present an effective conclusion.

6. Compile a list of references, or sources, to accompany your complete outline.

In this chapter you will learn how to organize your presentation. You will examine the three main parts of a speech: introduction, body, and conclusion; you will learn the functions of each part and how to effectively organize the content. Understanding the parts of a speech, the functions of each part, and ways to organize the entire message is essential to becoming a successful presenter.

Alan Perrault wanted to give a speech on geocaching, the GPS treasure-hunting game, which was a favorite personal activity. He was not sure whether his classmates knew about the game, so he began to informally talk about this activity before and after class. He learned that a couple of people had geocached in their hometowns, one had geocached near the campus, but most did not know what the term meant. From these interactions, Alan began to think about how he could structure his talk.

What would you suggest to Alan about the organization of his speech? Where should he start, and what information should he include? At the end of the chapter, we'll take another look at Alan's situation and how he decides to organize his speech.

How you organize a speech sends signals to audience members. Your speech will be more likely to accomplish its goals if you can gain and hold your audience's attention, make clear and smooth transitions between major sections, and end with a clear statement of what you want your audience to take away from your presentation. This chapter will teach you about organization by discussing the key elements of a speech—the introduction, body, and conclusion—as well as how to outline your speech effectively.

© Brand X Pictures/PunchStock RF

The Introduction

The **introduction,** the first part of your presentation, lets audiences assess you as a speaker. During your first few sentences, and certainly in the first few minutes of your speech, audience members decide whether to listen to you. They also decide whether your topic is important enough to hear. In those crucial early minutes, you can capture your audience's attention and keep their focus, or you can lose their attention—perhaps for the remainder of the presentation.

The five functions of an introduction are to gain the audience's attention, to arouse interest, to state the purpose or thesis of your speech, to establish your credibility, and to briefly forecast for listeners the organization of your speech and the way you will develop your ideas. You do not need to fulfill the functions in this order. Gaining audience attention often comes at the beginning, but maintaining attention is an important function throughout the speech. Forecasting the speech's organization often comes toward the end of an introduction, but it does not have to be last. Let us systematically explore the five functions and some examples of each.

Introduction
The first part of your presentation, in which you fulfill five functions.

GAINING AND MAINTAINING AUDIENCE ATTENTION

The first function of an introduction is to gain and maintain attention by involving your audience in your topic. Here are some suggestions:

1. *Bring to the presentation the object or person about which you are going to speak.* A student speaking on health foods brings a tray full of health foods, which he shares with the audience after the speech; a student speaking on weight lifting brings her 250-pound friend to demonstrate the moves during the speech.

2. *Invite your audience to participate.* Ask questions and invite audience members to raise their hands and answer. Or have the audience stand up and perform the exercise you are teaching them.

3. *Let your clothing relate to your presentation.* A nurse talking about the dangers of acute hepatitis wears a nurse's uniform; a construction worker dons a hard hat.

4. *Exercise your audience's imagination.* Have the audience members close their eyes and imagine they are poised on a ski slope, standing before a judge on a driving-while-intoxicated charge, or slipping into a cool Minnesota lake on a hot and humid day. Preston Gilderhus, a student in industrial engineering and management, presented a talk on the importance of bees. He began, "Imagine the world without apples, oranges, strawberries, or carrots. None of these foods would exist without bees."

5. *Start with sight or sound.* A student who gave a powerful presentation on motorcycle safety showed six slides as he talked about the importance of wearing a helmet while riding. Only one item appeared in color on each slide: a crushed or battered helmet that had been worn by someone who lived through a motorcycle accident. His words spoke of safety; the battered helmets reinforced the message.

6. *Arouse audience curiosity.* Five hundred white people gathered to hear a presentation on diversity. The speaker was a Chinese man dressed in traditional Chinese attire. He started his presentation by saying nothing; he just slowly scanned his audience. The audience, accustomed to speakers who start by speaking, was mystified by his quiet demeanor but exceedingly attentive. Then the speaker said, "Do you know how it feels to stand in front of a group this large and to see no one who looks like you?"

7. *Role-play.* A student invites an audience member to pretend to be a choking victim. The speaker then "saves" the victim by demonstrating the maneuver she is teaching the audience.

8. *Show a very short video.* A football player speaking on violence in that sport shows a short video of punt returns. He points out which players were deliberately trying to maim their opponents with face guards—as they have been taught to do.

9. *Present a brief quotation or have the audience read something you have provided.* One enterprising student handed every class member an official-looking letter right before his speech. Each letter was a personalized court summons for a moving violation detected by a police-owned spy camera at a busy intersection.

10. *State striking facts or statistics.* Emily Knilans, a first-year human development and family science student, introduced her speech on the importance of drinking water thus: "The human brain weighs about 3 pounds, about 2.4 of those pounds are water, and water contributes to all mental functions."

11. *Self-disclose.* Tell audience members something about yourself—related to the topic—that they would not otherwise know: "I took hard drugs for six years"; "I was an Eagle scout"; "I earn over $50,000 a year—legally."

12. *Tell a story, a narration.* A student told this story: The little boy asked his grandfather whether he was a hero, because the boy had heard that his grandpa fought in Vietnam when he was a young man. "No," said the grandfather, "I was not a hero, but I was in an entire battalion of heroes."

These suggestions for gaining and maintaining audience attention certainly are not the only possibilities available to you, but they have all been used successfully by other students. Your introduction should not simply imitate what you read in this edition of *Human Communication;* instead, think of ideas of your own that will work best for you and your audience.

Some words of caution about gaining and maintaining attention: no matter what method you use, avoid being overly dramatic. A student who pretended to cut himself and shot fake blood all over the front of the room got his teacher and his audience so upset that they could not listen to his presentation.

Always make sure your attention-getting strategy is related to your topic. Some speakers think every public speech must start with a joke, but this is a big mistake if you are not good at telling jokes or your audience is not interested in hearing them. Topically relevant jokes may be acceptable, but they are still just one of hundreds of ways a speaker can gain attention. Another overused device is writing something such as "s-e-x" on the chalkboard and then announcing your speech has nothing to do with sex—you just wanted to get the audience's attention. Your attention-getting strategy here has nothing to do with the topic. Finally, be wary of guests, animals, and PowerPoint, because all three can eliminate you from the speaking situation. They can all be effective to gain audience attention, but they must not become center stage while you and your message become background music.

AROUSING AUDIENCE INTEREST

The second function of an introduction is to arouse audience interest in the subject matter. The best way is to show clearly how the topic is related to the audience. A highly skilled speaker can adapt almost any topic to a given audience. Do you want to talk about collecting coins? Thousands of coins pass through each person's hands every year. Can you tell your audience how to spot a rare one? If you can arouse the audience's interest in currency, you will find it easier to encourage them to listen to your speech about the rare coins you have collected. Similarly, speeches about your life as a parent

One of the five main purposes of a speech introduction is to arouse audience interest by showing how the topic relates to them.

© Jeff Greenberg/The Image Works

of four, a camp counselor, or the manager of a business can be linked to audience interests. The following good example relates the topic to the audience; these words are quoted from a student speech on drinking and driving:

> Do you know what the leading cause of death is for people who attend this college? Some of you might think it is a disease that causes the most deaths—cancer, heart attacks, or AIDS. No, the leading cause of death among students at this college is car accidents. Not just ordinary car accidents, but accidents in which the driver has been drinking.

The speaker related her topic to the audience by linking a national problem to her own college. She prepared the audience to receive more information and ideas about this common problem.

STATING THE PURPOSE OR THESIS

The third function of an introduction is to state the purpose or thesis of your speech. Why? Because informative speeches invite learning, and learning is more likely to occur if you reveal to the audience what you want them to know. Consider the difficulty of listening to a history professor who spends 50 minutes telling you every detail and date related to the Crusades. Observe how much more easily you can listen to a professor who begins the lecture by stating what you are supposed to learn: "I want you to understand why the Crusades began, who the main participants were, and when the Crusades occurred."

Here are four examples of statements of purpose or thesis:

Thesis statement for a demonstration speech: "This afternoon I am going to demonstrate how you can mix three common household products to make your own antiseptic and reduce germs in your home."

Thesis statement for an informative speech: "Today I ask you to remember at least three of the five methods I will recommend to avoid identity theft."

Sample Introduction That Fulfills the Five Functions

Alan Perrault fulfilled the five functions of the introduction.

Introduction

I. *Attention getter:* Today, 1.54 million active geocaches exist around the globe.

II. *Listener relevance:* Geocaching is fun and it will allow you to visit new and interesting places. It is suitable for anyone, and the over 5 million geocachers worldwide include families with little kids all the way through older retirees.

III. *Speaker credibility:* I have been geocaching since I was 15 years old and I have nearly 200 finds to my name.

IV. *Thesis:* I am going to talk to you about the game of geocaching.

V. *Preview:* I will explain to you what geocaching is, how it works, and how you can get involved with it.

Thesis statement for a persuasive speech: "After you hear me today, you will be eager to join our movement to change the grading system at this college."

Thesis statement for an inspirational or motivational speech: "Our banquet tonight is to remind us of the sacrifice our soldiers made on our behalf."

In public speaking, as in education, audience members are more likely to learn and understand if you make your expectations clear. You can accomplish that goal by stating your purpose in the introduction. Sometimes in a persuasive speech you may wish to delay revealing your purpose until you have set the stage for audience acceptance. Under most circumstances, though—and especially in informative speeches—you should reveal your purpose or thesis in your introduction.

ESTABLISHING YOUR CREDIBILITY

The fourth function of an introduction is to describe any special qualifications you have to enhance your credibility. You can talk about your experience, your research, the experts you interviewed, and your own education and training in the subject. Although you should be wary about self-praise, you need not be reserved in stating why you can speak about the topic with authority. Here is an example of establishing credibility through self-disclosure:

You can probably tell from my fingernails that my day job is repairing automobiles, a job I have held at the same dealership for over 12 years. I have repaired thousands of cars. That is why I want to tell you today why you and your insurance company have to pay such high prices for repair.

For more information about establishing source credibility, see the chapter on being credible and using evidence.

sizing things up

Clarity Behaviors Inventory

The first step in understanding how to sound organized when presenting information is to learn how others do this. As college students, you have the opportunity to watch teachers present information nearly every day. Below are 12 statements describing things a teacher might do. Select a teacher from another class, and think of that teacher when responding to the statements. Or consider another student who has already presented in your class. Use the following scale to respond:

1 = Strongly disagree
2 = Disagree
3 = Neither agree nor disagree
4 = Agree
5 = Strongly agree

1. The speaker verbally stresses important issues presented in the presentation.
2. Written examples of topics covered in the presentation are provided in the form of handouts or visual materials (PowerPoint, dry-erase board, or chalkboard).
3. The organization of the talk is given to me in written form, either on paper or as part of a visual aid, such as an overhead or the chalkboard.
4. The speaker tells us what definitions, explanations, or conclusions are important to make note of.
5. The speaker explains how we are supposed to see relationships between topics covered in the presentation.
6. The speaker provides us with written descriptions of the most important things in the presentation.
7. The speaker explains when he or she is presenting something that is important for us to know.
8. The speaker provides us with written or visual definitions, explanations, or conclusions of topics covered in the presentation.
9. The speaker verbally identifies examples that illustrate concepts we are supposed to learn from the talk.
10. Written explanations of how ideas in the presentation fit together are presented on the chalkboard, on the overhead, on PowerPoint, or in handouts.
11. The speaker explains when he or she is providing an important definition of a concept.

This exercise can measure both oral and written clarity. A guide for interpreting your responses appears at the end of the chapter.

Source: Adapted from Titsworth, S., Novak, D., Hunt, S., & Meyer, K. (2004). The effects of teacher clarity on affective and cognitive learning: A causal model of clear teaching behaviors. International Communication Association, May, New Orleans, LA. Used by permission of the author.

FORECASTING DEVELOPMENT AND ORGANIZATION

The fifth function of an introduction is to forecast the organization and development of the presentation. The forecast provides a preview of the main points you plan to cover. Audience members feel more comfortable when they know what to expect. You can help by revealing your plan for the speech. Are you going to discuss a problem and its solution? Are you going to make three main arguments with supporting materials? Let your audience know what you plan to do early in your speech. Emily Knilans, the student who was quoted earlier, stated, "I will discuss what water does for our bodies and the differences between drinking bottled water and drinking tap water." Another student asserted, "Today I plan to present three good reasons why race should be a factor in college admissions."

The Body

Most speakers begin composing their presentations with the body rather than the introduction, because they need to know the content of the presentation to write an effective introduction.

The **body** of a presentation is the largest portion of the presentation, in which you place your arguments and ideas, your evidence and examples, your proofs and illustrations, and your stories and testimonials. Since you usually do not have time to state in a presentation everything you know about a subject, you need to decide what information to include in the

body
The largest part of the presentation, which contains the arguments, evidence, and main content.

body and what to exclude. Because the material you will use may not all be of equal importance, you need to decide placement—first, last, or in the middle. Generally, the most important information should be placed first or last. Audiences remember information in these positions more easily than they recall information in the middle of the body. Selecting, prioritizing, and organizing are three skills that you will use in developing the body of your speech.

Just as the introduction of a speech has certain functions to fulfill, so does the body. These are its main functions:

1. Increase what an audience knows about a topic (informative presentation)

2. Change an audience's attitudes or actions about a topic (persuasive presentation)

3. Present a limited number of arguments, stories, and/or ideas

4. Provide support for your arguments and/or ideas

5. Indicate the sources of your information, arguments, and supporting materials

You already know something about organization. Every sentence you utter is organized. The words are arranged according to rules of syntax for the English language. Even when you are in conversation, you organize your speech. The first statement you make is often more general than that which follows. For instance, you might say, "I don't like that candidate for Congress," after which you might say why you don't like her. You probably don't start by stating a specific fact, such as her voting record, her position on healthcare, or the issue that her personal life has been reported on the gossip pages. Likewise, when we compose a speech, we tend to limit what we say, prioritize our points, and back them as necessary with support—all organized according to principles we have either subconsciously learned (such as the rules of syntax) or consciously studied (such as the rules of organization).

building **behaviors**

Crafting an Effective Introduction: Things to Avoid

Here are some tips for strengthening your introduction by avoiding some common mistakes. Once you've drafted your introduction, check it against this list.

- Do not start talking until you are up in front and settled. Starting your speech on the way up to the lectern is bad form.

- Do not say negative things about you or your abilities: "I'm not used to public speaking," "I've never done this before," "I couldn't be more nervous than I am right now." You are supposed to build your credibility in the introduction, not give an audience more doubts about your ability.

- Do not let your nonverbal unease overcome your message. Crossing your legs, refusing to look at the audience, jingling the change in your pocket, repeatedly pushing your hair off your face—all of these signal to the audience your lack of confidence. So act confident even if you are not.

- Do not say negative things about your message: "I didn't have much time to prepare this speech," "I couldn't find much information on my topic," or "I really don't know much about this issue." Do the best you can to convey your message, but do not tell the audience to disregard your message.

THE PRINCIPLES OF OUTLINING

An **outline** is a written plan that uses symbols, margins, and content to reveal the order, importance, and substance of your speech. An outline shows the sequence of your arguments or main points, indicates their relative importance, and states the content of your arguments, main points, and subpoints. The outline is a simplified, abstract version of your speech.

Why should you learn how to outline? Here are three good reasons:

- Outlining is a skill that can be used to develop written compositions, to write notes in class, and to compose speeches.

- Outlining reinforces important skills, such as determining what is most important, what arguments and evidence will work best with this audience, and roughly how much time and effort will go into each part of your presentation.

outline
A written plan that uses symbols, margins, and content to reveal the order, importance, and substance of a presentation.

Creating an outline will help you structure your speech in the most effective way possible.

© Ingram Publishing RF

- Outlining encourages you to speak conversationally, because you do not have every word in front of you.

  You will find that learning how to outline can provide you with a useful tool in your classes and at work. Outlining is versatile and easy to learn as long as you keep six principles in mind:

- *Principle 1: Link outline to purpose.* All the items of information in your outline should be directly related to your purpose and long-range goal. The immediate purpose, you will recall, is what you expect to achieve *on the day of your presentation.* You might want the audience to be able to distinguish between a row house and a townhouse, to rent a particular DVD, or to talk with others about a topic. All these purposes can be achieved shortly after the audience hears about the idea. Remember that the long-range goal is what you expect to achieve by your message *in the days, months, or years ahead.* You may be talking about a candidate two months before the election, but you want your audience to vote a certain way at that future date. You may want to push people to be more tolerant toward persons of your race, gender, sexual preference, or religion, but tolerance is more likely to develop over time than instantly—so your goal is long-range.

- *Principle 2: Your outline is an abstract of the message you will deliver.* As a simplification, the outline should be less than every word you will speak but should include all important points and supporting materials. Some instructors say an outline should be about one-third the length of the actual presentation, if the message were in manuscript form. However, you should ask what your instructor expects, because some instructors like to see a very complete outline, whereas others prefer a brief outline. Nonetheless, even a complete outline is not a manuscript but an abstract of the talk you intend to deliver, a plan that includes the important arguments or information you intend to present.

- *Principle 3: Each outline part is a single idea.* That is, the outline should consist of single units of information, usually in the form of complete sentences that express a single idea:

  I. Government regulation of handguns should be implemented to reduce the number of murders in this country.

     A. Half the murders in the United States are committed by criminals using handguns.

     B. Half the handgun deaths in the United States are caused by relatives, friends, or acquaintances of the victim.

- *Principle 4: Your outline symbols signal importance.* In the portion of a sample outline that follows, the **main points,** or most important points, are indicated by Roman numerals, such as I, II, III, IV, and V. The number of main points in a 5- to 10-minute message, or even a longer presentation, should be limited to the number you can reasonably cover, explain, or prove in the time permitted. Most five-minute messages have from one to three main points. Even hour-long presentations must have a limited number of main points, because most audiences are unable to remember more than seven main points.

  Subpoints, less important points supporting the main points, are indicated by capital letters, such as A, B, C, D, and E. Ordinarily, two subpoints under a main point are regarded as the minimum if any subpoints are to be presented. Like main points, subpoints should be limited in number; otherwise, the audience may lose sight of your main points. A good guideline is to present two or three of your best pieces of supporting material in support of each main point.

main points
The most important points in a presentation; indicated by Roman numerals in an outline.

subpoints
The points in a presentation that support the main points; indicated by capital letters in an outline.

Sample Partial Outline Illustrating the Principles of Outlining

II. In the search for a cure, James Thomson in 1998 was the first biologist to isolate human embryonic stem cells.

    A. The goal of this research is to use stem cells to replace cells that have failed in the human body.

    B. Congress passed a bill in October 1998 prohibiting experimentation with embryonic stem cells except under very limited circumstances.

    C. Congress banned funding for any experimentation that would harm embryos.

III. People favoring stem cell research demonstrate that the prohibition is unnecessarily keeping us from medical advances.

    A. Experts estimate that 400,000 embryos already exist in fertility clinics.

    B. Most of the existing embryos are discarded if they are not donated to science.

> Principle 1: Outline links all major points to purpose.
>
> Principle 2: Outline simplifies and reduces presentation to series of related sentences.
>
> Principle 3: Each item in outline is one sentence.
>
> Principle 4: Symbols (I, II, and A, B, etc.) indicate main and subordinate ideas.
>
> Principle 5: Margins (far left for main points and indented for subordinate points) indicate importance.
>
> Principle 6: Each item is in parallel form.

- *Principle 5: Your outline margins signal importance.* The margins of your outline are coordinated with the symbols assigned to the outline items, so the main points all have the same left margin, the subpoints all have a slightly larger left margin, and sub-subpoints have a still larger one. The larger the margin on the left, the less important the item is to your purpose. Amber Rasche presented a speech on why we need embryonic stem cell research. A portion of her outline is presented later in this chapter to illustrate the relationship of main points and subpoints in the outline.

- *Principle 6: Use parallel form.* **Parallel form** relies on the consistent use of complete sentences, clauses, phrases, or words, but not a mixture of these. Hacker and Sommers, in their text on writing, explain, "Readers expect items in a series to appear in parallel grammatical form."[1] So do listeners. Most teachers prefer an outline consisting entirely of complete sentences, because such an outline reveals the speaker's message more completely. The outline on stem cell research is composed entirely of complete sentences; the form is parallel because no dependent clauses, phrases, or single words appear.

parallel form
The consistent use of complete sentences, clauses, phrases, or words in an outline.

THE ROUGH DRAFT

Before you begin composing your outline, you can save time and energy by (1) selecting a topic that is appropriate for you, your audience, your purpose, and the situation; (2) finding arguments, examples, illustrations, quotations, stories, and other supporting materials from your experience, from written and visual resources, and from other people; and (3) narrowing your topic, so that you can select the best materials from a large supply

Blogging
by Daniel Kalis

Introduction

My immediate purpose is to help my audience understand the origins, present practice, and future of blogging.

> Rough draft can have sentences, phrases, or just a word or two to indicate your overall plan for presentation

> Rough draft should be easy to change as you decide what to keep and what to discard based on what you can find about topic.

> Rough draft is an early plan containing cues about what you want to say.

I.   What is blogging and what is its importance now and in the future?

    A. What is blogging?

    B. Why is it important?

II. History

    A. Origin

        1. When?

        2. Who?

    B. Original uses

III. Present

    A. Reasons for popularity

    B. Complications

IV. Future

    A. Trends

    B. Genres

V.   Conclusion: Blogging is growing exponentially because of its many possibilities.

of available items (see the chapter on topic selection and audience analysis and the chapter on being credible and using evidence).

rough draft
The preliminary organization of the outline of a presentation.

Once you have gathered materials consistent with your purpose, you can begin by developing a **rough draft** of your outline—a preliminary organization of the outline. The most efficient way to develop a rough draft is to choose a limited number of main points important for your purpose and your audience.

Next, you should see what materials you have from your experience, from written and visual resources, and from other people to support these main ideas, including facts, statistics, testimony, and examples. What arguments, illustrations, and supporting materials will be most likely to have an impact on the audience? Sometimes speakers get so involved in a topic that they select mainly those items that interest them. In public speaking you should select the items likely to have the maximum impact on the audience, not on you.

Composing an outline for a speech is a process. Even professional speechwriters may have to make important changes to their first draft. Some of the questions you need to consider as you revise your rough draft follow:

1. Are your main points consistent with your purpose?

2. Do your subpoints and sub-subpoints relate to your main points?

3. Are the items in your outline the best possible ones for this audience, for this topic, for you, for the purpose, and for the occasion?

4. Does your outline follow the principles of outlining?

Even after you have rewritten your rough draft, you would be wise to have another person—perhaps a classmate—examine your outline and provide an opinion about its content and correctness.

The sample outline for a speech on blogging is an example of what a rough draft of a speech looks like.

A rough draft of a speech does not necessarily follow parallel form, nor is it as complete as the sentence outline, which often develops out of the rough draft. Mostly, the rough draft provides an overview so that you can see how the parts of the speech—the main points and subpoints—fit together. When you are ready to finalize your outline, you have several options. However, the sentence outline is preferred by many communication instructors.

THE SENTENCE OUTLINE

The sentence outline does not have all the words that will occur in the delivered speech, but it does provide a complete guide to the content. A **sentence outline** consists entirely of complete sentences. It shows in sentence form your order of presentation; what kinds of arguments, supporting material, and evidence you plan to use; and where you plan to place them. A look at your outline indicates strengths and weaknesses. You might note, for instance, that you have insufficient information about one main point or a surplus of information on another.

sentence outline
An outline consisting entirely of complete sentences.

In addition to creating the sentence outline itself, you may want to make notes on the functions being served by each part of your outline. For example, where are you trying to gain and maintain attention? Where are you trying to back up a major argument with supporting materials, such as statistics, testimony, or specific instances? A sentence outline, along with side notes indicating functions, is a blueprint for your speech. The sentence outline can strengthen your speech performance by helping you present evidence or supporting materials that will make sense to audience members and will help you inform or persuade them.

The sample sentence outline in this section is based on a student's speech. The immediate purpose of the presentation was to explain the reasons students should eat

Why All College Students Should Eat Breakfast
by Michael Burns

A sentence outline consists of complete sentences. It shows the order of the presentation as well as the arguments and supporting material you intend to use.

Introduction

I. Many people choose to sleep 30 minutes longer every day rather than take the time to eat breakfast.

    A. How many of you ate breakfast this morning? Your cup of coffee does not count. (*show of hands*)

CONTINUED

    B. College students who eat breakfast perform better in classes and are healthier.

    C. Eating breakfast should be a part of all college students' daily schedules.

Body

II. There are many reasons eating breakfast is beneficial.

    A. Breakfast is a great way to jump-start your metabolism and your day.

    B. Students who eat breakfast are healthier than students who don't eat breakfast.

       1. WebMD reports that people who eat breakfast are less overweight than people who don't eat breakfast.

       2. The Florida Department of Citrus claims that people who eat a breakfast that includes a glass of orange juice have a stronger immune system, but this might not be an impartial source.

    C. Students who eat breakfast also perform better in school.

       1. Mayo Clinic doctors have reported that people who eat breakfast regularly have more energy and are able to focus longer on tasks.

       2. The American Dietetic Association claims that students who eat breakfast are more likely to have better concentration and problem-solving skills than students who don't eat breakfast.

Conclusion

III. As college students, we need to eat breakfast daily.

    A. Eating breakfast every day will make us healthier.

    B. Eating breakfast every day will improve our performance in classes.

    C. Eating breakfast should be just as an important to our daily schedules as taking a shower.

breakfast. The action goal of the speech was to persuade classmates to get in the habit of eating breakfast every day. Notice that every entry in the outline is a sentence.

THE KEY-WORD OUTLINE

Using a manuscript for your entire speech may invite you to become too dependent on the manuscript. Too much attention to notes reduces your eye contact and minimizes your attention to audience responses. Nonetheless, you can become very proficient at reading from a manuscript on which you have highlighted the important words, phrases, and quotations. A sentence outline may be superior to a manuscript in that it forces you to extemporize, to maintain eye contact, and to respond to audience feedback. Key words and phrases can also be underlined or highlighted on a sentence outline. An alternative

engaging **diversity**

Different Cultures Use Different Organizational Patterns

The dominant culture in North America embraces linear organizational patterns that move from a distinct beginning to a middle and to an end, that tend to state early and boldly who the speaker is and what the main point is, and that are rather detailed in structure with main points, subpoints, and even sub-subpoints. Do not assume that other cultures are the same. For example, in some Pacific Rim cultures, speakers start their presentations by suggesting they are inadequate rather than building up their credibility in an introduction. By doing so, they are showing deference to the audience and demonstrating respect. Some Native American groups fill their messages with colorful imagery, metaphors, and illustrative stories instead of generating arguments and evidence. African Americans, among other groups, hit on a recurring refrain with a pattern of organization that keeps circling back to a main point with many related narratives between each repetition. When addressing people from cultures different from your own, you should be aware of how they like to organize their messages. You might intersperse your organizational pattern with some elements of your audience's preferred organizational patterns.

Source: Michael Burns

method is simply to use a **key-word outline,** an outline consisting of important words or phrases to remind you of the content of the speech.

A key-word outline shrinks the ideas in a speech considerably more than does a sentence outline. It ordinarily consists of important words and phrases, but it can also include

key-word outline
An outline consisting of important words or phrases to remind you of the content of the presentation.

The Youth Vote
by Amanda Peterson

Introduction

    I. Politicians ignore youth vote

        A. Mostly 18- to 24-year-olds don't vote

        B. Statistics on voting

        C. Forecast of the reasons

Body

    II. Youth apathetic to politics

        A. Sports & beer more interesting

        B. Don't know who represents them

    III. Politics unappealing

        A. Partisanship

        B. Political scandals

Conclusion

    IV. What solution?

        A. More focus on youth

        B. More attention on campus

A key word outline consists of important words or phrases to help remind the speaker of the content of the speech. It may also include key statistics and quotations.

building **behaviors**

Tips for Using Note Cards

A key-word outline fits easily on 3- by 5-inch or 4- by 6-inch note cards or on 8½- by 11-inch paper. If you choose note cards, the following suggestions may be useful:

1. Write instructions to yourself on your note cards. For instance, if you are supposed to write the title of your speech and your name on the chalkboard before your presentation begins, then you can write that instruction on the top of your first card.

2. Write on one side of the cards only. To use more cards with your key-word outline on one side only is better than to write front and back, which is more likely to result in confusion.

3. Number your note cards on the top so that you can keep them in order. If you drop them, you can quickly reassemble them.

4. Write out items that might be difficult to remember. Extended quotations, difficult names, unfamiliar terms, and statistics are items you may want to include on your note cards to reduce the chances of error.

5. Practice delivering your presentation at least two times using your note cards. Effective delivery may be difficult to achieve if you have to fumble with unfamiliar cards.

6. Write clearly and legibly.

organizational patterns
Arrangements of the contents of a presentation.

time-sequence pattern
A method of organization in which the presenter explains a sequence of events in chronological order.

communicating
creatively

Online Brainstorming

As you engage in topic selection and organization for your presentation, you may find it useful to use online brainstorming tools. A general Internet search for "online brainstorming" will yield numerous sites that you can use to storyboard and visually map your ideas. Some programs use visual elements like sticky notes and word clouds. Others contain forums that allow you to collaborate with other students and your teacher by posting your thoughts on a common topic. You can also brainstorm outside class at your convenience, testing ideas with others in a safe environment. Take advantage of online programs that allow you to work individually to map out your thoughts or collaborate with others to share ideas and receive valuable feedback.

statistics or quotations that are long or difficult to remember. The sample key-word outline came from a student's speech about the youth vote. Notice how the key-word format reduces the content to the bare essentials.

ORGANIZATIONAL PATTERNS

You can outline the body of a presentation using a number of **organizational patterns,** arrangements of the contents of the message. Exactly which pattern of organization is most appropriate for your presentation depends in part on your purpose and on the nature of your material. For instance, if your purpose is to present a solution to a problem, your purpose lends itself well to the problem/solution organizational pattern. If your material focuses on events that occurred over time, then it might be most easily outlined within a time-sequence pattern.

In this section we will examine four organizational patterns, prototypes from which a skilled presenter can construct many others. Keep in mind that a number of organizational patterns may appear in the same message: an overall problem/solution organization may have within it a time-sequence pattern that explains the history of the problem.

The Time-Sequence Pattern

The **time-sequence pattern** is a method of organization in which the presenter explains a sequence of events in chronological order. Most frequently seen in informative presentations, this pattern can serve in presentations that consider the past, present, and future of an idea, an issue, a plan, or a project. It is most useful for such topics as

How the Salvation Army Began	The Future of International Space Exploration
The Naming of a Team	The Development of Drugs for Treating HIV

Any topic that requires attention to events, incidents, or steps that take place over time is appropriate for this pattern of organization. Following is a brief outline of a composition organized in a time-sequence pattern.

How Ford Drove the Auto Industry
by Jared Fougner

Purpose: I plan to highlight the history of the Ford Motor Company in the United States from its beginnings to today, so my audience will be informed about this important background in a truly American industry.

Introduction

I. I've been interested in the automobile industry for many years, but until the recent financial troubles I never thought much about the vital role that the first mass-production automobile company, Ford, had in our industrial base.

   A. Automobiles play a vital role in all our lives.

   B. Automobiles are important to the economy.

   C. The Ford Motor Company illustrates the dynamic nature of the automobile market.

Body

II. Henry Ford started the Industrial Revolution in this country with the mass production of autos, and his company continued to be a key player in the auto industry in its early, middle, and later years.

   A. In the early years Ford experimented, developed mass production, and created cars ahead of their time.

      1. Henry Ford ran the first experimental car, the Quadricycle, down Detroit streets in 1896.

      2. Dr. Ernst Pfennig of Chicago purchased the first Ford vehicle in 1903.

   B. In the middle years Ford produced some of the nation's best-selling vehicles.

      1. Ford released the F-series pickup trucks in 1948 that even today outnumber all competitors.

      2. Ford launched the Taurus, another top seller, in 1986.

   C. In modern times Ford innovated and competed in an ever-tightening market.

      1. In 2000 Ford innovated with a Taurus Flex Fuel Vehicle.

      2. In 2005 Ford innovated with the Escape Hybrid.

      3. Today, Ford offers electric and hybrid automobiles, and the new EcoBoost engine which combines V8 power with V6 efficiency.

CONTINUED

Marginal annotations:

- Relates source credibility
- Announces topic
- Relates topic to audience
- Reveals purpose
- Shows organization
- Forecasts chronological order
- Introduces part I: early years
- Offers two examples
- Introduces part II: middle years
- Offers two examples
- Introduces part III: modern times
- Offers three examples

Conclusion

Summarizes topic

III. Ford Motor Company was an industry pioneer that evolved over the years and contributed mightily to our daily life.

Signals ending with review

A. Now you know that Henry Ford started the Industrial Revolution in this country with the mass production of autos.

Offers example of effect

B. With the advent of mass-produced cars came a need for an extensive system of hard-surface roads, highways, and interstates that changed the face of the United States.

Fulfills purpose

C. I hope that my look backward at one U.S. industry gives you new appreciation of Ford's contribution to our society.

The Cause/Effect Pattern

cause/effect pattern
A method of organization in which the presenter first explains the causes of an event, a problem, or an issue and then discusses its consequences, results, or effects.

In using a **cause/effect pattern,** the presenter first explains the causes of an event, a problem, or an issue and then discusses its consequences, results, or effects. The presentation may be cause–effect, effect–cause, or even effect–effect. A presentation on inflation that uses the cause/effect pattern might review the causes of inflation, such as low productivity, and then review the effects of inflation, such as high unemployment and interest rates. The cause/effect pattern is often used in informative presentations that seek to explain an issue. This pattern differs from the problem/solution pattern in that the cause/effect pattern does not necessarily reveal what to do about a problem; instead, the organization allows for full explanation of an issue. The outline for a speech on the effects of smoking is an example of the cause/effect pattern.

Confessions of a Smoker
by Linzey Crockett

Purpose: This speech by a confessed smoker notes the effects of smoking on the health of the smoker, an effect that includes early death.

Introduction

Relates source credibility

I. I'm a guy from South Chicago who has smoked at least 10 or more cigarettes a day for the past 15 years, a habit that will greatly increase my chances of getting lung cancer.

Gains attention

Uses cause/effect argument

A. Smoking cigarettes is an addiction that is exceedingly difficult to beat.

Offers fact

B. I've been in denial for years about how smoking is damaging my lungs.

Gives personal testimony

C. Today I will talk with you about the effects of smoking on the human body because I want you to know how lucky you are if you don't smoke and how threatened you are if you do.

Provides purpose

Relates topic to audience

Body

II. Smoking has physiological effects on heart and blood.

Provides main argument on causes

A. Smoking increases the heart rate.

B. Smoking increases blood pressure but slows the blood flow by constricting arteries and veins.

Offers supporting facts

C. Smoking increases your chances of both heart attack and stroke.

Relates serious effects

III. Carbon monoxide increases while oxygen depletes when you smoke.

States second argument

A. When you inhale a cigarette, carbon monoxide immediately flows throughout the body to make the heart and lungs work harder.

Offers supporting facts

B. Oxygen has difficulty reaching the extremities.

IV. As the cigarette burns close to your mouth the dangerous toxins concentrate in the cigarette butt.

States third argument

A. Tobacco tar is a known carcinogen, a cancer-producing agent.

Offers supporting facts

B. Nicotine from tobacco can increase cholesterol levels, which corrode the arterial system.

Conclusion

V. Smoking cigarettes can and will lead to pulmonary problems like lung cancer and emphysema, diseases that lead to an early death.

Provides cause/effect argument

A. Smoking affects heart rate and blood pressure, which makes the smoker vulnerable to heart attack and stroke.

Summarizes argument

B. Toxins like tobacco tar and nicotine increase cholesterol and contribute to cardiovascular disease, a result of smoking and major cause of premature death.

Reviews facts

C. I hope you now know considerably more about the physiological effects of smoking and why the habit is dangerous.

Restates purpose

The cause/effect pattern of organization is common in fields as varied as medicine (tobacco causes cancer), economics (when a recession ends, corporate profits rise, the economy improves, and inflation increases), and education (people with a college education nearly double their annual earnings).

The Problem/Solution Pattern

The third pattern of organization, used most often in persuasive presentations, is the **problem/solution pattern,** in which the presenter describes a problem and proposes a solution. A message based on this pattern can be divided into two distinct parts, with an optional third part in which the presenter meets any anticipated objections to the proposed solution.

The problem/solution pattern can contain other patterns. For example, you might discuss the problem in time-sequence order, and you might discuss the solution using a topical-sequence pattern. Some examples of problem/solution topics follow:

> Reducing Fat in Your Diet   Helping the Homeless
>
> A New Way to Stop Smoking   Eliminating Nuclear Waste

Each example implies both a problem and a solution.

The problem/solution pattern of organization requires careful audience analysis, because you have to decide how much time and effort to spend on each portion of the speech. Is the audience already familiar with the problem? If so, you might be able to discuss the problem briefly, with a few reminders to the audience of the problem's seriousness or importance. On the other hand, the problem may be so complex that you cannot cover both the problem and the solution in a single presentation. In that case you may have found a topic that requires both a problem presentation and a solution presentation. The outline for the speech on "Routine Body Shrinking" illustrates the organizational pattern of a problem/solution speech.

problem/solution pattern
A method of organization in which the presenter describes a problem and proposes a solution to that problem.

Routine Body Shrinking
by Greg Heller

Relates topic to speaker and establishes source credibility

Purpose: This presentation will persuade the audience to start a steady and well-planned exercise routine with positive, beneficial, and healthy results.

Introduction

Gains attention

I.   For years I was a fat guy, but since 2005 I have lost 130 pounds (the equivalent of another person) by simply starting and maintaining an exercise routine.

Relates topic to audience

   A. My personal experience will help you see the benefits of a well-planned routine to lose weight.

Announces topic

Reveals organization

B. My personal experience will reveal the effects of an exercise routine and the real benefits, so you can have the same kind of success without much stress.

                                                    Announces purpose

Body

II. Over the last decade many high-quality studies have shown the benefits of exercise.

                                                    States first argument

  A. Regular exercise increases stamina, agility, coordination, and balance.

  B. Physical activity promotes a healthier lifestyle.

                                           Offers two points to support claim

III. What did a well-planned workout regimen do for me?

  A. I lost weight and gained a normal metabolism.

                                           States second argument

  B. I could run long distances and remain alert all day.

  C. I felt much better about myself and how I looked.

                                           Offers three points to support claim

Conclusion

IV. Launching and sustaining a well-structured exercise routine yields benefits uncovered in studies and demonstrated in my own life.

                                           Summary/review

  A. No longer obese, my new body is evidence of the effects of a structured workout routine.

                                          Offers ethos: personal proof

  B. Now that you know the benefits, have heard about the studies, and see me in the flesh (actually a lot less flesh), you should consider an exercise routine for a healthier self.

                                           States action purpose

The Topical-Sequence Pattern

The **topical-sequence pattern,** used in both informative and persuasive presentations, emphasizes the major reasons the audience should accept a point of view by addressing the advantages, disadvantages, qualities, and types of a person, place, or thing. This pattern can be used to explain to audience members why you want them to adopt a certain point of view. It is appropriate when you have three to five points to make, such as three reasons people should buy used cars, four of the main benefits of studying speech, or five characteristics of a good football player. The topical-sequence pattern of organization is among the most versatile. The topical-sequence pattern can be seen in the outline for a speech informing the audience about global warming.

topical-sequence pattern
A method of organization that emphasizes the major reasons an audience should accept a point of view by addressing the advantages, disadvantages, qualities, and types of a person, place, or thing.

Global Warming: What Can You Do?
by Emily Holt

Purpose: This speech informs by exploring the negative effects of global warming and persuades the audience to take steps to avoid even more damage to the Earth.

Introduction

Relates speaker to topic

I. Always interested in the natural world and the out-of-doors with Mother Nature, I study global warming and passionately spread the word on how to reduce the harmful effects.

Relates topic to audience

   A. The impacts of global warming on the environment and on human life affect us all.

Defines key term

   B. "Global warming" refers to the warm blanket of carbon dioxide that now envelops the earth with more CO_2 than in the past 650,000 years.

Forecasts organization
States purpose

   C. I hope that by the end of this presentation you will understand the magnitude of the problem and feel confident that you can make a positive difference in helping planet Earth.

Body

Provides first argument & overview

II. As a direct consequence of human activity the average global temperature rises, causing glacial melting, Arctic ice shrinkage, and rising sea levels.

Includes facts to support argument

   A. Since 1980, glacial melting has increased rapidly, threatening the existence of global glaciers.

   B. Since the end of the nineteenth century (the 1800s) the total surface area of glaciers has decreased by 50%.

Uses prediction to support argument

   C. Rising ocean levels—an estimated 6 feet over the next 100 years (or sooner)—will be catastrophic to coastal regions and waterways where most humans live.

Provides second main argument

III. You can make smart choices in your daily life, choices that will affect your contribution to reducing global warming.

Offers three choices

   A. One smart choice is to buy at a farmers' market to avoid shipping costs and to obtain fresher food.

Provides possible actions

   B. Another smart choice is to buy a fuel-efficient car, because such vehicles leave a smaller carbon footprint.

    C. Unplug unused electronics, because they drain energy unnecessarily.

Relates intended outcomes

Conclusion

    IV. We have looked at the issue of global warming, explored some evidence of global warming's existence, and looked at some ways that you as an individual or as a family can decrease CO_2 and help reduce global warming.

Provides summary/review and intended result

TRANSITIONS AND SIGNPOSTS

So far, we have examined organization in its broadest sense. However, we also need to look more closely at the design of the presentation by examining the elements that connect the parts of a speech—transitions and signposts.

A **transition** is a bridge between sections of a message that helps a presenter move smoothly from one idea to another. Transitions also relax the audience momentarily. A typical transition is a brief flashback and a brief forecast that tell your audience when you are moving from one main point to another.

transition
A bridge between sections of a presentation that helps the presenter move smoothly from one idea to another.

The most important transitions are between the introduction and the body, between the main points of the body, and between the body and the conclusion of the presentation. Other transitions can appear between the main heading and main points, between main points and subpoints, between subpoints and sub-subpoints, between examples, and between visual aids and the point being illustrated. They can review, preview, or even be an internal summary, but they always explain the relationship between one idea and another. Transitions are the mortar between the building blocks of the speech. Without them cracks appear, and the structure is less solid. Table 1 gives examples of transitions.

Signposts are ways in which a presenter signals to an audience where the presentation is going. Signposts, as the name implies, are like road signs that tell a driver there is a curve, bump, or rough road ahead; they are a warning, a sign that the presenter is

signposts
Ways in which a presenter signals to an audience where the presentation is going.

Table 1 Examples of Transitions

Transition from one main point to another: "Now that we have seen why computers are coming down in cost, let us look next at why software is so expensive."

Transition from a main point to a visual aid: "I have explained that higher education is becoming more and more expensive. This bar graph will show exactly how expensive it has become over the past five years."

Transition that includes a review, an internal summary, and a preview: "You have heard that suntanning ages the skin, and I have shown you pictures of a Buddhist monk and a nighttime bartender who hardly ever exposed themselves to direct sunlight. Now I want to show you a picture of a 35-year-old woman who spent most of her life working in direct sunlight."

> **Table 2** Examples of Signposts
>
> "First, I will illustrate . . ."
>
> "Look at this bar graph . . ."
>
> "See what you think of this evidence . . ."
>
> "A second idea is . . ."
>
> "Another reason for . . ."
>
> "Finally, we will . . ."

making a move. Whereas transitions are often a sentence or two, signposts can be as brief as a few words. Transitions review, state a relationship, and forecast; signposts merely point.

You'll want to avoid using signposts that are too blatant: "This is my introduction," "Here is my third main point," or "This is my conclusion." More experienced presenters choose more subtle but equally clear means of signposting: "Let me begin by showing you . . . ," "A third reason for avoiding the sun is . . . ," or "The best inference you can draw from what I have told you is . . ." Table 2 gives examples of signposts.

Transitions and signposts help presenters map a message for the audience. Transitions explain the relationships in the message by reflecting backward and forward. Signposts point more briefly to what the presenter is going to do at the moment. Both transitions and signposts help bind the message into a unified whole.

The Conclusion

conclusion
The part that finishes the presentation by fulfilling the four functions of an ending.

Like the introduction, the **conclusion** fulfills specific functions. These four functions need not occur in the order shown here, but they are all normally fulfilled in the last minutes of a presentation:

1. Forewarn the audience that you are about to finish.
2. Remind the audience of your central idea and the main points of your presentation.
3. Specify what the audience should think or do in response to your speech.
4. End the speech in a manner that makes audience members want to think and do as you recommend.

Let us examine these functions of a conclusion in greater detail.

brakelight function
A forewarning to the audience that the end of the presentation is near.

The first function, the **brakelight function,** warns the audience that the end of the presentation is near. Can you tell when a song is about to end? Do you know when someone in a conversation is about to complete a story? Can you tell in a TV drama when the narrative is drawing to a close? The answer to these questions is usually yes, because you get verbal and nonverbal signals that songs, stories, and dramas are about to end.

How do you use the brakelight function in a presentation? One student signaled the end of her speech by stating that her time was up: "Five minutes is hardly time to consider all the complications of this issue . . ." Another said, "Thus men have the potential for much greater role flexibility than our society encourages . . ." The word *thus,* like *therefore,* signals the conclusion of a logical argument and indicates that the argument is drawing to a close.

You can fulfill the second function of a conclusion—reminding the audience of your central idea or the main points in your message—by restating the main points, summarizing them briefly, or selecting the most important point for special treatment. Elizabeth Nnoko ended her persuasive speech on legalizing drug purchases from Canada by briefly summarizing her message:

> We have discussed the rising cost of prescription drugs, the problem with Medicare, myth and reality concerning importation of prescription drugs, and solutions that can be implemented to solve this issue.

• An effective way to conclude a speech is with an inspirational statement.

© The Star-Ledger/Tim Farrell/The Image Works

The third function of a conclusion is to specify what you expect audience members to do as a result of your presentation. Do you want the audience to simply remember a few of your important points? Then tell them one last time the points you think are worth remembering. Do you want the audience to write down the argument they found most convincing, sign a petition, or talk to their friends? If so, state what you would regard as an appropriate response to your presentation. One student's presentation on unions concluded with the slogan "Buy the union label," specifying what she expected of the audience.

The fourth function of a conclusion is to provide a "clincher," a memorable statement that encourages listeners to think and do as you recommend. You can conclude with a rhetorical question: "Knowing what you know now, will you feel safe riding with a driver who has had a few drinks?"; an interesting statement: "When you are making the choice between bottled and tap, just remember that there is no such thing as 'new' water; the water we drink today is the same water the dinosaurs drank, so whatever you choose, you'll be choosing well"; a quotation: "As John F. Kennedy said, 'Forgive your enemies, but never forget their names' "[2]; a literary passage: "We conclude with the words of Ralph Waldo Emerson, who said, 'It is one light which beams out of a thousand stars; it is one soul which animates all men' "[3]; or an action: a tennis player demonstrates proper form for serving the ball.

Some cautions about conclusions: in ending a presentation, as in initiating one, you need to avoid being overly dramatic. Do not behave in a way that will offend members of your audience, create high tension, or frighten listeners. A better idea is to conclude your presentation with an inspirational statement, words that make audience members glad they spent the time and energy listening to you. One student delivered a single line at the end of his talk on using seat belts: "It is not who is right in a traffic accident that really counts," he said, "it is who is left." That conclusion was clever and memorable, it provided a brief summary, and it was an intelligent and safe way to end a presentation.

Following are two sample conclusions that fulfill the four functions described in this section. The first is from Danelle Hopkins, a political science major, from her speech about No Child Left Behind legislation. The second is from Alan Perrault, from his speech about geocaching that was described at the beginning of the chapter.

building behaviors

Crafting an Effective Conclusion: Things to Avoid
Once you've drafted your conclusion, check it against this list of things to avoid in a speech conclusion.

• Do not just end abruptly with no forewarning.

• Remind the audience of your main points but do not provide a detailed replay of everything you did in the speech.

• Do not say negative things about your own presentation: "Well, I guess that didn't go so well," "Probably I should have done more research," or "I sure blew that assignment."

• Do not let your own nonverbal communication signal a poor presentation by letting your voice trail off at the end, by dropping your arms and looking defeated, or by walking off to your seat as you finish.

Danelle Hopkins fulfilled the four functions of a conclusion

Uses brakelight function: warns that ending is near

Reminds audience of main points: summary

Specifies what the audience should do

Ends by recommending an action

Alan Perrault fulfilled the four functions of a conclusion

Sample Conclusions That Fulfill the Four Functions

Sample Conclusion 1

I. From what I have told you about No Child Left Behind, it is obvious that the program needs to be reformed.

II. I told you about the problems associated with No Child Left Behind, informed you about a proposed reform to the program, and let you know how you can help.

III. Please contact your congressional representatives—I have provided you with their e-mail addresses and their phone numbers.

IV. If nothing is done about No Child Left Behind, it might be that no children will be left behind. But the real problem is that no child might get ahead.

Sample Conclusion 2

I. *Brakelight function:* I do not want to overwhelm you with too many details about geocaching.

II. *Summary:* Today I told you about the sport of geocaching. I explained to you what geocaching is, how it works, and how you can get involved.

III. *Specific audience action:* I hope that this information might inspire you to learn more about this sport.

IV. *Clincher:* If current trends continue, we will likely see the 2,000,000th active geocache by the end of 2012. (*put up graph showing cache numbers and trend line*)

The References

references
A list of sources used in a presentation.

When you have completed your outline, you may be asked to provide a list of **references,** or the sources you used in your presentation. The main idea behind a reference list is to inform others of what sources you used for your speech and to enable them to check those sources for themselves. Each entry in your references should be written according to a uniform style. Several accepted style manuals can answer your questions about the correct format: *The Publication Manual of the American Psychological Association* (APA), *The MLA Handbook,* and *The Chicago Manual of Style.* Since some teachers prefer MLA and others prefer APA, you should ask your instructor's preference. You can learn more about APA style at www.apastyle.org and more about MLA style at www.mla.org/style. Because it is so efficient to find examples of the two styles on the Internet, we do not provide the correct forms for these sources here.

An example of a reference list on the importance of water, used in a speech by Emily Knilans, is provided below. Note that Emily used the APA style manual and that she included many online sources. Style manuals like APA are regularly updated. Make sure you are using the most current edition of any style manual.

References

Baskind, C. (2010, March 15). *5 reasons not to drink bottled water.* Retrieved September 27, 2011 from the Mother Nature Network website http://www.mnn.com/food/healthy-eating/stories/5-reasons-not-to-drink-bottled-water

Brain Statistics Galore. (2011). *Fun facts about the brain.* Retrieved October 13, 2011 from the Brain Health and Puzzles website http://www.brainhealthandpuzzles.com/fun_facts_about_the_brain.html

Culligan Water Company. (2011). *Common water problems.* Retrieved September 27, 2011 from the Culligan website http://northernplainsculligan.com/at-home-or-work/common-water-problems

Drinking Water Research Foundation. (2011). *Water and your health.* Retrieved September 26, 2011 from the Drinking Water Research Foundation website http://www.thefactsaboutwater.org/health/

Education Database Online. (2011). *The facts about bottled water.* Retrieved September 26, 2011 from the Education Database Online website http://www.onlineeducation.net/bottled_water

Environmental Protection Agency (EPA). (2009, December). *Water on tap: What you need to know.* Retrieved September 27, 2011 from the EPA, office of water website http://www.epa.gov/ogwdw/wot/pdfs/book_waterontap_full.pdf

Environmental Protection Agency (EPA). (2010, October 12). *Is bottled water safer than tap water?* Retrieved September 26, 2011 from the Environmental Protection Agency website http://safewater.supportportal.com/link/portal/23002/23015/Article/18873/Is-bottled-water-safer-than-tap-water

Friday, L. (2011, March 24). *Bottled vs. tap: Which tastes better?* Retrieved September 27, 2011 from the BU Today website http://www.bu.edu/today/2011/bottled-vs-tap-which-tastes-better/

Howard, B. (2003, December 9). *Despite the hype, bottled water is neither cleaner nor greener than tap water.* Retrieved September 27, 2011 from the Common Dreams website http://www.commondreams.org/headlines03/1209-10.htm

Klessig, L. (2004). *Bottled water industry.* Retrieved September 27, 2011 from the Water is life website http://academic.evergreen.edu/g/grossmaz/klessill/

Mayo Clinic Staff. (2011). *Water: How much should you drink every day?* Retrieved September 27, 2011 from the Mayo Clinic website http://www.mayoclinic.com/health/water/NU00283

Stossel, J. (2005, May 6). *Is bottled water better than tap?* Retrieved September 27, 2011 from the ABC website http://abcnews.go.com/2020/Health/story?id=728070&page=1

The facts about the global drinking water crisis. (2010). Retrieved September 27, 2011 from the Blue Planet Network website http://blueplanetnetwork.org/water/facts

be ready... for what's next

Organizing the Body of the Speech

Conducting an audience analysis can help you organize the body of your speech because you can adapt your presentation to fit your audience's knowledge of your topic. You don't want to spend too much time explaining what your audience already knows while neglecting information that would help audience members better understand your topic.

As Alan Perrault studied this chapter and thought about his audience's knowledge of geocaching, he decided to organize his speech around the topics of what geocaching is, what a person needs to geocache, and finally, how to get involved in geocaching.

I. What is a geocache?

   A. The basic geocache is a container with a log book and items to trade, known as "swag," that is hidden somewhere.

   B. Cache sizes can range from micro, the size of a music earbud, to large, which is typically an ammo box or ice cream bucket. (*show geocache pictures*)

   C. The larger caches will usually have items that you can trade. With these the general rule is to trade items of equal monetary value.

   D. The log book contains a listing of every person who has found the cache. When you find a cache, you sign and date the log.

   E. The log book is usually a small notebook in larger caches and a strip of paper in micro caches.

   Transition: Now that you know what a geocache is, how do you find one?

II. How do you find a geocache?

   A. There are only two things you need to find a geocache.

      1. You need a free account at geocaching.com.

      2. You also need a GPS.

      3. If you have a smartphone, you may be able to use that with a geocaching or GPS app, instead of an actual GPS.

   B. When you sign up for a geocaching.com account, you will choose a geocaching nickname. This is what you will use to sign a cache's log.

   C. Once you are signed up, do a search for your city or zip code to locate a nearby cache.

      1. On each cache's page, there are attributes for the cache's terrain and difficulty.

      2. It usually works best if your first cache has low ratings for both these.

   Transition: There is a whole world of caches available for you to find. Here is a quick overview.

III. Where can you find geocaches?

   A. Geocaches can be found all around the world (*map slide*); there are ~140 caches hidden within 5 miles of the campus. (Groundspeak, 2011). (*Fargo-Moorhead slide*)

   B. Coordinates for every active geocache can be found on geocaching.com.

   C. Many caches are hidden to bring attention to a place of interest.

   D. (*Pictures of some locations I've found caches*)

Can you think of another way that Alan could have organized his talk? Using the material you discovered in this chapter, how might you organize an informative or a persuasive speech?

Chapter Review & Study Guide

Summary

In this chapter, you learned the following:

1. An effective introduction fulfills five functions, which can occur in any order:

    - It gains and maintains audience attention.
    - It arouses audience interest in the topic.
    - It states the purpose of the presentation.
    - It establishes the presenter's credibility.
    - It forecasts the organization and development of the presentation.

2. An effective outline for a presentation follows six principles:

    - It relates the information presented to the immediate purpose and long-range goal.
    - It is an abstract of the message you will deliver.
    - It expresses ideas in single units of information.
    - It indicates the importance of items with rank-ordered symbols.
    - It provides margins that indicate the importance of each entry visually.
    - It states entries in parallel form (such as complete sentences, as in this list).

3. The most frequently used patterns of organization in public presentations are

    - Time-sequence pattern, or chronology, with items presented serially over time.

    - Cause/effect pattern, which posits a cause that results in some effect.
    - Problem/solution pattern, which poses a problem followed by a suggested solution.
    - Topical-sequence pattern, with items listed as a limited number of qualities or characteristics.

4. Transitions and signposts link ideas and indicate direction to the audience.

5. An effective conclusion fulfills certain functions:

    - It forewarns listeners that the presentation is about to end.
    - It reminds the audience of the central idea and main points of your presentation.
    - It specifies what you expect from the audience as a result of the presentation.
    - It ends the presentation in a manner that encourages the audience to think and act as you recommend.

6. Often a list of references, or sources, accompanies the complete outline.

Key Terms

Body
Brakelight function
Cause/effect pattern
Conclusion
Introduction
Key-word outline
Main points

Organizational patterns
Outline
Parallel form
Problem/solution pattern
References
Rough draft
Sentence outline

Signposts
Subpoints
Time-sequence pattern
Topical-sequence pattern
Transition

Study Questions

1. Which function of the introduction shows how the topic is related to the audience?
   a. gaining and maintaining audience attention
   b. arousing audience interest
   c. stating the purpose or thesis
   d. establishing speaker qualifications

2. Stating your purpose in the introduction
   a. is necessary because informative speeches do not invite learning, and this is your only opportunity to explain.
   b. is unnecessary, because the audience will learn of the purpose in the body of the speech.
   c. is not appropriate, because you will lose an element of surprise in the body of the speech.
   d. is important, because audience members are more likely to learn and understand if your expectations are clear.

3. When developing the body of a speech, you must
   a. select, prioritize, and organize information.
   b. write your introduction first.
   c. use as much information as possible.
   d. utilize sources but not cite them.

4. Which of the following statements is *not* true with regard to outlining?
   a. It uses symbols, margins, and content to reveal the order, importance, and substance of a presentation.
   b. All items of information in your outline do not need to be directly related to the speech's purpose and long-range goal.
   c. It encourages a conversational speaking tone, because not every word is in front of you.
   d. Items should appear in parallel form.

5. Which type of outline consists mostly of important words or phrases but not complex information?
   a. main point
   b. sentence
   c. key-word
   d. cause/effect pattern

6. If you were giving a speech about the parking problem at your university with possible means to resolve it, which organizational pattern would be best?
   a. time-sequence
   b. cause/effect
   c. problem/solution
   d. topical-sequence

7. When a presenter explains a progression of events in chronological order, he or she is most likely using which organizational pattern?
   a. time-sequence
   b. cause/effect
   c. problem/solution
   d. topical-sequence

8. Which of the following helps speakers move from one idea to another by reviewing, stating a relationship, and forecasting?
   a. transitions
   b. signposts
   c. subpoints
   d. goals

9. Reminding the audience of the speech's central idea and main points, specifying what is expected of audience members, and ending soundly are functions of the
   a. introduction.
   b. transitions.
   c. brakelight.
   d. conclusion.

10. A reference list is
    a. a list of the sources that you might have considered to use in your presentation.
    b. ideas that you do not want to forget as you are preparing your presentation.
    c. a list of sources organized as books, articles, interviews, and other sources.
    d. sources that you actually used in your presentation.

Answers:

1. (b); 2. (d); 3. (a); 4. (b); 5. (c); 6. (c); 7. (a); 8. (a); 9. (d); 10. (d)

Critical Thinking

1. Using the suggestions from the text, how would you begin your speech in order to gain the audience's attention if your speech topic was movies? Your university? Problems of the world, such as war, famine, or poverty? Why did you choose these methods?

2. What happens on morning talk shows when the hosts wish to change subjects? Do they transition smoothly or simply announce the next topic? As a listener, which do you prefer?

Sizing Things Up Scoring and Interpretation

Clarity Behaviors Inventory

This chapter helps you learn how to organize presentations. A significant body of literature in communication and education addresses the issue of "clarity" in academic settings. Although nearly all of this research approaches clarity from the perspective of the teacher—how to present clear lessons to students—this research is directly translatable to other types of speaking situations. The Clarity Behaviors Inventory (CBI) was developed by one of the authors and his colleagues to assess students' perceptions of teachers' clarity. You can use this survey to analyze the clarity of one of your other teachers. You should *not* identify the teacher you are rating. As you compare your teacher's score with those from your classmates, discuss some of the things those teachers do that likely results in differences in scores. How can you learn from this to influence how you deliver your speeches?

The CBI is used to assess teachers' clarity in both written and oral form. Calculate scores for both dimensions of clarity by averaging responses to the following items:

- *Written clarity:* items 2, 3, 6, 8, 10, and 12
- *Verbal clarity:* items 1, 4, 5, 7, 9, and 11

In both cases, higher values indicate higher levels of clarity. You can also average all items on the survey to obtain an overall assessment of clarity. An average score of 1 or 2 indicates low clarity, and an average of 4 or 5 indicates high clarity.

References

1. Hacker, D., & Sommers, N. (2011). *A writer's reference* (7th ed.). Boston: Bedford Books of St. Martin's Press, 63.

2. O'Brien, D. (2005). *How to develop a brilliant memory week by week: 52 proven ways to enhance your memory skills.* London: Duncan Baird Publishers.

3. Emerson, R., & Porte, J. (1983). *Essays & lectures.* New York: Literary Classics of the U.S.

© Monty Rakusen/Cultura/Getty Images RF

effective delivery *and* use of visual aids

Jim Katt, University of Central Florida

When you have read and thought about this chapter, you will be able to:

1. Name the four delivery styles and explain the advantages and disadvantages of each.

2. Understand the problems with speaking from a manuscript.

3. Understand how a speaker's delivery can affect the audience's message processing.

4. Understand the importance of eye contact.

5. Describe the effect of poor delivery on speaker credibility (ethos).

6. Define the term *visual aid* from a functional perspective.

7. Describe the ways that visual aids can help you communicate more clearly with your audience.

8. Describe the characteristics of effective visual aids.

9. Understand the advantages and disadvantages of the various types of visual aids.

10. Demonstrate the use of PowerPoint in a way that establishes the proper relationship between you and your visuals.

11. Be able to incorporate underused techniques when using PowerPoint.

When you are called upon to give a presentation, no matter how much thought you put into the content of the message, it will not be effective unless it is delivered well. This chapter explores the four types of delivery, some of the disadvantages and benefits of each, and how to use presentation aids most effectively. You will learn how delivery and use of presentation aids can enhance a presentation, enhance your own credibility, and increase your audience's understanding, acceptance and retention of the message.

When you are making a presentation to an audience, your audience has five senses with which to receive your message. Of the five, three have limited use in public speaking: touch, taste, and smell. Yes, there have been presentations where the audience was able to feel the texture of the fabric sample that was passed around, or was treated to some tasty samples of Greek pastry, or got a whiff of freshly baked bread, but most of the time, speakers use the channels of sound and sight. Of course, having something worthwhile to say, mounting sound rhetorical arguments, and creating a well-organized, compelling message are important aspects of any presentation. But no matter how well-conceived your message is, it won't be an effective communication unless you can effectively translate your message into sounds and sights. This chapter takes a look at both.

Delivery

It seems safe to assume that for as long as there have been people, there has been public speaking. It is also probably true that for as long as there has been public speaking, people have been giving each other advice on delivery: the manner in which one presents a speech. Many public speaking textbooks offer very particular rules about the do's and don't's of delivery, but too often the emphasis on oratorical prescriptions causes speakers to lose sight of more basic elements of the presentation. Instead of jumping directly to "What do you need to do to deliver your presentation effectively?", we must first answer the question, "How do you want your audience to be different after experiencing your presentation?" Some might respond, "Oh, I don't want anyone to be different at all. I just want them to listen to what I have to say." But why do you want people to listen? Most of the time, an honest answer to that question involves some combination of three outcomes. As a speaker, you might want your audience to 1) know something they didn't know before, or 2) feel about something differently than they felt before, or 3) do something differently than they have done it before. So in most cases, we do want our audience to be different after we have spoken to them; we want them to know, feel, or behave differently (or some combination of the three).

We bring up this point in the context of speech delivery because it helps us take a practical approach. From this perspective, delivery is not a set of rules to follow, but rather a means to an end—we should do those things that help us accomplish our goals (to help our audience know, feel, or behave differently) and avoid doing those things that get in the way of accomplishing our communicative goals. In the next few paragraphs, we will discuss some of the decisions that you as a presenter will have to make about your delivery, and encourage you to keep your communicative goals in mind when making those decisions.

COMMUNICATION VS. PERFORMANCE ORIENTATION

Accomplishing your speaking goals can be facilitated or harmed by your orientation to delivering a speech. Many speakers put undue pressure on themselves by seeing their presentation as a performance and seeing their audience as a group of critics, just waiting for the speaker to make an oratorical mistake. For speakers with a **performance orientation,** perfection is the goal (Motley, 1997).

performance orientation
Seeing your presentation as a performance and your audience as critics.

Most of you, at one time or another, have watched television coverage of women's gymnastics at the Olympic Games. This competition may represent the epitome of a performance orientation. Let's use the vault as an example. These amazing young athletes speed down the runway, spring from the vault, and literally fly through the air while executing a dizzying sequence of twists and turns. You say to yourself, "How can anyone do those things?" But then the color commentator states gravely, "Well, she had excellent elevation, but she bent her knee on her take-off, over-rotated on her third twist, and had her toes over-pointed on her landing; the judges will take off points for each of these and she'll be effectively out of the competition." In other words, her lifetime of practice and preparation have all been for naught because when it counted most, she was less than perfect. The quest for perfection is cold-hearted.

Some speakers imagine their presentation requires the same type of perfection. They feel their audience is just waiting to criticize them, and that any imperfection will result in total failure. But that simply isn't true. Audiences aren't subtracting (or awarding) style points. The only real concern audiences have is that listening to the presentation is worthwhile for them. They are hoping to learn something, or to feel something, or to be inspired to do something, and it is doubtful they will even notice your mistakes unless your mistakes are so egregious or frequent that they interfere with your speech being worthwhile.

communication orientation
Your focus as a speaker is to achieve your communicative goals.

A more helpful orientation is a **communication orientation**, where your focus as a speaker is simply to achieve your communicative goals (Motley, 1997). It gets back to what we discussed earlier: helping your audience to know or understand something differently, stirring your audience to feel about something differently, or motivating your audience to do something differently than they did before. If you accomplish your communicative goals, your presentation is a success, and no one will remember whether or not you "over-rotated."

· Instead of thinking of a presentation as a performance, imagine it to be more like an expanded conversation you have every day with friends or co-workers.

Another attitude that will help you maintain a communication orientation is thinking of your speech as merely an expanded version of the type of conversation you have everyday with friends, family, or at work. When you have something you want to share—a great movie experience, your latest tale of road rage, your take on how to make the perfect peanut butter and jelly sandwich, or the latest juicy gossip—you talk about it in conversations with others. While you're telling your story, you are doing most of the talking and your co-conversationalists are acting as your audience. You become part of their audience when they are telling their stories. Making a presentation is not fundamentally different. Over 70 years ago, public speaking scholar James Winans offered the following advice:

I wish you to see that speech-making, even in the most public place, is a normal act which calls for no strange, artificial methods, but only for an extension and development of that most familiar act, conversation. Should you grasp this idea you will be saved much wasted effort and unnecessary worry and effort (as cited in McCroskey, 2001, p. 274).

In spite of the fact that Winan's advice has been often repeated, many speakers still see public speaking from a performance orientation. For them, speech delivery is a terribly difficult process, one at which they are destined to fail. If we instead see public speaking as the natural extension of the conversations we engage in daily, we realize we are not attempting something new and dangerous, we are just enlarging what we already know how to do. One scholar put it simply, "Public speaking is **enlarged conversations**. It should be enlarged enough to fill the room" (Brigance, 1961).

Delivery Style

After adopting a communication orientation, one of the first decisions a speaker must make is what style of delivery to choose. Most experts acknowledge four basic delivery styles: impromptu, manuscript, memorized, and extemporaneous. Let's explain and consider each of them.

An **impromptu** delivery is when speakers have little or no preparation and essentially make up the speech as they go along. It is an exercise in improvisation. Many students' worst nightmare is that a teacher will ask them to stand in front of the class without preparation and talk on some spontaneously assigned topic. It is the ultimate in being put on the spot. But while being able to "wing it" can be a useful skill, it isn't appropriate for most speaking occasions. Impromptu speeches tend to be disorganized, ambiguous, and wandering. In real life speaking situations, most audiences want you to be clear, concise, and well-prepared.

Another option is a **manuscript** delivery, where the speaker writes the entire presentation word-for-word, like a written paper, except using a tone and language that are appropriate for speaking rather than reading. To deliver the manuscript speech, the speaker simply reads aloud what is written. Unlike an impromptu speech, the manuscript delivery style provides the opportunity to organize and craft the speech carefully. A manuscript delivery is necessary for occasions when the exact wording is important. For example, let's pretend you work for the U.S. Department of State and are going to be speaking to the United Nations. Although you have written and will deliver your speech in English, your words will be translated into dozens of other languages. In all likelihood, the State Department would require you to submit your manuscript ahead of time so their translators could be sure that what you were saying could be accurately translated. If, for example, you used an English idiom that when translated into Sudanese became an ethnic slur, they would have you choose another phrase—one that translates more accurately. Once your manuscript was thoroughly examined and edited, you would be expected to deliver it *exactly* as written, lest you inadvertently offend the leaders of some other country. Most of us, however, never speak in this sort of situation, so a manuscript delivery is unnecessary and often problematic, because most speakers who read from manuscripts also tend to have poor eye contact, lack vocal variety, and commit more verbal errors (more on this a little later).

Another type of delivery is a **memorized** speech. The speaker writes the speech as a manuscript, but instead of reading it to the audience, memorizes it and then recites it from memory. This is the appropriate style for times when exact words are important but scripts are inappropriate. Stage actors, for example, need to speak their lines precisely because other actors (as well as the technical production personnel) are using the words to cue their actions and responses. Since actors cannot carry scripts around while acting, they must memorize their lines. For public speakers, memorizing solves the eye contact problem associated with manuscript speeches, but the memorization process is time-consuming. Unlike the actor, who has other actors' lines to serve as prompts, the memorized speech is a soliloquy. Forgetting what to say next is a real danger; if interrupted, many speakers find themselves unable to pick up where they left off. (Try reciting the Pledge of Allegiance starting with "America . . ." without mentally going back to the beginning.)

impromptu delivery
A speech that has little or no preparation time and is made up along the way.

manuscript delivery
A speech that is written word-for-word using a tone and language that are appropriate for speaking rather than reading.

memorized delivery
A speech is written as a manuscript and then delivered from memory.

This brings us to the fourth style, **extemporaneous** delivery. In an extemporaneous delivery, the speaker has practiced the speech (but not memorized it), and the speaker uses some form of speaking notes (but not a full-text manuscript). The speaker is able to talk in a natural manner, while still being well-prepared and well-organized. In a way, it is the best of the three other styles. Like an impromptu delivery, it allows for some spontaneity, but doesn't require improvisation, and does allow preparation and practice. Like a manuscript delivery, there is the comfort of having written notes to refer to, but without the difficulty of reading word-for-word while trying to maintain eye contact, vocal variety, and fluency. Like a memorized speech, the speaker will probably recall the wording of some key phrases, or perhaps the introduction and conclusion from having practiced the speech, but there is no pressure to have the entire text memorized, and no danger of drawing a blank (because of the notes). An extemporaneous delivery is the most effective delivery style for most speeches and the easiest for inexperienced speakers to use proficiently. Properly used, this style will serve you well for college as well as business presentations.

What's Wrong with Using a Manuscript?

Most experts recommend using an extemporaneous delivery unless a particular speaking situation requires another style, but some speakers are drawn to a manuscript delivery despite advice to the contrary. Many people fear not knowing what to say when giving a speech. "I'm afraid I'll forget everything and just stand there, looking like an idiot. I know I won't forget how to read, so I'll just read my speech." Although many find it comforting to have that manuscript in front of them while speaking, there is a problem. Speaking *effectively* from a manuscript is extremely difficult, and to be good at it takes years of practice. The vast majority of speakers (including this author, and you, if you haven't had years of experience) are not skilled at delivering from a manuscript and so their attempts at manuscript speeches suffer in several ways.

First, eye contact suffers. Establishing and maintaining a relationship with the audience is essential for effective public speaking and it is nearly impossible to establish and maintain that relationship without maintaining eye contact. Unfortunately, it is also nearly impossible to maintain eye contact while reading from a script. That's where the practice comes in. After delivering hundreds of written speeches, some speakers are able to master the art of looking at their audience most of the time and only glancing down at their scripts occasionally. Most of us lack that skill, however, and in spite of intentions to the contrary, end up looking down at the script most of the time and only occasionally glancing up at our audience.

If that weren't bad enough, many speakers also become monotone in their delivery when reading from a manuscript. In normal conversation, we use all sorts of vocal inflections without even being aware of doing so. Our voice gets higher and lower, louder and softer, and faster and slower—our speech is naturally animated. But when reading aloud (unless we have had extensive practice), we tend to concentrate so much on getting the words right that we lose most of our vocal variety and become monotone.

Verbal mistakes (also known as **non-fluencies**), such as false starts, mispronunciations, or excessive ah's and um's, are another problem that plagues many manuscript speeches. One of the reasons people are drawn to having a manuscript is that they feel they will make fewer verbal mistakes. But often, just the opposite is true. Once again, reading aloud *fluently* is a skill that requires practice. Most beginning speakers actually have more non-fluencies when reading from a manuscript than they do when speaking extemporaneously. Although using a manuscript may have started out as a plan to avoid mistakes and embarrassment, such speeches are usually doomed to be boring and difficult to follow because the speaker is looking down, speaking without much vocal variety, and committing a lot of verbal mistakes.

Delivery and Message Processing

Some speech teachers have a list of specific public speaking "no-no's" involving the delivery of a speech. For example, one training method is to have everyone in the audience rap on the table each time an "um" or "ah" slips out of the speaker's mouth. Apparently, this helps speakers break the habit of using **vocalized pauses** (the official name for um's and ah's). Some teachers promote some very specific rules for gesturing, demanding different types of gestures for specific speaking situations and suggesting that the use of any other type of gesture would be *wrong*. Other delivery "no-no's" might include: moving around too much, or not moving around enough; exhibiting poor posture while speaking; or failing to vary the pitch and volume of one's voice. Concentrating on not breaking these oratorical rules breeds a performance orientation. If we have adopted a communication orientation, we can see that all of these delivery issues are examples of sender variables, which from an Elaboration Likelihood Model perspective, would be considered peripheral cues. The ELM suggests that when a topic is perceived to be relevant, the audience's focus is drawn away from these behaviors in favor of the message itself. This might lead us to believe that as long as our audience is motivated, delivery doesn't matter. But as you may recall from our discussion of the ELM, there are two factors that determine whether audience members are likely to engage in effortful processing of a message. The relevance of the message provides motivation to process, but the other factor is ability—the receiver must be *able* to process the message. This is where delivery comes in. Good delivery cannot make an audience more able to process your message, but poor delivery can interfere with message processing. If delivery faults are severe enough or frequent enough to be a distraction, they may act as a hindrance to the audience's ability to elaborate on the message—even a relevant message. We have all endured presentations from speakers who have a bad habit of saying "ah" or "um" before practically every phrase they utter. If the audience perceives the message to be relevant, they may listen through the vocalized pauses for a while, but eventually the constant barrage of ah's and um's draws their attention away from the message and becomes a barrier to message processing. So, the problem is not that throwing in an occasional vocalized pause is an oratorical sin. However, when the ah's and um's are frequent enough to be distracting, they can interfere with message processing.

Even delivery elements that are normally considered "good" can be distracting when overused. For example, if the setting permits, moving around a bit while speaking can help foster a sense of closeness with your audience. Some speakers, however, pace back and forth quickly and constantly, creating the impression that they may wear out a portion of the floor. In these cases, there is a danger the audience will focus on the pacing instead of the message. If other bodily movements, such as shifting your weight, fiddling with your ring, or pushing back your hair, occur only occasionally during your presentation, they probably won't even be noticed by your audience. But if they occur over and over while you speak, there is a good chance your audience will be focused on your movements rather than your message.

How to avoid a distracting delivery? Rather than worry about all the distracting things you *might* be doing (most of which you probably do not have a problem with), ask a friend to give you a report on your delivery the next time you make a presentation. If your friend identifies distracting behaviors in your delivery, work on eliminating them. It goes back to the statement made earlier in this chapter: do those things that help you accomplish your communicative goals and avoid doing those things that get in the way.

vocalized pauses
Filler words such as "um" and "ah".

When you have a conversation with your friends, you make eye contact. It's just as important when you're giving a presentation.

© Shutterstock/Rido

Eye Contact

Many public speaking experts believe eye contact is the most important element of speech delivery. Making that human-to-human connection is an important part of any communication transaction, but especially so in the context of public speaking. One prominent scholar puts it this way, "Direct eye contact contributes more to the establishment of a circular response between speaker and audience than does any other element of delivery" (McCroskey, 2001, p. 278). That circular response is vital to the communication transaction. It is the way an audience decides what to make of the speaker, and the way the speaker gauges the effectiveness of what he or she is saying. Another scholar suggests eye contact amounts to much more than the speaker and audience looking each other in the eye:

> Their looking-into-the-eye is only an outward sign of an inward state of mind. Actually, they are trying to look each other in the mind. This is the mental attitude of a good public speaker, no matter how large the audience or how small. His manner will vary to fit the occasion. His posture, action, and voice may change to fit the size of the audience and the formality of the occasion. But one thing does not change: his direct looking-the-audience-in-the-mind mode of communication (Brigance, 1962, p. 76).

Beginning speakers may find it difficult to look directly at their audiences and endure their audiences looking back at them. But with very little practice, this discomfort fades. Experienced speakers are uncomfortable when they *cannot* make eye contact with their audiences. You may find it helpful to first look for a friendly face to make eye contact with (Motley, 1997), but once you feel a little more comfortable, begin to look at the others in your audience as well. It is helpful to remind yourself that pubic speaking is just an expanded conversation. Recall what happens when you are having a conversation with a small group of friends. You look at them. They look at you. It would be awkward to do otherwise. When speaking to a larger group, do what you do in smaller conversations; look at your audience.

Delivery and Credibility

We also talked about credibility, also called ethos, which is an audience's perception of a message-sender's competence, trustworthiness, and goodwill. We generally think about competence as topic expertise—does the speaker know what he or she is talking about? But an audience's perception of a speaker's competence may also be influenced by the speaker's delivery expertise. Remember, credibility is the audience's perception of the speaker; speakers whose delivery is less than competent cast doubt as to their competence in general. The good news is that your delivery doesn't have to be perfect for you to be perceived as competent, but several studies that have compared the ethos of speakers with very poor delivery with speakers with good delivery found that speakers with poor delivery are consistently perceived as having less credibility (McCroskey, 2001). Apparently, part of being perceived as someone who knows what you're is talking about begins with sounding and looking like you know what you're talking about. Of course, if you really don't know what you are talking about, a smooth delivery won't help much. But when you *do* know what you're talking about, don't allow poor delivery to impugn your aura of competence.

Using Visual Aids Effectively

Today, visual aids seem to pop up in almost every speech. PowerPoint slides, flip charts, diagrams, objects, and video clips increasingly find their way into presentations. These visual augmentations are supposed to help the presenter deliver the message to the audience. Unfortunately, visual aids are often poorly conceived and fail to help speakers communicate more clearly. To the contrary, they often get in the way of an otherwise clear presentation. But used well, visual aids can enhance the effectiveness of a presentation. For the rest of this chapter, we'll look at how to use visual aids effectively. While your most important visual is yourself, our discussion will focus on the use of *other* visual elements in your speeches. But it is appropriate to be reminded of the importance of ourselves as visuals, because we want to be sure the other visuals you present don't take too much attention away from the most important element in your presentation—you.

Defining Visual Aids

Visual aids are visual elements that help (aid) your audience receive your message. It is important to remember that the visual aid, whether it takes the form of an object, a poster, or some sort of projected image, is not the message, and not the messenger; it is just your helper. If, when speaking, you treat the visual aid like it is more important than you are, your audience is likely to begin to feel that it is more important than you. It is unfortunate when that happens, because ultimately they would have been able to relate more to you, the person, than they will ever relate to your object, your poster, or your projected image.

visual aids
Visual elements that help your audience receive your message.

Ways Visual Aids Help Us Communicate More Effectively

If used appropriately, visual aids can assist you in getting your message across in several ways. Let's discuss some of those ways.

ATTRACT AUDIENCE ATTENTION

Visuals attract the audience's attention. Hold up an object or project a slide and all eyes will be on it. For a speaker, this is a two-edged sword. Drawing your audience's attention away from their daydreaming or looking around the room is a good thing, but drawing your audience's attention away from you, the presenter, is only worthwhile if the visual they're drawn to conveys (or helps to convey) your message. This is one reason it is unwise to display visual aids throughout the entire speech. When you need to draw attention to something visual, use a visual aid. The rest of the time, put the visual aids away and let the audience pay attention to the presenter.

EMPHASIZE KEY POINTS

Because visuals draw attention, they can be used to emphasize key concepts. When your audience can see as well as hear certain key points, they are likely to remember them (Katt, Murdock, Butler, & Pryor, 2008; Vogel, Dickson, & Lehman, 1986). A well-constructed bullet list can help your audience see your main points and how they relate to one another. A compelling photograph may stay in your audience's memories far longer than your words. But it's important to realize that this effect can backfire if overused. We have all fallen victim to presenters who have almost the entire text of their speeches written out on PowerPoint slides or overhead transparencies, and then proceed to read to us what we are seeing on the screen. This technique fails for several reasons. First, everything in the speech can't be a key point. Someone once noted that there cannot be peaks without valleys. The same logic goes for messages. If you were composing a written message you might bold

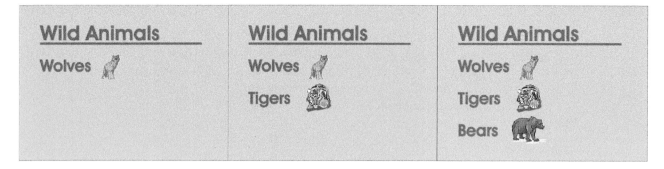

Revealing one bullet at a time helps make your speech clearer to your audience.

a key word, for emphasis. But if you bold *all* the words, you end up emphasizing nothing. Secondly, the audience can read for themselves, so it's patronizing to read to them. Finally, when everything is on the screen, the audience gets the idea that *you* aren't very important, since you don't seem to add any value to the transaction. When that happens, you throw away the high-touch impact of your presence. And if you don't add anything to the presentation, you're wasting your audience's time. You could have emailed your slides to them, if that's all you had. Judicious use of visuals for emphasis can be effective in helping your audience know and remember those key concepts.

SHOW THE RELATIONSHIP BETWEEN POINTS

When you read a book, there are sentences, and paragraphs, and sections, and chapters to help you know how the information goes together. When you listen to someone speak, it can be difficult to know what goes with what. There are some aural things (like using clear transitions and signposts) that you can do to make the organization of your speech clearer to your audience. Visuals can also be used for this purpose. A concise bullet list, for example, provides a visual indication of how one point relates to the next, and if you reveal the bullet points one at a time, it helps your audience realize when you are moving from one point to the next.

SIMPLIFY NUMERIC INFORMATION

Graphic representation of numeric data helps your audience make sense of the information.

Most people learned numbers visually. We learned to recognize them visually, and we learned to add, subtract, multiply, and divide them visually. So it's little wonder that when we receive a barrage of numeric information orally, it is difficult to follow. When

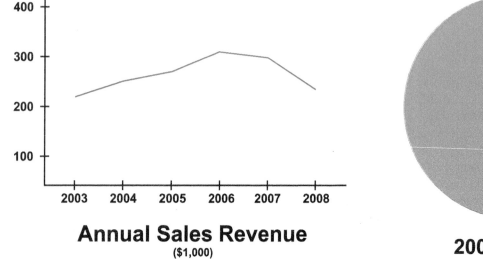

Annual Sales Revenue
($1,000)

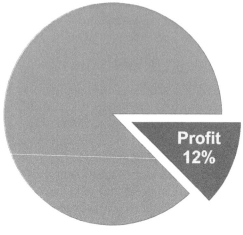

2009 Revenue

• A picture can take a general idea and quickly make it specific.

hearing numeric data, many people resort to mentally visualizing the numerals to make sense of them. Properly designed visual aids can make things easier on our audiences. Either by showing them the numbers, or by providing a graphic representation of the values the numbers represent, speakers can make life easier for their audiences, and be more effective presenters.

MAKE EXAMPLES MORE SPECIFIC

Perhaps your speech is about your camp counselor who first got you interested in astronomy and inspired you to work hard, get good grades, and go to college to become a rocket-scientist. There would be stories to tell and touching anecdotes to include in your speech, but a photograph of that counselor (maybe even one with you in the shot), would go a long way in helping your audience feel like they *knew* that person, instead of just knowing some things about her. Perhaps it is not a technique that works for every speech, but sometimes a well-placed picture can take an example from general to specific in a hurry. I once heard a young woman give a speech about her job driving a huge, off-road dump truck at a coal mining site. She mentioned several times that the truck was very large, but it wasn't until she showed the picture of her standing next to the truck (the top of her head came only to the middle of the wheel) that the audience really got a sense of how large the truck really was. Saying "large" provided a general idea; showing the truck, with her as a reference, made it specific.

ILLUSTRATE DIFFICULT-TO-DESCRIBE OBJECTS OR SCENES

Some things are just difficult to put into words. If you wanted to describe a location on the other side of the campus, you could talk about how to get there, or what it was near, or where it was relative to some central feature of the campus—or you could show them a campus map with the location highlighted. Some things are just easier to show than to tell; that's where a good visual aid can be a real helper.

• Maps can quickly illustrate locations that are difficult to describe.

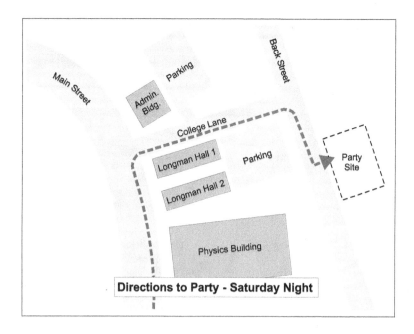

ILLUSTRATE SYMBOLIC RELATIONSHIPS

A drawing or diagram is often symbolic rather than literal. Suppose you were giving a speech about interpersonal communication and you needed to describe the importance of each person's experiences as they relate to the shared experiences between two people in a relationship. You could talk it through, but it is a fairly abstract concept that might become clearer if you introduced a diagram that helped your audience visualize the concept.

Of course people don't literally walk around with big circles of experience that intersect other people's circles, but the circles provide a symbolic way of representing the experiential relationship.

So visual aids can help speakers attract an audience's attention, emphasize key points, show relationships between points, simplify numeric information, make examples more specific, illustrate things that are difficult-to-describe, or create symbolic relationships. But this isn't always the case. Frequently, speakers employ visual elements that

• Drawings can simplify complex concepts.

fail to accomplish any of these functions. In an attempt to avoid having that happen to us, let's examine some of the characteristics of effective visual aids.

Characteristics of Effective Visual Aids

EFFECTIVE VISUAL AIDS ARE VISIBLE

Of course, it wouldn't make any sense to have an invisible visual aid, but some speakers create visual aids that might as well be invisible because they are not *large* enough, or not *legible*. Ideally, visual aids are not just visible; they are *easy* for the audience to see. If the visuals involve text, the letters must be large enough for everyone to see easily. We'll discuss this more in the PowerPoint portion of this chapter, but I recommend that projected visuals (either PowerPoint or overhead transparencies) be set in no less than 24-point type. That means that *all* text, even captions, labels, and citations, should be at least 24-point. If you are creating a poster or flip chart, the "correct" size will depend on how large the room is. For small rooms (seating 30 people or fewer) a minimum text size of 1½ inches is suggested, with titles at least twice as large (Hamilton, 1996).

If your visual aid is an object, it needs to be large enough for all to see. One sure way to annoy your audience is to hold up a small object and then say, "Well, you probably can't see this, but. . . ." Besides the obvious dysfunction of a visual aid the audience can't really see, the act of showing them the "too small" object can send the unintended message that you really don't care that much about whether or not the audience receives your message clearly. And if they get the idea you don't care, there really isn't any reason for them to care either. If the thing you are talking about is too small, figure out a way to enlarge it for your audience. Often, the easiest method is to find (or take) a digital picture of the object and make the image into a PowerPoint slide. In that case, you might still show the actual object, so they can see how small it is, but use the PowerPoint slide to allow them to visually examine the object.

**Mint Mark
(Denver Mint)**

A PowerPoint slide of a small object can help your audience see it in detail.

© Getty Images/
iStockphoto/Kary Niewenhuis

Today, most college students have grown up with computers and graphic programs like Power-Point. It wasn't that long ago when the most common student visual aid was created with poster board and markers. That put a lot of pressure on the creator to write legibly, so the audience could actually read what was written on the poster. One would think computers would solve the legibility problem, but presenters have found new, computerized ways to make even computer-generated visuals illegible. The PowerPoint section of this chapter will cover this issue at some length, but at this point, let's remind ourselves that *legible*, like *large*, is not about making text *possible* to read; it's about making it *easy* to read. Avoid decorative fonts and choose font colors that contrast with the background colors. Old English or script fonts are the modern version of illegible, along with green text over a blue background.

This lithograph, Waterfall (1961), by M.C. Escher, creates an "impossible illusion" by taking advantage of our perceptual predispositions.

EFFECTIVE VISUAL AIDS ARE NON-DISTRACTING

A good visual aid can draw the audience's attention to key points, but a poor visual aid can draw their attention away from the speaker's message. Some speakers allow their visual aids to be more disruptive than instructive. This unfortunate situation can be avoided by following two guidelines.

First, keep the visual aid out of sight when not in use. Suppose your speech included a reference to the art of M.C. Escher. What if, at the beginning of your speech, you set up an easel with a poster-sized reproduction of one of Escher's optical illusions and then started in on your introduction? Do you think the audience would be paying attention to what you were saying? Most of them would be engrossed in the picture, trying to figure out how the illusion works. In this case, your visual serves as a distraction rather than an aid. The solution is to keep it out of sight until you are ready to use it. In the case of a poster on an easel, just bring a sheet of white poster board to cover the visual until you're ready for it. If you are using an overhead transparency, leave the projector turned off until its time comes. If you are using PowerPoint, display a black slide or use the "B" key (as explained later in this chapter). When you are finished referring to your visual, put it back out of sight, using the same method.

Second, keep the visual aid in your possession if at all possible. There may be occasions where a pass-around visual aid is necessary, but try to avoid those situations. The pass-around visual aid inevitably draws attention away from the presentation as it snakes its way through the audience. And from the perspective of the individuals in the audience, the pass-around is received too early or too late for everyone except the lucky one or two who happen to have it exactly when it's being referred to.

EFFECTIVE VISUAL AIDS ARE SIMPLE AND CLEAR

Because visuals naturally draw attention, it is important to have the attention focused on something that helps communicate your message. Sometimes speakers include too much visual information and leave their audience confused instead of enlightened. As the story goes, someone viewed one of Michelangelo's sculptures, a stunning lion, just after the artist

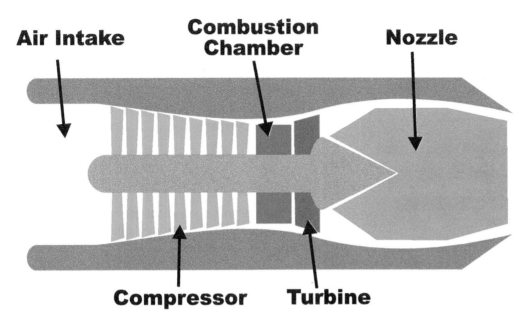

Air Intake **Combustion Chamber** **Nozzle**

Compressor **Turbine**

Good illustrations only include the elements you want to discuss.

had completed it. The observer asked Michelangelo how he was able to create such a beautiful lion from a block of stone. The artist thought a moment, then said he studied the blank stone until he could "see" the lion inside it. Then, he continued, it was simply a matter of removing all the stone that wasn't the lion. Of course! That explains why everyone who is skillful with a chisel can't create timeless art. It only works for those who can "see the lion." A student gave a speech on jet engines. He explained that there were really only five major components of a jet engine: the air intake, compressor, combustion chambers, turbine, and the exhaust nozzle. That seemed simple enough to his audience. Then he projected an overhead slide that must have been copied from an aircraft repair manual. The illustration showed every nut, bolt, and washer in a commercial airliner's jet engine, along with part numbers and arrows to connect the part numbers to the parts. It was an incredibly complex visual. As the speaker frantically pointed to various areas in the mass of parts that he claimed corresponded to the five basic components, the audience became confused, quickly gave up trying to understand, and soon tuned out the speaker and his message. Metaphorically speaking, this speaker was guilty of displaying the block of stone and expecting his audience to see the lion within. Good visual aids have nothing extraneous that needs to be chipped away. Good illustrations show the elements that are being explained and nothing else.

Showing the audience more than you are prepared to explain is, at the least, an annoyance, and, at the most, reason for them to give up on your message altogether.

EFFECTIVE VISUAL AIDS ARE FUNCTIONAL

Some students include visual aids in their presentations because their professor has required them to do so. While adherence to the requirements of the assignment is a good thing, a visual aid that has no communicative purpose is not. Remember the definition at the beginning of the chapter: visual aids are visual elements that help your audience receive your message. If your visual aid doesn't help get your message across, it's not really a visual aid. A student who presented a speech about his job building and selling computers held up a computer mouse at the end of his speech. He said, "By the way, here's a mouse. Most of the computers I sold came with a mouse." What communicative purpose did that visual serve? Was there nothing else in his message that could have been communicated more effectively with the help of a visual aid? During the course of his speech, he mentioned that the systems he built offered more features for less money than the brand-name computers. He might have created a visual that pictured one of his computer systems next to a brand-name system. He could have listed the pertinent specifications of each along with the prices, reinforcing his claim that the computers he built were a better value than the brand-name computers. That sort of visual aid would have served a communicative purpose. The mouse did not. In this case, it didn't even fulfill the requirement to have a visual aid—his professor refused to give him credit for a non-functional visual aid.

Types of Visual Aids

OBJECTS OR MODELS

Often, showing your audience "the thing" that you are talking about goes a long way toward making your speech more effective. Of course, some things are too large or too small, but many objects are portable enough to bring with you and still large enough to see. Often, objects can be used effectively with other visuals. For example, if you were giving a speech that included describing the parts located on the motherboard of a computer, you might bring in an actual motherboard, so your audience gets sense of its overall size, and also have a series of projected pictures that show the individual parts, which would be too small for them to see on the motherboard. Objects can be helpful in a *literal* sense—showing the audience how big the motherboard is—or in a *symbolic* sense.

A student speaking about his job as a server in a restaurant used a waiter's wallet (the leather or plastic folder containing the bill that servers bring to the table) as a symbol of ongoing feedback from customers that is reflected by the size of the tips. "Some employees are evaluated once a year," he said. "Servers are evaluated every day, and the results show up here, in this wallet." The audience members already knew what the wallet looked like, so it wasn't informative in the usual sense, but the speaker made it into a symbol of the evaluative nature of tips. Each time he referred to one of the customer service aspects of his job, he held up the wallet, reminding the audience that being a waiter (and earning tips) is all about customer service. It was an effective—and symbolic—visual.

Some objects would be helpful visual aids, but they are too large, too expensive, or too dangerous to bring with you. In these cases, models or facsimiles may be the answer. The space shuttle is too large, too expensive, and too dangerous to bring with you, but a model might provide a more compelling visual than a drawing or a picture. The young woman who spoke about the huge truck she drove couldn't bring the truck, but the picture she brought got her message across. Also, beware of safety regulations, particularly for college presentations. When you give that speech about bow hunting, you'll want to bring in a *picture* of your cross bow and leave the real thing at home.

POSTERS OR FLIP CHARTS

Posters and flip charts are only useful for relatively small audiences, but they have some advantages. They are inexpensive, they do not require special lighting, and they are completely low-tech, so they aren't subject to the technical problems that often plague Power-Point presentations. They do have problems of their own, however. First, if the posters or flip charts are hand drawn, care must be taken to make them legible—not just decipherable, but *easy* to read. As we mentioned previously, text should be no smaller than 1½ inches high and titles should be at least twice as large. Second, some thought needs to go into how they are going to be supported (literally, what's going to hold them up). Poster boards balanced on the chalk tray of a blackboard will almost always fall down in the middle of your presentation. In the same manner, masking tape doesn't really stick to a chalkboard—at least not for long. Some tapes can also damage paint or wall coverings, which leaves you making a bad impression with whoever is hosting the event. Pushpins are effective, providing you bring them and there is a "pinable" surface available. Easels also work well, if the visual is stiff enough not to bend over during your speech. The biggest reason speakers have poster support problems is that they fail to carefully think through the issue *before* their speeches. This isn't rocket science, just one of those cases where an ounce of prevention really *is* better than a pound of cure. Finally, posters should look *professional*. If it looks like an elementary school student scribbled it together moments before your speech, your credibility can be damaged.

OVERHEAD TRANSPARENCIES

The venerable overhead transparency projector is often scornfully viewed by speakers who increasingly prefer to use projected computer images like PowerPoint. While it is true that presentation software has many advantages over its low-tech predecessor, there are still some merits in using overhead transparencies. First is that overheads can be projected effectively in rooms that are too bright for computer video projectors to work properly. The most important advantage, however, is dependability. About the only thing that can go wrong with the overhead projector is the bulb burning out. Many projectors have spare lamps built into them, making them extremely dependable. Even though projecting PowerPoint is hardly cutting-edge technology, there is a lot that *can* go wrong. Murphy's Law suggests than anything that *can* go wrong *will* go wrong, so overhead transparencies provide fewer opportunities for Murphy to interfere with your speech. Many professional speakers who use PowerPoint as their primary presentational aid carry overhead transparencies of key slides just in case disaster strikes.

Although overhead transparencies are not used very much these days, it is still a good idea to know how to use this old, but reliable visual aid. There are "Tips for Projecting Overhead Transparencies" listed at the end of this chapter. You would do well to read the tips carefully, just in case you ever find yourself needing to make a low-tech presentation.

POWERPOINT

Presentation software, such as Microsoft's PowerPoint, has become a standard tool of the workplace, something everyone is expected to know how to use—like word-processing or email. In many ways, this is a good thing. Visual information that was once displayed on poster boards, flip charts, or overhead transparencies now can be easily and clearly presented with the help of PowerPoint or one of the competing presentation software packages. A well-designed set of PowerPoint slides can provide visual support to a spoken message and allow the speaker to devote only a minimal amount of his or her attention to displaying the visuals.

PowerPoint is a tool, and like any tool, it can be misused. The experienced carpenter can use saws and chisels to create fine furniture. However, those same tools, badly used, can turn good lumber into worthless scraps of wood. In the realm of carpentry, even the less-than-skillful carpenter generally realizes his or her mistakes and doesn't try to assemble the mis-crafted pieces into furniture. Unfortunately, in the realm of presentations, ill-fashioned PowerPoint slides often fail to go to into the trash and instead become part of the presentation—to the detriment of both presenter and audience. Are there any among us who have not been the victims of some of the following varieties of PowerPoint abuse?

- Speakers who include nearly everything they say on the slides, and spend most of their "presentation" reading the slides to the audience

- Speakers who turn their backs to their audiences, face the screen, and read the slides.

- Presentations where every new bullet point or graphic object flies into view in a distracting, annoying manner
- Presentations where the annoying fly-ins are accompanied by even more annoying sound effects
- Speakers who turn the lights out on themselves, their voices becoming disembodied, mystery narrators for their slides
- Text slides that are difficult to read because the text is too small, they are too wordy, poorly laid out, or the color of the lettering blends into the background
- Illustrations, charts, and graphs contain so much information that it is difficult to find the point of the message.

- There are many ways that PowerPoint can distract from your message.

© Image Source

Using PowerPoint Effectively

There are many books and Web sites that explain how to create slides and operate PowerPoint software, but very few resources offer guidance on how to effectively integrate PowerPoint visuals into a presentation. The remainder of this chapter concerns using PowerPoint effectively and avoiding PowerPoint abuse.

WHO'S THE PRESENTER AND WHO'S THE HELPER?

One way to avoid PowerPoint abuse is to be clear about your role and PowerPoint's role in your presentation. It is easy, and sometimes more comfortable, to think of PowerPoint as the presenter and you as the helper/technician/projectionist, but to do so relinquishes the power of face-to-face communication. You are the human being—the living, breathing, thinking, feeling person who can relate to and communicate with other humans in much a more powerful way than any arrangement of ones and zeros and pixels. You are the speaker—the communicator, the person in charge of the presentation. PowerPoint can be a great helper, but be careful not to let it take over your role as presenter. Here are some things you can do to help keep you and PowerPoint in a proper relationship.

MAINTAIN EYE CONTACT WITH YOUR AUDIENCE

During your presentation, maintain eye contact with your audience, not with your PowerPoint slides. It's okay to sneak a quick peak at the screen every so often, just to make sure it's working, but when you find yourself looking at the screen most of the time and at your audience only occasionally, you are (non-verbally) telling your audience that PowerPoint is the presenter and you are just the narrator. Keeping your eyes off the screen is easier said than done. When all of your audience is looking at the screen, it is tempting to join them. But when you do so, you relinquish your role as the presenter. Fight the temptation.

SHOW VISUALS ONLY WHEN THEY ADD SOMETHING TO YOUR SPEECH

Realize that you do not have to display an image on the screen at all times. It's okay to turn the screen off when you don't need it. In fact, building in some PowerPoint down time during your speech is desirable. After all, the PowerPoint images are usually larger and more colorful than you are. It is easy for your audience to become immersed in what's on the screen behind you and forget about *you*. Actors refer to this process as being "upstaged."

In a theater, the part of the stage closest to the audience is referred to as downstage, while the area farthest away from the audience is upstage. If, while an actor is delivering lines downstage, actors behind him capture the audience's attention by making distracting movements, the distracters are guilty of "upstaging" the actor. A good director will not allow that to happen. When you are making a presentation, you are your own director, and you need to be careful not to allow yourself to be upstaged by your own PowerPoint.

Building in some time where PowerPoint is dark allows your audience to re-connect with you, the presenter. Because it is so easy to create PowerPoint slides, presenters often include slides that are not really necessary. Did you ever use poster board and markers to create a visual aid for some high school or middle school presentation? In those cases, would you ever go to the trouble of preparing a poster that said "Introduction" to hold up during the first part of your presentation? Most of us would not, yet speakers using PowerPoint do it all the time. In doing so, they not only miss an opportunity to connect with their audience, they demonstrate to their audience that the images shown on the screen may not be all that important. If the audience gets the idea that *you* aren't very important (because you are constantly being upstaged by PowerPoint), and that your PowerPoint isn't very important either (because information like "Introduction" isn't really useful), they will likely tune you *and* your PowerPoint out, and let their minds wander elsewhere.

The solution is to display PowerPoint images only when they add something to your speech. The rest of the time, when a visual aid is not essential to your message, turn PowerPoint off and take advantage of having your audience's undivided attention. Techniques for making PowerPoint "fade to black" are discussed later in this chapter.

DRAW ATTENTION TO THE CONTENT, NOT THE PACKAGE

Your audience only has a limited amount of attention. The more they divide their attention, the less of it is focused on any one thing. While you are making a presentation, you want your audience to be attending to your *message*. What you say and do is an important part of your message, so you want your audience to be paying attention to *you*. But it's actually a little more complicated than that. What if you were giving a presentation on wireless widgets and decided to wear an orange and purple striped jump suit? That would certainly get your audience's attention, but would they be paying attention to your wireless widgets or your wardrobe? In fact, all of the attention they gave to your outfit would be attention that did *not* go to your message. So you want your audience to pay attention to the parts of "you" that are your message, and not be distracted by other aspects of "you."

The words and images on your PowerPoint slides are also part of your message, but presenters often make the mistake of dressing their messages up in ways that draw attention to the package instead of the content. When text or images fly onto the screen from all directions, the movement is at best distracting and at worst distracting *and* annoying. Either way, the audience is paying attention to the animation effect instead of the content. I find it troubling that the newer versions of PowerPoint have included a category of animation effects labeled "exciting." Do we really want the method by which our content appears on the screen to be exciting? Wouldn't it be more effective if our *content* was the exciting part? Art curators know how to frame paintings and photographs in ways that draw the viewers' attention to the picture, not the frame. Speakers using visuals must strive to accomplish the same result.

Use animation effects with extreme caution. For most situations, choose "appear" as the desired effect. If you simply must have things fly in, choose one of the subtle moves and use that same move throughout your presentation. Mixing up animation effects encourages your audience to pay attention to the effects—attention that would be better directed to the message.

PowerPoint also allows you to have sound effects accompany slide changes or animation effects. Although many presenters become infatuated with sound effects, the inclusion of sound rarely helps communicate the message and often distracts and annoys the audience. Sound effects should only be used on those rare occasions when they help convey the message. Using sounds as attention-getters only draws attention away from you and your message.

MAKE YOUR VISUALS EASY FOR YOUR AUDIENCE TO RECEIVE

Some experts suggest that effective visuals should be designed so the viewer can absorb the information in no more than six seconds (Hamilton, 1996). This means text slides must be easy to read. Many authors have written lists of guidelines for creating text visuals, most of which come down to limiting the amount of text and presenting it in the most easy-to-read manner. To that end, I suggest the following:

- maximum six bullet points per slide with 1.5 line spacing between each bullet point
- maximum six words per bullet phrase with 1.0 line spacing between phrases
- minimum 24 point text font size
- use phrases, not sentences
- use uppercase and lowercase text; ALL UPPERCASE IS DIFFICULT TO READ
- use simple typeface fonts such as Calibri or Ariel
- use simple animations = "appear"
- use simple bullets versus numbering sequence
- **use BOLD**, *italics*, <u>underline</u> = for emphasis only
- use high contrast colors between text and background
- avoid red-green color scheme for color-blinded audience members
- use realistic pictures, graphs and clip art to enhance audience understanding

Paying attention to these simple rules will result in slides that are easier to read. If, when a slide appears on the screen, it looks like it will require some mental energy to decode the information, audience members are likely to either fall into a reading mode (which necessitates ignoring the aural message), or simply tune out the visual altogether. Either way, the visual aid is not aiding the communication process. On easy-to-read text slides, the information jumps off the screen, and the audience does not feel they have to exert significant mental effort to interpret it.

Slides with graphics should also be comprehensible in six seconds. One common mistake that results in difficult-to-comprehend graphics is the inclusion of too much information Charts and graphs are efficient ways of displaying a lot of information, but we must be careful not to display more than the audience can reasonably comprehend. A single chart that makes several points can be difficult for audiences to follow. One chart that illustrates one point is usually a better way to go. Also, most presentations do not require a lot of charts and graphs (although that doesn't stop some speakers from including them anyway). Pick just one or two that clearly illustrate the points being made.

Illustrations and diagrams can also suffer from information overload. Illustrations downloaded from the Internet often include more detail than the presenter intends to cover. While it is tempting to use the overloaded illustration and just ignore the extraneous information, there is a good chance that your audience will be distracted by the unexplained items. A good rule of thumb is never to show something you are not going to talk about. This might mean a little extra work. You may have to apply some electronic "White-Out" to the unwanted items, or you may have to create a new, simplified diagram or illustration. Expending the extra effort, however, is a good habit to acquire. Presenters are rarely accused of being too clear, and displaying unsuitable images may convey to your audience that you do not value them sufficiently to create graphics that might actually help them understand and remember your message.

Effective graphic slides are also well identified. This includes **titles**, which tell the audience what they are looking at in general, and **labels**, which identify and call attention to specific items within the slide. PowerPoint makes it easy to highlight elements electronically, eliminating the need for presenters to use fingers, sticks, or laser pens to point out items while presenting. Highlighting and labeling are excellent examples of how PowerPoint's drawing and animation features can be used to focus the audience's attention on the message rather than distract from it. When using complex graphics, it is also possible to have PowerPoint reveal portions of the graphic one at a time, so that the audience does not have to try to comprehend the entire graphic all at once. Some tips for labeling and highlighting are provided later in this chapter.

titles
Describe the general focus of a graphic slide.

labels
Identify specific elements of a graphic slide.

The bottom line is that when your visuals are unclear or difficult to comprehend, your audience is faced with the decision of either devoting a lot of attention to your visuals (at the expense of attending to your oral message), or tuning out your visuals (which usually involves tuning you out as well). In either case, the PowerPoint has taken over your presentation.

Underused PowerPoint Techniques

MAKING POWERPOINT "FADE TO BLACK" DURING A PRESENTATION

It's difficult to make PowerPoint actually "fade," but it is easy to have the screen go dark. As we discussed earlier, there are often times when visuals aren't required, and it would be better to give PowerPoint a rest. Having the screen go black accomplishes just that, and there are two techniques for achieving a black screen.

Create a Black Slide

A black slide is a slide with a black background and no text or graphics. When you project it, there is nothing to project, so the effect is the same as if you have turned the projector off. At the end of this chapter there are instructions for creating a black slide—it's not difficult. Many presenters begin their presentations with a black slide. This allows them to connect with their audience during the introduction of the presentation. Later, when a visual image is required, a simple slide advance will display the first image. Black slides work best when you have places in the presentation where you *know* you want to give PowerPoint a rest. Inserting the black slide will make it impossible for you to forget to give the graphics a break.

Use the "B" Key

Sometimes, in the course of making a presentation, you might want to go to black in a place where you had not planned to do so. The more spontaneous way to achieve a black screen is simply to touch the "B" key (the letter "B" on the keyboard, just above the middle of the space bar). It's easy to remember—"B" for black or "B" for blank. When you touch the key, the screen goes black. When you touch it again, your slides come back on, just where you left off. Be aware that this feature only works when you are in the presentation (slide show) mode.

Whether you do so by using black slides or the "B" key, giving PowerPoint some time off during your presentation is a good idea. The slides you show will be more effective if you show only the slides that add something to your presentation.

USING CUSTOM ANIMATION FOR YOUR BULLET LISTS

One useful feature of PowerPoint is the ability to have your bullet points revealed one at a time. This keeps your audience from reading ahead and pondering the points you have not yet covered. Sometimes you may have a list that has main points and sub points.

- Main Point 1
- Main Point 2
  - Sub Point 2.1
  - Sub Point 2.2
  - Sub Point 2.3
- Main Point 3

You may have the sub points revealed along with the main point, or have each sub point revealed separately. Choose the way that helps you present your message most clearly. At the end of this chapter are instructions for adjusting PowerPoint's animation settings. What's most important is that you have PowerPoint animate your slides the way that is most helpful for *your* presentation. If the default settings are not helpful for your presentation, change them. You're in charge.

HIGHLIGHTING PORTIONS OF A SLIDE

Earlier we talked about the need to highlight or point out specific elements on a picture or diagram. There are a number of ways of accomplishing this, but the instructions at the end of this chapter offer one of the more foolproof methods that does not require a lot of advanced PowerPoint knowledge. You can use this highlighting technique on charts, graphs, pictures, or diagrams. You can also add labels to go along with your highlights.

For example, if you are talking about the state of Florida, you might display a simple map (as shown above). When you want your audience to know where Orlando is located, you might add a star to highlight the location and a label to make it clear what

Highlighting a slide is a simple technique to clarify your message.

Original Slide

Highlighted Slide

you are highlighting. This simple technique uses the power of PowerPoint to help make your message clearer.

PowerPoint Recap

The use of PowerPoint can either help or hinder your presentation. It is a wonderful tool that can help you create and present effective visuals, but it can also be used to produce distracting images that overload and annoy your audience. How you use it is your decision, but bear in mind that *you* are the presenter and PowerPoint is your helper. This means *you* (not PowerPoint) are the most important element in your presentation. This means PowerPoint can (and should) go away when it's not needed. This means your slides must be designed in ways that emphasize the content, not the package. This means your audience should never feel like they are the victims of PowerPoint abuse.

Final Thoughts on the Effective Use of Visual Aids

Whatever type of visual aids you use, it is important to practice your speech with the visual aids—preferably in the location where you will be speaking. Whether your plan is to hold up an object, use a poster on an easel, project overhead transparencies, or utilize PowerPoint, practice can make the difference between success and failure. We have all witnessed presentations where problems with visuals not only distracted the audience, but distracted the speaker. Objects that prove to be unexpectedly difficult to hold, posters that slide off their easels, overhead transparencies that are projected upside-down (or backwards), or PowerPoint files that the computer refuses to read are the sorts of occurrences that every speaker dreads. But, in most cases, these potential disasters can be avoided with a little preparation. Lack of preparedness can add unnecessary stress to your speaking situation. Visual elements that you have practiced using, that you feel confident using, can help *reduce* anxiety. Do yourself and your audience the favor of practicing your presentation with your visual aids.

Visual aids can make your speeches more interesting, more memorable, and more effective—or not. The key is making the visual elements help you communicate your message more clearly. Don't fall into the trap of including visual elements just because everyone else has visuals, or because they're fun, or because you hope they will make your speech seem more professional. Let form follow function. Use visuals when they help your audience receive your message clearly, and put them away when they do not.

Chapter Addendum

CREATING A BLACK SLIDE IN POWERPOINT

These instructions will vary slightly depending on which version of PowerPoint you are using, but the basic technique remains the same. **Instructions will vary based on the version of PowerPoint you are using.**

1. Create a new, blank slide (Insert > New Slide > if you have a choice of layouts, choose "blank").
2. Go into the slide editing, or "normal" view, if you are not already in it (View > Normal).
3. Right click anywhere on the slide. A menu will appear.
4. From the menu, choose "Background." A dialog window will appear.
5. Activate the pull-down menu located in the lower part of the "Background fill" box. Color boxes will appear.

6. Click the black box. You will be returned to the "Background" window.

7. Check the "Omit background graphics from master" box.

8. Click "Apply." Caution: Do not click "Apply to all."

You have created a black slide. To create additional black slides, go into the "Slide Sorter" view, and select (single click) your black slide. While holding down the "Control" key, drag your existing black slide to wherever you need an additional black slide. PowerPoint will place a copy of your black slide in the new location, and leave the original where it was.

ADJUSTING THE ANIMATION OF BULLET LISTS IN POWERPOINT

PowerPoint makes it fairly easy to set up the animations, although the exact instructions differ from version to version. The instructions below should give you the basic idea. **Instructions will vary based on the version of PowerPoint you are using.**

1. Create a bullet list with sub points by pressing the *Tab* key before typing the first word of the sub point. PowerPoint will automatically indent and add a "sub" bullet. (To return to another main point, press *Shift + Tab*.)

2. From the "Slide Show" menu, choose "Custom Animation." A "Custom Animation" pane should appear on the right side of the PowerPoint desktop.

3. Click anywhere on your bullet list to select the bullet list text as the element you wish to animate. A box should appear around your bullet list, indicating it has been selected.

4. Click the "Add Effect" button in the "Custom Animation" pane. A sub menu will appear.

5. Select "Entrance" from the sub menu.

6. A list of effects should appear. Locate and click on "Appear."

7. You'll notice that numbers appear in gray boxes to the left of each of your bullet points. These indicate which items will appear on each successive click. (All of the items labeled one will appear on the first click, all of the items labeled two on the second click, etc.) If you want each point and its sub points to appear at the same time, skip to step 10.

8. If you want each point and each sub point to appear separately, activate the drop-down menu in the "Custom Animation" pane labeled "Start" and select "On Click."

9. Notice that the gray boxes have been re-numbered, indicating that each sub point now requires a separate click.

10. Note: If the numbers in the gray boxes do not reflect the order of appearance you desire, click on the double down arrow in the large box in the "Custom Animation" pane. This will allow you to view the controls for each of your bullet points and change them to suit your needs.

11. From the "Slide Show" menu, choose "View Show" to test the animation.

HIGHLIGHTING PORTIONS OF A POWERPOINT SLIDE

The exercise below will highlight some text, but the same technique can be used for any visual. **Instructions will vary based on the version of PowerPoint you are using.**

1. Launch the PowerPoint program

2. If a "Create New Presentation Using" window comes up, choose "Blank Presentation." If not, drop down the "file" menu and choose "new."

3. A "Choose Auto Layout" window will appear, select the "title slide" layout and click "OK."

4. Click where it says "Click to add title." Type your first name, middle initial and last name.

For the sake of practice, let's assume that you wanted to call attention to your middle initial in a presentation. The following steps show how to highlight the initial.

5. Enter the "Slide Sorter" view of PowerPoint (view > slide sorter).

6. Click on the thumbnail of the slide you just created. A box should appear around the slide, indicating you have selected it.

7. While holding down the Control Key, click on the slide, drag to the right, and release. You should now have two copies of your slide.

8. Double-click the second slide. This should take you to the "slide editing" (or "Normal") view.

9. Drop down the "View" menu, select "Toolbars," and be sure the "Drawing" toolbar is checked.

10. On the "Drawing" toolbar (usually near the bottom of your desktop) there are several drawing tools. One is called the "line tool." Its icon is a diagonal line. Click on the "line tool" icon.

11. Position your cursor just under the left side of your middle initial.

12. Click and drag to the right, underlining your initial, and release. A line should appear. (Don't be concerned that it is not very attention-getting. We'll work on that.)

13. Your line should have little circles on each end, indicating that it is "selected." If it is not selected, select it by single-clicking on the line.

14. Locate the "Line Style" tool on the "Drawing" toolbar. Its icon is four horizontal lines of increasing thickness. Clicking on the icon opens a window of line style choices. Choose a thick line, like "6 pt." Your line should become thicker.

15. Locate the "Line Color" tool on the "Drawing" toolbar. Its icon is a brush painting a thick line. Just to the right of the icon is a down arrowhead. Click on the arrowhead. A window with several color boxes should appear. You may choose one of those boxes or click "More Line Colors" to reveal more choices. Choose a bright color, like red, and click "OK." You should now have a thick, red line below your middle initial.

16. Return to the "Slide Sorter" view (View > Slide Sorter). Notice that you have two identical slides, except that the second one has your middle initial underlined.

17. Click on the first slide.

18. Drop down the "Slide Show" menu and select "View Show." Your first slide should appear in full-screen, presentation mode.

19. Press the spacebar once to advance the slide and notice what happens. You are advancing to the next slide, but because everything except the underline is the same, it appears that the underline has been added to the original slide.

This is a very basic example of highlighting. There are other drawing tools besides the line tool. For example, you could use the rectangle tool or the oval tool to highlight something. *Tip: When you create closed shapes like ovals and rectangles, PowerPoint defaults to drawing a filled (colored-in) object. To remove the fill, click the down arrowhead next to the "Fill Color" (paint bucket) icon, and choose "No Fill."*

Alternatively, it is possible to make highlights and labels "appear" by using animations, but often it is easier and quicker to simply copy the slides and add the highlights to the copies. The copy technique is also more likely to work correctly on all versions of PowerPoint, while animations sometimes work differently from one version to another.

TIPS FOR PROJECTING OVERHEAD TRANSPARENCIES

There are a few things to bear in mind when using overhead transparencies. First, when creating the transparencies, follow the same rules for text visuals that you would for designing PowerPoint slides. This includes trying to keep the text size at least 24 point. Speakers will sometimes photocopy a page of a book onto a transparency. This almost always makes a poor visual, with text so small that the audience either cannot read it or will not be willing to put forth the effort to read it. Projecting a bad visual doesn't make it a good visual—it just increases the number of people who can see that it's bad.

The overhead projector will project either a landscape or portrait slide, but nearly all screens are oriented for landscape, so compose your slide in the landscape format. Also, be careful with colors. Many of the inks used in inkjet printers are opaque rather than translucent. Since light must shine through the transparency for a color to be projected, opaque colors end up looking black when projected. The best practice is to test your slides prior to your presentation.

Getting the projector positioned and focused is a fairly simple matter, but should be taken care of prior to your speech. The following hints and a little practice should be all you need to use an overhead projector effectively.

- **Image size** – is determined by the distance of the projector from the screen (the farther away, the larger your image will be). Be sure the projector is far enough away to produce an image that is big enough to be seen by everyone.

- **Focus** – is adjusted by the knob near the lens-head. Check focus prior to your presentation.

- **Vertical position of image** – The lens-head tilts to allow you to move the image up or down on the screen. Adjust tilt prior to your presentation.

- **Orientation of slide** – If you are standing behind the projector (your back to the screen), place the slide on the glass with the same orientation as if you were reading it (upper left at the upper left, etc.).

- **Position slide with the projector OFF** – Whenever possible, turn the projector off to position or change slides. Spare your audience the distraction of watching you set up the next slide.

- **Avoid "giant hand"** – Using your finger to point to things on the transparency can have a King Kong effect. If it is necessary to point to items on the slide, use a pencil, pen or other small pointer.

- **Eye contact** – Avoid turning toward, or talking to, the screen. Maintain eye contact with your audience.

- **Find a good place to stand** – You'll want to avoid standing in the projector beam (and thus casting a distracting shadow on the screen), or blocking part of your audience's view. This is one of the biggest disadvantages of overhead projector use. It is often difficult to find a place that doesn't obstruct someone's view. Stepping back to a position next to the screen is often the only solution—if you are using speaker's notes, be sure to take them with you when you step back.

- **Turn the projector off** – when not in use.

Chapter Review & Study Guide

Summary

In this chapter you learned the following:

1. Approaching your presentation with a communication orientation instead of a performance orientation will help you understand that it is more like an expanded conversation than a great oratorical performance.

2. There are four types of delivery.

   - An impromptu speech has little or no preparation.

   - A manuscript speech is written word-for-word and then read to the audience. While it can be the most accurate, this type of delivery tends to lead to poor eye contact, lack of vocal variety and be prone to more verbal errors.

   - A memorized speech is first written like a manuscript, and then memorized word-for-word. Forgetting what to say next makes this type of delivery undesirable for most speakers.

   - An extemporaneous speech allows the speaker to be more spontaneous. It has the advantage of being thoroughly practiced without being memorized, and carefully constructed notes give the speaker peace of mind. An extemporaneous delivery is the best strategy for most speaking occasions.

3. Delivery flaws, such as non-fluencies, can distract our audience and reduce their ability to process our message. On the other hand, "good" delivery that is overdone can also reduce the likelihood that they will hear our message. Rather than worrying about distracting things you *might* be doing, have a friend observe you, and later tell you if you did anything that was distracting.

4. You wouldn't have a conversation with your friends or coworkers without making eye contact with them. It is equally important to maintain eye contact when you are giving a presentation.

5. Looking and sounding like you know what you're talking about, i.e., good delivery, will increase your credibility with your audience.

6. Visual aids can help you communicate more effectively by

   - Attracting audience attention

   - Emphasizing key points

   - Showing the relationship between points

   - Simplifying numeric information

   - Making examples more specific

   - Illustrating difficult-to-describe objects or scenes

   - Illustrating symbolic relationships

7. To be effective, visual aids must be visible, non-distracting, simple and serve a function.

8. While the most important visual element in your presentation is *you,* other visual elements include objects, models, posters, flip charts, and overhead transparencies. All require thought, planning, and caution.

9. Presentation software, such as PowerPoint, when used with care, can add value to your presentation; however, it's important to remember that *you* are the presenter and PowerPoint is the helper.

Key Terms

communication orientation	non-fluencies	B key
extemporaneous delivery	performance orientation	Objects (as visual aids)
impromptu delivery	titles	Flip charts
labels	visual aids	Overhead transparencies
manuscript delivery	vocalized pauses	Models
memorized delivery	PowerPoint	Black slides
		Posters

Study Questions

1. The advantage of having a communication orientation toward a presentation instead of a performance orientation is

   a. You will see your audience as critics.
   b. It helps you focus on your goals as a communicator.
   c. You will see that giving a presentation is distinctly different than having a conversation with your friends.
   d. You will be able to focus on your delivery flaws.

2. The disadvantage of an impromptu speech is

   a. It doesn't allow for much preparation.
   b. It is not spontaneous.
   c. It makes the speaker's voice sound unnatural.
   d. It tends to sound memorized.

3. The mode of delivery that may be the most accurate is

   a. Impromptu
   b. Extemporaneous
   c. Manuscript
   d. Memorized

4. False starts, mispronunciations and excessive um's and ah's are known as

   a. Labels
   b. Sender variables
   c. Vocal variety
   d. Non-fluencies

5. One might think of eye contact between audience and speaker as

   a. Impossible to do well
   b. Looking each other in the mind
   c. Only possible in small groups
   d. Only appropriate in informal settings

6. Visual aids should

   a. Be in the audience's view at all times
   b. Illustrate every point in your speech
   c. Serve a communicative purpose
   d. Be passed around the room so everyone can see them

7. Which of the following is *not* an example of PowerPoint abuse

   a. Leaving the lights on
   b. Having your entire presentation on the slides
   c. Using distracting animation
   d. Using elaborate fonts

8. Building blank slides into a PowerPoint presentation

   a. Makes most presentations too long
   b. Allows you to re-connect with your audience
   c. Makes it look like you're including unnecessary slides
   d. Is too complicated for most computer users to do

Answers:
1. (b); 2. (a); 3. (c); 4. (d); 5. (b); 6. (c); 7. (a); 8. (b)

Critical Thinking

1. Think about the visual aids you see speakers use when making presentations in your classes or at work. How do they help or hinder your learning?

2. Think about a presentation you saw that annoyed you. What advice from this chapter could have helped the presenter make a more effective (less annoying) presentation?

References

1. Brigance, W. N. (1961). *Speech: Itstechniques and disciplines in a free society* (2nd ed.). New York: Appleton-Century-Crofts.

2. Hamilton, C. (1996). *Successful Public Speaking.* Belmont, CA: Wadsworth.

3. Katt, J., Murdock, J., Butler, J., & Pryor, B. (2008). Establishing best practices for the use of PowerPoint as a presentation aid. *Human Communication. 11,* 193–200.

4. McCroskey, J. C. (2001). *An introduction to rhetorical communication* (8th ed.). Needham Heights, MA: Allyn & Bacon.

5. Motely, M. T. (1997). *Overcoming your fear of public speaking.* Boston, MA: Houghton Mifflin.

6. Nesmith, M. (1984). *Megatrends.* New York: Warner.

7. Vogel, D., Dickson, G., & Lehman, J. (1986). *Persuasion and the role of visual presentation support: The UM/3M study* (MISRC-WP-86-11), Minneapolis, MN: University of Minnesota, Management Information Systems Research Center.

8. Pubsley, L. (2010). Design an effective PowerPoint presentation. *Education for Primary Care, 21*(1), 51-53.

14

persuasive presentations

Burt Pryor, University of Central Florida

When you have read and thought about this chapter, you will be able to:

1. Define the concept of persuasion.

2. Discuss the influence of the Elaboration Likelihood Model.

3. Discuss how the central and peripheral routes allow persuasion to occur.

4. Understand the effect of source, message, channel, and receiver on receivers' likelihood to elaborate.

5. Define the three types of persuasive effects.

6. Explain how one-sided versus two-sided messages, inoculation theory, use of statistical and story evidence, and fear appeals can make messages more persuasive.

7. Understand how source characteristics, message-related peripheral cues, and sequential request strategies influence persuasion.

The role of persuasion in everyday life is pervasive, vitally important, and central to human endeavor. In this chapter, you will learn about the persuasion process. This chapter examines how the primary components of the process—source, message, channel, and receiver—contribute to persuasive effects. We present the research and applications through the lens of the most comprehensive theory in the study of persuasion, the Elaboration Likelihood Model (ELM). It is our hope that your new understanding of the persuasion process will benefit you as a persuader, and as a consumer and evaluator of the continual stream of the persuasive messages that are directed your way.

Why Is the Study of Persuasion Important?

Persuasion is so much a routine part of our lives that most of us are probably not aware of its pervasiveness unless it is called to our attention. Literally everyone is in the business of persuasion. If you were to keep a log of every persuasion attempt that you encountered in a given day as a persuader, receiver, or observer, you would soon realize the necessity of having that log available wherever you went. Think of those who practice persuasion professionally: advertisers, attorneys, politicians, educators (including the authors of the message you are reading right now), clergy, salespeople (including telemarketers), media consultants, managers, coaches—even engineers. The list is practically endless. We receive direct mail ads on a daily basis, the so-called "junk mail." Pratkanis & Aronson (2001) reported that adults are exposed to an average of 750 television ads per week. We are also bombarded with advertising through other media, including newspapers, magazines, radio and the Internet. When we are driving in our cars, the persuasive messages on the radio, billboards, and bumper stickers permeate our consciousness. Even our clothing carries persuasive messages. Hats and T-shirts display the logos and slogans of manufacturers, and our casual clothing is commonly decorated with designer labels. Add to this the daily interpersonal influences involving parents, couples, children, friends, and relatives, and one begins to see that we humans are constant participants in this process we call persuasion. Because of its central role in our daily lives, it is an understatement to say it makes sense to study persuasion. A better understanding of the persuasion process, from the perspectives of both the persuader and the one being persuaded, will have far-reaching personal and professional benefits.

DEFINING THE CONCEPT OF PERSUASION

Persuasion is the process by which attitudes or behaviors are influenced as a result of receiving a message (Anderson & Pryor, 1992). However, definitions of persuasion vary according to whether they recognize *unintentional influence* as persuasion. For example, let's assume you plan an "informative" presentation about recycling programs, including their costs and benefits. Though your purpose may only be to inform, it is quite plausible that your discussion about the long-term benefits of recycling on the environment may influence your audience's attitudes and even their behaviors involving recycling. So, your "informative" message might also persuade the receivers. A broad definition of persuasion might include this type of unintentional persuasion.

> **Persuasion**
> The process by which attitudes or behaviors are influenced as a result of receiving a message.

Narrower definitions of persuasion typically limit what we call persuasion to situations that include an intentional persuader. It should be noted that those who espouse the "intentional" model of persuasion do not argue that people's minds and behaviors are never changed without an intentional persuader. They just believe that attitude or behavior change without an intentional persuader should not be classified as persuasion. Most of the research on persuasion works from this narrower definition of persuasion.

It is also important to distinguish between coercion, which is based on reward and punishment power and receivers' lack of perceived choice, and persuasion, which is based on information power. The statement, "Give me your money, or I will shoot you" allows the receiver little choice in light of the punishment for refusing to give up the money. The lack of perceived choice is what separates persuasion from coercion. So, if you are thinking that a gun threat is pretty persuasive, it isn't. It is, however, pretty coercive.

This chapter focuses on strategies that persuaders can implement to increase their odds of success. The strategies are derived from systematic research conducted by social scientists over the past few decades that has led to a better understanding of cause-effect relationships in persuasion. These relationships center on how various characteristics of the source (speaker or writer), message, channel, and receiver influence persuasive effects. We will begin by examining some of these relationships within the framework of the most comprehensive theory yet developed in the field of persuasion, the Elaboration Likelihood Model, also known as the ELM (Petty & Cacioppo, 1986).

THE ELABORATION LIKELIHOOD MODEL

As suggested by its name, the Elaboration Likelihood Model predicts the likelihood that receivers will "elaborate" (process, think about, evaluate) a message under various circumstances. The ELM suggests that people want to make "correct" decisions about how to respond to persuasive messages, but cannot possibly scrutinize every persuasive message that comes their way. Sometimes we engage in effortful, elaborative processing; other times, we may choose not to mentally elaborate on the message. According to the ELM and its research findings, the two major determinants of the extent to which receivers engage in message elaboration are their motivation and ability to process the message. Those who are motivated (they really want to process a message) and are able (they can process a message) tend to engage in elaborative message processing. Those who lack motivation or ability tend to process the message superficially.

TWO ROUTES TO PERSUASION: CENTRAL AND PERIPHERAL

central route processing Persuasion achieved by the quality of the arguments in a message.

peripheral route processing Influence based upon factors outside of the quality of the message.

The ELM identifies two main routes to persuasion—the **central route** and the **peripheral route**. Essentially, the central route involves persuasion achieved by the quality of the arguments in the message, while peripheral route persuasion occurs when receivers are influenced by factors other than argument quality (e.g., speaker expertise or attractiveness). The ELM holds that receivers will focus on the message arguments to the extent that they are both *motivated* and *able* to process the message. Central route persuasion, then, relies on high message elaboration.

On the other hand, to the extent that receivers are lacking in either motivation or ability to process the message, persuasion will succeed or fail based on factors outside the message. These are called *peripheral cues*. As demonstrated earlier, we are inundated with persuasive messages on a continual basis. We simply do not have the time or energy to thoroughly process every message

Figure 1

The central/peripheral routes to persuasion are not an either/or relationship. Instead, they represent a continuum.

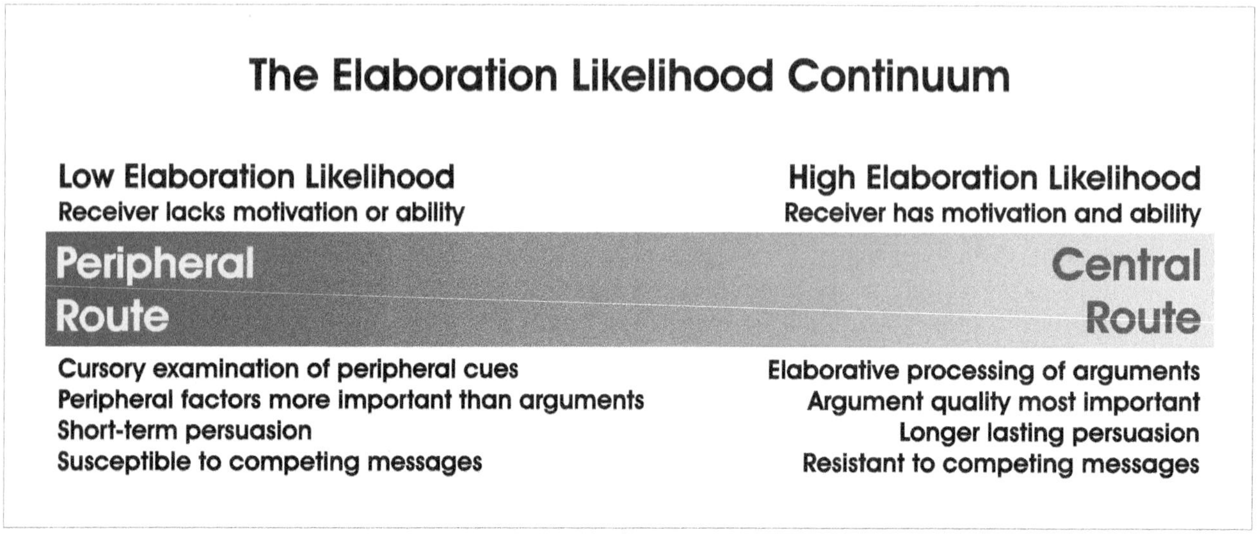

The Elaboration Likelihood Continuum

Low Elaboration Likelihood
Receiver lacks motivation or ability

High Elaboration Likelihood
Receiver has motivation and ability

Peripheral Route

Central Route

Cursory examination of peripheral cues
Peripheral factors more important than arguments
Short-term persuasion
Susceptible to competing messages

Elaborative processing of arguments
Argument quality most important
Longer lasting persuasion
Resistant to competing messages

that comes our way, lest we pull our cars to side of the road to make sure we carefully consider every billboard. Think of it as literally "paying" attention: it costs us time and energy to process a message. Consequently, we use decision rules, or mental shortcuts, in response to many persuasive messages, particularly those we perceive as low in relevance or consequence for our daily lives. We often quickly accept or reject persuasive appeals, from advertisements to issues of national scope, on the basis of peripheral cues—such as whether or not we like the speaker, or how expert we perceive the speaker to be—without even examining the arguments the speaker presents.

It is important to note, though, that the central-peripheral distinction represents a continuum, not an "either/or" relationship. It is not a matter of using one route or the other exclusively, but of relying more on the central route than the peripheral route in some situations, and more on the peripheral route than the central route in others.

WHAT ELM RESEARCH OFFERS PERSUADERS

The ELM has spawned a body of research about how numerous factors affect the likelihood of message elaboration. The research has shown two main advantages of central route over peripheral route persuasion. Because it is more grounded in substantive attitude and belief modification than persuasion achieved through the peripheral route, central route persuasion is (1) longer lasting, and (2) more resistant to subsequent competing messages (Petty & Cacioppo, 1986). Since receivers will process the message more thoroughly when they are using the central route, it makes sense that a speaker must use high quality arguments to be successful.

Consider a situation where receivers are highly motivated and able to scrutinize the message, but the message contains weak arguments. For example, "We should raise the drinking age to 23 because several prominent politicians think it is a good idea and some think it will curb alcohol sales." If the audience consists of college age people, the persuader would likely be better off if they processed the message *less* thoroughly, because thorough processing of weak arguments only accentuates receivers' negative responses to the message. The critical point here is that strategically increasing receivers' attention to a set of arguments is not always a good thing. It's a good idea only if the receivers perceive the arguments to be strong.

Central Route Factors: Things That Make Elaboration More Likely

We have already stated that receivers engage in effortful information processing (elaboration) of a message when they are both motivated and able. This section introduces some of the factors that have been shown to make elaboration more likely. These include characteristics of the speaker, elements of the message, the use of multiple channels, and the attitudes and perceptions of the receivers. Once we've examined the research, we will explore some practical applications you can use as a persuader.

SOURCE CHARACTERISTICS

Source Expertise

Source expertise refers to receivers' perceptions of the source's (persuader's) knowledge, qualifications, and competence. Although source expertise has its most direct impact on persuasion as a peripheral cue (discussed in detail later in this chapter), it can affect receivers' motivation and thus be a factor in determining how much elaboration receivers will engage in. Source expertise has little effect on information processing of highly relevant messages because receivers are already motivated to process the message;

source expertise
Receivers' perceptions of the persuader's knowledge, qualifications and competence.

however, some studies (e.g., Petty & Cacioppo, 1984) have shown that expert sources increase receivers' motivation to process messages when issue relevance is moderate or ambiguous. Petty & Cacioppo (1986) explain that when receivers are not sure whether a message merits their attention, "characteristics of the message source can help a person decide if the message is worth thinking about" (p. 206).

Number of Sources and Arguments

Harkins and Petty (1981) examined the effects of multiple sources/multiple arguments on receivers' message processing and attitude change. Participants listened to messages from one speaker or from three speakers that utilized one argument or three different

arguments. The combination of three speakers, each with a different strong argument, produced more positive thoughts about the issue and more persuasion than any of the other conditions. Harkins and Petty concluded that each time the participants heard the voice of a new speaker (changing stimulus) they were re-stimulated to process the message. Since the arguments were strong, this increased attention to the message resulted in more favorable thoughts and more persuasion. Had the arguments been weak, the ELM would predict the increased processing brought by multiple sources and multiple arguments would only increase receivers' negative thoughts, decreasing persuasion in comparison to the other conditions.

· Listeners are more likely to process a message from an expert source.

© Ariel Skelley/Blend Images LLC

The relationship between attention and stimulus variety has been well documented in social science research. Vernon (1962, p. 183) concluded from early research that "normal consciousness, perception, and thought can be maintained only in a constantly changing environment." It has been said that variety is the "spice of life." This research suggests that adding a little of that spice to your presentation might help motivate your audience to more thoughtfully process your message.

MESSAGE CHARACTERISTICS

ELM research has identified several message characteristics that affect receivers' motivation and ability to process information. Among those that have received research attention are forewarning of persuasive intent and message repetition.

Forewarning and Resistance to Persuasion

You have probably heard someone say that "forewarned is forearmed." In other words, if we know something is coming, a hurricane, cutback in work hours, or the need to make repairs on a declining old car, we will be more likely to prepare for it. In the case of persuasive messages, this statement should be amended to say that forewarned is forearmed, but only if (1) the issue is personally relevant to the receiver, (2) the message is intended to change attitudes (not create or reinforce attitudes), and (3) the receivers have at least a few minutes to arm themselves. Sometimes we receive warnings that we are soon to be the target of a persuasion attempt. A friend may warn you that a mutual acquaintance plans to talk to you about joining a pyramid business scheme; your mother may alert you that she and Dad want to sit down with you to discuss your progress toward graduation; a company may alert you that a salesperson will be "in your area" next week. The ELM research shows that these warnings can render you more, or less, susceptible to influence, depending on the three factors listed above.

Participants in research by Petty and Cacioppo (1977) listened to a live class presentation in which a speaker, identified as psychologist from the testing center, presented strong arguments for initiating comprehensive exams as a graduation requirement. Since a previous survey had shown that students were against this policy change, the message constituted an attempt to change attitudes. In various classes, the students were either informed (warned) about the persuasive intent of the impending presentation five minutes prior to the speaker's arrival, told of the intent as the speaker was introduced, or not warned at all. Only the group that received the five-minute warning resisted being persuaded. The data showed that they had spent the time following the warning thinking of counterarguments to the anticipated presentation. The forewarning had motivated them to do so. For this group, forewarned was forearmed. Since the participants who were warned immediately prior to the presentation had no time to develop their defenses, they were persuaded, along with the unwarned group, by the strong arguments.

Forewarning and Increased Persuasion

At other times, forewarning can lead to increased persuasion. For example, when issue relevance is low, receivers are less motivated to devote efforts to building ammunition to defend against the anticipated message. This is particularly true in interpersonal situations where friendship and harmony may take priority over rejecting someone's influence attempt on a topic of low importance (see Cialdini, Levy, Herman, Kozlowski, & Petty, 1976). Another situation where warning may heighten susceptibility to persuasion is when issue relevance is high, but the position taken is consistent with the receiver's attitude. Under such circumstances, the ELM would predict that the warning would cause receivers to experience mostly positive thoughts in anticipation of the message, leading to increased susceptibility to attitude reinforcement.

Message Repetition

Persuaders often use repetition for purposes of clarifying, reminding, or reinforcing message effects. This tactic is most common in advertising, where the same commercial airs repeatedly until it reaches the **wear-out point** for its audience. Virtually all persuaders—the clergy, attorneys, parents, teachers and students—employ message repetition in their efforts to influence listeners. ELM research, including its applied studies in advertising, has yielded consistent results on the effects of message repetition on information processing and persuasion. With messages that initially produce positive responses to a set of strong arguments, or to a novel, clever commercial, the repetition effects follow an inverted U-shaped pattern. That is, positive thoughts and persuasion increase up to a wear-out point, then decrease as receivers begin to tire of the message. Wear-out points vary, largely as a function of the complexity and novelty of messages, but the pattern does not. At some point, even the cleverest commercial begins to lose its appeal.

In an experiment by Cacioppo and Petty (1979), participants listened to strong arguments that advocated increasing tuition to facilitate hiring more faculty, offering more classes, and other student-oriented improvements. Each participant listened to the message one, three, or five times. Participants who heard the message once generated mostly positive thoughts and were influenced by the strong arguments. Attitude change and the number of positive thoughts increased in the three-repetition condition, but decreased with five repetitions. Petty and Cacioppo reasoned that repeating the message three times increased receivers' ability to think about the strong argument, but five repetitions was too much, causing feelings of boredom and tedium.

wear-out point
The point at which a repeated persuasive message loses its effectiveness.

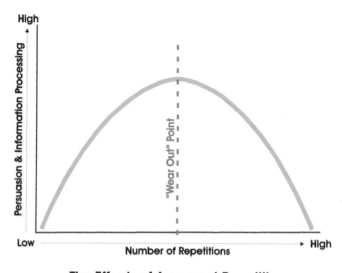

The Effects of Argument Repetition

Figure 2

Positive thoughts and persuasion increase up to a wear-out point, then decrease as receivers begin to tire of the message.

A subsequent study by Petty and Cacioppo (1985) showed that three repetitions of weak arguments increased receivers' negative thoughts and reduced attitude change. Repetition of the weak arguments gave participants more opportunity to recognize just how weak the arguments were.

CHANNEL OPTIONS

Information processing is also affected by whether the message is transmitted through written or spoken channels. Research (e.g., Chaiken & Eagly, 1976) indicates that when messages are complex, written versions are more persuasive than spoken versions. This finding has been attributed to greater comprehension of complex or difficult material when receivers can process (read) the message at their own pace. In ELM terms, the written channel increases receivers' ability to process the message; however, one does not have the opportunity to slow down or revisit material when they are listening to a speaker. Since the receivers' re-reading of material is actually a form of message repetition, one could infer from this research that, when dealing with complex spoken messages, using an alternate channel to provide some form of repetition might increase the audience's ability to elaborate on the message.

RECEIVER CHARACTERISTICS AND INFORMATION PROCESSING

Receiver's Initial Position

The receiver's initial position on a topic determines which of three types of persuasive effects are possible. The three main types of persuasive effects are (1) creating a new attitude, (2) reinforcing an existing attitude or behavior, and (3) changing an attitude and/or behavior.

The three types of persuasive effects are:
· create a new attitude
· reinforce an existing attitude or behavior
· change an attitude or behavior.

When the receiver has had no previous exposure to a topic, the effects of a persuasive message are to **create a new attitude.** The new attitude may also lead to new behavior. Examples of this type of persuasion include consumers seeing an advertisement for a new product, jurors hearing initial evidence in a court case, or employers interviewing a job candidate or seeing a candidate's resume for the first time. The new attitudes toward the product, defendant, or job candidate will likely affect the receiver's behaviors when making a decision about purchasing the product, voting for guilt or innocence, or hiring the applicant.

The majority of persuasive messages that we pay attention to involve the second type of persuasive effect: **reinforcement of an existing attitude.** This is because people tend to place themselves in environments where others' viewpoints and messages coincide with their own attitudes. Republicans would usually rather listen to Republican candidates for office; Democrats prefer listening to Democrats; we attend to messages that reinforce our own religious views; we'd rather watch our favorite team play while surrounded by supporters of that team. People attend church, political rallies, and fundraisers for a favored charity, knowing that the persuasive messages they will hear will be reinforcing, consistent with their own views. Social scientists refer to our tendency to place ourselves in "likeminded" situations as **selective exposure.** This may be seen as a defense mechanism that helps us avoid the psychological discomfort of listening to messages that conflict with our views.

The third type of persuasive effect involves **attitude or behavior change.** Despite our preference for information that supports our views, we often come into contact with competing views. You might hate minivans, but you will have a difficult time avoiding every minivan commercial. You might disagree with a television host's position on a political candidate, but you watch the show because you do like the featured guest's views. When receivers are exposed to competing views, they sometimes engage in **selective attention** as a defense. In other words, receivers can still avoid a message by not paying attention to it. Message positions that are in conflict with listeners' attitudes must overcome the selective attention barrier. As you will see in the following sections, there are numerous strategies that can be used to motivate receivers to attend to a message.

selective exposure
The tendency to place ourselves in environments with others who think as we do.

selective attention
Receivers avoid a message by not paying attention to it.

Receiver's Involvement (Relevance)

Perhaps the most important determinant of the amount of effort audience members will expend to process a message is their involvement in the issue. When receivers perceive that a message is personally relevant and that the information being presented has useful or important implications for their lives, they tend to pay close attention, processing the information carefully and discerning the strengths and weaknesses of the arguments. This has been shown in numerous experiments. Let's examine one experiment by ELM researchers Petty and Cacioppo.

People will listen to messages they perceive as personally relevant.

Petty and Cacioppo (1979) developed persuasive messages of high quality and low quality that argued for instituting required senior comprehensive exams. The high quality message contained eight strong arguments. The low quality message contained eight weak arguments. The participants in the experiment were asked to listen to either the high or low quality message and then complete a questionnaire on which they recorded their attitudes toward the issue. They were also tested to determine how much effort they had put into processing the messages.

Half of the participants (in both the high and low quality conditions) were told the exams were being considered for their university (high involvement). The other half were told the exams were being considered for a different, far-away university (low involvement). Participants who were led to believe *they* would be the ones taking the exams evaluated the messages more carefully. Because the message was personally relevant, they were motivated to pay close attention. Accordingly, they were very aware of the weaknesses in the low

Applying What the Research Tells Us about the Effects of Source, Message, Channel, and Receiver Factors on the Likelihood to Elaborate

- You will certainly want to be viewed as a knowledgeable and expert source in both formal and informal persuasion situations.
  - Perceptions of your expertise will directly enhance speech effects mostly when issue relevance is *low* for receivers.
- An important indirect effect of source expertise occurs when issue relevance is *moderate*. Under these conditions, your demonstrated **expertise** will motivate receivers to process the message more actively. By this point, you know what that means for the impact of argument quality. Anything that increases receivers' active processing of the message also increases the importance of argument quality. The perceived relevance of most issues is likely to vary from person to person. For example, a presentation on the value of mastering a second language may be highly relevant to some audience members, but moderately or minimally relevant to others. It seems reasonable to suggest that many issues will not be seen as particularly high or low, but will fall into the moderate relevance range for some receivers. Your demonstrated expertise will enhance the motivation to process the message for those people.
- Presenting the actual arguments of **multiple sources**, rather than relying on just one source, not only varies the stimulus, but also has the potential to increase message credibility by showing the message recipients that several different sources have independently arrived at a similar position or conclusion. So, it is advantageous to cite several different, respected sources to reinforce your argument.
- You would not want your receivers to have prior knowledge of your intent if you were planning to try to change their attitudes on an issue important to them. Whether it takes the form of telling audience members about your topic or even inadvertently displaying your PowerPoint slides while setting up for a presentation, **forewarning** could provide the chance for receivers to build defenses in the form of thoughts that are negative to your purpose. On the other hand, it is probably best to reveal your intent in advance of presenting a message that will coincide with receivers' attitudes.
- Organizing persuasive messages to provide moderate **repetition** of strong arguments is an effective strategy. One way to apply this strategy is to introduce or preview strong arguments in an introduction, develop them in the body of the presentation, and then include them in a summary. Although there is no formula for calculating the best use of repetition, it is likely that the wear-out point will be higher for messages that are complex or novel.

- Use **alternate channels** to provide repetition. While you would rely primarily on the spoken channel in a presentation, repetition can be accomplished by reinforcing your message with presentational aids, such as PowerPoint or other means of displaying key points in written form. Assuming your message is of high quality, such repetition should produce an increase in receivers' positive thoughts and persuasion. Of course, too much repetition can bore or annoy your audience, so you should be careful not to overdo it.

- Consideration should be given to your receivers' **initial position** on the issue. Will you be attempting to create a new attitude, reinforce an existing attitude, or change an existing attitude? Note that the same message has the potential to produce all three effects, depending on the controversial level of the issue and the receivers' initial position.

- Your receivers' perceptions of the **relevance** of your message may be the most important factor in determining their motivation to elaborate on your message. Perceptions of relevance will increase your listeners' motivation to process the message, but be sure your message contains high quality arguments. Speakers who pique listeners' interests, but then provide weak arguments that cause listeners to rehearse negative thoughts in their minds, are likely to succeed only in increasing opposition to their position.

quality message, but also very aware of the strong points in the high quality message. Responses to the questionnaire showed that these highly involved participants responded more positively to the strong message, and were more persuaded than participants who thought the exams were intended for students at another university. But, the highly involved participants listed a greater number of negative thoughts and were *less persuaded* than the participants with low involvement when the arguments were of low quality.

It is important to note that it is the audience's perception of relevance, not the "actual" relevance of the message that counts when it comes to providing motivation to elaborate. In the examples cited above, it is unlikely that perceptions differed from reality; comprehensive tests being considered for *your* university are relevant to you and you would be unlikely to perceive otherwise. Conversely, comprehensive tests being considered for some other university would have nothing to do with you and you would be unlikely to perceive the topic as relevant. But what about all of the topics that are potentially relevant to your audience, but not necessarily perceived to be relevant? For example, it may be true that global warming *should* be relevant to everyone, but many do not perceive it to be relevant. Although the research is still evolving in this area, Katt (2004) found that for some topics, even a single statement explaining why a topic is relevant can increase receivers' perceptions of relevance, and based on previous ELM research, we would expect increased perceptions of relevance to be accompanied by increased elaborative message processing.

Argument Quality: How to Plan a Strong Message

Our discussion of the persuasion research has so far centered on characteristics of source, channel, receiver, and message that affect the likelihood receivers will actively process the message. The ELM research shows that if you increase receivers' processing by employing one or more of these characteristics, the receivers will be persuaded based primarily on the quality of your arguments. Increased processing leads to more persuasion when the arguments are strong, but decreased persuasion if the arguments are weak. The arguments used in the ELM research were all pre-tested to validate that the strong arguments elicited mostly positive thoughts from receivers and the weak arguments produced mostly negative thoughts. But what was it about the "strong" messages that made them stronger than the "weak" messages? We must look at research outside the ELM for answers to this question.

Research on one-sided versus two-sided messages, inoculation theory, use of statistical and story evidence, and fear appeals has identified strategies that can make a message more persuasive. While the research in these areas has not been conducted within the ELM framework, the ELM would suggest that effective message strategies would have their greatest impact when motivation and ability (and thus the likelihood for central route processing) are high.

ONE-SIDED VERSUS TWO-SIDED MESSAGES

message-sidedness
One-sided messages
provide only the
arguments that support
your message; two-sided
nonrefutational
messages provide
counter-arguments but
do not refute those
arguments; two-sided
refutational messages
provide and refute
counter arguments.

Suppose a university board of directors sought to create positive public perceptions regarding a tuition increase. In terms of the "**message-sidedness**" research, the board could develop a campaign based on any of three strategies. These include the **one-sided, two-sided nonrefutational,** and **two-sided refutational approaches.** One-sided messages provide only the arguments that support one's position, never acknowledging competing views. If the board was to adopt the one-sided strategy, they would cite all the benefits the tuition hike would provide to students, e.g., more summer classes, more parking facilities, availability of more sections of required classes at varied times of day.

Alternatively, they would go one step further by using the two-sided nonrefutational approach. Here, the board would continue to emphasize the benefits of the increase, but would also present reasons why some constituents may react negatively to it, e.g., "Some may feel the increase is too much, but let's look again at what you get for your money."Notice that the opposing view (counterargument), that the increase is too much, was not directly refuted. The two-sided nonrefutational strategy identifies opposing views, then tries to overcome them with additional one-sided arguments. Research has generally shown twosided nonrefutational strategies to be less persuasive than one-sided messages. One possible explanation for this is that identifying competing arguments but failing to show they can be refuted lends additional credence to those competing views.

The two-sided refutational approach has been shown to be the most effective of the message-sidedness strategies (see Allen, 1991; O'Keefe, 1999). Were the board to adopt this message strategy in their efforts to influence public perceptions, they would not only identify specific competing arguments, but would also attempt to directly refute them. For example, after acknowledging that some may feel the proposed increase is too much, they might compare the increase with rising costs of products and services, the cost of living index, or higher tuition rates at other schools as evidence that the higher tuition rate is still a bargain in today's market.

INOCULATION THEORY: RESISTANCE TO PERSUASION

As the above heading states, this section deals with *resistance* to persuasion, not persuasion. Much of the work on resistance to persuasion has been conducted within a theory known as Inoculation Theory (McGuire, 1964; see Szabo & Pfau, 2002 for a review and analysis of research on this theory). This research is closely related to the message-sidedness research, as it deals with the effectiveness of one-sided versus two-sided refutational messages in conferring resistance to subsequent counter-persuasion. Going back to the tuition increase issue, let's assume that the board of directors used the one-sided strategy, giving only the arguments in support of the increase. Let's assume further that in the days and weeks following the release of their messages, the target audience is exposed to competing views from other sources. Even if the board's campaign had been successful in inducing somewhat favorable perceptions regarding the increase, they would not have prepared receivers to resist the "counterattacks." Would these same audience members have been better able to resist the counter-persuasion had the campaign identified and refuted the arguments they subsequently heard? The research tells us that they would.

Two-sided refutational messages "inoculate" receivers, making them better able to resist counter-persuasion similar to the way that a biological inoculation helps us to better resist certain diseases. The research findings show that receivers who are first given a twosided refutational message rate subsequent, opposing arguments as less credible than receivers who are first exposed to a one-sided message (see Pryor & Steinfatt, 1978, for further explanation).

EVIDENCE: STATISTICS VERSUS STORIES

As you might expect, the research has shown clearly that citing evidence to support one's claims increases persuasiveness (Maurin, 2000). The two main types of evidence are statistical and story evidence. Statistical evidence is usually based on averages or percentages from a sample of many, while story evidence is based on a single case. For example, if you were trying to persuade a person or group about the need for organ donations, you could support your contention by providing statistics showing the national shortage of available organs, or you could develop a story about a person who went through a long and lifethreatening wait for an organ transplant. While statistical evidence may be seen as more valid than a single story, receivers may be more attentive to an interesting story that supports a point. The question of whether statistical or story evidence is most effective has been extensively researched. Some studies have concluded that statistical evidence is superior (e.g., Hoeken, 1999), some show an advantage for story evidence (e.g., Koballa, 1986), while still others (e.g., Krupat, Smith, Leach, & Jackson, 1997) report no difference. At this point, the best conclusion is that both types of evidence are more effective than no evidence, but there is no consistent advantage to one over the other.

FEAR APEALS

The use of fear appeals as a persuasive strategy is a common practice. Advertisers suggest that if we fail to buy the their brand of tires, we are risking the safety of our families, anti-cigarette ads depict the dire consequences of nicotine addiction, and public service ads ("Click it or ticket") threaten that the police will be ticketing us if we are caught not wearing our seatbelts. Parents, managers, and relationship partners sometimes resort to threats in their efforts to persuade. Do fear appeals work? The answer is not a simple yes or no, but the research does provide guidelines about how best to use fear as a persuasion tactic.

Though researchers have been interested in fear appeals for decades, the most consistent and useful findings have grown out of a theory developed by Witte (1992) known as the Extended Parallel Process Model (EPPM). The EPPM holds that the persuasiveness of a fear appeal hinges on receivers' parallel processing about the threat and the solution offered in the message. According to the EPPM, receivers assess the threat in two ways, including (1) the severity of the consequences of not following the source's recommendations and (2) the likelihood that they, personally, would fall prey to those consequences. Receivers are also said to consider the solution in two ways, including assessments about (1) whether the recommended solution would work, and (2) whether they are capable of following the recommendation. Research has been supportive of the theory (see, for example, Regan, 2001; Witte, Cameron & McKeon, 1998).

Fear appeals require a convincing threat and an effective solution.

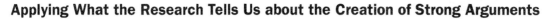

Applying What the Research Tells Us about the Creation of Strong Arguments

- Should you use a **one-sided** or **two-sided** message? The research evidence is clear. You are best advised to use the two-sided refutational strategy in a persuasive speech. You may need to do some research to identify the potential counterarguments and how best to refute them, but your efforts should enhance the persuasiveness of your speech.

- **Inoculation theory** suggests that knowing both sides of an argument makes one less susceptible to being "un-persuaded." Persuasion practitioners can benefit from the use of two-sided refutational messages, not only in terms of increased persuasiveness, but also from the perspective of inducing resistance to counter-persuasion. One-sided messages do not prepare receivers to resist counter- persuasion.

- Though the research has focused primarily on whether **statistical** or **story evidence** is more persuasive, the best approach might be to use both. This would take advantage of both the interest value of story evidence, and the validity value of statistical evidence. In any case, you will be more persuasive if your claims are supported by evidence.

- Notice the next time you hear **fear appeals** whether the Extended Parallel Process Model (EPPM) guidelines seem to be met. This will help you understand and apply the EPPM. If you are planning to use fear in a persuasive presentation, make sure that you carefully consider each of the four steps in the model. It is essential that you provide a high quality solution, meaning that receivers are convinced both that the solution will work, and that they are capable of applying the solution. Research has also shown that when fear is aroused without a high quality solution, receivers may defensively avoid thinking about the message (see Regan, 2001). There is psychological discomfort in being shown a problem for which no good solution is given. Consider a physician who uses a fear message in an effort to motivate obese patients to follow a certain diet. If the patients believe that the diet is good, but they personally could not stick to it, the fear message could cause the patients to avoid dealing with the problem (fear control).

An example will help clarify the EPPM terminology. Mass media campaigns on various health and safety issues sometimes incorporate fear appeals. Assume that such a campaign uses a fear appeal strategy in an effort to persuade people to always wear seatbelts. Following the EPPM guidelines, the messages would need to demonstrate both the likelihood and severity of the threat. Statistical evidence could be used to show receivers (1) the likelihood that they will be involved in a car crash at some point in their lives, and (2) the possible increased severity of the consequences of being in a crash while not wearing a seatbelt. The severity issue could be demonstrated with story and statistical evidence, and perhaps some photos. If the messages are successful in convincing the receivers of the severity and likelihood of the threat, campaign success in persuading people to wear seatbelts will depend on convincing the target audience members that (1) seatbelts do work to reduce injury, and (2) they are capable of wearing a seatbelt every time they travel by car. Such a campaign may have to deal with misconceptions ("I'll be trapped in my seatbelt in a bad crash") and concerns ("Seatbelts wrinkle my clothes") by using two-sided refutational arguments.

Peripheral Route Persuasion Cues

To reiterate our earlier explanation, when we lack either motivation or ability to engage in effortful processing, we rely more on simple decision rules, called peripheral cues, to determine responses to persuasive messages. Use of these cues provides us with decision shortcuts made necessary by our increasingly busy lives. In most situations, we would probably choose to make the case that our topic is relevant and then back up our position with strong arguments, hoping our receivers would take the trouble to engage in elaborative processing and rely primarily on the central route to react to our message. But even our best efforts cannot guarantee that each message recipient will focus on our arguments. At least part of their attention will fall on peripheral cues, so it is also important make those elements of our presentation as persuasive as possible. The peripheral cues that will be covered in this section include characteristics of the source, message-related peripheral cues, and compliance-gaining strategies that place the receiver in a position of reliance on decision rules.

SOURCE CHARACTERISTICS

Credibility

Source credibility has been defined as "the image held of a communicator at a given time" (Andersen & Clevenger, 1963, p. 59). This definition captures two important characteristics of the concept. First, any source of information will hold varying levels of credibility for different receivers, depending on how those receivers evaluate the expertise and character of the source. While one receiver may believe that a certain presidential candidate is extremely competent and of high moral character, others may question that candidate's competence, character, or both. The words "image held" in this definition mean that the receiver assigns source credibility. The second important feature of the definition is contained in the words "at a given time." This phrase makes the point that a speaker's credibility can fluctuate over time even in the eyes of the same receiver. If a star athlete or politician behaves in a way that you feel shows bad character, your assessment of that person's character may be lowered. If a physician misdiagnoses your illness, you may revise you evaluation of that physician's expertise. Research has identified expertise (competence) and character (trustworthiness) as the two main components of speaker credibility (see, for example, McCroskey, 1966). From these examples, you can see that speaker credibility, including both the expertise and character components, is a dynamic variable, with the potential for favorable and unfavorable fluctuations.

> **source credibility**
> The image held of a communicator by a receiver at a given time.

Both the competence and character dimensions of source credibility have been shown to affect persuasion (for a review of this research, see O'Keefe, 2002). Petty, Cacioppo, and Goldman (1981) demonstrated that source effects have their greatest impact when issue relevance is low. Consistent with ELM predictions, when participants in the experiment thought the issue advocated in the message *would not* affect them (low relevance), they were more influenced by source expertise, the peripheral persuasion cue, than by the argument quality. Because the receivers thought they would be unaffected by the issue, they put less effort into processing the message. As a result, they were not as tuned in to the strengths and weaknesses of the arguments. Instead, the participants with low involvement used source expertise as a shortcut to determine their responses to the message. As you should now be able to predict, the receivers who thought the issue *would* affect them (high relevance) were motivated to carefully process the message and were more influenced by the quality of the arguments than by speaker expertise. Because they engaged in effortful processing, they noticed the quality of the argument and were more persuaded by strong arguments than weak arguments.

How to Build Your Credibility

How can you build your credibility as a speaker or writer in the persuasion process? Strategies for developing receivers' perceptions of expertise and character may be classified as message factors or delivery factors.

Building Credibility through Message Factors

Use of strategies outlined in the previous section on argument quality will serve to demonstrate your expertise on the issue at hand. For example, use of evidence and two-sided messages show that you have made efforts to research the issue, and that you are communicating from a position of knowledge and understanding regarding the topic. This lets your receivers know that if you are not an expert on your topic, then you are relying on those who are. Informing receivers of your own issue-relevant experience is another effective message strategy for enhancing your expertise. For example, if you were attempting to convince someone that yoga is an excellent workout option, your expertise would be judged higher if you were a yoga instructor, or had been practicing yoga over a period of time, than if you had limited experience with yoga.

Regarding character ratings, research has also shown that when the position you take appears to be self-serving, receivers may question your sincerity. One of your authors witnessed a student speech that compared the virtues of various vacuum cleaners. The speaker consistently portrayed one of the brands as superior to the others. When questioned by the class following the speech, it was revealed that the speaker currently held a sales job with that company. Research on "vested interest" has shown that speakers are viewed as more trustworthy when they appear to speak from unbiased positions (see, for example, Peters, Covello, & McCallum, 1997).

Building Credibility through Delivery Factors

Regarding spoken presentations, certain delivery characteristics also affect ratings of speakers' expertise. Monotone speech (Addington, 1968), and nonfluent speech, including vocalized pauses, such as "um," "uh," and "you know," word repetitions, and pronunciation corrections (Bledsoe, 1984), appear to damage ratings of speakers' expertise. Studies have shown that maintaining eye contact with the audience throughout most of the speech has a favorable impact on expertise ratings (see, for example, Wagner, 1999).

Research also shows that certain delivery characteristics are related to ratings of a speaker's trustworthiness. Pearce and Conklin (1971) reported that a conversational delivery style produced higher ratings of honesty and trustworthiness than a highly dynamic style. The authors speculated that extreme levels of dynamism, marked by wide variations in pitch and loudness, might lead to perceptions of affectation and manipulative intent. Late-night infomercials are filled with examples of this. Accordingly, the more moderate levels of dynamism that define the conversational style evoke more favorable ratings of a speaker's genuineness and trustworthiness. Too little dynamism, as exhibited in monotone speech, lowers ratings of a speaker's trustworthiness (Addington, 1968). As was the case with expertise, research shows that nonfluencies and lack of eye contact are detrimental to ratings of trustworthiness.

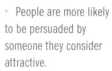

People are more likely to be persuaded by someone they consider attractive.

© Shutterstock/antoniodiaz

Source Attractiveness

Research indicates that physical attractiveness correlates positively with persuasiveness. Cialdini (2001), cites "halo effects" as one explanation. "Research shows that we automatically assign to good-looking individuals such favorable traits as kindness, honesty, and intelligence (148)." Whether the issue is getting the best paying jobs (Hamermesh & Biddle, 1994), a jury's decision on a defendant (see Downs & Lyons, 1990), or dating preferences in speed-dating contexts (Kurzban & Weeden, 2005), both males and females show a bias for attractive others.

In one study of attractiveness effects on persuasion, Chaiken (1979) measured the success of 68 college student speakers in persuading their peers to support a new policy regarding the university's food plan. Judges rated the attractiveness of each speaker, based on photographs and videotaped speeches. Chaiken reported that the 34 most attractive speakers were significantly more persuasive than the 34 least attractive speakers, regardless of whether the receivers were male or female. This result is consistent with other research on the topic (see Knapp & Hall, 2002). Research has also shown that attractive people tend to be more liked (see O'Keefe, 2002). Increased liking appears to be another reason why attractive people have more social influence than less attractive people.

Clothing also contributes to perceptions of attractiveness. Since dress has been shown to affect ratings of both competence and character, it follows that dress can serve as a peripheral persuasion cue. Mills and Aronson (1965) used clothing and makeup to make a female speaker appear attractive (fashionable clothing and make-up), or unattractive (poorly fitted clothing, no make-up). Though the speaker and speech were the same in each case, the attractive condition obtained greater persuasion. Similar findings have been reached in other studies (see Knapp & Hall, 2002).

Source Similarity

Source similarity is another important peripheral cue. Research has consistently demonstrated that similarity breeds liking (see O'Keefe, 2002). For example, Byrne (1961) asked participants to complete a questionnaire about their beliefs on various issues, and then evaluate another participant on the basis of their responses to the questions. The evaluators' responses showed a distinct preference for others who displayed beliefs that were highly similar to their own. Concluding from research on the connection between similarity and liking, Cialdini (2001) stated "those who want us to like them so that we

Applying What the Research Tells Us about the Effects of Peripheral Speaker Characteristics on Persuasion

- If your message is perceived to be relevant and understandable, your receivers will be more likely to focus more on your **message** (central route) than on peripheral factors such as your appearance, your credibility, or their perceptions of you being likeable or similar to them. But, even in high relevance situations, they will pay some attention to the peripheral elements, so you would do well to consider them.

- You can build your **credibility** in the eyes of your receivers with high quality messages and good delivery. Conscientious preparation of the message content and practice are necessary in delivering presentations. Practice until you can deliver your message fluently, while maintaining eye contact with the audience throughout most of the presentation.

- In cases where receivers do not perceive your message as relevant, they may use your **appearance** as a peripheral persuasion cue. Th e research tells us that in such situations, a neat, clean appearance with appropriate dress will contribute to your credibility and persuasiveness.

- Persuaders can take advantage of the peripheral cue effects of **similarity** and **liking** by demonstrating what they and the audience have in common. Similarities in dress, demographics, experiences, and interests have all been shown to contribute to liking (Cialdini, 2001).

will comply with them can accomplish that purpose by appearing similar to us in a wide variety of ways" (p. 150). Like all peripheral cues, we would expect attractiveness and similarity to be less important when the receivers are engaged in elaborative processing, but because central and peripheral routes are not mutually exclusive, we would do well to pay attention to any factors that may affect our persuasiveness.

MESSAGE-RELATED FACTORS AS PERIPHERAL PERSUASION CUES

Conformity Effect

Asch (1951) published a series of experiments on what he called the conformity effect. In Asch's experiments, participants were asked to look at several straight lines projected on a screen. Each participant was asked to pick out which lines were the same lengths. When performing this task alone, everyone correctly identified which lines were the same lengths. In another treatment however, participants were asked the same question aft er they witnessed others (who were secretly in collusion with Asch) give a wrong answer. Nearly all participants who witnessed one or two others give the wrong answer still answered correctly themselves, but an amazing thing happened when the number of people giving the same wrong answer reached three. At that point, one-third of the participants "conformed" by giving the same wrong answer. Subjects no longer trusted their ability to judge line lengths when their perceptions were threatened by the judgments of three others. No additional conformity effects were observed as the number of confederates was further increased. Summing up this and other research on the conformity effect, Cialdini (2001, p. 100) concluded: "Whether the question is what to do with the empty popcorn box in a movie theater, how fast to drive on a certain stretch of the highway, or how to eat the chicken at a dinner party, the actions of those around us will be important guides in defining the answer."

Scarcity

Persuasion practitioners, particularly in the areas of marketing and advertising, are constantly telling us that certain offers or opportunities will be available only until a specified deadline, or that supplies are limited in regard to a certain item. These familiar strategies are applications of the "scarcity principle" that Cialdini (2001) argues is a powerful compliance motivator. In Cialdini's words, " . . . opportunities seem more valuable to us when they are less available" (p. 205). Consider a difficult to find toy at Christmas, a rare coin, a ticket to a sold-out event, or a soon to expire 20% off coupon. Realization of the scarcity of the opportunity and the possibility of losing it seem to increase perceptions of the desirability of that item or opportunity. Stories of the frenzied behavior of shoppers on quests for limited supply bargains are common around the holidays and at liquidation sales at stores that are going out of business.

The use of time and supply limits are so commonplace in advertising that we may not even be aware of the tug on our purchasing intentions and behavior, but the effects are undeniable. Viewers of television shopping channels routinely respond to time limits and a continually decreasing supply of the item. Faced with a 1:00 p.m. deadline, Macy's customers rushed to use $10 coupons on the Friday after Thanksgiving, 2008. Car dealership sales events "end at the close of business on Sunday," and price reductions on a multitude of products, services, and opportunities are advertised with time and/or quantity limits. Scarcity effects can even be fatal, as witnessed at Wal-Mart's day after-Thanksgiving sale in 2008. About 2000 people waited outside the Wal-Mart doors before the 5:00 a.m. opening on that day. Among the bargain prices and limited supply items they would compete for that day were plasma televisions, digital cameras and a $9

Incredible Hulk DVD. When the doors opened, the crowd's fervor to claim the sale merchandise was so strong that a 34-yearold Wal-Mart employee was trampled to death and at least four other people, including a pregnant woman, were taken to the hospital with injuries. One woman who witnessed the incident reported that when the shoppers were told the store was closing because of the death, people began yelling that they had been in line since Thanksgiving morning. "They just kept shopping," she said (Long, 2008).

Research has supported the stark anecdotal evidence of the power of scarcity effects. For example, Worchel, Lee, and Adewole (1975) asked participants to taste a chocolate chip cookie from a jar containing either two or 10 cookies. Participants rated the cookies more positively when they were aware they were getting one of just two remaining cookies. The bias for the two-cookie condition increased when it was presented in a slightly different way. This time, a jar of 10 cookies was taken away and replaced with a jar of two cookies. Witnessing the dwindling supply of cookies apparently caused the participants to value them even more.

· Shoppers can be persuaded to compete for items they believe to be scarce.

© Floresco Productions/age fotostock

Sequential Request Strategies as Peripheral Cues

Compliance-gaining strategies are persuasion techniques that rely on decision rules, not quality arguments, for their success. Persuasion practitioners employ these techniques when the main goal is to elicit desired behaviors (compliance) rather than to change attitudes. An understanding of three compliance techniques is valuable for persuaders and potential persuadees.

Foot-in-the-Door Strategy (FID)

The FID strategy is so labeled because its practitioner first tries to get a "foot-in- the-door" by getting the receiver to comply with a simple, small request. Once that is accomplished, the persuader attempts to capitalize on the initial commitment by getting the receiver to agree to a second, larger request. The first request is a tactic to increase the chances of getting compliance with the real behavior that the persuader wants. The effectiveness of this strategy has been documented in numerous experiments (see Cialdini, 2001). For example, Freedman and Fraser (1966) showed that California homeowners were more likely to agree to place a

four-by-six foot "Be a Safe Driver" sign on their front lawns to support Safe Driver Week if they had previously agreed to sign a petition or display a window sticker in support of the cause. The FID strategy is predicated on the premium people place on remaining consistent with their commitments, a principle most of us learn from our parents early in life. If we make a commitment to do something, we are taught, it is our responsibility to keep it. Persuasion practitioners take advantage of this belief with the FID strategy. In one application of this strategy, Sherman (1980) reported a 700% increase in American

· Many salespeople use compliance-gaining strategies to persuade potential customers.

Cancer Society collection volunteers by individuals who, a few days earlier, had answered yes to a survey question that asked them to predict what they would say if asked to donate three hours of their time to this organization.

Door-in-the-Face (DIF)

The DIF strategy employs the opposite sequence of requests. Practitioners first ask for a large "favor" that they know will be refused. The goal is to then get the receiver to compromise by agreeing to a smaller request. Research has shown DIF to be an effective technique. For example, Cialdini and Ascani (1976) reported that college students who had previously been asked to donate blood regularly for two years were more likely to agree to donate blood once than students who were simply asked to donate once. Various explanations have been offered for the effectiveness of DIF, including perceptual contrast (the second request seems smaller when you are first exposed to the large request), guilt about refusing the first request, or compromise. The effects are probably best explained by a combination of these factors.

Low-Ball

Another compliance strategy that relies on the power of commitment is called the low-ball technique. In this strategy, the persuader tries to elicit a commitment from the receiver before revealing all of the "costs." For example, after inducing a customer to commit to a deal at a certain price, a car salesperson might add on a dealer fee of several hundred dollars. Or, you might agree to assume an office with a school organization, only to find out afterwards that the job requires far more time than you thought. The research indicates that your initial commitment makes it less likely that you will reverse your decision. For example, Cialdini, Cacioppo, Bassett, and Miller (1978) obtained greater compliance from students asked to participate in a 7:00 a.m. experiment when they obtained a commitment to participate before informing the students of the time than when students were told "up front" of the early starting time.

Applying What the Research Tells Us about Other Peripheral Route Factors

- Even when you do everything you can to increase your receivers' motivation and ability to engage in elaborative processing of your message, there may be some who are unwilling to expend the mental effort and are looking for a shortcut to help them decide whether or not to accept your position. Available research suggests several elements that might serve as mental shortcuts for those who are unwilling, or unable, to thoroughly process the message.

- People have a tendency to go along with the crowd. You may be able to employ the **conformity effect** by citing evidence that a majority of others who are similar to your receiver(s) have complied with your request. For example, in helping with a blood donation campaign on campus, you may be able to show prospective donors that numerous similar others, e.g., other students, members of the fraternity/sorority system, same major, have already signed up to donate.

- The **scarcity strategy** refers to messages that alert receivers of time or quantity limitations regarding the availability of a product, service, or opportunity. Persuasion practitioners can often find ways to apply the strategy to fit their own circumstances. For example, one student who worked at a movie rental store reported that DVD rentals of certain movies lagged when there was too much supply. In the eyes of at least some customers, if all 12 copies of a movie were still on the shelf, the movie must not be very good. This student reported that re-arranging the "supply" so that it appeared that only a few of the 12 copies were still available produced an increase in rentals. It appears the movies were viewed as more desirable when the apparent dwindling supply made the loss of the opportunity more preeminent, just like the cookies in the Worchel et.al. (1975) experiment. Note that this application takes advantage of both the scarcity and conformity strategies.

- We have all experienced each of these **sequential request strategies,** as both persuaders and as the ones being persuaded. Your agreement to complete a brief telephone survey may have led to your compliance with a request for an "obligation-free" trial of a product or service (**foot-in-thedoor**); your refusal to loan a friend $50 may have resulted in a $20 loan (**door- in-the-face**); and you have probably agreed to help out on a project that later required a much larger commitment than you were initially led to expect (**low-ball**). You may be able to design ways to apply one or more of these techniques. For example, in a presentation, you might ask audience members to promise themselves they will take certain actions (private commitment), or you might ask for a public commitment, such as signing a petition. In any case, you must keep ethical considerations in mind when using these compliance strategies. Th e same strategy (FID, for example) can be used for ethical purposes—persuading your out-of-shape friend to visit the fitness center just once, or unethical purposes—the drug dealer who convinces your nephew to try cocaine "just one time."

Chapter Review & Study Guide

Summary

in this chapter, you learned the following:

1. The results of a large body of research help us understand the process of persuasion and provide strategies for increasing our effectiveness as persuasive communicators.

2. The Elaboration Likelihood Model helps us understand that people who have sufficient motivation and ability tend to engage in effortful processing of messages.
   - This message scrutiny results in their reacting positively to strong arguments and negatively to weak arguments.
   - Whether we are attempting to persuade an audience of one or many, we would do well to create relevant and understandable messages that proffer the strongest possible arguments to increase the likelihood for elaboration.

3. The likelihood for elaboration can also be influenced by
   - source factors (expertise and use of outside sources)
   - channel factors (the use of the visual channel to enhance the audience's ability to process the message)
   - message factors (forewarning and repetition)
   - receiver factors (their initial position or their level of involvement with the topic)

- Of these, receivers' perceptions of the relevance of the message may be the most important determinant of the likelihood for elaboration.

4. Receivers who engage in elaborative processing are persuaded mainly by strong arguments.

5. We also discussed strategies for making messages strong:
   - The appropriate use of one- and two-sided messages
   - The use of statistical or anecdotal evidence
   - The use of fear appeals

6. Because the central/peripheral distinction is not an eitheror proposition, and we cannot be sure that all receivers will be sufficiently motivated and able to process a given message, we should also pay attention to peripheral cues.
   - Credibility, attractiveness, and similarity are some of the source characteristics that may serve as peripheral cues.
   - The message can also contain elements that may serve as peripheral cues, such as appeals to our audience's need for conformity, perceptions of scarcity, and the use of sequential request strategies.

Key Terms

Argument quality
Central route processing
Conformity effect
Door-in-the-face
Elaboration Likelihood Model
Extended Parallel Process Model
Foot-in-the-door
Forewarning
Inoculation Theory

Intentional model of persuasion
Low-ball
One-sided messages
Peripheral cues
Peripheral route processing
Receiver involvement (relevance)
Scarcity
Selective attention
Selective exposure

Sequential-request strategies
Source attractiveness
Source credibility
Source expertise
Source similarity
Two-sided nonrefutational messages
Two-sided refutational messages
Wear-out point

Study Questions

1. The "wear-out" point on commercial advertisements:

   a. is three repetitions
   b. is five repetitions
   c. increases with the novelty and complexity of the ad
   d. decreases with the novelty and complexity of the ad

2. In the central route to persuasion, attitude change is predicted

   a. more by argument quality than by source factors
   b. more by source expertise than argument quality
   c. more by the number of arguments (quantity) than argument quality
   d. more by source attractiveness than argument quality

3. Receivers are more likely to take the central route to persuasion when

   a. they view the message as personally relevant
   b. they view the message as personally irrelevant
   c. they believe the message is of high relevance to the source
   d. they believe the message is of low relevance to the source

4. Compared to persuasion resulting from peripheral factors, persuasion resulting from central route processing is

   a. more enduring (lasting)
   b. more resistant to counter-persuasion
   c. less enduring and less resistant to counterpersuasion
   d. both a and b are true

5. According to the ELM, when the message is of high relevance to receivers

   a. persuasion will increase
   b. persuasion will decrease
   c. persuasion may increase or decrease, depending on argument quality
   d. persuasion is not affected by message relevance

6. High message relevance (as opposed to low message relevance)

   a. decreases receivers' processing
   b. increases receivers' processing
   c. has no effect on the amount of processing
   d. processing only if repetition is used in the message

7. Which of the following should produce the most persuasion, assuming high quality arguments and high issue relevance?

   a. three sources, one (same) argument each
   b. three sources, each with a different argument
   c. one source, three different arguments
   d. one source, one argument

8. The order of effectiveness (persuasiveness) of one-sided and two-sided messages is generally as follows: (from most to least effective)

   a. two-sided refutational, one-sided, two-sided nonrefutational
   b. two-sided refutational, two-sided nonrefutational, one-sided
   c. one-sided, two-sided refutational, two-sided nonrefutational
   d. two-sided nonrefutational, two-sided refutational, one-sided

9. The Parallel Processes in Witte's EPPM are

   a. attitude and behavior change
   b. message comprehension and acceptance
   c. the likelihood and severity of the consequences
   d. fear control and danger control

10. Inducing the receiver to comply with an initial, small request, then later asking for a larger commitment is known as:

    a. Door-in-the-face   c. Inoculation
    b. Foot-in-the-door   d. Badgering

Answers:

1. (c); 2. (a); 3. (a); 4. (d); 5. (c); 6. (b); 7. (b); 8. (a); 9. (d); 10. (b)

Critical Thinking

1. Analyze several television advertisements for different products for the use of central and peripheral route strategies. Which route seems to be emphasized in each advertisement? Evaluate the potential effectiveness of each ad for high and low involved receivers.

2. Think of one example for each of the following peripheral cues in which you were a participant as a persuader or receiver: similarity, conformity, scarcity, FID, DIF, low-ball.

References

1. Addington, D. (1968). The relationship of selected vocal characteristics to personality perception. *Speech Monographs*, 35, 492–503.

2. Allen, M. (1991). Meta-analysis comparing the persuasiveness of one-sided and two-sided messages. *Western Journal of Speech Communication*, 55, 390–404.

3. Andersen, K., & Clevenger, T. (1963). A summary of experimental research in ethos. *Speech Monographs*, 30, 59–78.

4. Andersen, S., & Pryor, B. (1992). *Speech fundamentals: A contemporary approach*. Needham Heights, MA: Ginn Press.

5. Asch, S. (1951). Effects of group pressure upon the modification of and distortion of judgment. In H. Guetzhow (Ed.), *Groups, leadership, and men*. Pittsburgh: Carnegie.

6. Bledsoe, D. (1984). *Nonfluencies and distraction theory: A proattitudinal approach*. Unpublished masters thesis, University of Central Florida.

7. Byrne, D. (1961). Interpersonal attraction and attitude similarity. *Journal of Abnormal and Social Psychology*, 62, 713–715.

8. Cacioppo, J. T., & Petty, R.E. (1979). Effects of message repetition and position on responses, recall, and persuasion. *Journal of Personality andSocial Psychology*, 37, 97–109.

9. Cacioppo, J. T., & Petty, R.E. (1982). The need for cognition. *Journal of Personality and Social Psychology*, 42, 116–131.

10. Cacioppo, J. T., & Petty, R.E. (1984). The need for cognition: Relationship to attitudinal processes. In R. McGlynn, J. Maddux, C. Stoltenberg, and J. Harvey (Eds.), *Social perception in clinical and counseling psychology*. Lubbock: Texas Tech Press.

11. Cacioppo, J. T., & Petty, R. E. (1985). Central and peripheral routes to persuasion: The role of message repetition. In A. Mitchell, & L. Alwitt (Eds.), *Psychological processes andadvertising effects*. Hillsdale, NJ: Erlbaum.

12. Chaiken, S. (1979). Communicator physical attractiveness and persuasion. *Journal of Personality and Social Psychology*, 37, 1387–1397.

13. Chaiken, S., & Eagly, A.H. (1976). Communication modality as a determinant of message persuasiveness and message comprehensibility. *Journal of Personality and Social Psychology*, 39, 752–766.

14. Cialdini, R. (2001). *Influence: Science and practice*. Boston: Allyn and Bacon.

15. Cialdini, R., & Ascani, K. (1976). Test of a concession procedure for inducing verbal, behavioral, and further compliance with a request to give blood. *Journal of Applied Psychology*, 61, 295–300.

16. Cialdini, R. B., Levy, A., Herman, P., Koslowski, L., & Petty, R.E. (1976). Elastic shifts of opinion: Determinants of direction and durability. *Journal of Personality and Social Psychology*, 34, 663–672.

17. Cialdini, R. B., Cacioppo, J. R., Bassett, R., & Miller, J. A. (1978). The low-ball procedure for producing compliance: Commitment then cost. *Journal of Personality and SocialPsychology*, 36, 463–476.

18. Downs, A.C., & Lyons, P.M. (1990). Natural observations of the links between attractiveness and initial legal judgments. *Personality and Social Psychology Bulletin*, 17, 541–547.

19. Freedman, J., & Fraser, S. (1966). Compliance without pressure: The foot-in-the-door technique. *Journal of Personality and Social Psychology*, 4, 195–202.

20. Hamermesh, D. S., & Biddle, J.E. (1994). Beauty and the labor market. *American Economic Review*, 84, 1174– 1194.

21. Harkins, S. G., & Petty, R. E. (1981). The multiple source effect in persuasion: The effects of distraction. *Personality and Social PsychologyBulletin*, 7, 627–635.

22. Hoeken, H. (1999). The perceived and actual persuasiveness of different types of inductive arguments. In F. van Eemeren, R. Grootendorst, J. Blair, & C. Willard, (Eds.), *Proceedings of the fourth international conference of the International Society for the Study of Argumentation* (pp. 353–357). Amsterdam: Sic Sat.

23. Katt, J. (2004, November). *Infl uencing perceptions of relevance*. Paper presented at the annual conference of the National Communication Association, Chicago, IL.

24. Knapp, M., & Hall, J. (2002). Nonverbal communication in human interaction. Fort Worth: Harcourt Brace.

25. Koballa, T. (1986). Persuading teachers to reexamine the innovative elementary science programs of yesterday: The effect of anecdotal versus data-summary communications. *Journal of Research in Science Teaching*, 23, 437–449.

26. Krupat, E., Smith, R., Leach, C., & Jackson, M. (1997). Generalizing from atypical cases: How general a tendency? *Basic and Applied Psychology*, 19, 345–361.

27. Kurzban, R., & Weeden, J. (2005). HurryDate: Mate preferences in action. *Evolution and Human Behavior*, 227–244.

28. Long, C. (2008). Sought: Wal-Mart shoppers who trampled NY worker. *Associated Press*, http:// news.yahoo .com/s/ ap/20081129/ap_on_re_us/ wal_mart_ death/print;_ylt= Aqy5vJg . . .

29. Maurin, P. (2000). *The effects of statistical and story evidence on attitudechange*. Unpublished masters thesis, University of Central Florida.

30. McCroskey, J. C. (1966). Scales for measurement of ethos. *Speech Monographs*, 33, 65–72.

31. McGuire, W. J. (1964). Inducing resistance to persuasion: Some contemporary approaches. In L. Berkowitz (Ed.), *Advances in experimental social psychology*, (Vol.1). New York: Academic Press.

32. Mills, J., & Aronson, E., (1965). Opinion change as a function of the communicator's attractiveness and desire to influence. *Journal of Personality and Social Psychology*, 1, 173–177.

33. O'Keefe, D. (1999). How to handle opposing arguments in persuasive messages. A meta-analytic review of the effects of one-sided and twosided messages. *Communication Yearbook*, 22, 209–249.

34. O'Keefe, D. (2002). *Persuasion: Theory and research*. Thousand Oaks, CA: Sage.

35. Pearce, W. B., & Conklin, F, (1971). Nonverbal vocalic communication and perceptions of a speaker. *Speech Monographs*, 38, 235–241.

36. Peters, R., Covello, V., & McCallum, D. (1997). The determinants of trust and credibility in environmental risk communication: An empirical study. *Risk Analysis*, 17, 43–54.

37. Petty, R. E., & Cacioppo, J. T. (1977). Forewarning, cognitive responding, and resistance to persuasion. *Journal of Personality and Social Psychology*, 35, 645–655.

38. Petty, R. E., & Cacioppo, J. T. (1979). Issue involvement can increase or decrea se persuasion by enhancing message-relevant cognitive responses. *Journal of Personality and Social Psychology*, 37, 1915–1926.

39. Petty, R. E., & Cacioppo, J. T. (1984). Source factors and the elaboration likelihood model of persuasion. *Advances in Consumer Research*, 11, 668–672.

40. Petty, R. E., & Cacioppo, J. T. (1984). The effects of involvement on responses to argument quality and quantity: Central and peripheral route to persuasion. *Journal of Personalityand Social Psychology*, 46, 69–81.

41. Petty, R. E., & Cacioppo, J. T. (1986). *Communication and persuasion:Central and peripheral routes to attitudechange*. New York: Springer-Verlag.

42. Petty, R. E., Cacioppo, J. T., & Goldman, R. (1981). Personal involvement as a determinant of argument-based persuasion. *Journal of Personality and Social Psychology*, 41, 847–855.

43. Pratkanis, A., & Aronson, E. (2002). *The age of propaganda: The everyday use and abuse of persuasion*. New York: W.H. Freeman & Co.

44. Pryor, B., & Steinfatt, T. M. (1978). The effects of initial belief level on inoculation theory and its proposed mechanism. *Human Communication Research*, 4, 217–230.

45. Regan, N., (2001). *Fear appeals andhealth communication: The effects of threat and efficacy on intentions to modify behavior*. Unpublished masters thesis, University of Central Florida.

46. Sereno, K. K., & Hawkins, G. J. (1967). The effects of variations in speakers' nonfluency upon audience ratings of attitude toward the speech topic and speakers' credibility. *Speech Monographs*, 34, 58–64.

47. Sherman, S. (1980). On the self-erasing nature of errors of prediction. *Journal of Personality and Social Psychology*, 39, 211–221.

48. Szabo, E., & Pfau, M. (2002). Nuances in inoculation: Theory and applications. In J. Dillard & M. Pfau (Eds.), *The persuasion handbook: Developments in theory and practice*. Thousand Oaks, CA: Sage.

49. Vernon, M. (1962). The psychology of perception. Baltimore: Penguin Books.

50. Wagner, T. (1999). *Effects of various levels of speakers' eye contact onreceivers' assessments of the speakerand the speech*. Unpublished masters thesis, University of Central Florida.

51. Witte, K. (1992). Putting the fear back in fear appeals: The extended parallel process model. *Communication Monographs*, 59, 329–349.

52. Witte, K., Berkowitz, J., Cameron, K., & McKeon, J. (1998). Preventing the spread of genital warts: Using fear appeals to promote self-protective behaviors. *Health Education and Behavior*, 25, 571–585.

Communicating In Our Technological World

Jim Katt

Technology is Everywhere

Technology has become ubiquitous in our society today. We enjoy the benefits of all of the technology that works for us and suffer the annoyance of all the technology that doesn't. For better or worse, technology has permeated nearly every part of our lives.

Given the expanding role of technology, it is not surprising that most professions require specialized, technical knowledge. And while it is certainly important to have that specialized knowledge, the knowledge is not fully useful to us unless we have the ability to communicate our unique knowledge to others. During our college years, most of us spend a lot more time acquiring new knowledge than we do acquiring the ability to share that knowledge. This is particularly true of students in the science and engineering disciplines, whose crowded curricula offer only limited opportunities to study ways of communicating effectively. Yet, often it is the students of those disciplines that most need to study communication. Scientists and engineers end up knowing the most technical, specialized information and are often the ones least able to communicate in ways that are clear, concise, and compelling. This problem becomes more serious as technology becomes more complex and specialized.

More than Ever

Today, more than ever, communication skills are essential for those in professions that involve technology. There are a number of reasons why this is so.

First, there is simply more to know than there once was. Humankind has succeeded in discovering more and more knowledge, while discarding very little. As a result, it is more difficult for any one person to know all there is to know about anything. This means we all have to rely more on others (and they on us) to know what we don't. This type of collaboration, however, only works if the parties involved can communicate clearly with one another.

Second, the growth of technology has led to more specialization. There was a time, for example, when all electrical engineers knew the same sorts of things. That made it fairly easy for one electrical engineer to communicate with another electrical engineer. Today the electrical engineer specializing in nanotechnology may find she has little in common with an electrical engineer specializing in power systems. The result of this increased specialization is that, even within a single discipline, communication has become a more difficult task, and communicating effectively requires more skill.

A third reason for the increased emphasis on communication skills has to do with a shift in the make-up of work teams. Computers have provided a common denominator between specialties. Consider the publishing business, for example. There have always been writers and editors, graphic artists, photographers, typesetters and printers. But, until recently they were set apart by the tools that they used. Writers and editors used typewriters, while graphic artists used paper and pen. Photographers used cameras and film, chemicals to process the film, and photographic paper to display the images. Typesetters used linotype machines to cast lines of type in lead, while printers were the masters of ink and the presses. Although these specialties still exist, in many cases they now all use the same tool - the computer. This convergence around the one's and zero's of computing allows a smaller workforce, one where the production teams are no longer specialists of one type, but rather groups of different specialists working together. This reconfiguration of work teams can result in greater efficiency, creativity, and quality, but requires close and effective communication among the diverse team members.

What Employers Want

The increased need for communication skills has not gone unnoticed by those whose hire people in technical professions. Companies who hire engineers, scientists, and other specialists are looking for people who not only know their stuff, but also have the ability to communicate what they know. While writing the book, *Technically Speaking,* co-author Stephan Ihde (Ihde, Katt, & Bosley, 2000) interviewed executives from a number of companies that employ engineers and other technical professionals. Their responses could be summed up in one statement: "We are looking for people who can communicate what they know to others." People who communicate more effectively simply do better in the workplace. Dr. E. H. Dowell, former Dean of the School of Engineering at Duke University, echoes that sentiment:

> I have often seen engineers who are adept at communications enjoy a considerable advantage over those who are not. On the other hand, I have seen engineers whose technical skills are superior fail to communicate their ideas effectively, and then find out that their ideas do not receive the attention they deserve. (1999, p. 3)

Why Speech?

For people aspiring for a job that involves technology, it's important to learn about communication. But why speech? In ancient times speech was the primary mode of communication because there were not a lot of other choices. In Aristotle's time there were no printing presses, no sound recordings, no telephone, no telegraph, and certainly no television or internet. Those who wished to voice their opinion did so with their voices, in public. As those who spoke most effectively enjoyed the most influence. The ability to speak effectively was essential to being successful.

Today, we have many modalities of communication. Our communication technologies have broken down the barriers of time and distance. Still, face-to-face communication remains an essential channel. A live human being speaking to others who are present in the same location is a powerful phenomenon. There is something in that human transaction that cannot be replaced by technology. One could argue that technology has provided so many impersonal methods of exchanging information, face-to-face communication has even more impact because of its relative rarity. Two decades ago, author Michael Nesmith

(1984) predicted that the growth of technology, "high tech," would result in people spending more of their time interacting with computers and other machines and less time interacting with people. Nesmith further predicted that this lack of human interaction would increase the significance of those times when people did communicate in a face-to-face, "high touch" setting. Certainly, not everything has to be communicated orally. Our workplaces and our society are enriched by the variety of communication methods that are now available. But there are times when the most effective way of communicating a message is to have one human stand in front of a group of other humans and speak. In the business world, presentations are a way of life. One must approach the study of public speaking thinking this will be useful *when* I need to make presentations, not *if* I need to make presentations. In addition, students who intend to pursue careers in technical fields need to understand that not only will there be presentations to make, but there will be presentations to make to non-technical audiences. This necessitates not only being able to speak effectively to groups of people, but also to be able to make complex, technical information understandable to those with non-technical (or different-technical) backgrounds.

References

1. Dowell, E. (1999). "From the Dean: To get ahead, engineers must calculate and communicate." *DukEngineer,* 61 (2), 3–5

2. Ihde, S., Katt, J. and Bosley, A. (2000). *Technically Speaking.* Kendall/Hunt: Dubuque, IA.

3. Nesmith, Michael (1984). *Megatrends.* Warner: New York.

Glossary

A

accommodation goal The marginalized group manages to keep its identity while striving for positive relationships with the dominant culture.

active perception Perception in which your mind selects, organizes, and interprets that which you sense.

adaptors Nonverbal movements that usually involve the unintended touching or manipulating of our bodies or artifacts to fulfill some physical or psychological need.

affect displays Nonverbal movements of the face and body used to show emotion.

affection The emotion of caring for others and/or being cared for.

ageist language Language that denigrates people for being young or old.

aggressiveness The assertion of one's rights at the expense of others and caring about one's own needs but no one else's.

amoral The process of communication is ethically neutral.

analogy A comparison of things in some respects, especially in position or function, that are otherwise dissimilar.

and stress group harmony.

argumentativeness The quality or state of being argumentative; synonymous with contentiousness or combativeness.

articulation Coordinating one's mouth, tongue, and teeth to make words understandable to others.

artifacts Ornaments or adornments you display that hold communicative potential.

assigned groups Groups that evolve out of a hierarchy whereby individuals are assigned membership to the group.

assimilation goal The marginalized group attempts to fit in with the dominant group.

attractiveness A concept that includes physical attractiveness, how desirable a person is to work with, and how much "social value" the person has for others.

autocratic leaders Leaders who maintain strict control over their group.

B

bargaining The process in which two or more parties attempt to reach an agreement on what each should give and receive in a transaction between them.

behavioral flexibility The ability to alter behavior to adapt to new situations and to relate in new ways when necessary.

bibliographic references Complete citations that appear in the "references" or "works cited" section of your speech outline.

body The largest part of the presentation, which contains the arguments, evidence, and main content.

boundary spanner An individual who shares information between groups and establishes strategic vision for collaboration.

brakelight function A forewarning to the audience that the end of the presentation is near.

C

cause/effect pattern A method of organization in which the presenter first explains the causes of an event, a problem, or an issue and then discusses its consequences, results, or effects.

celebrity testimony Statements made by a public figure who is known to the audience.

central route processing Persuasion achieved by the quality of the arguments in a message.

central route processing Receivers mentally elaborate on the elements of your message and carefully scrutinize your arguments and evidence.

channel The means through which the message is sent.

chronemics Also called temporal communication; the way people organize and use time and the messages that are created because of their organization and use of that time.

chronological résumé A document that organizes your credentials over time.

cliché An expression that has lost originality and force through overuse.

closure The tendency to fill in missing information in order to complete an otherwise incomplete figure or statement.

code sensitivity The ability to use the verbal and nonverbal language appropriate to the cultural norms of the individual with whom you are communicating.

collectivist cultures Cultures that value the group over the individual.

collectivistic cultures Cultures that discourage individual assertiveness and stress group harmony.

common ground The degree to which the speaker's values, beliefs, attitudes, and interests are shared with the audience; an aspect of credibilty.

communibiology The study of the biological bases of human communication.

communication apprehension Fear and avoidance of communication with other people.

communication networks Patterns of relationships through which information flows in an organization.

communication orientation Your focus as a speaker is to achieve your communicative goals.

competence The degree to which the speaker is perceived as skilled, qualified, experienced, authoritative, reliable, and informed; an aspect of credibility.

complementarity The idea that we sometimes bond with people whose strengths are our weaknesses.

complementary relationships Relationships in which each person supplies something the other person or persons lack.

complementing Using nonverbal and verbal codes to add meaning to each other and to expand the meaning of either message alone.

compliance-gaining Attempts made by a source of messages to influence a target "to perform some desired behavior that the target otherwise might not perform."

compliance-resisting The refusal of targets of influence messages to comply with requests.

conclusion The part that finishes the presentation by fulfilling the four functions of an ending.

concrete language Words and statements that are specific rather than abstract or vague.

connotative meaning An individualized or personalized meaning of a word, which may be emotionally laden.

Connotative meaning the implied meaning of a word based upon its use within a given context.

content curation The collection and storage of documents and other multimedia from the web, covering a specified topic.

contradicting Sending verbal and nonverbal messages that conflict.

contradictions In dialectic theory, the idea that each person in a relationship might have two opposing desires for maintaining the relationship.

control The ability to influence our environment.

cover letter A short letter introducing you and your résumé to an interviewer.

criteria The standards by which a group must judge potential solutions.

cultural relativism The belief that another culture should be judged by its own context rather than measured against your culture.

culture A unique combination of rituals, religious beliefs, ways of thinking, and ways of behaving that unify a group of people.

culture The socially transmitted behavior patterns, beliefs, attitudes, and values of a particular period, class, community, or population.

customer service encounter The moment of interaction between the customer and the firm.

D

dating Specifying when you made an observation, since everything changes over time.

deceptive communication The practice of deliberately making somebody believe things that are not true.

decode The process of assigning meaning to others' words in order to translate them into thoughts of your own.

defensiveness The response that occurs when a person feels attacked.

deficiency needs Basic human needs, which must be satisfied before higher-order needs can be met. They include needs for food, water, air, physical safety, belongingness and love, and self-esteem and social esteem.

definitions Determinations of meaning through description, simplification, examples, analysis, comparison, explanation, or illustration.

democratic leaders Leaders who encourage members to participate in group decisions.

denotative meaning The agreed-upon meaning or dictionary meaning of a word.

Denotative meaning The literal or explicit definition of a word

descriptiveness The practice of describing observed behavior or phenomena instead of offering personal reactions or judgments.

designated leader Someone who has been appointed or elected to a leadership position.

dialectic The tension that exists between two conflicting or interacting forces, elements, or ideas.

dominant culture A culture determined by who has the power and influence in traditional social structures like politics, religious institutions, schools, and businesses; in the United States the dominant culture is white, male, able-bodied, straight, married, and employed.

downward communication Messages flowing from superiors to subordinates.

dynamism The extent to which the speaker is perceived as bold, active, energetic, strong, empathic, and assertive; an aspect of credibility.

E

economic orientation Organizations that manufacture products and/or offer services for consumers.

elaboration The degree to which a receiver scrutinizes a message.

emblems Nonverbal movements that substitute for words and phrases.

emergent groups Groups resulting from environmental conditions leading to the formation of a cohesive group of individuals.

emergent leader Someone who becomes an informal leader by exerting influence toward the achievement of a group's goal but does not hold the formal position or role of leader.

emotional labor Jobs in which employees are expected to display certain feelings in order to satisfy organizational role expectations.

emphasizing The use of nonverbal cues to strengthen verbal messages.

encode The process of translating your thoughts into words.

enunciation Combining pronunciation and articulation to produce a word with clarity and distinction.

environment The situation or context in which the transaction takes place.

environmental reinforcers Factors within our environment that contribute to our fear of speaking.

ethnocentrism The belief that your own group or culture is superior to other groups or cultures.

ethos The receiver's perception of a sender's competence and trustworthiness; credibility.

euphemism A more polite, pleasant expression used instead of a socially unacceptable form.

examples Specific instances used to illustrate your point.

expert testimony Statements made by someone who has special knowledge or expertise about an issue or idea.

explanation A clarification of what something is or how it works.

extemporaneous delivery A speech is practiced thoroughly, but not memorized, using speaker's notes, not a manuscript.

F

figure The focal point of your attention.

first impression An initial opinion about people upon meeting them.

formal communication Messages that follow prescribed channels of communication through-out the organization.

formal role Also called positional role; an assigned role based on an individual's position or title within a group.

frozen evaluation An assessment of a concept that does not change over time.

functional résumé A document that organizes your credentials by type of function performed.

G

gender identity How you feel about and express your gender.

gender-biased language Language that privileges a certain gender over another.

generalized anxiety Feelings of anxiety associated with communication in nearly all situations.

genetic contributors Combinations of inherited tendencies that may exert influences on our behavioral preferences.

ground The background against which your focused attention occurs.

group climate The emotional tone or atmosphere members create within the group.

group conflict An expressed struggle between two or more members of a group.

group culture The socially negotiated system of rules that guide group behavior.

group decision support system (GDSS) An interactive network of computers with specialized software, allowing users to generate solutions for unstructured problems.

groupthink An unintended outcome of cohesion in which the desire for cohesion and agreement takes precedence over critical analysis and discussion.

growth needs Higher-order human needs, which can be satisfied only after deficiency needs have been met. They include self-actualization (the process of fully realizing one's potential), knowledge and understanding, and aesthetic needs.

H

heterosexist language Language that implies that everyone is heterosexual.

heuristics Mental shortcuts used to make decisions—for instance, evaluating sources.

horizontal communication Messages between members of an organization who have equal power.

hostile work environment sexual harassment Conditions in the workplace that are sexually offensive, intimidating, or hostile and that affect an individual's ability to perform his or her job.

hurtful messages Messages that create emotional pain or upset.

I

illustrators Nonverbal movements that accompany or reinforce verbal messages.

immediacy Communication behaviors intended to create perceptions of psychological closeness with others.

impression management Sharing personal details in order to present an idealized self.

impromptu delivery A speech that has little or no preparation time and is made up along the way.

in-group A group that people belong to that gives them a source of pride, self-esteem, and sense of belonging to a social world.

inclusion The state of being involved with others; a human need.

incremental plagiarism The intentional or unintentional use of information from one or more sources without fully divulging how much information is directly quoted.

indexing Identifying the uniqueness of objects, events, and people.

individualistic cultures Cultures that value individual freedom, choice, uniqueness, and independence.

individualistic cultures Societies that stress individual assertiveness over group harmony.

inflection The variety or changes in pitch.

informal communication Interactions that do not follow the formal upward and downward structures of the organization but emerge out of less formal interactions among organizational members.

informal role Also called behavioral role; a role that is developed spontaneously within a group.

integration orientation Organizations that help mediate and resolve discord among members of society.

interaction management Establishing a smooth pattern of interaction that allows a clear flow between topics and ideas.

intercultural communication The exchange of information between individuals who are unalike culturally.

intergroup perspective The theory that emphasizes the ways in which people in a social interaction identify and categorize themselves or others in terms of group membership and how these categorizations shape perceptions and interactions with others.

internal references Brief notations indicating a bibliographic reference that contains the details you are using in your speech.

interpersonal communication The process of using messages to generate meaning between at least two people in a situation that allows mutual opportunities for both speaking and listening.

interpersonal relationships Associations between at least two people who are interdependent, who use some consistent patterns of interaction, and who have interacted for an extended period of time.

interpretive perception Perception that involves a blend of internal states and external stimuli.

introduction The first part of your presentation, in which you fulfill five functions.

J

jargon Language particular to a specific profession, work group, or culture and not meant to be understood by outsiders.

job description A document that defines a job in terms of its content and scope.

journalism The communication of news, information about events in our communities, our nation, and our world; and commentary.

K

key-word outline An outline consisting of important words or phrases to remind you of the content of the presentation.

kinesics The study of bodily movements, including posture, gestures, and facial expressions.

kinesics The study of body movement and facial expressions.

L

labels Identify specific elements of a graphic slide.

laissez-faire leaders Leaders who take almost no initiative in structuring a group discussion.

language A collection of symbols, letters, or words with arbitrary meanings that are governed by rules and used to communicate.

lay testimony Statements made by an ordinary person that substantiate or support what you say.

leadership A process of using communication to influence the behaviors and attitudes of others to meet group goals.

learned helplessness A person feels unable to predict whether a behavior will result in a reward or punishment, therefore he or she avoids the behavior all together if possible.

listening The process of receiving, attending to, and assigning meaning to aural and visual stimuli.

logos Logical appeals.

M

main points The most important points in a presentation; indicated by Roman numerals in an outline.

maintenance functions Behaviors that focus on the interpersonal relationships among group members.

manuscript delivery A speech that is written word-for-word using a tone and language that are appropriate for speaking rather than reading.

mass-media communication The process of using messages to generate meaning in a mediated system, between a source and a large number of unseen receivers.

memorized delivery A speech is written as a manuscript and then delivered from memory.

message The message the speaker *intends* to send.

message-sidedness One-sided messages provide only the arguments that support your message; two-sided nonrefutational messages provide counter-arguments but do not refute those arguments; two-sided refutational messages provide and refute counter arguments.

N

narratives Stories to illustrate an important point.

negative self-talk Destructive self-criticism.

non-dominant culture A term that includes people of color, women, gays/lesbians/bisexuals, people with disabilities, the lower/working class, the unemployed, the underemployed, the bankrupt, the young, and the elderly.

non-fluencies Verbal mistakes such as false starts, mispronunciations or excessive ah's and um's.

nonverbal codes Messages consisting of symbols that are not words, including nonword vocalizations.

nonverbal communication The process of using messages other than words to create meaning with others.

nonword sounds Sounds like "mmh," "huh," and "ahh," as well as the pauses or the absence of sounds used for effect.

norms Informal rules for group interaction created and sustained through communication.

O

objectics Also called object language; the study of the human use of clothing and artifacts as nonverbal codes.

objective statement An articulation of your goals.

On-time The time schedule that compartmentalizes time to meet personal needs, separates task and social dimensions, and points to the future.

operational definition A definition that identifies something by revealing how it works, how it is made, or what it consists of.

organization The grouping of stimuli into meaningful units or wholes.

organizational communication The communication that is necessary to form and maintain an organization.

organizational communication The ways in which groups of people both maintain structure and order through their symbolic interactions and allow individual actors the freedom to accomplish their goals.

organizational communities Groups of similar businesses or clubs that have common interests and become networked together to provide mutual support and resources.

organizational patterns Arrangements of the contents of a presentation.

organizations Social collectives, or groups of people, in which activities are coordinated to achieve both individual and collective goals.

out-group A group of people excluded from another group with higher status; a group marginalized by the dominant culture.

outline A written plan that uses symbols, margins, and content to reveal the order, importance, and substance of a presentation.

P

paralinguistic features The nonword sounds and nonword characteristics of language, such as pitch, volume, rate, and quality.

parallel form The consistent use of complete sentences, clauses, phrases, or words in an outline.

paraphrasing Restating another person's message by rephrasing the content or intent of the message.

pathos Emotional appeals.

pattern-maintenance orientation Organizations that promote cultural and educational regularity and development within society.

perception checking A process of describing, interpreting, and verifying that helps us understand another person and his or her message more accurately.

perception The process of using the senses to acquire information about the surrounding environment or situation.

perceptual constancy The idea that your past experiences lead you to see the world in a way that is difficult to change; your initial perceptions persist.

performance orientation Seeing your presentation as a performance and your audience as critics.

peripheral route processing Influence based upon factors outside of the quality of the message.

peripheral route processing Receivers give brief attention to the message without elaborated thought.

personal brand Your personal attributes and values that can be consistently communicated to others.

personal experience Your own life as a source of information.

personal identity Perception of what makes an individual unique with regard to various personality characteristics, interests, and values.

personal idioms Unique forms of expression and language understood only by individual couples.

personal network A web of contacts and relationships that can help you gain job leads and can provide referrals.

Persuasion The process by which attitudes or behaviors are influenced as a result of receiving a message.

pervasiveness Communication takes place wherever humans are together because people tend to look

for meaning, even when a message is not deliberately sent.

phatic communication Communication that is used to establish a mood of sociability rather than to communicate important information or ideas.

pitch The highness or lowness of the voice.

plagiarism The intentional use of information from another source without crediting the source.

political orientation Organizations that generate and distribute power and control within society.

power Interpersonal influence that forms the basis for group leadership.

pragmatics The study of language as it is used in a social context, including its effect on the communicators.

prejudice A negative attitude toward a group of people just because they are who they are.

prejudice An unfavorable predisposition about an individual because of his or her membership in a stereotyped group.

problem/solution pattern A method of organization in which the presenter describes a problem and proposes a solution to that problem.

profanity A type of swearing that uses indecent words or phrases.

pronunciation Saying a word correctly or incorrectly.

proxemics The study of the human use of space and distance.

proximity The location, distance, or range between persons and things.

proximity The principle that objects physically close to each other will be perceived as a unit or group.

public speaking The process of using messages to generate meanings in a situation in which a single source transmits a message to a number of receivers.

Q

quality The unique resonance of the voice, such as huskiness, nasality, raspiness, or whininess.

quid pro quo sexual harassment A situation in which an employee is offered a reward or is threatened with punishment based on his or her participation in a sexual activity.

R

racist language Language that insults a group because of its race or ethnicity.

rate The pace of your speech.

receivers The audience to whom the message is delivered.

reference librarian A librarian specifically trained to help you find sources of information.

references A list of sources used in a presentation.

reflexivity Being self-aware and learning from interactions with the intent of improving future interactions.

regionalisms Words and phrases specific to a particular region or part of the country.

regulating Using nonverbal codes to monitor and control interactions with others.

regulators Nonverbal movements that control the flow or pace of communication.

relational deterioration The stage in a relationship in which the prior bond disintegrates.

relational development The initial stage in a relationship that moves a couple from meeting to mating.

relational maintenance The stage in a relationship after a couple has bonded and in which they engage in the process of keeping the relationship together.

relationship-oriented groups Groups that are usually long-term and exist to meet our needs for inclusion and affection.

repeating Sending the same message both verbally and nonverbally.

responsiveness The idea that we tend to select our friends and loved ones from people who demonstrate positive interest in us.

rituals Formalized patterns of actions or words followed regularly.

role A consistent pattern of interaction or behavior exhibited over time.

role The part you play in various social contexts.

rough draft The preliminary organization of the outline of a presentation.

S

Sapir-Whorf hypothesis A theory that our perception of reality is determined by our thought processes, our thought processes are limited by our language, and therefore language shapes our reality and our behaviors.

search engine A program on the Internet that allows users to search for information.

selective attention Receivers avoid a message by not paying attention to it.

selective attention The tendency, when you expose yourself to information and ideas, to focus on certain cues and ignore others.

selective exposure The tendency to expose yourself to information that reinforces, rather than contradicts, your beliefs or opinions.

selective exposure The tendency to place ourselves in environments with others who think as we do.

selective perception The tendency to see, hear, and believe only what you want to see, hear, and believe.

selective retention The tendency to remember better the things that reinforce your beliefs than those that oppose them.

self-centered functions Behaviors that serve the needs of the individual at the expense of the group.

self-disclosure The process of making intentional revelations about yourself that others would be unlikely to know and that generally constitute private, sensitive, or confidential information.

self-talk Silent communications with oneself that influence our perceptions of reality.

semantics The study of the way humans use language to evoke meaning in others.

sentence outline An outline consisting entirely of complete sentences.

separation goal The marginalized group relates as exclusively as possible with its own group and as little as possible with the dominant group.

sexual harassment Unwelcome, unsolicited, repeated behavior of a sexual nature.

signposts Ways in which a presenter signals to an audience where the presentation is going.

silence The lack of sound.

similarity The idea that our friends and loved ones are usually people who like or dislike the same things we do.

similarity The principle that elements are grouped together because they share attributes, such as size, color, or shape.

slang Informal, casual language used among equals with words typically unsuitable for more formal contexts.

sleeper effect A change of audience opinion caused by the separation of the message content from its source over a period of time.

small group communication Communication that takes place among three or more individuals who are interdependent, share goals, identify with one another and interact.

small-group communication Interaction among three to nine people working together to achieve an interdependent goal.

Sometime The time schedule that views time as "contextually based and relationally oriented."

source credibility The audience's perception of your effectiveness as a speaker.

source credibility The image held of a communicator by a receiver at a given time.

source expertise Receivers' perceptions of the persuader's knowledge, qualifications and competence.

source The person initiating the communication.

stakeholders Groups of people who have an interest in the actions of an organization.

statistics Numbers that summarize numerical information or compare quantities.

stereotype A generalization about some group of people that oversimplifies their culture.

stereotyping Making a hasty generalization about a group based on a judgment about an individual from that group.

strategic ambiguity The purposeful use of symbols to allow multiple interpretations of messages.

subjective perception Your uniquely constructed meaning attributed to sensed stimuli.

subpoints The points in a presentation that support the main points; indicated by capital letters in an outline.

substituting Using nonverbal codes instead of verbal codes.

supporting material Information you can use to substantiate your arguments and to clarify your position.

supportive communication Listening with empathy, acknowledging others' feelings, and engaging in dialogue to help others maintain a sense of personal control.

surveys Studies in which a limited number of questions are answered by a sample of the population to discover opinions on issues.

symbolic interactionism The process in which the self develops through the messages and feedback received from others.

symmetrical relationships Relationships in which participants mirror each other or are highly similar.

syntax The way in which words are arranged to form phrases and sentences.

T

tactile communication The use of touch in communication.

task functions Behaviors that are directly relevant to the group's purpose and that affect the group's productivity.

task-oriented groups Also called secondary groups; groups formed for the purpose of completing tasks, such as solving problems or making decisions.

testimonial evidence Written or oral statements of others' experience used by a speaker to substantiate or clarify a point.

The three types of persuasive effects are:
· create a new attitude
· reinforce an existing attitude or behavior
· change an attitude or behavior.

time-sequence pattern A method of organization in which the presenter explains a sequence of events in chronological order.

titles Describe the general focus of a graphic slide.

topical-sequence pattern A method of organization that emphasizes the major reasons an audience should accept a point of view by addressing the advantages, disadvantages, qualities, and types of a person, place, or thing.

transition A bridge between sections of a presentation that helps the presenter move smoothly from one idea to another.

trustworthiness The degree to which the speaker is perceived as honest, fair, sincere, friendly, honorable, and kind; an aspect of credibility.

two-sided argument A source advocating one position presents an argument from the opposite viewpoint and then goes on to refute that argument.

U

uncertainty-accepting cultures Cultures that tolerate ambiguity, uncertainty, and diversity.

uncertainty-rejecting cultures Cultures that have difficulty with ambiguity, uncertainty, and diversity.

upward communication Messages flowing from subordinates to superiors.

V

verbal citations Oral explanations of who the source is, how recent the information is, and what the source's qualifications are.

visual aids Visual elements that help your audience receive your message.

vocal cues All of the oral aspects of sound except words themselves.

vocalized pauses Filler words such as "um" and "ah".

volume The loudness or softness of the voice.

W

wear-out point The point at which a repeated persuasive message loses its effectiveness.

within-group diversity The presence of observable and/or implicit differences among group members.

Index

Please note that **bolded** page numbers indicate defined terms.